A Concordance To The Works Of Thomas Kyd, Volume 15, Part 1

Charles Crawford

Materialien zur Kunde

des

älteren Englischen Dramas

Materialien zur Kunde

des älteren

Englischen Dramas

UNTER MITWIRKUNG DER HERREN

F. S. Boas-London, A. Brandl-Berlin, R. Brotanek-Wien, F. I. Carpenter-Chicago, G. B. Churchill-Amherst, Ch. Crawford-London, W. Creizenach-Krakau, E. Eckhardt-Freiburg i. B., A. Feuillerat-Rennes, R. Fischer-Innsbruck, W. W. Greg-London, F. Holthausen-Kiel, J. Hoops-Heidelberg, W. Keller-Jena, R. B. Mc Kerrow-London, G. L. Kittredge-Cambridge, Mass., E. Koeppel-Strassburg, H. Logeman-Gent, J. M. Manly-Chicago, G. Sarrazin-Breslau, L. Proescholdt-Friedrichsdorf, A. Schröer-Cöln, G. C. Moore Smith-Sheffield, G. Gregory Smith-Belfast, A. E. H. Swaen-Groningen, A. H. Thorndike-Evanston, Ill., A. Wagner-Halle a. S.

BEGRUENDET UND HERAUSGEGEBEN

VON

W. Bang

o. ö. Professor der Englischen Philologie an der Universität Louvain

BAND XV ERSTER TEIL : A Concordance to the Works of Thomas Kyd by Ch. Crawford.

LOUVAIN
A. UYSTPRUYST

LEIPZIG
O. HARRASSOWITZ

LONDON
David NUTT

1906

A

CONCORDANCE

TO THE WORKS OF THOMAS KYD

BY

Ch. Crawford.

LOUVAIN
A. UYSTPRUYST

LEIPZIG
O. HARRASSOWITZ

LONDON
DAVID NUTT

1906

PREFACE.

My main object in compiling this concordance was to enable others to test the accuracy or otherwise of my conclusion that the anonymous play of *Arden of Feversham* is a work by Thomas Kyd. My views and the evidence upon which they are founded are set forth in a paper which I contributed to the *Jahrbuch der Deutschen Shakespeare-Gesellschaft*, 1903. As I found that the vocabulary, phrasing, and general resemblances between *Arden* and *Soliman and Perseda* and the pamphlet entitled *The Murder of John Brewen* were much closer than any I could find after comparing the play with the rest of Kyd's known work, I have placed all quotations from it between passages cited from the pieces named. I hope this arrangement will be found useful by students who may wish to investigate the question.

I have endeavoured as far as possible to make the concordance perfect, and have not spared myself in doing so. Fortunately, I had to hand Professor F. S. Boas' edition of Kyd's works, which follows the original spelling. I have adhered to this spelling throughout, and have reproduced Professor Boas' punctuation. All leading words that are spelt in modern form are indicated by the first letter only.

It has always seemed to me to be a cumbersome method in concordances to cite many references ; and, personally, I have often experienced mental distress when I found I had to carry in my mind the act and scene as well as the number of the line where a passage was to be looked for. To avoid this circumlocution, which causes unnecessary disturbance to one's thoughts, I have numbered the lines in each play or prose-piece throughout without breaks. A Key to the numbering will be found in the front of the volume. Here let me say, that I have made no departure from the counting of the lines as recorded in Professor Boas' Kyd or in the Rev. Ronald Gower's version of *Arden of Feversham*. I have merely ignored divisions : my end-number in each case will be found to agree with the total arrived at after adding together the lines of all the scenes or pages in the several works. All that is needed to make the concordance easy for immediate use is to number the first line of each page in accordance with the Key, a task that should only occupy about half-an-hour of the student's time.

As regards arrangement, the singular form of leading words appears first ; next come words in the possessive case ; and then plurals.

Words such as 'gainst, 'mongst, &c., are placed under their unabbreviated forms ; and the latter parts of hyphenated words are recorded at the end of each list. Wherever necessary, too, words employed in a sense different from the ordinary usage will also be found at the ends of the lists.

The concordance includes everything supposed to have been written by Kyd ; that is, every scrap of verse or prose printed in Professor Boas' book, including *Tychbornes Elegie*, and excepting only the German version of *The Spanish Tragedie*, and, of course, the *Fragments of a Theological Disputation* quoted by Professor Boas in his Introduction, pp. cx to cxiii. Even marginal notes are given, and these are distinguished from the text by having placed after the line-numbers a small « a ».

The volume will include, as an appendix, a concordance to Professor Edward Dowden's version of *Hamlet*, as printed in *The Arden Shakespeare*, published by Messrs Methuen and Co, 36, Essex Street, Strand, London ; and mingled with it will be found a further corcordance to the 1603 quarto of the same play, this latter reproducing the original spelling and punctuation. These two texts of *Hamlet* have been carefully collated with the First Folio play ; and the more important variations in all three will be duly recorded. It is hoped that this addition will result in lightening the labour of those who are interested in investigating the claim of Kyd to the *Ur-Hamlet* on which it is fairly evident Shakespeare founded his great tragedy. In any case, a concordance to the quarto play cannot but be useful to all students of the Elizabethan drama.

My most grateful thanks are given to Professor Bang for much encouragement, and the trouble he has put himself to in the publishing of this work.

Charles CRAWFORD.

ABBREVIATIONS USED.

The version of Kyd's work followed in this concordance is that edited by Professor Frederick S. Boas, and published by The Clarendon Press Oxford, 1901. *Arden of Feversham* was copied from the Reverend Ronald Bayne's edition of the play published in 1897 by Messrs J. M. Dent and Co., Aldine House, London.

Puck = Letter to Sir John Puckering.
ST = The Spanish Tragedie.
STA = The Spanish Tragedie Additions.
ST Bal. = The Spanish Tragedie Ballad.
SP = Soliman and Perseda.
Cor. = Cornelia.
HP Ind. = Index to The Housholders Philosophie.
HP = The Housholders Philosophie.
JB = The Murder of John Brewen.
Eng. Parn. = England's Parnassus.
Jer. = The First Part of Jeronimo.
VPJ = Verses of Prayse and Joye.
Ard. = Arden of Feversham.

WORDS OMITTED.

Conivrationem — V. P. J. Title C. hexasticon
Fallow — Ard. 1361 flowers do sometimes spring in f. lands
Gildest — Cor. 1903 O radiant Sunne that slightly guildst our dayes

---0---

KEY TO THE KYD CONCORDANGE.

PAGE IN BOAS	SUBJECT	TOP LINE
Intr.	Letter to Sir John Puckering	
CVIII	»	1
CIX	»	21
CX	»	60
1	The Spanish Tragedie	Title
4	»	1
5	»	20
6	»	56
7	»	90
8	»	123
9	»	156
10	»	189
11	»	220
12	»	251
13	»	289
14	»	321
15	»	358
16	»	387
17	»	421
18	»	456
19	»	489
20	»	521
1	»	553
2	»	580
3	»	614
4	»	649
5	»	684
6	»	714
7	»	746
8	»	778
9	»	813
30	»	844
1	»	874
2	»	904
3	»	937
4	»	973
5	»	1003
6	»	1022
7	»	1053
8	»	1083
9	»	1114
40	»	1143
1	»	1178
2	»	1208
3	»	1235
4	»	1263
5	»	1295
6	»	1326
7	»	1360
8	»	1391
9	»	1418
50	»	1452
1	»	1487
2	»	1522
3	»	1553

PAGE IN BOAS	SUBJECT	TOP LINE
4	The Spanish Tragedie, cont	1590
5	»	1620
6	»	1647
7	»	1681
8	»	1717
9	»	1744
60	»	1777
1	»	1807
2	»	1836
3	»	1869
4	»	1904
5	»	1937
6	»	1971
7	»	2008
8	»	2041
9	»	2082
70	»	2114
1	»	2145
2	»	2174
3	»	2205
4	»	2235
5	»	2270
6	»	2299
7	»	2333
8	»	2368
9	»	2398
80	»	2432
1	»	2457
2	»	2485
3	»	2520
4	»	2553
5	»	2589
6	»	2622
7	»	2656
8	»	2681
9	»	2713
90	»	2743
1	»	2770
2	»	2805
3	»	2840
4	»	2875
5	»	2910
6	»	2943
7	»	2983
8	»	3010
9	»	3048
101	Cornelia	Title
2	»	Dedicat
3	»	Argum
105	»	1
6	»	28
7	»	65
8	»	102
9	»	142

PAGE IN BOAS	SUBJECT	TOP LINE
110	Cornelia, cont	180
1	»	215
2	»	248
3	»	286
4	»	324
5	»	364
6	»	404
7	»	442
8	»	480
9	»	517
120	»	554
1	»	594
2	»	631
3	»	663
4	»	699
5	»	737
6	»	774
7	»	810
8	»	848
9	»	882
130	»	917
1	»	951
2	»	989
3	»	1024
4	»	1059
5	»	1092
6	»	1132
7	»	1172
8	»	1211
9	»	1249
140	»	1286
1	»	1324
2	»	1359
3	»	1397
4	»	1436
5	»	1474
6	»	1509
7	»	1545
8	»	1577
9	»	1608
150	»	1643
1	»	1683
2	»	1723
3	»	1761
4	»	1799
5	»	1838
6	»	1874
7	»	1912
8	»	1952
9	»	1989
160	»	2027
1	Soliman & Perseda	Title
164	»	1
5	»	21

KEY TO THE KYD CONCORDANCE

PAGE IN BOAS	SUBJECT	TOP LINE	PAGE IN BOAS	SUBJECT	TOP LINE	PAGE IN BOAS	SUBJECT	TOP LINE
166	Soliman & Perseda, Contd	57	231	The Housholders Philosophie	Title	292	The Murder of John Brewen, Contd	180
7	»	95		»	Dedicaton	3	»	220
8	»	129		»	Index	294	England's Parnassus	1
9	»	161	234	»	1		Add, as line 15,	
170	»	197	5	»	24		« He liveth long that lives	
1	»	231	6	»	64		victorious. »	
2	»	268	7	»	97	295	The First Part of Jeronimo	Title
3	»	299	8	»	127	298	»	1
4	»	330		»	Pamphlet	9	»	19
5	»	361	239	»	1	300	»	55
6	»	393	240	»	27	1	»	89
7	»	426	1	»	67	2	»	125
8	»	460	2	»	105	3	»	152
9	»	494	3	»	144	4	»	187
180	»	530	4	»	188	5	»	215
1	»	568	5	»	223	6	»	246
2	»	604	6	»	263	7	»	276
3	»	638	7	»	302	8	»	307
4	»	667	8	»	340	9	»	338
5	»	703	9	»	380	310	»	370
6	»	738	250	»	418	1	»	394
7	»	772	1	»	458	2	»	424
8	»	812	2	»	498	3	»	455
9	»	847	3	»	538	4	»	493
190	»	881	4	»	576	5	»	530
1	»	908	5	»	616	6	»	566
2	»	945	6	»	656	7	»	596
3	»	981	7	»	694	8	»	628
4	»	1011	8	»	734	9	»	661
5	»	1047	9	»	773	320	»	693
6	»	1082	260	»	811	1	»	723
7	»	1110	1	»	850	2	»	757
8	»	1144	2	»	890	3	»	793
9	»	1179	3	»	930	4	»	819
200	»	1217	4	»	967	5	»	847
1	»	1253	5	»	1007	6	»	881
2	»	1282	6	»	1047	7	»	915
3	»	1314	7	»	1084	8	»	944
4	»	1340	8	»	1124	9	»	969
5	»	1372	9	»	1164	330	»	994
6	»	1401	270	»	1204	1	»	1023
7	»	1437	1	»	1244	2	»	1050
8	»	1473	2	»	1284	3	»	1076
9	»	1509	3	»	1324	4	»	1104
210	»	1544	4	»	1364	5	»	1136
1	»	1583	5	»	1402	6	»	1164
2	»	1623	6	»	1442	7	»	1189
3	»	1654	7	»	1482			
4	»	1689	8	»	1522	339	Verses of Prayse and Joye	Title
5	»	1724	9	»	1562		»	1
6	»	1753	280	»	1602	340	»	15
7	»	1788	1	»	1640	1	»	51
8	»	1821	2	»	1682	2	»	83
9	»	1857	3	»	1722	343	The Ballad of The Spanish Tragedie	Title
220	»	1893	4	»	1760	4	»	1
1	»	1926	285	The Murder of John Brewen	Title	5	»	25
2	»	1956		»	Pamphlet	6	»	69
3	»	1990	287	»	1	7	»	109
4	»	2027	8	»	26		»	153
5	»	2059	9	»	64			
6	»	2093	290	»	102			
7	»	2128	1	»	142			
8	»	2164						
9	»	2197						

KEY TO THE KYD CONCORDANCE,

PAGE IN DENT	SUBJECT	TOP LINE	PAGE IN DENT	SUBJECT	TOP LINE	PAGE IN DENT	SUBJECT	TOP LINE
1	Arden of Feversham,	1	37	Arden of Feversham, cont⁴	872	73	Arden of Feversham. cont⁴	1685
2	»	15	8	»	898	4	»	1708
3	»	41	9	»	926	5	»	1732
4	»	65	40	»	951	6	»	1756
5	»	90	1	»	972	7	»	1774
6	»	114	2	»	988	8	»	1800
7	»	140	3	»	1011	9	»	1827
8	»	165	4	»	1036	80	»	1848
9	»	188	5	»	1062	1	»	1874
10	»	215	6	»	1083	2	»	1897
1	»	243	7	»	1107	3	»	1913
2	»	267	8	»	1134	4	»	1929
3	»	291	9	»	1152	5	»	1954
4	»	314	50	»	1178	6	»	1977
5	»	341	1	»	1196	7	»	2003
6	»	366	2	»	1220	8	»	2028
7	»	391	3	»	1241	9	»	2054
8	»	416	4	»	1267	90	»	2079
9	»	442	5	»	1294	1	»	2103
20	»	466	6	»	1321	2	»	2128
1	»	493	7	»	1349	3	»	2151
2	»	518	8	»	1374	4	»	2171
3	»	541	9	»	1391	5	»	2193
4	»	567	60	»	1417	6	»	2217
5	»	592	1	»	1437	7	»	2242
6	»	618	2	»	1463	8	»	2262
7	»	641	3	»	1487	9	»	2285
8	»	654	4	»	1510	100	»	2309
9	»	681	5	»	1533	1	»	2334
30	»	709	6	»	1538	2	»	2346
1	»	734	7	»	1552	3	»	2365
2	»	759	8	»	1576	4	»	2381
3	»	776	9	»	1598	5	»	2399
4	»	799	70	»	1621	6	»	2420
5	»	819	1	»	1644		»	
6	»	845	2	»	1664			

A.

Jer. 225 heere is a slave just *a.* the stampe I wish
STA 2968 hee might *a.* come to weare the crowne of Spaine

Abactae.

HP 1322 Inde, ubi prima quies medio jam noctis *a.*

Abandon.

SP 724 therefore be blithe, sweet love, *a.* feare

Abandoned.

SP 1579 then let him live abandond and forlorne

Abashed.

HP 201 are more abasht with the company of women

Abbey.

Ard. 5 all the lands of the *a.* of Feversham
Ard. 294 the *a.* lands, whereof you are now possessed
Ard. 461 of all the lands of the *a.* of Feversham
Ard. 482 he shall wish the *a.* lands had rested still
Ard. 536 from whom my husband had the *a.* land
Ard. 737 hath highly wronged me about the *a.* land
Ard. 2040 that done, bear him behind the *a.*
Ard. 2198 I saw him walking behind the *a.* even now
Ard. 2297 behind the *a.* there he lies murdered

Abel.

JB 10 the blood of the just *A.* cried most shrill

Abhor.

Cor. 1139 that thys hand (though Caesar blood *a.*)
Ard. 141 as I *a.* him and love only thee
Cor. 1034 mischaunce, that every man abhors
Ard. 54 though this abhors from reason, yet I'll try it

Abhorring.

Cor. 1527 and (*a.* blood) at last pardon'd all offences

Abide.

Cor. 414 (enlarg'd) to drowne the payne it did *a.*
Cor. 907 mongst whom there dooth *a.* all treason
ST 266 will both *a.* the censure of my doome?
Ard. 1393 or dare *a.* the noise the dag will make
JB 79 neither could she *a.* to be called after his name

Abideth.

HP 105 a Courtier in Rome, and that yet *a.* there

Ability.

HP 1306 necessary and fitt for the *a.* and credite of her house

Abject.

Jer. 1120 O *a.* prince, what, doost thou yeild to two?

Able.

HP 235 of *a.* and sufficient yeeres
HP 848 in wares if they be *a.*, they may shew themselves
HP 1341 not rych that was not *a.* to maintaine an Armie
Jer. 23 *a.* to ravish even my sence away
Jer. 773 speech; tis *a.* to infect a vertuous eare
ST 2807 were she *a.*, thus she would revenge thy treacheries

Aboard.

Jer. 176 are all things abord?
Jer. 404 our selfe in person will see thee safe aboard

Aboarding.

SP 200 even to the verge of golde, aboording Spaine (Boas, abounding)

Abode.

HP 72 no neede to doubt of your *a.*

Abolish.

Ard. 768 Ah, Mistress Susan, *a.* that paltry painter

Abominable.

HP 227 (which is most abhominable)

Abound.

HP 1466 where things superfluously abounde

Aboundant see Abundant.

Aboundeth.

VPJ 8 and everywhere *a.* godly love

HP 383 fruits, whereof Autumn most *a.*
HP 798 that first age *a.* in naturall heate

Abounding.

Cor. 1911 worne with mishaps, yet in mishaps *a.*
SP 200 even to the verge of golde *a.* Spaine (Qq. golde, aboording *etc*)

About.

HP 1 *a.* that time of the yeere that
HP 7 and turning me *a.*, I beheld a little kidde
HP 89 *a.* the which were prettie lodgings
HP 150 and then he decks his boord *a.* with meats
HP 408 it the[n] began *a.* the Spring
HP 478 with the dysease of those that are *a.* us
HP 481 *a.* that time that Charles the fift
HP 1254 eyther from the Countrey, or bought *a.* in Markets
Cor. Arg. 32 reduc'd the Townes and places there-*a.*
Cor. 929 and round *a.* the wronged people leape
Cor. 1216 a fore-game fecht *a.* for civill discord
Cor. 1481 maintaine a watchfull guard *a.* your gate
Cor. 1550 purest blood *a.* the heart
Cor. 1647 leaving theyr crannyes to goe search *a.*
Cor. 1743 fly forth as thicke as moates *a.* the Sunne
Cor. 1790 marcht through the battaile (laying still *a.* him)
Jer. 584 tis all *a.* the court in every eare
Jer. 630 tis all *a.* the Court Andreas come
Jer. 708 questioned me? bout love?
Jer. 1023 tis now *a.* the heavy dread of battaile
Jer. 1189 looke well *a.* thee, imbrace them
ST Bal 79 then frantickly I ran *a.*
ST Bal 99 that frantickly I ran *a.*
ST 212 goe, let them march once more *a.* these walles
ST 610 by force, or faire meanes will I cast *a.*
ST 993 and learne by whom all this was brought *a.*
ST 1370 and be advisde that none be there *a.*
ST 1613 dauncing *a.* his newly healed wounds
ST 1900 stand from *a.* me
ST 3044 hang Balthazar *a.* Chimeras neck
SP 578 shouldst come *a.* the person of a King
SP 871 why then, lets make us ready, and *a.* it.
SP 953 I doe not love to preach with a haulter *a.* my necke
SP 993 weele lay the ports and havens round *a.*
SP 1016 my maister wore the chaine *a.* his necke
SP 1038 so will I soare *a.* the Turkish land
SP 1322 *a.* it then
SP 1498 and all the Graces smiling round *a.* her
SP 1718 and ile stay heere *a.* my maisters busines
SP 1721 tis noisd *a.* that Brusor is sent to fetch
SP 1723 therefore ile *a.* it straight
Ard. 70 instead of him, caught me *a.* the neck
Ard. 418 I am glad he is gone; he was *a.* to stay
Ard. 572 to London, for to bring his death *a.*
Ard. 675 to London, Will, *a.* a piece of service
Ard. 694 a mutchado, which he wound *a.* his ear
Ard. 737 hath highly wronged me *a.* the Abbey land
Ard. 1089 Greene, get you gone, and linger here *a.*
Ard. 1102 were't not a serious thing we go about
Ard. 1164 that sees a lion foraging *a.*
Ard. 1166 he pries *a.* with timorous suspect
Ard. 1498 I have divers matters to talk with you *a.*
Ard. 1770 about the plat of ground which
Ard. 1932 the notches of his tallies and beat them *a.* his head
Ard. 1934 and carried him *a.* the fields on a coltstaff.
Ard. 2003 this night I rose and walked *a.* the chamber
Ard. 2317 and look *a.* this chamber where we are
Ard. 2384 *a.* a letter I brought from Master Greene
JB 87 free accesse to practise with her *a.* the murther

JB 127 hee began to waxe very ill *a.* the stomack

Above.

HP 80 divers roomes and stories, one *a.* another

HP 302 as that *a.* all the rest is wherof we have spoken

HP 1040 but, *a.* the rest, to have a speciall care

HP 1078 but *a.* all, me thinks, the Charitie of Maisters

HP 1284 amongst whom she shall have one *a.* the rest

HP 1370 ought *a.* all things to be diligent heerein

HP 1432 most naturall *a.* the rest must

Cor. 1 vouchsafe Immortals, and (*a.* the rest) great Jupiter

Cor. 1582 mongst whom *a.* the rest, that moves me most

Jer. 383 why should my face, thats placed *a.* my mind

Jer. 409 affect? *a.* affection, for her breast is

Jer. 829 prove honor to sore *a.* the pitch of love

Jer. 1124 Andrea slaine, thanks to the stars *a.*

Jer. 1138 the powers *a.* have writ it downe in marble leaves

ST 3046 repining at our joyes that are *a.*

SP 1059 like to the wings of lightning from *a.*

SP 1601 petition to Cupid to plague you *a.* all other

SP 2189 but I, that have power in earth and heaven *a.*

Ard. 84 he will not stay *a.* a month at most

Ard. 147 I'll see he shall not live *a.* a week

Ard. 699 a worsted stocking rent *a.* the shoe

Ard. 1303 that would have stated me *a.* thy state

Ard. 2428 but this *a.* the rest is to be noted

JB 75 maried to Brewen *a.* three dayes, whe[n] she put

JB 185 one day *a.* the rest most earnest with him to

Abraham-coloured.

SP 2006 the eldest sonne of Pryam, that *a.* Troian?

Abridged.

SP 1100 and by that chalenge I abridgde his life

Abroad.

HP 1286 though the Maister or Mistres be abroade

Cor. 732 I mov'd mine head, and flonge abroade mine armes

Cor. 1278 his glory, spred abroade by Fame

Jer. 294 go, tell it Abrod now

ST 1299 why? because he walkt *a.* so late

ST 1522 where shall I run to breath *a.* my woes

Ard. 2192 because her husband is *a.* so late

Ard. 2238 and there are many false knaves *a.*

Abruptly.

ST 2260 lips murmure sad words *a.* broken off

Absence.

HP 924 in the *a.* of their Maisters record the things commaunded

Jer. 179 be in my *a.* my deare selfe, chast selfe

ST 677 least *a.* make her thinke thou dost amisse

ST 911 my husbands *a.* makes my heart to throb

SP 1543 and from whose *a.* I derived my sorrow

Ard. 765 so I, mourning for your *a.*, do walk

JB 120 this sly shift she devised to have his *a.*

Absent.

HP 211 *a.* and imployed otherwise

HP 645 (beeing *a.* for a season from his wife)

Cor. 416 (to *a.* me from thys hatefull light)

Jer. 559 Jeronimo lives much *a.* from the Court

Jer. 560 and being *a.* there, lives from report

ST 1706 to *a.* your selfe, and give his fury place

Absistam.

ST 1009 At tamen *a.* properato cedere letho

Absolute.

HP 1546 Kings, Tyrants, and other *a.* Princes

HP 1598 said to have no end or *a.* determination

Absolutely.

HP 979 our plain distinction that *a.* will resolve thee

Abstain.

HP 646 he cannot abstaine from pleasures of the flesh

Abstracts.

ST 2617 and heere, my Lords, are severall *a.* drawne

Abstulit.

HP 564 Ille meos, primus qui me sibi junxit, Amores *a.*

Abundance.

HP 163 I have aboundaunce of every thing

HP 334 all sorts of fruite in great aboundance

HP 1249 great aboundaunce of the yere and fruitfulnes of seasons

HP 1496 where in most aboundaunce, where in lesse

Abundant.

Jer. 981 O aboundant joy

Abuse.

Cor. 1030 power and will t'*a.* the vulgar wanting skill

Cor. 1597 and, Madam, let not griefe *a.* your wisdom

ST 1014 and they *a.* fair Bel-imperia

ST 1662 and with extreames *a.* my company

SP 284 take you the Latins part? ile *a.* you to

SP 808 couldst thou *a.* my true simplicitie

SP 1590 what was it but *a.* of Fortunes gift?

SP 1592 what was it but *a.* of Loves commaund?

SP 1594 what was it but *a.* of heavens that gave her me?

Abused.

HP 1177 or *a.* by his Factor, beeing a Merchaunt

HP 1595 it is used beyond the proper use, and so *a.*

Ard. 508 so fair a creature should be so *a.*

Ard. 1870 poor wench *a.* by thy misgovernment!

Abusest.

SP 283 Thou *a.* the phrase of the Latine

Ard. 1105 I tell thee thee, Shakebag, thou *a.* me

Abuseth.

STA 2091 but reason *a.* me, and there's the torment

Abutting.

Ard. 1140; see **Butting**

Aby.

SP 1982 thou shalt abie for both your trecheries

Accent.

Jer. 51 if friendly phraises, honied speech, bewitching *a.*

Accept.

HP 67 necessity now bound me to *a.* his courtesie

HP 77 the more shall I *a.* of it

SP 71 which to effect, *a.* this carkanet

SP 78 *a.* this ring to equall it

SP 2099 I loved thee deerelie, and *a.* thy kisse

Acceptable.

HP 242 was more *a.* to the Sonne than

HP 310 pleasing to the sences or *a.* to the minde

HP 398 most *a.* to the Housekeeper

HP 475 it shall be very *a.* unto mee to heare

Access.

Cor. 677 to whom in doubtfull things we seeke accesse

ST 2401 because you have not accesse unto the King

JB 87 free accesse to practise with her about the murther

Accident.

HP 583 by some *a.* of Fortune, a man marrieth a

Cor. 649 but what disastrous or hard *a.*

Cor. 1617 and what disastrous *a.* did breake

ST 1575 of everie *a.* I neere could finde till now

ST 1009 what *a.* hath hapt Hieronimo?

SP 917 to cross me with this haplesse accedent?

SP 1549 by this one accedent I well perceive that

Ard. 875 this *a.* of meeting him in Paul's

Cor. 345 the wide worlds *a.* are apt to change

Accidental.

HP 1161 some expence which (beeing accidentall) cannot

Accited *see* **'Cited.**

Accompanied.
HP 589 which honor is not yet *a.* with reverence
HP 786 and is as easily *a.* with love
HP 951 the mind also of Servaunts is *a.* with reason
HP 1782 arose and *a.* me unworthy to the Chamber
ST 1691 by being found so meanely *a.*
SP 275 O heaven, she comes, *a.* with a child
Accompanies.
Cor. 96 hatred *a.* prosperitie
Ard. 1014 woes *a.* this gentle gentleman !
Accompany.
ST 2305 *a.* thy friend with thine extremities
Accomplish.
SP 637 I did *a.* on Haleb and Amurath
Ard. 950 I will *a.* all I have revealed
Accomplished.
HP 75 so well *a.* an Hoste
HP 513 have easely accomplisht what he
Cor. Ded. 15 a fitter present for a Patronesse so well *a.*
Cor. Arg. 2 as much accomplisht with the graces of the bodie
Accomplishment.
SP 390 so yong, and of such good *a.*
Accord.
SP 377 *a.* to his request, brave man at armes
According.
HP Ded. yet truely set *a.* to the sence
HP 243 and he, *a.* to my remembraunce
HP 417 *a.* to the motion of the *Primum mobile*
HP 418 or *a.* to the motion of the Sun
HP 424 *a.* therefore to the motions of the Sun
HP 425 *a.* to the motion of the *Primum mobile*
HP 430 *a.* to the custome of nature
HP 450 *a.* to the Cosmographicall dyscription of some
HP 602 (*a.* to the testimony of Hesiodus)
HP 775 punish her *a.* to the Lawes
HP 1017 fare as *a.* to the season shall be happilye purveighed
HP 1163 though they be divers *a.* to the variety of Countreys
HP 1256 in severall places *a.* to their natures
HP 1372 *a.* to their quallitie
HP 1437 distinguished *a.* to the distinction of Beastes
HP 1538 living well, *a.* to his estate
HP 1607 Number is reputed either *a.* to the formall or materiall beeing
HP 1681 *a.* as God commaunded the first man
Cor. 299 (*a.* to th' encountring passages)
Jer. 792 *a.* [to] your gratious, dread Comand
SP 372 *a.* to the proclimation made
SP 1043 faire Love, *a.* unto thy commaund
Accordingly.
JB 222 this was *a.* performed, and they were executed
Account.
HP 404 Doctors of the Hebrues, and Christians of great *a.*
HP 587 and not only to *a.* her his companion in love
HP 715 the more convenient it is that they *a.* of it
HP 1049 spoile thinges otherwise of value and *a.*
HP 1189 as other meane things, or things of more *a.*
HP 1297 keeping just *a.* of things that are to be accounted
HP 1472 if they were small, were base and but of vile *a.*
Cor. 1097 they care not for us, nor *a.* of men
ST 545 the third and last, not least in our *a.*
SP 1168 Christians *a.* our Turkish race but barbarous
SP 1652 the Turkes, whom they *a.* for barbarous
Accounted.
HP 107 in these quarters highly are accou[n]ted
HP 109 knowne, and not *a.* of ?
HP 1182 that which is *a.*, (as gold or silver coyned)

HP 1297 keeping just account of things that are to be *a.*
Accoustrements.
Cor. 2000 careles of Arte, or rich *a.*
Accrebbe.
HP 1341 Scemó la notte, quanto il giorno *a.*
Accumulate.
HP 1597 multiply or accumulat infinite and excessive profits
Accurse.
SP 2121 ah no, the heavens did neuer more *a.* me
Accursed.
Cor. 178 which, where it lights, doth show the Land accurst
Cor. 208 *a.* Catives, wretches that wee are
Cor. 1079 *a.* Rome, that arm'st against thy selfe a Tyrants rage
Cor. 1091 O Rome, *a.* Rome, thou murdrest us
Jer. 697 why speaks not this *a.*, damned villaine ?
Jer. 710 object mine eies met was that most accurst
Jer. 716 others take charg of that *a.* villaine
Jer. 737 wherefore didst thou this *a.* deed ?
Jer. 743 say, slave, how came this *a.* evill ?
ST 1060 and let him die for this *a.* deed
ST 1096 *a.* wretch, to intimate these ills
ST 1562 and actors in th' *a.* Tragedie
ST 1624 *a.* brother, unkinde murderer
ST 2687 *a.* complot of my miserie
ST 2843 but night, the coverer of *a.* crimes
ST 2870 with these, O, these *a.* murderers
ST 2903 *a.* wretch, why staiest thou him
SP 599 *a.* Amurath, that for a worthlesse cause
SP 1273 *a.* chaine, unfortunate Perseda
SP 1274 *a.* chaine, unfortunate Lucina
SP 1977 *a.* Soliman, prophane Alcaron
SP 2068 thou wicked tirant, thou murtherer, *a.* homicide
Ard. 1861 *a.* to link in liking with a frantic man !
JB 66 and this *a.* Parker
JB 203 and accurst be I, if I trust thee or hazard my life
Accusations.
SP 1865 what answerest thou unto their *a.* ?
Ard. 1472 to encounter all their *a.*
Accuse.
Jer. 543 do you *a.* me so, kind Isabella ?
ST 1165 to *a.* thy brother, had he beene the meane ?
ST 1170 that thou by this Lorenzo shouldst *a.*
SP 920 and to acuse fell Fortune, Love, and Death
SP 1627 ready to *a.* him of treason
SP 1876 to moane Perseda, and *a.* my friend
Ard. 382 cannot I be ill but you'll *a.* yourself ?
Ard. 2406 leave to *a.* each other now
JB 7 albeit there was none in the world to *a.* Caine
Puck 41 I in no sort can *a.* nor will excuse by reson of
Puck 80 whom I cold justlie *a.* of that damnable offence
Accused.
ST 1074 or for thy meed hast falsely me accusde
Puck 73 their lyves that herein have *a.* me
Accustom.
HP 799 aboundeth in naturall heate, he accustome them to cold
Accustomed.
HP 61 the compasse whereunto it was *a.*
HP 836 so hardly or severely as the Lacedemonians were *a.*
HP 1003 as in great houses it hath beene *a.*
HP 1181 that which is accustomd to be numbred by Algorisme
HP 1383 *a.* to be attended on by many servants
Cor. 1394 (to conquering *a.*)
Ace.
Ard. 2148 one *a.*, or else I lose the game
Acheron.
Cor. 506 I am an offring fit for *A.*

Cor. 768 downe by the fearefull gates of *A*.
ST 19 to passe the flowing streame of *A*.
ST 2441 to combate, *A*. and Erebus,
ST 3006 or to the loathsome pool of *A*.
ST 3050 let him be dragde through boyling *A*.
Achieve.
SP 111 from whence Ile borrow what I do atchieve
Achillas.
Cor. Arg. 12 murdred by *A*. and Septimius the Romaine
Cor. 946 Photis and false *A*. he beheadded
Achilles.
HP Ind. 1 *A*. is not to bee imitated of a noble man
HP 837 or as Achylles of Chyro was
HP 841 yet was not *A*. such an one in his conditions
ST 49 and *A*. Mermedons do scoure the plaine
SP 2008 that well knit Accill[es] ? dead
Acknowledge.
HP 69 I had rather *a*. this favour
Acknown.
Cor. 450 but ours of others will not be acknowne
A'clock *see* **O'clock.**
Acquaint.
HP 1383 as hee that dooth *a*. his studie with the use of Poetry
ST 474 in plaine tearmes *a*. her with your love
STA 1199 all's one, Hieronimo, *a*. me with it
Ard. 579 what ! to *a*. each stranger with our drifts
Acquaintance.
Puck 20 my first *a*. wth this Marlowe, rose upon
Acquainted.
HP 35 you are not well *a*. with the waie
HP 1634 industrie : wherewith Usury can never be *a*.
Jer. 591 *a*. with our drift ?
Ard. 687 thou art *a*. with such companions
Acquittal.
ST 1100 to make a quittall for thy discontent.
Acquittance.
Jer. 1050 and give you *a*. with a wound or two
Ard. 842 but forbearance is no *a*.
Acquitting.
Cor. 1513 that of care *a*. us
Across.
Cor. 1752 runnes crosse the Squadrons with a smokie brand
Ard. 96 gallop with Arden 'cross the Ocean
Act.
Jer. 161 shape frightful conceit beyond the intent of *a*.
Jer. 732 and by that slave this purple *a*. was done.
Jer. 1054 for by this *a*. I hold thy arm devine
ST Bal 125 then for to *a*. this Tragedy, I gave
ST 2619 and *a*. it as occasion's offred you
ST 2648 must *a*. his parte in unknowne languages
SP 1724 what hast thou done in this latter *a*. ?
SP 2202 in this last *a*. note but the deedes of Death
Ard. 747 as if he had been condemned by an *a*. of Parliament
Jer. 853 whose servile acts live in their graves
ST 2764 how well he acts his amourous passion
SP 7 and what are Tragedies but acts of death ?
Acted.
Jer. 430 till this be *a*. I in passion burne
Jer. 905 part that must be *a*. on the feeldes greene stage
ST 2577 to have been *a*. by Gentlemen and schollers too
STA 2979 now do I applaud what I have *a*.
Acting.
ST 2558 as but to grace me with your *a*. it
ST 2742 for nothing wants but *a*. of revenge
Action.
HP Ind. 4 *a*. distinguished

HP 776 happily employed better in some other *a*.
HP 906 if he chaunce to faile in *a*., co[m]lines, or utteraunce
HP 1103 but the Servaunt is Instrument of the *a*.
HP 1106 a lively and several instrument of *a*.
Jer. 1168 use *a*., if you will, but not in voice
ST 2153 Sir, an *a*. — Of Batterie ?
ST 2155 no, sir, mine is an *a*. of the Case
ST 2642 they would performe any thing in *a*.
JB 52 she concluded, on condition he would let his *a*. fal
VPJ 10 everlasting fame attend on thee in all thine actions
HP 487 turne the eyes of all the world upon theyr actions
HP 588 (in dyvers actions of publique aparance)
HP 741 cause or procure shamefastnes in all her actions
HP 1107 of actions, some are placed in care of families
ST 2143 that I should plead their several actions ?
ST 2158 that I should plead your severall actions ?
Actionis.
HP 1105 is Animatum *a*. et Instrumentum seperabile
Actor.
ST 2889 author and *a*. in this Tragedie
SP 28 whose cheefest *a*. was my sable dart
SP 1741 the historie prooves me cheefe *a*. in this tragedie
ST 1562 and actors in th' accursed Tragedie
ST 2892 as any of the Actors gone before
SP 38 Why stay we then ? Lets give the Actors leave
SP 624 hath in the Actors showne the greatest power ?
Ard. 1249 chief actors to Arden's overthrow
Adam.
Ard. 105 and here comes *A*. of the Flower-de-luce
Ard. 107 how now, *A*., what is the news with you ?
Ard. 121 stay, *A*., stay ; thou wert wont to be my friend
Ard. 1953 Mosbie, Franklin, Bradshaw, *A*. Fowle, with divers
JB 6 The onelye sonnes of the first man, *A*.
Adamant.
ST 75 the walles of brasse, the gates of *a*.
ST 2760 whose eies compell, like powrefull *A*.
SP 249 whereby I purchased the surname of Pities adomant
SP 859 no more can flie then iron can *A*.
SP 1479 my thoughts are like pillers of *A*.
Ard. 1687 no, let our love be rocks of *a*.
Adamantic.
Jer. 605 I may possess an adimanticke power
Add.
ST 622 now to these favours will I adde reward
ST 1708 that were to adde more fewell to your fire
SP 91 and *a*. fresh courage to my fainting limmes
Ard. 2055 will *a*. unwonted courage to my thought
Jer. 1148 my boy ads treble comfort to my age
SP 1113 Ads but a trouble to my brothers ghoasts
Added.
HP (Title) with a Table *a*. thereunto of all the
HP 1385 for Poesy hath never more spirit *a*. to it
Addens.
HP 1326 Noctem *a*. operi, famulasque ad lumina longo
Adding.
HP 1331 And *a*. so unto her labors some part of the night
ST 109 that, *a*. all the pleasure of thy newes
ST 3032 *a*. sweet pleasure to eternall daies
Additions.
Jer. 295 but see you put no new aditions to it
Addressed.
Ard. 1471 *a*. herself to encounter all their accusations
Adieu.
Jer. 189 tis fixed upon my hart ; adew, soules friend
Jer. 960 Adew. — Adew. — Lets meet. — Tis meete we did
Ard. 2167 we have our gold ; Mistress Alice, *a*.

Adigat.
HP 581 Vel pater omnipotens *a.* me fulmine ad umbras
Adjacent.
HP 1216 or whether any Springs or Ryvers be *a.*
Adjoineth.
HP 1046 adjoyneth worth, and bettereth things by Nature base
Adjoining.
SP 926 if into any stay adjoyning Rhodes
Adjudge.
ST 301 seeks him whome fates adjuge to miserie
Adjuged.
Cor. 767 where, when it is by Aeacus adjudg'd
ST 619 for which thou wert adjug'd to punishment
Administration.
HP 1109 some stretch further and extend to civil *a.*
Admirable.
SP 272 the reflecting eye of that *a.* comet Perseda
Admiration.
HP 557 nor without great *a.* should Dydo have
Admire.
VPJ 11 this makes thy friends, this makes thy foes *a.*
ST 285 whome I *a.* and love for chivalrie
Admired.
HP 461 to be praised and *a.* for your speeches
Admiring.
HP 1398 seene it without disdayne and diverslie *a.* it
Admit.
Cor. 231 *a.* me passage to th' infernall Lake
ST 1214 *a.* he have not, his conditions such, as feare
SP 1477 how dooth thy heart *a.* the pure affection of
Admittance.
SP 1700 incrochest upon my familiaritie without speciall *a.* ?
Admonition.
HP 881 the Maister to give them *a.*
HP 880 with wages, meate, work, and *a.*, then
Ado.
HP 1534 cannot with much a doe pierce the out side
Ard. 1930 I made no more *a.*, but went to the clerk
JB 49 made no more adoe but arested her for the jewels
A-doors.
STA 1990 deare Hieronimo, come in a doores
STA 2034 Pedro, Jaques, goe in a doores ; Isabella, goe
STA 2088 goe in a doores, I say
Adopted.
SP 1209 and be great Solimans *a.* friend
Adore.
Cor. 1043 in hope he shall his wish obtaine, doth thee *a.*
Cor. 1282 all after ages shall *a.*
Cor. 1514 (who at last *a.* him thus)
SP 203 him we *a.*, and in his name I crie, Mahomet
SP 1657 I, fearing they would *a.* me for a God
Adorn.
HP 686 shee is so desirous to adorne and beautifie her bodie
Cor. 2014 adorne and grace his graceles Enemy ?
HP 657 no collour better graceth or adornes a womans cheekes
Adorned.
HP 626 is *a.* with those vertues
HP 688 the bodies of the Male be more *a.* then the Females
Cor. 678 by whom our family hath bene adorn'd
SP 1452 and so adornd with beauties miracle
SP 1586 the other so *a.* with grace and modestie
SP 2015 I am *a.* with natures gifts
Adorning.
HP 1383 grace and comlines in beautifying and *a.* things
Advance.
HP 1363 that in some sort she shall advaunce herselfe

ST 674 I can more *a.* thy state then she
SP 484 didst thou *a.* me for my greater fall ?
Advantage.
HP 1486 whe[n] they may utter them unto theyr most *a.*
HP 1491 wherin he shall much advauntage him and hys
ST 407 taking *a.* of his foes distresse
STA 2081 looking upon him by the *a.* of my torch
ST 2121 but in extreames *a.* hath no time
ST 2344 a small *a.* makes a water breach
ST 2846 to take *a.* in my Garden plot upon
SP 294 and at his best *a.* stole away
Ard. 956 and takes *a.* for to eat him up
ST 1393 eares, that lye too open to advantages
Ard. 1304 forslowed advantages, and spurned at time
Adventure.
ST 1263 it is no dreame that I *a.* for
Ard. 2056 make me the first that shall *a.* on him
Ard. 2376 and run full blank at all adventures
Adverse.
Cor. Arg. 28 he was assailed, beaten and assaulted by the *a.* Fleete
Cor. 1868 where th' *a.* Navie, sent to scoure the seas
Adversities.
Cor. 1019 fickle in our *a.*
Adversity.
Cor. 293 clowdes of adversitie will cover you
Advertise.
SP 476 least publike rumour might *a.* her
Advertised.
HP 778 he shall never neede to be *a.* by us
HP 1175 beeing well *a.* and instructed
Advice.
Jer. 337 we have with best advise thought of our state
ST 771 yet heerein shall she follow my *a.*
Advise.
HP 22 I would *a.* you, if it please you, to
HP 31 you shall *a.* your selfe
HP 204 wel that you begin to *a.* your selfe
HP 816 so yet I thinke good to *a.* thee that
HP 860 *a.* and counsell that thou bring them upp in
HP 1233 if (like a good husband) thou *a.* thee and consider it
ST 774 *a.* thy King to make this marriage up
ST 1168 *a.* thee therefore, be not credulous
ST 1669 *a.* you better, Bel-imperia
ST 2991 heere, and *a.* thee that thou write the troth
SP 470 I *a.* you meddle with no chaines of mine
Advised.
HP 989 they advisde to carry with them to the field
HP 1178 as I have said that he ought to be *a.*
HP 1695 those things whereof I have *a.* thee
Jer. 785 our setled Judgment hath *a.* us what
ST 1370 and be advisde that none be there about
ST 1893 Hieronimo, you are not well advisde
ST 2447 for thou art ill advisde to sleepe away what
JB 193 I would be twice *a.* how I did wed with such a
Cor. 1387 that (ill advis'd) repined at my glory
Advocate.
HP 243 an honest advocat to pleade my cause
ST 2146 there is not any *A.* in Spaine that can
Aeacus.
Cor. 767 where, when it is by *A.* adjudg'd
ST 33 sate Minos, Eacus, and Rhadamant
ST 41 why then, said Eacus, convay him hence
ST 2232 goe backe, my sonne, complaine to Eacus
Aeneades.
HP 559 thus in the book of Virgils Aeneidos

Aeneas

HP 820 in that same booke of his Aeneidos maketh mention
Cor. 1506 and faire Venus, thou of whom the Eneades are come

Aeneas.

HP 268 Virgil likewise inducith A. that in
HP 284 Virgil, speaking of A. soldiours

Aeolus.

SP 1033 but, Eolus and Neptune, let him go

Aequinoctial *see* **Equinoctial.**

Aesop's.

Cor. 816 lyke morall Esops mysled Country swaine
Ard. 1414 I pray you, sirs, list to A. talk

Aetas.

HP 662ᵃ formam populabitur a.

Aether.

ST 103 O multum dilecte Deo, tibi militat a.

Aetna.

ST 1709 your fire, who burnt like Aetne for Andreas losse
SP 2177 and boyles, like Etna, in my frying guts

Afeared.

Cor. 771 to walke by night, or make the wise afeard
Cor. 1640 but, being afeard to loose so fit a place
Jer. 548 if it were not so, you would not be afeard to

Affable.

SP 2135 kinde, euen to his foes, gentle and a.

Affairs.

HP 1004 the Baylieffe, to whom the Toun affaires belong
HP 1112 to write and mannedge some of their affaires
HP 1769 usd and exercised in affaires of more estate
Cor. Arg. 8 the incertaine successe of those affaires
Cor. Arg. 18 after he had ordred the affayres of Egipt
Cor. 1096 they leave to see into the worlds affaires
ST 1030 as Fortune toyleth in the affaires of Kings
SP 1764 great affaires, importuning health and wealth of Soliman
Ard. 83 no longer there till my a. be done
Ard. 777 stand you here loitering, knowing my a.

Affect.

Jer. 408 do you a. my sister ?
Jer. 400 a. ? above affection, for her breast is

Affecting.

HP 1087 good servants, liking and a. of their Maisters

Affection.

Jer. 326 my masters love, peace, and a.
Jer. 409 affect ? above a., for her breast is
Jer. 415 on whom my Sister Bellimperia casts her a.
SP 682 to coole a. with our woords and lookes
SP 1311 and cloake a. with hir modestie
SP 1478 the pure a. of great Soliman ?
SP 1540 what words in a. doe I see ?
SP 792 shouldst pawne my true affections pledge to
SP 1610 that I may plead in your affections cause
HP 633 compell affections to be subject unto reason
HP 652 amongst which three affectio[n]s Feare is
Cor. 156 but in commaunding our affections
Jer. 751 for her affections were all firmly planted in
SP 1526 that cannot governe private fond affections ?

Affectionate.

HP Dedic. your worships most a. T. K.

Affirmed.

Puck. 17 toching that opinion, affirmd by Marlowe to be his

Afflict.

Cor. 1495 the feare of evill doth a. us more then
SP 1184 least with the discourse thou shouldst a. thy selfe

Afflicted.

Cor. 896 and out-rag'd over an a. soule

Afflictions.

Cor. Ded. 2 traveld with th' a. of the minde

ST 2916 avenged with greater far than these a.
STA 2939 revenged with greater far then these a.

Afford.

Cor. 338 what end (O race of Scipio) will the Fates a. your
Cor. 648 a. no hope of future happinesse
Cor. 1758 which in her rage free passage doth a.
Jer. 184 I could a. [it] well, didst thou stay here
Jer. 633 so slack in murder not to a. me notice
ST 2921 what lesser libertie can Kings affoord then
ST 2922 then harmeles silence ? then affoord it me
SP 1359 the greatest honor Fortune could affoord
Cor. Ded. 3 then which the world affoords no greater misery
Jer. 14 and more, what speech afords, Ile speak in drops
ST 812 with greatest pleasure that our Court affords
ST 2135 thy tung to milder speeches then thy spirit affords
SP 1328 if you resist, expect what warre affordes

Affordeth.

HP 618 that ponderous and heavie loade which our humanity a.

Affranius.

Cor. 1104 A. and Faustus murdred dyed

Affray *see* **Fray.**

Affright.

Cor. 56 and whom (save heaven) nothing could afright
Cor. 867 and when the man that had afright the earth
ST 1601 good Madam, a. not thus yourselfe
ST 1661 first, to a. me with thy weapons drawne
SP 2167 a. me not with sorrowes and laments

Affront.

Cor. 1898 he durst a. me and my warlike bands
Cor. 808 the men, the Ships, wher-with poore Rome affronts him

A-fire.

STA 2084 the house is a., the house is a.
Ard. 1658 then looks he as if his house were a.

A-foot.

HP 30 seeing him a foote

Afore.

SP 1069 a bout at cuffes, a. you and I part

Afore-God.

STA 2048 Bazardo, afore-god, an excellent fellow

Aforesaid.

ST 60 on the right hand side was ready way unto the foresaid fields
SP 309 & 310 I, the a. Basilisco

Afraid.

Cor. 1897 beeing a. t'attend the mercy of his
Ard. 108 be not a. ; my husband is now from home
Ard. 2194 and she, poor soul, is a. he should be hurt
Ard. 2307 I was so a. I knew not what I did

A-fresh.

Cor. 1835 he that had hap to scape, doth helpe a. to

Afric.

HP Ind. 91 harts not bredde in Affrick
HP 268 Aeneas that in Affrick slew seaven Harts
HP 270 for in Affrick are no Harts bred
Cor. Arg. 17 and occupied the greater part of Afrique
Cor. Arg. 26 a Towne in Affrique at the devotion of Caesar
Cor. Arg. 35 these crosse events and haples newes of Affrique
Cor. 136 what interest had they to Afferique ?
Cor. 482 that Romes high worth to Affrique did extend
Cor. 674 and bring from Affrique to our Capitoll
Cor. 682 and that my Father now (in th' Affrique wars)
Cor. 1185 both Gaule and Affrique perrish by his warres
Cor. 1503 that from sable Affrique brings conquests
Cor. 1601 an hoste of men to Affrique meanely Arm'd
Cor. 1974 through the slaughter th'Affrique seas were dide
SP 197 the desert plaines of Affricke have I staind

African.
Cor. 679 and graced with the name of Affrican
Cor. 1397 discent of Affrican (so fam'd for Armes)
Affric-walls.
Cor. 1969 when thwarting Destinie at Affrique walls did
After.
VPJ (2nd Title) a. the apprehension and execution of Babington
HP 154 neede not mervaile if, I, a. their fashion
HP 170 a. the manner of our petit Countries
HP 248 backt a. the manner of mynced meate
HP 250 drest, a. our Countrey fashion, with Larde
HP 268 where, a. the judgment of some, it shold
HP 474 who a. a while returning, I beganne
HP 549 as a. that the bande that tyes the
HP 1060 a. the imitation of Virgil, who, before he
HP 1329 a. midnight did the woman wake
Cor. Arg. 6 Pompey the great, who (three yeeres a.)
Cor. Arg. 14 a. which, shee retyred herselfe to Rome
Cor. Arg. 16 of those that survived a. the battaile
Cor. Arg. 18 a. he had ordred the affayres of Egipt
Cor. Arg. 20 and there (a. many light encounters) was
Cor. 60 (a martiall people madding a. Armes)
Cor. 271 oathes made in marriage, and a. broke
Cor. 590 forsaken as before, yet a. are re-edified
Cor. 916 due punishment succeeds not alwaies a. an offence
Cor. 1170 and shortly a. (backt with wintered souldiers
Cor. 1409 to see theyr Caesar, a. dangers past
Cor. 1949 my hard mishap in marrying a. thee
ST 432 for a. him thou hast deserved it best
ST 540 he a. was created Duke of Yorke
ST 785 he shall enjoy the kingdome a. us
STA 963 if it should proove my sonne now a. all
STA 2067 then, sir, a. some violent noyse, bring
ST 2226 tushe, no ; run a. catch me if you can
ST 2469 but a. them doth Himen hie as fast
ST 2995 hope that Spaine expected a. my discease
SP 463 that am to make inquirie a, it
SP 486 in hunting a. praise, I lost my love
SP 541 a. so many valiant Bassowes slaine
SP 556 a. his Highnes sweares it shall be so ?
SP 1002 a. my most hearty commendations
SP 1014 a. we had got the chaine in mummery
SP 1219 but ever a. thy continuall friend
SP 1309 but I will a. my delitious love
SP 1686 came like a coward stealing a. me
SP 1717 I will a. to take revenge
SP 1784 and a. make repentance of the deed
SP 2140 and a. tempt so vertuous a woman ?
Ard. 286 and he shalt die within an hour a.
Ard. 1122 but rust and canker a. I have sworn
Ard. 1191 speak, milksop slave, and never a. speak
Ard. 1246 and a. smother him to have his wax
Ard. 1487 my man's coming a., but
Ard. 1580 so, fair weather a. you
Ard. 1896 ay, a. he had reviled him
Ard. 1927 I have pierced one barrel a. another
Ard. 2133 thou ne'er shalt see me more a. this night
Ard. 2432 two years and more a. the deed was done
JB (Title) two yeares a. the murther was committed
JB 73 a. which deede done, Parker promised to
JB 78 lay not with him a. the first night of
JB 80 neither could she abide to be called a. his name
JB 88 the Wednesday a. she was married she
JB 126 within a pretty while a. hee had eaten his
JB 133 and immediatlie a. he began to vomet exceedingly
JB 153 immediatly a. he had eaten it, he dyed

JB 160 within a small space a. her husband was dead
JB 180 the space of two yeares a. her husband was dead
JB 207 poyson, and a. thy direction I did minister it unto him
JB 217 to be delivered of her childe, and a. brought back
JB 224 two yeares and a halfe a. the murder was committed
After-ages.
Cor. 1282 all after ages shall adore
After-aid.
Cor. 1209 to make an Armie for his after-ayde against
After-good.
Cor. 15 which to preserve (unto our after good) our fathers
After-harms.
Cor. 196 head-long to runne and reck no after harmes
After-times.
ST 2492 be not a historie to after times
Afterward.
HP 326 a. Homer calleth it black
HP 331 and a., beeing begun to by him, I pledged
HP 431 things are first ingendred and a. corrupted
HP 875 and a. called servaunts a seruando
HP 1200 a. (by the lawe of man) was money invented
Cor. Arg. 5 a. she tooke to second husbande Pompey
Cor. 2032 and a. (both wanting strength and moysture
STA 2982 first take my tongue, and a. my hart
JB 53 and not to think ever the worse of her a.
HP 1561 afterwards devided and begueathed amongst his
HP 1568 and, afterwards, disrobed of their Purple
ST 2932 first take my tung, and afterwards my heart
Ard. 1109 and afterwards attempt me when thou darest
Ard. 1146 and afterwards go hearken for the flood
After-years.
VPJ 47 thy ill spent youth thine after yeares hath nipt
Again.
HP 207 and the good man of the house beganne againe
HP 1059 The Ploughman takes his weapons once againe
HP 1132 must many times be redd and redd a. by thee
HP 1245 againe he may keepe his mony by him
HP 1272 a., there are some things, which (beeing dryed)
HP 1484 retaileth them or selleth them againe
Cor. 257 by calling Hymen once more back againe
Cor. 464 to ferry those that must be fetcht againe
Cor. 593 engendreth fountaines, whence againe those
Cor. 615 and chastest Lucrece once againe
Cor. 669 not (once againe) returne our Senators
Cor. 672 will they not once againe encourage them
Cor. 773 descends to hell, with hope to rise againe
Cor. 800 forbeare to tempt the enemy againe
Cor. 1017 she fleres againe, I know not how, still to beguile
Cor. 1531 doth oppose himselfe agen bloody minded, cruell men
Cor. 1875 which being sore beaten, till it brake agen
Jer. 193 Ile call him back againe
Jer. 400 we have fresh sperits that can renew it againe
Jer. 789 we have fresh spirites that can renew it againe
Jer. 816 you came but now, [and] must you part agen ?
Jer. 840 The drum agen. — Hath that more power then I ?
Jer. 860 let thers be equall to quit yours againe
Jer. 986 go, search agen ; bring him, or neare returne
Jer. 1020 mingle your selfe againe amidst the army
ST (Title) The Spanish Tragedie : or, Hieronimo is mad againe
ST 467 then with conceite enlarge your selfe againe
ST 646 but if thou dally once againe, thou diest
ST 803 then once againe farewell, my Lord
STA 965 let me looke againe. O God, confusion
ST 2823 and in a minute starting up againe
SP 837 if I can but get the Chaine againe
SP 991 why, ile be heere, as soone as ever I come a.

SP 1032 dreadfull Neptune, bring him backe againe
SP 1082 why, wilt thou stay till I come againe?
SP 1107 and lift him up, and throw him downe againe
SP 1371 rackt up in ashes, revives againe to flames
SP 1624 fetch him backe againe, under couler of
SP 1631 come thou againe ; but let the lady stay
SP 1722 Brusor is sent to fetch my maister back againe
SP 1732 againe I made him to recall his passions
SP 1739 Brusor is sent to fetch him back againe
SP 1951 because I now am Christian againe
SP 2154 Captaine, is Rhodes recovered againe?
Ard. 85 come a. within a day or two, or else I die
Ard. 396 lest that in tears I answer the a.
Ard. 570 and repossess his former lands a.
Ard. 646 a rogue as he, lives not a. upon the earth
Ard. 831 but, were my consent to give a., we
Ard. 1090 and at some hour hence come to us a.
Ard. 1125 and let me never draw a sword a.
Ard. 1200 ay, to my former happy life a.
Ard. 1353 be clear a., I'll ne'er more trouble thee
Ard. 1956 ah, gentle Michael, run thou back a.
Ard. 2028 and if he e'er go forth a., blame me
Ard. 2179 ay, well, if Arden were alive a.
Ard. 2279 peace, fool, the snow will cover them a.
Ard. 2280 but it had done before we came back a.
JB 13 blood-sheader should have his blood justly shed a.
JB 44 to demaund his golde and jewels againe
JB 46 requested that he might have his gifts againe
JB 107 while she put the posnet on the fire againe
JB 121 and by the time he came againe she had made
JB 144 the next morning she came to him againe
JB 181 at length he got her with child againe

Against.

HP 87 directly a. the Gate whereby wee entred
HP 416 the Sunne goes a. the *Primum mobile*
HP 805 to indurat and harden them a. the cold
HP 987 assembled an Armie of me[n] a. theyr servants
HP 1458 which the Knights of Malta have a. the Barbarians
HP 1463 a. the title of good Husbandry
Cor. Arg. 4 the disconfiture of the Romains a. the Parthians
Cor. Arg. 18 a. all whom Caesar (after he had ordred the
Cor. 3 that if (provok'd a. us by our evils) you
Cor. 125 and shew Gods wrath a. a cruell soule
Cor. 146 a. this Citty, ritch of violence?
Cor. 359 I saw a. poore Sylla proud Cynna
Cor. 420 exclaime and bellow forth a. the Gods
Cor. 458 a. th'inevitable dart of Death?
Cor. 529 to force us doe that goes a. our hart
Cor. 686 oppose themselves a. us in theyr wrath
Cor. 814 the sword which murdrer-like a. thy selfe he drawes
Cor. 830 a. the Samnites, Sabins, and fierce Latins?
Cor. 986 his wrath a. you t'will exasperate
Cor. 1079 that arm'st a. thy selfe a Tyrants rage
Cor. 1161 a. both Cynnas host and Marius
Cor. 1203 he rashly styrd a. us without cause
Cor. 1205 a. a harmeles Nation, kindly given
Cor. 1210 an Armie for his after-ayde a. the Romains
Cor. 1408 and in route a. thy gates they rushe
Jer. 289 intent a. the vertuous rivers of his life
ST 135 marcht forth a. him with our Musketiers
ST 411 I with my hand set foorth a. the Prince
ST 853 but first my lookes shall combat a. thine
ST 1097 a. the life and reputation of
ST 1402 were it not sin a. secrecie, I would say
ST 2237 for just revenge a. the murderers
ST 2336 and he exclaime a. thee to the King

ST 3034 a. the rest how shall my hate be showne?
SP 162 a. the light foote Irish have I served
SP 192 a. the Sophy in three pitched fields
SP 259 although it go a. my starres to jest, yet
SP 954 for this once, ile be honest a. my will
SP 1196 when they should gase a. the glorious Sunne
SP 1240 a. the Persians, or the barbarous Moore
SP 1249 nor shalt thou war a. thy Countrimen
SP 1334 shall strengthen us a. your insolence
SP 1628 of treason doone a. your mightines
SP 1864 thou seest what witnes hath produced a. thee
SP 2073 harbour a wicked thought a. the spotlesse life of
Ard. 312 the statute makes a. artificers
Ard. 742 stab him as he stands pissing a. a wall
Ard. 838 standing a. a stall, watching Arden's coming
Ard. 1271 discharged a. a ruinated wall
Ard. 634 but a. when shall I have it?
Ard. 941 the doors I'll leave unlocked a. you come
Ard. 2026 see all things ready, Alice, a. we come
JB 65 such a hatred in her heart a. her new made choyce
JB 78 conceived such deadly hatred a. him
JB 136 never mystrusting the trecherie wrought a. him
JB 159 rather then to any malice conceaved a. her husband
Cor. 538 of certaine courage gainst incertaine chaunce
Cor. 804 cryme that gainst the heavens might bee imagined
Cor. 1050 gainst one whose power and cause is best
Cor. 1082 thy chyldren gainst thy children thou hast arm'd
Cor. 1412 that gainst my will I have maintaind this warre
Cor. 1610 are heapt with rage and horror gainst this house
Cor. 1960 opposing of thy freatfull jelosie gainst his mishap
Jer. 508 say, gainst Lorenzo and the divell, little
Jer. 528 Thy assured friend gainst Lorenzo and the divell
Jer. 839 this scarfe shall be my charme gainst foes and hell
Jer. 951 a Generall defiance gainst Portugale
Jer. 952 breath our Lord General gainst the Spaniards
ST 345 my hart growne hard gainst mischiefes battery
SP 508 how he hath borne him gainst the Christians
SP 867 rather than ile seeke justice gainst the Dame

Agamemnon.

HP 262 for the banquets of A., as we read
HP 903 represents the person of A., Atreus, or

Age.

Eng. Parn 3 Under a tyrant, to consume ones a.
HP Ind. 9 a. in marriage to be lookt unto
HP 11 a youth of eighteene or twenty yeeres of a.
HP 116 he was a man of midle a.
HP 236 are arived and come unto their a.
HP 470 (loaden both with a. and with experience)
HP 579 in two speciall things to be considered — Estate and A.
HP 599 passing to the a., I say that the Husband
HP 609 as the beginning of the ones a. match not with
HP 783 that first and tender a. of infancie
HP 794 but that first a. past over
HP 798 that first a. aboundeth in naturall heate
HP 1301 I speake of choyse wynes which get strength with a.
Jer. 30 a. ushers honor ; tis no shame ; confesse
Jer. 98 Lorenzo is not drempt on in this a.
Jer. 205 this lazy a., that yeelds me no imployments
Jer. 461 & 462 Tis a villainus a. this
Jer. 511 Signeor Andrea, tis a villainus a. this
Jer. 1148 my boy ads treble comfort to my a.
ST Bal 15 a. with silvered haires my aged head had overspred
ST. Bal. 149 thus when in a. I sought to rest
ST 1421 this toyles my body. this consumeth a.
STA 1769 makes them looke olde, before they meet with a.
ST 1825 imperfection of his a. doth make him dote

ST 2093 what *a*. hath ever heard such monstrous deeds?
SP 180 at foureteene yeeres of *a*. was I made Knight
SP 798 soone cropt with *a*. or with infirmities?
SP 962 ah, Ferdinand, the stay of my old *a*.
SP 1127 his name Erastus, not twentie yeares of *a*.
SP 1914 although his *a*. did plead for innocence
SP 2165 before his *a*., hath seene his mellowed yeares
SP 386 Oh, the pollicie of this *a*. is wonderfull
SP 376 charactered with ages print upon thy warlike face
Cor. 1282 all after ages shall adore

Aged.
Cor. 1706 and *a*. Senators in sad discourse
ST Bal. 16 age with silvered haires my *a*. head had overspred
STA 1943 and — now his *a*. yeeres should sleepe in rest

Agent.
SP 1671 had left some other to be his *a*. here
SP 1707 and I left heere to be their *a*.?
Puck 64 I was neither *a*. nor consenting therunto

Ager's.
Ard. 296 Greene, one of Sir Antony *A*. men

Aggravate.
Cor. 1591 will agravate my former misery

Aggrieved.
ST 2400 I hear you find your selfe agrieved at my Sonne

Aghast.
Cor. 1826 as with the sight doth make the sound agast

Aglets.
STA 1972 those Starres that gaze upon her face, are agglots on her sleeve

Agnoscit.
Puck 43 ex minimo vestigio artifex *a*. artificem

Ago.
Cor. 377 where so long agoe Heavens did theyr favors
Cor. 922 els had my life beene long agoe expired
Jer. 351 but three minutes agoe was thy full friend
SP 1398 no, no; my hope full long agoe was lost
Ard. 2283 I saw him come into your house an hour *a*.

Agony.
SP 945 now am I growing into a doubtful *a*.
SP 1683 what suddaine agonie was that?
Ard. 1791 I speak it in an *a*. of spirit

Agree.
Cor. 1560 with their humor can *a*.
Jer. 472 what, write him « honest Lord » ? ile not *a*.
ST Bal. 111 to see me with his foes *a*.
ST 275 appoint the sum, as you shall both *a*.
Ard. 1218 why, I'll *a*. to anything you'll have me

Agreeable.
HP 858 discipline may conforme and be *a*. therewith

Agreed.
Jer. 394 *a*., right valliant prince
Jer. 922 *a*.
Jer. 942 can we be foes, and all so well *a*.?
Ard. 1923 unless she have *a*. with me first
Ard. 571 on this we 'greed, and he is ridden straight to

Agrestibus.
HP 1062 Dicendum et quae sint duris *a*. arma

Agunt.
Puck 72 *a*. ut viri boni esse videant?

Ah.
ST 1597 *a*., but none of them wil purge the hart
ST 2245 *a*., ruthlesse fate, that favour thus transformes
ST 2246 *a*., my good Lord, I am not your yong Sonne
ST 2706 *a*. nay, thou doest delay their deaths
ST 2777 *a*., my Erasto, welcome to Perseda
ST 2781 *a*., Bashaw, heere is love betwixt Erasto and

SP 116 *a*., my Erastus, there are Europes Knights
SP 483 *a*., treacherous Fortune, enemy to Love
SP 499 *a*. no, great losses sildome are restord
SP 502 *a*., but my love is cerimonious
SP 535 *a*., Soliman, whose name hath shakt thy foes
SP 592 *a*., that my rich imperiall Diadem
SP 601 *a*., what is dearer bond then brotherhood?
SP 607 *a*., Amurath, why wert thou so unkind
SP 708 *a*., false Erastus, how am I betraid
SP 726 *a*., false Erastus, full of treacherie
SP 748 *a*., that my moyst and cloud compacted braine
SP 753 *a*., false Erastus, how had I misdoone
SP 777 *a*., how thine eyes can forge alluring lookes
SP 791 *a*., false Erastus, how had I misdone
SP 813 *a*. stay, my sweete Perseda ; heare me speake
SP 840 *a*., Love, and if thou beest of heavenly power
SP 853 *a*., vertuous Lampes of ever turning heavens
SP 858 *a*., were she not Perseda, whom my heart
SP 912 *a*., fickle and blind guidresse of the world
SP 918 *a*., if but time and place would give me leave
SP 932 *a*., hard attempt, to tempt a foe for ayde
SP 962 *a*., Ferdinand, the stay of my old age
SP 964 *a*., loving cousen, how art thou misdone by
SP 965 by false Erastus — *a*. no, by treacherie
SP 1026 *a*., stay, no more ; for I can heere no more
SP 1030 *a*., poore Erastus, how thy starres malign
SP 1288 for whom weep you ? — *a*., for Fernandos dying
SP 1289 for whom mourne you ? — *a*., for Erastus flying
SP 1297 *a*., how unpleasant is mirth to melancholy
SP 1425 *a*., gratious Soliman, now showe thy love
SP 1541 *a*., pardon me, great Soliman, for this is she
SP 1795 *a*. that Perseda were not half so faire
SP 1889 *a*., poore Erastus, art thou dead already?
SP 1961 *a*. no ; my nightly dreames foretould me this
SP 1966 but strangled? *a*., double death to me
SP 2034 *a*., Brusor, see where thy Lucina lyes
SP 2071 *a*., perjur'd and inhumaine Soliman
SP 2077 *a*., wicked tirant, in that one mans death
SP 2082 *a*., foolish man, therein thou art deceived
SP 2096 what, my Perseda? *a*., what have I done?
SP 2103 *a*., let me kisse thee too, before I dye
SP 2111 *a*., Perseda, how shall I mourne for thee?
SP 2113 *a*. heavens, that hitherto have smilde on me
SP 2121 *a*. no, the heavens did never more accurse me
SP 2137 *a*., was he so?
SP 2164 *a*., Janisaries, now dyes your Emperour
SP 2175 *a*., now I feele the paper tould me true
Ard. 227 *a*., would we could !
Ard. 265 *a*., that thou couldst be secret
Ard. 319 *a*., Master Arden, you have injured me
Ard. 402 *a*., if thou love me, gentle Arden, stay
Ard. 488 *a*., Master Greene, God knows how I am used
Ard. 493 *a*., Master Greene, be it spoken in secret here
Ard. 605 *a*., Master Clarke, it resteth at my grant
Ard. 751 *a*., that I might be set a work thus
Ard. 767 *a*., Mistress Susan, abolish that paltry painter
Ard. 913 *a*., Will —
Ard. 957 *a*., harmless Arden, how hast thou misdone
Ard. 989 *a*., Franklin, Franklin, when I think on this
Ard. 1003 here, here it lies, *a*. Franklin, here it lies
Ard. 1011 *a*., what a hell is fretful jealousy !
Ard. 1057 he comes, he comes ! *a*., Master Franklin, help !
Ard. 1209 *a*., Mosbie !
Ard. 1363 *a*., how you women can insinuate
Ard. 1381 *a*., would it were ! Then comes my happy hour
Ard. 1428 *a*., might I see him stretching forth his limbs

Ard. 1839 *a.*, Mosbie ! perjured beast ! bear this and all !
Ard. 1843 *a.*, Arden, what folly blinded thee ?
Ard. 1846 *a.*, jealous harebrained man, what hast thou done !
Ard. 1861 *a.* me accursed to link in liking with
Ard. 1946 *a.*, gentle Michael, art thou sure they're friends ?
Ard. 1956 *a.*, gentle Michael, run thou back again
Ard. 1965 *a.*, gentlemen, how missed you of your
Ard. 1987 *a.*, sirs, had he yesternight been slain
Ard. 1998 *a.*, say not so ; for when I saw thee hurt
Ard. 2059 *a.*, would he now were here that it might open !
Ard. 2150 *a.*, Master Arden, « now I can take you »
Ard. 2158 *a.*, that villain will betray us all
Ard. 2187 *a.*, but I cannot ! was he not slain by me ?
Ard. 2197 *a.*, Master Greene, did you see my husband lately ?
Ard. 2222 *a.*, neighbours, a sudden qualm came o'er my heart
Ard. 2296 *a.*, by whom ? Master Franklin, can you tell ?
Ard. 2305 *a.*, Michael, through this thy negligence thou hast
Ard. 2328 *a.*, Master Franklin, God and heaven can tell
Ard. 2394 *a.*, but for thee I had never been a strumpet
Ard. 2399 *a.*, gentle brother, wherefore should I die ?
JB 132 « *a.* », quoth her husband, « now I feele my selfe sicke
Aid.
HP Ind. 2 ayde amongst Servants for the
HP 230 expect and approve that ayde and comfort
Cor. 19 desiring Armes to ayde our Capitoll
Cor. 524 we aske Deaths ayde to end lifes wretchednes
Cor. 1068 implor'd thine ayde
Cor. 1130 not to be subject, but to ayde his right
SP 932 ah, hard attempt, to tempt a foe for ayde
SP 1104 and give him aide and succour in distresse
Cor. 1209 to make an Armie for his after-ayde against
Ail.
Ard. 2191 how now, Mistress Arden ? what *a.* you weep ?
SP 709 what ailes you, madam, that your colour changes ?
Ard. 2221 what ails you, woman, to cry so suddenly ?
Aim.
HP 814 Their horses fit for service and their archery for aime
Cor. 1249 why cry you ayme, and see us used thus ?
Jer. 481 and canst not aime at Figurative speech ?
ST 595 I, but her hopes aime at some other end
ST 1263 and let me shift for taking of mine aime
SP 579 must I give aime to this presumption ?
Jer. 106 I hate Andrea, cause he aimes at honor
Jer. 668 aymes at some fatall pointed tragedy
Aimed.
Cor. 584 so they with equall pace be aim'd
Cor. 1172 he aym'd at us, bent to exterminate who ever
Aimedst.
Jer. 703 I, villiane, for thou aym[ed]st at this true hart
Aiming.
ST 394 for glorious cause still *a.* at the fairest
Air.
HP 5 where, seeing the ayre wexe blacke
HP 801ᵃ because, the hygh parts of the ayre being cold
HP 1215 by the exhalation of whose evill vapours the ayre becommeth filthy
HP 1218 may gather vertue to refine and purge the ayre
Cor. 175 which with their noisome fall corrupt the ayre
Cor. 914 the plaints of men opprest doe pierce the ayre
Cor. 1732 the ayre (that thickned with theyr thundring cryes)
Cor. 1742 the shyvered Launces (ratling in the ayre)
Cor. 1995 and presse the ayre with your continuall plaints
Jer. 597 trust not the open aire, for aire is breath
ST Bal. 80 filling the ayre with mournefull groanes
ST 145 and shivered Launces darke the troubled aire
ST 1389 I list not trust the Aire with utterance of

ST 1524 mine exclaimes, that have surcharged the aire
ST 1533 passions, that winged mount, and, hovering in the aire;
ST 2851 I heare his dismall out-cry eccho in the aire
SP 221 as the aire to the fowle, or the marine moisture to
Ard. 1078 ay, by my faith ; the *a.* is very cold
ST 2691 an Easterne winde, commixt with noisome aires
Air-bred.
SP 1194 as ayre bred Eagles, if they once perceive that
Airy.
Cor. 733 but his airie spirit beguiled mine embrasements
Ard. 94 O that some *a.* spirit would in the shape and
Ajax.
ST 2822 the death of *A.* or some Romaine peere
SP 2009 where is that furious *A.*, the sonne of Telamon
Alablaster.
SP 1502 her milke white necke, that *A.* tower ?
Alack.
Jer. 1135 betweene the stroke, but now *a.* must die
STA 1968 alacke, when mischiefe doth it knowes not what
A-land.
SP 1852 we came aland, not minding for to returne
SP 1855 but ere we could summon him a land
Alarm.
Cor. 1850 to come upon them with a fresh alarme
Cor. 385 for oft he search't amongst the fierce allarms
SP 1936 my troubled eares are deft with loves alarmes
Alarum.
Jer. 875 weele be as shrill as you : strike a larum, drum
Jer. 977 I am wars tuter ; strike a larum, drum
Alas.
Cor. 68 but Rome (*a.*) what helps it that thou ty'dst the
Cor. 147 tis not enough (*a.*) our power t'extend
Cor. 252 *a.*, thou shouldst, thou shouldst, Cornelia, have
Cor. 319 *a.*, and here-withall what holpe it thee that
Cor. 392 *a.*, my sorrow would be so much lesse
Cor. 431 *a.*, must I, must I my selfe be murderer
Cor. 684 but wretched that I am, *a.*, I feare
Cor. 910 *a.*, that profits nought
Cor. 2003 *a.*, what shall I doe ? O deere companions
Jer. 140 *a.*, that Spaine cannot of peace forbeare
Jer. 360 allas, that Spaine should correct Portugal
Jer. 1034 *a.* ; war knows I am to proud a scholler grown
Jer. 1146 *a.*, I pitty Bellimperias eies
ST 481 *a.*, my Lord, these are but words of course
ST 635 *a.*, my Lord, since Don Andreas death
ST 891 *a.*, it is Horatio, my sweet sonne
ST 1412 *a.*, poore Pedringano, I am in a sorte sorie for thee
ST 1476 *a.*, sir, you are a foot too low to reach it
STA 2031 *a.*, sir, I had no more but he
ST 2221 *a.*, my lease, it cost me ten pound, and
ST 2238 *a.*, my L[ord], whence springs this troubled speech ?
ST 2358 *a.*, how easie is it for him to erre
SP 1306 alasse, how could I ? for his man no sooner
SP 1649 *a.*, the Christians are but very shallow in
SP 1880 *a.*, how can he but be short, whose tongue
Ard. 189 and, out *a.* ! made shipwreck of mine honour
Ard. 484 *a.*, poor gentleman, I pity you
Ard. 2247 *a.*, I counsel ! fear frights away my wits
Ard. 2267 *a.*, Mistress Arden, the watch will take me here
JB 100 *a.*, husband (quoth she), if I could not find
JB 109 « out, alasse, » quoth she, « I have spilt a measse
Albeit.
HP 69 *a.*, (quoth he) I had rather
HP 103 *a.*, he hath spent the greater part of his time
HP 184 for, *a.* they be sweet of savour
HP 200 for *a.* I knowe that

HP 306 *a.* happilie the manner of their
HP 487 *a.* that for their greatnes
HP 547 *a.*, for some other respect, it ought rather
HP 642 but *a.* Chastitie or Shamefastnes be not
HP 682 for *a.* superfluous pompe be fitter for a stage
HP 687 for *a.* we see that Nature in other creatures
HP 697 beards, which *a.* they becom men
HP 746 *a.* I beleeve that there was never
HP 891 *a.* the Lawes and usages of men are variable and divers
HP 950 *a.* there is no more reason in it then in the other
HP 1118 *a.* in those good worldes of the Romaine Common wealth
HP 1351 and *a.* the Greekes observed not so much decorum
HP 1395 which, *a.* of it selfe it beare no great semblance of credit
HP 1611 *a.* in respect of the partition or devision it seeme
HP 1618 for *a.* the number of mony bee not formall
HP 1745 *a.* they onely differ not in form, but are
HP 1753 for *a.* wee differ farre from those of elder times
HP 1777 *a.* somethings unspoken of might be revived
Ard. 429 why so it shall, Mosbie, *a.* he live
JB 7 and *a.* there was none in the world to accuse Caine
JB 34 *a.* he had the good will and favour of al her friends
JB 58 *a.* it proved the worst bargain that ever
Albion.
ST 525 who, when King Stephen bore sway in *A.*
ST 535 was Edmund, Earle of Kent in *A.*
ST 554 and made them bow their knees to *A.*
Alcario.
Jer. 239 *A.*, the Duke Medinas sonne
Jer. 443 shall show all Don Andrea, not *A.*
Jer. 677 it is *A.*, Duke Medinas son
Jer. 679 *A.* slaine? hast thou beguild me, sword?
Jer. 683 who names *A.* slaine? it is *A.*
Jer. 696 that was *A.*, my shapes counterfet
Jer. 731 my leedge, *A.*, Duke Medinas son
Jer. 733 who names *A.* slaine? aie me, tis he
Jer. 747 that haples, bleeding Lord *A.*
Alcides.
ST 2205 getting by force, as once *A.* did
SP 1080 I tell thee, if *A.* lived this day
SP 2003 let me see: where is that *A.*, surnamed Hercules
Alcinous.
HP 1350 the daughter of Alcinoe, the King of Phaeaces
Alcoran.
SP 513 for by the holy Alcaron I sweare
SP 552 sweare upon the Alcaron religiously that
SP 1859 both lay your hands upon the Alcaron
SP 1971 two great Knights of the post swore upon the Alcaron
SP 1977 accursed Soliman, prophane Alcaron
Alderman.
JB 212 carried before *A.* Howard to be examined
Aldersgate.
Ard. 743 he is now at London, in *A.* Street
Ard. 940 this night come to his house at *A.*
Ale.
Ard. 1651 half drowned with new *a.* overnight
Aleagement.
SP 836 yet this is some aleagement to my sorrow [So Qq. —
   Boas, *aleavement.*]
Alecto.
Cor. 1797 as when *A.*, in the lowest hell, doth breathe
Alehouse.
Ard. 445 in London many *a.* ruffians keep
Ard. 1140 at the *a.* butting Arden's house
Ard. 1937 all the tenpenny-alehouses-men would stand
Alexander.
SP 1511 brought *A.* from warre to banquetting

SP 2011 where is tipsie *A.*, that great cup conquerour
Alexandria.
SP 1439 Augustus sparde rich *A.* for Arrius sake
Alexandro.
Jer. 922 proud *A.*, thou art mine
Jer. 961 *A.*
ST 353 *A.*, that here counterfeits under the colour
ST 1075 nay, *A.*, if thou menace me
ST 1098 against the life and reputation of noble *A.*
ST 1112 wherein hath *A.* used thee ill?
ST 1124 and, *A.*, let us honor thee with
ST 1129 come, *A.*, keepe us companie
ST 1036 I had not thought that Alexandros hart
ST 1043 then Alexandros purpose to the Prince
ST 1049 procrastinating Alexandros death
ST 1107 thus falsly betray Lord Alexandros life?
ST 1115 for not for Alexandros injuries, but for reward
Algorism.
HP 1182 that which is accustomd to be numbred by Algorisme
Alice.
Ard. 56 How! *A.*!
Ard. 65 this night, sweet *A.*, thou hast killed my heart
Ard. 78 Mistress *A.*, I heard you name him once or twice
Ard. 81 I must to London, sweet *A.*, presently
Ard. 87 I cannot long be from thee, gentle *A.*
Ard. 91 meanwhile prepare our breakfast, gentle *A.*
Ard. 109 he whom you wot of, Mosbie, Mistress *A.*
Ard. 206 ungentle and unkind *A.*, now I see
Ard. 225 to London, *A.*? if thou'lt be ruled by me
Ard. 234 sweet *A.*, he shall draw thy counterfeit
Ard. 278 enough sweet *A.*; thy kind words makes me melt
Ard. 300 *A.*, make ready my breakfast, I must hence
Ard. 367 not wholesome; didst thou make it, *A.*?
Ard. 381 why, gentle *A.*, cannot I be ill but you'll
Ard. 395 I know it, sweet *A.*; cease to complain
Ard. 409 and so farewell, sweet *A.*, till we meet next
Ard. 420 ay, *A.*, and it was cunningly performed
Ard. 440 well proved, Mistress *A.*; yet by your leave
Ard. 448 *A.*, what's he that comes yonder?
Ard. 507 now trust me, Mistress *A.*, it grieveth me
Ard. 538 how now, *A.*, what's the news?
Ard. 540 tell me, *A.*, how have you dealt
Ard. 551 now, *A.*, let's hear thy news
Ard. 576 but trust me, *A.*, I take it passing ill
Ard. 590 then, sweet *A.*, let it pass: I have a drift
Ard. 626 well questioned, *A.*; Clarke, how answer you that?
Ard. 636 now, *A.*, let's in and see what cheer you keep
Ard. 854 and sweet *A.* Arden, with a lap of crowns
Ard. 1258 I may not trust you, *A.*: you have
Ard. 1264 how now, *A.*? what, sad and passionate?
Ard. 1273 ungentle *A.*, thy sorrow is my sore
Ard. 1367 I will forget thy quarrel, gentle *A.*
Ard. 1370 soft, *A.*, here comes somebody
Ard. 1571 farewell, sweet *A.*, we mind to sup with thee
Ard. 1874 pardon me, sweet *A.*, and forgive this fault!
Ard. 1887 content thee, sweet *A.*, thou shalt have thy will
Ard. 2007 faith, *A.*, no longer than this night
Ard. 2026 see all things ready, *A.*, against we come
Ard. 2097 *A.*, bid him welcome; he and I are friends
Ard. 2118 and, gentle Mistress *A.*, seeing you are so stout
Ard. 2121 why, *A.*! how can I do too much for him
Ard. 2139 come, *A.*, is our supper ready yet?
Ard. 2151 Mosbie! Michael! *A.*! what will you do?
Ard. 2167 we have our gold; Mistress *A.*, adieu
Ard. 2189 it shall not long torment thee, gentle *A.*
Ard. 2253 how now, *A.*, whither will you bear him?

Ard. 2268 tell me, sweet A., how shall I escape?
Ard. 2271 until to-morrow, sweet A., now farewell
Ard. 2273 be resolute, Mistress A., betray us not

Alike.
HP 852 al a. or both togeather
HP 1749 the manner and facultie of eyther is a.
Jer. 416 you are in stature like him, speech a.
ST 117 both menacing a. with daring showes
ST 398 their strength a., their strokes both dangerous

Aliquis.
ST 997 O a. mihi quas pulchrum ver &c

Alium.
HP 1665 Et unum a. excedere per artem et naturam

Alive.
Cor. Arg. 28 and for hee woulde not fall a. into the hands of
Cor. 864 honored with true devotion, both a. and dead
Cor. 995 fling mee a. into a Lyons denn
Cor. 1809 nor example of any of theyr leaders left a.
Ard. 2179 ay, well, if Arden were a. again

All.
Eng. Parn. 11 Honour indeede, and a. things yeeld to death
VPJ 4 a. other princes thou must over-peere
VPJ 10 everlasting fame attend on thee in a. thine actions
VPJ 18 health of thy Countrey, helpe to a. our harmes
VPJ 24 and al my good is but vaine hope of gaine
HP (Title) a. the notable thinges
HP Ded. Health and a. Happines
HP Ind. 60 Earth, universall nurse of a. thinges
HP 96 furnished with a. sorts of daintie fruits
HP 166 with wheate and a. kind of graine
HP 186 and not discovered on al sides to the Sunne
HP 208 all my deerest thinges
HP 244 I hunted not a. in vaine to day
HP 302 as that above a. the rest is wherof
HP 309 al things, either pleasing to the sences or
HP 315 a. of them have some kind of sweetnes
HP 334 a. sorts of fruite in great aboundance
HP 383 most aboundeth of a. other seasons
HP 394 but a. his meats are mard
HP 410 and hath a. his parts so uniforme as in it
HP 419 a. thinges contained in thys our variable and
HP 422 and is indeede the father of a. living things
HP 486 turne the eyes of a. the world upon theyr actions
HP 529 a. the good and a. the evill incident to life
HP 537 the like communitie shoulde be in a. offices
HP 538 in a. offices and a. operations
HP 572 a desire most naturall in a. reasonable creatures
HP 574 but once in a. theyr life beene tyed with that band
HP 603 receive and retaine a. formes of customes
HP 702 of a. the other Gods were most fayre
HP 710 disrobing themselves of a. theyr other ornaments
HP 727 that she be forwarde with the first at a. dauncings
HP 740 cause or procure shamefastnes in a. her actions
HP 758 Lay doun with him upo[n] the grasse al covered with a clowde
HP 849 unfurnished of a. or one of these professions
HP 852 al alike or both togeather
HP 853 al this part of education and bringing up of Children
HP 904 in Purple and glistering a. in Golde and precious stones
HP 965 and a. those others of whom we reade
HP 1010 it shall suffise thee to provide one for a.
HP 1030 and generallie a., in such busines as
HP 1078 but above a., me thinks, the Charitie of Maisters
HP 1095 he keepeth a. the instruments of houshold occupied
HP 1097 wherin he differeth from a. the other instruments
HP 1170 that hee take the like notice of a.

HP 1206 Arteficiall riches may a. those things be called
HP 1229 a. which conditions, as they much increase
HP 1243 a. which he may easily doo
HP 1259 a. which a good huswife well considering
HP 1280 that a. her houshold corne be some ground for bread
HP 1290 of houshold necessaries as a. things els
HP 1292 should so provide that a. things whatsoever
HP 1354 forbad the Mistres of the house a. other works
HP 1370 ought above a. things to be diligent heerein
HP 1377 al the Images and formes of visible and
HP 1423 the art of housekeeping and getting is not a. one
HP 1434 the Earth is the naturall and universall Mother of us a.
HP 1461 exchaungeth the profit of a. those things
HP 1493 the nature, goodnes, and value of a. things
HP 1562 to live well and civilly with a.
HP 1600 a. those meanes and members work that
HP 1614 things of a. kinds that cannot be devided are
HP 1636 a Rebell and resister of a. humaine orders
HP 1700 practise is in the end imposed to a. instructions
HP 1709 instructed you in a. hys institutions
HP 1713 Whether houshold care or housholde government be a. one
Cor. Ded. 25 and another of the night in wishing you a. happines
Cor. Ded. 27 yours Honors in a. humblenes. T. K.
Cor. 8 be pour'd on me, that one may die for a.
Cor. 25 t'is thou that train'st us into a. these errors
Cor. 76 but as a bayte for pride (which spoiles us a.)
Cor. 117 and almost yoked a. the world beside
Cor. 119 Rome and the earth are waxen a. as one
Cor. 122 and even that yoke, that wont to tame a. others
Cor. 142 the lyves or lyberties of a. those Nations
Cor. 163 a further plague will pester a. the land
Cor. 205 were a. too little to reward thy wrath
Cor. 206 nor a. the plagues that fierie Pluto hath
Cor. 215 a. sad and desolate our Citty lyes
Cor. 245 yee gods (at whose arbitrament a. stand)
Cor. 291 and a. your hopes with hap may be effected
Cor. 320 that even in a. the corners of the earth
Cor. 327 destinie (envious of a. thine honors) gave thee mee
Cor. 382 O haples wife, thus ominous to a.
Cor. 438 the servitude that causeth a. our cares
Cor. 443 if a. the world were in the like distresse
Cor. 448 then when they see their woes not worst of a.
Cor. 474 a. things are subject to Deaths tiranny
Cor. 563 a. fortunes, a. felicities, upon their motion doe
Cor. 567 that cover all this earthly round
Cor. 626 may light upon them once for a.
Cor. 647 and whose first fortunes (fild with a. distresse)
Cor. 663 under his outrage now are a. our goods
Cor. 707 with a ghastly looke, a. pale and brawne-falne
Cor. 787 for thou, that wont'st to tame and conquer a.
Cor. 810 a. the powre we raise turnes but to our misfortune
Cor. 908 there dooth abide a. treason, luxurie, and homicide
Cor. 970 a. these, nor anything we can devise
Cor. 974 tyme calmeth a. things
Cor. 1143 exceeds a. loves, and deerer is by farre
Cor. 1243 commaunds the world, and brideleth a. the earth
Cor. 1276 were a. the world his foes before
Cor. 1282 a. after ages shall adore
Cor. 1300 for high Jove that guideth a., when he
Cor. 1306 therefore he, whom a. men feare, feareth
Cor. 1307 feareth a. men every where
Cor. 1333 now a. the world (wel-nye) doth stoope to Rome
Cor. 1354 the sea, the earth, and a. is almost ours
Cor. 1371 Caesar doth tryumph over a. the world
Cor. 1372 and a. they scarcely conquered a nooke

Cor. 1383 have a. been urg'd to yeeld to my commaund
Cor. 1460 what, shall I slay them a. that I suspect?
Cor. 1462 rather I will my lyfe and a. neglect
Cor. 1473 but for thy friends and Country a. too-short
Cor. 1516 from our walls a. woes to cleere
Cor. 1528 pardon'd a. offences past
Cor. 1599 O no, for a. is lost
Cor. 1664 well ,forth to field they marched a. at once
Cor. 1674 meane-while our Emperor (at a. poynts arm'd)
Cor. 1685 that we must a. live free, or friendly die
Cor. 1719 thys sayd, his Army crying a. at once
Cor. 1816 the field was fild with a. confusion
Cor. 1834 but put them a. (remorceles) to the sword
Cor. 1887 since a. our hopes are by the Gods beguil'd
Cor. 1921 then a. the Captives in th' infernall Court
Cor. 1937 whose ende, sith it hath ended a. my joyes
Cor. 1938 O heavens, at least permit of a. these plagues
Cor. 1940 sith in this widdow-hood of a. my hopes
Cor. 2005 widdowed of a. my hopes, my haps, my husbands
Jer. 2 by a. the dewe and customary rights
Jer. 13 Ile empty a. my vaines to serve your wars
Jer. 52 well tuned mellody, and a. sweet guifts of nature
Jer. 76 you ha no tricks, you ha none of a. their slights
Jer. 142 and yet this is not a. : I know you are to hot
Jer. 160 my lives happines, the joy of a. my being
Jer. 176 are a. things abord?
Jer. 186 be woman in a. partes, save in thy eies
Jer. 190 a. honor on Andreas steps attende
Jer. 253 deny his gifts, be a. composd of hate
Jer. 313 but, boy, feare not, I will out stretch them al.
Jer. 318 and do him a. the honor that belonges him
Jer. 350 and a. the peeres of Portugalle the like
Jer. 351 then thus a. Spaine, which but three minutes agoe
Jer. 372 for a. Spaines wealth lde not graspe hands
Jer. 386 I am a. vext. — I care not
Jer. 421 proportiond in a. parts — nay, twins his own
Jer. 431 a. fals out for the purpose : a hits jumpe
Jer. 434 true, true ; a. to the purpose
Jer. 443 shall show a. Don Andrea, not Alcario
Jer. 458 elce had my pen no cause to write at a.
Jer. 584 tis a. about the court in every eare
Jer. 623 at first they cried a. war, as men
Jer. 625 at which I thundered words a. clad in profe
Jer. 630 tis a. about the Court Andreas come
Jer. 633 not to afford me notice a. this while
Jer. 666 an omynous horror a. my vaines doth strike
Jer. 682 strew a. the galleries with gobbits round
Jer. 701 I will resolve you a. this strange, strang thing
Jer. 711 which, I much feare me, by a. signes pretends
Jer. 745 to tell you a. without a tedious toong
Jer. 751 her affections were a. firmly planted in
Jer. 758 and in a. parts disguised, as there you see
Jer. 849 let a. the tribute that proud Spaine receavd
Jer. 850 of a. those captive Portugales deceased
Jer. 857 indeed your a. that may be termed reveng
Jer. 859 and a. those wounds that you receive of Spaine
Jer. 868 and a. that gold thou hadst from Portugale
Jer. 873 a. they have receaved they back must pay
Jer. 884 tall as an English gallows, uper beam and a.
Jer. 896 shall paye deere trybute, even there lives and a.
Jer. 925 or thine, or thine, or a. at once
Jer. 927 thy valiansie, and a that thou holdst great
Jer. 941 Do you the like. — And you a., and we
Jer. 942 can we be foes, and a. so well agreed?
Jer. 958 I am a. fire, Andrea
Jer. 972 be a. as fortunate as heavens blest host

Jer. 974 ride [home] a. Conquerours, when the fight is done
Jer. 984 O for a voise shriller then a. the trumpets
Jer. 989 by a. that thou holdst deere upon this earth
Jer. 991 now death doth heap his goods up a. at once
Jer. 1053 inherit within my bosome, a. I have is thine
Jer. 1117 I could whip al these, were there hose downe
Jer. 1145 smeard with foes bloud, a. for the maisters honer
Jer. 1153 give him my blessing, and then a. is done
Jer. 1160 see, he points at his owne hearse — mark, a.
Jer. 1192 your welcome, a., as I am a Gentleman
Jer. 1195 I hope thers never a Jew among you a.
ST Bal. 4 thinking your griefes a. griefes exceede
ST Bal. 56 enters my bower a. in the night
ST Bal. 142 uppon me a. they straight did run
ST 8 for there in prime and pride of a. my yeeres
ST 71 and a. foule sinnes with torments overwhelmd
ST 93 a. wel, my soveraigne Liege, except some few
ST 109 that, adding a. the pleasure of thy newes
ST 154 in a. this turmoyle, three long houres and more
ST 172 when he was taken, a. the rest they fled
ST 199 that a. (except three hundred or few more)
ST 278 Horatios house were small for a. his traine
ST 478 on whose perfection a. my thoughts attend
ST 589 and being worthles, a. my labours lost
ST 599 I, but I feare she cannot love at a.
ST 611 to finde the truth of a. this question out
ST 632 for she reposeth a. her trust in thee
ST 660 I sweare to both. by him that made us a.
ST 669 let this be a. that thou shalt doe for me
ST 715 where riding a. at ease she may repaire
ST 731 why stands Horatio speecheles a. this while?
ST 738 dangers of death, and pleasures none at a.
ST 802 and shall be sent with a. convenient speed
ST 814 if she give back, a. this will come to naught
ST 836 I feare no more ; love now is a. my thoughts
ST 887 a man hangd up and a. the murderers gone
STA 931 true, a. Spaine takes note of it
STA 938 syrha, sirha, Ile know the trueth of a.
STA 963 if it should proove my sonne now after a.
STA 967 drop a. your stinges at once in my cold bosome
ST 1015 on whom I doted more then a. the world
ST 1016 because she lov'd me more then a. the world
ST 1241 the complot thou hast cast of a. these practises
ST 1274 besides, this place is free from a. suspect
ST 1307 and doe your worst, for I defie you a.
ST 1407 and al presuming of his pardon from hence
ST 1417 for a. our wrongs, can compasse no redresse
ST 1422 that onely I to a. men just must be
ST 1594 or tyre them a. with my revenging threats
ST 1651 but that's a. one
ST 1653 salve a. suspitions, onely sooth me up
ST 1719 too pollitick for me, past a. compare
STA 1746 nor as you thinke ; you'r wide a.
STA 1793 and so doth bring confusion to them a.
ST 1904 to be avenged on you a. for this
STA 1939 when man and bird and beast are a. at rest
STA 1965 when as the Sun-God rides in a. his glorie
STA 1971 and a. those Starres that gaze upon her face
STA 2022 God hath engrossed a. justice in his hands
STA 2033 But a. is one
STA 2060 nay, it should crie ; but a. is one
STA 2064 that euer lived in a. Spaine
ST 2122 and therefore a. times fit not for revenge
ST 2127 that ignorantly I will let a. slip
ST 2185 I, this, and that, and a. of them are thine
ST 2186 for a. as one are our extremeties

ST 2262 and *a.* this sorrow riseth for thy Sonne
ST 2267 a song, three parts in one, but *a.* of discords fram'd
ST 2278 and welcome *a.* his honorable traine
ST 2345 and no man lives that long contenteth *a.*
ST 2373 but not too fast, least heate and *a.* be done
ST 2426 freends, quoth he? see, Ile be freends with you *a.*
ST 2510 and *a.* the Saintes doe sit soliciting for
ST 2544 is this *a.* ?
ST 2545 I, this is *a.*
ST 2588 whose beauty ravished *a.* that her behelde
ST 2629 as *a.* the world shall say
ST 2638 my Lords, *a.* this must be perfourmed
ST 2654 in courtly French shall *a.* her phraises be
ST 2657 and hardly shall we *a.* be understood
ST 2659 shall prove the intention, and *a.* was good
ST 2714 where's your fellows, that you take *a.* this paine ?
ST 2716 to look that *a.* things may goe well
ST 2738 *a.* woe begone for him, hath slaine her selfe
ST 2766 that's because his minde runs *a.* on Bel-imperia
ST 2820 and that we doo as *a.* Tragedians doo
ST 2837 *a.* fled, faild, died, yea, *a.* decaide with this
ST 2930 and therefore in despight of *a.* thy threats
STA 2936 I, *a.* are dead ; not one of them survive
STA 2939 see, here's a goodly nowse will hold them *a.*
STA 2947 Ide give them *a.*, I, and my soule to boote
STA 2978 rowle *a.* the world within thy pitchie cloud
ST 2909 I am the next, the neerest, last of *a.*
ST 3032 blaspheming Gods and *a.* their holy names
SP 129 the Prince and all the outlandish Gentlemen are ready
SP 164 our word of courage *a.* the world hath heard
SP 212 so are *a.* blades with me : behold my instance
SP 242 [I], *a.* on foote, like an Herculian offspring
SP 363 muske, he said, *a.* his kindred smelt so
SP 370 brave Gentlemen, by *a.* your free consents
SP 396 and thankes unto you *a.*, brave worthy sirs
SP 398 Erastus will be dutifull in *a.*
SP 443 it was worth more then thou and *a.* thy kin are worth
SP 493 and lost with hir is *a.* my happinesse
SP 520 that Key will serve to open *a.* the gates
SP 534 make an universall Campe of *a.* his scattered legions
SP 598 and live in servile bondage *a.* my dayes
SP 623 now, Death and Fortune, which of *a.* us three
SP 648 whereon depended *a.* his hope and joy
SP 664 my words, my lookes, my thoughts are *a.* on thee
SP 670 when shall the gates of heaven stand *a.* wide ope[n]
SP 689 *a.* the world loves, none hates but envie
SP 690 *a.* haile, brave Cavelere
SP 744 my tongue to tell my woes is *a.* to weake
SP 774 which if I doe, *a.* vengeance light on me
SP 779 are there no honest drops in *a.* thy cheekes
SP 789 that in thee *a.* their influence dooth change
SP 812 and *a.* my former love is turnd to hate
SP 826 and they are *a.* as false as thou thy selfe
SP 921 for *a.* these three conspire my tragedie
SP 931 renownd for *a.* heroyicall and kingly vertues
SP 943 farewell, Perseda, dearest of them *a.*
SP 944 dearer to me then *a.* the world besides
SP 949 *a.* the while I weare this chaine
SP 951 hetherto *a.* goes well ; but, if I be taken
SP 953 of *a.* things I doe not love to preach with a haulter
SP 960 I, I ; I see his body *a.* to soone
SP 1062 and *a.* to late repents his surquedry
SP 1065 to be a laughing stock to *a.* the towne
SP 1078 Ile combat thee, my body *a.* unarmd
SP 1087 a disgrace to *a.* my chivalrie to combate one so base
SP 1132 he might have borne me through out *a.* the world

SP 1139 *a.* the Knights that there incountred him
SP 1156 more brave Souldiers then *a.* that Ile will beare
SP 1188 know thou that Rhodes, nor *a.* that Rhodes containes
SP 1203 then this, my gratious Lord, is *a.* I crave
SP 1265 will you have them *a.* at once ?
SP 1332 your Lord usurps in *a.* that he possesseth
SP 1389 past *a.* compare. and more then my desart
SP 1408 nor *a.* my faire intreats and blandishments?
SP 1421 Rhodes is taken, and *a.* the men are slaine
SP 1423 I, there it is : now *a.* my friends are slaine
SP 1428 but by my selfe lament me once for *a.*
SP 1431 go, then, go spend thy mournings *a.* at once
SP 1441 *a.* Rhodes is yoakt, and stoopes to Soliman
SP 1448 this present pleaseth more then *a.* the rest
SP 1498 and *a.* the Graces smiling round about her
SP 1505 now she is *a.* covered, my Lord
SP 1542 for whom I mourned more then for *a.* Rhodes
SP 1575 mervaile not that *a.* if hast I wish you to depart
SP 1596 *a.* three have decreed that I shall love her still
SP 1691 petition to Cupid to plague you above *a.* other
SP 1705 do you not know that they are *a.* friends
SP 1783 we will returne with *a.* speede possible
SP 1810 yes, thou, and I, and *a.* of us betray him
SP 1813 I heere protest by heavens uuto you *a.* that
SP 1828 began to question us of *a.* sorts of fire-workes
SP 1832 *a.* this is yours, quoth he, if you consent to
SP 1854 we made *a.* knowne unto great Soliman
SP 1858 that *a.* is true that heere you have declard
SP 1872 such favour send *a.* Turkes, I pray God
SP 1885 loe, this is *a.* ; and thus I leave to speake
SP 1934 lets saile to Rhodes with *a.* convenient speede
SP 1989 theres a reward for *a.* thy treasons past
SP 2040 and *a.* to soone be turnd to Tragedies
SP 2050 great Soliman, Lord of *a.* the world
SP 2051 thou art not Lord of *a.* ; Rhodes is not thine
SP 2069 for whome hell gapes, and *a.* the ugly feendes do waite
SP 2124 when Brusor lives that was the cause of *a.* ?
SP 2153 spoile *a.*, kill *a.* ; let none escape your furie
SP 2174 and let one Epitaph containe us *a.*
SP 2200 by wasting *a.* I conquer *a.* the world
Ard. (Title) and the shamefull end of *a.* murderers
Ard. 5 *a.* the lands of the Abbey of Feversham
Ard. 51 and lie with me at London *a.* this term
Ard. 132 do, and one day I'll make amends for *a.*
Ard. 162 what needs *a.* this ? I say that Susan's thine
Ard. 186 is this the end of *a.* thy solemn oaths ?
Ard. 264 you shall command my life, my skill, and *a.*
Ard. 282 and yet in taste not to be found at *a.*
Ard. 330 that she knows, and *a.* the world shall see
Ard. 344 when *a.* the knights and gentlemen of Kent
Ard. 348 upon whose general bruit *a.* honour hangs
Ard. 359 and I will lie at London *a.* this term
Ard. 454 yet *a.* my labour is not spent in vain
Ard. 461 of *a.* the lands of the Abbey of Feversham
Ard. 462 so that *a.* former grants are cut off
Ard. 465 this is *a.*, Mistress Arden ; is it true or no ?
Ard. 492 why, *a.* Kent knows your parentage and what you are
Ard. 513 shall set you free from *a.* this discontent
Ard. 533 good fortune follow *a.* your forward thoughts
Ard. 536 *a.* this goes well : Mosbie I long for thee
Ard. 537 to let thee know *a.* that I have contrived
Ard. 545 go to her, Clarke ; she's *a.* alone within
Ard. 559 I told him *a.*, whereat he stormed amain
Ard. 591 I have a drift will quiet *a.*
Ard. 650 *a.* the camp feared him for his villainy
Ard. 700 a livery cloak, but *a.* the lace was off

Ard. 734 thy mother, thy sister, thy brother, or *a.* thy kin
Ard. 785 a crew of harlots, *a.* in love, forsooth
Ard. 793 zounds, I'll kill them *a.* three
Ard. 820 if you get you not away *a.* the sooner
Ard. 823 look to your signs, for I'll pull them down *a.*
Ard. 915 sith thou hast sworn, we dare discover *a.*
Ard. 980 I will accomplish *a.* I have revealed
Ard. 997 bear your woes, twice doubled *a.*, with patience
Ard. 1070 are the doors fast locked and *a.* things safe ?
Ard. 1073 ne'er trust me but the doors were *a.* unlocked
Ard. 1153 and summoned *a.* my parts to sweet repose
Ard. 1193 for here I swear, by heaven and earth and *a.*
Ard. 1213 your penance, to feast us *a.* at the Salutation
Ard. 1294 and made me slanderous to *a.* my kin
Ard. 1298 and *a.* the causes that enchanted me !
Ard. 1308 whose dowry would have weighed down *a.* thy wealth
Ard. 1342 wilt thou not look ? is *a.* thy love o'erwhelmed ?
Ard. 1350 weigh *a.* thy good turns with this little fault
Ard. 1402 than either thou or *a.* thy kin are worth
Ard. 1418 Arden escapes us, and deceives us *a.*
Ard. 1472 to encounter *a.* their accusations
Ard. 1502 thou wilt be hanged in Kent, when *a.* is done
Ard. 1505 I think thou ne'er said'st prayer in *a.* thy life
Ard. 1512 the devil break *a.* your necks at four miles'end !
Ard. 1522 ay, in health towards Feversham, to shame us *a.*
Ard. 1530 and if *a.* the Cheinies in the world say no
Ard. 1536 let us go, and tell her *a.* the matter
Ard. 1586 how doth my mistress and *a.* at home?
Ard. 1588 ay, how doth she and *a.* the rest ?
Ard. 1619 if *a.* the rest do fail, will catch
Ard. 1636 and buries *a.* his haughty pride in dust
Ard. 1698 and then *a.* our labour's lost
Ard. 1737 zounds, I was ne'er so toiled in *a.* my life
Ard. 1804 and *a.* the sailors praying on their knees
Ard. 1839 perjured beast ! bear this and *a.* !
Ard. 1851 *a.* for a worthless kiss and joining arms
Ard. 1861 no, ears and *a.* were witched ; ah me
Ard. 1928 by the ears till *a.* his beer hath run out
Ard. 1931 went to the clerk and cut *a.* the notches of his tallies
Ard. 1937 *a.* the tenpenny-alehouses-men would stand
Ard. 1949 and railed on Franklin that was cause of *a.*
Ard. 2017 but what of *a.* this ? how shall he be slain ?
Ard. 2026 see *a.* things ready, Alice, against we come
Ard. 2158 ah, that villain will betray us *a.*
Ard. 2178 how now ? what's the matter ? is *a.* well ?
Ard. 2210 I fear me, Michael, *a.* will be bewrayed
Ard. 2233 I like not this ; I pray God *a.* be well
Ard. 2260 the Mayor and *a.* the watch are coming
Ard. 2277 as we went, it snowed *a.* the way
Ard. 2306 thou hast betrayed and undone us *a.*
Ard. 2329 I loved him more than *a.* the world beside
Ard. 2376 and run full blank at *a.* adventures
Ard. 2413 let my death make amends for *a.* my sins
Ard. 2419 to speedy execution with them *a.* !
JB 35 the good will and favour of al her friends and kinsfolk
JB 139 left the poysoned man *a.* alone that whole night longe
JB 140 *a.* that night was he extreame sicke
JB 142 vomiting till his intrailes were *a.* shrunke and broken
JB 177 did she not as he would have her in *a.* things
JB 224 the Lord give *a.* men grace by their example to
Puck. 68 in *a.* humillitie & in the feare of god
Puck. 84 Yo^r L^ps most humble in *a.* duties, Th. Kydde
STA 1199 all's one, Hieronimo, acquaint me with it
ST 1324 that als revealed to Hieronimo
Ard. 1589 all's well but Susan ; she is sick
Jer. 578 so legd, so facst, so speecht, so *a.* in *a.*

SP 1152 and, *a.* in *a.*, their deedes heroicall
SP 2136 affable ; and, *a.* in *a.*, his deeds heroyacall

All-amazed.
Cor. 711 but all amaz'd, with fearefull, hollow eyes

Allay.
ST 1420 to know the cause that may my cares *a.* ?
SP 2156 yet that alayes the furie of my paine

Alle.
HP 1340 Come la nobil Greca ch' *a.* tele sue

Allegiance.
SP 1853 and, as our duty and aleageance bound us

Allevement.
SP 836 yet this is some aleagement to my sorrow [So Qq. —
      Boas : aleavement]

Alley.
STA 2073 bring me thorow allie and allye

Allow.
Cor. 1015 and of no labour will *a.*,

Allowed.
HP 193 to shew that I *a.* of that he spake
HP 1629 may have some sufficient gaine *a.*

All-powerless.
Cor. 809 all powreles give proud Caesars wrath free passage

All-raging.
Cor. 1872 *a.* mad to rig his better Vessels

All-to.
Ard. 696 a watchet satin doublet *a.* torn

Allure.
Jer. 118 him with a goulden baite will I *a.*
Cor. 933 and by the traynes, where-with he us allures

Alluring.
SP 777 ah, how thine eyes can forge *a.* lookes

All-wrathful.
Jer. 1131 when his all wrathfull sword did basely point at

Ally.
SP 909 whose neere alye he was and cheefe delight

Allying.
Cor. Arg. 17 *a.* himselfe to Juba King of Numidia

Almains.
Cor. 1202 the restfull Allmaynes with his crueltie he rashly styrd

Almighty.
HP 491 the providence of our *a.* God.
HP 566 Or that th'almightie would with lightning drive me to

Almost.
HP 197 but he then, *a.* at a staie, said
HP 264 old Nestor at the[m] *a.* as a Parasite
HP 705 call him Phoebus with these Epythetons *a.* co[n]tinually
Cor. 117 and *a.* yoked all the world beside
Cor. 406 in mine armes he *a.* felt the poygnard
Cor. 1354 the sea, the earth, and all is *a.* ours
Cor. 1384 that hath *a.* made an universall conquest
Cor. 1764 one while the top doth *a.* touch the earth
Jer. 887 what, have I *a.* quited you ?
SP 547 the ones a Lyon *a.* brought to death
Ard. 811 zounds, draw, Shakebag, I am *a.* killed
Ard. 1007 *a.* ten.
Ard. 1375 'tis *a.* supper-time, thou shalt stay with us
Ard. 1475 come, we are *a.* now at Rainham Down
Ard. 1677 I am *a.* stifled with this fog
Ard. 1683 here, Shakebag, *a.* in hell's mouth
Ard. 1703 help, Will, help, I am *a.* drowned
Puck 55 whom I have servd *a.* theis iij. yeres nowe

Aloft.
HP 1228 if *a.*, where it lyes in prospect, or below in some valley

Alone.
Eng. Parn. 12 (Vertue excepted) which *a.* survives

Jer. 272 let mee *a*. ; Ile turne him to a ghoast
ST 441 I. goe, Horatio, leave me heere *a*.
ST 490 let me *a*., l'le scatter them my selfe
ST 1228 let me *a*. ; ile send to him to meet the Prince
ST 1500 let them *a*. till some other time
SP 641 nay, one *a*. to honor his beloved
SP 1899 thy soule shall not go mourning hence *a*.
SP 1902 nor shall her death *a*. suffice for his
Ard. 494 I never live good day with him *a*.
Ard. 545 go to her, Clarke ; she's all *a*. within
Ard. 765 when she hath lost her mate, sitteth *a*.
Ard. 1142 and then let me *a*. to handle him
Ard. 1745 let me *a*. ; it most concerns my state
Ard. 2236 leave that to my charge, let me *a*.
Ard. 2243 you know I do not love to be *a*.
JB 139 left the poysoned man all *a*. that whole night longe

Alonely.
Cor. 1489 is not *a*. happy in this world

Along.
Cor. 1407 th'impatient people runne *a*. the streets
Cor. 1630 coasting *a*. and following by the foote
ST 291 and tribute paiment gone *a*. with him ?
STA 2074 still with a distracted countenance going a long
ST 3004 and let the winde and tide hall me *a*. to
SP 199 *a*. the coasts held by the Portinguize
SP 439 yet stay, Ile ride *a*. with thee my selfe
Ard. 128 to come this morning but *a*. my door
Ard. 1488 my honest friend that came *a*. with me
Ard. 1497 and bring your honest friend *a*. with you ?
Ard. 1537 let her go *a*. with us
Ard. 1539 and us the more for bringing her *a*.
Ard. 1828 wronged, in that we did not carry her *a*.
Ard. 1890 come thou thyself, and go *a*. with me
Ard. 2025 come, Master Greene, go you *a*. with me
Ard. 2302 ay, so they shall : come you *a*. with us

Aloof.
ST 2695 shall stand aloofe and looking at it, tell

Aloud.
ST 1591 and cry *a*. for justice through the Court
Ard. 1161 crying *a*., « Thou art the game we seek »

Alps.
Cor. 1722 lyke Northern windes that beate the horned **Alpes**
Cor. 1762 as on the Alpes the sharpe Nor-North-east wind

Already.
HP 956 they having alreadye so much temperaunce and
Cor. 221 Latium (alreadie quaild) will be destroyd
Cor. 249 *a*. wander under your commaunds
Cor. 704 eyes, *a*. tyerd and loaden with my teares
Cor. 803 that fiercely burnes a house *a*. fired
Cor. 855 and many a Romaine sword *a*. drawne
Cor. 1593 or wherefore am I not *a*. dead ?
Cor. 1671 them that *a*. dream'd of death or flight
ST 562 I think our councell is *a*. set
ST 606 I have *a*. found a stratageme
ST 795 that is perfourmd alreadie, my good Lord
ST 801 between us theres a price *a*. pitcht
ST 866 O sir, forbeare : your valour is *a*. tride
ST 1374 tell him his pardon is *a*. signde
ST 2285 *a*. is betroth'd to Balthazar
ST 2528 for why the plots *a*. in mine head
ST 2610 for I *a*. have conceited that
SP 1337 the breach thats made *a*. on the other side
SP 1534 and joyne their hands, whose hearts are knit *a*. ?
SP 1672 faith, I am wearie of the office alreadie
SP 1692 now sir, Cupid, seeing you alreadie hurt before
SP 1837 because we were alreadie in his gallyes

SP 1889 ah, poore Erastus, art thou dead *a*. ?
Ard. 204 and matched *a*. with a gentleman
Ard. 813 zounds, I am tame enough *a*.
Ard. 1028 is he himself *a*. in his bed ?
Puck. 45 of my religion & life I have alredie geven some instance

Alta.
HP 823 ite per *a*. Dindyma

Altars.
Cor. 1126 their temples, A., and theyr Images

Alter.
ST 1232 when thinges shall *a*., as I hope they wil
SP 1523 unlesse my state shall *a*. by my will
Ard. 1567 that time nor place nor persons *a*. me
Ard. 1823 happy the change that alters for the best !

Alteration.
HP 895 either by *a*. of time or variety of customes

Altered.
HP 786 if the mylke *a*. not the bodies
SP 952 I marry, sir, then the case is *a*., I, and haltered to
SP 1391 what pleaseth the eye, when the sence is *a*. ?

Although.
HP 263 *a*., by the opinion of Lucian, they
HP 278 *a*. they be of great nourishment, yet
HP 1583 *a*. it be impertinent to Husbandry and housekeeping
Cor. 1326 can live content, *a*. unknowne
ST Bal. 108 *a*. in heart I never meant
ST 225 young prince, *a*. thy fathers hard misdeedes
ST 268 nor I, *a*. I sit beside my right
ST 522 *a*. I sound not well the misterie
ST 767 *a*. she coy it as becomes her kinde
ST 821 *a*. my fainting hart controles my soule
ST 874 *a*. his life were still ambituous proud
ST 1884 *a*. he send not that his Sonne returne
ST 2460 nor dies Revenge, *a*. he sleepe awhile
ST 2501 *a*. I beare it out for fashions sake
SP 259 *a*. it go against my starres to jest, yet
SP 1659 *a*. in time perhaps I might aspire to
SP 1763 *a*. to me you never come to soone ?
SP 1914 *a*. his age did plead for innocence
Ard. 1241 but needs must on, *a*. to danger's gate
Ard. 1772 *a*. the rent of it be very small
Ard. 1778 *a*. the rent of it was ever mine
Ard. 1826 *a*., most bounteous and liberal
Ard. 2088 *a*. I wished you to be reconciled
JB 13 of which law, *a*. no man is ignorant, and
JB 28 who, *a*. hee was better beloved, yet
JB 63 *a*. she could not any way amend it
JB 66 *a*. he was not as then in estate to
JB 71 and *a*. she often refused to work his death
JB 76 and *a*. the honest young man loved hir tenderly
JB 156 honest woman, *a*. through her youth she knew not
JB 162 *a*. she since confessed it was not
JB 199 *a*. I never found any by thee
Puck. 21 *a*. his L\[p\] never knewe his service
Puck. 47 *a*. p[er]haps my paines and undeserved tortures

Alto.
HP 938 Di lei, ch' *a*. vestigio

Altogether.
HP 1387 the one ordered with the other may altogeather consent

Altra.
HP 1653 E perchè l'usuriere[e] *a*. via tiene

Altro.
HP 1655 Dispregia, poichè in *a*. pon la spene

Always.
HP 130 alwaies hath beene used to strangers
HP 185 hanging alwaies on the earth and

HP 1187 for Landes are not alwaies let at one rate
HP 1373 she shall alwaies have them ready and at hand
HP 1557 to be considered alwaies in respect of him that
HP 1509 alwaies worketh to a certaine set and
Cor. 108 as if inconstant Chaunce were alwaies one
Cor. 509 Death's alwaies ready, and our time is knowne
Cor. 916 due punishment succeedes not alwaies after an offence
Cor. 1570 for their wound is alwaies one
ST Bal. 72 it allwayes at my hart is kept
ST Bal. 100 and of my sonne did allwayes cry
STA 1788 they doe not alwayes scape, that is some comfort
SP 727 I alwayes told you that such coward knights
SP 1405 why, how now, Erastus, alwaies in thy dumpes?
Ard. 1485 your honour's a. ! bound to do you service

Amain.
Cor. 807 till it finde a trayne to seaze upon, and then it flames
    amaine
Ard. 559 I told him all, whereat he stormed a.
Ard. 1467 watching the drops that fell a. from thence

Amariores.
HP 318 Inger mi calices a.

Amazed.
Cor. 306 thou saw'st the trembling earth with horror mazed?
Cor. 711 but all amaz'd, with fearefull, hollow eyes
ST Bal. 64 I stood forlorne, as one amased in his minde
Ard. 1986 faith, I was so a., I could not strike

Amazement.
Jer. 626 which strooke a. to their pauled speeche

Ambages.
ST 473 let goe these a., and in plaine tearmes acquaint

Ambassador.
Jer. 77 so, so, Andrea must be sent imbassador ?
Jer. 97 Andreas gone embassador
Jer. 143 to full of spleene for an imbassador
Jer. 236 thou knowest Andreas gone embassador
Jer. 316 an embas[sador], my Lord, is new arived from Spaine
Jer. 320 welcom, worthy lord, Spaines choyse embassador
Jer. 413 you know Andreas gone embassador
Jer. 448 to Don Andrea, Spaines embassador ?
Jer. 580 welcome, faire Lord, worthy embassador
Jer. 981 when first thou camst embassador
ST 289 is our embassadour dispatcht for Spaine ?
ST 494 to feast the Portingall Embassadour
ST 497 to welcome hither our Embassadour
ST 556 which hath pleasde both the Embassador and me
ST 1082 Embassadour, what news hath urg'd
ST 1851 now shew, Embassadour, what our Viceroy saith
ST 1928 and, Brother, now bring in the Embassador
ST 2537 at the entertainement of the Embassadour
Jer. 653 welcome home, Lord embassador
ST 499 see, Lord Embassadour, how Spaine intreats
ST 773 then Lord Embassadour of Portingale
ST 1936 on then, and heare you, Lord Embassadour
Jer. 83 we make thee our Lord hie imbassador

Ambition.
Cor. 24 poysoned A. (rooted in high mindes)
Cor. 944 whose fell a. (founded first in blood)
Cor. 1167 nor urg'd by ought but his a.
Cor. 1192 who (monster-like) wyth his a. hath
Cor. 1199 which with a. now he ruinates
Cor. 1418 but destinie revers'd th'effect of theyr a.
ST 321 my late a. hath distaind my faith
Jer. 101 Ambitions plumes, that florish in our court

Ambitious
Cor. 132 what right had our a. auncestors
Cor. 373 till thys a. Tyrants time

Cor. 1131 but if (envenom'd with a. thoughts)
Jer. 1080 Ile top thy head for that a. word
ST 373 but thy a. thought shall breake thy necke
ST 748 a. villaine, how his boldenes growes
STA 2018 O a. begger, wouldest thou have that

Ambitious-proud.
ST 874 although his life were still ambituous proud

Ambrosia.
SP 1461 lips of pure Corall, breathing Ambrosie

Ambush.
SP 1108 and heere and there in a. Death will stand

Amen.
JB 115 « mary, A., » quoth she

Amend.
HP 1707 thereof to certefie mee and a. it
ST 2862 with *God amende that mad Hieronimo*
Ard. 993 she will a., and so your griefs will cease
JB 64 although she could not any way a. it
Cor. 1206 to whom we should do well (for some amends)
SP 706 why then the mends is made, and we still friends
Ard. 132 do, and one day I'll make amends for all
Ard. 818 what 'mends shall I have for my broken head ?
Ard. 819 marry, this 'mends, that if you get you not away
Ard. 1902 a fault confessed is more than half amends
Ard. 2413 let my death make amends for all my sins
JB 198 refusest to make amends for thy fault

Amended.
ST (Title) newly corrected, a., and enlarged with new Additions
Ard. 1455 I have been often so, and soon a.

Amiable.
ST 808 the Prince is a. and loves her well

Amicitia.
Puck 27 Digni sunt a. quib[us] in ipsis inest

Amid.
SP 505 as stormes that fall a. a sun shine day
SP 1040 and then and there fall downe a. his armes

Amidst.
Cor. 394 had hee a. huge troopes of Armed men beene
Jer. 1020 mingle your selfe againe a. the army
ST 32 not farre from hence, a. ten thousand soules
ST 349 Don Balthazar, a. the thickest troupes
ST 393 your worthy chivalier a. the thikst
ST 899 a. these darke and deathfull shades
ST 985 then will I joy a. my discontent
ST 1023 seated a. so many helpeles doubts
ST 1664 a. a crue of thy confederates
SP 1662 a. their Church they bound me to a piller
SP 2188 miserie a. his greatest joy and jollitie

Amilcars.
Cor. 1980 the Hannons, the A., Asdrubals

Amiss.
ST 677 least absence make her thinke thou dost amisse
SP 2185 for Solimans too much amisse, this day shall be
Ard. 591 a drift will quiet all, whatever is a.
Ard. 2224 I know something's a., he is not well

Amity.
Cor. 959 nay, he was mov'd with former amitie
Jer. 380 woundes will tie an everlasting setled a.
Jer. 943 why, man, in war thers bleeding a.
ST 750 where first we vowd a mutuall amitie

Among.
Cor. 1529 for high Jove the heavens a.
Jer. 1195 I hope thers never a Jew a. you all
STA 1767 reccons his parents a. the rancke of fooles
ST 2338 or what a scandale wert a. the Kings, to
SP 176 welcome, Castilian, too a. the rest

SP 1638 I will go sit *a.* my learned Euenukes
Ard. 501 there, forsooth, he revels it *a.* such filthy ones
Ard. 1136 't would make a peasant swear *a.* his boys
Ard. 1235 and sought to build my nest *a.* the clouds
JB 189 and a shame *a.* my neighbours
Jer. 916 this should not be mong men of vertuous sprit

Amongst.

VPJ 87 God graunt thee long *a.* us breathe
HP Ind. 2 ayde *a.* Servants for the
HP 98 *a.* the woods and in a Countrey Towne
HP 652 *a.* which three affectio[n]s Feare is
HP 973 conflict *a.* the Romains which they called Cyvill warre
HP 1021 *a.* which, those relicts and fragme[n]ts of
HP 1074 love and courtesie entreats not thus *a.* them
HP 1109 (*a.* who[m] I wish thee to be numbred)
HP 1283 *a.* whom she shall have one above the rest
HP 1350 the daughter of *Alcinoe,* the King of *Phaeaces, a.* them
HP 1561 devided and bequeathed *a.* his Children
HP 1758 *a.* the houses of the Dukes of Savoy
Cor. Arg. 21 was a fierce and furious battaile given *a.* them
Cor. 192 *a.* the forward Souldiers first discend
Cor. 242 you that *a.* the darksome mansions of
Cor. 385 for oft he search't *a.* the fierce allarms
Cor. 708 in tryumph borne *a.* the conquering Romans
Cor. 797 and Juba, that *a.* the Mores did raigne
Cor. 839 to serve no stranger, but *a.* us one that
Cor. 859 *a.* the rest of mine extreame mishaps
Cor. 1573 *a.* so many wracks as I have suffred
Cor. 1813 make forth *a.* the flock, that scattered flyes
Jer. 250 his bounty *a.* souldiers sokes him dry
ST 22 I might not sit *a.* his passengers
ST 351 *a.* the rest I saw him, hand to hand
ST 796 *a.* the rest of what you have in charge
ST 1392 the winde convay our words *a.* unfreendly eares
SP 105 *a.* these worthies will Erastus troupe
SP 106 though like a Gnat *a.* a hive of Bees
Ard. 666 domineer'd with it *a.* good fellows
Ard. 1228 and he but pines *a.* his delicates, whose
Puck 14 *a.* those waste and idle papers
Puck 32 nombred *a.* the best conditions of men
VPJ 1 mongst spyny cares sprong up now at the last
Cor. 907 a hatefull race, mongst whom there dooth abide
Cor. 1582 mongst whom above the rest, that moves me most
Cor. 1908 that mongst the spirits th'infernall Lakes may
Cor. 1929 but mongst the rest, what horrible offence, what
ST 2644 seene the like in Paris, mongst the French Tragedians

Amor.

HP 682ᵃ Ovid De med. faciei Certus *a.* moru[m] est

Amores.

HP 563 Ille meos, primus qui me sibi junxit, *A.* abstulit

Amorous.

HP 757 with love and lovely termes and *a.* games
Jer. 832 silken charme, tyed with an *a.* knot
ST 2764 how well he acts his amourous passion
SP 270 glances of many *a.* girles, or rather ladies

Amurath.

SP 524 say, brother *A.*, and Haleb, say
SP 568 now for thy chastisement know, *A.*
SP 588 no, *A.*, for murthering him thou dyest
SP 599 accursed *A.*, that for a worthlesse cause
SP 602 yet, *A.*, thou wert my brother too
SP 657 I did accomplish on Haleb and *A.*

An. [*also see* **And.**]

Ard. 895 nay, *a.* you be offended, I'll be gone
Ard. 1135 he were a villain, *a.* he would not swear
Ard. 2208 or, *a.* thou sayest the word, let us sit down too

Ancestor.

Cor. 481 brave Scipio, your famous auncestor
Cor. 92 thou vaunt'st not of thine Auncestors in vaine
Cor. 132 what right had our ambitious auncestors
Cor. 259 have made thine auncesters and thee renound
Cor. 1711 to shew as worthy of our auncesters
Cor. 2007 and of the joyes mine auncestors enjoy'd
SP 1341 now let their soules tell sorrie tidings to their *a.*

Anchor.

Cor. Arg. 27 where (lying at *a.*) he was assailed
Cor. 1870 at *a.*, slightly shipt, besieg'd, betraide by winde

Ancient.

HP 291 of the auncient times of Noble men
HP 473 the auncient Gentlewoman, giving thanks, arose
HP 712 an auncient custome, as we read of Hellen in Euripides.
HP 942 the authority of Hesiodus, that auncient Poet
Cor. 121 of th'*a.* freedom wherein we were borne
Cor. 371 which peaceably retain'd her auncient state
Cor. 498 whose auncient beautie, worth and weapons
Cor. 967 nor auncient lawes, nor nuptiall chast desire
Cor. 1128 suffer not his *a.* liberty to be represt
Cor. 1669 he showes that auncient souldiers need not feare
Cor. 1686 for my part (being an auncient Senator
Cor. 1698 our goods, our honors, and our auncient lawes
ST 2421 house, the Duke of Castile, Ciprians *a.* seat
SP 1510 the self same musick that in auncient daies brought

And. [*also see* **An.**]

ST 1380 open 't not, *a.* if thou lovest thy life
ST 1738 nay, *a.* you argue things so cunningly, weele goe
ST 2141 Petitioners, that are importunate, *a.* it shall please: you, sir
ST 2568 in faith, Hieronimo, *a.* you be in earnest
SP 1267 the Governour will hang you, *a.* he catch you
Ard. 120 nay, *a.* you be so impatient, I'll be gone

Andrea.

Jer. (Title) and the life and death of Don Andraea
Jer. 57 Oh, heeres a Lad of mettle, stout Don *A.*
Jer. 70 pray, king, pray, peeres, let it be Don *A.*
Jer. 77 so, so, *A.* must be sent imbassador ?
Jer. 82 then, Don *A.* —
Jer. 94 farwel then, Don *A.* ; to thy chargde
Jer. 97 Andreas gone embassador
Jer. 106 I hate *A.*, cause he aimes at honor
Jer. 155 O deere *A.*, pray, lets have no wars
Jer. 169 but will you indeed, *A.* ?
Jer. 249 indeede *A.* is but poore, though honorable
Jer. 257 at his returne to Spaine, Ile murder Don *A.*
Jer. 271 come then, how ere it hap, *A.* shall be crost
Jer. 277 murder *A.* ? O Inhumain practis
Jer. 281 murder *A.* ? honest lord ? Impious villayns
Jer. 287 Ile dispatch letters to don *A.*
Jer. 290 murder *A.* ?
Jer. 304 murder *A.* ? What bloud sucking slave
Jer. 321 brave, stout *A.*, for soe I gesse thee
Jer. 327 and we receve them, and thee, worthy *A.*
Jer. 336 thus much returne unto thy King, *A.*
Jer. 365 meete, Don *A.* ? Yes, in the battles Bowels
Jer. 373 meet, Don *A.* ? I tell thee, noble spirit
Jer. 406 remember, Don *A.*, that we meet
Jer. 413 you know Andreas gone embassador
Jer. 443 all Don *A.*, not Alcario
Jer. 448 to Don *A.*, Spaines embassador ?
Jer. 459 « Signeor *A.* », say
Jer. 460 « Signeor *A.* »
Jer. 511 « Signeor *A.*, tis a villainus age this »
Jer. 553 love to *A.*, I, even to his very bosome

Jer. 571 that Don A. may prevent his death
Jer. 574 you are as like A., part for part, as he
Jer. 581 worthy embassador, brave Don A.
Jer. 583 what, have you given it out A. is returnd?
Jer. 614 welcome, brave Don A., Spaines best of sperit
Jer. 619 welcom, my lifes selfe forme, deere Don A.
Jer. 622 what newes, A.? treats it peace or war?
Jer. 630 tis all about the Court Andreas come
Jer. 650 now lives A., now A. dies
Jer. 652 Lazarotto has kild me in stead of A.
Jer. 657 why, Don, Don A.
Jer. 660 I, Don A., or else Don the devill
Jer. 669 son Horatio, see A. slaine
Jer. 670 A. slaine? then, weapon, clyng my brest
Jer. 672 lives Don A.?
Jer. 689 who names A. slaine? O, tis A.
Jer. 694 A. lives: O let not death beguile thee
Jer. 695 are you A.?
Jer. 707 was it not you, A., questioned me?
Jer. 709 belike twas false A., for
Jer. 723 ha, A., the foore runner of these newes?
Jer. 725 ha, A., speake; what newes from Portugale?
Jer. 740 A. had line there, he walkt upright
Jer. 755 to kill A., which hire kild himselfe
Jer. 761 I tooke him for A., downe he fell
Jer. 803 wheres our lord generall, Lorenzo, stout A.
Jer. 926 I bind thee, Don A., by thy honer
Jer. 938 therefore, A., as thou tenderst fame
Jer. 958 I am all fire, A.
Jer. 969 valliant A., fortunate Lorenzo
Jer. 983 can you not find [me] Don A. forth?
Jer. 987 valliant A., by thy worthy bloud
Jer. 993 might I now and A. in one fight make
Jer. 995 whose that? A.?
Jer. 1027 I have sweat much, yet cannot find him. — A.
Jer. 1070 could I meete A., now my blouds a tiptoe
Jer. 1077 A., we meet in bloud now
Jer. 1090 my harts friend, O my A. slaine
Jer. 1124 A. slaine, thanks to the stars above
ST 5 my name was Don A.; my discent
ST 86 then know, A., that thou art ariv'd where
ST 156 till Don A. with his brave Launciers
ST 162 and in that conflict was A. slaine
ST 445 had he not loved A. as he did
ST 567 be still, A.; ere we go from hence
ST 1628 A., O A., that thou sawest
ST 1689 disgrace which you for Don A. had indurde
ST 2380 it is not now as when A. liv'd
ST 2444 such fearefull sights, as poore A. sees
ST 2456 content thy selfe, A.; though I sleepe, yet
ST 2463 beholde, A., for an instance, how
Jer. 120 to be Andreas death at his retourne
Jer. 124 Andreas Himens draught shall be in bloud
Jer. 190 all honor on Andreas steps attende
Jer. 212 the love betwixt Bellimperia and Andreas bosome?
Jer. 236 thou knowest Andreas gone embassador
Jer. 306 what, harping still upon Andreas death?
Jer. 420 I have a suit just of Andreas cullers
Jer. 435 moreover, I will buze Andreas landing
Jer. 577 I could not think you but Andreas selfe
Jer. 705 this letter came not to Andreas hands
Jer. 752 firmly planted in Don Andreas bosome
Jer. 757 he tooke Andreas shape unknowne to me
Jer. 843 Andreas bosome bears away my hart
Jer. 985 shriller then all the trumpets, to pierce Andreas ears
Jer. 1093 and fetch Andreas ransome fourth thy vaines

Jer. 1155 Don Andreas ghoast salutes me, see, embraces me
Jer. 1182 spent upon the Funerall of Andreas dust
ST Bal. 28 her love Andreas woofull fate
ST 386 relate the circumstance of Don Andreas death
ST 400 enuying at Andreas praise and worth
ST 409 and left not till Andreas life was done
ST 414 but then was Don Andreas carkasse lost?
ST 443 yet what availes to waile Andreas death
ST 450 Ile love Horatio, my Andreas freend
ST 618 for thy conveiance in Andreas love
ST 634 I meane, whome loves she in Andreas place?
ST 635 alas, my Lord, since Don Andreas death
ST 1703 your first favourite Don Andreas death
ST 1709 who burnt like Ætne for Andreas losse

Andromache.
SP 136 fortune as the good A. wisht valiant Hector

Anew.
ST Bal. 165 whose death I could a. bewayle
ST 1432 for I had written to my Lord a.

Angel.
Jer. 1058 had not Horatio plaid some Angels part
HP 493 whose dignity doth come so neere the Angels
Jer. 714 angels of heaven forefend it
Jer. 825 why it would raise spleene in the host of Angels
Ard. 729 I'll give you twenty angels for your pains
Ard. 730 how? twenty angels? give my fellow
Ard. 731 give my fellow George Shakebag and me twenty angels?
Ard. 739 will you kill him? here's the angels down
Ard. 807 how can I miss him, when I think on the forty angels
Ard. 1089 I would have crammed in angels in thy fist

Anger.
SP 293 he saw my a. figured in my brow
Ard. 1277 it is not love that loves to a. love
Ard. 1513 zounds, I could kill myself for very a.!

Angry.
Cor. 1014 one while shee bends her a. browe
Jer. 826 enough to make [the] tranquile saints of a. stuffe
ST 2566 nay, be not angrie, good Hieronimo
SP 1595 and therefore angrie heavens will be revengd
SP 1781 be not angrie for that I carry thy beloved from thee
Ard. 114 but tell me, is he a. or displeased?
Ard. 2104 I pray you be not a. or displeased

Anguish.
Cor. 1930 O see mine a.; haplie seeing it

Animal.
HP 927 so that a servaunt may be called A. rationale
HP 1671 that God is a. sempiternum et optimum

Animatum.
HP 1105 is A. actionis et Instrumentum seperabile

Animatus.
HP 1098 they are Inanima, things without soule, he is A.

Anne.
JB 23 a proper young woman named A. Welles
JB 80 still to be termed A. Welles as she was before
JB 148 ‹ well A., › quoth, hee, ‹ stay with mee now

Annexed.
VPJ (Title) whereunto is a. Tychbornes Lamentation
HP 1711 more might be annext to that which he hath uttered

Annorum.
ST 999 Aut si qui faciunt a. oblivia

Annoy.
VPJ 88 God shield thee from a.
Cor. 340 and we have time to burie our a.?
ST 718 that pleasure followes paine, and blisse a.
ST Bal. 3 feeding on nought but dire annoyes

Annoyance.

HP 1677 touching the hurt or annoyaunce of Nature
Ard. 1453 the *a.* of the dust or else
Annoyed.
HP 1514 may not thereby be anoyd or hyndered
Annoyeth.
HP 1050 as sluttishness *a.* and impayreth it
Anoint.
Cor. 1214 annoynt theyr sinewes fit for wrestling
Cor. 1759 that with our blood she may annoynt her sword
Anon.
HP 8 surchargd, pursued, and *a.* overtaken
HP 113 and *a.* there came the Father
SP 2016 a giddie goddesse that now giueth and *a.* taketh
Ard. 299 that question we'll decide *a.*
Ard. 2193 is't nothing else ? tush, he'll be here *a.*
Ard. 2202 fear you not, he'll come *a.* ; meantime
Another.
HP Ind.3 for the helpe and ease of one *a.*
HP 80 divers roomes and stories, one above *a.*
HP 88 *a.* Gate, and thereby we descended
HP 110 there mette us *a.* youth of lesse yeeres
HP 114 a footeman and *a.* servitor
HP 177 there is an other garden full of all sorts of
HP 355 which the labour of *a.* time hath yielded
HP 553 imagined the soule did passe from one unto *a.*
HP 554 as dooth the Pilgrim passing from one lodging to *a.*
HP 1033 doone by him that hath *a.* charge
HP 1040 nowe to one, nowe to *a.*
HP 1070 and *a.* hath more day then work
HP 1071 one should so helpe *a.* as wee see
HP 1258 one while set in the Sunne, *a.* while in the winde
HP 1285 shall keepe one keye, and she *a.*
HP 1450 one asked *a.* whether he were a Pyrat or a Rover
HP 1501 the league and traffique that one Cittie hath with *a.*
HP 1501 one Province or Countrey with *a.*
HP 1680 that the corruption of one bee the generation of *a.*
Cor. Ded. 25 and *a.* of the night in wishing you all happines
Cor. 127 doe that to *a.*, which our selves dysdaine
Cor. 298 one while the hart, *a.* while the liver
Cor. 395 beene wounded by *a.* any waie
Cor. 451 yet one mans sorrow will *a.* tutch
Cor. 581 reformes *a.* thing thereby
Cor. 627 and let *a.* Brutus rise
Cor. 1016 *a.* while she fleres againe, I know not how
Cor. 1536 when they heare *a.* prais'd
Cor. 1654 *a.* while we softly sally foorth
Cor. 1829 here one new wounded helps *a.* dying
Cor. 1865 but as one mischiefe drawes *a.* on
Jer. 219 from friers that nurse whores there goes *a.* path
Jer. 223 yet starve the needy swarmes, *a.* path
Jer. 1082 *a.* over mine : let them both meete
ST 128 they brought *a.* wing to incounter us
ST 541 this is *a.* speciall argument
ST 727 dye, hart ; *a.* joyes what thou deservest
ST 1247 and thus one ill *a.* must expulse
ST 2570 Ile make one. — And I, *a.*
SP 781 calst thou me love, and lovest *a.* better ?
SP 1530 this seat I keep voide for *a.* friend
SP 1611 one woman may do much to win *a.*
Ard. 633 and softly as *a.* work I paint
Ard. 842 *a.* time we'll do it, I warrant thee
Ard. 1159 and at the noise *a.* herdman came
Ard. 1260 and will extirpen me to plant *a.*
Ard. 1315 and put *a.* sight upon these eyes
Ard. 1608 such *a.* word will cost you a cuff
Ard. 1669 but yet my wife has *a.* moon

Ard. 1670 *a.* moon ?
Ard. 1689 weather to run away with *a.* man's wife
Ard. 1927 I have pierced one barrel after *a.*
JB 123 one for herselfe, and *a.* for a little boye
JB 148 « stay in the house one night, till you had gotten *a.* ? »
Cor. 97 for one man grieveth at anothers good
Cor. 453 anothers teares draw teares fro forth our eyes
Cor. 1966 and careful of anothers tiranny
Answer.
VPJ (Title) and an aunswere to the same
HP 125 to whom his Sonne made aunswer thus
HP 1388 altogeather consent, or musically aunswer crosse
Jer. 10 and that shall answere gratefully for me
Jer. 342 we shall not *a.* at next birth our fathers fawltes
Jer. 348 is this thy *a.*, Portingalle ?
Jer. 349 a royal *a.* to, which Ile maintaine
Jer. 395 then, Portugale, this is thy resolute answere ?
Jer. 982 « tis said we shall not answere at next birth »
Jer. 1018 I call thee by thy right name, answere me
ST 477 in whose faire answere lyes my remedy
ST 743 write loving lines, ile answere loving lines
ST 1306 what ere he be, ile answere him and you
ST 2329 to my sorrow, I have been ashamed to answere
SP 2017 I am wise, but quiddits will not *a.* death
Ard. 396 lest that in tears I *a.* thee again
Ard. 458 or can with safety, I will *a.* you
Ard. 626 well questioned, Alice ; Clarke, how *a.* you that ?
Ard. 682 and I am bound to *a.* at the 'size
Ard. 857 « such yearly tribute will I *a.* thee »
Ard. 1395 I pray thee, Shakebag, let this *a.* thee
Ard. 1463 her *a.* then ? I wonder how she looked
Ard. 2358 study not for an *a.* ; look not down
JB 47 made answere that he should stay for it
Answerable.
HP 1168 that what be reapes be aunswerable unto that he sowed
JB 166 whose welcome was *a.* to his desier ?
Answered.
HP 308 heere I aunswered that the Wines were
HP 330 having aunswered thus, I tasted of a cup of
HP 1728 but therunto he aunswered thus
JB 131 she *a.* « I » ; so likewise said the childe
JB 191 was nothing moved therewith, but churlishly *a.*
JB 193 *a.* shee had never been strumpet but for him
Answerest.
SP 1865 what *a.* thou unto their accusations ?
Antarctic.
HP 438 it must followe that the Pole Antartick is
Ante.
HP 562 A., pudor, quam te violem aut tua jura resolvam
Antiperistasis.
HP 801 causing that which the Philosophers call A.
HP 801ᵃ A., where heate expels cold
Antipodes.
HP 440 approcheth neerer unto our A.
Antiquities.
HP 871 *a.* written of housekeeping and government of families.
Antiquity.
HP 701 and Love by the judiciall figures of antiquitie hath
Cor. 2010 (a house of honour and antiquitie
Antony.
Cor. 1402 now therefore let us tryumph, Anthony
Cor. 1431 why, Anthony, what would you wish mee doe ?
Cor. 1438 whom fear'st thou then, Mark Anthony ?
Cor. 1470 no, Anthony, Death cannot injure us
Cor. 2011 usurpt in wrong by lawlesse Anthony ?
Ard. 296 Greene, one of Sir A. Ager's men

Ard. 680 saying he served Sir A. Cooke

Any.
HP 25 then in a. other place nigh thereabouts
HP 34 not to arrogat anie superioritie, but as
HP 195 then a. other thing
HP 214 « I cannot « (quoth I) » in anie sort commend
HP 288 without a. noisome or superfluous fulness
HP 533 so that when a. part of the bodie grieveth us
HP 551 that the soule can hee conjoynd with a. other body
HP 784 infancie, apt to be molded of a. fashion
HP 834 for if a. there be valiant, many of the
HP 949 holdeth and disposeth a. sort of weapon
HP 1214 lye neere or far fro[m] a. Cittie
HP 1214 if they joyne to a. standing Lake or Poole
HP 1216 or whether a. Springs or Ryvers be adjacent
HP 1220 whether upon the bancks to a. navigable water
HP 1225 neere to a. high way or common street
HP 1248 he heares or feareth a. dearth or scarcitie
HP 1280 as there shalbe no misse of a. other meats
HP 1303 should be first dronk or sold if thou have a. quantitie
HP 1316 may furnish a. sufficie[n]t house or dwelling
HP 1544 too too much and immoderate for a. one in Praeneste
HP 1549 ought not to exceede the rest in a. such condition
HP 1554 so a Citizen of a. Cittie whatsoever
HP 1563 neither resteth anie more for me to say
HP 1590 neither receive we a. benefit thereof
HP 1621 gathered togeather then anie other thing
Cor. Arg. 3 and the vertues of the minde as ever a. was
Cor. 333 worse than Megera, worse than a. plague
Cor. 395 beene wounded by another a. waie
Cor. 542 the resolute at a. time have stayed
Cor. 1424 by a. others greatnes be o're-ruld
Cor. 1809 nor example of a. of theyr leaders left alive
Jer. 547 there is no written name of a. Lady
ST 239 yet free from bearing a. servile yoake
ST 613 hath your Lordship a. service to command me?
ST 825 and let us know if a. make approch
ST 894 O speak, if a. sparke of life remaine
ST 1058 to yield me hope of a. of her mould
ST 1355 tis hard to trust unto a multitude, or a. one
ST 1599 nor a. phisick to recure the dead
ST 1666 where none might come at me, nor I at a.
ST 1675 as you, or a., need to rescue it?
STA 2067 in a. case observe that
ST 2146 there is not a. Advocate in Spaine that can
ST 2318 thou wouldst be loath that a. fault of thine
ST 2542 or a. such like pleasing motion
ST 2892 as a. of the Actors gone before
SP 213 infringeth the temper of a. blade
SP 908 flie, Erastus, ere the Governour have a. newes
SP 926 if into a. stay adjoyning Rhodes
SP 1195 perceive that a. of their broode but close their sight
SP 1812 why then to thee, or unto a. else, I heere protest
Ard. 19 can a. grief be half so great as this?
Ard. 48 in a. case be not too jealous
Ard. 111 in a. case you may not visit him
Ard. 178 and let not him nor a. know thy drifts
Ard. 237 for thou, or I, or a. other else
Ard. 249 why, sir, I'll do it for you at a. time
Ard. 285 or a. kind of broth that he shall eat
Ard. 485 and woe is me that a. man should want!
Ard. 630 as nothing can any way offend my sight
Ard. 632 that for a crown he'll murder a. man
Ard. 637 yet thy friend to do thee a. good I can
Ard. 796 nay, sirs, touch not his man in a. case
Ard. 918 whatever shall betide to a. of us

Ard. 1026 was never a. lived and bare it so
Ard. 1061 speak, Michael: hath a. injured thee?
Ard. 1173 God grant this vision bedeem me a. good
Ard. 1432 brawl not when I am gone in a. case
Ard. 1695 why, didst thou hear a.?
Ard. 1761 to part from a. thing may do thee good
Ard. 1824 see in a. case you make no speech of
Ard. 1968 thou dost me wrong; I did as much as a.
Ard. 2022 but come not forth before in a. case
Ard. 2272 and see you confess nothing in a. case
Ard. 2289 why, Master Mayor, think you I harbour a. such?
JB 63 although she could not a. way amend it
JB 92 without a. swelling of the body
JB 112 « but it grieves me that a. good thing should so »
JB 154 no person as then suspecting a. manner of evil
JB 158 ignorance rather then to a. malice conceaved against
JB 173 held hee up but his finger at a. time
JB 199 « although I never found a. by thee »
Puck 67 by enie waie incensd yor L^ps to
Puck 79 if I knewe eny whom I cold justlie accuse of that

Anything.
HP 162 that I send to the Cittie for any thing necessarie
HP 1705 for if anie thing be said that in your opinion may
HP 1708 for anie thing that I can see, your father
Cor. 970 all these, nor a. we can devise
Jer. 119 (for Courtiers wil doe any thing for gould)
Jer. 1159 O my pale friende, wert thou a. but a ghoast
ST 2642 they would performe any thing in action
ST 2647 whats that, Hieronimo? forget not any thing
SP 1206 I, that, or any thing thou shalt desire
Ard. 164 or a. that you will have me do
Ard. 167 I'll ne'er confess that you know a.
Ard. 1218 why, I'll agree to a. you'll have me
JB 167 she durst not denie him a. he requested
JB 214 neither would the woman confesse a. till

Apace.
HP 1347 « Upon a wel devided loome thy wife doth weave a. »
SP 1932 and wooes a. in Solimans behalfe

Apart.
HP 858 I will lay a part this argument
Cor. 1164 he layd a. the powre that he had got

Apennines.
SP 1463 neck, whiter then the snowie Apenines

Apollo.
HP 702 so Bacchus, so A., who of all the other Gods were most fayre

Apostrophe.
VPJ (Title) Ad serenissimam reginam, Elizabetham, A.

Appalled see 'Palled.

Apparel.
HP Ind. 10 Apparrell for Women
HP 1093 serves to feede, apparrell, and keepe cleane the rest
Jer. 885 devourer of apparell, thou huge swallower
Ard. 695 what a. had he?

Apparelled.
HP 682 with convenient ornaments should be sufficiently a.
HP 723 that she may goe a. as others
HP 903 apparrelled in Purple and glistering all in Golde

Apparently.
Ard 935 sith you have urged me so a.

Appeal.
SP 1808 why, then appeale to him, when thou shalt know
SP 1811 no, no; in this case no appeale shall serve
Ard. 320 I do a. to God and to the world

Appear.
Cor. 760 which eaths appeare in sadde and strange disguises

Cor. 1515 he a peaceful starre appeare
ST 198 whereby by demonstration shall appeare
ST 548 as by his Scutchin plainely may appeare
STA 1766 the more unsquard, unbevelled he appeares
Ard. 2175 the more I strive, the more the blood appears !
Appearance.
HP 588 (in dyvers actions of publique aparance)
ST 2249 to make a. before grim Mynos and
HP Ind. 116 people regard aparances
Appeareth.
HP 1320 as a. by these verses in the Booke of Virgill
HP 1334 in which verses it a. that he spake
HP 1338 to princely Ladies, as a. by these verses
Appease.
Cor. 1948 but, sacred ghost, a. thine ire, and see
Jer. 112 for such complexions best a. my pride
Appeased.
Cor. 9 oft hath such sacrafice appeas'd your ires
Jer. 907 let trybute be apeased and so stayed
Ard. 340 the deadly hatred of my heart's a.
Appertain.
HP 668 those things chiefely which appertaine to women
HP 1316 and other instruments that appertaine to weaving
HP 1521 that appertaine unto familiar or publique cares
HP Ind. 61 education of Children as well appertaines to
HP 500 this that rather appertaines to thee
HP 1726 appertaines to one and the selfesame Mason
Appetites.
HP 929 as mens a. by participation with the
HP 931 our a. receyve within themselves the forme of
HP 1291 not unpleasant to the a. of those he
Applaud.
VPJ 7 for this, thy people publikely applaude
Cor. 1720 with joyfull tokens did applaude his speeches
STA 2979 now do I a. what I have acted
Applied.
HP 801a it is a. to well water, which is
HP 1117 friendship which by Aristotle is a. in the highest
HP 1603 Number as touching Number, not aplied to materiall
   things
HP 1605 is not considered to be otherwise a.
HP 1608 a collection of a summe, not a. to things numbred
HP 1619 as that which is applyed to Gold and Silver
Applies.
HP 1764 wholy hee a. him to his housholde care
ST 2509 why then I see that heaven a. our drift
Apply.
HP 1572 to a. himselfe unto that kind of gayne
HP 1773 may endevour and a. themselves to serve in
ST 1632 constraine my selfe to patience, and a. me to the time
Appoint.
ST 275 a. the sum, as you shall both agree
ST 746 but, gratious Madame, then a. the field
ST 1283 for heere did Don Lorenzos Page a. that thou
ST 2099 for mortall men may not a. their time
SP 1867 now it resteth I a. thy death
Ard. 925 thy office is but to a. the place
JB 192 answered, shee should not a. him when to marrie
Appointed.
Cor. 532 we seeke to shorten our a. race
ST 2874 who therefore was a. to the part
ST 2880 solie a. to that tragicke part
Appointment.
HP 1197 money which was first found out by mans a.
ST 2286 and by a. and our condiscent
Apportioned.

HP 607 heate is not aportioned unto superfluous moisture
HP 1539 they ought to be a. to him that hath them
Apprehend.
Ard. 2287 I have the Council's warrant to a. him
Ard. 2338 and seek for Mosbie, and a. him too
Ard. 2366 and get the Council's warrant to a. them
Ard. 2378 the constable had twenty warrants to a. me
Apprehended.
ST 1331 he that is a. for the fact
Apprehension.
VPJ (Title) after the a. and execution of Babington
Jer. 1156 it is your love that shapes this apprehention
STA 960 weake a. gives but weake beleife
ST 1271 as for the feare of a., I know
Approach.
Jer. 603 that, when I a. within the presence of
Jer. 611 see, where she makes approch
ST 34 to whome no sooner gar. I make approch
ST 136 and stopt the malice of his fell approch
ST 825 and let us know if any make approch
Ard. 1151 whistly watching for the herd's a.
Approacheth.
HP 429 removing foregoes not, but aprocheth us
HP 432 the Sun removing out of Aries, it approcheth unto us
HP 440 approcheth neerer unto our Antipodes
Appropriate.
HP 502 (a thing most needful and a. to housekeeping)
Approve.
HP 230 expect and a. that ayde and comfort
Cor. 1683 wherein our Country shall a. our love
SP 2084 which to approve, Ile come to combate thee
HP 657 excellently approves that no collour better graceth
Approved.
HP 1743 if that be true which is a. by Socrates
Cor. 1620 and their desire to be approov'd in Armes
Jer. 82 my aproved leedge
ST 1452 dispatch : the faults a. and confest
SP 101 each one of these approved combatants
SP 155 by thy approved valour in the field
SP 217 being approoved weaker than this lim
SP 379 unmaske thyself, thou well approoved knight
SP 405 should bide the shock of such approoved knights
SP 2002 a brave Cavelere, but my aprooved foeman
Ard. 1465 and at the instant so a. upon her
Apt.
HP 232 that a. forme of speech used by Lucretius
HP 601 a woman is more a. to child-bearing in youth
HP 784 infancie. a. to be molded of any fashion
HP 923 Beastes whom Nature hath also framed a. to learne
HP 971 as onely makes them a. and ready to obey
HP 1115 capable of fashions, or a. to studie or contemplat
HP 1444 but hath framed men, that are a. to obey
Cor. 345 the wide worlds accidents are a. to change
Apter.
Cor. 170 but to forgive the a. that they be
Aptly.
HP 284 therefore'it was a. said of Virgil
Aquitain.
HP 803 nations, and especially those of Aquitan and
Arabian.
Cor. 63 The Greek, Th' A., Macedons or Medes
Arbitrament.
Cor. 245 yee gods (at whose a. all stand)
Arbour.
ST 1685 and unexpected, in an a. there, found
Ard. 954 through the thicket of an a. brake

Archers.
SP 99 and English *A.*, hardy men at armes
Archery.
HP 814 « Their horses fit for service and their *a.* for aime »
Architect.
HP 1517 the *A.* erect and builde with as much exelency
HP 1727 the selfsame Mason, Carpenter, or *A.*
Architecture.
HP 167 the use of *A.*, and other
Arden.
Ard. (Title) the lamentable and true tragedie of M. *A.*
Ard. 1 *A.*, cheer up thy spirits, and droop no more !
Ard. 73 *A.*, leave to urge her over-far
Ard. 85 a month ? ay me ! sweet *A.*, come again
Ard. 96 gallop with *A.* 'cross the Ocean
Ard. 194 decree to murder *A.* in the night ?
Ard. 198 *A.*, to me was dearer than my soul
Ard. 233 that *A.* may, by gazing on it, perish
Ard. 242 *A.*, I know, will come and show it me
Ard. 276 enjoy thee still, then *A.* should not die
Ard. 293 Master *A.*, being at London yesternight
Ard. 307 *A.*, I thought not on her, I came to thee
Ard. 319 ah, Master *A.*, you have injured me
Ard. 325 *A.*, now thou hast belched and vomited
Ard. 331 sweet *A.*, pardon me, I could not choose
Ard. 334 and, *A.*, though I now frequent thy house
Ard. 392 God will revenge it, *A.*, if thou dost
Ard. 399 *A.* shall go to London in my arms
Ard. 402 ah, if thou love me, gentle *A.*, stay
Ard. 451 Mistress *A.*, you are well met
Ard. 465 this is all, Mistress *A.* ; is it true or no ?
Ard. 470 pardon me, Mistress *A.*, I must speak
Ard. 489 why, Mistress *A.*, can the crabbed churl
Ard. 547 thank you, Mistress *A.*, I will in
Ard. 637 I hope, now Master *A.* is from home
Ard. 718 carry this letter to Mistress *A.* of Feversham
Ard. 736 *A.* of Feversham hath highly wronged me
Ard. 798 the first is *A.*, and that's his man
Ard. 824 as by this means *A.* hath escaped
Ard. 841 and in the tumult *A.* escaped us and
Ard. 846 where *A.* may be met with handsomely
Ard. 854 and sweet Alice *A.*, with a lap of crowns
Ard. 873 on *A.* so much pity would I take
Ard. 888 where supped Master *A.* ?
Ard. 957 ah, harmless *A.*, how hast thou misdone
Ard. 971 I am resolved, and *A.* needs must die
Ard. 992 gentle *A.*, leave this sad lament
Ard. 1004 that will not out till wretched *A.* dies
Ard. 1088 and *A.* sent to everlasting night
Ard. 1242 then, *A.*, perish thou by that decree
Ard. 1256 yet Mistress *A.* lives ; but she's myself
Ard. 1259 you have supplanted *A.* for my sake
Ard. 1280 thou knowest how dearly *A.* loved me
Ard. 1418 *A.* escapes us, and deceives us all
Ard. 1482 what, Master *A.* ? you are well met
Ard. 1510 come, Master *A.*, let us be going
Ard. 1517 *A.*, thou hast wondrous holy luck
Ard. 1520 for by this bullet *A.* might not die
Ard. 1533 ay, and excuse ourselves to Mistress *A.*
Ard. 1620 if all the rest do fail, will catch Master *A.*
Ard. 1697 my life for thine, 'twas *A.*, and his companion
Ard. 1729 what, is the deed done ? is *A.* dead ?
Ard. 1746 ay, Mistress *A.*, this will serve the turn
Ard. 1769 Master *A.*, I am now bound to the sea
Ard. 1787 nay, then, I'll tempt thee, *A.*, do thy worst
Ard. 1807 vengeance on *A.* or some misevent

Ard. 1816 I think so, Master *A.*
Ard. 1844 I may thank you, Mistress *A.*, for this wound
Ard. 1845 ah, *A.*, what folly blinded thee ?
Ard. 1892 why, Master *A.* ! know you what you do ?
Ard. 1943 hence, Will ! here comes Mistress *A.*
Ard. 1964 Mistress *A.*, Dick Greene and I do mean to
Ard. 1969 nay then, Mistress *A.*, I'll tell you how it was
Ard. 1983 with that comes *A.*, with his arming sword
Ard. 1997 ay, Mistress *A.*, this is your favour
Ard. 2000 took the weapon thou let'st fall, and run at *A.*
Ard. 2015 I'll fetch Master *A.* home, and we like friends
Ard. 2093 Master *A.*, methinks your wife would
Ard. 2110 pardon me, Master *A.* ; I'll away
Ard. 2113 I pray you, Master *A.*, let me go
Ard. 2132 yet, *A.*, I protest to thee by heaven
Ard. 2150 ah, Master *A.*, « now I can take you »
Ard. 2179 ay, well, if *A.* were alive again
Ard. 2191 had now, Mistress *A.* ? what ail you weep ?
Ard. 2196 now, Mistress *A.*, lack you any guests ?
Ard. 2219 Mistress *A.*, here's to your husband
Ard. 2227 fear not, Mistress *A.*, he's well enough
Ard. 2249 sweet *A.*, smeared in blood and filthy gore
Ard. 2267 alas, Mistress *A.*, the watch will take me here
Ard. 2285 Mistress *A.*, know you not one that is
Ard. 2295 *A.*, thy husband and my friend, is slain
Ard. 2346 see, Mistress *A.*, where your husband lies
Ard. 2348 *A.*, sweet husband, what shall I say ?
Ard. 2352 forgive me *A.* : I repent me now
Ard. 2354 rise up. sweet *A.*, and enjoy thy love
Ard. 2382 Mistress *A.*, you are now going to God
Ard. 2385 I pray you, Mistress *A.*, speak the truth
Ard. 2410 bear Mistress *A.* unto Canterbury
Ard. 2429 *A.* lay murdered in that plot of ground
Ard. 140 fear the biting speech of men, nor Arden's looks
Ard. 468 are void for term of Master Arden's life
Ard. 581 to make it open unto Arden's self
Ard. 794 the other is Franklin, Arden's dearest friend
Ard. 827 why, sirs, Arden's as well as I
Ard. 838 standing against a stall, watching Arden's coming
Ard. 863 as I to finish Arden's tragedy
Ard. 866 till Arden's heart be panting in my hand
Ard. 878 whose earth may swallow up this Arden's blood
Ard. 922 to give an end to Arden's life on earth
Ard. 936 I have vowed my master Arden's death
Ard. 1140 at the alehouse butting Arden's house
Ard. 1249 chief actors to Arden's overthrow
Ard. 1250 when they shall see me sit in Arden's seat
Ard. 1292 to honest Arden's wife, not Arden's honest wife
Ard. 1642 i'the broom, close watching Arden's coming
Ard. 2002 shall never close till Arden's be shut up
Ard. 2060 I shall no more be closed in Arden's arms
Ard. 2420 thus have you seen the truth of Arden's death
Argomento.
HP 915 Nudo di judicio e povero d'*a.*
Argue.
ST 1738 nay, and you *a.* things so cunningly, weele goe
ST 2477 then *a.* not, for thou hast thy request
ST 463 that argues that he lives in libertie
SP 1163 his habite argues him a Christian
Argueth.
HP 1475 in other places where hee *a.* like a Cittizen
Ard. 2320 which *a.* he was murdered in this room
Argument.
HP 242 my *a.* was more acceptable to the Sonne
HP 858 I will lay a part this *a.*
HP 916 « Naked of judgment, and poore of *a.* »

HP 983 it is a great *a.* of basenes that servile fortune
Jer. 283 the greatest *a.* and sign that I begot thee
Jer. 828 by that *a.* you firmly prove honor to
ST 177 and for some *a.* of more to come, take this
ST 341 this is another speciall *a.*
ST 551 this is an *a.* for our Viceroy
ST 1878 it is an *a.* of honorable care to
ST 2583 you will but let us know the *A.*
ST 2719 this is the *a.* of what we shew
ST 2752 this is the *a.* of that they shew
SP 738 this is good *a.* of thy true love
SP 1024 for perfect *a.* that he was true
HP 670 condemnd as arguments of much unshamefastnes
ST 656 full fraught with lines and arguments of love
Ard. 1461 and many other assured arguments

Arguto.
HP 1346 *A.* conjux percurrit pectine telas

Ariadne's.
ST 1723 of those thy tresses, Ariadnes twines

Aries.
HP 432 the Sun removing out of *A.*, it approcheth unto us
HP 434 when the world began, the Sun was in *A.*

Aright.
SP 844 for, if report but blazen her *a.*

Arise.
Cor. 565 and from the starres doth still *a.*

Ariseth.
HP 1241 and with the mony that *a.* thereof to buy

Aristippus-like.
SP 564 thou, Aristippus like, didst flatter him

Aristophanes.
HP 1743 if that be true which is approved by Socrates to *A.*

Aristotle.
HP 654 said of *A.* that Shamefastnes, which merits no praise in man
HP 803 as we read in *A.*, to wash their newe borne
HP 1117 friendship which by *A.* is applied in the highest
HP 1641 not onely beene condemned by *A.*, but
HP 1644 a sentence put by *A.* in his booke de Phisicis
HP 1671 it is also said by *A.* that God is
HP 1749 a pamphlet that is dedicated to *A.*
HP 1656 « If Aristotles phisicks thou peruse »
HP 1779 part out of Aristotles Bookes and the rest

Arm.
Cor. 1160 did arme himselfe (but in his owne defence)
ST 1231 and ile goe arme my selfe to meet him there
SP 386 he shall helpe your husband to arme his head
SP 733 goe thou foorthwith, arme thee from top to toe
SP 768 thy lookes did arme me, not my coate of steele
Cor. 1830 here lay an arme, and there a leg lay shiver'd
Jer. 680 arme, hast thou slaine thy bountifull, kind lord ?
Jer. 830 lend me thy loving and thy warlicke arme
Jer. 978 O valiant boy ; stroake with a Giants arme
Jer. 1054 for by this act I hold thy *a.* devine
Jer. 1099 this arme neare met so strong a courage
Jer. 1130 heaven and this arme once saved thee from thy foe
ST 206 held him by th' arme, as partner of the prize ?
ST 250 let goe his arme, upon our priviledge
ST 425 this scarfe I pluckt from off his liveles arme
STA 1776 the very arme that did hold up our house
STA 1780 when his strong arme unhorsd the proud Prince Balthazar
STA 2009 in my shirt, and my gowne under myne arme
ST 2265 leane on my arme : I thee, thou me shalt stay
SP 214 the vigour of this arme infringeth the temper of
SP 257 hee that will try me, let him waft me with his arme

SP 344 it is the fury of his horse, not the strength of his **arme**
SP 1008 how got he this from of Lucinas arme ?
SP 2085 my wrathfull arme shall chastise and rebuke
Ard. 1124 lop not away his leg, his *a.*, or both
Ard. 1996 sweet Mosbie, hide thy *a.*, it kills my heart
Ard. 1751 marching *a.* in *a.*, like loving friends
HP 372 woulde nestle in the armes of her Husband
Cor. 405 I saw him, I was there, and in mine armes he
Cor. 419 (with armes to heaven uprear'd) I gan exclaime
Cor. 428 with folded armes I sadly sitte and weepe
Cor. 732 I mov'd mine head, and flonge abroade mine armes
Cor. 752 and, thinking to embrace him, opte mine armes
Cor. 779 didst extend thy conquering armes beyond the Ocean
Jer. 1190 my armes are of the shortest
ST 151 there legs and armes lye bleeding on the grasse
ST 417 I tooke him up, and wound him in mine armes
ST 857 my twining armes shall yoake and make thee yeeld
ST 858 nay then, my armes are large and strong withall
SP 1040 and then and there fall downe amid his armes
SP 1772 my armes should frame mine oares to crosse the seas
SP 1935 for till I fould Perseda in mine armes, my
Ard. 399 Arden shall go to London in my arms
Ard. 1553 could once have drawn you from these arms of mine
Ard. 1837 untwine those arms
Ard. 1851 all for a worthless kiss and joining arms
Ard. 1837 when we joined arms, and when I kissed his cheek ?
Ard. 1990 kissed thee, too, and hugged thee in my arms
Ard. 2060 I shall no more be closed in Arden's arms
Ard. 2062 Mosbie's arms shall compass me, and
Cor. 19 desiring Armes to ayde our Capitoll
Cor. 60 (a martiall people madding after Armes)
Cor. 194 to excite to Armes the troopes enraged with
Cor. 893 for yee have basely broke the Law of Armes
Cor. 1138 beares the selfe-same Armes to be aveng'd on hym
Cor. 1397 discent of Affrican (so fam'd for Armes)
Cor. 1540 was enforc'd to take up Armes
Cor. 1620 and their desire to be approov'd in Armes
Jer. 802 are up in armes, glittering in steel
ST 259 inforct by nature and by law of armes
ST 335 that were a breach to common law of armes
ST 350 to winne renowne did wondrous feats of armes
SP 103 are hither come to try their force in armes
SP 152 to grace thy nuptials with their deeds at armes
SP 189 not for thy lay, but for thy worth in armes
SP 640 each one by armes to honor his beloved
SP 652 the fond Bragardo, to presume to armes
SP 1225 and now from armes to counsell sit thee downe
SP 1585 the one so renownd for armes and curtesie
Ard. 1730 what could a blinded man perform in arms ?
Cor. 1605 where are our Legions ? where our men at Armes ?
Cor. 1807 our men at Armes (in briefe) begin to flye
ST 163 brave man at armes, but weake to Balthazar
SP 1149 brave men at armes, and friendly out of armes
SP 158 in Scotland was I made a Knight at armes

Arma.
HP 826 Idaeae ; sinite *a.* viris, et cedite ferro
HP 1062 Dicendum et quae sint duris agrestibus *a.*
HP 1065 cerealiaque *a.* expediunt fessi rerum
ST 147 *A.* sonant armis vir petiturque viro

Armed.
Cor. 193 arm'd with his blood-besmeard keene Coutelace
Cor. 394 had hee amidst huge troopes of *A.* men beene
Cor. 1082 thy chyldren gainst thy children thou hast arm'd
Cor. 1124 then (arm'd) to save their freedom and their fame ?
Cor. 1661 an hoste of men to Affrique meanely Arm'd
Cor. 1674 meane-while our Emperor (at all poynts arm'd)

ST 523 the first arm'd knight that hung his Scutchin up
SP 857 jealousie had armd her tongue with malice
SP 1028 my heart had arm'd my tongue with injury

Armest.
Cor. 1079 that arm'st against thy selfe a Tyrants rage

Armi.
HP 1058 L'avaro Zappator l'a. riprende

Armies.
HP 975 the A. which the Soldane gathered of slaves
HP 1346 to muster and maintaine A. becommeth Kings, Tyrants
Cor. 1766 so did the A. presse and charge each other
Cor. 1802 theyr warlike A. (last lockt foote to foote)
ST 115 there met our a. in their proud aray
ST 348 when both the a. were in battell joynd
ST 392 when both our A. were enjoynd in fight
SP 1343 the Turkish a. did [oer-throw] in Christendome
Cor. 1393 with eyther A. murdred souldiers gore

Arming-sword.
Ard. 1983 with that comes Arden with his arming sword

Armis.
ST 147 Arma sonant a. vir petiturque viro
ST 678 why so : Tam a. quam ingenio

Armour.
HP 832 « leave a. then to such as Souldiers be »
Cor. 1633 with heavy Armor on theyr hardned backs
Cor. 1659 and quickly claps his rustie A. on
Cor. 1723 the clattring A., buskling as they paced
Cor. 1730 the Darts and Arrowes on theyr A. glaunced
Cor. 1734 the fire in sparks fro forth theyr A. flew
Cor. 1745 they hewe their A., and they cleave their casks
Cor. 1842 they layd aside theyr A., and at last
Jer. 833 prove inchaunted a. being charmed by love
ST 281 to him we yeeld the a. of the Prince
SP 88 over mine a. will I hang this chaine
ST 402 she, she her selfe, disguisde in armours maske

Armourer.
HP 1419 as the A. doth the curasse
SP 1048 marrie, sir, in an Armorours shop, where

Armoury.
HP 1410 be well resembled to the Armorie of Venice
HP 1415 compared it to some higher matter then an Armorie

Army.
HP 987 assembled an Armie of me[n] against theyr servants
HP 1413 in manner of an Armie
HP 1541 not rych that was not able to maintaine an Armie
Cor. Arg. 11 his purpose was to have reenforc'd a newe Armie
Cor. Arg. 22 seeing himselfe subdued and his Armie scattered
Cor. 1209 to make an Armie for his after-ayde against
Cor. 1400 till he lost his scattred Armie
Cor. 1653 to ease our A., if it should retyre
Cor. 1719 thys sayd, his A. crying all at once
Jer. 376 to single thee out of the gasping armye
Jer. 965 to pierce Andreas ears throgh the hot a.
Jer. 1020 mingle your selfe againe amidst the a.
ST 549 he with a puissant armie came to Spaine
Cor. 1107 our Army's broken, and the Lybian Beares devoure

Arose.
HP 473 the auncient Gentlewoman, giving thanks, a.
HP 1782 a. and accompanied me unworthy to the Chamber
Cor. 1729 clowde, a., and over-shadowed horse and man
Ard. 840 whereupon a. a brawl, and in the tumult

Arpin's.
Cor. 1059 so noble Marius, Arpins friend

Arraigned.
Ard. 711 and shall be a. the next 'size
JB 219 both araigned and condemned for the murder at the

Arrant.
JB 199 « out, a. queane » (quoth he), « thou wouldst
JB 204 « why, thou a. beast » (quoth shee), « what did

Array.
ST 115 there met our armies in their proud aray

Arrest.
SP 1802 I a. you in the Kings name
SP 1804 what thinks Lord Brusor of this strange a. ?

Arrested.
JB 49 made no more adoe but arested her for the jewels

Arrius'.
SP 1439 Augustus sparde rich Alexandria for Arrius sake

Arrived.
HP 57 wee arived on the side of the Ryver
HP 236 their Parents are arived and come unto their age
Cor. 1863 now had he thought to have ariv'd in Spayne
Jer. 316 an embas[sador], my Lord, is new arived from Spaine
ST 86 thou art ariv'd where thou shalt see
ST 526 a. with five and twenty thousand men

Arrogance.
Cor. 612 (with a. and rage enflam'd)

Arrogate.
HP 33 not to arrogat anie superioritie, but as your guide

Arrow.
HP 58 swifter then which never ranne arrowe from
Cor. 1730 the Darts and Arrowes on theyr Armour glaunced
SP 876 foole that went to shoote, and left his arrowes behinde
him ?
Ard. 1798 for curses are like arrows shot upright

Ars.
HP 1376a A. memoratina

Art.
VPJ 13 honour'd a., Princely behaviour, zeale to good
HP Ind. 5 arte of weaving honourable
HP 1318 and not without reason was this arte first
HP 1337 so much worth it seemeth that this arte hath
HP 1385 with the greatest arte and industrie
HP 1417 whether this arte of encreasing be housekeeping
HP 1423 the a. of housekeeping and getting is not all one
HP 1515 every arte dooth infinitly seeke the end it purposeth
HP 1528 in every arte the instruments should be proportioned
HP 1658 that arte doth Nature imitate and use
HP 1660 so that our arte is Neipce to God by kind »
HP 1669 Nature and arte (her follower) they despise
HP 1673 which nature is imitated of our arte
HP 1675 for arte depending upon Nature, shee is as it were
HP 1676 he that offendeth arte offendeth God
HP 1681 exercise the arte according as God commaunded
Cor. 592 cut from a spring by chaunce or arte
Cor. 2000 careles of Arte, or rich accoustrements
STA 2065 stretch thine Arte, and let their beardes be of
SP 756 Ile frame my selfe to his dissembling a.
Ard. 611 you could compound by a. a crucifix impoisoned
HP 1522 the instruments of some arts are not infinit

Arte.
HP 1647 Che l'a. vostra quella, quanto puote
HP 1649 Si che vostr' a. a Dio quasi e' Nipote

Artem.
HP 1666 Et unum alium excedere per a. et naturam

Artes.
Cor. 2038 Non prosunt Domino, quae prosunt omnibus, A. —
Tho. Kyd

Article.
HP 405 beeing no A. of our beliefe
ST 1095 these are his highnes farther articles
ST 1852 hath hee receiv'd the articles we sent ?

ST 2294 have upon thine articles confirmed thy motion
Articulated.
ST 1126 to end those thinges a. heere
Artifex.
Puck 43 ex minimo vestigio a. agnoscit artificem
Artificem.
Puck 44 ex minimo vestigio artifex agnoscit a.
Artificer.
HP 1524 if they were infinit in number, the A. could not know
  them
Ard. 1296 a mean a., that low-born name
Ard. 1384 O no, I am a base a.
HP Ind. 6 Artificers defined
HP 1101 and is also different fro[m] Artificers
HP 1102 Artificers are Instruments of those things which
  properly they call workmanship
Ard. 312 the statute makes against artificers
Artificial.
HP Ind. 11 arteficiall riches, what
HP 660 artificiall Oyles and dawbings which they use
HP 665 to recover it with slime or artificiall coullered trash
HP 1194 that is artificiall or naturall, of living things
HP 1195 Arteficiall are moveables or houshold implements
HP 1206 Arteficiall riches may all those things be called
HP 1634 an arteficiall gayne, a corrupter of a Common wealth
HP 1683 it is not artificiall that money shoulde bring forth money
Artificially.
HP 92 Trees, verie orderlie and a. disposed
HP 1388 as hath arteficially beene used by orators
As.
ST Bal. 86 a. then a Letter there I did espy
Ascend.
Cor. 144 whose mournfull cryes and shreekes to heaven a.
Cor. 1466 a. to heaven upon my winged deeds
Ascended.
HP 82 and there they a. by double staires
Ascribed.
HP 1337 been ascribd or attributed to privat huswifes
Asdrubals.
Cor. 1980 the Hannons, the Amilcars, A.
Ashamed.
HP 764 beeing a. of her selfe, a Clowde shoulde bee sent to
Jer. 449 fie : I am a shamed to see it
STA 958 away, I am a.
ST 2328 to my sorrow, I have been a. to answere
ST 2416 my Lord, I am a. it should be said
Ard. 1017 a. to gaze upon the open world
Ashes.
Jer. 912 to make their a. perjorde and unjust
Jer. 1188 Andreas dust, those once his valliant a.
SP 1570 fire, that lay with honours hand rackt up in a.
Ashore.
HP 129 whence soever he be, hee is welcome here a shore
Ashy.
Cor. 878 the ashie reliques of his haples bones
Asia.
Cor. 134 to enter A. ? What, were they the heires to
SP 196 [and] marcht [a] conquerour through A.
Aside.
HP 734 so bold and hardy that she lay a. honest shame
Cor. 369 yet Sylla, shaking tyrannie a., return'd due honors
Cor. 1842 they layd a. theyr Armour, and at last
ST 865 my Lord away with her, take her a.
SP 420 Page, set a. the jesture of my enemy
SP 2132 then tell me, (his treasons set a.) what was Erastus
Ard. 371 I cannot speak or cast a. my eye

Ask.
HP 1451 as though it were no injurie to aske him
Cor. 524 we aske Deaths ayde to end lifes wretchednes
Cor. 525 we neither ought to urge nor aske a thing
ST 231 and cards once dealt, it bootes not aske, why so ?
STA 1993 I doe not cry : aske Pedro, and aske Jaques
ST 2228 to aske for justice in this upper earth
SP 1202 aske what thou wilt ; it shall be graunted thee
Ard. 122 a. Mosbie how I have incurred his wrath
Ard. 267 you know not me that a. such questions
Ard. 292 Master Mosbie, a. him the question yourself
Ard. 607 but, so you'll grant me one thing I shall a.
Ard. 1050 methinks I hear them a. where Michael is
Ard. 1387 then a. me if my nose be on my face
Ard. 1779 sirrah, you that a. these questions
Ard. 1806 and a. of God, whate'er betide of me
ST 1424 your office askes a care to punish such as
Ard. 2331 speaks as it falls, and asks me why I did it
Askance.
Cor. 315 t' have lookt a-skance, and see so many Kings to
Asked.
HP 123 a. him whence I was
HP 1449 one a. another whether he were a Pyrat or a Rover
ST 2567 the Prince but a. a question
SP 362 when it was askt him where he had that muske
SP 1284 had I not askt it, my friend had not departed
Ard. 1462 her husband a. her whether it were not so
JB 95 kindly shee a. her husband how he did
JB 97 and a. if he would have that colde morning
JB 146 she a. him if he would have her forsworne
Asketh.
ST 837 why sit we not ? for pleasure a. ease
ST 1185 he a. for my Lady Bel-imperia
Askew.
SP 1199 for looking but a scue at heavens bright eye
Asleep.
ST 756 the gentle Nightingale shall carroll us asleepe
Ard. 67 't is like I was a. when I named him
Ard. 766 ↄ one day I fell a. and lost my master's pantofles ›
Ard. 1062 as I fell a., upon the threshold
Aspect.
HP 11 tall of stature, of a good a., well proportioned
ST 479 on whose a. mine eyes finde beauties bowre
Aspics.
Cor. 901 let A., Serpents, Snakes, and Lybian Beares
Aspire.
SP 1660 I might a. to purchase Godhead
Aspiring.
ST Bal. 20 prickt forth by fames a. wings
Ass.
Jer. 738 because I was an asse, a villainus asse
SP 1667 that doone, they set me on a milke white Asse
Assail.
SP 346 that I might assaile thy maister
Assailed.
Cor. Arg. 27 he was a., beaten and assaulted by the adverse
  Fleete
Ard. 1451 so fierce a qualm yet ne'er a. me
Assault.
Cor. Arg. 11 and give a second a. to Caesar
Cor. 64 once dare t'a. it, or attempt to lift theyr
Cor. 402 slaine trayterouslie, without a. in warre
Cor. 823 and feareles kept us from th' a. of foes
Cor. 1390 proov'd to his losse, but even in one a.
Cor. 1673 that they o're-layd them in the first a.
SP 1253 prepare a fleet to a. and conquer Rhodes

SP 2152 souldiers, *a.* the towne on every side
Assaulted.
Cor. Arg. 27 he was assailed, beaten and *a.* by the adverse Fleete
Cor. 1159 Sylla (*a.* by the enemie) did arme
Assemble.
HP 726 where other honest women and those of credit doo *a.*
Assembled.
HP 986 having *a.* an Armie of me[n] against
Cor. Arg. 16 *a.* new forces, and occupied the
SP 102 *a.* from severall corners of the world
SP 143 *a.* heere in thirsty honors cause
SP 509 that are *a.* there to try their valour
Assemblies.
Eng. Parn.7 flyes the light of Parliaments and state *a.*
HP 728 dauncings, Comedies, and other such *a.*
Assembly.
ST 2337 what honour wert in this assemblie
ST 2361 and wondrous plausible to that *a.*
Assertion.
SP 213 infringeth the temper of any blade, quoth my *a.*
Assist.
HP 938 to rescue many times and *a.* their Maisters
Ard. 1121 ne'er let this sword *a.* me when I need
Assistance.
Jer. 602 0, immortall powers, lend your *a.*
Assize.
Ard. 682 and I am bound to answer at the 'size
Ard. 712 and shall be arraigned the next 'size
Assuage.
Cor. 1063 did prove thy furie in the end, which nought could
  swage
Cor. 1189 or th' Ocean (whom no pitty can asswage)
SP 1641 I may assuage, but never quench loves fire
Assuetis.
HP 824 ubi *a.* biforem dat tibia cantum
Assurance.
Cor. 526 wherein we see so much assuraunce lyes
Cor. 1482 what more *a.* may our state defend
SP 992 but for *A.* that he may not scape
Puck 37 ffor more *a.* that I was not of that vile opinion
Assure.
Cor. Ded. 22 I will *a.* your Ladiship my next Sommers better
  travell
Cor. 1463 nor labour I my vaine life to *a.*
Cor. 1612 *a.* your selfe that Scipio bravely dyed
ST Bal. 5 *a.* yourselves it is not so
STA 935 which doe *a.* me he cannot be short lived
ST 1341 *a.* thee, Don Lorenzo, he shall dye
ST 1365 and what we may, let him *a.* him of
ST 2535 why, my good Lords, *a.* your selves of me
ST 2543 *a.* your selfe, it would content them well
ST 2560 *a.* you it will proove most passing strange
ST 2663 *a.* your selfe, shall make the matter knowne
SP 40 why, when, Perseda? wilt thou not *a.* me?
SP 868 but this *a.* your selves, it must be mine
Ard. 1447 I do *a.* you, sir, you task me much
Ard. 1813 but I *a.* you I ne'er did him wrong
Cor. 956 his owne estate more firmely he assures.
ST 2490 beliefe assures thee to be causeles slaughtered
Assured.
HP 1414 I am well *a.* he would have compared
Cor. Ded. 9 and perfectly assur'd of your honourable favours
Cor. 1163 and of his safety throughly was assur'd
Cor. 1270 and he that in his soule assur'd hath
Cor. 1891 by whom I am assurde this hap to have
Jer. 507 « Thy *a.* friend », say, « gainst Lorenzo and

Jer. 528 « Thy *a.* friend gainst Lorenzo and
Jer. 866 I am asured of your forwardnes
ST 1636 thou art assurde that thou sawest him dead?
ST 2111 yet shalt thou be *a.* of a tombe
SP 58 as if my thoughts had been *a.* true
SP 510 but more to be well *a.* by him
SP 722 0, be assur'd, tis far from noble thoughts to
SP 1186 but (as a token) that we are assurde
SP 1200 Erastus, to make thee well assurde how well
SP 1809 and be *a.* that I betray thee not
Ard. 1461 and many other *a.* arguments
Assuredly.
HP 402 as indeede wee may assuredlie beleeve it did
Assuring.
Puck 79 *a.* yor good Lp that if I knewe eny
Asti.
HP 1759 those Governours of *A.*, Vercellis
Astonish.
SP 1060 I with a martiall looke *a.* him
Astonished.
Cor. 750 for tis a trueth that hath astonisht me
JB 51 was so *a.* and dismayed that she
Asunder.
Ard. 1638 which time nor place nor tempest can *a.*
HP 1372 not things composedly but seperat and placd in sonder
Ate.
Ard. 1454 meat you *a.* at dinner cannot brook with you
Atheism.
Puck 8 that yor Lp holds me in concerning Atheisme
Atheist.
Puck 35 to cleere my self of being thought an *A.*
Athenians.
Cor. 1288 for so the two *A.*, that
Atreus.
HP 905 represents the person of Agamemnon, *A.*, or
Attained.
HP 218 wherunto me thinks your Sonne heere hath *a.*
Attempt.
Cor. Ded. 6 *a.* the dedication of so rough, unpollished
Cor. 64 or *a.* to lift theyr humbled heads
Cor. 726 that (being yet sav'd) he may *a.* no more
Cor. 1267 but resolutely to *a.* what may
Cor. 1625 he would *a.* the entrance on our barrs
Jer. 1031 of a daring message, and a proud *a.*?
ST 132 did with his Cornet bravely make *a.*
ST 1135 if this inhumane and barberous *a.*
ST 1400 that, they are most forbidden, they will soonest *a.*
SP 932 ah, hard *a.*, to tempt a foe for ayde
SP 1192 thoughts should dare *a.*, or but creepe neere my heart
SP 2226 that Death shall die, if he *a.* her end
Ard. 534 and whosoever doth *a.* the deed
Ard. 853 offering me service for my high *a.*
Ard. 1109 and afterwards *a.* me when thou darest
Ard. 37 attempts to violate my dear wife's chastity
Attempted.
Cor. 194 *a.* to excite to Armes the troopes
Attempting.
ST 1262 give but success to mine *a.* spirit
Attend.
VPJ 10 good fortune and an everlasting fame *a.* on thee
HP 813 « But bigger growne, they tende the chase »
Cor. Arg. 7 there to attende the incertaine successe of
Cor. 318 t'*a.* thy mercy in this morneful state?
Cor. 1483 then love of those that doe on us *a.*?
Cor. 1898 (beeing afraid t'*a.* the mercy of his
Jer. 190 all honor on Andreas steps attende

ST 478 on whose perfection all my thoughts *a.*
ST 496 then heere it fits us to *a.* the King
ST 676 goe and *a.* her, as thy custome is
ST 1282 heere, Serberine, *a.* and stay thy pace
ST 1378 thou with his pardon shalt *a.* him still
STA 1959 we are your servants that *a.* you, sir
STA 1961 you bid us light them, and *a.* you here
ST 2098 then stay, Hieronimo, *a.* their will
ST 2769 let then Perseda on your grace *a.*
SP 675 where thou in joy and pleasure must *a.*
SP 1272 for now I must *a.* the Emperour
Attendance.
Jer. 104 giving *a.*, that were once attended
Attended.
HP 114 on horsebacke, *a.* with a footeman
HP 474 arose, and was *a.* by her Sonnes
HP 1336 accustomed to be *a.* on by many servants
Jer. 104 giving attendance, that were once *a.*
Attendeth.
Cor. 722 such hap (as ours) *a.* on my sonnes
Attending.
HP 14 gave it to a pesaunt *a.* on him
Attention.
HP 197 to harken to their speeches with *a.*
Attire.
ST 2623 and, Madame, you must *a.* your selfe like Phoebe
Attired.
Ard. 1867 if well *a.*, thou thinks I will be gadding
Attributed.
HP 540 the name of Consort or Felow is to be *a.* to
HP 541 as to the Soule it hath beene heretofore *a.*
HP 684 notwithstanding herein much may be *a.* to use
HP 805 which custome is by Virgil *a.* to the Latins
HP 1318 first *a.* to Minerva, goddesse of wysedome
HP 1388 been ascribd or *a.* to privat huswifes
Audience.
ST 1407 scorne the *a.*, and descant on the hangman
ST 2824 revive to please too morrowes *a.*
Audit.
Ard. 1086 as loth to give due *a.* to the hour
Augment.
HP 506 good husbandry did much *a.* it
SP 1569 this title so augments her beautie, as the fire
Augmented.
HP 119 his dignity was much *a.*
Augustus.
SP 1438 *A.* sparde rich Alexandria for Arrius sake
Ausis.
VPJ 59 sed *a.* et sceleri retulit turba
Ausonian.
Cor. 180 warre, that hath sought Th' *A.* fame to reare
Cor. 1053 that with *A.* blood did die our warlike field
Austerity.
HP 882 uttered with more austeritie and signiorising termes
Author.
ST 87 where thou shalt see the *a.* of thy death
ST 341 my Soveraign, pardon the *a.* of ill newes
ST 916 O, wheres the *a.* of this endles woe?
ST 917 to know the *a.* were some ease of greife
ST 988 time is the *a.* both of truth and right
ST 2889 *a.* and actor in this Tragedie
ST 2715 O sir, it is for the authors credit to
ST Bal. 154 the authors of this bloody fetch
Authority.
HP 106 whose valour and authoritie in these quarters
HP 490 with the *a.* of theyr examples

HP 667 the rule and authoritie of the Husband to be moderate
HP 942 the *a.* of Hesiodus, that auncient Poet
Jer. 102 severe *a.* has dasht with justice
Jer. 558 as the faire cheeke of high *a.*
Autumn.
HP Ind. 7 *A.* more copious of fruites then the spring time
HP Ind. 8 *A.*, wherfore judged the best of other seasons
HP Ind. 21 comodities of the Spring and of *A.*
HP Ind. 84 grapes gathered in *A.*
HP Ind. 53 delights of the Spring and of Autumne
HP 341 me thinks no time may be compared to *A.*
HP 377 the Spring and *A.* are not to be touched
HP 381 co[m]pare *A.* and the Spring togeather
HP 382 the springe so farre inferior to *A.*
HP 383 fruits, whereof *A.* most aboundeth
HP 385 other hath *A.* onely proper to his season
HP 396 *A.* is the most noble and best season of the yeere
HP 445 this that is *A.* to us is their Springtime
Cor. 355 to whom mylde Autumne doth earths treasure bring
Cor. 980 I breathe an Autumne forth of fiery sighes
Cor. 1011 more inconstant in their kinde then Autumne blasts
SP 536 as withered leaves with Autume throwen downe
Autumnal.
HP 443 the world began in the *A.* aequinoctial
Avail.
Jer. 53 cannot availe or win him to it
ST 2524 and ought that may effect for thine availe
Cor. 457 what boote your teares, or what availes your sorrow
Cor. 470 weeping availes not : therefore doe I weepe
ST 448 yet what availes to waile Andreas death
ST 2130 nor ought availes it me to menace them who
Availing.
VPJ 41 thy crop of corne is tares *a.* naughts
Avanzar.
HP 1652 Prender sua vita & *a.* la gente
Avaro.
HP 1058 L'*a.* Zappator l'armi riprende
Avenged.
Cor. 270 that care to be aveng'd of Lovers othes
Cor. 1138 beares the selfe-same Armes to be aveng'd on hym
ST 1072 my guiltles death will be aveng'd on thee
ST 1904 to be *a.* on you all for this
ST 2915 upon whose soules may heavens be yet *a.*
Avernus'.
ST 29 that leades to fell Avernus ougly waves
Avoid.
ST 1245 thus must we worke that will avoide distrust
Ard. 632 so put I rhubarb to *a.* the smell
Awake.
ST 2439 *A.*, Erichtho ; Cerberus, *a.*
ST 2445 Revenge, *a.*
ST 2446 *a.* ? for why?
ST 2447 *a.*, Revenge ; for thou art ill advisde to
ST 2450 *a.*, Revenge, if love, as love hath had
ST 2454 *a.*, Revenge, or we are woe begone
ST 2466 *a.*, Revenge ; reveale this misterie
Ard. 68 for being *a.* he comes not in my thoughts
Ard. 1031 *a.* me with the echo of their strokes
Ard. 1170 so, trust me, Franklin, when I did *a.*
Cor. 638 the Country-wench unto her worke awakes
Ard. 59 had I been wake, you had not risen so soon
Awaked.
HP 373 is by him forsaken and *a.*
Ard. 1175 who being *a.* with the noise he made
Awards.
ST 267 I crave no better then your grace *a.*

Aware.
ST 756 shall carroll us asleepe, ere we be ware
Away.
HP 473 the Servants tooke *a.*
HP 711 they use yet in some place of Italie to cut *a.* theyr hayre
HP 755 Homer faigned that Juno, taking *a.* Venus garter
HP 1269 drawes *a.* theyr moysture
Cor. 253 did first beare Armes, and bare *a.* my love
Cor. 1008 when shee hath heap't her gifts on us, *a.* shee flies
Cor. 1971 when forcefull weapons fiercely tooke *a.* their
Cor. 2016 sold at a pike, and borne *a.* by strangers?
Jer. 23 able to ravish even my sence *a.*
Jer. 302 in, gentle soule; Ile not bee long *a.*
Jer. 446 this speedy letter must *a.* to night
Jer. 760 by that sly shift, to steale *a.* her troth
Jer. 764 beare him *a.* to execution
Jer. 771 *a.* with him
Jer. 774 *a.* with him, I will not heare him speake
Jer. 843 Andreas bosome bears *a.* my hart
ST 377 *a.* with him; his sight is second hell
ST 865 my Lord *a.* with her, take her aside
ST 877 come, stop her mouth; *a.* with her
STA 958 *a.*, I am ashamed
ST 1383 A. — I goe, my Lord, I runne
ST 1469 I pray, sir, dispatch; the day goes *a.*
ST 1650 heard me say sufficient reason why she kept *a.*
ST 1826 come, lets *a.* to seek my Lord the Duke
ST 1838 *a.*, Hieronimo; to him be gone
ST 1850 and heere, I heere — there goes the hare *a.*
ST 1894 *a.*, Lorenzo, hinder me no more
ST 1897 *a.*, Ile rip the bowels of the earth
ST 2448 to sleepe *a.* what thou art warnd to watch
SP 294 and at his best advantage stole *a.*
SP 470 get you *a.*, sirra. I advise you
SP 712 why then, farewell: Fernando, lets *a.*
SP 946 to run *a.* with this Chaine, or deliver it
SP 949 if I run *a.* with it, I may live upon credit
SP 1237 I speake not this to shrinke *a.* for feare
SP 1261 to drive *a.* this melancholly moode
SP 1385 *a.*, begone
SP 1589 repent that ere I gave *a.* my hearts desire
SP 1698 beare of some blowes when you run *a.* in a fraye
SP 2028 and he can doe lesse that cannot runne *a.*
Ard. 92 for yet ere noon we'll take horse and *a.*
Ard. 93 ere noon he means to take horse and *a.*!
Ard. 173 for I will rid mine elder brother *a.*
Ard. 180 *a.*, I say, and talk not to me now
Ard. 269 and fain would have your husband made *a.*
Ard. 397 come, leave this dallying, and let us *a.*
Ard. 502 as counsels him to make *a.* his wife
Ard. 568 by some device to make *a.* the churl
Ard. 654 how now, fellow Bradshaw? whither *a.* so early?
Ard. 792 come but a turn or two, and then *a.*
Ard. 804 to the Blackfriars, and there take water and *a.*
Ard. 817 is 't nothing else? come, Franklin, let's *a.*
Ard. 820 if you get you not *a.* all the sooner
Ard. 1008 see, see, how runs *a.* the weary time!
Ard. 1029 he is, and fain would have the light *a.*
Ard. 1124 lop not *a.* his leg. his arm, or both
Ard. 1202 he locked the gates, and brought *a.* the keys
Ard. 1205 for with the tide my master will *a.*
Ard. 1337 see, Mosbie, I will tear *a.* the leaves
Ard. 1542 the season fits; come, Franklin, let's *a.*
Ard. 1562 if I should go, our house would run *a.*
Ard. 1647 we have great haste; I pray thee, come *a.*
Ard. 1678 stifled with this fog; come, let's *a.*

Ard. 1688 weather to run *a.* with another man's wife
Ard. 1941 and his lattice borne *a.* the next night
Ard. 1973 hurts the slave; with that he slinks *a.*
Ard. 1993 and stab him in the crowd, and steal *a.*
Ard. 2110 pardon me, Master Arden; I'll *a.*
Ard. 2172 and, Susan, fetch water and wash *a.* this blood
Ard. 2174 but with my nails I'll scrape *a.* the blood
Ard. 2235 how shall I do to rid the rest *a.*?
Ard. 2247 alas, I counsel! fear frights *a.* my wits
Ard. 2381 come, make haste and bring *a.* the prisoners
JB 69 continually urged her to make him *a.*
JB 113 that any good thing should so unluckily be cast *a.* ▸
Awful.
Puck 80 that damnable offence to the awefull Matie of god
A-work.
Ard. 752 be set a work thus through the year
Awry.
Ard. 372 but he imagines I have stepped *a.*
Ay.
Cor. 882 ayh-me, what see I?
Jer. 733 who names Alcario slaine? aie me, tis he
ST 909 *a.* me most wretched, that have lost my joy
STA 923 aye me, Hieronimo, sweet husband, speake
STA 930 aye me, he raves, sweet Hieronimo
ST 2795 *a.* me, Erasto; see, Solyman, Erastoes slaine
SP 775 aye me, how gracelesse are these wicked men
Ard. 85 a month? *a.* me! sweet Arden, come again
B.
Babes.
HP 811 ‹A painful people by our byrth, for first our *b.* we bring›
Babington.
VPJ (Title) and execution of *B.*, Tychborne, Salisburie, and
Babingtoni.
VPJ (Title) In nefariam *B.* caeterorumque
Babylon.
ST 2671 now shall I see the fall of *B.*
Bacchi.
HP 285 Implentur veteris *B.* pinguisque ferina[e]
Bacchus.
HP 702 so *B.*, so Apollo, who of all the other Gods were most fayre
Back.
Cor. Arg. 26 that drave him backe to Hippon
Cor. 105 O fooles, looke *b.* and see the roling stone
Cor. 257 by calling Hymen once more *b.* againe
Cor. 314 beat backe like flyes before a storme of hayle?
Cor. 1136 he render not the Empyre *b.* to Rome
Cor. 1345 backe to thy grass-greene bancks to welcom us
Jer. 193 Ile call him *b.* againe
Jer. 384 these three years detained and kept *b.*
Jer. 873 all they have receaved they *b.* must pay
ST 226 in keeping *b.* the tribute that he owes
ST 416 nor stept I *b.* till I recoverd him
ST 814 if she give *b.*, all this will come to naught
ST 832 the starres, thou seest, hold backe their twinckling shine
ST 1854 *b.*, seest thou not the King is busie?
ST 2232 goe backe, my sonne, complaine to Eacus
ST 2325 still keepst him *b.*, and seeks to crosse his sute
ST 2346 busie to keepe *b.* him and his supplications
SP 757 desire perswades me on, feare puls me *b.*
SP 1032 dreadfull Neptune, bring him backe againe
SP 1056 thinkes he bare cannon shot can keepe me *b.*?
SP 1277 returne him *b.*, faire starres, or let me die
SP 1278 returne him backe, fair heavens, or let me die
SP 1319 if we be beaten backe, weele come to you
SP 1504 and peeces flying backe will wound my selfe
SP 1624 fetch him backe againe, under couler of

SP 1722 Brusor is sent to fetch my maister *b*. againe
SP 1739 Brusor is sent to fetch him *b*. againe
SP 1773 and should the seas turne tide to force me backe
SP 1942 what meanes made you to steale backe to Rhodes ?
Ard. 53 but, being kept *b*., straight grow outrageous
Ard. 63 would pull her by the purple mantle *b*.
Ard. 1143 sirrah, get you *b*. to Billingsgate
Ard. 1435 'twere best that I went *b*. to Rochester
Ard. 1439 well, get you *b*. to Rochester ; but
Ard. 1736 at their coming *b*. meet with them once more
Ard. 1750 soon, when my husband is returning *b*.
Ard. 1936 ah, gentle Michael, run thou *b*. again
Ard. 2280 but it had done before we came *b*. again
JB 218 and after brought *b*. to prison
ST 820 I follow thee, my love, and will not backe
Ard. 714 I'll *b*. and tell him who robbed him
Ard. 1240 I cannot *b*., but needs must on
Cor. 159 upon thy backe (where miserie doth sit)
Cor. 560 or on her nurse-like backe sustaines
Jer. 417 and had you but his vestment on your backe
ST 355 discharged his Pistoll at the Princes *b*.
Ard. 97 and throw him from his *b*. into the waves !
Cor. 1633 with heavy Armor on theyr hardned backs
Cor. 1786 with bristled backs, and fire-sparkling eyes
Jer. 1038 to have me borne upon the backs of men
STA 1779 he had not seene the backe of nineteene yeere
Ard. 772 « as a plaster of pitch to a galled horse-*b*. »

Backbone.
SP 424 my back bone, my channell bone, and

Back-door.
SP 1694 wish you to have an eye to the back dore
Ard. 2264 out at the *b*., over the pile of wood

Backed.
Cor. 1170 (backt with wintered souldiers us'd to conquering)
ST 1612 backt with a troup of fiery Cherubins
Ard. 34 for where he by the Lord Protector *b*.

Backwards.
Ard. 2315 *b*. and forwards may you see the print

Bacon.
STA 1760 a young *B*., or a fine little smooth Horse-colt should

Bad.
Cor. 338 in good or *b*. as to continue it
Jer. 719 the King may thinke my newes is a *b*. guest
ST Bal. 93 by Lorenzos *b*. intent I hindred was
SP 1840 the rest I dare not speake, it is so *b*.
Ard. 651 I warrant you he bears so *b*. a mind
Ard. 701 'twas *b*., but yet it served to hide the plate
Ard. 1282 and then — conceal the rest, for 'tis too *b*.
Ard. 1310 this certain good I lost for changing *b*.

Bad [= Bade.]
Jer. 793 I *b*. defiance with a vengfull hand
ST 82 and *b*. thee lead me through the gates of Horn
SP 469 a chaine, sir, a chaine, that your man *b*. me crie
SP 567 but gave my censure, as his highnesse *b*.
SP 1023 delivered me the chaine, and *b*. me give it you
SP 1946 flouds of teares for your depart, he *b*. me follow him

Badger.
Jer. 556 the *B*. feeds not till the Lyons served

Bags.
Ard. 221 my saving husband hoards up *b*. of gold

Bailed.
Ard. 1936 and *b*. whom I list with my sword and buckler

Bailiff.
HP 1003 the Baylieffe, to whom the Toun affaires belong
HP 1010 that may be Stewarde, Horsekeeper, and Bailieffe
HP 1176 he cannot be deceived by his Bailieffe

Bait.
Cor. 76 but as a bayte for pride (which spoiles us all)
Jer. 118 him with a goulden baite will I allure
Ard. 756 let us be going, and we'll *b*. at Rochester

Baked.
HP 248 some was roste, some was backt

Baker's.
HP 1064 also he termes the Bakers instruments weapons

Baking.
HP 1068 to fetch the watrie, rotten Corne, and *b*. weapons
HP 1268 *b*. of some kinds of flesh or fish

Baleful.
ST 1810 whose balefull humours if you but upholde
Ard. 624 the colours being *b*. and impoisoned

Ball.
STA 1792 violence leapes foorth like thunder wrapt in a *b*. of fire
SP 2 why, what is Love but Fortunes tenis-*b*. ?

Ballace.
STA 1751 doth serve to *b*. these light creatures we call Women

Balm.
ST 1491 it may be, in that box is balme for both
SP 998 and honored with Balme and funerall

Balthazar.
Jer. 317 son Balthezer, we pray, do you goe meet him
Jer. 364 Prince Balthezer, shalles meete ?
Jer. 796 Baltheser, his son, grew Violent
Jer. 863 Prince Balthezer, as you say, so say we
Jer. 890 no, Prince Balthezer, I have desired
Jer. 897 Prince Balthezer, I know your valiant sperit
Jer. 1006 where might I find this vallorous Balthezer ?
Jer. 1015 Prince Balthezer, Portugals valliant heire
Jer. 1028 Andrea. — Prince Balthezer
Jer. 1076 Balthezer, Prince Balthezer
Jer. 1091 price of him in princely bloud, Prince Balthezer
ST Bal. 22 that he Prince Baltazer Captive brings
ST Bal. 31 then more to vexe Prince Baltazer
ST Bal. 55 Prince Baltazer with his compeeres
ST Bal. 115 when Bloody Baltazar enters in
ST Bal. 127 sweete Bellimperia Baltazar killes
ST 88 Don *B*., the Prince of Portingale
ST 159 but *B*., the Portingales young Prince
ST 223 welcome Don *B*. ; welcome Nephew
ST 236 I, *B*., if he observe this truce
ST 282 how likes Don *B*. of this device ?
ST 349 Don *B*., amidst the thickest troupes
ST 357 and therewithall Don *B*. fell doune
ST 366 wherein had *B*. offended thee
ST 379 if *B*. be dead, he shall not live
ST 395 by yong *B*. encountred
ST 406 then yong Don *B*. with ruthles rage
ST 452 and where Don *B*. that slew my love
ST 500 their prisoner *B*., thy Viceroyes sonne
ST 503 supposing that Don *B*. is slaine
ST 505 you see, my Lord, how *B*. is slaine
ST 637 preferring him before Prince *B*.
ST 681 how likes Prince *B*. this stratageme ?
ST 784 and if by *B*. she have a Sonne
ST 794 but wheres Prince *B*. to take his leave ?
ST 871 O, save him, brother ; save him, *B*.
ST 873 but *B*. loves Bel-imperia
STA 925 and said he would goe visit *B*.
ST 1012 I lookt that *B*. should have been slaine
ST 1021 Ile shew thee *B*. in heavy case
ST 1042 when he in Campe consorted *B*.
ST 1083 know, Soveraigne L[ord], that *B*. doth live
ST 1084 what saiest thou ? liveth *B*. our sonne ?

ST 1157 revenge thy selfe on *B.* and him
ST 1563 wast thou, Lorenzo, *B.* and thou
ST 1580 and *B.*, bane to thy soule and me
ST 1713 looke on thy love, behold yong *B.*
ST 1734 then, faire, let *B.* your keeper be
ST 1735 no, *B.* doth feare as well as we
ST 1741 wends poore, oppressed *B.*
STA 1780 when his strong arme unhorsd the proud Prince *B.*
ST 1848 and *B.*, Ile be with thee to bring, and thee
ST 1875 there will he give his Crowne to *B.*
ST 1880 and wondrous zeale to *B.* his sonne
ST 1914 the ransome of the yong Prince *B.*
ST 1930 the match twixt *B.* and Bel-imperia
ST 2285 already is betroth'd to *B.*
ST 2298 faire Bel-imperia, with my *B.*
ST 2313 for her, my Lord, whom *B.* doth love
ST 2375 welcome, *B.*, welcome, brave Prince
ST 2383 but, *B.*, heere comes Hieronimo
ST 2423 but heere, before Prince *B.* and me
ST 2727 what, are you ready, *B.* ?
ST 2729 well doon, *B.*, hang up the Title
ST 2762 see, Vice-roy, that is *B.*, your sonne
ST 2841 the hate : Lorenzo, and yong *B.*
ST 2857 if thou canst weepe upon thy *B.*
ST 2877 so, Vice-roy, was this *B.*, thy Sonne
ST 2897 we are betraide ; my *B.* is slaine
ST 2908 why hast thou murdered my *B.* ?
ST 2913 slaine, and by Lorenzo and that *B.*
ST 2919 for by her hand my *B.* was slaine
STA 2951 for by her hand my *B.* was slaine
STA 2956 and by Lorenzo and that *B.* am I
ST 3007 to weep my want for my sweet *B.*
ST 3015 Prince *B.* by Bel-imperia stabd
ST 3044 hang *B.* about Chimeras neck
ST 2364 come, Bel-imperia, Balthazars content
Ban.
Ard. 1299 nay, if you *b.*, let me breathe curses forth
Band.
HP 549 the bande that tyes the body and the soule togeather
HP 555 divorced by death from that first *b.* of Matrimonie
HP 574 but once in all theyr life beene tyed with that *b.*
ST 1872 to knit a sure inextricable *b.* of kingly love
ST 2160 and heere is my *b.*
HP 582 cannot be consorted well under the bands of wedlock
HP 647 if hee himselfe doo not first violate the bandes
Cor. 256 goe break the bands by calling Hymen once more
Cor. 275 untye the bands that sacred Hymen knyt
Cor. 1398 he durst affront me and my warlike bands
Cor. 1818 the feeble bands that yet were left entyre
Band *see* **Bond.**
Bandying.
Cor. 85 equals are ever *b.* for the best
Bane.
ST Bal. 69 swearing to worke their woefull baine
ST 1580 and Balthazar, *b.* to thy soule and me
SP 119 let not my beauty prick thee to thy *b.*
SP 173 his weapons point impoysoned for my *b.*
Banish.
Ard. 1785 I'll *b.* pity if thou use me thus
Banished.
SP 1204 that, being banisht from my native soile
Banishment.
SP 1101 and forst Erastus into *b.*
Bankrupt.
ST 1895 for thou hast made me *b.* of my blisse
Banks.

HP 1219 whether upon the bancks to any navigable water
Cor. 1345 backe to thy grass-greene bancks to welcom us
Banned.
ST Bal. 66 and cur'sd and bann'd each thing was there
ST 1586 and band with bitter execrations be the day
Banner.
Jer. 1144 Ile kisse this little ensigne, this soft *b.*
Bannerets.
Cor. 874 Seggs, that with the winde dyd wave like *b.*
Banquet.
ST 520 to grace our *b.* with some pompous jest
HP 262 for the banquets of Agamemnon, as we read
Banqueting.
ST 566 nothing but league, and love and *b.*
SP 1511 brought Alexander from warre to banquetting
Bar.
Jer. 772 your highnes may doe well to barre his speech
Cor. 1625 he would attempt the entrance on our barrs
Barbarian.
SP 95 the Moore upon his hot *B.* horse
HP 1458 against the Barbarians and Turkes
Barbarous.
Cor. 890 O *b.*, inhumaine, hatefull traytors
ST 1135 if this inhumane and barberous attempt
SP 961 what *b.* villaine ist that rifles him ?
SP 1168 account our Turkish race but *b.*
SP 1240 against the Persians, or the *b.* Moore
SP 1652 the Turkes, whom they account for *b.*
Bare.
VPJ 46 thy faith *b.* fruit as thou hadst faithles beene
HP 266 the companions of Ulisses *b.* not so many mishaps
Cor. 255 did first beare Armes, and *b.* away my love
SP 163 and in my skinne *b.* tokens of their skenes
SP 1655 and in procession *b.* me to the Church
Ard. (Title) who for the love she *b.* to one Mosbie, hyred
Ard. 1026 was never any lived and *b.* it so
HP 1616 much more may riches multiply that consist in *b.* money
ST 1400 by my *b.* honesty, heeres nothing but the *b.* emptie box
SP 1056 thinkes he *b.* cannon shot can keepe me back ?
Ard. 693 his chin was *b.*, but on his upper lip a
Ard. 1775 leave in Feversham, God knows, needy and *b.*
Ard. 698 a pair of thread-*b.* velvet hose, seam reut
Barely.
HP 971 they want vertue, whereof they taste but *b.*
Bargain.
HP 1251 became rich with a bargaine that he made for Oyle
Ard. 884 but that a *b.* is a *b.*, and so forth
Ard. 1665 thereby lies a *b.*, and you shall not
JB 58 the worst *b.* that ever he made in his life
Bargained.
HP 1483 *b.* for the commodities of a Countrey
Bark.
SP 322 better a Dog fawne on me, then barke
Barking.
ST 3005 to Silla's *b.* and untamed gulfe
Barns.
Jer. 221 from farmers that crack *b.* with stuffing corne
Barrel.
Ard. 1927 I have pierced one *b.* after another
Barren.
ST 2689 *b.* the earth, and bliselesse whosover immagines
Barricade.
Cor. 388 hee gave his bodie (as a *B.*) for Romes defence
Cor. 1637 dig and cast new Trenches, and plant strong Barricades
Barter.
HP 1228 or such as use to bartre or exchange

Base.
HP 29 (judging him to be of no *b*. or meane condicion)
HP 581 a noble woman matching with a man of *b*. estate
HP 731 wherewith *b*. slaves or servaunts are kept under
HP 735 a kind of feare distinguished from servile *b*. feare
HP 788 the Nurses bceing ordinary *b*. persons
HP 914 but *b*. of mind, grosse of understanding, and
HP 1047 bettereth things by Nature *b*. and filthie
HP 1334 it appeareth that he spake not of *b*. women
HP 1471 that Merchandize, if they were small, were *b*.
Cor. 23 endure a million of *b*. controls
Cor. 530 twere more then *b*. in us to dread his dart
Cor. 1119 plaine in their Tombes of our *b*. cowardise?
Cor. 1241 O *b*. indignitie : a beardles youth, whom
Cor. 1577 whose coates of steele *b*. Death hath stolne into
Jer. 338 and find it much dishonord by *b*. homage
Jer. 340 by our forfathers *b*. captivitie
Jer. 344 that which they lost by *b*. Captivitie, we
Jer. 347 hee is a *b*. King that payes rent for his throne
Jer. 819 to be denide our honor, why, twere *b*.
Jer. 846 to seet you free from *b*. captivity
Jer. 848 seene as a *b*. blush upon your free borne cheeks
Jer. 934 showes that what they lost by *b*. Captivity
Jer. 1085 my foes are *b*., and slay me cowardly
Jer. 1106 O *b*. renowne, tis easie to seize those
Jer. 1116 Lorenzo, thou doost boast of *b*. renowne
ST 1255 and better its that *b*. companions dye
ST 1317 that by those *b*. confederates in our fault
ST 2803 as thy butcher is pittilesse and *b*.
SP 533 a common presse of *b*. superfluous Turkes
SP 538 let not thy Souldiers sound a *b*. retire
SP 577 it is not meete that one so *b*. as thou
SP 1088 a disgrace to all my chivalrie to combate one so *b*.
Ard. 26 who, by *b*. brokage getting some small stock
Ard. 199 *b*. peasant, get thee gone, and boast
Ard. 306 she's no companion for so *b*. a groom
Ard. 342 as for the *b*. terms I gave thee late
Ard. 660 a corporal, and thou but a *b*. mercenary groom?
Ard. 788 wilt thou be married to so *b*. a trull?
Ard. 1000 then that *b*. Mosbie doth usurp my room
Ard. 1334 O no, I am a *b*. artificer
Basely.
Cor. 401 but *b*. slaine, slaine trayterouslie
Cor. 620 *b*. seen by shameles rape to be defilde
Cor. 895 for yee have *b*. broke the Law of Armes
Jer. 1131 his all wrathfull sword did *b*. point
Base-minded.
Ard. 324 a cheating steward, and *b*. peasant?
Baseness.
HP 984 it is a great argument of basenes that
Cor. 439 besides the basenes wherein we are yoked
ST 1583 woe to thy basenes and captivitie
Bashaw.
ST 2595 her had this *B*. long solicited
ST 2604 what then became of him that was the *B*.?
ST 2753 *B*., that Rhodes is ours, yield heavens the honour
ST 2781 ah, *B*., heere is love betwixt Erasto and
ST 2872 and to this end the *B*. I became
ST 2594 one of his Bashawes whom he held full deere
ST 2601 and, to escape the Bashawes tirannie, did stab
SP 518 call home my Bassowes and my men of war
SP 541 after so many valiant Bassowes slaine
Basilisco.
SP 205 now, Signeur *B*., you we know
SP 211 why Signeur *B*., is it a she sword?
SP 309 & 310 I, the aforesaid *B*.

SP 1290 why, Lady, is not *B*. here?
SP 1291 why, Lady, dooth not *B*. live?
SP 1665 but thinke you *B*. squicht for that?
SP 1937 now, signior *B*., which like you, the
SP 1983 *B*., dooest thou love me? speake
SP 2025 but I love *B*., as one I hould more worthy
SP 2208 wheres *B*., but in my triumph?
SP 1370 and lastly Love made Basiliscos tongue to
SP 1653 having forehard of Basiliscoes worth
Basilisk.
Ard. 215 so looks the traveller to the *b*.
Basolus.
SP 1675 why, I meant nothing but a *B*. manus
Basso *see* **Bashaw.**
Bastard.
Cor. 21 our *b*. harts lye idely sighing
Cor. 624 as tyrannie shall yoke our basterd harts
Cor. 851 or think'st thou Romains beare such *b*. harts
Basterà.
ST 1395 Intendo io : quel mi *b*.
Bastinadoes.
HP 990 many whips and bastonadoes
Batchelors.
JB 26 Batchelers, of good friends, and well esteemed
Bate.
Jer. 357 Ile not *b*. an inch of courage nor a haire of fate
Bated.
HP 1342 that *b*. in the night as much as she had woven by day
Bathe.
Cor. 845 nor shalt thou *b*. thee longer in our blood
Cor. 2031 may trickling *b*. your generous sweet cynders
Bathed.
Cor. 650 hath bath'd your blubbred eyes in bitter teares
Bathing.
ST 1820 *b*. him in boyling lead and blood of innocents
Battalions.
Cor. 1804 they fiercely open both *B*.
Battery.
ST 345 my hart growne hard gainst mischiefes *b*.
Ard. 1766 or make no *b*. in his flinty breast
ST 2154 Sir, an Action. — Of Batterie?
Battle.
Cor. Arg. 16 of those that survived after the battaile
Cor. Arg. 20 was a fierce and furious battaile given amongst them
Cor. 313 so many enemies in battaile ranged
Cor. 900 pestered with battaile, famine, and perpetuall plagues
Cor. 1790 marcht through the battaile (laying still about him)
Jer. 157 souldiers that were maimde in the last battaile
Jer. 1010 and single me out of the mistie battaile
Jer. 1023 tis now about the heavy dread of battaile
Jer. 1061 lets to the battaile once more ; we may meete
ST 108 unfolde in breefe discourse your forme of battell
ST 133 to breake the order of our battell rankes
ST 157 in their maine battell made so great a breach
ST 348 when both the armies were in battell joynd
SP 1150 courteous in peace, in battell dangerous
SP 1241 Erastus will be formost in the battaile
Jer. 365 meete, Don Andrea? Yes, in the battles Bowels
Jer. 928 to meete me single in the battailes heat
ST 188 for tis thy Sonne that winnes this battels prize
Cor. 189 and Canpe to Canpe did endlesse battailes wage
Cor. 1370 and fought more battailes then the best of them
Cor. 1650 even so our battails, scattred on the sands
Cor. 1736 the battels lockt (with bristle-poynted speares)
Cor. 1855 their battailes scattred, and their Ensignes taken
Jer. 1048 paid tribute as well ; then battailes had bin staid

ST 128 our battels both were pitcht in squadron forme
ST 138 both battailes joyne and fall to handie blowes
SP 198 and there in three set battles fought
Battlements.
Cor. 1334 O lofty towres, O stately *b.*
Bawd.
Jer. 232 makes the punck wanton and the *b.* to winke
Bawdy-house.
SP 449 lost her selfe betwixt a taverne and a bawdie house
Ard. 1923 the bawdy-houses have paid me tribute
Bay.
SP 331 the baye horse with the blew taile, and the
Cor. 312 thy Helmet deckt with coronets of Bayes ?
Bazardo.
STA 2047 you have heard of my painting : my name's *B.*
STA 2048 *B.*, afore-god, an excellent fellow
Bazulto.
ST 2173 supplication of Don *B.* for his murdred Sonne ᵣ
ST 2176 but mine, or thine, *B.*, be content
Beadroll.
Cor. 421 a bedroll of outragious blasphemies
Bead's-man.
Ard. 1504 I am your bedesman, bound to pray for you
Beam.
Jer. 884 tall as an English gallows, uper *b.* and all
Cor. 1355 where the bright Sun with his neyghbor beames doth
SP 383 least that the sun should tan them with his beames
SP 1457 faire lockes, resembling Phoebus radiant beames
SP 109 as the glasse that takes the Sun-beames burning
Ard. 232 shall, with the beams that issue from his sight
Bear.
HP 211 for want of one to beare her company
HP 1398 albeit of it selfe it beare no great semblance of credit
HP 1625 the force of reason that it seemes to beare
Cor. 41 while th' earth, that gron'd to beare their carkasses
Cor. 445 O, but men beare mis-fortunes with more ease
Cor. 851 or think'st thou Romains beare such bastard harts
Cor. 1142 the love that men theyr Country and theyr birth-right beare
Cor. 1234 meekely beare the rider but by force
Cor. 1565 fire-brands in their brests they beare
Cor. 1983 for even those fields that mourn'd to beare their bodies
Jer. 764 beare him away to execution
Jer. 1138 in purple I will beare thee to my private tent
ST 284 that Don Horatio beare us company
ST 529 to beare the yoake of the English Monarchie
ST 542 that Portingale may daine to beare our yoake
ST 995 and beare him in from out this cursed place
ST 1917 this is the love that Fathers beare their Sonnes
STA 2006 it grew a gallowes, and did beare our sonne
ST 2132 will beare me downe with their nobilitie
ST 2150 now must I beare a face of gravitie
ST 2235 Hieronimo will beare thee company
ST 2501 although I beare it out for fashions sake
ST 2996 beare his body hence, that we may mourne
SP 218 may very well beare a feminine Epitheton
SP 300 a Typhon, to beare up Peleon or Ossa ?
SP 440 and Ile beare you company
SP 619 and beare my joyes on either side of me
SP 873 feare not for money, man, ile beare the Boxe
SP 1064 and thus I beare him thorough every·streete
SP 1156 more brave Souldiers then all that Ile will beare
SP 1697 serve to beare of some blowes when you run away
SP 1846 Rhodes must no longer beare the turkish yoake
SP 1990 yet dare I beare her hence, to do thee good
SP 2041 go, Brusor, beare her to thy private tent

Ard. 123 *b.* him from me these pair of silver dice
Ard. 404 go, if thou wilt, I'll *b.* it as I may
Ard. 697 the inner side did *b.* the greater show
Ard. 996 let your comfort be that others *b.* your woes
Ard. 1188 I'll *b.* you company
Ard. 1215 and, Michael, you shall *b.* no news of this tide
Ard. 1407 it is not for mine honour to *b.* this
Ard. 1839 perjured beast ! *b.* this and all !
Ard. 2040 that done, *b.* him behind the Abbey
Ard. 2171 Mosbie, go thou and *b.* them company
Ard. 2253 how now, Alice, whither will you *b.* him ?
Ard. 2364 but wherefore stay we ? Come and *b.* me hence
Ard. 2408 *b.* Mosbie and his sister to London straight
Ard. 2410 *b.* Mistress Arden unto Canterbury
Ard. 2415 but *b.* me hence, for I have lived too long
HP 1289 where the Steward or Butler beares the keyes
Cor. 658 and stil (unsatisfide) more hatred beares
Cor. 984 yes, newes of Caesars death that medcyn beares
Cor. 1137 beares the selfe-same Armes to be aveng'd
Jer. 843 Andreas bosome beares away my hart
SP 276 whose chin beares no impression of manhood
Ard. 651 I warrant you he bears so bad a mind
Ard. 1976 bears his sword-point half a yard out of danger
Cor. 901 let Aspics, Serpents, Snakes, and Lybian Beares
Cor. 1107 Lybian Beares devoure the bodies of our Cittizens
Cor. 1608 Lyons and Beares, are theyr best Sepulchers
Beard.
HP Ind. 95 Love figured without a bearde
HP 118 the whiteness of his hayre and *b.*
Cor. 712 hys hayre and *b.* deform'd with blood and sweat
Jer. 30 confesse, *B.*, thou art fifty full, not a haire lesse
Jer. 878 thou very little longer then thy *b.*
Jer. 1109 now, by my *b.*, you lie
ST 263 so Hares may pull dead Lyons by the *b.*
ST 2730 our scene is Rhodes : — what, is your *b.* on ?
HP 697 neyther are their faces shadowed with beards
HP 703 most fayre, were decyphered without beards
STA 2066 and let their beardes be of Judas his owne collour
Ard. 1753 and boldly *b.* and brave him to his teeth
Bearded.
HP 700 and farre more lovely then those of *b.* men
Beardless.
Cor. 1241 a beardles youth, whom King Nicomedes could
Bearest.
ST 2478 is this the love thou bearst Horatio ?
Bearing.
ST 239 yet free from *b.* any servile yoake
ST 2890 *b.* his latest fortune in his fist
SP 96 *b.* in his face the empresse of a noble warriour
SP 622 *b.* in either hand his hearts decay
Ard. 644 a knave chiefly for *b.* the other company
Puck 20 rose upon his *b.* name to serve my Lo
HP 601 a woman is more apt to child-*b.* in youth
SP 1943 the mightie pinky-ey'd, brand *b.* God
Beast.
ST 363 false, unkinde, unthankfull, traiterous *b.*
ST 581 then *b.*, or bird, or tree, or stony wall
STA 1939 when man and bird and *b.* are all at rest
Ard. 1839 ah, Mosbie ! perjured *b.* ! bear this and all !
Ard. 1840 and yet no horned *b.* ; the horns are thine
Ard. 1898 reviled him by the injurious name of perjured·*b.*
JB 204 ‹ why, thou arrant *b.* › (quoth shee), ‹ what did
HP Ind. 55 instruction of Servauntes and of Beastes
HP 278 but the flesh of wild Beasts, although
HP 281 Swine, or other Beastes that fatneth by the hande
HP 283 Beasts that commonly are stald and foddered

HP 922 they differ from Horses, Mules, and other Beastes
HP 946 differeth much from that wherwith we governe Beasts
HP 947 that enstruction or kinde of teaching Beastes
HP 1436 the nourishments and foode that we receive of Beastes
HP 1437 distinguished according to the distinction of Beastes
HP 1438 for of Beastes some are tame and compynable
HP 1084 bruite beasts rejoyce to see their Maisters cheerish them
HP 1443 that Nature hath engendred not onely bruite Beasts

Beastliness.

HP 1048 beastlines and filth corrupt, disgrace, and spoile thinges

Beat.

Cor. 314 *b.* backe like flyes before a storme of hayle ?
Cor. 652 why doe you beate your brests ? why mourne you so ?
Cor. 1722 lyke Northern windes that beate the horned Alpes
Cor. 1852 to beate them downe as fierce as thundring flints
Cor. 1996 beate at your Ivorie breasts, and let your robes
ST 1534 *b.* at the windowes of the brightest heavens
STA 1955 *b.* at the bushes, stampe our grandam earth
Ard. 1429 as I have seen them *b.* their wings ere now !
Ard. 1932 the notches of his tallies and *b.* them about his head
Ard. 1979 he shall never *b.* me from this ward
ST 141 it beats upon the rampiers of huge rocks

Beaten.

Cor. Arg. 27 he was assailed, *b.* and assaulted by the adverse Fleete
Cor. 85 thy sides sore *b.*, and thy hatches broke
Cor. 1875 which being sore *b.*, till it brake agen
ST 170 but straight the Prince was *b.* from his horse
SP 1319 if we be *b.* backe, weele come to you
Ard. 820 you shall be well *b.* and sent to the Counter
Ard. 1319 and now the rain hath *b.* off thy gilt

Beating.

HP 13 *b.* and crying out upon the doggs

Beauteous.

Cor. 1342 O beautious Tyber, with thine easie streames
SP 692 except Persedas beautious excellence

Beauties.

SP 702 we Ladies stand upon our *b.* much

Beautified.

HP 624 *b.* with many faire and necessary vertues

Beautify.

HP 686 by nature shee is so desirous to adorne and beautifie her bodie

Beautifying.

HP 1382 grace and comlines in *b.* and adorning things

Beauty.

HP Ind. 12 beautie more regarded in a Woman then a Man
HP Ind. 13 *b.* forced by painting insupportable in a woman
HP 694 more regard to the *b.* of the Female then the Male
HP 714 more regard then Nature hath had to the *b.* of women
Cor. 498 whose auncient beautie, worth and weapons
Cor. 1500 with the beautie of thy rayes
Jer. 749 was a huge dotar on Bellimperias beautye
ST 1722 tis of thy beautie, then, that conquers Kings
ST 2369 wherein my hope and heavens faire beautie lies
ST 2588 whose *b.* ravished all that her behelde
ST 2797 faire Queene of beautie, let not favour die
ST 2799 griefe, that with Persedaes beautie is encreast
SP 113 thy *b.* yet shall make me knowne ere night
SP 119 let not my *b.* prick thee to thy bane
SP 688 whom women loue for vertue, men for bewty
SP 716 no, no ; her beautie far surpasseth mine
SP 760 thy *b.* did defend me, not my force
SP 797 whats *b.* but a blast, soone cropt
SP 1357 their lives priviledge hangs on their beautie
SP 1569 this title so augments her beautie, as the fire

SP 1731 made him praise love, and [his] captives beautie
SP 1820 but bright Persedaes beautie stops my tongue
SP 2090 but [die] maintaining of Persedas beautie
SP 2145 and on thy beautie [lie] still contemplate
Ard. 332 I could not choose, her *b.* fired my heart !
Ard. 1309 whose *b.* and demeanour far exceeded thee
Ard. 1602 and spoil her *b.* with blotting
ST 479 on whose aspect mine eyes finde beauties bowre
ST 504 so am I slaine, by beauties tirannie
ST 598 yet might she love me as her beauties thrall
SP 1452 and so adornd with beauties miracle
SP 1729 and made great Soliman, sweete beauties thrall

Beaver.

SP 339 and my *B.* closd for this encounter

Became.

HP Ind. 135 howe hee *b.* rich
HP 37 heere I *b.* silent
HP 193 here he *b.* silent, and I, to shew that
HP 1251 suddainly *b.* rich with a bargaine that he made
ST 694 and by my yeelding I *b.* his slave
ST 2604 what then *b.* of him that was the Bashaw ?
ST 2872 and to this end the Bashaw I *b.*
SP 1956 so I *b.* a Turke to follow her
JB 168 and *b.* so jelious that, had she lookt but
ST 420 and sighed and sorrowed as *b.* a freend
ST 362 where then *b.* the carkasse of my Sonne ?

Because.

HP 34 *b.* perhaps you are not well acquainted
HP 174 *b.* beyond this Orchard, wherein
HP 183 but *b.* I deeme them scarce
HP 198 said, *b.* his wife was wanting
HP 275 « *B.* » (quoth I) « they are of great
HP 279 *b.* they be much exercised and stirring
HP 300 *b.* they were made of the Grapes that
HP 321 this was not *b.* the Poet desired
HP 322 but *b.* olde Wine, loosing the sweetnes
HP 414 *b.* that is the right side whereof the
HP 415 but *b.* the motion of the Sunne goes
HP 445 *b.* this that is Autumn to us is their
HP 477 but, *b.* it would bee greevous unto me to
HP 523 *b.* the care of reasonable thinges is
HP 600 not onelie *b.* a woman is more apt to
HP 602 but *b.* (according to the testimony of Hesiodus)
HP 666 but *b.* it behoveth the rule and authoritie of
HP 769 *b.* it is most unseemlie in them
HP 792 *b.* the Mother is chieflie knowne and
HP 801ᵃ *b.*, the hygh parts of the ayre being cold
HP 815 *b.* to us that have not used it it seemes extreame
HP 853 but *b.* al this part of education and
HP 855 *b.* it is wholie pollitique that
HP 891 but *b.* (albeit the Lawes and usages of men
HP 901 *b.* the people that onely have regarde to exterior
HP 942 and *b.* the authority of Hesiodus
HP 970 *b.* they want vertue, whereof they taste
HP 974 *b.* it was begunne and stirred up by servaunts
HP 1024 but *b.* a family well fedde and truely paid
HP 1069 but *b.* it sometime happeneth that one is
HP 1093 *b.* he keepeth all the instruments of houshold occupied
HP 1126 but *b.* that use of service as wee talkt of
HP 1135 and nowe *b.* we have sufficiently spoken
HP 1138 and *b.* there hath beene nothing left out that
HP 1145 *b.* the encrease is as proper to the Maister
HP 1198 *b.* we may live without it, as they dyd
HP 1311 *b.* such busines are not to be manedged
HP 1418 a Minister, *b.* it ministreth the Instruments
HP 1469 *b.* it growes not other-where so plentiously

HP 1570 but *b*. the Husbandman and
HP 1586 it is not naturall, *b*. it doth pervert the proper use
HP 1603 infinitly, *b*. Number as touching Number, not
HP 1614 *b*. things of all kinds that cannot be
HP 1666 Now *b*. the Usurers doo wander otherwise
HP 1681 *b*. it doth not exercise the arte
HP 1718 *b*. the care of Princes Halles belongeth not to
Cor. 580 *b*. the matter that remaines reformes
Cor. 616 (*b*. her name dishonored stood)
Cor. 933 Ile downe with joy : *b*., before I died, mine eyes
Cor. 947 that was *b*. that, Pompey being theyr freend
Cor. 958 *b*. hymselfe of life did not bereave him
Cor. 1085 *b*. thou ever hatedst Monarchie
Cor. 1957 *b*. thy husband did revive the lights of thy
Jer. 738 *b*. I was an asse, a villainus asse
ST Bal. 32 *b*. he slewe her chiefest friend
ST Bal. 81 *b*. I had not yet found out the murtherers
ST Bal. 120 *b*. I knew twould worke their woe
ST Bal. 128 *b*. be slew her dearest friend
ST 370 perchance, *b*. thou art Terseraes Lord
ST 1016 *b*. she lov'd me more then all the world
ST 1290 why ? *b*. he walkt abroad so late
ST 2401 *b*. you have not accesse unto the King
ST 2766 that's because his minde runs all on Bel-imperia
SP 252 I have no word, *b*. no countrey
SP 358 *b*. he would not be put to carve, he wore
SP 831 *b*. that Fortune made the fault, not Love
SP 832 *b*. I lost the pretious Carcanet
SP 1300 *b*. that, when Erastus spake my name
SP 1712 thats *b*. you were out of the way
SP 1837 *b*. we were alreadie in his gallyes
SP 1951 *b*. I now am Christian againe
SP 2079 dyed he *b*. his worth obscured thine ?
Ard. 134 *b*. my husband is so jealous
Ard. 618 though I am loth, *b*. it toucheth life
Ard. 661 *b*. you are a goldsmith and have a little plate
Ard. 899 *b*. I think you love your mistress better
Ard. 1216 *b*. they two may be in Rainham Down
Ard. 1445 *b*. I would not view the massacre
Ard. 1601 *b*. you painters make but a painting table of
Ard. 1911 and yet, *b*. his wife is the instrument
Ard. 2177 *b*. I blush not at my husband's death
Ard. 2192 *b*. her husband is abroad so late
HP 153 contents the world, cause faire they seeme
Cor. 224 (cause I cannot dry your ceaselesse springs)
Cor. 280 (cause hee sees that I am thine)
Jer. 106 I hate Andrea, cause he aimes at honor
ST 1219 and cause I know thee secret as my soule

Beck.
HP 15 and at a *b*. of the youth gat him swiftly on before
HP 1088 understand the[m] at a *b*., and obey them at a winck of the eye

Beckons.
Jer. 838 harke, the drum beckens me ; sweet deere, farwell

Become.
VPJ 74 their bed *b*. their grave
HP 610 *b*. unable and unfit for generation
HP 733 *b*. so bold and hardy that she lay aside
HP 819 as they *b*. such milke sops as were those Phrygians
HP 844 may *b*. good members of the Cittie where
HP 850 *b*. not werish and of a womanish
HP 930 with the light of understanding *b*. reasonable
HP 940 so that I see I am *b*. hir liege man
HP 952 is accompanied with reason, and may *b*. discipline
HP 1025 may with idlenes and ease *b*. pestilent
HP 1272 (beeing dryed) wold *b*. both hard and naught to eate

HP 1300 the longer they are kept *b*. so much the better
HP 1552 may *b*. so grosse and large in time
HP 1621 and so by covetous desire to *b*. infinit
Cor. 589 *b*. forsaken as before, yet after
Cor. 1688 the world should see me to *b*. a slave
Jer. 292 strang newes : Lorenzo is becom an honest man
Jer. 297 Lorenzo is *b*. an honnest man »
ST 1494 is your roaguerie *b*. an office with a knaves name ?
ST 1717 brother, you are *b*. an Oratour
Ard. 29 is now *b*. the steward of his house
Ard. 1097 how now, Will ? *b*. a precisian ?
Ard. 1607 put horns to them to make them *b*. sheep
HP 365 in the Summer the daie becomes victor
HP 697 beards, which albeit they becom men
HP 864 practises of mind and body as *b*. them
ST 186 these words, these deeds, *b*. thy person well
ST 767 although she coy it as becomes her kinde

Becomest.
Cor. 89 but touch, thou straight becomst a spoyle to Neptune

Becometh.
HP 801 the complexion of the child becommeth strong and lustie
HP 1215 the ayre becommeth filthy and infected
HP 1346 to muster and maintaine Armies becommeth Kings, Tyrants

Bed.
VPJ 74 their *b*. become their grave
HP 1784 in a very soft *b*. I bequeathed my bones to rest
Cor. 705 came glyding by my *b*. the ghost of Pompey
Cor. 1958 did revive the lights of thy forsaken *b*.
ST 878 what out-cries pluck me from my naked *b*.
ST 893 O was it thou that call'dst me from my *b*. ?
ST 1300 come sir, you had bene better kept your *b*.
SP 356 he goes many times supperles to *b*., and yet
Ard. 40 shall on the *b*. which he thinks to defile
Ard. 907 to further Mosbie to your mistress' *b*.
Ard. 1009 come, Master Franklin, shall we go to *b*. ?
Ard. 1027 my master would desire you come to *b*.
Ard. 1028 is he himself already in his *b*. ?
Ard. 1075 get you to *b*., and if you love my favour
Ard. 1077 come, Master Franklin, let us go to *b*.
Ard. 1118 the white-livered peasant is gone to *b*.
Ard. 1200 being in *b*., he did bethink himself
Ard. 1236 each gentle stirry gale doth shake my *b*.
Ard. 1261 'tis fearful sleeping in a serpent's *b*.
JB 81 and to excuse her from his *b*., she sayd
JB 135 then he requested her to have him to *b*.
VPJ 65 crowne, scepter, roiall marriage *b*.
HP 648 violate the bandes by so defiling of the marriage bedde
Cor. 285 whom once I had receiv'd in marriage *b*.
SP 72 my Grandame on her death *b*. gave it me
SP 674 and Cupid bring me to thy nuptiall *b*.
Ard. 2359 his purse and girdle found at thy bed's head
HP 1033 the Chamberlaine make the bedds and brush
Ard. 1145 first go make the *b*., and afterwards
Jer. 427 both wed, *b*., and boord her ?

Bedeem.
Ard. 1173 God grant this vision *b*. me any good

Bedesman, *see* **Bead's-man.**

Bedew.
Cor. 222 and wil ye needs *b*. my dead-grown joyes

Bedroll, *see* **Beadroll.**

Beef.
HP Ind. 14 beefe at feasts, more used for fashion then foode
HP Ind. 15 beefe sought for and desired by Ulysses Servants
HP 256 as for Beefe and such like, I holde it rather a trouble
HP 261 none other flesh eaten then Beefe, Porke

HP 267 de**s**ire of Feisants or Partrich, but to feede upon Beefe

Beer.

Ard. 1374 go in, Bradshaw ; call for a cup of *b*.
Ard. 1928 by the ears till all his *b*. hath run out
Ard. 2218 sirrah Michael, give's a cup of *b*.

Bees.

HP 174 some store of hyves for *B*.
SP 106 though like a Gnat amongst a hive of *B*.
Ard. 1247 such *b*. as Greene must never live to sting

Befall.

Cor. 7 els let the mischiefe that should them *b*.
ST Bal. 35 but marke what then did straight *b*.
ST 280 and that just guerdon may *b*. desert
ST 2998 that he may be entom'd, what ere *b*.
SP 1860 the most dishonour that could ere *b*.
Ard. 562 stab him, whatsoever did *b*. himself

Befallen.

SP 938 and let her know what hath *b*. me

Befell.

Cor. 179 and nere did good, where ever it *b*.

Befits.

Cor. 1480 as *b*. your state, maintaine a

Before.

VPJ (Title) in the Tower *b*. his Execution
HP 16 at a beck of the youth gat him swiftly on *b*.
HP 20 the River that runneth *b*. the Cittie
HP 33 and thether will I goe *b*.
HP 80 *b*. the house there was a little Court
HP 114 and another servitor that rode *b*.
HP 217 *b*. themselves were come unto their groweth
HP 305 *b*. the time of Grape-gathering
HP 412 ryght nor left, under nor over, *b*. nor behind
HP 470 a few yeeres *b*. his death
HP 499 *b*. I shall surrender this that rather
HP 610 so that one of them *b*. the other become
HP 766 Jove had not the[n] so much desire towards her as *b*.
HP 962 *B*. his maister, whom he likes
HP 1060 Virgil, who, *b*. he had called those instruments weapons
HP 1143 the care of wealth or substance, as we said *b*.
Cor. Arg. 13 *b*. her eyes, and in the presence of his young Sonne
Cor. 20 yea, come they are, and, fiery as *b*.
Cor. 314 beat backe like flyes *b*. a storme of hayle ?
Cor. 484 fought, *b*. the fearefull Carthagenian walls
Cor. 528 (to fright us) sette pale death *b*. our eyes
Cor. 589 become forsaken as *b*., yet after
Cor. 727 to venge the valure that is tryde *b*.
Cor. 791 thy cheeks with teares besprent, *b*. the victor
Cor. 933 Ile downe with joy : because, *b*. I died, mine eyes
Cor. 1000 for I had died *b*. the fall of Rome
Cor. 1276 were all the world his foes *b*.
Cor. 1578 and in thys direful warre *b*. mine eyes
Cor. 1634 where *b*. faire Tapsus, he made his Pyoners
Cor. 1715 may perrish in the presse *b*. our faces
Cor. 1814 the flock, that scattered flyes *b*. the Shepheard
Cor. 1878 *b*. the foe and in theyr Captaines presence
Cor. 2001 that with the gold and pearle we us'd *b*.
Cor. 2022 but if I die, *b*. I have entomb'd my
Jer. 268 sould to newe, *b*. the first are thoroughly cold
Jer. 475 what went *b*. ? thou hast put me out
Jer. 535 who, I ? *b*. your grace it must not be
Jer. 700 *b*. the King I will resolve you all
Jer. 806 trample the fields *b*. you ?
Jer. 874 what, are you braving us *b*. we come ?
Jer. 906 *b*. the evening deawes quench the sunnes rage
Jer. 1122 Ile to the King *b*., and let him know

ST Bal. 161 the Kinges, that scorn'd my griefes *b*.
ST 196 to shew themselves *b*. your Majestie
ST 403 (as Pallas was *b*. proud Pergamus)
ST 495 things were in readines *b*. I came
ST 636 I have no credit with her as *b*.
ST 657 preferring him *b*. Prince Balthazar
ST 880 which never danger yet could daunt *b*. ?
ST 976 sweet lovely Rose, ill pluckt *b*. thy time
ST 1280 and ward so neare the Duke his brothers house *b*.
ST 1305 Hieronimo ? carry me *b*. whom you will
STA 1769 makes them looke olde, *b*. they meet with age
STA 2042 is there no trickes that comes *b*. thine eies ?
ST 2151 for thus I usde, *b*. my Marshalship
ST 2250 appearance *b*. grim Mynos and just Radamant
ST 2423 but heere, *b*. Prince Balthazar and me
ST 2892 as any of the Actors gone *b*.
SP 80 it is no boot, for that was thine *b*.
SP 296 I must talke with you *b*. you goe
SP 297 O, if thou beest magnanimious, eome *b*. me
SP 827 hard doome of death, *b*. my case be knowne
SP 955 *b*. I goe, Ile be so bolde as to
ST 1226 *b*. thy comming I vowd to conquer Rhodes
SP 1568 now is she fairer then she was *b*.
SP 1750 that was *b*. he knew thee to be mine
SP 1835 what have we heer ? my maister *b*. the Marshall ?
SP 1875 yet give me leave, *b*. my life shall end
SP 2007 yet kisse me, gentle love, *b*. thou die
SP 2103 ah, let me kisse thee too, *b*. I dye
SP 2112 faire springing Rose, ill pluckt *b*. thy time
SP 2157 yet that alayes the furie of my paine *b*. I die
SP 2165 *b*. his age hath seene his mellowed yeares
SP 2224 whom Death did feare *b*. her life began
Ard. 196 *b*. I saw that falsehood look of thine
Ard. 423 why, he's as well now as he was *b*.
Ard. 467 and whatsoever leases were *b*. are void
Ard. 526 shall be intitled as they were *b*.
Ard. 553 *b*. I can begin to tell my tale
Ard. 717 *b*. you go, let me intreat you
Ard. 1010 I pray you, go *b*. : I'll follow you
Ard. 1137 that ne'er durst say *b*. but « yea » and « no »
Ard. 1217 be in Rainham Down *b*. your master
Ard. 1576 why, I pray you, let us go *b*.
Ard. 1580 *b*. you lies Black Will and Shakebag
Ard. 1629 and life shall end *b*. my love depart
Ard. 1645 go *b*. to the boat, and I will follow you
Ard. 1817 now that our horses are gone home *b*.
Ard. 2022 but come not forth *b*. in any case
Ard. 2075 stand *b*. the counting-house door
Aad. 2280 but it had done *b*. we came back again
JB 1 *b*. the sight of the eternall God
JB 14 that we see it put in execution daylie *b*. our eyes
JB 50 that had never *b*. been in the like daunger
JB 54 and this *b*. good witnes she vowed to performe
JB 81 still to be termed Anne Welles as she was *b*.
JB 90 as Parker had *b*. given direction
JB 98 (for it was the weeke *b*. shrovetide)
JB 124 but her husbands she had poysoned as *b*.
JB 129 « you were well *b*. you went forth, were you not ? »
JB 211 carried *b*. Alderman Howard to be examined
JB 212 and the man *b*. Justice Younge, who stoode
JB 221 the man to be hanged in the same place *b*. her **eyes**
Ard. 197 'fore I was tangled with thy 'ticing speech

Beforehand.

Jer. 504 « especially being warned before hand »
Jer. 523 especially being warnd *b*.

Beg.

ST 3021 now will I *b.* at lovely Proserpine, that, by
SP 1673 that rid a pilgrimage to *b.* cakebread?
Ard. 168 being a maid, may *b.* me from the gallows
Ard. 477 nor cares he though young gentlemen do *b.*

Began.
HP 6 to raine, I *b.* to set spurs to my Horse
HP 139 and then he *b.* thus
HP 207 and the good man of the house beganne againe
HP 289 and the olde man *b.* thus
HP 335 hee *b.* thus to reason
HP 402 that in this season the world *b.*
HP 408 it the[n] *b.* about the Spring
HP 427 seeke in what season it is like the world *b.*
HP 428 that it then *b.* when the Sun
HP 434 when the world *b.*, the Sun was in Aries
HP 439 the world *b.* in that season
HP 443 the world *b.* in the Autumnal aequinoctial
HP 444 it would follow that it *b.* in the Spring
HP 455 beganne earnestlie to looke upon me, and said
HP 475 who after a while returning, I beganne
HP 480 the good olde man *b.* thus
HP 485 and *b.* to reason with me thus
Cor. 1774 and fought as freshly as they first beganne
ST 78 whereat faire Proserpine *b.* to smile
ST 358 and when he fell, then we *b.* to flie
STA 2002 the infant and the humaine sap *b.* to wither
ST 2171 with incke bewray what blood *b.* in me
SP 238 insomuch that my Steed *b.* to faint
SP 1827 his Cabine doore fast shut, he first *b.*
SP 2224 whom Death did feare before her life *b.*
Ard. 1982 Mosbie, perceiving this, *b.* to faint
JB 127 hee *b.* to waxe very ill about the stomack
JB 133 immediatlie after he *b.* to vomet exceedingly
Cor. 361 flesh'd so long, till they gan tiranize the Towne
Cor. 419 (with armes to heaven uprear'd) I gan exclaime
Cor. 698 now gan to cast her sable mantle off
Cor. 703 gan close the windowes of my watchfull eyes
Cor. 820 till (waxen warme) it nimbly gan to styr
Cor. 1889 they gan retyre, where Juba was encampt
ST 34 to whome no sooner gan I make approch
ST 2593 then gan he break his passions to a freend
Ard. 61 often chid the morning when it 'gan to peep

Begat.
Ard. 1232 my daily toil *b.* me night's repose

Beget.
HP 1678 it is not naturall that money should *b.* or

Beggar.
HP 582 or, contrarily, a Gentleman with a Begger
STA 2018 O ambitious begger, wouldest thou have that
SP 454 where he hath but ten pence of a begger
Ard. 1358 we beggars must not breathe where gentles are

Begged.
ST 79 and begd that onely she might give my doome
Ard. 1561 no, *b.* favour merits little thanks

Begin.
HP 204 wel that you *b.* to advise your selfe
HP 221 when the youth of their sonnes *b.* to flourish
HP 517 now, to *b.*, I say thus
HP 567 Ere I to lose or violate my chastity beginne
Cor. 717 thys solemne tale he sadly did *b.*
Cor. 1652 one while at Tapsus we *b.* t'entrench
Cor. 1807 our men at Armes (in briefe) *b.* to flye
ST 127 from out our rearward to *b.* the fight
ST 850 then thus *b.* our wars: put forth thy hand
ST 1428 but come, for that we came for: lets *b.*
ST 3056 Ile there *b.* their endles Tragedie

SP 589 Oh, Haleb, how shall I *b.* to mourne
SP 590 or how shall I *b.* to shed salt teares
Ard. 553 before I can *b.* to tell my tale
Ard. 1754 when words grow hot and blows *b.* to rise
Ard. 2119 seeing you are so stout, you shall *b.*!
Cor. 1340 how your Empire and your praise begins
Cor. 1646 that come to forrage when the cold begins
Cor. 1799 begins a fresh remembrance of our former sins
Jer. 639 the evening to begins to slubber day
ST 813 now that the night begins with sable wings
ST 1149 early begins to regester my dreames
SP 1928 and now begins my pleasant Comedie
SP 2067 and thus my tale begins: thou wicked tirant
HP 1330 and she gins the ymbers up to rake
ST 752 our howre shall be when Vesper ginnes to rise
SP 2150 for now I feele the poyson gins to worke

Beginner.
SP 391 thrive, faire *b.*, as this time doth promise

Beginneth.
HP 429 it *b.* with generation, not with
HP 441 and *b.* generation in those parts of

Beginning.
HP 407 (the world *b.*, as it is supposed)
HP 411 there can bee perceived neither *b.* nor ende
HP 415 whereof the motion hath his *b.*
HP 432 giveth *b.* to the generation and
HP 446 the *b.* of the motion should be taken
HP 1164 those compasses which gave begining to Geometry in
    Egypt
Cor. 566 both their *b.* and their end
Cor. 585 showes their *b.* by their last
JB 3 yet from the *b.* we may evidently see
HP 609 as the *b.* of the ones age match not

Begone.
Cor. 1569 wretches, they are woe-*b.*
ST 2738 all woe *b.* for him, hath slaine her selfe
Ard. 1025 so woe-*b.*, so inily charged with woe

Begot.
Jer. 284 sign that I *b.* thee, for it showes thou art mine
STA 1748 a thing *b.* within a paire of minutes, thereabout

Beguile.
HP 943 Hesiodus, that auncient Poet, shall not *b.* thee
Cor. 264 bewitcht my life, and did *b.* my love
Cor. 1018 she fleres againe, I know not how, still to *b.*
Jer. 694 Andrea lives: O let not death *b.* thee
Ard. 1020 sometimes he seeketh to *b.* his grief
Jer. 49 Oh, a polyticke speech beguiles the eares of foes
Ard. 1476 your pretty tale beguiles the weary way

Beguiled.
HP 375 these if I be not *b.*, are the
HP 1670 For in their Gold their hope *b.* lies
Cor. 289 byd you beware for feare you be beguild
Cor. 734 but his airie spirit *b.* mine embrasements
Cor. 777 some false Daemon that beguild your sight
Cor. 1887 since all our hopes are by the Gods beguil'd
Jer. 679 Alcario slaine? hast thou beguild me, sword?

Beguiling.
Ard. 1156 and rounded me with that *b.* home

Begun.
VPJ 44 t'obscure thy light unluckelie *b.*
HP Ind. 47 civill warres *b.* by Servants
HP 331 beeing *b.* to by him, I pledged him of a Cup
HP 974 it was begunne and stirred up by servants
Cor. 172 that we continue our offence begunne
Cor. 500 but whatsoe're hath been *b.*, must end
Jer. 797 grew Violent, and wished the fight begune

ST Bal. 106 to stay the rumour then begone
ST 408 did finish what his Halberdiers *b.*
Ard. 1108 go forward now in that we have *b.*
Ard. 1419 Why, he *b.* — And thou shalt find I'll end
Ard. 1854 though *b.* in sport, yet ends in blood !
Cor. 1510 by his tryumphs new *b.*
ST 906 to leese thy life ere life was new *b.* ?
ST 2371 love, which, new *b.*, can shew no brighter yet

Behalf.

ST 2334 the K[ing] my brothers care in his behalfe
SP 736 and thou in my behalfe shalt work revenge
SP 1932 and wooes apace in Solimans behalfe
SP 1980 hast thou for this, in Solimans behalfe

Behave.

ST Bal. 24 did so *b.* him in the fielde that
JB 156 she knew not as then how to *b.* her selfe to

Behaviour.

VPJ 13 honour'd art, Princely *b.*, zeale to good
HP 842 propose him or his *b.* for theyr example
JB 24 her good *b.* and other commendable qualities

Beheaded.

Cor. 946 Photis and false Achillas he beheadded

Beheld.

HP 8 I *b.* a little Kidde surchargd, pursued, and
HP 27 whilst he thus spake, I stedfastly *b.* him
Cor. 709 at his feete *b.* great Emperors fast bound
Cor. 1025 behelde her never over night lye calmely downe
Cor. 1376 *b.* the swift Rheyn under-run mine Ensignes
Cor. 1579 *b.* theyr corses scattred on the plaines
Cor. 1846 when he *b.* his people so discomfited
Jer. 600 within this walke have I *b.* her
ST 1040 no ; for, my Lord, had you behelde the traine
ST 1088 these eies *b.*, and these my followers
ST 1585 what have I heard, what have mine eies behelde ?
ST 1812 whose rockie cliffes when you have once behelde
ST 2588 whose beauty ravished all that her beheelde

Behest.

SP 1232 to whose *b.* I vowe obedience

Behind.

HP 412 ryght nor left, vnder nor over, before nor *b.*
Cor. 789 now shalt thou march (thy hands fast bound *b.* thee)
ST 1224 thou knowest tis heere hard by behinde the house
ST 1236 at S. Luigis Parke, behinde the house
ST 2682 that I will have there behinde a curtaine
SP 876 went to shoote, and left his arrowes behinde him ?
SP 1379 wherfore stay we ? thers more *b.*
SP 1693 a greater punishment to hurt you *b.*
SP 1695 sooth thou sayest, I must be fenced behinde
Ard. 1240 is hedged *b.* me that I cannot back
Ard. 1460 her glove brought in which there she left *b.*
Ard. 1563 or else be stolen ; therefore I'll stay *b.*
Ard. 1577 whilst he stays *b.* to seek his purse
Ard. 1614 stayed you *b.* your master to this end ?
Ard. 1829 for sure she grieved that she was left *b.*
Ard. 2037 that I may come *b.* him cunningly
Ard. 2040 that done, bear him *b.* the Abbey
Ard. 2198 I saw him walking *b.* the Abbey even now
Ard. 2297 *b.* the Abbey there he lies murdered

Behold.

HP 491 as we *b.* the providence of our almighty God
HP 1046 is not onelie pleasing or delightfull to beholde
Cor. 1111 and mournfull we *b.* him bravely mounted
Cor. 1874 *b.*, his owne was fiercely set upon
Cor. 2012 shall I *b.* the sumptuous ornaments
Jer. 550 pray you, let me *b.* it
ST Bal. 139 but when they did *b.* this thing

ST 1713 looke on thy love, *b.* yong Balthazar
STA 1957 yet cannot I *b.* my sonne Horatio
STA 2079 *b.* a man hanging, and tottering, and tottering
ST 2191 *b.* the sorrowes and the sad laments that
ST 2463 beholde, Andrea, for an instance, how
ST 2798 but with a gratious eye *b.* his griefe
ST 2830 beholde the reason urging me to this
ST 2864 and heere beholde this bloudie hand-kercher
ST 2888 and, Princes, now beholde Hieronimo
SP 212 so are all blades with me : *b.* my instance
SP 265 and with impartiall eyes *b.* your deedes
SP 266 to *b.* the faire demeanor of these
SP 273 I will place her to *b.* my triumphes
JB 175 so haule and pull her as was pittie to *b.*

Beholding.

SP 262 he is *b.* to you greatly, sir

Behoof.

SP 1800 yet must his bloud be spilt for my behoofe

Behoves.

HP 1163 it behooves that he himself have seene and
ST 1174 and of his death *b.* me be reveng'd
ST 2739 behooves thee then, Hieronimo, to be reveng'd
Ard. 2256 well, it *b.* us to be circumspect

Behoveth.

HP 667 it *b.* the rule and authoritie of the
HP 1167 it also behooveth that he knowe that
HP 1424 for the one it behooveth to provide

Being.

HP 1607 Number is reputed either according to the formall or materiall beeing
Cor. 1655 and wakefull Caesar that doth watch our *b.*
Jer. 160 my lives happines, the joy of all my *b.*

Belched.

Ard. 325 thou hast *b.* and vomited the

Beldam.

Jer. 110 night, that yawning Beldam with her Jettie skin

Beleaguer.

SP 519 and so beleager Rhodes by sea and land

Beleagured.

SP 2021 hath beleagred Rhodes, whose chieftaine is a woman

Beleagureth.

SP 268 I am melancholy : an humor of Venus belegereth me

Belgia.

SP 226 a sore drought in some part of *B.*

Belief.

HP 405 beeing no Article of our beliefe
STA 960 weake apprehension gives but weake beleife
ST 2489 both my letters and thine own beliefe assures
Ard. 1181 some one in twenty may incur *b.*

Believe.

HP 402 as indeede wee may assuredlie beleeve it did
HP 746 I beleeve that there was never greater sweet
HP 1085 how much more may we beleeve that men
HP 1733 I beleeve that private house of mine should
Cor. 268 but if (as some *b.*) in heaven or hell be
Cor. 653 and *b.* it grieves me that I know not
Cor. 1177 *b.* it not ; he bought it deere, you know
Jer. 183 beleeve it, Bellimperia, tis as common to weepe
ST 1916 beleeve me, Nephew, we are sorie fort
ST 2355 my gracious father, beleeve me, so he doth
Ard. 152 there's no such matter, Michael ; *b.* it not
Ard. 1832 for I *b.* she'll strive to mend our cheer
Ard. 2201 *b.* me I saw him not since morning
JB 215 made to beleeve that Parker had bewrayed the

Believed.

HP 400 (if the troth reported of him may but be beleeved)

Ard. 1328 which too incredulous I ne'er *b*.
Believing.
ST 2516 my feare and care in not beleeving it
Belike.
Jer. 709 *b*. twas false Andrea, for the first
ST 465 your prison then, *b*., is your conceit
SP 1857 *b*. he thought we had bewrayd his treasons
Bel-imperia.
Jer. 128 thats Bellimperia
Jer. 150 sweet Bellimperia
Jer. 166 true, Madam Bellimperia, thats his taske
Jer. 178 then, Bellimperia, I take leave : Horatio
Jer. 180 what, playing the woman, Bellimperia ?
Jer. 183 beleeve it, Bellimperia, tis as common to weepe at
Jer. 212 the love betwixt Bellimperia and Andreas bosome ?
Jer. 240 dotes on your Sister, Bellimperia
Jer. 269 so Bellimperia ; for this is common
Jer. 414 on whom my Sister Bellimperia casts her
Jer. 616 but see, my Sister Bellimperia comes
Jer. 628 but, maddam Bellimperia, leave we this
Jer. 691 looke to my Sister, Bellimperia
Jer. 692 raise up my deere love, Bellimperia
Jer. 708 Bout love ? — No, Bellimperia
Jer. 1086 farewell deere, dearest Bellimperia
ST Bal.(Title) the lamentable murders of Horatio and Bellimperia
ST Bal. 89 which Bellimperia foorth had flung from
ST Bal. 109 sweete Bellimperia comes to me
ST Bal. 127 sweete Bellimperia Baltazar killes
ST Bal. 132 but Bellimperia ends her life
ST (Title) the lamentable end of Don Horatio, and Belimperia ; with
ST 11 which hight sweet *B*. by name
ST 89 depriv'd of life by *B*.
ST 437 humbly to serve faire *B*.
ST 572 my Lord, though *B*. seeme thus coy
ST 631 whome loves my sister *B*. ?
ST 647 if Madame *B*. be in love
ST 666 be still conceald from *B*.
ST 766 what saies your daughter *B*. ?
ST 806 to winne faire *B*. from her will
ST 818 come, *B*., let us to the bower
ST 843 for joy that *B*. sits in sight
ST 873 but Balthazar loves *B*.
ST 1014 and they abuse fair *B*.
ST 1160 and better fare then *B*. doth
ST 1164 or what might moove thee, *B*.
ST 1180 close, if I can, with *B*., to listen more
ST 1185 he asketh for my Lady *B*.
ST 1249 this slie inquiry of Hieronimo for *B*.
ST 1634 come, Madame *B*., this may not be
ST 1669 advise you better, *B*.
ST 1681 have patience. *B*. ; heare the rest
ST 1686 found *B*. with Horatio
ST 1712 but, *B*. see the gentle Prince
ST 1730 Tis I that love. — Whome ? — *B*.
ST 1731 But I that feare. — Whome ? — *B*.
ST 1866 the marriage of his Princely Sonne with *B*.
ST 1876 and make a Queene of *B*.
ST 1930 the match twixt Balthazar and *B*.
ST 2208 faire *B*., with my Balthazar
ST 2313 She is thy Sister ? — Who, *B*. ?
ST 2364 come, *B*., Balthazars content
ST 2377 and welcome, *B*.. How now, girle ?
ST 2507 that *B*., vowes such revenge
ST 2513 pardon, O pardon, *B*.
ST 2530 how now, Hieronimo ? what, courting *B*. ?

ST 2653 I know that *B*. hath practised the French
ST 2747 who, *B*. ?
ST 2765 I, *B*. hath taught him that
ST 2766 that's because his minde runs all on *B*.
ST 2811 but *B*. plaies Perseda well
ST 2812 were this in earnest, *B*., you
ST 2842 the love : my sonne to *B*.
ST 2878 that Soliman which *B*., in person
ST 2882 poore *B*. mist her part in this
ST 2918 that was thy daughter *B*.
STA 2950 that was thy daughter *B*.
ST 3015 Prince Balthazar by *B*. stabd
ST 3018 my *B*. falne as Dido fell
ST 3029 Ile lead my *B*. to those joyes that
Jer. 263 I will make way to Bellimperias eies
Jer. 637 this gallery leads to Bellimperias lodging
Jer. 749 was a huge dotar on Bellimperias beautye
Jer. 1146 alas, I pitty Bellimperias eies
ST 479 and worne it for his Bel-imperias sake
ST 484 be sure while Bel-imperias life endures
ST 446 he could not sit in Bel-imperias thoughts
ST 582 but wherefore blot I Bel-imperias name ?
ST 698 which slie deceits smooth Bel-imperias eares
ST 1571 that Bel-imperias Letter was not fainde
Bell'ingannus'.
HP 745 the kysses of Bell'ingannus Paramour seemed sweeter
Bellona.
Cor. 1755 *B*., fiered with a quenchles rage, runnes
ST 143 now while *B*. rageth heere and there
Bellow.
Cor. 420 exclaime and *b*. forth against the Gods
Bells.
STA 2076 the Belles towling, the Owle shriking
Belly.
JB 184 for feare her neighbours should perceave her great bellie
Belong.
HP 1004 the Baylieffe, to whom the Toun affaires *b*.
HP 1053 that *b*. unto his office
HP 1032 everie thing that belongs to the keeping of a house
Cor. 1257 nor ought doth Brutus that to Brute belongs
Jer. 318 and do him all the honor that belonges him
Belonged.
Cor. 1538 so wrong'd of the honor him belong'd
Belongeth.
HP 1138 nothing left out that *b*. to a Husband
HP 1171 all whatsoever els *b*. to husbandry
HP 1367 that it *b*. to the wife to keepe
HP 1718 the care of Princes Halles *b*. not to private men
Belonging.
HP 503 touching things *b*. to good government
Beloved.
HP 739 O my *b*. father in law whom I have hourely feard
Cor. 1485 then theirs whom we offend, and once belov'd
ST Bal. 27 to relate the death of her *b*. friend
ST 448 till I revenge the death of my *b*. ?
STA 932 besides, he is so generally *b*.
ST 1031 that would be feard, yet feare to be *b*.
ST 1173 deare was the life of my *b*. Sonne
ST 1866 with Bel-imperia, thy *b*. Neece
ST 2207 to solemnize the marriage of thy *b*. Neece
ST 2679 where thus they murdered my *b*. sonne
ST 2774 that he may see Perseda my *b*.
ST 2997 mourne the losse of our *b*. brothers death
SP 640 each one by armes to honor his *b*.
SP 641 nay, one alone to honor his *b*.
SP 1778 I will stay with you, from Brusor my *b*.

SP 1782 angrie for that I carry thy *b.* from thee
SP 1869 for that thou wert *b.* of Soliman
JB 25 was *b.* of divers young men, especially of two
JB 29 who, although hee was better *b.*, yet
ST 325 and with their blood, my joy and best *b.*
ST 326 my best *b.*, my sweete and onely Sonne
SP 1535 see where he comes, my other best *b.*
SP 1536/7 my sweete and best *b.*

Below.
HP 1229 or *b.* in some valley, where it may be overflowne
Cor. 2037 encrease the number of the ghosts be-low

Ben.
HP 1645 E se tu *b.* la tua fisica note

Bending.
Jer. 506 *b.* in the hams like an old Courtier
Jer. 524 *b.* in the hams enough, like a Gentleman usher ?
SP 531 *b.* them upon a paltrie Ile of small defence

Bends.
Cor. 1014 one while shee *b.* her angry browe
ST 1625 why *b.* thou thus thy minde to martir me ?
ST 1882 that *b.* his liking to my daughter thus

Benefit.
HP 1518 to make his *b.* of things unto their uttermost
HP 1590 neither receive we any *b.* thereof
ST 1094 For both our honors and thy benefite
SP 1197 heavens brought thee hether for our *b.*
HP 1366 considering that those benefits are small

Benign.
SP 260 yet to gratulate this benigne Prince

Bent.
HP 1089 at a winck of the eye, or *b.* of the brow
Cor. 1172 he aym'd at us, *b.* to exterminate who ever
Cor. 1618 so many people *b.* so much to fight
Cor. 1803 stooping their heads low *b.* to tosse theyr staves
SP 6 Melpomene is wholy *b.* to tragedies discourse
Ard. 1160 with falchion drawn, and *b.* it at my breast

Beona.
HP 1400 returning from Paris and comming by *B.*

Bequeath.
HP 1697 I will bestowe them and *b.* thee them in writing

Bequeathed.
HP 1561 devided and *b.* amongst his Children
HP 1784 in a very soft bed I *b.* my bones to rest
Jer. 810 farwell, brave Lords ; my wishes are bequeathd

Berayed.
Ard. 1739 how cams't thou so *b* ?

Bereave.
Cor. 866 when I saw the murdring Egiptians *b.* his lyfe
Cor. 958 because hymselfe of life did not *b.* him
Cor. 1906 *b.* my lyfe, or lying strangle me
ST 306 yes, Fortune may *b.* me of my Crowne
SP 915 thou didst *b.* me of my dearest love
SP 1891 for to *b.* Erastus life from him

Bereaved.
ST Bal. 74 finding her sonne bereav'd of breath
ST Bal. 159 and eke my selfe bereav'd of life
ST 2705 whose hatefull wrath berev'd him of his breath

Bereaving.
Cor. 1945 hath given blessed rest for lifes *b.*

Berecynthia.
HP 825 Tympana vos buxusque voca[n]t *B.* matris

Berecyntian.
HP 831 Cebiles *B.* pypes and Tymberils, you see, do call

Bereft.
HP 910 hath beene deposed or *b.* of his dignitie
Cor. 2006 and last, not least, *b.* of my best Father

ST 2685 heere lay my blisse, and heere my blisse *b.*
SP 2191 but I *b.* them both of love and life

Bergamo.
HP 49 *B.*, a Cittye situate in Lombardy

Beseech.
HP 479 I *b.* you commaund your Sons to sitte
Cor. Ded. 18 I shall *b.* your Honour to repaire with
Ard. 1492 I *b.* your honour pardon me
Ard. 1788 God, I *b.* thee, show some miracle
Puck 68 I shall besech in all humillitie & in the

Beseemed.
ST 2349 passions that ill beseemde the presence of a King

Beseeming.
HP 93 every other ornament *b.* the lodging of a Gentleman
HP 763 things more *b.* a Lover then a Wife

Beseems.
ST 2284 (for it beseemes us now that it be knowne)

Beset.
Cor. 1714 that this brave Tyrant, valiantly *b.*, may
Ard. 1065 *b.* with murderer thieves that came to rifle me

Beshrew.
Jer. 476 beshrow thy impudence or insolence

Beside.
Cor. 117 and almost yoked all the world *b.*
ST 268 nor I, although I sit *b.* my right
ST 792 wilt please your grace command me ought *b.* ?
SP 425 *b.* two dossen small inferior bones
SP 1367 *b.*, I sat on valiant Brusors tongue
Ard. 2329 I loved him more than all the world *b.*
JB 106 having set the porringer doune *b.* her
HP 218 besides, the fathers ought to exceede their
HP 384 besides that, whatsoever fruite Sommer hath
HP 429 besides, it beginneth with generation
HP 785 besides, if the mylke altered not the bodies
HP 989 (besides their weapons) many whips
HP 1049 besides, Cleanlines increaseth and preserveth the
HP 1265 besides, many sorts of fruits that
HP 1294 besides she shold busie herselfe in viewing and
HP 1478 besides those things whereof they exercized trafique
HP 1629 besides the value of mony of some Country coyne
Cor. 438 besides the servitude that causeth all our cares
Cor. 439 besides the basenes wherein we are yoked
Cor. 440 besides the losse of good men dead and gone
Cor. 1444 besides theyr lives, I did theyr goods restore
Jer. 429 besids, within these few daies heele returne
ST 667 besides, your Honors liberalitie deserves
ST 778 besides that she is daughter and half heire
STA 932 besides, he is so generally beloved
ST 1274 besides, this place is free from all suspect
ST 2661 and with a strange and wondrous shew besides
SP 651 besides Love hath inforst a foole
SP 944 dearer to me then all the world besides
Ard. 906 we know besides that you have ta'en your oath
Ard. 2379 besides that, I robbed him and his man once
Puck 29 besides he was intemp[er]ate & of a cruel hart

Besiege.
Cor. 46 that we will come thy borders to *b.*
Jer. 47 oft besiedge the eares of rough heawn tyrants

Besieged.
Cor. 400 with pike in hand upon a Forte besieg'd
Cor. 1871 besieg'd, betraide by winde, by land, by sea

Besmeared.
Cor. 609 (with haples brothers blood besmear'd)
ST 981 seest thou this handkercher besmerd with blood ?
Cor. 193 arm'd with his blood-besmeard keene Coutelace

Besprent.

Cor. 790 thy head hung downe, thy cheeks with teares *b*.
Best.
HP Ind. 8 judged the *b*. of other seasons
HP 1482 and thereof maketh their *b*.
Cor. 35 equals are ever bandying for the *b*.
Cor. 150 or that we proudly doe what lyke us *b*.
Cor. 1050 gainst one whose power and cause is *b*.
Cor. 1298 their glorie equall with the *b*.
Cor. 1370 and fought more battailes then the *b*. of them
Cor. 1587 but hope the *b*., and harken to his newes
Cor. 1608 Lyons and Beares, are theyr *b*. Sepulchers
Cor. 1772 and thrice the *b*. of both was faine to breathe
Cor. 1876 ended the lives of his *b*. fighting men
Cor. 2006 and last, not least, bereft of my *b*. Father
Jer. 86 discharg the waight of your command with *b*. respect
Jer. 112 for such complexions *b*. appease my pride
Jer. 244 great gifts and gold have the *b*. toong to move
Jer. 319 father, my *b*. indevour shall obay you
Jer. 337 we have with *b*. advise thought of our state
Jer. 614 welcome, brave Don Andrea, Spaines *b*. of sperit
Jer. 1098 honors in bloud *b*. swim
ST 53 to dome him as *b*. seemes his Majestie
ST 277 for thine estate *b*. fitteth such a guest
ST 432 for after him thou hast deserved it *b*.
ST 442 for sollitude *b*. fits my cheereles mood
ST 560 but welcome are you to the *b*. we have
ST 1056 Yet hope the *b*. — Tis heaven is my hope
ST 1926 tis *b*. that we see further in it first
ST 2118 which under kindeship wilbe cloked *b*.
ST 2625 which to your discretion shall seeme *b*.
SP 294 and at his *b*. advantage stole away
SP 371 this knight unknowne hath *b*. demeand himself
SP 455 let them paie that *b*. may, as the Lawyers use their
SP 482 Ile doe the *b*. I can to finde your chaine
SP 511 how I *b*. may lay my never failing siege
SP 946 a doubtful agony, what I were *b*. to do
SP 1049 where you had not *b*. go to him
SP 1210 the least of these surpasse my *b*. desart
SP 1552 they love each other *b*. : what then should follow
SP 1938 which like you, the Turkish or our nation *b*.?
SP 2064 to use as to thy liking shall seeme *b*.
SP 2215 for powerfull Death *b*. fitteth Tragedies
Ard. 102 and therefore Mosbie's title is the *b*.
Ard. 370 you were *b*. to say I would have poisoned you
Ard. 585 I did it for the *b*.
Ard. 805 why, that's the *b*. ; but see thou miss him not
Ard. 808 'tis very late ; I were *b*. shut up my stall
Ard. 1178 it may be so, God frame it to the *b*.
Ard. 1390 you were *b*. swear me on the interrogatories
Ard. 1435 'twere *b*. that I went back to Rochester
Ard. 1674 ay, but you had not *b*. to meddle with
Ard. 1823 happy the change that alters for the *b*.!
Ard. 1906 I know my wife counsels me for the *b*.
Puck 32 nombred amongst the *b*. conditions of men
Best-beloved.
ST 325 and with their blood, my joy and best beloved
ST 326 my best beloved, my sweete and onely Sonne
SP 1535 see where he comes, my other best beloved
SP 1536/7 my sweete and best beloved
Best-cheap.
HP 1497 where they are helde deerest, and where best cheape
Bestir.
ST 2708 and none but I bestirre me — to no ende
Bestow.
HP 1696 I will bestowe them and bequeath thee them in writing
Cor. 378 heavens did theyr favors lavishly *b*.

ST 220 we will *b*. on every souldier two duckets
Bestowed.
Jer. 132 what, not to have honor *b*. on me ?
SP 10 a tale wherein she lately hath *b*. the huskie humour of
JB 40 golde and jewels, which he willingly *b*. upon her
Bestoweth.
HP 1513 and so much time and labour onely hee *b*.
Bethink.
ST 2733 *b*. thy selfe, Hieronimo, recall thy wits
Ard. 845 and let us *b*. us on some other place
Ard. 877 let us *b*. us of some other place
Ard. 1200 being in bed, he did *b*. himself
Ard. 1640 and let us *b*. us what we have to do
Bethought.
Jer. 396 we have *b*. us what tribute is
Betide.
HP 959 civill broyle or other troubles that may often *b*. them
HP 1159 losses which by chaunce or Fortune may *b*. him
ST 2767 what ever joy earth yields, *b*. your Majestie
SP 1860 foule death *b*. me, if I sweare not true
Ard. 918 whatever shall *b*. to any of us
Ard. 1806 and ask of God, whate'er *b*. of me
Betided.
Cor. 351 we must not thinke a miserie *b*. will never cease
Cor. 1681 and to endure what ere betyded them
Betook.
Cor. Arg. 22 he betooke himselfe. with some small troope, to
Betray.
ST 367 that thou shouldst thus *b*. him to our foes ?
ST 1107 thus falsly *b*. Lord Alexandros life ?
SP 927 they will *b*. me to Phylippos hands
SP 1000 I must betraie my maister ?
SP 1809 and be assured that I *b*. thee not
SP 1810 yes, thou, and I, and all of us *b*. him
Ard. 2158 ah, that villain will *b*. us all
Ard. 2160 why, dost thou think I will *b*. myself ?
Ard. 2266 that is the next way to *b*. myself
Ard. 2273 be resolute, Mistress Alice, *b*. us not
Betrayed.
Cor. 1871 besieg'd, betraide by winde, by land, by sea
ST 382 deceived the King, betraid mine enemy
ST 864 whose there. Pedringano ? We are betraide
ST 977 faire worthy sonne, not conquerd, but betraid
ST 1166 Hieronimo, beware, thou art betraide
ST 1319 we are betraide to old Hieronimo
ST 1320 betraide, Lorenzo ? tush, it cannot be
ST 2897 we are betraide ; my Balthazar is slaine
SP 708 ah, false Erastus, how am I betraid
SP 2078 thou hast betrayde the flower of Christendome
Ard. 2306 thou hast *b*. and undone us all
Betraying.
Ard. 960 now must I quittance with *b*. thee.
Betrothed.
ST 2285 already is betroth'd to Balthazar
ST 2586 he was *b*., and wedded at the length
Better.
HP 32 whether you were *b*. to passe on or staie
HP 603 she can *b*. receive and retaine all formes
HP 657 no collour *b*. graceth or adornes a womans
HP 671 he can practise no way *b*. to dyswade her
HP 864 and may *b*. their estate with praise
HP 885 of one that *b*. may content him
HP 950 disposeth any sort of weapon *b*. then the left
HP 1300 the longer they are kept become so much the *b*.
HP 1368 as things preserved may the *b*. be disposed
HP 1495 grow the *b*., and in which the worse

HP 1605 but for thy *b.* understanding what we say, know
Cor. Ded. 23 my next Sommers *b.* travell with the Tragedy of Portia
Cor. 384 Pompey could not die a *b.* death
Cor. 1486 *b.* it is to die then be suspitious
Cor. 1598 haply the newes is *b.* then the noyse
Cor. 1872 all raging mad to rig his *b.* Vessels
Jer. 237 the *b.* ther is oppertunity
Jer. 997 ha, Vullupo? — No ; but a *b.*
ST 267 I crave no *b.* then your grace awards
ST 297 this *b.* fits a wretches endles moane
ST 299 and therefore *b.* then my state deserves
ST 776 I know no *b.* meanes to make us freends
ST 1160 and *b.* fare then Bel-imperia doth
ST 1255 and *b.* its that base companions dye
ST 1300 come sir, you had bene *b.* kept your bed
ST 1669 advise you *b.*, Bel-imperia
ST 1705 and *b.* wast for you, being in disgrace
STA 2090 I am never *b.* then when I am mad
ST 2631 Hieronimo, methinkes a Comedie were *b.*
ST 2813 you would be *b.* to my Sonne then so
SP 120 *b.* sit still then rise and overtane
SP 322 *b.* a Dog fawne on me, then barke
SP 368 olde laughing ; it will be *b.* then the Fox in the hole for me
SP 613 might I not *b.* spare one joy then both?
SP 781 calst thou me love, and lovest another *b.*?
SP 1351 I love them both, I know not which the *b.*
SP 1620 is it not *b.* that Erastus die
SP 1747 brought Soliman from worse to *b.*
SP 2037 and yet we usd Perseda little *b.*
Ard. 25 a botcher, and no *b.* at the first
Ard. 280 some other poison would do *b.* far
Ard. 393 for never woman loved her husband *b.*
Ard. 899 because I think you love your mistress *b.*
Ard. 1209 why now, Greene, 'tis *b.* now nor e'er it was
Ard. 1420 I do but slip it until *b.* time
Ard. 1687 unless my feet see *b.* than my eyes
Ard. 1688 didst thou ever see *b.* weather to
Ard. 1833 why, there's no *b.* creatures in the world
Ard. 1981 nay, 'tis *b.* than a sconce, for I have tried it
JB 29 who, although hee was *b.* beloved, yet
JB 82 till he had gotten her a *b.* house
JB 120 that she might the *b.* performe hir wicked intent
Puck 82 as I wold request yᵉ Lᵖˢ *b.* thoughts
Better-cheap.
HP 1243 now and then when they are better cheape
Bettered.
HP 1706 if anie thing be said that in your opinion may be *b.*
Bettereth.
HP 1047 *b.* things by Nature base and filthie
Between.
HP 780 devided so betweene the Father and the Mother
Jer. 1135 O then stept heaven and I betweene the stroke
ST 169 not long betweene these twaine the fight indurde
ST 801 *b.* us theres a price already pitcht
ST 1273 will stand betweene me and ensuing harmes
ST 1547 you will stand *b.* the gallowes and me?
SP 1532 so shall I joy betweene two captive friends
JB 39 had, upon a promise *b.* them, receaved of Brewen
JB 209 spoken betweene them in vehemencie of spirite
Jer. 609 and hem perswasion tweene her snowy paps
Betwixt.
HP Ind. 50 difference *b.* Exchaunge and Usury
HP Ind. 53 difference *b.* the instruction of
HP Ind. 58 distinction of nobilitie *b.* man and wife

HP 4 rode *b.* Novara and Vercellis
HP 840 the woorthines *b.* Winter and Sommer
HP 854 slothfull and sleepie *b.* idlenes and eating
HP 857 the difference *b.* the day and night
HP 592 hath ordeined *b.* men and women
HP 1115 *b.* them and their Maisters can be
HP 1127 utterly extinguished *b.* Maisters and Servants
HP 1144 and is devided *b.* the Master and Mistresse
HP 1622 yet *b.* Exchange and Usury there is some difference
Cor. Arg. 6 the civill warres *b.* him and Caesar
Jer. 212 the love *b.* Bellimperia and Andreas bosome?
ST 14 forcing divorce *b.* my love and me
ST 620 I stood *b.* thee and thy punishment
ST 1874 league *b.* the Crownes of Spaine and Portingale
ST 2784 love *b.* Erasto and faire Perseda
SP 449 lost her selfe *b.* a taverne and a bawdie house
Ard. 1287 forget, I pray thee, what hath passed *b.* us
Ard. 2147 to prevent that, creep *b.* my legs
HP Ind. 33 how it is to bee devided twixt
HP 772 love which ought to bee twixt man and wife
Cor. 243 twixt sighes, and sobs, and teares, do
ST 72 twixt these two waies I trod the middle path
ST 1574 now may I make compare twixt hers and this
ST 1836 and twixt his teeth he holdes a fire-brand
ST 1930 the match twixt Balthazar and Bel-imperia
ST 2182 this was a token twixt thy soule and me
SP 1465 twixt which a vale leads to the Elisian shades
Ard. 15 love-letters pass 'twixt Mosbie and my wife
Ard. 1891 and be a mediator 'twixt us two
Ard. 1904 work crosses and debates 'twixt man and wife
Bewail.
ST Bal. 165 whose death I could anew bewayle
ST 3045 and let him there bewaile his bloudy love
SP 2043 and with our teares bewaile her obsequies
Bewailed.
Cor. 42 bewail'd th' insatiat humors of them both
Cor. 937 Caesar bewail'd his death
ST 1882 whose death he had so solemnely bewailde
Beware.
Cor. 289 byd you *b.* for feare you be beguild
Cor. 547 daughter, *b.* how you provoke the heavens
Cor. 985 Madam, *b.* ; for, should hee heare of thys
Jer. 297 *b.*, *b.* ; for honesty, spoken in
ST 1166 Hieronimo, *b.*, thou art betraide
ST 1652 then in your love *b.*, deale cunningly
ST 1857 Hieronimo *b.* ; goe by, goe by
Bewitch.
Jer. 251 and therefore great gifts may *b.* her eie
Jer. 606 and so *b.* her with my honied speech
Bewitched.
Cor. 264 bewitcht my life, and did beguile my love
SP 1366 with a looke orespred with teares, *b.* Solyman
Ard. 1297 I was *b.* : woe worth the hapless hour
Ard. 1312 I was *b.*, — that is no theme of thine
Ard. 1910 poor gentleman, how soon he is *b.* !
Bewitching.
Jer. 51 if friendly phraises, honied speech, *b.* accent
Bewray.
ST 342 and Ile *b.* the fortune of thy Sonne
ST 1181 to listen more, but nothing to *b.*
ST 2171 with incke *b.* what blood began in me
Bewrayed.
SP 1857 belike he thought we had bewrayd his treasons
Ard. 1106 why, thy speech *b.* an inly kind of fear
Ard. 2210 I fear me, Michael, all will be *b.*
JB. 215 made to beleeve that Parker had *b.* the matter

Beyond.
HP 174 *b*. this Orchard, wherein you see
HP 1595 it is used *b*. the proper use, and so abused
Cor. 779 didst extend thy conquering armes *b*. the Ocean
Jer. 161 shape frightful conceit *b*. the intent of act
SP 419 *b*. the course of Titans burning raies
Bibam.
ST 1002 Ipse *b*. quicquid meditatur saga veneni
Bid.
HP 1287 and to *b*. a stranger drinke
Cor. 289 byd you beware for feare you be beguild
Jer. 356 I *b*. you sudden warres
STA 940 and *b*. my sonne Horatio to come home
ST 1235 and *b*. him forthwith meet the Prince and me
ST 1239 *b*. him not faile. — I fly, my Lord
ST 1260 now, Pedringano, *b*. thy Pistoll holde
ST 1371 *b*. him be merry still, but secret
ST 1373 *b*. him not doubt of his deliverie
ST 1375 and thereon *b*. him boldely be resolved
ST 1641 and *b*. him let my Sister be enlarg'd
STA 1961 you *b*. us light them, and attend you here
STA 1963 was I so mad to *b*. you light your torches now?
STA 2009 *b*. him come in, and paint some comfort
SP 131 *b*. my men bring my horse, and a dosen staves
SP 438 page, run, *b*. the surgion bring his incision
SP 473 to crie the chaine, when I *b*. thou shouldst not?
SP 474 *b*. thee onely underhand make privie inquirie
SP 849 and *b*. them bring some store of crownes with them
Ard. 127 and *b*. him, if his love do not decline
Ard. 1348 when I have *b*. thee hear or see or speak
Ard. 1958 *b*. Mosbie steal from him and come to me
Ard. 1962 and *b*. him lay it on, spare for no cost
Ard. 1963 nay, and there be such cheer, we will *b*. ourselves
Ard. 2097 Alice, *b*. him welcome; he and I are friends
Ard. 2099 but I had rather die than *b*. him welcome
Ard. 2103 I'll *b*. him welcome, seeing you'll have it so
Ard. 2203 you may do well to *b*. his guests sit down
Ard. 2244 go, Susan, and *b*. thy brother come
ST 628 my bounden duety bids me tell the truth
ST 1346 and thus experience bids the wise to deale
ST 1420 for heere lyes that which bids me to be gone
SP 1903 and bids me kill those bloudie witnesses
SP 2049 why, what art thou that boldlie bids us yeeld?
Ard. 1528 and bids him to a feast to his house at Shorlow
Bidden.
SP 357 last night he was *b*. to a gentlewomans to supper
Bide.
Cor. 588 were desert fields where none would byde
SP 405 should *b*. the shock of such approved knights
Biforem.
HP 824 Dindyma, ubi assuetis *b*. dat tibia cantum
Big.
Jer. 854 should raise spleens *b*. as a cannon bullet
Jer. 879 speake not such *b*. words
Ard. 1595 of a lordaine, too, as *b*. as yourself
Big-boned.
SP 98 the sudden Frenchman, and the bigbon'd Dane
Bigger.
HP 843 « But *b*. growne, they tende the chase »
Big-swoln.
Jer. 56 stretch his mouth wider with big swolne phrases
Billingsgate.
Ard. 1143 sirrah, get you back to B.
Billows.
Cor. 81 when foming billowes feele the Northern blasts
Bills.

Ard. 2281 are coming towards our house with glaives and *b*.
Bind.
Jer. 248 not spare an oath without a jewell to *b*. it fast
Jer. 926 I *b*. thee, Don Andrea, by thy honer
ST 1069 binde him, and burne his body in those flames
SP 1175 so his deserts binds me to speake for him
Bindeth.
HP 231 their due, and nature *b*. children unto
Bird.
ST 581 then beast, or *b*., or tree, or stony wall
ST 1287 heere comes the *b*. that I must ceaze upon
ST 1349 and sees not that wherewith the *b*. was limde
STA 1939 when man and *b*. and beast are all at rest
Ard. 1423 lime well your twigs to catch this wary *b*.
HP 277 nourishment which Birds cannot yeelde
ST 754 there none shall heare us but the harmeless birds
ST 842 harke, Madame, how the birds record by night
SP 1991 no, let her lie, a prey to ravening birds
Birth.
HP 74 neither of ignoble *b*. nor meane capacitie
HP 584 a man marrieth a woman of so high a *b*.
HP 811 « A painful people by our byrth, for first our babes we bring »
Cor. 283 that I receiv'd from heaven at my *b*.
Jer. 342 answer at next *b*. our fathers fawltes in heaven
Jer. 932 « tis said we shall not answere at next *b*. »
ST 1584 woe to thy *b*., thy body, and thy soule
SP 1434 well, well, Erastus, Rhodes may blesse thy *b*.
Ard. 36 I am by *b*. a gentleman of blood
Ard. 490 respects he not your *b*., your
Birth-hour.
Ard. 921 marked in my *b*. by the destinies
Birth-right.
Cor. 1142 the love that men theyr Country and theyr *b*. beare
Bit.
Cor. 1233 the stiffneckt horses champe not on the *b*.
ST Bal. 146 even with my teeth I *b*. my tongue
Bite.
Ard. 1330 I'll *b*. my tongue if it speak bitterly
Biting.
Ard. 139 shall neither fear the *b*. speech of men
Biting-bridle.
Cor. 329 deeds might (with a byting brydle) bee restraind
Bitten.
ST 2984 Vice-roy, he hath *b*. foorth his tung
Ard. 935 the hunger-*b*. wolf o'erpries his haunt
Bitter.
HP Ind. 18 Catullus, why he called Wine bytter
HP 319 « Pray fill with *b*. wines »
HP 321 not because the Poet desired *b*. Wyne
HP 324 that sharp and heddie taste which be calleth *b*.
HP 325 as it was called *b*. by Catullus
Cor. Ded. 19 those so *b*. times and privie broken passions
Cor. 403 and *b*. chaunce decreed to have me there
Cor. 650 hath bath'd your blubbred eyes in *b*. teares
Cor. 869 o're whom I shed full many a *b*. teare
Cor. 1121 poynt at us in theyr *b*. teares, and say
Cor. 1628 but when he saw his wiles nor *b*. words
Jer. 55 and be as *b*. as physitions drugs
ST Bal. 36 to turne my sweete to *b*. gall
ST 1586 and band with *b*. execrations be the day
SP 645 a sweet renowne, but mixt with *b*. sorrow
Ard. 398 forbear to wound me with that *b*. word
Ard. 1224 and nips me as the *b*. north-east wind
Ard. 1382 till then my bliss is mixed with *b*. gall
Ard. 1797 fie, *b*. knave, bridle thine envious tongue

Ard. 1801 as oft I have in many a *b.* storm
JB 61 and with *b.* speeches so taunted and checkt her
Bitterest.
ST 1121 but with the *b.* torments and extreames
Bitterly.
Ard. 1330 I'll bite my tongue if it speak *b.*
Bitterness.
HP 322 none to whom bitternes is not unpleasant
Cor. 1188 th' infectious plague, and Famins bitternes
Blab.
Jer. 799 hell : tho he *b.* there, the diveles will not tell
Jer. 1164 no, youle *b.* secrets then
Ard. 135 and these my narrow-prying neighbours *b.*
Black.
HP 5 where, seeing the ayre wexe blacke, and
HP 326 afterward Homer calleth it *b.*
STA 956 that such a blacke deede of mischiefe should be done
ST 2240 sweet boy, how art thou chang'd in deaths *b.* shade
ST 2248 sent from the emptie Kingdome of blacke night
ST 2621 a Turkish cappe, a *b.* mustacio, and a Fauchion
SP 1406 still in *b.* habite fitting funerall ?
SP 1449 were their garments turned from *b.* to white
Ard. 1080 *b.* night hath hid the pleasures of the day
Ard. 1082 and with the *b.* fold of her cloudy robe
Ard. 2061 like the snakes of *b.* Tisiphone sting me
Ard. (Title) two desperat ruffins, Blackwill and Shakbag
Ard. 647 *B.* Will is his name
Ard. 747 if once *B.* Will and I swear his death
Ard. 859 with which *B.* Will was never tainted yet
Ard. 891 how now, Master Shakebag ? what, *B.* Will !
Ard. 1039 that grim-faced fellow, pitiless *B.* Will
Ard. 1051 and pitiless *B.* Will cries : « Stab the slave ! »
Ard. 1501 what ! *B.* Will ? for whose purse wait you ?
Ard. 1581 before you lies *B.* Will and Shakebag
Ard. 1641 *B.* Will and Shakebag I have placed i' the broom
Ard. 1723 his name is *B.* Will
Ard. 1728 *B.* Will and Shakebag, what make you here ?
Ard. 1920 silver noses for saying, « There goes *B.* Will ! »
Ard. 2008 *B.* Will and Shakebag, will you two perform
Ard. 2018 why, *B.* Will and Shakebag locked within the
Ard. 2029 come, *B.* Will, that in mine eyes art fair
Ard. 2078 *B.* Will is locked within to do the deed
Ard. 2090 *B.* Will and Greene are his companions
Ard. 2285 know you not one that is called *B.* Will ?
Ard. 2362 I hired *B.* Will and Shakebag, ruffians both
Ard. 2421 as for the ruffians, Shakebag and *B.* Will
Ard. 2425 *B.* Will was burned in Flushing on a stage
Blacker.
Jer. 226 whose Incke-soules *b.* then his name
Black-faced.
Ard. 1481 or will this *b.* evening have a shower ?
Blackfriars.
Ard. 803 then to the *B.*, and there take water
Blade.
Cor. 367 did (with his *b.*) commit more murther then Rome ever
SP 215 infringeth the temper of any *b.*
SP 216 and thereby gather that this *b.*, being
SP 307/8 by the contents of this *b.*
SP 1233 sheath my slaughtering *b.* in the deare bowels of
SP 212 I, and so are all blades with me : behold
Ard. 1921 I have cracked as many blades as thou hast nuts
Blame.
HP 653 Feare is as worthy of praise as *b.*
Jer. 973 but *b.* me not, Ide have Horatio most
ST Bal. 9 and now her flattering smiles I *b.*
ST 583 it is my fault, not she that merites *b.*

SP 828 my judge unjust, and yet I cannot *b.* her
SP 830 myselfe in fault, and yet not worthie *b.*
Ard. 79 thereof came it, and therefore *b.* not me
Ard. 2028 and if he e'er go forth again, *b.* me
Ard. 2069 then *b.* not me that slay a silly man
JB 9 have walked securely and without *b.*
Blamed.
HP 1449 in the olde time prayeng or robberye was not to be *b.*
Cor. 1194 souldiers with such reproch should not be blam'd
Blandishments.
ST 712 thus in the midst of loves faire *b.*
SP 1408 nor all my faire intreats and *b.* ?
Blank.
Ard. 2376 and run full *b.* at all adventures
Blasphemest.
SP 278 peace, Infant, thou *b.*
Blasphemies.
Cor. 421 a bedroll of outragious *b.*
Blaspheming.
ST 3052 *b.* Gods and all their holy names
Blast.
ST 2692 shall *b.* the plants and the yong saplings
SP 797 whats beauty but a *b.*, soone cropt
Ard. 1634 but that it shakes with every blast of wind
Cor. 81 when foming billowes feele the Northern blasts
Cor. 1011 more inconstant in their kinde then Autumne blasts
SP 750 but scalding sighes, like blasts of boisterous windes
Blasted.
ST 2243 spring with withered winter to be *b.* thus ?
Blaze.
Cor. 802 Caesar is like a brightlie flaming *b.*
Blazen.
HP 462 happily *b.* mine estimation or sufficiencie
SP 844 for, if report but blazen her aright
Blear.
HP 1343 « woven by day, to bleare her sutors sight »
Cor. 1022 that (blynd herselfe) can bleare our eyes
Bleared.
ST 368 wast Spanish gold that *b.* so thine eyes
Bled.
Ard. 1948 when Mosbie *b.*, he even wept for sorrow
Bleed.
Jer. 14 Ile *b.* for you ; and more, what speech afords
Jer. 286 to prevent those that would make vertue *b.*
Jer. 685 not see, but make the wrong man *b.* ?
Jer. 763 to make the heire of honor melt and bleede
Jer. 923 Ile make thee *b.*
Jer. 1128 that I could die, wert but to *b.* with thee
Ard. 2349 the more I sound his name, the more he bleeds
Bleeding.
Cor. 1102 and launc'd hys *b.* wound into the sea
Jer. 662 reare up the *b.* body to the light
Jer. 720 a bad guest, when the first object is a *b.* brest
Jer. 727 why then, that *b.* object doth presage
Jer. 747 that haples, *b.* Lord Alcario
Jer. 895 and receive the somes of many a *b.* hart
Jer. 943 why, man, in war thers *b.* amity
ST 151 there legs and armes lye *b.* on the grasse
ST 983 seest thou those wounds that yet are *b.* fresh ?
ST 2866 I weeping dipt within the river of his *b.* wounds
Bless.
Cor. 740 and blesse me with my Pompeys company ?
Cor. 1704 that they will blesse our holy purposes
Jer. 814 and heaven blesse you, my father, in this fight
ST 1540 O Lord, sir : God blesse you, sir : the man, sir
STA 2015 God blesse you, sir

STA 2054 « God blesse thee, my sweet sonne »
SP 1434 well, well, Erastus, Rhodes may blesse thy birth
SP 1473 then, sweeting, blesse me with a cheerefull looke
Blessed.
Cor. 1076 and till the time that they are dead, is no man blest
Cor. 1291 shall live for valiant prowesse blest
Cor. 1945 Death hath given b. rest for lifes bereaving
Jer. 22 O fortunate houre, b. mynuit, happy day
Jer. 671 live, truest friend, for ever loved and blest
Jer. 835 it may put by the sword, and so be blest
Jer. 972 be all as fortunate as heavens blest host
Jer. 1056 no, my deere selfe, for I was blest by thee
ST 101 then blest be heaven, and guider of the heavens
STA 2016 how, where, or by what meanes should I be blest?
Blessing.
Jer. 1153 give him my b., and then all is done
Blew.
Ard. 1158 with that he b. an evil-sounding horn
Blind.
Cor. 840 one that with b. frenzie buildeth up his throne?
Cor. 1022 that (blynd herselfe) can bleare our eyes
Jer. 753 unwise he still pursued it with b. lovers eies
ST 311 Fortune is blinde, and sees not my deserts
SP 603 if wilfull folly did not b. mine eyes
SP 705 love makes him blinde, and blinde can judge no coulours
SP 912 ah, fickle and b. guidresse of the world
SP 1380 though Love winke, Loves not starke blinde
Ard. 613 that whoso look upon it should wax b.
Ard. 1360 and I too b. to judge him otherwise
Ard. 1702 come, let us go on like a couple of b. pilgrims
Blinded.
Ard. 1730 what could a b. man perform in arms?
Ard. 1845 ah, Arden, what folly b. thee?
Blindfold.
SP 818 where none scape wrackt but blindfould Marriners?
Blindly.
Cor. 106 whereon she b. lighting sets her foote
Cor. 153 then he that b. toyleth for a shade
Bliss.
Cor. 155 our blysse consists not in possessions
ST 13 Deaths winter nipt the blossomes of my blisse
ST 571 their joyes to paine, their blisse to miserie
ST 718 that pleasure followes paine, and blisse annoy
ST 724 that sweetest blisse is crowne of loves desire
ST 1895 for thou hast made me bankrupt of my blisse
ST 2365 my sorrowes ease and soveraigne of my blisse
ST 2835 heere lay my blisse, and heere my blisse bereft
ST 2836 but hope, hart, treasure, joy, and blisse
SP 668 O never may Ferdinando lack such blisse
SP 1456 that her captivitie may turne to blisse
SP 1753 to worke each others blisse and hearts delight
SP 2186 this day shall be the peryod of my blisse
Ard. 1382 till then my b. is mixed with bitter gall
Blissful.
VPJ 81 raigne, live, and blisfull dayes enjoy
ST 112 we may reward thy blissfull chivalrie
ST 2759 Perseda, blisfull lampe of Excellence
SP 676 a blisful war with me, thy chiefest friend?
Blissless.
ST 2689 and bliselesse whosoever immagines not to
Blithe.
SP 724 therefore be b., sweet love, abandon feare
Block.
SP 2142 Janisaries take him straight unto the b.
Ard. 137 but, if I live, that b. shall be removed
Blood.

Eng. Parn. 5 Whose cursed Courts with bloud and incest swell
Cor. 16 our fathers hazarded their derest b.
Cor. 31 soyl'dst our Infant Towne with guiltles b.
Cor. 40 and with their b. made marsh the parched plaines
Cor. 43 that as much b. in wilfull follie spent
Cor. 226 make the b. fro forth my branch-like vaines
Cor. 297 no sooner tutcheth then it taints the b.
Cor. 362 and spilt such store of b. in every street
Cor. 397 his noble Roman b. mixt with his enemies
Cor. 407 whereat my b. stopt in my stragling vaines
Cor. 504 would Death had steept his dart in Lernas b.
Cor. 609 (with haples brothers b. besmear'd)
Cor. 618 and make a river of her b.
Cor. 673 to fill our fields with b. of enemies
Cor. 681 title be not expired in Cornelias b.
Cor. 712 hys hayre and beard deform'd with b. and sweat
Cor. 784 Rome, thou art tam'd, and th' earth, dewd with thy bloode
Cor. 842 if yet our harts retaine one drop of b.
Cor. 845 nor shalt thou bathe thee longer in our b.
Cor. 868 earth, did homage to it with his deerest b.
Cor. 928 to see his tired corse lye toyling in his b.
Cor. 944 whose fell ambition (founded first in b.)
Cor. 968 respect of b., or (that which most should move)
Cor. 1055 that with Ausonian b. did die our warlike field
Cor. 1083 and thinkst not of the rivers of theyr bloode
Cor. 1090 employest our lives, and lavishest our b.
Cor. 1139 and that thys hand (though Caesar b. abhor)
Cor. 1145 if this brave care be nourisht in your b.
Cor. 1225 but know, while Cassius hath one drop of b.
Cor. 1264 who prodigally spends his b.
Cor. 1413 nor thirsted I for conquests bought with b.
Cor. 1527 and (abhorring b.) at last pardon'd all offences
Cor. 1550 and to choller doth convart purest b. about the heart
Cor. 1584 and Death, that sees the Nobles b. so rife
Cor. 1746 till streames of b. like Rivers fill the downes
.Cor. 1754 encourageth the over-forward hands to bloode and death
Cor. 1759 that with our b. she may annoynt her sword
Cor. 1780 theyr jawbones dy'd with foming froth and b.
Cor. 1792 who nicely did but dyp his speare in b.
Cor. 1822 dismembred bodies drowning in theyr b.
Cor. 1824 whose b., as from a spunge, or bunche of Grapes crusht
Cor. 1843 would melt with nothing but theyr deerest b.
Cor. 1881 and by the foe fulfild with fire and b.
Cor. 1885 looking upon his weapon, dide with b.
Cor. 1895 that fro the wound the smoky b. ran bubling
Cor. 1915 and feede your selves with mine enflamed b.
Jer. 79 Ile wake the Court, or startle out some bloud
Jer. 93 let them keep coine, pay tribute with their b.
Jer. 124 Andreas Himens draught shall be in bloud
Jer. 162 I know thy love is vigilant ore my bloud
Jer. 354 thou shalt pay trybute, Portugalle, with b.
Jer. 374 Ide wade up to the knees in bloud
Jer. 379 when we have drunke hot bloud together
Jer. 391 heere let the rising of our hot bloud set
Jer. 713 to light upon my bloud
Jer. 807 thers time enough to let out bloud enough
Jer. 821 even as necessary as our bloud
Jer. 899 yet, O prince, be not confirmed in blud
Jer. 959 ile quench thee, prince, with thy own bloud
Jer. 987 valliant Andrea, by thy worthy bloud
Jer. 990 sweat now to find me in the hight of bloud
Jer. 992 and crams his store house to the top with bloud
Jer. 1022 now wounds are wide, and bloud is very deepe
Jer. 1076 and no meane bloud shall quit it

Jer. 1077 Andrea, we meete in bloud now
Jer. 1078 I, in valliant bloud of Don Rogeroes sheding
Jer. 1091 Ile have the price of him in princely bloud
Jer. 1098 honors in bloud best swim
Jer. 1114 with my bloud dispence, untill my leedge shall
Jer. 1145 this soft banner, smeard with foes bloud
ST Bal. 68 I dipt a napkin in his *b.*
ST Bal 129 and I Lorenzos *b.* did spill
ST 324 and with my treasure my peoples *b.*
ST 325 and with their *b.*, my joy and best beloved
ST 374 I, this was it that made thee spill his bloud
ST 375 but Ile now weare it till thy bloud be spilt
ST 897 beene glutted with thy harmeles *b.*
ST 981 seest thou this handkercher besmerd with *b.* ?
ST 1427 who, when he lived, deserved my dearest *b.*
ST 1448 for *b.* with *b.* shall, while I sit as judge, be satisfied
ST 1589 when naught but *b.* will satisfie my woes ?
ST 1821 bathing him in boyling lead and *b.* of innocents
STA 1987 had he been framed of naught but *b.* and death
ST 2171 with incke bewray what *b.* began in me
ST 2181 and when I dyde it in thy deerest *b.*
ST 2224 shew me one drop of bloud fall from the same
ST 2471 and blowes them out, and quencheth them with *b.*
ST 3010 when *b.* and sorrow finnish my desires
SP 185 or end the period of my youth in *b.*
SP 198 staind with *b.* of Moores, and there
SP 542 whose bloud hath bin manured to their earth
SP 600 in *b.* hath shortned our sweet Halebs dayes
SP 612 withould thy hand from heaping bloud on bloud ?
SP 1329 mischiefe, murther, bloud, and extremitie
SP 1800 yet must his bloud be spilt for my behoofe
Ard. 43 smeared in the channels of his lustful *b.*
Ard. 832 I value every drop of my *b.* at a French crown
Ard. 878 whose earth may swallow up this Arden's *b.*
Ard. 1448 a heavy *b.* is gathered at my heart
Ard. 1834 though begun in sport, yet ends in *b.* !
Ard. 1988 for every drop of his detested *b.*
Ard. 2172 and, Susan, fetch water and wash away this *b.*
Ard. 2173 the *b.* cleaveth to the ground and will not out
Ard. 2174 but with my nails I'll scrape away the *b.*
Ard. 2180 in vain we strive, for here his *b.* remains
Ard. 2249 smeared in *b.* and filthy gore
Ard. 2309 it is the pig's *b.* we had to supper
Ard. 2318 and you shall find part of his guiltless *b.*
Ard. 2322 see, see ! his *b.* ! it is too manifest
Ard. 2325 it is his *b.*, which, strumpet, thou hast shed
Ard. 2350 this *b.* condemns me, and in gushing forth speakes as
    it falls
Ard. 2391 Christ, whose *b.* must save me for the *b.* I shed
Ard. 2418 my *b.* be on his head that gave the sentence
JB 9 yet the *b.* of the just Abel cried most shrill
JB 13 *b.*-sheader should have his *b.* justly shed again
JB 227 for bloud is an unceassant crier in the eares of the Lord
Jer. 1070 could I meete Andrea, now my blouds a tiptoe
Jer. 74 noble spyrits, gallant bloods
Jer. 858 now let your blouds be liberall as the sea
Jer. 981 like Orenges, and squeese their blouds out
HP 900 were hee of the Kings bloode, is neverthelesse a servaunt
Ard. 36 I am by birth a gentleman of *b.*
Blood-besmeared.
Cor. 193 arm'd with his blood-besmeard keene Coutelace
Blood-shedder.
JB 12 a Lawe that the cruel and unjust blood-sheader should
Blood-sucking.
Jer. 304 what bloud sucking slave could choke bright honor
Blood-thirsting.

Cor. 1718 and he (*b.*) wallow in his owne
Blood-thirsty.
Cor. 1750 blood-thirstie Discord, with her snakie hayre
Bloody.
VPJ 69 but, as their purpose *b.* was, so
Cor. 177 or *b.* warre (of other woes the worst)
Cor. 183 which yet, to sack us, toyles in *b.* sweat
Cor. 404 decreed to have me there, to see this *b.* deed
Cor. 1183 hee is not *b.*
Cor. 1188 but by *b.* jarres he hath unpeopled most part of
Cor. 1269 and *b.* Tyrants rage prevent
Cor. 1435 doe bring their treasons to a *b.* end
ST Bal. 115 when *B.* Baltazar enters in
ST Bal. 135 I shew'd my sonne with *b.* wounds
ST Bal. 154 the authors of this *b.* fetch
ST 61 where lovers live and bloudie Martialists
ST 65 where bloudie furies shakes their whips of steele
ST 322 my breach of faith occasiond bloudie warres
ST 323 those bloudie warres have spent my treasure
ST 898 and left thy bloudie corpes dishonoured heere
ST 1155 ‹ for want of incke receive this bloudie writ ›
ST 1508 murder, O bloudy monster, God forbid a fault so foule
STA 1940 save those that watch for rape and *b.* murder
ST 2864 and heere beholde this bloudie hand-kercher
ST 2868 and never hath it left my *b.* hart
ST 2905 speake, traitour ; damned, bloudy murderer, speak
ST 3045 and let him there bewaile his bloudy love
SP 11 the huskie humour of her bloudy quill
SP 1903 bids me kill those bleudie witnesses
SP 1922 by making knowne our bloudy practises
Ard. 844 I pray thee, Will, make clean thy *b.* brow
Ard. 865 from hence ne'er will I wash this *b.* stain
Ard. 892 how chance your face is so *b.* ?
Ard. 1040 and Shakebag, stern in *b.* stratagem
Bloody-minded.
Cor. 1532 doth oppose himselfe agen bloody minded, cruell men
Blossom.
ST 2685 a bough, a branch, a blossome, nor a leafe
SP 1420 faire blossome, likely to have proved good fruite
ST 13 Deaths winter nipt the blossomes of my blisse
Ard. 1225 doth check the tender blossoms in the spring
Blot.
ST 233 his colours ceaz'd, a *b.* unto his name
ST 582 but wherefore *b.* I Bel-imperias name ?
Blotting.
Ard. 1603 and spoil her beauty with *b.*
Blow.
Jer. 90 too insulting waves, who at one *b.*
Jer. 946 to gaine that name, ile give the deepest blowe
Ard. 176 when he may have it for a right down *b.*
Jer. 48 of rough heawn tyrants more then blowes
Jer. 356 I bid you sudden warres. — I, sudden blowes
ST 138 both battailes joyne and fall to handie blowes
SP 148 that exercise their war with friendly blowes
SP 480 what you want in shooes, ile give ye in blowes
SP 1494 strike, strike ; thy words pierce deeper then thy blows
SP 1697 beare of some blowes when you run away in a fraye
Ard. 496 hard words and blows to mend the match withal
Ard. 1754 when words grow hot and blows begin to rise
ST 921 *b.* sighes, and raise an everlasting storme
SP 250 rough wordes blowe my choller
ST 2471 and blowes them out, and quencheth them with blood
Blowing.
STA 2076 the Starres extinct, the Windes *b.*
Blown.
SP 1037 my ship shall be borne with teares, and blowne with sighs

Jer. 598 aire is breath, and breath-*b.* words raise care
ST 1645 which, as a nine daies wonder, being ore-blowne
Blubbered.
Cor. 650 hath bath'd your blubbred eyes in bitter teares
Cor. 1702 with blubbred eyes and handes to heaven uprear'd
Blue.
SP 331 the baye horse with the blew taile, and the
Blush.
Jer. 11 let not my youthfull *b.* impare my vallor
Jer. 848 seene as a base *b.* upon your free borne cheeks
STA 946 nay, *b.* not, man
SP 780 to check thy fraudfull countenance with a *b.* ?
Ard. 600 you make her *b.*
Ard. 1288 for how I *b.* and tremble at the thoughts !
Ard. 2177 because I *b.* not at my husband's death
Blushing.
HP 874 that she *b.* held downe her head
Ard. 988 is deeply trenched in my *b.* brow
Jer. 170 by this, and by this lip *b.* kisse
Blustering.
ST 1526 the blustring winds, conspiring with my words
Boar.
HP 252 « this wilde boare » (quoth the good man) » was taken
Board.
HP 143 « Hyed home at night and fild his bord with delicats
   unbought »
HP 150 « And then he decks his boord about with »
HP 1016 such as shall be set upon thyne owne boorde
Jer. 427 both wed, bed, and boord her ?
SP 1830 spredding on the boord a huge heape of our
Ard. 2372 at last be fain to go on *b.* some hoy
Boast.
Jer. 1116 Lorenzo, thou doost *b.* of base renowne
Ard. 200 and *b.* not of thy conquest over me
Boasting.
HP 1452 Virgill having regard brought in Numa *b.* thus
Boat.
Jer. 1165 by Charons *b.*, I will not
Jer. 1177 Charon, a bote ; Charon, Charon
Ard. 1645 go before to the *b.*, and I will follow you
Ard. 2371 in some oyster-*b.* at last be fain to go
Boatman.
ST 20 but churlish Charon, only *b.* there
Bode.
SP 174 and yet my starres did *b.* my victory
ST 1250 and this suspition boads a further ill
Ard. 1096 this drowsiness in me bodes little good
Bodies.
HP 368 we may sufficiently restore our *b.*
HP 638 the *b.* of the Male be more adorned
HP 786 if the mylke altered not the *b.* and
HP 1071 as wee see by use in our owne *b.*
Cor. 182 (now growne so great with Souldiers *b.* that
Cor. 548 in our *b.* (as a tower of strength) have plac'd our soules
Cor. 1086 now o're our *b.* (tumbled on heapes,)
Cor. 1108 Lybian Beares devoure the *b.* of our Cittizens
Cor. 1190 though they containe dead *b.* numberles
Cor. 1822 dismembred *b.* drowning in theyr blood
Cor. 1857 to see the passage choakt with *b.* of the dead
Cor. 1983 for even those fields that mourn'd to beare their *b.*
Cor. 1986 and on theyr Tombes we heape our *b.*
SP 1410 for what are friends but one minde in two *b.* ?
SP 2193 their soules are knit, though bodyes be disjoynd
SP 2195 their *b.* buried, yet they honour me
JB 19 soules and the destructions of their *b.* on earth
Bodkin.

Ard. 313 use your *b.*, your Spanish needle
Body.
HP Ind. 17 bodie wedded to the soule
HP Ind. 26 like that of the *b.* and the soule
HP Ind. 115 practises of minde and *b.*, howe to be used
HP 518 two thinges, that is his *b.* and hys goods
HP 522 and first of hys *b.* rather then hys goods
HP 532 communicats her operations with the bodie
HP 532 and the *b.* with the soule
HP 533 when any part of the bodie grieveth us
HP 535 followes the infirmities or weakenes of the bodie
HP 539 like to that which the *b.* hath with the soule
HP 547 said that the soule was espoused to the bodie
HP 550 the bande that tyes the *b.* and the soule togeather
HP 551 that the soule can bee conjoynd with any other *b.*
HP 629 as a Servant doth his Maister, or the bodye the mind
HP 681 her bodie with convenient ornaments should be
HP 687 by nature shee is so desirous to adorne and beautifie
   her bodie
HP 852 exercise themselves in practise of the mind and *b.*
HP 864 most commendable practises of mind and *b.*
HP 995 neither fitte for warre in minde nor *b.*
HP 1100 the hand is fastned and united to the bodie
HP 1575 busied in those exercises of the bodie
Cor. Arg. 2 as much accomplisht with the graces of the bodie
Cor. 296 like poyson that (once lighting in the *b.*)
Cor. 388 hee gave his bodie (as a Barricade) for Romes defence
Cor. 417 I would have plung'd my *b.* in the Sea
Cor. 620 a seate should builde within a *b.*, basely
Cor. 764 for when our soule the *b.* hath disgaged
Cor. 857 and thy dismembred *b.* (stab'd and torne)
Cor. 875 and layd his *b.* to be burn'd thereon
Cor. 924 will fire his shamefull bodie with their flames
Cor. 1226 blood, to feede this worthles *b.* that you see
Jer. 303 as short my *b.*, short shall be my stay
Jer. 662 reare up the bleeding *b.* to the light
Jer. 675 who is the owner of this red, melting *b.* ?
Jer. 715 some take up the bodie ; others take charg
ST 150 heere falles a *b.* scindred from his head
ST 701 thus hath he tane my *b.* by his force
ST 1069 binde him, and burne his *b.* in those flames
ST 1304 helpe me here to bring the murdred *b.* with us too
ST 1421 this toyles my *b.*, this consumeth age
ST 1490 that that is good for the *b.* is likewise good for the soule
ST 1519 but let his *b.* be unburied
ST 1584 woe to thy birth, thy *b.*, and thy soule
ST 2096 go, beare his *b.* hence, that we may mourne
SP 89 and, when long combat makes my *b.* faint
SP 244 my *b.* distilled such dewy showers of swet
SP 959 see, where his *b.* lyes
SP 960 I, I ; I see his *b.* all to soone
SP 997 my selfe will see the *b.* borne from hence
SP 1078 Ile combat thee, my *b.* all unarmd
SP 2125 come Brusor, helpe to lift her bodie up
SP 2168 and when my soule from *b.* shall depart
SP 2172 that my *b.* with Persedas be interd
Ard. 42 whilst on the planchers pants his weary *b.*
Ard. 1223 feebles my *b.* by excess of drink
Ard. 2166 first lay the *b.* in the counting-house
Ard. 2251 come, Susan, help to lift his *b.* forth
Ard. 2270 but first convey the *b.* to the fields
Ard. 2330 bring me to him, let me see his *b.*
JB 92 without any swelling of the *b.*, or other signe
Cor. 228 and spunge my bodies heate of moisture so
Ard. 2431 in the grass his body's print was seen two years
Boiled.

HP 251 the one roasted, the other boyled

Boiling.
ST 70 and perjurde wightes scalded in boyling lead
ST 1821 bathing him in boyling lead and blood of innocents
ST 3050 let him be dragde through boyling Acheron

Boils.
SP 2177 and boyles, like Etna, in my frying guts

Boisterous.
Cor. 80 a ship, at random wandring in a boistrous Sea
SP 750 but scalding sighes, like blasts of *b.* windes

Bold.
HP 733 so *b.* and hardy that she lay aside honest shame
HP 1314 that without noysomnes or filthines she may be bolde
to touch
Jer. 117 whose hands are washt in rape, and murders bould
SP 472 how durst thou be so bould to crie the chaine
SP 758 tush, I will to her ; innocence is bould
SP 953 Ile be so bolde as to dive into this Gentlemans pocket
SP 1890 what bould presumer durst be so resolved
Ard. 1680 let us have some more of your *b.* yeomanry
JB 166 and so bould in the end he grew with her that

Boldly.
HP 510 (let me *b.* say thus much to thee, my Son)
HP 676 desirous to content their Husbands I may *b.* speake
ST 1375 and thereon bid him boldely be resolved
SP 838 I bouldly then shall let Perseda know
SP 1102 whats he that thus bouldly enters in ?
SP 2049 why, what art thou that boldlie bids us yeeld ?
Ard. 1753 and *b.* beard and brave him to his teeth

Boldness.
ST 748 ambitious villaine, how his boldenes growes

Bolstered.
Ard. 1044 methinks I see them with their *b.* hair

Bolton.
Ard. 174 and then the farm of *B.* is mine own

Bond.
ST 2219 & 2220 save my *b.*
ST 740 but such a warre, as breakes no *b.* of peace
SP 601 ah, what is dearer *b.* then brotherhood ?

Bond, *see* **Band.**

Bondage.
Cor. 516 can *b.* true nobility exclude ?
Cor. 838 into the *b.* where (enthrald) we pine ?
SP 598 and live in servile *b.* all my dayes

Bondman.
SP 984 thou art a *b.*, and wouldst faine be free ?

Bond-slave.
Eng. Parn. 1 Time is a bondslave to eternitie

Bone.
Ard. 1253 I can cast a *b.* to make these curs
Ard. 1415 whilst two stout dogs were striving for a *b.*
HP 1784 in a very soft bed I bequeathed my bones to rest
Cor. 878 the ashie reliques of his haples bones
Cor. 882 bones which (in extreames) an earthen Urne containeth
Cor. 1187 are full of dead mens bones by Caesar slayne
Cor. 2034 the happie vessels that enclose your bones
SP 543 whose bones hath made their deep waies passable
SP 425 beside two dossen small inferior bones
SP 423 I, villaine, I have broke my shin *b.*
SP 424 my back *b.*, my channell *b.*, and my thigh *b.*

Boned.
SP 98 the sudden Frenchman, and the bigbon'd Dane

Boni.
Puck 72 agunt ut viri *b.* esse videant ?

Bonnet.
SP 1950 your turkish *b.* is not on your head ?

Bonny.
Ard. 2161 in Southwark dwells a *b.* northern lass

Book.
HP (Title) contained in this Booke
HP 558 thus in the *b.* of Virgils Aeneidos
HP 820 in that same booke of his Aeneidos maketh mention
HP 1134 perticularize none, but refer thee to the booke
HP 1320 as appeareth by these verses in the Booke of Virgill
HP 1470 and heereof speaketh Tully in his Booke of Offices
HP 1644 a sentence put by Aristotle in his booke de Phisicis
HP 1702 discourse, gathered by him into a little Booke
STA 1983 she should have shone : Search thou the booke
SP 144 the brass leaved booke of never wasting perpetuitie
HP 1779 part out of Aristotles Bookes and the rest
Ard. 546 Michael my man is clean out of her books
JB 36 but no man was so high in her books as Parker
Ard. 1333 burn this prayer-*b.*, where I here use the

Book-keeper.
ST 2751 heere, brother, you shall be the booke-keeper

Boon.
SP 1212 Erastus, now thou hast obtaind thy boone
SP 1520 graunt [me] one boone that I shall crave of thee

Boot.
Cor. 457 what boote your teares, or what availes your sorrow
ST 1461 Ile not change without *b.*, thats flat
STA 2947 Ide give them all, I, and my soule to boote
SP 79 receive my hart to boote ; it is no *b.*, for
SP 80 it is no *b.*, for that was thine before
ST 231 and cards once dealt, it bootes not aske, why so ?
ST 475 what bootes complaint, when thers no remedy ?
SP 1874 what bootes complaining wheres no remedy ?

Booties.
Ard. 1399 but, should I brag what *b.* I have took

Bootless.
ST 2818 happely you thinke (but booteles are your thoughts)
Ard. 2361 it *b.* is to swear thou didst it not

Booty.
Ard. 2164 I'll make *b.* of the quean even to her smock

Borders.
Cor. 46 that we will come thy *b.* to besiege

Bore.
ST 525 who, when King Stephen *b.* sway in Albion
STA 2004 at last it grewe, and grewe, and *b.*, and *b.*
STA 2007 it *b.* thy fruit and mine : O wicked, wicked plant
ST 2467 the two first the nuptiall torches boare
SP 770 thy favours *b.* me, not my light foote Steed

Born.
HP 47 « I was borne » (quoth I) « in Naples
HP 898 some are naturally borne to commande, and others to
obey
HP 899 and hee that is borne to obey, were hee of the
HP 969 Servaunts are properly those that are borne to obey
Cor. 121 of th'ancient freedom wherein we were borne
Cor. 886 O poore Cornelia, borne to be distrest
Cor. 1287 shall we then, that are men and Romains borne
STA 1755 being borne, it poutes, cryes, and breeds teeth
SP 207 you are a Rutter borne in Germanie
Puck 67 to reduce himself to that he was not borne unto
HP 804 to wash their newe borne Children in the Rivers
Jer. 937 our courages are new borne, our vallors bred
Cor. 676 then, home-borne houshold gods, and ye good spirits
Cor. 1243 brave Romaine Souldiers, sterne-borne sons of Mars
Cor. 1375 and those brave Germains, true borne Martialists
Cor. 1892 that, being free borne, I shall not die a slave
Jer. 848 as a base blush upon your free borne cheeks
Jer. 862 to live like captives, or as free borne die ?

Ard. 1296 a mean artificer, that low-*b*. name

Borne.

Cor. 707 not in tryumph *b*. amongst the conquering Romans
Cor. 858 dragd through the streets, disdained to bee *b*.
Cor. 2016 sold at a pike, and *b*. away by strangers?
Jer. 1038 to have me *b*. upon the backs of men
SP 508 how he hath *b*. him gainst the Christians
SP 997 my selfe will see the body *b*. from hence
SP 1037 my ship shall be *b*. with teares, and
SP 1132 he might have *b*. me through out all the world
Ard. 1941 and his lattice *b*. away the next night
SP 324 coucht too hie, and their steeds ill *b*.

Borrow.

Jer. 346 we borow nought ; our kingdome is our owne
SP 111 from whence Ile *b*. what I do atchieve

Borrowed.

ST 409 pay that you *b*. and recover it

Bosom.

Cor. 293 fraught with change of plagues is mine infected bosome
Jer. 63 in placing me next unto his royall bosome
Jer. 212 the love betwixt Bellimperia and Andreas bosome?
Jer. 553 love to Andrea, I, even to his very bosome
Jer. 752 firmly planted in Don Andreas bosome
Jer. 843 Andreas *b*. bears away my hart
Jer. 1053 couldst thou inherit within my bosome
STA 955 can thy soft bosome intertaine a thought
STA 967 drop all your stinges at once in my cold bosome
SP 1041 and in his bosome there power foorth my soule
Cor. 1990 valing your Christall eyes to your fair bosoms
Jer. 855 big as a cannon bullet within your bosomes
Jer. 902 bosomes that yet firmely move without disturbed spleenes
Jer. 126 I faith, my deare bosome, to take solemne leave
Jer. 1089 my other soule, my bosome, my harts friend

Bosphoron.

SP 1844 lyes hard by us heere in *B*. ?

Botcher.

Ard. 25 a *b*., and no better at the first
Ard. 316 and mark my words, you goodman *b*.
Ard. 321 why, canst thou deny thou wert a *b*. once?

Both.

HP 121 reverence which I thought fitting *b*. his yeres and
HP 640 wherwith *b*. the one and the other of them may
HP 852 al alike or *b*. togeather
HP 1178 advised, *b*. of the quantity and quallitie of
HP 1273 become *b*. hard and naught to eate without some
HP 1283 *b*. to the men and mayd servants used for those
HP 1352 *b*. greater and more curious observers of such things
HP 1593 it is thought *b*. necessary and commodious
HP 1672 of whom *b*. heaven and Nature doe depend
HP 1744 a Tragedie and Comedie bee bothe the worke of one
Cor. Ded. 4 which *b*. requireth cunning, rest and oportunity
Cor. Arg. 37 to redouble *b*. her teares and lamentations
Cor. 42 bewail'd th' insatiat humors of them *b*.
Cor. 70 what helps thee now t'have tam'd *b*. land and Sea?
Cor. 72 the Morne and Mid-day *b*. by East and West
Cor. 95 now we are hated *b*. of Gods and men?
Cor. 145 importuning *b*. vengeance and defence against
Cor. 251 I, that am but one, (yet once *b*. theyrs) survive
Cor. 276 els onely I am cause of *b*. theyr wraths
Cor. 387 till, fraught with yeeres and honor *b*. at once
Cor. 475 *b*. Clownes and Kings one self-same course must run
Cor. 485 *b*. brothers, and *b*. warrs fierce lightning fiers
Cor. 487 hath hid them *b*. embowel'd in the earth
Cor. 566 *b*. their beginning and their end
Cor. 569 have *b*. theyr rising and theyr fall

Cor. 798 nowe you, whom *b*. the gods and Fortunes grace
Cor. 815 and violates *b*. God and Natures lawes
Cor. 862 *b*. in his life and at hys latest houre
Cor. 864 honored with true devotion, *b*. alive and dead
Cor. 1114 so Rome to Caesar yeelds *b*. powre and pelfe
Cor. 1161 against *b*. Cynnas host and Marius
Cor. 1574 so many wracks as I have suffred *b*. by Land
Cor. 1772 and thrice the best of *b*. was faine to breathe
Cor. 1789 *b*. comfort and encourage his to fight
Cor. 1804 they fiercely open *b*. Battalions
Cor. 1942 for, *b*. my husbands and my Father gone
Cor. 2013 (which *b*. the world and Fortune heapt on him)
Cor. 2032 and afterward (*b*. wanting strength and moysture
Jer. 152 you have *b*. proud spirits and *b*. will strive to aspire
Jer. 308 and make them *b*. stand like too politique sots
Jer. 427 in this disguise I may *b*. wed, bed, and
Jer. 624 resolved to loose *b*. life and honor at one cast
Jer. 729 whats he that lies there slaine, or hurt, or *b*. ?
Jer. 914 they swore to Spaine, *b*. for themselves and you
Jer. 1083 let them *b*. meete in crimson tinctures shine
Jer. 1119 the vanquisht yeilds to *b*., to you [the] first
ST 38 this Knight (quoth he) *b*. liv'd and died in love
ST 40 and, by warres fortune, lost *b*. love and life
ST 116 *b*. furnish well, *b*. full of hope and feare
ST 117 *b*. menacing alike with daring showes
ST 118 *b*. vaunting sundry colours of device
ST 119 *b*. cheerly sounding trumpets, drums, and fifes
ST 120 *b*. raising dreadfull clamors to the skie
ST 123 our battels *b*. were pitcht in squadron forme
ST 138 *b*. battailes joyne and fall to handie blowes
ST 256 and truth to say, I yeeld myselfe to *b*.
ST 266 will *b*. abide the censure of my doome?
ST 270 you *b*. deserve, and *b*. shall have reward
ST 275 appoint the sum, as you shall *b*. agree
ST 328 the cause was mine ; I might have died for *b*.
ST 348 when *b*. the armies were in battell joynd
ST 392 when *b*. our Armies were enjoynd in fight
ST 398 their strength alike, their strokes *b*. dangerous
ST 431 but now weare thou it *b*. for him and me
ST 516 we *b*. are freends ; tribute is paid
ST 531 that which may comfort *b*. your King and you
ST 536 which hath pleasde *b*. the Embassador and me
ST 633 speake, man, and gaine *b*. freendship and reward
ST 660 I sweare to *b*., by him that made us all
ST 680 but golde doth more then either of them *b*.
ST 682 *b*. well and ill : it makes me glad and sad
ST 729 heare still, mine eares, to heare them *b*. lament
ST 810 she *b*. will wrong her owne estate and ours
ST 988 time is the author *b*. of truth and right
ST 1028 as we *b*. doubt and dread our overthrow
ST 1094 (For *b*. our honors and thy benefite)
ST 1315 nor you, nor me, my Lord, but *b*. in one
ST 1491 it may be, in that box is balme for *b*.
ST 1573 *b*. her, my selfe, Horatio, and themselves
ST 1727 to love and feare, and *b*. at once, my Lord
ST 2489 *b*. my letters and thine own beliefe assures
ST 2909 why hast thou butchered *b*. my children thus?
ST 3017 *b*. done to death by olde Hieronimo
SP 3 nay, what are you *b*., but subjects unto Death?
SP 20 nay then, it seemes, you *b*. doo misse the marke
SP 142 brave Knights of Christendome, and Turkish *b*.
SP 332 and the silver knight are *b*. downe
SP 367 overthrowne him and his Curtall *b*. to the ground
SP 613 might I not better spare one joy then *b*. ?
SP 684 so *b*. our hearts are still combind in one
SP 761 is come to joyne *b*. hearts in union

SP 771 therefore to thee I owe *b.* love and life
SP 1137 *b.* to have seene and tride his valour
SP 1292 am not I worth *b.* these for whom you mourne ?
SP 1294 or if you gladly would injoy me *b.*
SP 1296 and I will pay you *b.* your sound delight
SP 1533 and yet my selfe be captive to them *b.*
SP 1551 I love them *b.*, I know not which the better
SP 1553 that I conquer *b.* by my deserts
SP 1556 and *b.* give me your hands
SP 1559 so well I love you *b.*
SP 1786 she curse me not ; and so farewell to *b.*
SP 1859 *b.* lay your hands upon the Alcaron
SP 1862 mischiefe and death shall light upon you *b.*
SP 1982 thou shalt abie for *b.* your trecheries
SP 2190 stung them *b.* with never failing love •
SP 2191 but I bereft them *b.* of love and life
Ard. 157 can *b.* write and read and make rhyme too
Ard. 193 did we not *b.* decree to murder Arden
Ard. 310 revenge it on the proudest of you *b.*
Ard. 582 and bring thyself and me to ruin *b.*
Ard. 1118 and laughs us *b.* to scorn
Ard. 1124 lop not away his leg, his arm, or *b.*
Ard. 1284 and published in the world to *b.* our shames
Ard. 1416 there comes a cur and stole it from them *b.*
Ard. 1555 my deserts or your desires decay, or *b.*
Ard. 1751 you and I *b.* marching arm in arm
Ard. 1852 *b.* done but merrily to try thy patience
Ard. 1947 why, I saw them when they *b.* shook hands
Ard. 1970 when he should have lockéd with *b.* his hilts
Ard. 1985 ay, but I wonder why you *b.* stood still
Ard. 2308 I thought I had thrown them *b.* into the well
Ard. 2362 I hired Black Will and Shakebag, ruffians *b.*
JB 40 receaved of Brewen *b.* golde and jewels
JB 218 then shee and Parker were *b.* araigned and
Bottom.
Jer. 494 « and honesty in the bottome of a seller »
Jer. 517 « and honesty in the bottome of a seller »
ST 607 to sound the bottome of this doubtfull theame
Bough.
ST 2685 a *b.*, a branch, a blossome, nor a leafe
Cor. 1518 his warlike browes still be deckt with Lawrel boughes
ST 2680 doune with these branches and these loathsome bowes
Ard. 1234 but since I climbed the top-*b.* of the tree
Bought.
HP 1254 eyther from the Countrey, or *b.* about in Markets
Cor. 1177 believe it not ; he *b.* it deere, you know
Cor. 1413 nor thirsted I for conquests *b.* with blood
ST 1605 *b.* you a whistle and a whipstalke too
Ard. 1120 as dear as ever coistril *b.* so little sport
Ard. 1777 that which he craves i dearly *b.* of him
JB 91 the varlet had *b.* a strong deadly poyson
JB 170 the price thereof, and have *b.* her merrement deerely
Boulogne.
Ard. 648 at *B.* he and I were fellow-soldiers
Ard. 659 was not thou and I fellow-soldiers at *B.*
Ard. 1408 why, Shakebag, I did serve the king at *B.*
Bound.
HP 67 necessity now *b.* me to accept his courtesie
Cor. 710 great Emperors fast *b.* in chaynes of brasse
Cor. 789 now shalt thou march (thy hands fast *b.* behind thee)
ST 1000 let him unbinde thee that is *b.* to death
SP 731 and bring him *b.* for thee to tread upon
SP 1050 I am in honor *b.* to combat him
SP 1068 I am *b.*, in paine of my maisters displeasure
SP 1304 I brought not *b.* unto her Erastus
SP 1400 if not destroide, yet *b.* and captivate

SP 1662 amidst their Church they *b.* me to a piller
SP 1853 and, as our duty and aleageance *b.* us
SP 1870 thou shalt foorthwith be *b.* unto that post
Ard. 682 and I am *b.* to answer at the 'size
Ard. 1485 your honour's always ! *b.* to do you service
Ard. 1490 ay, my good lord, and highly *b.* to you
Ard. 1504 I am your bedesman, *b.* to pray for you
ST 114 their frontiers, leaning on each others *b.*
Cor. 115 as with their losse we did our bounds enlarge
Cor. 138 within the bounds of further Brittanie ?
Cor. 184 t'enlarge the bounds of conquering Thessalie
Cor. 596 that oft exceede their wonted bounds
Jer. 84 your highnes cirkels me with honors boundes
ST 62 but either sort containd within his bounds
Ard. 1769 Master Arden, I am now *b.* to the sea
Bounden.
ST 628 my *b.* duety bids me tell the truth
Bounding.
ST 142 and gapes to swallow neighbour *b.* landes
Bounteous.
SP 1444 but straight reward thee with a *b.* largesse
Ard. 1826 although most *b.* and liberal
Bountiful.
Jer. 680 arme, hast thou slaine thy bountifull, kind lord ?
Bounty.
Jer. 4 my knee sings thanks unto your highnes bountie
Jer. 250 his *b.* amongst souldiers sokes him dry
Jer. 440 Lorenzoes *b.* I do more enfould then
SP 1172 and liberall hands to such as merit bountie
Bout.
Jer. 1001 what ere you be, ile have a *b.* with you
SP 1069 to have a *b.* at cuffes, afore you and I part
SP 1073 I must have a *b.* with you, sir, thats flat
'Bout, *see* **About.**
Bow.
HP 59 arrowe fro forth the strongest *b.* of Parthia
ST 554 and made them *b.* their knees to Albion
ST 2137 thy Cappe to curtesie, and thy knee to *b.*
Bowels.
Jer. 89 tempests, or the vexed *b.* of too insulting waves
Jer. 279 I should have ponyarded the Villaynes *b.*
Jer. 365 meete, Don Andrea ? Yes, in the battles *B.*
Jer. 809 tribute shall flow out of their *b.*
ST 1897 away, Ile rip the *b.* of the earth
SP 1234 blade in the deare *b.* of my countrimen
Bower.
ST Bal. 56 enters my *b.* all in the night
ST 479 on whose aspect mine eyes finde beauties bowre
ST 749 then be thy fathers pleasant *b.* the field
ST 818 come, Bel-imperia, let us to the *b.*
ST 888 and in my *b.*, to lay the guilt on me
ST 904 the vilde prophaner of this sacred *b.* ?
ST 3011 Horatio murdered in his Fathers *b.*
Ard. 2067 from her watery *b.* fling down Endymion
ST 838 the more thou sitst within these leavy bowers
Bowl.
Jer. 587 I tooke a boule and quaft a health to him
Ard. 703 since we trolled the *b.* at Sittingburgh
Cor. 583 the roundnes of two boules cross-cast
Box.
ST 1379 shew him this boxe, tell him his pardons in't
ST 1396 my Maister hath forbidden me to looke in this *b.*
ST 1401 heeres nothing but the bare emptie *b.*
ST 1404 and tell him his pardon is in this boxe
ST 1410 pointing my finger at this boxe
ST 1478 sirra, dost see yonder boy with the *b.* in his hand ?-

ST 1486 what hath he in his boxe, as thou thinkst?
ST 1491 it may be, in that *b.* is balme for both
SP 850 foure Visards, foure Gownes, a boxe, and a Drumme
SP 873 feare not for money, man, ile beare the Boxe
SP 1015 lost our *b.* in counter cambio
Ard. 383 Franklin, thou hast a *b.* of mithridate

Boy.
HP 702 hath beene portraied like a *B.*
Jer. 5 come hether, *b.* Horatio ; fould thy joynts
Jer. 16 well spoke, my *b.* ; and on thy fathers side
Jer. 274 come hether, *b.* Horatio, didst thou here them ?
Jer. 282 I like thy true hart, *b.* ; thou lovest thy friend
Jer. 307 have courage, *b.* : I shall prevent their plots
Jer. 313 but, *b.*, feare not, I will out stretch them al
Jer. 506 *b.* Horatio, write « leave » bending in the hams
Jer. 518 true, *b.* : thers a morall in that   '
Jer. 563 *b.*, thy mothers jealous of my love
Jer. 812 O, my sweet *b.*, heaven shield thee still from care
Jer. 948 I hope, *b.*, thou wilt gaine a brother too
Jer. 967 I, I, Don Pedro, my *b.* shall meete thee
Jer. 978 O valiant *b.* ; stroake with a Giants arme his
Jer. 982 never had father a more happier *b.*
Jer. 1098 lug with him, *b.* ; honors in bloud best swim
Jer. 1121 content thee, *b.* ; thou shalt sustaine no wrong
Jer. 1148 my *b.* ads treble comfort to my age
ST 910 in leesing my Horatio, my sweet *b.*
ST 1237 this evening, *b.* — I goe, my Lord
ST 1357 *B.* — My Lord
ST 1366 fellow, be gone ; my *b.* shall follow thee
ST 1368 *b.*, goe, convay this purse to Pedringano
ST 1431 gramercy, *b.*, but it was time to come
ST 1478 sirra, dost see yonder *b.* with the box in his hand ?
ST 1635 *b.*, talke no further ; thus farre things goe well
ST 2233 gentle *b.*, be gone, for justice is exiled
ST 2240 sweet *b.*, how art thou chang'd in deaths black shade
ST 2848 there mercilesse they butcherd up my *b.*
Ard. 839 a *b.* let down his shop-window and broke his head
JB 123 a little boye which she brought with her
STA 1984 in my boyes face there was a kind of grace
Ard. 1136 'twould make a peasant swear among his boys

Brabble.
Ard. 1615 have you no other time to brable in

Brabbling.
Ard. 815 'tis nothing but some brabling paltry fray

Brace.
Jer. 273 farewell, true *b.* of villaynes

Bradshaw.
Ard. 654 how now, fellow *B.* ? whither away so early ?
Ard. 658 why, *B.*, was not thou and I fellow-soldiers
Ard. 669 good neighbour *B.*, you are too proud
Ard. 707 sirrah *B.*, what wilt thou give him that
Ard. 722 farewell, *B.* ; I'll drink no water
Ard. 1371 how now, *B.*, what's the news with you ?
Ard. 1374 go in, *B.* ; call for a cup of beer
Ard. 1378 « we thank our neighbour *B.* — Yours, Richard
   Greene »
Ard. 1953 Mosbie, Franklin, *B.*, Adam Fowle, with divers
Ard. 2204 ay, so they shall ; Master *B.*, sit you there
Ard. 2237 'tis very late, Master *B.*
Ard 2412 Michael and *B.* in Feversham must suffer death

Brag.
SP 354 it is a world to heere the foole prate and *b.*
Ard. 1399 but, should I *b.* what booties I have took
Ard. 1409 and thou canst *b.* of nothing that

Bragardo.
SP 632 the fond *B.*, to presume to armes

Bragginest.
SP 352 take the braginst knave in Christendom with thee

Brain.
SP 748 ah, that my moyst and cloud compacted braine
Ard. 1222 continual trouble of my moody *b.*
Ard. 1650 like to a good companion's smoky *b.*
Cor. 1828 and on the earth theyr braines lye trembling

Brain-sick.
ST 2861 and rated me for brainsicke lunacie

Brake.
Cor. 730 (setled in my vaines) *b.* up my slumber
Ard. 419 but did you mark me then how I *b.* off?
STA 1954 looke on each tree, and search through every *b.*
Ard. 934 through the thicket of an arbour *b.*
Ard. 1167 throughout the thorny casements of the *b.*

Bramble-bush.
Ard. 1676 scratch you by the face with my *b.*

Branch.
ST 2683 a bough, a *b.*, a blossome, nor a leafe

Branched.
HP 689 the Hart with his fayre and bushie braunched hornes

Branches.
ST 2680 doune with these *b.* and these loathsome bowes

Branch-like.
Cor. 226 then make the blood fro forth my *b.* vaines

Brand.
Cor. 1752 runnes crosse the Squadrons with a smokie *b.*
Cor. 1512 fierce warrs quenches fire-*b.*
ST 1836 and twixt his teeth he holdes a fire-*b.*
SP 1947 he with his fier *b.* parted the seas
Cor. 1565 fire-brands in their brests they beare

Brand-bearing.
SP 1943 the mightie pinky-ey'd, brand bearing God

Brandished.
Cor. 502 with brandisht dart doth make the passage free
ST 690 first, in his hand be *b.* a sword

Brass.
HP 1408 Pewter so set uppe, the Brasse and yron works so bright
Cor. 710 great Emperors fast bound in chaynes of brasse
Jer. 1167 secrets in hell are lockt with doores of brasse
ST 75 the walles of brasse, the gates of adamant
ST 1835 a judge upon a seat of steele and molten brasse

Brass-leaved.
SP 144 the brass leaved booke of never wasting perpetuitie

Brave.
Cor. 48 for those *b.* souldiers, that were (sometime) wont
Cor. 481 *b.* Scipio, your famous auncestor
Cor. 742 and such a number of *b.* regiments
Cor. 1145 if this *b.* care be nourisht in your blood
Cor. 1245 *b.* Romaine Souldiers, sterne-borne sons of Mars
Cor. 1336 and you my *b.* walls, bright heavens masonrie
Cor. 1375 and those *b.* Germains, true borne Martialists
Cor. 1386 and that *b.* warrier, my brother in law
Cor. 1405 come on, *b.* Caesar, and crowne thy head
Cor. 1662 but such as had *b.* spirits, and
Cor. 1684 *b.* Romains, know this is the day and houre
Cor. 1710 on then, *b.* men, my fellowes and Romes friends
Cor. 1714 that this *b.* Tyrant, valiantly beset, may
Cor. 1859 losse, and souspirable death of so *b.* souldiers
Jer. 321 *b.*, stout Andrea, for soe I gesse thee
Jer. 581 worthy embassador, *b.* Don Andrea
Jer. 614 welcome, *b.* Don Andrea, Spaines best of sperit
Jer. 810 farewell, *b.* Lords ; my wishes are bequeathd
ST 156 till Don Andrea with his *b.* Launciers
ST 163 *b.* man at armes, but weake to Balthazar
ST 214 conferre and talke with our *b.* prisoner

Braved (continued)

ST 547 *b.* John of Gaunt, the Duke of Lancaster
STA 2091 when I am mad : then methinkes I am a *b.* fellow
ST 2277 welcome, *b.* Vice-roy, to the Court of Spaine
ST 2376 welcome, *b.* Prince, the pledge of Castiles peace
SP 14 the historie of *b.* Erastus and his Rodian Dame ?
SP 142 *b.* Knights of Christendome, and Turkish both
SP 149 *b.* Prince of Cipris, and our sonne in law
SP 179 what is thy word of courage, *b.* man of Spaine ?
SP 191 what is thy noted word of charge, *b.* Turke ?
SP 263 mount, ye *b.* Lordings, forwards to the tilt
SP 335 he is a *b.* warrriour
SP 370 *b.* Gentlemen, by all your free consents
SP 377 accord to his request, *b.* man at armes
SP 380 I long to see thy face, *b.* warriour
SP 396 and thankes unto you all, *b.* worthy sirs
SP 690 all haile, *b.* Cavelere. God morrow, Madam
SP 695 to have so *b.* a champion to hir Squire
SP 1149 *b.* men at armes, and friendly out of armes
SP 1154 for eyther Rhodes shall be *b.* Solymans, or
SP 1314 *b.* prince of Cipris, and our sonne in law
SP 2002 a *b.* Cavelere, but my aprooved foeman
SP 2012 or Pompey that *b.* warriour ? dead
SP 190 upon the first *b.* of thine enemy
SP 209 what is your *b.* upon the enemy ?
SP 266 forward, *b.* Ladies, place you to behold the
Ard. 1753 and boldly beard and *b.* him to his teeth
Ard. 2083 that's *b..* I'll go fetch the tables

Braved.

Jer. 1032 you *b.* me, Don, within my Fathers court

Bravely.

Cor. 390 *b.* he died, and (haplie) takes it ill that
Cor. 628 *b.* to fight in Romes defence
Cor. 1263 *b.* to doe his country good
Cor. 1612 assure your selfe that Scipio *b.* dyed
Cor. 1668 *b.* to fight for honor of the day
Cor. 1773 and thrice recomforted they *b.* ranne
Cor. 1879 dye *b.*, with their fauchins in their fists
ST 132 did with his Cornet *b.* make attempt
Cor. 1111 and mournfull we behold him *b.* mounted
ST 2810 olde Marshall, this was *b.* done
Ard. 30 and *b.* jets it in his silken gown
Ard. 2034 ay, and that *b.*, too. Mark my device

Bravery.

Ard. 1971 he in a *b.* flourished o'er his head

Bravest.

Cor. 793 thy *b.* Captaines, whose coragious harts

Braving.

Jer. 874 what, are you *b.* us before we come ?

Brawl.

Ard. 840 whereupon arose a *b.*, and in the tumult
Ard. 1432 but *b.* not when I am gone in any case

Brawn-fallen.

Cor. 707 with a ghastly looke, all pale and brawne-falne

Brazen.

ST 1530 and broken through the *b.* gates of hell
ST 1818 there, in a *b.* Caldron fixt by Jove

Breach.

Cor. 401 upon a Forte besieg'd, defending of a *b.*
ST 157 in their maine battel made so great a *b.*
SP 1336 let us to the *b.* thats made already
ST 322 my *b.* of faith occasiond bloudie warres
ST 335 that were a *b.* to common law of armes
ST 2344 a small advantage makes a water *b.*

Bread.

HP 1281 corne be some ground for *b.*, and othersome made
HP 1683 in the sweate of thy face thou shalt eate thy *b.*

Break.

Cor. 256 goe *b.* the bands by calling Hymen once more
Cor. 413 did raving strive to breake the prison ope
Cor. 1168 did breake into the hart of Italie
Cor. 1617 and what disastrous accident did breake
Cor. 1805 cleave, breake, and raging tempest-like o're turne
Cor. 1875 which being sore beaten, till it brake agen
Jer. 1067 and *b.* our haughty sculs downe to our feete
ST 133 to breake the order of our battell rankes
ST 373 but thy ambitious thought shall breake thy necke
ST 1471 if you doo, I may chance to *b.* your olde custome
ST 1472 for I am like to *b.* your yong necke
ST 1475 pray God. I be not preserved to breake your knaves pate
ST 2898 breake ope the doores ; runne, save Hieronimo
SP 745 I must unclaspe me, or my heart will breake
SP 1503 twill breake the edge of my keene Semitor
Ard. 1037 oath, for Susan's sake, the which I may not *b.*
Ard. 1314 but I will *b.* thy spells and exorcisms
Ard. 1512 the devil *b.* all your necks at four miles' end !
Jer. 611 breake of, my Lord : see, where she makes approch
ST 2816 heere breake we off our sundrie languages
Ard. 253 make heavenly gods *b.* off their nectar draughts
ST 295 for deepest cares *b.* never into teares
ST 2593 then gan be *b.* his passions to a freend
Puck 73 sure to breake [thro] their lewde designes
ST 740 but such a warre, as breakes no bond of peace
ST 1348 I set the trap : he breakes the worthles twigs
Ard. 1272 breaks my relenting heart in thousand pieces

Breakfast.

Ard. 91 meanwhile prepare our *b.*, gentle Alice
Ard. 300 Alice, make ready my *b.*, I must hence
Ard. 361 husband, sit down ; your *b.* will be cold

Breaking.

HP 651 from *b.* of her faith unto her Husbande
Cor. 1860 he spurrs his horse, and (*b.* through the presse)

Breast.

Cor. 410 my frightfull hart (stund in my stone-cold *b.*)
Cor. 1101 Scipio hath wrencht a sword into hys brest
Cor. 1551 which (ore-flowing of their brest)
Cor. 1562 spightfull hate so pecks their brest
Cor. 1798 doth breathe new heate within Orestes brest
Cor. 1886 sighing he sets it to his brest, and said
Jer. 207 I have mischiefe within my *b.*
Jer. 332 to put your brest in mind of tribute due
Jer. 409 her *b.* is my lives treasure
Jer. 670 Andrea slaine ? then, weapon, clyng my brest
Jer. 678 I know him by this mould upon his brest
Jer. 720 a bad guest, when the first object is a bleeding brest
Jer. 827 you have ore wrought the chiding of my brest
Jer. 1065 witnes the naked truth upon my *b.*
ST 447 but how can love find harbour in my brest
ST 480 in whose translucent brest my hart is lodgde
ST 757 and, singing with the prickle at her *b.*
ST 2711 and with this weapon will I wound the brest
ST 2712 the haplesse brest, that gave Horatio suck
SP 76 even in thy brest doo I elect my rest
SP 720 at last have perest through thy tralucent brest
SP 1759 they shall lie buried in Persedas brest
Ard. 47 to race the flint walls of a woman's *b.*
Ard. 283 suck venom to his *b.* and slay himself
Ard. 924 whose edge must search the closet of his *b.*
Ard. 1030 conflicting thoughts, encamped in my *b.*
Ard. 1160 with falchion drawn, and bent it at my *b.*
Ard. 1267 but I will dam that fire in my *b.*
Ard. 1275 to wound a *b.* where lies a heart that
Ard. 1531 I'll have a bullet in his *b.* to-morrow

Ard. 1766 or make no battery in his flinty *b.*
Cor. 652 why doe you beate your brests? why mourne you so?
Cor. 1565 fire-brands in their brests they beare
Cor. 1996 beate at your Ivorie breasts, and let your robes
SP 784 if heavens were just, men should have open brests
SP 1464 brests, like two overflowing Fountaines
Jer. 430 I have hard of your honor, gentle brest

Breasted.
Jer. 275 O my true brested father

Breath.
VPJ 86 through thee we draw our *b.* with joy
Cor. 541 for heaven it selfe, nor hels infectious *b.*
Cor. 1321 surprizd, doth coward poison quaile their *b.*, or
Jer. 572 and know his enemy by his envious *b.*
Jer. 598 trust not the open aire, for aire is *b.*
Jer. 1088 I keepe her faver longer then my *b.*
ST Bal. 74 finding her sonne bereav'd of *b.*
ST 1841 or this, and then thou needst not take thy breth
ST 2705 whose hatefull wrath berev'd him of his *b.*
ST 2838 from forth these wounds came *b.* that gave me life
SP 1902 the *b.* dooth murmure softly from his lips

Breath-blown.
Jer. 598 aire is breath, and *b.* words raise care

Breathe.
VPJ 87 God graunt thee long amongst us *b.*
Cor. 980 I *b.* an Autumne forth of fiery sighes
Cor. 1772 and thrice the best of both was faine to *b.*
Cor. 1798 doth *b.* new heate within Orestes brest
Jer. 820 why, twere base to breath and live
Jer. 950 breath like your name, a Generall defiance
Jer. 952 the like breath our Lord General gainst
ST 1522 where shall I run to breath abroad my woes
SP 515 and let the Sophie breath, and from the
Ard. 1299 nay, if you ban, let me *b.* curses forth
Ard. 1338 we beggars must not *b.* where gentles are
Cor. 174 that breaths her heavie poisons downe to hell
ST 2261 by force of windie sighes thy spirit breathes

Breathed.
Jer. 770 the most notorious rogue that ever breathd
Jer. 811 a nobler ranke of sperits never breathd
ST 165 breathd out proud vauntes, sounding to our reproch

Breathedst.
Jer. 1127 I loved thee so entirely, when thou *b.*

Breathing.
SP 1461 lips of pure Corall, *b.* Ambrosie
SP 2001 hath deprived Erastus trunke from *b.* vitalitie

Bred.
HP Ind. 91 harts not bredde in Affrick
HP 270 for in Affrick are no Harts *b.*
Jer. 937 our courages are new borne. our vallors *b.*
STA 1750 a lump *b.* up in darkenesse, and doth
SP 1194 as ayre *b.* Eagles, if they once perceive that

Breed.
Cor. 902 Tygers and Lyons, *b.* with you for ever
Jer. 957 this will but breede a muteny in the campe
ST 1657 concealde that els would *b.* unrest
ST 2650 that it may *b.* the more varietie
Jer. 742 breeds in my soule an everlasting terror
ST 1249 this slie inquiry of Hieronimo for Bel-imperia breeds suspition
ST 1340 this their dissention breeds a greater doubt
STA 1755 being borne, it poutes, cryes, and breeds teeth

Breeding.
HP 1025 pestilent, *b.* evill thoughts, and bringing forth

Brennus.
Cor. 1169 and lyke rude *B.* brought his men to field

Brethren.
SP 658 the worthy *b.* of great Soliman
JB 5 but two *b.* living in the world

Brewen.
JB (Title) murthering of John *B.*, Goldsmith of London
JB (2nd Title) the murder of John *B.*, Goldsmith of London
JB 28 the one of them was called John *B.*
JB 32 so came it to passe by *B.*, who
JB 40 receaved of *B.* both golde and jewels
JB 55 *B.* was hereof very joyfull, and
JB 63 that she repented the promise she made to *B.*
JB 73 she consented by his direction to poyson *B.*
JB 75 not been maried to *B.* above three dayes, whe[n]
JB 65 it turned to Brewens death and destruction

Brewer's.
Ard. 1929 a *b.* cart was like to have run over me

Bride.
HP 1405 as if it were the chamber of a new maryed *B.*
Jer. 111 tis she I hug as mine effeminate *b.*
SP 1566 give me a crowne, to crowne the *b.* withall

Bridge.
Jer. 375 Ide make a *b.* of Spanish carkases

Bridle.
SP 349 why, my Page stands holding him by the *b.*
HP 726 nor on the other side to give her the *b.* of libertie
Cor. 101 to brydle time with reason as we should
SP 610 *b.* the fond intemperance of thy tongue?
Ard. 1797 fie, bitter knave, *b.* thine envious tongue
Cor. 329 deeds might (with a byting brydle) bee restraind

Bridleth.
Cor. 1243 commaunds the world, and brideleth all the earth

Bridling.
Cor. 1404 for brideling those that dyd maligne our glory

Brief.
ST 107 unfolde in breefe discourse your forme of battell
SP 257 to be briefe, hee that will try me, let him waft me
SP 1842 the rest, and worst will I discourse in briefe

Bright.
HP 1045 shine like Silver, or looke as *b.* as Christall
HP 1054 as the Souldiour hath to see his weapons to be *b.*
HP 1408 Pewter so set uppe, the Brasse and yron works so *b.*
Cor. 1338 and you brave walls, *b.* heavens masonrie
Cor. 1355 be't where the *b.* Sun with his neyghbor beames
Jer. 305 could choke *b.* honor in a skabard grave?
SP 631 and by the world's *b.* eye first brought to light
SP 713 say, worlds *b.* starre, whence springs this suddaine change?
SP 1199 for looking but a scue at heavens *b.* eye
SP 1820 but *b.* Persedaes beautie stops my tongue
Cor. 1788 Caesar, whose kinglike lookes, like day *b.* starrs
Cor. 603 the sun-*b.* crowne, that now the Tyrans head doth
ST 2368 and cleare them up with those thy sunne *b.* eyes

Brighter.
ST 2371 love, which, new begun, can shew no *b.* yet

Brightest.
Jer. 441 then the greatest mine of Indians *b.* gold
ST 1534 beat at the windowes of the *b.* heavens
SP 1460 quick lampelike eyes, like heavens two *b.* orbes

Brightly.
Cor. 802 Caesar is like a brightlie flaming blaze
Cor. 1690 this sword you see (which *b.* shone)
ST 2468 as *b.* burning as the mid-daies sunne

Brightness.
ST 816 to over-cloud the brightnes of the Sunne

Brightsome.
SP 29 nor will I up into the *b.* sphere

Brim.
Ard. 388 would it were full of poison to the *b.*
Bring.
HP 796 as oftentimes they *b.* them up too delicately
HP 811 A painfull people by our byrth, for first our babes we *b.*
HP 818 *b.* them up under so soft and easie discipline
HP 835 *b.* them up so hardly or severely as the Lacedemonians
HP 838 that thou shouldest *b.* the[m] up so fiercely
HP 843 teach and *b.* up thy Children as they may become
HP 856 howe he is to educate and *b.* up his Children
HP 861 that thou *b.* them upp in the feare and love of God
HP 978 record and *b.* to mind our plain distinction
HP 1678 beget or *b.* forth money without corruption
HP 1684 it is not artificiall that money shoulde *b.* forth money
Cor. 353 to whom mylde Autumne doth earths treasure *b.*
Cor. 674 and *b.* from Affrique to our Capitoll
Cor. 880 1 *b.* to faire Cornelia to interr
Cor. 1284 shall *b.* the fairest flowers that grow in Rome
Cor. 1435 doe *b.* their treasons to a bloody end
Cor. 1456 good deeds the cruelst hart to kindnes *b.*
Jer. 986 go, search agen ; *b.* him, or neare returne
ST Bal. 41 which for to *b.* well to effect
ST Bal. 167 for murther God will *b.* to light
ST 218 *b.* hether the young Prince of Portingale
ST 989 and time will *b.* this trecherie to light
ST 1059 why linger ye ? *b.* forth that daring feend
ST 1304 helpe me here to *b.* the murdred body with us too
ST 1430 *b.* forth the Prisoner, for the Court is set
ST 1642 and *b.* her hither straight
STA 1793 and so doth *b.* confusion to them all
ST 1890 and *b.* my Sonne to shew his deadly wounds
ST 1928 and. Brother, now *b.* in the Embassador
STA 2014 and then they hate them that did *b.* them up
STA 2068 *b.* me foorth in my shirt, and my
STA 2073 *b.* me foorth, *b.* me thorow allie and allye
STA 2092 at the last, sir, bringe me to one of the murderers
ST 2728 *b.* a chaire and cushion for the King
STA 2962 what, dost thou mocke us, slave ? *b.* torturs forth
SP 131 bid my men *b.* my horse, and a dosen staves
SP 438 Page, run, bid the surgion *b.* his incision
SP 674 and Cupid *b.* me to thy nuptiall bed
SP 711 weele *b.* you home
SP 731 and *b.* him bound for thee to tread upon
SP 849 and bid them *b.* some store of crownes with them
SP 988 learne where Erastus is, and *b.* me word
SP 995 that he that can *b.* foorth the murtherer
SP 1032 dreadfull Neptune, *b.* him backe againe
SP 1045 seeke him, finde him, *b.* him to my sight
SP 1640 for till that Brusor *b.* me my desire
SP 1779 till he *b.* backe Erastus unto you
SP 1893 Lord Marshall, *b.* them hether
Ard. 119 unless that thou wouldst *b.* me to my love
Ard. 572 to London, for to *b.* his death about
Ard. 582 and *b.* thyself and me to ruin both
Ard. 679 which one did *b.* and sold it at my shop
Ard. 1497 and *b.* your honest friend along with you ?
Ard. 1932 sent me to *b.* you word that Mosbie
Ard. 2087 husband, what mean you to *b.* Mosbie home ?
Ard. 2093 but wherefore do you *b.* him hither now ?
Ard. 2242 *b.* them to the doors, but do not stay
Ard. 2330 but *b.* me to him, let me see his body
Ard. 2331 *b.* that villain and Mosbie's sister too
Ard. 2381 come, make haste and *b.* away the prisoners
JB 171 yea, to [such] slaverie and subjection did be *b.* her
JB 227 yet at length the Lorde will *b.* it out
Cor. 1503 that from sable Affrique brings conquests

ST Bal. 22 that he Prince Baltazer Captive brings
SP 680 brings in the spring with many gladsome flowers
SP 1762 what hastie news brings you so soone to Rhodes
Ard. 106 I hope he brings me tidings of my love
ST 1848 Ile be with thee to *b.*, and thee, Lorenzo
Bringeth.
HP 353 fruite it *b.* forth for spoile of weather
Bringing.
HP Ind. 30 customs in *b.* up of Children
HP 793 commended by the *b.* of her children up
HP 853 this part of education and *b.* up of Children
HP 1026 breeding evill thoughts, and *b.* forth worse works
Ard. 1539 and us the more for *b.* her along
Bristled.
Cor. 408 mine haire grew *b.*, like a thornie grove
Cor. 1786 with *b.* backs, and fire-sparkling eyes
Bristle-pointed.
Cor. 1736 the battels lockt (with bristle-poynted speares)
Britany.
Cor. 138 within the bounds of further Brittanie ?
Britons.
Cor. 1377 the Brittaines (lockt within a watry Realme)
Broil.
HP 959 in the perill of some civill broyle or other troubles
Cor. 441 what one he is that in this broile hath bin
Cor. 6 and save the rest in these tempestious broiles
Cor. 799 hath sav'd from danger in these furious broyles
SP 515 and from the Russian broiles call home my
Brokage.
Ard. 26 who, by base *b.* getting some small stock
Broke.
Cor. 85 thy sides sore beaten, and thy hatches *b.*
Cor. 253 have *b.* the sacred thred that tyde thee heere
Cor. 271 oathes made in marriage, and after *b.*
Cor. 893 for yee have basely *b.* the Law of Armes
Cor. 952 he will not let his statues be *b.*
Cor. 954 his owne from beeing *b.* he doth defend
SP 423 I, villaine, I have *b.* my shin bone
Ard. 703 where I broke the tapster's head
Ard. 836 I pray thee, how came thy head *b.* ?
Ard. 837 why, thou seest it is *b.*, dost thou not ?
Ard. 839 boy let down his shop-window and *b.* his head
Ard. 2342 and *b.* her neck, and cut her tapster's throat
Broken.
Cor. Ded. 20 those so bitter times and privie *b.* passions
Cor. 1107 our Army's *b.*, and the Lybian Beares devoure
ST 1530 and *b.* through the brazen gates of hell
ST 1532 with *b.* sighes and restles passions
ST 2260 lips murmure sad words abruptly *b.* off
Ard. 818 what 'mends shall I have for my *b.* head ?
Ard. 823 Shakebag, my *b.* head grieves me not
Ard. 849 tush, I have *b.* five hundred oaths !
Ard. 1935 I have *b.* a sergeant's head with his own mace
JB 142 vomiting till his intrailes were all shrunke and *b.*
Cor. 637 the wandring Swallow with her *b.* song
Broker.
Jer. 467 & 468 ‹ or a *B.* ›
Jer. 513 as an Ostler, or a Serjant, or a *b.*
Jer. 219 from brokers stals, from rich that die and
Brood.
SP 1195 perceive that any of their broode but close their sight
Brook.
ST 2863 how can you *b.* our plaies Catastrophe ?
Ard. 1454 meat you ate at dinner cannot *b.* with you
Ard. 862 ne'er longed so much to see a running *b.*
Broom.

Ard. 1641 Black Will and Shakebag I have placed i' the *b*.
Broom-close.
Ard. 1581 in the broom close, too close for you
Broth.
Ard. 281 ay, such as might be put into his *b*.
Ard. 285 or any kind of *b*. that he shall eat
Ard. 366 something in this *b*. that is not wholesome
Ard. 425 that might have given the *b*. some dainty taste
Brother.
HP 104 a *B* that hath long beene a Courtier in Rome
HP 300 rather appertaines to thee then to thy *B*.
Jer. 252 heeres no fine villainie, no damn[e]d *b*.
Jer. 945 gives me the deepest wound, Ile call him *b*.
Jer. 948 I hope, boy, thou wilt gaine a *b*. too
ST 106 thanks to my loving *b*. of Castile
ST 512 *B*., sit downe ; and, Nephew, take your place
ST 765 *B*. of Castile, to the Princes love what saies
ST 779 heire unto our *b*. heere, Don Ciprian
ST 805 now, *b*., you must take some little paines
ST 1156 me hath my haples *b*. hid from thee
ST 1165 to accuse thy *b*., had he beene the meane ?
ST 1624 accursed *b*., unkinde murderer
ST 1659 thou art no *b*., but an enemy
ST 1698 you (gentle *b*.) forged this for my sake
ST 1717 *b*., you are become an Oratour
ST 1732 feare your selfe ? — I, *B*. — How ?
ST 1877 *b*., how like you this our Vice-roies love ?
ST 1918 but gentle *b*.; goe give to him this golde
ST 1928 and, *B*., now bring in the Embassador
ST 2270 go, *B*., it is the Duke of Castiles cause
ST 2304 see, *b*., see, how nature strives in him
ST 2731 heere, *b*., you shall be the booke-keeper
ST 2776 tell me, *b*., what part plaies he ?
ST 2896 *B*., my Nephew and thy sonne are slaine
ST 2992 looke to my *b*., save Hieronimo
ST 2994 my *b*., and the whole succeeding hope that
SP 524 say, *b*. Amurath, and Haleb, say
SP 531 didst thou not heare our *b*. sweare
SP 565 not like my *b*., or a man of worth
SP 602 yet, Amurath, thou wert my *b*. too
SP 617 justice that makes the *b*. Butcher of his *b*.
Ard. 178 for I will rid mine elder *b*. away
Ard. 263 then, *b*., to requite this courtesy
Ard. 734 thy mother, thy sister, thy *b*., or all thy kin
Ard. 2244 go, Susan, and bid thy *b*. come
Ard. 2250 my *b*., you, and I shall rue this deed
Ard. 2399 ah, gentle *b*., wherefore should I die ?
Ard. 2403 if your *b*. and my mistress had not
ST 594 yet might she love me as her brother's freend
ST 1280 so neare the Duke his brothers house
ST 2333 seest thou not the K[ing] my brothers care in
ST 2997 mourne the losse of our beloved brothers death
SP 585 villaine, thy brothers grones do call for thee
HP 226 for many times they are companions and brothers
Cor. 485 both brothers, and both warrs fierce lightning fiers
SP 1117 in controversie touching the Ile of Rhodes my brothers
     dyde
Cor. 31 with guiltles blood by brothers hands out-lanched
Cor. 609 (with haples brothers blood besmear'd)
SP 147 and be our tilting like two brothers sportes
SP 1113 ads but a trouble to my brothers ghoasts
Brotherhood.
Jer. 947 nay, then, if brother-hood by strokes come dewe
SP 601 ah, what is dearer bond then *b*. ?
Brother-in-law.
Cor. 1386 and that brave warrier, my brother in law

Brought.
HP Ind. 35 thinges that are *b*. into the house
HP 111 that *b*. worde of his Father's comming
HP 297 which are *b*. over heere to us
HP 384 whatsoever fruite Sommer hath *b*. forth
HP 719 and *b*. up in good discipline
HP 1287 be *b*. from his Ferme or Mannor in the Countrey
HP 1253 such things whatsoever as are *b*. into the house
HP 1348 not onely *b*. Penelope and Circes in the number of
HP 1429 *b*. forth by Nature for mans use and service
HP 1432 Virgill having regard *b*. in Numa boasting thus
Cor. 695 God graunt these dreames to good effect bee *b*.
Cor. 1169 and lyke rude Brennus *b*. his men to field
Cor. 1660 *b*. at first an hoste of men to Affrique
Jer. 585 and my invention *b*. to me for newes
Jer. 686 yur fault, my lord ; you *b*. noe word
ST 73 which *b*. me to the faire Elizian greene
ST 126 I *b*. a squadron of our readiest shot
ST 128 they *b*. another wing to incounter us
ST 160 *b*. rescue and encouragde them to stay
ST 404 *b*. in a fresh supply of Halberdiers
ST 412 and *b*. him prisoner from his Halberdiers
ST 993 and learne by whom all this was *b*. about
SP 547 the ones a Lyon almost *b*. to death
SP 631 and by the world's bright eye first *b*. to light
SP 636 Fortune, that first by chance *b*. them together
SP 872 what store of Crownes have you *b*. ?
SP 1098 meane time, I *b*. Fernando on the way
SP 1165 tell me, man, what madnes *b*. thee hether ?
SP 1183 the cause that *b*. thee hether
SP 1187 heavens *b*. thee hether for our benefit
SP 1257 till thou hast *b*. Rhodes in subjection
SP 1304 I *b*. not bound unto her Erastus
SP 1511 *b*. Alexander from warre to banquetting
SP 1725 I *b*. Perseda to the presence of Soliman
SP 1736 and *b*. him home unto his native land
SP 1747 that so *b*. Soliman from worse to better
Ard. 491 your honourable friends, nor what you *b*. ?
Ard. 1202 he locked the gates, and *b*. away the keys
Ard. 1460 her glove *b*. in which there she left behind
Ard. 1794 or else be *b*. for men to wonder at
Ard. 2282 Master Mayor, have you *b*. my husband home ?
Ard. 2384 about a letter I *b*. from Master Greene
Ard. 2387 you *b*. me such a letter, but I dare swear
JB 123 a little boye which she *b*. with her
JB 218 and after *b*. back to prison
Broughtest.
ST 1011 broughtst thou me hether to encrease my paine ?
Brow.
HP 1089 at a winck of the eye, or bent of the *b*.
Cor. 1014 one while shee bends her angry browe
Jer. 1184 homeward with victory to crowne Spaines *b*.
SP 293 he saw my anger figured in my *b*.
SP 504 within forst furrowes of her clowding *b*.
Ard. 844 I pray thee, Will, make clean thy bloody *b*.
Ard. 988 is deeply trenched in my blushing *b*.
Cor. 1517 his warlike browes still be deckt with Lawrel boughes
Jer. 795 I, and returned it with menasing browes
Ard. 691 with mighty furrows in his stormy brows
Jer. 116 upon whose eie browes hangs damnation
STA 2067 and let their eie-browes juttie over
SP 1459 small pensild eye browes, like two glorious rainbowes
Bruit.
Cor. 1340 to bruite the prayses of our conquests past ?
Ard. 348 upon whose general *b*. all honour hangs
Brush.

HP 1035 the Chamberlaine make the bedds and *b.*

Brusor.

SP 201 hath *B.* led a valiant troope of Turkes

SP 507 I long till *B.* be returnde from Rhodes

SP 1118 tell me, *B.*, whats the newes at Rhodes?

SP 1134 these praises, *B.*, touch me to the heart

SP 1145 *B.*, tell me now, how did the Christians

SP 1153 then tell me, *B.*, how is Rhodes fenst?

SP 1252 *B.*, goe levie men

SP 1256 *B.*, be gon : and see not Soliman till thou

SP 1453 heere, *B.*, this kinde Turtle shall be thine

SP 1495 *B.*, hide her, for her lookes withould me

SP 1496 O *B.*, thou hast not hid her lippes

SP 1501 O *B.*, seest thou not her milke white necke

SP 1508 harke, *B.*, she cals on Christ

SP 1604 pleaseth your Majestie to heare *B.* speake?

SP 1630 O fine devise ; *B.*, get thee gone

SP 1636 *B.*, be gone ; for till thou come I languish

SP 1640 for till that *B.* bring me my desire

SP 1721 that *B.* is sent to fetch my maister back

SP 1737 subornd *B.* with envious rage to counsell Soliman

SP 1739 *B.* is sent to fetch him back againe

SP 1760 welcome, Lord *B.* — And, Lucina, to

SP 1778 I will stay with you, from *B.* my beloved

SP 1780 Lord *B.*, come ; tis time that we were gon

SP 1804 what thinks Lord *B.* of this strange arrest?

SP 1911 and, *B.*, see Erastus be interd with honour

SP 1920 *B.*, as thou lovest me, stab in the marshall

SP 1933 then, *B.*, come ; and with some few men

SP 1972 was *B.* by? — 1

SP 2034 ah, *B.*, see where thy Lucina lyes

SP 2038 nay, gentle *B.*, stay thy teares a while

SP 2041 go, *B.*, beare her to thy private tent

SP 2124 when *B.* lives that was the cause of all?

SP 2125 come *B.*, helpe to lift her bodie up

SP 2210 wheres valiant *R.*, but in my triumph?

SP 1367 beside, I sat on valiant Brusors tongue

SP 1377 why, Brusors victorie was Fortunes gift

SP 1415 and ile impart to thee our Brusors newes

SP 1442 first, thanks to heaven ; and next to Brusors valour

SP 1727 and gave Lucina into Brusors hands

Brute.

Cor. 1257 nor ought doth Brutus that to *B.* belongs

Brute-beasts.

HP 1084 bruite beasts rejoyce to see their Maisters cheerish them

HP 1442 that Nature hath engendred not onely bruite Beasts

Brutus.

HP 1357 by Collatyn, by *B.*, and Tarquinius

Cor. 17 yet *B.* Manlius, hardie Scevola

Cor. 827 and let another *B.* rise

Cor. 1116 but, *B.*, shall we dissolutelie sitte, and see

Cor. 1127 to see (for one) that *B.* suffer not

Cor. 1137 see that *B.* thys day beares the selfe-same Armes to

Cor. 1158 Caesar and Sylla, *B.*, be not like

Cor. 1175 (deere *B.*) thinke you Caesar such a chyld

Cor. 1223 no, *B.*, never looke to see that day

Cor. 1231 *B.*, I cannot serve nor see Rome yok'd

Cor. 1248 O, *B.*, speake ; O say, Servilius, why

Cor. 1250 but *B.* lives, and sees, and knowes, and feeles that

Cor. 1253 the sonne, of noble *B.*, hys great Grandfather

Cor. 1257 nor ought doth *B.* that to Brute belongs

Bubbling.

Cor. 1895 that fro the wound the smoky blood ran bubling

Buckler.

SP 703 herein, Lucina, let me *b.* him

SP 704 not Mars himselfe had eare so faire a *B.*

Ard. 962 and *b.* thee from ill-intending foes

Ard. 1936 and bailed whom I list with my sword and *b.*

Ard. 1980 a *b.* in a skilful hand is as good as a

Ard. 2375 and had not I with my *b.* covered my head

Buds.

HP 827 your robes are dyed with Saffron and with glistring purple *b.*

Ard. 187 is this the fruit thy reconcilement *b.*?

Ard. 976 and couch dishonour as dishonour *b.*

Bugs.

ST 3036 where none but furies, *b.*, and tortures dwell

Ard. 1098 sleep, when *b.* and fears shall kill our courages

Build.

HP 1517 and builde with as much exelency and perfection

Cor. 619 scorning her soule a seate should builde within

Jer. 220 from rich that die and *b.* no hospitals

Jer. 595 *b.* a foundation surest, when

Ard. 1235 and sought to *b.* my nest among the clouds

Buildest.

Cor. 1088 thou buildst thy kingdom, and thou seat'st thy King

Buildeth.

Cor. 840 one that with blind frenzie *b.* up his throne?

Built.

ST 1816 murderers have *b.* a habitation for their cursed soules

Ard. 1631 like to a pillar *b.* of many stones

Bulk.

Jer. 207 mischiefe within my breast, more then my bulke can hold

Jer. 314 my minds a giant, though my bulke be small

Bull.

ST 574 in time the sauvage *B.* sustaines the yoake

Cor. 1738 dash together like two lustie Bulls

Bullet.

SP 183 to change a *b.* with our swift flight shot

SP 1057 wherfore serves my targe of proofe but for the *b.*?

SP 2030 mine is no more, and a *b.* may pearce it

Ard. 1520 for by this *b.* Arden might not die

Ard. 1531 I'll have a *b.* in his breast to-morrow

ST 144 thicke stormes of bullets ran like winters haile

Jer. 854 should raise spleens big as a cannon *b.*

Ard. 1413 and he supposed a cannon-*b.* hit him

Bunch.

Cor. 1824 whose blood, as from a spunge, or bunche of Grapes crusht

Buon.

HP 961 Ch' innanzi a *b.* signor fa servo forte

Burden.

ST 2213 then sound the *b.* of thy sore harts greife

Burial.

ST 21 said that my rites of buriall not performde

ST 2113 heaven covereth him that hath no buriall

Buried.

Cor. 182 with Souldiers bodies that were *b.* there

ST 388 and in his death hath *b.* my delights

SP 1268 Ferdinando is *b.* ; your friends commend them to you

SP 1759 they shall lie *b.* in Persedas brest

SP 2195 their bodies *b.*, yet they honour me

JB 154 was *b.*, no person as then suspecting

Buries.

Ard. 1636 and *b.* all his haughty pride in dust

Burn.

Cor. 1151 we stay too-long : I burne till I be there

Jer. 430 till this be acted I in passion burne

ST 1069 binde him, and burne his body in those flames

STA 1966 then we burne day light

ST 2372 new kindled flames should burne as morning sun

ST 2683 and *b*. the roots from whence the rest is sprung
Ard. 1335 and *b*. this prayer-book, where I here use
Cor. 803 blaze that fiercely burnes a house already fired
Ard. 1266 fire divided burns with lesser force

Burned.
Cor. 875 and layd his body to be burn'd thereon
ST 1709 fire, who burnt like Ætne for Andreas losse
STA 1967 let it be burnt ; night is a murderous slut
Ard. 2411 where her sentence is she must be burnt
Ard. 2425 Black Will was *b*. in Flushing on a stage
JB (Title) for which fact she was *b*., and he hanged in
JB 220 the woman had judgement to be *b*. in Smythfield

Burning.
Cor. 1769 with *b*. hate let each at other flie
ST 2468 as brightly *b*. as the mid-daies sunne
SP 109 that takes the Sun-beames *b*. with his force
SP 419 beyond the course of Titans *b*. raies
SP 677 full fraught with love and *b*. with desire
SP 1801 such is the force of marrow *b*. love

Burst.
SP 422 ho, God save you, sir, Have you *b*. your shin ?
Ard. 1270 such deep pathaires, like to a cannon's *b*.
JB 134 straines as if his lungs would *b*. in pieces

Bursting.
Ard. 209 which even in *b*. forth consumes itself

Bury.
Cor. 340 and we have time to burie our annoy ?
ST 640 thy death shall *b*. what thy life conceales
SP 978 to fetch the Sexten to *b*. him, I thinke
SP 1161 it eyther shall be mine, or burie me

Bush.
Ard. 1163 like one obscured in a little *b*.
STA 1935 beat at the bushes, stampe our grandam earth
Ard. 1676 scratch you by the face with my bramble-*b*.

Bushy.
HP 689 the Hart with his fayre and bushie braunched hornes

Busied.
HP 1574 *b*. in those exercises of the bodie
HP 1762 that is *b*. and employed in office for the
ST 1729 of more import then womens wits are to be *b*. with

Business.
HP Ind. 113 orders in housholde busines
HP 741 shamefastnes in all her actions and busines of her life
HP 996 labor, countrey busines, and household exercise
HP 1001 to whom the busines of the stable and of horses
HP 1031 in such busines as thou canst not severallie set them
HP 1108 in care of families and housholde busines
HP 1143 the duetie of a Huswife and of womens busines
HP 1311 such busines are not to be manedged and handled by
ST 1856 who is he that interrupts our busines ?
SP 1718 and ile stay heere about my maisters busines
Ard. 403 yet, if thy *b*. be of great import
Ard. 778 what haste my *b*. craves to send to Kent ?
Ard. 781 and do ye slack his *b*. for your own ?

Buskling.
Cor. 1723 the clattring Armour, *b*. as they paced

Busy.
HP 1293 she shold busie herselfe in viewing and surveighing
HP 1360 the lesse she may dysdaine to busie herselfe
ST 1854 back, seest thou not the King is busie ?
ST 2346 busie to keepe back him and his supplications
JB 3 how busie the divell hath beene to provoke

But.
HP 57 little more then halfe a mile *b*. wee arived on the
ST Bal. 145 *b*. that I would not tell it then. even with my teeth I
ST 433 *b*. for thy kindnes in his life and death

Butcher.
ST 907 O wicked *b*., what so ere thou wert
ST 2803 as thy *b*. is pittilesse and base
SP 617 justice that makes the brother *B*. of his brother
SP 2122 then when they made me *B*. of my love

Butchered.
ST 2848 there mercilesse they butcherd up my boy
ST 2909 why hast thou *b*. both my children thus ?
SP 2035 butcherd dispightfullie without the walles
Ard. 1793 either there be *b*. by thy dearest friends

Butler.
HP 1289 where the Steward or *B*. beares the keyes

Butting.
Ard. 1140 at the alehouse *b*. Arden's house

Buxusque.
HP 825 Tympana vos *b*. voca[n]t Berecynthia matris

Buy.
HP 1174 to be enformed how they *b*. or sell
HP 1241 and with the mony that ariseth thereof to *b*.
STA 2020 all the undelved mynes cannot *b*. an ounce of justice
Ard. 1119 and he shall *b*. his merriment as dear as
Ard. 2213 but to prevent the worst, I'll *b*. some ratsbane

Buying.
HP 1203 made the entercourse of *b*. and selling very easie
HP 1307 profit gathered by the *b*., selling, or exchanging

Buz.
Jer. 435 moreover, I will buze Andreas landing

By.
Ard. 1129 hated and spit at by the goers-*b*.
ST Bal. 98 and tolde the King then *b*. and *b*.

C.

Cabin-door.
SP 1827 his Cabine doore fast shut, he first began to

Cabinet.
SP 1824 he sent for me into his *C*.

Cadat.
ST 303 Qui jacet in terra non habet unde *c*.
STA 2980 Nunc iners *c*. manus

Caeca.
ST 1003 Quicquid & herbarum vi *c*. nenia nectit

Caesar.
Cor. Arg. 7 the civill warres betwixt him and *C*.
Cor. Arg. 11 and give a second assault to *C*.
Cor. Arg. 18 against all whom *C*. (after he had ordred the
Cor. Arg. 27 a Towne in Affrique at the devotion of *C*.
Cor. Arg. 31 *C*. (having finished these warres, and
Cor. 802 *C*. is like a brightlie flaming blaze
Cor. 843 *C*., thou shalt not vaunt thy conquest long
Cor. 915 yet *C*. liveth still
Cor. 937 *C*. bewail'd his death
Cor. 950 yet *C*. speakes of Pompey honourablie
Cor. 1069 now *C*., swolne with honors heate
Cor. 1114 so Rome to *C*. yeelds both powre and pelfe
Cor. 1115 and o're Rome *C*. raignes in Rome it selfe
Cor. 1129 I freely marcht with *C*. in hys warrs
Cor. 1139 and that thys hand (though *C*. blood abhor)
Cor. 1158 *C*. and Sylla, Brutus, be not like
Cor. 1166 where *C*., that in silence might have slept
Cor. 1175 (deere Brutus) thinke you *C*. such a chyld
Cor. 1179 but, Cassius, *C*. is not yet a King
Cor. 1187 are full of dead mens bones by *C*. slayne
Cor. 1224 for *C*. holdeth signiorie too deere
Cor. 1228 in spite of *C*., Cassius will be free
Cor. 1364 *C*. is now earthes fame, and Fortunes terror
Cor. 1369 *C*. hath tam'd more Nations, tane more Townes
Cor. 1371 *C*. doth tryumph over all the world

Cor. 1405 come on, brave C., and crowne thy head
Cor. 1409 to see theyr C., after dangers past
Cor. 1427 well, C., now they are discomfited, and
Cor. 1474 should C. lyve as long as Nestor dyd
Cor. 1537 C., a Cittizen so wrong'd of the honor
Cor. 1619 that wisely knewe his souldiers harts
Cor. 1655 and wakefull C. that doth watch
Cor. 1660 for true it is that C. brought
Cor. 1666 them C. soone and subt'ly sets in ranke
Cor. 1788 C., whose kinglike lookes, like day bright starrs
Cor. 1840 but there had C. eftsoones tyranniz'd
Cor. 2020 or C. triumph in thine infamie
Cor. 688 O no, our losse lyfts Caesars fortunes hyer
Cor. 809 all powreles give proud Caesars wrath free passage
Cor. 926 with Caesars death to end onr servitude
Cor. 948 they had determin'd once of Caesars end
Cor. 984 yes, newes of Caesars death that medcyn beares
Cor. 1003 that Caesars death shall satisfie his wrong
Cor. 1148 to sheathe our new-ground swords in Caesars throate?
Cor. 1191 are yet inferior to Caesars rage
Cor. 1217 civill discord, wrought by Caesars sleights
Cor. 1239 his owne disgrace, and Caesars violence
Cor. 1339 to see your Caesars matchles victories?
Cor. 1365 and Caesars worth hath staynd old souldiers prayses
Cor. 1419 and Caesars prayse increasd by theyr disgrace
Cor. 1461 els cannot Caesars Emporie endure
Cor. 1502 long preserve our Caesars life
Cor. 1955 enflam'dst so cruell a revenge in Caesars hart
Caetera.
HP 1785 Me mea, sic tua te ; c. mortis erunt
Caeterorumque.
VPJ (Title) In nefariam Babingtoni c.
Cain.
JB 8 to accuse Caine for so fowle a fact
Caitiffs.
Cor. 208 accursed Catives, wretches that wee are
Cakebread.
SP 1673 that rid a pilgrimage to beg c.?
Calabrian.
Cor. 1811 as in the faire C. fields when Wolves
Calamity.
Cor. 801 for feare you feele a third calamitie
Cor. 1962 where calamitie hath sojourn'd with such sorrow
Caldron.
ST 1818 there, in a brazen C. fixt by Jove
Calf.
STA 1758 why might not a man love a Calfe as well
Calices.
HP 318 Inger mi c. amariores
Call.
HP 165 parts or formes, c. them what you will
HP 328ᵃ which we c. redde Wine
HP 705 whereupon the Poets c. him Phoebus
HP 801 which the Philosophers c. Antiperistasis
HP 832 pypes and Tymberils, you see, do c. you thence
HP 903 then they doo in Tragedies of him they c. the King
HP 1102 which properly they c. workmanship
HP 1112 mannedge some of their affaires, and him they c. theyr Clerke
HP 1179 I c. not onely that Quantitie which
HP 1194 that c. I Quallity of substance, then, that
HP 1428 Natural I c. that which getteth the living out of
HP 1566 we may c. to mind that there were
HP 1761 unlesse be c. his government Civill
Cor. 1411 I c. to witnes heavens great Thunderer, that
Cor. 1627 and c. our souldiers cowards to theyr face

Jer. 26 in Rome they c. the fifty year the year of Jubily
Jer. 193 Ile c. him back againe
Jer. 693 O, be of comfort, sweet, c. in thy sperits
Jer. 945 gives me the deepest wound, Ile c. him brother
Jer. 945 then, prince, c. me so
Jer. 1018 I call thee by thy right name, answere me
ST 2363 goe one of you, and c. Hieronimo
ST 2396 nay, stay, Hieronimo — goe, c. him, sonne
SP 514 Ile c. my Souldiers home from Persia
SP 516 c. home my hardie, dauntlesse Janisaries
SP 518 c. home my Bassowes and my men of war
SP 530 not good pollicie to c. your forces home
SP 585 villaine, thy brothers grones do c. for thee
SP 1531 goe, Janisaries, c. in your Governour
SP 1755 when as we c. to minde forepassed greefes
Ard. 55 and c. her forth and presently take leave
Ard. 66 I heard thee c. on Mosbie in thy sleep
Ard. 244 this is the painter's house ; I'll c. him forth
Ard. 573 but c. you this good news ?
Ard. 682 you were glad to c. me ‹ fellow Will ›
Ard. 1058 c. on the neighbours, or we are but dead !
Ard. 1374 go in, Bradshaw ; c. for a cup of beer
Ard. 1755 I'll c. the cutters forth your tenement
Jer. 40 Marshall, our kingdome calles thee father
Jer. 534 and now he calls for wax to seale it
Jer. 1178 who cals so loud on Charon ?
ST 881 who cals Hieronimo ? speak, heere I am
ST 1886 Horatio, who cals Horatio ?
STA 2070 ‹ What noyse is this ? Who calls Hieronimo ? ›
SP 906 he lewdly lyes that cals me treacherous
SP 1508 harke, Brusor, she cals on Christ
Ard. 1059 what dismal outcry calls me from my rest ?
Ard. 1704 who's that that calls for help ?
Called.
HP Ind. 18 he c. Wine bytter
HP Ind. 85 Homer, why he c. Wine sweete and why bitter
HP 200 I will cause her to bee c.
HP 205 the Wife, beeing c., came and sat
HP 298 praysing Wine c. it Nigrum et dulce
HP 300 are c. Grecian wines, because they
HP 325 that it is c. sweete of Homer
HP 485 c. mee to him, and began to
HP 875 and afterward c. servaunts a servando
HP 911 neverthelesse be c. the Noble or the Gentleman
HP 927 so that a servaunt may be c. Animal rationale
HP 973 conflict amongst the Romains which they c. Cyvill warre
HP 1060 had c. those instruments weapons
HP 1094 the limns, which are also c. instruments
HP 1201 whereupon it was c. Numus of Νωμω
HP 1206 Arteficiall riches may all those things be c.
HP 1437 and that may well be c. Naturall gayne
HP 1464 trade or science is at this day commonlie c. Merchandize
HP 1503 which for the most part are c. Fayres or Marts
HP 1567 c. from the Plough and Carte to be Magistrates
HP 1585 the one is c. Exchaunge, the other Usurie
HP 1764 private that is segregat and not c. to office
STA 1786 and there is Nemesis, and Furies, and things c. whippes
SP 280 he did worse ; he cald that Ladie his
Ard. 1706 I came to help him that c. for help
Ard. 1860 c. I not help to set my husband free ?
Ard. 2285 know you not one that is c. Black Will ?
JB 28 the one of them was c. John Brewen
JB 79 neither could she abide to be c. after his name
Calledst.
ST 893 O was it thou that call'dst me from my bed ?
Callest.

SP 781 calst thou me love, and lovest another better?

Calleth.
HP 324 and heddie taste which he *c.* bitter
HP 326 afterward Homer *c.* it black
HP 1476 and *c.* that order of the Publicans most honest

Calling.
HP 724 goe apparelled as others of her *c.* doo
Cor. 257 by *c.* Hymen once more back againe

Calm.
Cor. 164 thou dost not seeke to calme heavens ireful king
Cor. 342 have faild in power to calme my passion

Calmed.
Cor. 396 it would have *c.* many of my sighes

Calmeth.
Cor. 974 tyme *c.* all things

Calmly.
Cor. 1026 over night lye calmely downe

Cambio.
SP 1015 and lost our box in counter *c.*

Came.
HP 30 a hyreling that *c.* with me
HP 43 I repent me not that I *c.* this waie
HP 113 anon there *c.* the Father
HP 115 immediately *c.* up the staires
HP 205 *c.* and sat her down
HP 699 youthes, uppon whose faces hayre never *c.*
Cor. 705 and loe (me thought) *c.* glyding by my bed
Cor. 1373 the Gauls, that *c.* to Tiber to carouse
Jer. 705 this letter *c.* not to Andreas hands
Jer. 743 say, slave, how *c.* this accursed evill?
Jer. 816 you *c.* but now, [and] must you part agen?
ST 125 but ere we joynd and *c.* to push of Pike
ST 495 things were in readines before I *c.*
ST 537 be *c.* likewise, and razed Lishon walles
ST 549 he with a puissant armie *c.* to Spaine
ST 1428 but come, for that we *c.* for : lets begin
ST 1684 now when I *c.*, consorted with the Prince
ST 2254 that *c.* for justice for my murdered Sonne
ST 2838 from forth these wounds *c.* breath that gave me life
SP 762 and till I *c.* whereas my love did dwell
SP 1686 *c.* like a coward stealing after me
SP 1873 I see this traine was plotted ere I *c.*
SP 1948 parted the seas, and we *c.* over drie-shod
SP 1978 Lucina, *c.* thy husband to this end
Ard. 76 now I remember whereupon it *c.*
Ard. 79 thereof *c.* it, and therefore blame not me
Ard. 307 Arden, I thought not on her, I *c.* to thee
Ard. 557 *c.* hither, railing, for to know the truth
Ard. 836 I pray thee, how *c.* thy head broke?
Ard. 1066 murderer thieves that *c.* to rifle me
Ard. 1159 and at the noise another herdman *c.*
Ard. 1488 my honest friend that *c.* along with me
Ard. 1706 I *c.* to help him that called for help
Ard. 1848 *c.* lovingly to meet thee on thy way
Ard. 1950 no sooner *c.* the surgeon in at doors
Ard. 2222 ah, neighbours, a sudden qualm *c.* o'er my heart
Ard. 2280 but it had done before we *c.* back again
Ard. 2337 I *c.* thither, thinking to have had harbour
JB 32 so *c.* it to passe by Brewen, who, not
JB 38 it *c.* to passe that this nice maiden
JB 121 and by the time he *c.* againe she had made
JB 143 the next morning she *c.* to him againe

Camest.
Jer. 931 when first thou camst embassador
Ard. 1739 how cam'st thou so berayed?

Camillus.

Cor. 18 Scevola, and stout *C.*, are returnd fro Stix

Camp.
Cor. 189 and Campe to Campe did endlesse battailes wage
Cor. 1644 and as a houshold Campe of creeping Emmets
Cor. 1679 and with a cheerefull looke surveigh'd the Campe
Jer. 937 this will but breede a muteny in the campe
ST 92 now say, L[ord] Generall, how fares our Campe?
ST 1042 when he in Campe consorted Balthazar
SP 553 make an universall Campe of all his scattered legions
Ard. 650 all the *c.* feared him for his villainy

Candle-light.
HP 1332 at their distaffe doth she hold her maids by candlelight
Ard. 1693 should never dine nor sup without *c.*

Candy.
HP 95 the Cupboorde charged with curious plates of Candie

Caniciem.
HP 1453 *C.* galea premimus, semperque recentes

Canker.
Ard. 1122 but rust and *c.* after I have sworn

Cannon.
SP 1052 hath planted a double *c.* in the doore
Ard. 1270 such deep pathaires, like to a cannon's burst

Cannon-bullet.
Jer. 854 should raise spleens big as a cannon bullet
Ard. 1418 and he supposed a *c.* hit him

Cannon-shot.
SP 1056 thinkes he bare cannon shot can keepe me back?

Canon.
SP 1952 for as the old Cannon saies very pretily

Canterbury.
Ard. 2410 beare Mistress Arden unto *C.*

Cantionem.
VPJ (Title) T. K. in Cygneam *C.* Chidiochi Tychborne

Cantum.
HP 824 Dindyma, ubi assuetis biforem dat tibia *c.*

Canzonet.
HP 546 Dante, who in his *C.* of Noblesse said

Cap.
ST 2137 thy Cappe to curtesie, and thy knee to bow
ST 2620 you must provide a Turkish cappe
STA 2075 and let my haire heave up my night-*c.*

Capable.
HP 920 that they may be *c.* of his commaundements
HP 969 who therfore are not *c.* of any office
HP 1115 *c.* of fashions, or apt to studie or contemplat

Capacity.
HP 74 neither of ignoble birth nor meane capacitie

Capessas.
VPJ 57 Quid non Papa ruens spondet, modo jussa *c.*?

Capital.
SP 1689 that you have lost a capitoll part of your Lady ware

Capitano.
HP 1413 Gnato, that disposd the household of his glorious Sig. *C.*

Capitol.
Cor. 19 desiring Armes to ayde our Capitoll
Cor. 674 and bring from Affrique to our Capitoll
Cor. 824 great Jupiter, to whom our *C.*
Cor. 1405 lets to the Capitoll
SP 1670 and viewd the Capitoll, and was Romes greatest glorie

Captain.
Jer. 1019 go, Captaine, passe the leaft wing squadron ; hie
SP 1207 thou shalt be Captaine of our Janisaries
SP 2134 Captaine, is Rhodes recovered againe?
Cor. 1878 before the foe and in theyr Captaines presence
Cor. 793 thy bravest Captaines, whose coragious harts

Cor. 1604 where is thine Emperor? — Where our Captaines are
Cor. 1629 could draw our Captaines to endanger us
Cor. 1978 content to count the ghosts of those great Captains
Cor. 2019 let not those Captains vainlie lie inter'd
ST 130 and Captaines strove to have their valours tride
ST 148 on every side drop Captaines to the ground
Captious.
SP 2018 to be c., vertuous, ingenious, are to be nothing
Captivate.
ST 702 and now by sleight would c. my soule
SP 1400 if not destroide, yet bound and c.
SP 1401 if c., then forst from holy faith
Captivated.
SP 271 I am now c. with the reflecting eye of
Captive.
Cor. 1401 and to shun the scorne of being taken c.
Jer. 850 of all those c. Portugales deceased
ST Bal. 22 that he Prince Baltazer C. brings
SP 1532 so shall I joy betweene two c. friends
SP 1533 and yet my selfe be c. to them both
SP 1731 made him praise love, and [his] captives beautie
Cor. 67 like Captives lyv'd eternally enchaynd
Cor. 1921 then all the Captives in th' infernall Court
Jer. 862 to live like captives, or as free borne die?
Captivity.
Jer. 340 by our forfathers base captivitie
Jer. 344 that which they lost by base Captivitie, we
Jer. 846 to seet you free from base c.
Jer. 864 to die with honor, scorne c.
Jer. 984 showes that what they lost by base C.
ST 591 I, but thats slaundred by captivitie
ST 1583 woe to thy basenes and captivitie
SP 1456 that her captivitie may turne to blisse
Car.
SP 2213 and they must wait upon the Carre of Death
SP 2221 fetch his imperiall Carre from deepest hell
Ard. 1541 path wherein he wont to guide his golden c.
HP 1221 may be transported easily in Carres or other carriages
Carbines.
ST 173 and our C. pursued them to the death
Carbo.
Cor. 360 proud Cynna, Marius, and C. flesh'd so long
Carcanet.
SP 71 which to effect, accept this carkanet
SP 107 know me by this thy pretious carkanet
SP 413 and please her with this C. of worth
SP 490 when she delivered me the Carkanet
SP 627 the Ring and Carkanet were Fortunes gifts
SP 647 I made him loose the pretious C.
SP 682 till when, receive this precious C.
SP 707 still friends? still foes; she weares my C.
SP 806 could nothing serve her but the C.
SP 833 I lost the pretious C. she gave me
Carcase.
Jer. 1126 come, noble rib of honor, valliant carcasse
ST 362 where then became the carkasse of my Sonne?
ST 414 but then was Don Andreas carkasse lost?
Cor. 41 while th' earth, that gron'd to beare theyr carcasses
Cor. 1428 and Crowes are feasted with theyr carcases
Jer. 375 Ide make a bridge of Spanish carkases
Cardinal.
HP 106 highlie favoured of the good Cardinall Vercellis
HP 108 of Italie ⟩ (quoth I) ⟨ is that good Cardinall knowne
Cards.
ST 231 and c. once dealt, it bootes not aske, why so?
Care.

HP Ind. 31 c. of housekeeping of divers sortes
HP Ind. 33 c. of Children, how it is to bee
HP Ind. 35 c. of the Huswife concerning thinges
HP Ind. 39 c. of houshold is
HP Ind. 40 c. of housekeeping as great to
HP Ind. 41 as is the c. of a Kingdome to a King
HP Ind. 43 c. of servaunts in their sicknes
HP Ind. 126 servaunts c. in maintayning of their working tooles
HP 471 government of his house and c. of his familie
HP 509 looked to my husbandry with so great c.
HP 517 the c. of a good householder is devided into two thinges
HP 523 the c. of reasonable thinges is more woorth
HP 525 to have c. in choosing of his wife
HP 779 the c. of them should be devided
HP 854 is, or ought to be, in a manner the c. of a Father
HP 1001 should the housholde c. bee commended
HP 1028 thy cheefe c. and the duetie of thy Steward shall be thys
HP 1040 but, above the rest, to have a speciall c.
HP 1052 such c. of scowring and keeping cleane those tooles
HP 1107 some are placed in c. of families and
HP 1143 the c. of wealth or substance, as we said
HP 1234 to the c. and regard that is (indeede) required
HP 1252 this shall bee the Husbands c.
HP 1298 neyther ought her c. only extend to the spending
HP 1304 her principall c. should be of Lynnen or of
HP 1486 the c. of opportunity to sell what is a mans owne
HP 1510 leaving the c. of them to Factors
HP 1511 the c. of the Husbandman or Housekeeper doth
HP 1514 bestoweth as his chiefe and principall c.
HP 1713 whether houshold c. or housholde government
HP 1718 the c. of Princes Halles belongeth not to private men
HP 1727 so shoulde the c. of either houskeeping be one
HP 1765 wholy hee applies him to his housholde c.
HP 1775 that so necessary c. of governing a Princes house
Cor. 270 that c. to be aveng'd of Lovers othes
Cor. 822 O gods, that once had c. of these our walls
Cor. 1097 they c. not for us, nor account of men
Cor. 1145 if this brave c. be nourisht in your blood
Cor. 1478 but Fortune and the heavens have c. of us
Cor. 1513 that of c. acquitting us
Cor. 1967 O Gods, that earst of Carthage tooke some c.
Cor. 2024 who will performe that c. in kindnes for me?
Jer. 386 I am all vext. — I c. not
Jer. 598 and breath-blown words raise c.
Jer. 812 O, my sweet boy, heaven shield thee still from c.
Jer. 924 I c. not whose
ST 1425 a c. to punish such as doe transgresse
ST 1487 faith, I cannot tell, nor I c. not greatly
STA 1768 strikes c. upon their heads with his mad ryots
ST 1879 an argument of honorable c. to keepe his freend
ST 2333 seest thou not the K[ing] my brothers c. in
ST 2496 whom they with c. and cost have tendred so
ST 2516 my feare and c. in not beleeving it
ST 2884 yet I of kindnes, and of c. to her
STA 2937 nay, then I c. not; come, and we shall be friends
SP 305 I c. not for that; wilt thou not swear?
Ard. 973 if love of me or c. of womanhood
Ard. 2027 take no c. for that; send you him home
Ard. 2212 I c. not though I be hanged ere night
Ard. 2344 I have the gold; what c. I though it be known!
Ard. 2417 faith, I c. not, seeing I die with Susan
VPJ 1 mongst spiny cares sprong up now at the last
VPJ 21 my prime of youth is but a frost of cares
HP Ind. 37 cares necessary for a housekeeper
HP 388 one of the cheefest cares the Housekeeper should have
HP 1522 that appertaine unto familiar or publique cares

Cor. 438 the servitude that causeth all our cares
Cor. 1035 and cares for crowned Emperors shee doth reserve
Cor. 1303 with huge cares doth crosse kings lives
ST 295 for deepest cares break never into teares
ST 1420 to know the cause that may my cares allay?
SP 746 but inward cares are most pent in with greefe
SP 749 could spend my cares in showers of weeping raine
Ard. 389 then should my cares and troubles have an end
Ard. 477 nor cares he though young gentlemen do beg
Puck 59 his loves and cares both towards hir sacred Matie
Cared.
Puck 15 waste and idle papers (wh^ch I carde not for)
Career.
Cor. 1810 had powre to stay them in this strange carrier
Careful.
HP 1037 the carefull Steward or surveighor of the house
HP 1570 the Husbandman and carefull housekeeper
Cor. 1966 and c. of anothers tiranny
SP 85 as carefull will I be to keepe this chaine
SP 1281 but why was I so carefull of the Chaine?
Ard. 480 as careless as he is c. for to get
Ard. 1021 and tels a story with his c. tongue
JB 182 she was carefull for the saving of her credit
Carefully.
HP 1309 if they be c. provided for and ordered
Careless.
HP 672 and carelesse of those that are faire with
Cor. 617 shall by herselfe be carelesse slaine
Cor. 1963 the people stood so careles of their conquered libertie
Cor. 2000 careles of Arte, or rich accoustrements
ST 2407 have tendred so, thus careles should be lost
SP 1282 but why was I so carelesse of the Chaine?
Ard. 480 value life as c. as he is careful for to get
Carelessly.
Cor. 1488 the quiet life, that carelesly is ledd, is
Care-oppressed.
Ard. 1015 now will he shake his c. head
Carezze.
ST 2437 Chi mi fa più c. che non suole
Carle.
Ard. 1767 I'll curse the c., and see what that will do
Ard. 1808 to show the world what wrong the c. hath done
Carol.
ST 756 the gentle Nightingale shall carroll us asleepe
Carouse.
Cor. 1373 the Gauls, that came to Tiber to c.
Carp.
HP Ded. let others carpe, tis your discretion that must
Carpenter.
HP 1727 the selfesame Mason, C., or Architect
Carriages.
HP 1222 transported easily in Carres or other c.
Carried.
HP 1499 carryed or recarried most conveniently
Ard. 1283 lest that my words be c. with the wind
Ard. 1715 will you have any letters c. to them?
Ard. 1934 and c. him about the fields on a coltstaff
Ard. 2313 murdered in this house and c. to the fields
JB 94 secretly caried with her to her husbands house
JB 211 c. before Alderman Howard to be examined
JB 217 then was she c. into the countrey to be
Carries.
ST 695 now, in his month he c. pleasing words
Carrieth.
HP 203 the custome of our Countrey, carieth a certain priviledge
Carrion.

Cor. 847 vomit it, like to a Curre that C. hath devour'd
Carry.
HP 989 they advisde to c. with them to the field
HP 1361 such things as carie meaner worth in showe
Cor. Arg. 9 and carrie her with him into Egipt
ST 1305 Hieronimo? c. me before whom you will
ST 1694 and c. you obscurely some where els
SP 117 that c. honour graven in their helmes
SP 879 go without the chaine, unlesse you carrie false dice
SP 1782 for that I c. thy beloved from thee
Ard. 718 to c. this letter to Mistress Arden
Ard. 1238 but whither doth contemplation c. me?
Ard. 1404 that c. a muscado in their tongue
Ard. 1597 go to, you c. an eye over Mistress Susan
Ard. 1828 wronged, in that we did not c. her along
Carrying.
SP 1785 that for my c. of Erastus hence she
Cart.
HP 1567 called from the Plough and Carte to be Magistrates
Cor. 133 auncestors (ignobly issued from the Carte and Plough)
Ard. 1929 a brewer's c. was like to have run over me
Carte.
HP 1646 Tu troverai non dopo molte c.
Carthage.
Cor. 116 C. and Sicily we have subdude
Cor. 496 C. can witnes, and thou, heavens handwork
Cor. 1967 O Gods, that earst of C. tooke some care
Carthaginian.
Cor. 484 fought, before the fearefull Carthagenian walls)
Carve.
SP 358 and, because he would not be put to c., he wore
Carved.
HP 246 he c. me of the daintiest morsels of
Casa.
HP 1131 writte[n] by Signior Giovanni della C.
Case.
Cor. 555 so, in this c., we ought not to surrender
Jer. 820 wars in such a c. is even as necessary as
ST 616 thus stands the c. : it is not long
ST 629 if c. it lye in me to tell the truth
ST 782 in c. the match goe forward, the tribute
ST 996 Ile say his dirge, singing fits not this c.
ST 1021 Ile shew thee Balthazar in heavy c.
STA 2067 in any c. observe that
SP 827 hard doome of death, before my c. be knowne
SP 952 marry, sir, then the c. is altered
SP 958 a plain c. : Qui tacet consitiri videtur
SP 1811 no, no ; in this c. no appeale shall serve
Ard. 48 in any c. be not too jealous
Ard. 111 in any c. you may not visit him
Ard. 580 chiefly in c. of murder, why, 'tis the way to
Ard. 796 nay, sirs, touch not his man in any c.
Ard. 1432 brawl not when I am gone in any c.
Ard. 1747 in c. we fall into a second fog
Ard. 1824 see in any c. you make no speech of
Ard. 2022 but come not forth before in any c.
Ard. 2272 and see you confess nothing in any c.
Ard. 2298 there he lies murdered in most piteous c.
JB 179 in this miserable c. hee kept her unmarried for
JB 187 « you see » (quoth she) « in what c. I am
ST 2142 that you should plead their cases to the King
ST 2155 no, sir, mine is an action of the C.
Casements.
Ard. 1167 throughout the thorny c. of the brake
Cashier.
HP 1285 (as the Maister hath his Stewarde or Cashur)

Casque.
Cor. 1676 were (warlike) lockt within a plumed caske
Cor. 1745 they hewe their Armour, and they cleave their casks
Cassius.
Cor. 1179 but. *C.*, Caesar is not yet a King
Cor. 1225 but know, while *C.* hath one drop of blood
Cor. 1228 in spite of Caesar, *C.* will be free
Cast.
HP 1409 *c.* such a delicat reflection
Cor. 698 now gan to *c.* her sable mantle off
Cor. 837 to *c.* so soone a state, so long defended, into
Cor. 1636 the self-same day to dig and *c.* new Trenches
STA 959 *c.* a more serious eye upon thy griefe
ST 1813 doth *c.* up filthy and detested fumes
Ard. 64 and *c.* her in the ocean to her love
Ard. 371 I cannot speak or *c.* aside my eye
Ard. 373 here's he that you *c.* in my teeth so oft
Ard. 379 wrong yourself and me to *c.* these doubts
Ard. 1018 now will he *c.* his eyes up towards the heavens
Ard. 1157 which late, methought, was pitched to *c.* the deer
Ard. 1233 I can *c.* a bone to make these curs
Ard. 1466 first did she *c.* her eyes down to the earth
JB 34 was still disdained and *c.* off, albeit he had
JB 107 her coat *c.* downe that messe which
JB 113 that any good thing should so unluckily be *c.* away ›
Cor. 1757 cuts, casts the ground, and madding makes a poole
Cor. 1867 and casts him up neere to the Coasts of Hyppon
Jer. 415 on whom my Sister Bellimperia casts her affection
Cor. 942 and *c.* the plot to catch him in the trap
ST 610 by force, or faire meanes will I *c.* about
ST 1240 the complot thou hast *c.* of all these practises
ST 1325 and therefore know that I have *c.* it thus
Jer. 624 resolved to loose both life and honor at one *c.*
Cor. 583 the roundnes of two boules cross-*c.*
Castile.
ST Bal. 103 The Duke of Castyle, hearing then how I
ST 106 thanks to my loving brother of *C.*
ST 550 and tooke our King of *C.* prisoner
ST 765 brother of *C.*, to the Princes love what saies
ST 804 farewell, my Lord of *C.*, and the rest
ST 2273 and greet the Duke of *C.*
ST 2421 house, the Duke of *C.*, Ciprians ancient seat
ST 3016 the Duke of *C.* and his wicked Sonne both done to death
Jer. 573 now, by the honor of Casteels true house
ST Bal. 25 the Duke of Castyles Daughter then
ST Bal. 86 the streets, hard by the Duke of Castiles house
ST 506 I frolike with the Duke of Castiles Sonne
STA 939 Jaques, runne to the Duke of Castiles presently
ST 1179 and harkening neere the Duke of Castiles house
ST 2270 go, Brother, it is the Duke of Castiles cause
ST 2376 welcome, brave Prince, the pledge of Castiles peace
Castilian.
SP 176 welcome, *C.*, too among the rest
Casting.
Cor. 713 *c.* a thyn course lynsel ore hys shoulders
Castle.
SP 989 I shall finde you at the *C.*, shall I not?
Ard. 1980 a buckler in a skilful hand is as good as a *c.*
Castum.
HP 1327 Exercet penso, *c.* ut servare cubile
Cat.
Ard. 1550 home is a wild *c.* to a wandering wit
STA 1069 and yonder pale faced Hee-*c.* there, the Moone
Catalogue.
HP (Title) A *C.* or Index of those things
Catastrophe.

Cor. Arg. 38 closeth the *C.* of this theyr Tragedie
Cor. 1939 that I may finish the *C.*
ST 2863 how can you brook our plaies *C.*?
Catch.
Cor. 942 and cast the plot to *c.* him in the trap
ST 1352 he runnes to kill whome I have holpe to *c.*
ST 2226 tushe, no; run after, *c.* me if you can
SP 1267 the Governour will hang you, and he *c.* you
Ard. 1423 lime well your twigs to *c.* this wary bird
Ard. 1620 if all the rest do fail, will *c.* Master Arden
Cates.
Ard. 1226 well fares the man, howe'er his *c.* do taste
Catiline's.
Cor. 835 or why from Catlins lewde conspiracies preserv'd
Cato.
Cor. 796 Petreus, *C.*, and Scipio are slaine
Cor. 1103 undaunted *C.* tore his entrails out
Catullus.
HP Ind. 18 *C.*, why he called Wine bytter
HP 326 as it was called bitter by *C.*
Candle.
JB 152 made him a *c.* with suger and other spices
Caught.
Cor. 1316 they have *c.* deserved skarrs
Ard. 70 instead of him, *c.* me about the neck
Caulas.
Puck 49 when lesse by farr hath dryven so many imo extra *c.*
Causa.
Puck 28 in ipsis inest *c.* cur diligantur
Cause.
HP 200 I will *c.* her to bee called
HP 224 and oft it is the *c.* that such regarde is
HP 246 an honest advocat to pleade my *c.*
HP 307 may also be the *c.* of their whitnes
HP 380 the one hath little *c.* to complaine of the other
HP 421 the Sunne, which is the *c.* of generation and
HP 512 hath beene the *c.* that I with
HP 740 onely *c.* or procure shamefastnes in
HP 964 and not without *c.* were Mylos servaunts
HP 1260 shold *c.* those that wyll not keepe to be
HP 1270 theyr moysture (that is *c.* of theyr corruption)
Cor. Arg. 36 shee tooke (as shee had *c.*) occasion to
Cor. 276 els onely I am *c.* of both theyr wraths
Cor. 655 O poore Cornelia, have not wee good *c.*
Cor. 992 yes, *c.* your death
Cor. 1050 gainst one whose power and *c.* is best
Cor. 1203 he rashly styrd against us without *c.*
Cor. 1263 represse, or kill out-right, this *c.* of our distresse
Cor. 1509 rather *c.* thy deerest sonne, by his
Cor. 1955 revenge in Caesars hart upon so slight a *c.*
Jer. 458 elce had my pen no *c.* to write at all
ST Bal. 12 then had not beene this *c.* of teares
ST Bal. 37 the *c.* why that his sister was unkinde
ST Bal. 46 his sister's love, the *c.* of strife
ST 328 the *c.* was mine; I might have died for both
ST 394 for glorious *c.* still aiming at the fairest
ST 602 some *c.* there is that lets you not be loved
ST 1163 what *c.* had they Horatio to maligne?
ST 1420 to know the *c.* that may my cares allay?
ST 1582 woe to the *c.* of these constrained warres
ST 1622 the *c.* of these my secret and
ST 1701 but whats the *c.* that you concealde me since?
ST 2163 come hether, father, let me know thy *c.*
ST 2164 O worthy sir, my *c.*, but slightly knowne, may
ST 2270 go, Brother, it is the Duke of Castiles *c.*
ST 2404 Hieronimo, I hope you have no *c.*

ST 2417 Hieronimo, I never gave you *c*.
ST 2536 you have given me *c*.; I, by my faith, have you
ST 2600 as *c*. of this, slew Soliman
ST 2840 the *c*. was love, whence grew this mortall hate
SP 143 assembled heere in thirsty honors *c*.
SP 159 where for my countries *c*. I chargde my Launce
SP 239 I, conjecturing the *c*. to be want of water, dismounted
SP 599 accursed Amurath, that for a worthlesse *c*.
SP 1182 Erastus, ile not yet urge to know the *c*.
SP 1248 whom I in honours *c*. have reft of life
SP 1572 remoove the *c*., and then the effect will die
SP 1576 there is an urgent *c*., but privie to my selfe
SP 1610 that I may plead in your affections *c*.
SP 1770 without inquirie what should be the *c*.
SP 2124 when Brusor lives that was the *c*. of all ?
SP 2139 first *c*. me murther such a worthy man
Ard. 343 I had *c*. to speak, when all the
Ard. 368 I did, and thats the *c*. it likes not you
Ard. 1169 but quakes and shivers, though the *c*. be gone
Ard. 1949 and railed on Franklin that was *c*. of all
Ard. 2109 and if I do not, sir, think I have *c*.
Ard. 2122 whose life I have endangered without *c*.?
Ard. 2268 and *c*. suspicion, where else would be none
JB 201 but for that *c*. I meane to keepe as long
Puck 34 dared in the greatest *c*., wch is to cleere my self of
Cor. 1197 yes, where the causes reasonable are
ST 2152 to plead in causes us Corrigidor
ST 2428 for divers causes it is fit for us that we be
Ard. 1298 and all the causes that enchanted me !
'Cause, *see* **Because.**
Caused.
HP 982 daungerous warres are *c*. and continued by such
Cor. Arg. 23 certaine shippes which he had *c*. to stay for him
Causeless.
ST 1630 and him for me thus causeles murdered
ST 2490 assures thee to be causeles slaughtered
ST 2522 that causles thus have murdered my sonne
Ard. 858 at last confesse how *c*. they have injured her
Causeth.
Cor. 438 the servitude that *c*. all our cares
Causing.
HP 800 *c*. that which the Philosophers call Antiperistasis
Cavalier.
SP 690 all haile, brave Cavelere. God morrow, Madam
SP 2002 a brave Cavelere, but my aprooved foeman
Cave.
Cor. 173 then from her lothsome *C*. doth Plague repaire
Cease.
Cor. 352 a miserie betided will never *c*.
Cor. 909 *c*. these laments
Jer. 818 nay, sweet love, *c*.
Jer. 953 now *c*. words ; I long to heare the
Jer. 1101 if thou beest valliant, *c*. these idle words
ST 990 meane while, good Isabella, *c*. thy plaints
SP 34 Ile stay my flight, and *c*. to turne my wheele
SP 1293 then take each one halfe of me, and *c*. to weepe
Ard. 357 and then. I hope, they 'll *c*., and at last confesse
Ard. 395 I know it, sweet Alice ; *c*. to complain
Ard. 993 she will amend, and so your griefs will *c*.
Ceased.
HP 454 and heere I *c*., when the olde man
Ceaseless.
Cor. 4 you needs wil plague us with your ceasles wroth
Cor. 225 (cause I cannot dry your ceaselesse springs)
Cor. 804 and, ceasles lanching out on everie side
Cor. 976 my griefe is lyke a Rock, whence (ceaseles) strayne

Cor. 1590 whose ceaseles griefe (which I am sorry for)
ST 1525 surcharged the aire with ceasles plaints
ST 2302 let me live a solitarie life, in ceaselesse praiers
Ceasing.
JB 141 never *c*. vomiting till his intcailes were all
Cedar.
SP 2023 but the shrub is safe when the *C*. shaketh
Cedere.
ST 1009 At tamen absistam properato *c*. letho
Cedite.
HP 826 Idaeae ; sinite arma viris, et *c*. ferro
Cees.
Jer. 452 eate Cues, drunk *C*., and cannot give a letter
Celebrate.
Jer. 96 lets in to *c*. our second feast
Celebration.
ST 790 in *c*. of the nuptiall day
Celestial.
Cor. 573 to practise stayes of this celestiall influence
SP 670 for celestiall Gods with gladsome lookes to gase
Cell.
Jer. 310 to hooke the divell from his flaming *c*.
Cellar.
Jer. 494 ‹ And honesty in the bottome of a seller ›
Jer. 517 and honesty in the bottome of a seller ›
HP 1043 walles and pavements, lofts and sellers
Cement.
Ard. 1633 nor with *c*. to fasten it in the joints
Censor.
ST 50 then Minos, mildest *c*. of the three
Censure.
HP 1730 so judicial as to *c*. that which you propose
ST 266 will both abide the *c*. of my doome ?
SP 264 myselfe will *c*. of your chivalrie
SP 567 but gave my *c*., as his highnesse bad
Ard. 1032 and I, a judge to *c*. either side
Puck 69 to *c*. me as I shall prove my self
Centre.
Cor. 462 and wandreth in the Center of the earth ?
ST 1044 that howerly coastes the center of the earth
Cerberus.
ST 30 there, pleasing *C*. with honied speech
ST 2439 awake, Erichtho ; *C*., awake
Cerealiaque.
HP 1065 *c*. arma expediunt fessi rerum
Ceremonies.
SP 1668 compassing me with goodly *c*.
Ceremonious.
SP 502 ah, but my love is cerimonious
Cererem.
HP 1065 Tum *C*. corruptam undis
Certain.
HP 203 the custome of our Countrey, carieth a *c*. priviledge
HP 1204 more certaine then when they onely used exchaunge
HP 1520 hath his desires of riches certaine and determinat
HP 1599 worketh to a certaine set and determinat ende
HP 1600 and to a certaine ende doo all those meanes and
HP 1615 that cannot be devided are of number certaine
Cor. Arg. 23 to certaine shippes which he had caused to stay
Cor. 538 of certaine courage gainst incertaine chaunce
Cor. 1094 that seeme to feare a certaine Thunderer
ST 1678 concerning certaine matters of estate
ST 1931 and that we may prefixe a certaine time
ST 2117 as by a secret, yet a certaine meane, which
Ard. 90 for I have *c*. goods there to unload
Ard. 1199 with *c*. gold knit in it, as he said

Ard. 1310 this *c.* good I lost for changing bad
Ard. 2019 shall at a *c.* watchword given rush forth
JB 53 to marrie him by a *c.* day, and to make him

Certes.

SP 271 but, *c.*, I am now captivated with the

Certified.

HP 1162 (to be *c.* of his substance and the value of his riches)

Certify.

HP 1707 thereof to certefie mee and amend it
Ard. 763 « this is to *c.* you that as the turtle true »

Certus.

HP 662ª Ovid De med. faciei *C.* amor moru[m]est

Chafe.

Jer. 851 turne into *c.*, and choke their insolence
Ard. 1534 O, how she'll *c.* when she hears of this !

Chain.

SP 85 as carefull will I be to keepe this chaine
SP 88 over mine armour will I hang this chaine
SP 441 come, sirra, let me see how finely youle cry this chaine
SP 458 crie the chayne for me Sub forma pauperis, for money
SP 461 hee must not know that thou cryest the Chaine for me
SP 469 a chaine, sir, a chaine, that your man bad me crie
SP 473 how durst thou be so bould to crie the chaine
SP 482 Ile doe the best I can to finde your chaine
SP 488 take thou the honor, and give me the chaine
SP 500 what, if my chaine shall never be restord ?
SP 649 and more then so ; for he that found the chaine
SP 650 even for that Chaine shall be deprived of life
SP 837 if I can but get the Chaine againe
SP 864 but, if we can, to win the chaine she weares
SP 879 loose your money, and go without the chaine
SP 904 dasell mine eyes, or ist Lucinas chaine ?
SP 905 lay downe the chaine that thou hast stole
SP 914 wast not enough when I had lost the Chaine
SP 937 take this chaine, and give it to Perseda
SP 946 to run away with this Chaine, or deliver it
SP 950 all the while I weare this chaine
SP 1014 after we had got the chaine in mummery
SP 1016 my maister wore the chaine about his necke
SP 1018 revil'd my maister, saying he stole the chaine
SP 1023 delivered me the chaine, and bad me give it you
SP 1091 Fortune, thou madest Fernando finde the chaine
SP 1269 Perseda hath the chaine, and is like to die for sorrow
SP 1273 accursed chaine, unfortunate Perseda
SP 1274 accursed chaine, unfortunate Lucina
SP 1281 but why was I so carefull of the Chaine ?
SP 1282 but why was I so carelesse of the Chaine ?
Cor. 710 great Emperors fast bound in chaynes of brasse
SP 471 I advise you meddle with no chaines of mine

Chained.

Cor. 412 my spirite (*c.* with impatient rage)

Chair.

VPJ 71 for chaire of state, a stage of shame
ST 2728 bring a chaire and cushion for the King
SP 1669 that day, me thought, I sat in Pompeyes Chaire
Ard. 2035 place Mosbie, being a stranger, in a *c.*

Chalices.

HP 320 Pray fill with bitter wines these challices of mine

Challenge.

ST 168 to *c.* forth that Prince in single fight
SP 182 what time a daring Rutter made a *c.*
SP 699 heres none but friends ; yet let me *c.* you for
SP 1099 to see and chalenge what Lucina lost
SP 1100 and by that chalenge I abridgde his life
Ard. 938 doth *c.* nought but good deserts of me

Challenged.

SP 1071 eagles are chalenged by paltry flyes
SP 1702 that petty pigmie that chalenged me at Rhodes

Challenger.

SP 185 hit the haughtie *c.*, and strooke him dead

Chamber.

HP 1404 as if it were the *c.* of a new maryed Bride
HP 1782 arose and accompanied me unworthy to the *C.*
Jer. 492 « O, that villainy should be found in the great *C.* »
Jer. 517 O that villainy should be found in the great *c.*
STA 928 he may be in his *c.*; some go see
Ard. 238 coming into the *c.* where it hangs, may die
Ard. 887 and I am going to prepare his *c.*
Ard. 945 leads directly to my master's *c.*
Ard. 2003 this night I rose and walked about the *c.*
Ard. 2317 and look about this *c.* where we are
Puck 19 by some occasion of oʳ wrytinge in one *c.*

Chamberlain.

HP 1034 the Chamberlaine make the bedds and brush

Chambly.

Ard. 2162 a bonny northern lass, the widow *C.*
Ard. 2334 the widow *C.* in her husband's days I kept

Champ.

Cor. 1233 « the stiffneckt horses champe not on the bit

Champant.

HP 1220 the bancks to any navigable water, or in a *c.* Countrey
Cor. 1748 and of a *C.* Land makes it a Quagmire

Champion.

Jer. 69 I am wars *C.*, and my fees are swords
SP 695 to have so brave a *c.* to hir Squire

Chance.

HP 906 where if he chaunce to faile in action, co[m]lines, or
HP 1159 losses which by chaunce or Fortune may betide him
Cor. 103 as if inconstant Chaunce were alwaies one
Cor. 124 a note of Chaunce that may the proude controle
Cor. 375 flattring Chaunce, that trayn'd his first designes
Cor. 403 and bitter chaunce decreed to have me there
Cor. 538 of certaine courage gainst incertaine chaunce
Cor. 592 cut from a spring by chaunce or arte
Cor. 606 if fortune chaunce but once to check
Cor. 1074 from chaunce is nothing franchized
Cor. 1098 for what we see is done, is done by chaunce
ST 310 such is the folly of dispightfull *c.*
ST 1026 but ever subject to the wheele of *c.*
ST 1471 if you doo, I may *c.* to break your olde custome
STA 2011 one knowes not what may *c.*
ST 2554 it was my *c.* to write a Tragedie
SP 430 but how *c.* his nose is slit ?
SP 636 Fortune, that first by *c.* brought them together
SP 694 marry, thrise happy is Persedas *c.*
SP 1373 how *c.* it then, that Love and Fortunes power
SP 1949 but how *c.*, your turkish bonnet is not
Ard. 891 God's dear lady, how *c.* your face is so bloody ?
Ard. 893 go to, sirrah ; there is a *c.* in it
Ard. 1196 but see the *c.* : Franklin and my master
Ard. 1701 and then we may *c.* meet with them
Puck 76 soe maie I chaunce wᵗʰ Paul to live &

Chancery.

Ard. 469 he hath the grant under the *C.* seal

Chandlers.

Ard. 1691 a fine world for *c.*, if this weather would last

Change.

Cor. 294 so (pestilently) fraught with *c.* of plagues is
Cor. 345 the wide worlds accidents are apt to *c.*
Cor. 376 may *c.* her lookes, and give the Tyrant over
ST 1460 Ile not *c.* without boot, thats flat
SP 21 did not I *c.* long love to sudden hate

SP 33 though Fortune have delight in *c.*
SP 81 and far more welcome is this *c.* to me
SP 183 a challenge to *c.* a bullet with our swift flight shot
SP 713 say, worlds bright starre, whence springs this suddaine *c.*?
SP 789 that in thee all their influence dooth *c.*
SP 869 by game, or *c.*, by one devise or other
SP 1487 and die thou shalt, unlesse thou *c.* thy minde
Ard. 1823 happy the *c.* that alters for the best!
SP 709 what ailes you, madam, that your colour changes?

Changed.
VPJ 73 their scepter to a halter changde
HP Ind. 106 Nature chaunged by Nurses Milke
HP 895 as the Lawes and dyfferences of Nature are not chaunged
HP 1594 when mony, then, is *c.* with mony
HP 1630 coyne beeing variable and often to be changd
ST 2240 sweet boy, how art thou chang'd in deaths black shade
SP 409 but my Lucina, how she *c.* her colour
SP 860 her late unkindnes would have *c.* my minde
Ard. 655 O Will, times are *c.* : no fellows now
Ard. 1289 what, are you *c.*?
Ard. 1820 greatly *c.* from the old humour

Changing.
HP 1186 which is often *c.* and incertaine
Ard. 1310 this certain good I lost for *c.* bad

Channel-bone.
SP 424 my back bone, my channell bone, and my thigh bone

Channels.
Ard. 43 smeared in the *c.* of his lustful blood

Chanting.
ST 1614 singing sweet hymnes and *c.* heavenly notes

Chap.
Jer. 115 whose famisht jawes look like the *c.* of death

Chaplets.
SP 673 with Rosie *c.* deck thy golden tresses

Character.
SP 224 I keep no table to *c.* my fore-passed conflicts
Jer. 929 where ile set downe, in caractors on thy flesh

Charactered.
SP 375 wrinckles time has *c.* with ages print

Charge.
HP 1033 doone by him that hath another *c.*
HP 1255 shall be wholy recommended to the wyves *c.*
Cor. 114 and tyerd our neighbour Countries so with *c.*
Jer. 87 cannot effect the vertue of your *c.*
Jer. 94 farwel then, Don Andrea ; to thy chargde
Jer. 330 I had in *c.*, at my depart from Spaine
Jer. 715 others take charg of that accursed villaine
ST 197 for so I gave in *c.* at my depart
ST 390 I nill refuse this heauie dolefull *c.*
ST 440 for so the Duke, your father, gave me *c.*
ST 796 amongst the rest of what you have in *c.*
SP 807 which, as my life, I gave to thee in *c.*?
Ard. 1809 this *c.* I'll leave with my distressful wife
Ard. 2236 leave that to my *c.*, let me alone
HP 1155 of his revenewes with the issue of his charges
SP 574 I *c.* thee, say wherein ; or else
Ard. 375 I *c.* thee speak to this mistrustful man
Puck 62 as for the libel laide unto my chardg I am resolved
Cor. 1680 exhorting them to *c.*, and fight like men
Cor. 1737 doe at the halfe pyke freely *c.* each other
Cor. 1766 so did the Armies presse and *c.* each other
SP 191 what is thy noted word of *c.*, brave Turke?

Charged.
HP 93 the Cupboorde *c.* with curious plates of Candie
HP 1070 that one is too much *c.* with labor
HP 1224 he must needs be chargde w[ith] sompter men

HP 1296 such things as she *c.* to be kept
HP 1536 and the family that he is *c.* withall
Cor. 1853 and lay them levell with the *c.* earth
ST 175 our Trumpeters were chargde to sound retreat
ST 1277 that we are thus expressly chargde to watch
SP 159 where for my countries cause I chargde my Launce
Ard. 1025 so woe-begone, so inly *c.* with woe
Puck 8 wch I was undeserved chargd wthall

Chariot.
Cor. 74 the golden Sunne, where ere he drive his glittring *C.*
Cor. 1112 bravely mounted (with stearne lookes) in his *C.*
Cor. 1357 or where his *C.* staies to stop the day
Cor. 1406 and crowne thy head, and mount thy *C.*
ST 24 and slakte his smoaking charriot in her floud

Charitable.
Jer. 283 O father, tis a *c.* deed to

Charity.
HP 1078 the Charitie of Maisters and love of Servants

Charlemagne.
SP 888 I, marrie, this showes that Charleman is come

Charles.
HP 481 that time that *C.* the fift desposed his Monarchie
HP 495 *C.* the fift, that thrise renowmed Emperor

Charm.
Jer. 831 arme, on which I knit this softe and silken charme
Jer. 839 this scarfe shall be my charme gainst foes and hell
Ard. 850 but wouldst thou *c.* me to effect this deed

Charmed.
Jer. 833 prove inchaunted armour being *c.* by love

Charon.
Cor. 463 Caron takes not paine to ferry those that
Jer. 1174 come, *C.*; come, hels Sculler, waft me ore
Jer. 1177 *C.*, a bote ; *C.*, *C.*
Jer. 1178 who cals so loud on *C.*?
ST 20 but churlish *C.*, only boatman there
ST 2443 o'er-ferried Caron to the fierie lakes
Jer. 1165 by Charons boat, I will not

Chase.
HP 813 « But bigger growne, they tende the *c.* »
Ard. 1545 it was no *c.* that made me rise so early
Cor. 157 and vices needfull chace farre from our harts
Cor. 348 or like the Sunne that hath the Night in chace
Cor. 1290 did freely *c.* vile servitude

Chased.
Cor. 1162 whom when he had discomfited and chas'd

Chaste.
HP 1333 « To keep her chast, and that her children wel maintaine »
Cor. 967 nor auncient lawes, nor nuptiall chast desire
Jer. 179 be in my absence my deare selfe, chast selfe
ST 2616 Perseda, *c.* and resolute
SP 2130 Was she not *c.*? — As is Pandora or Dianaes thoughts
Ard. 2066 had *c.* Diana kissed him, she like me

Chasten.
Cor. 152 and can with reason *c.* his desire

Chastest.
Cor. 615 and *c.* Lucrece once againe (because her

Chastest-seeming.
Jer. 247 gifts and giving will melt the chastest seeming female living

Chastise.
SP 730 that I with words and stripes may chastice him
SP 2086 shall *c.* and rebuke these injuries

Chastisement.
HP Ind. 44 *c.* toward servants
HP 873 labor, victuall, and *c.*
HP 878 this latter part of *c.* might well be left

Cor. 917 oftentimes tis for our *c*. that heaven
SP 568 now for thy *c*. know, Amurath
SP 1704 I owe him *c*. in Persedas quarrel

Chastity.
HP 587 « Ere I to lose or violate my *c*. beginne »
HP 640 to woman, Modestie and Chastitie
HP 642 albeit Chastitie or Shamefastnes be not properly the
HP 649 much confirme the womans chastitie
SP 801 and for her chastitie let others judge
SP 1981 with cunning wordes tempted my chastitie ?
Ard. 38 to violate my dear wife's *c*.
Ard. 45 to ease thy grief and save her *c*.

Che.
ST 1234 *C*. le Ieron. — My Lord. — Goe, sirra, to Serberine
ST 1394 Et quel *c*. voglio io, nessun lo sa

Cheap.
HP 1243 now and then when they are better cheape
HP 1497 where they are helde deerest, and where best cheape

Cheating.
Ard. 324 a *c*. steward, and base-minded peasant ?

Check.
Cor. 606 if fortune chaunce but once to *c*.
SP 780 to *c*. thy fraudfull countenance with a blush ?
Ard. 1225 as the bitter north-east wind doth *c*. the tender
   blossoms
Ard. 1457 ay, where the gentleman did *c*. his wife

Checked.
JB 62 and with bitter speeches so taunted and checkt her

Checking.
SP 936 by *c*. his outragious insolence

Cheek.
Jer. 558 as the faire cheeke of high authority
Jer. 1158 now he would kisse my cheeke. O my pale friende
SP 436 O, touch not the cheeke of my Palphrey
Ard. 1857 when we joined armes, and when I kissed his *c*. ?
HP 658 no collour better graceth or adornes a womans cheekes
Cor. 790 thy head hung downe, thy cheeks with teares besprent
Cor. 1991 raine showres of greefe upon your Rose-like cheeks
Jer. 848 as a base blush upon your free borne cheeks
ST 2258 thy eies are gum'd with teares, thy cheekes are wan
SP 779 are there no honest drops in all thy cheekes ?
SP 1462 cheekes, where the Rose and Lillie are in combate

Cheer.
ST 510 now come and sit with us, and taste our cheere
Ard. 638 let's in and see what *c*. you keep
Ard. 1742 here's to pay for a fire and good *c*.
Ard. 1825 make no speech of the *c*. we had
Ard. 1832 for I believe she'll strive to mend our *c*.
Ard. 1963 nay, and there be such *c*., we will bid ourselves
Ard. 1 Arden, *c*. up thy spirits, and droop no more !
Ard. 715 this cheers my heart ; Master Greene, I'll leave you

Cheerful.
Cor. 631 the cheerefull Cock (the sad nights comforter)
Cor. 1679 and with a cheerefull looke surveigh'd the Campe
ST 95 but what portends thy *c*. countenance
SP 1473 then, sweeting, blesse me with a cheerefull looke
Ard. 575 'twere *c*. news to hear the churl were dead

Cheerless.
ST 442 for sollitude best fits my cheereles mood

Cheerly.
ST 119 both *c*. sounding trumpets, drums, and fifes
Ard. 586 well, seeing 'tis done, *c*. let it pass

Cheese-house.
Jer. 519 to say, knavery in the Court and honesty in a cheese house

Cheinies.
Ard. 1530 and, if all the *C*. in the world say no

Cheiny.
Ard. 678 of late Lord *C*. lost some plate
Ard. 688 now, Lord *C*. solemnly vows, if law
Ard. 713 let Lord *C*. seek Jack Fitten forth
Ard. 1525 comes my Lord *C*. to prevent his death
Ard. 1527 the Lord *C*. hath preserved him
Ard. 1547 to dine with my Lord *C*.
Ard. 1579 to the Isle of Sheppy to my Lord Cheiny's
Ard. 1713 that went to dine at my Lord Cheiny's
Ard. 1825 the cheer we had at my Lord Cheiny's

Cherish.
HP 1084 bruite beasts rejoyce to see their Maisters cheerish
   them

Cherubins.
ST 1612 backt with a troup of fiery *C*.

Chest.
Ard. 155 the which I hear the wench keeps in her *c*.

Chevalier.
ST 393 your worthy chivalier amidst the thikst

Chid.
Ard. 61 have often *c*. the morning when it 'gan to peep

Chiding.
Jer. 827 you have ore wrought the *c*. of my brest

Chidiochi.
VPJ (Title) T. K. in Cygneam Cantionem *C*. Tychborne

Chief.
HP 1028 thy cheefe care and the duetie of thy Steward shall be
HP 1514 bestoweth as his chiefe and principall care
HP 1694 my chiefe desire that thou record effectually those
ST Bal. 33 she chose my sonne for her chiefe flower
ST 131 Don Pedro, their chiefe Horsemens Corlonell
ST 711 (two chiefe contents, where more cannot be had)
SP 194 have I been chiefe commaunder of an hoast
SP 909 whose neere alye he was and cheefe delight
SP 963 and cheefe remainder of our progenie
SP 1741 the historie prooves me cheefe actor in this tragedie
Ard. 1249 *c*. actors to Arden's overthrow

Chiefest. '
HP 388 one of the cheefest cares the Housekeeper should have
ST Bal. 32 because he slewe her *c*. friend
ST Bal. 70 that so had spoyl'd my *c*. good
ST 2390 who at the marriage was the cheefest guest
SP 28 whose cheefest actor was my sable dart
SP 485 in dalying war, I lost my *c*. peace
SP 676 a blisful war with me, thy *c*. friend ?

Chiefly.
HP 417 ought chiefly to be taken according to
HP 420 chiefely depende upon the motion of the Sunne
HP 668 those things chiefely which appertaine to women
HP 792 is chieflie knowne and commended by the
Cor. Ded. 5 but chiefely, that I would attempt the dedication of
ST 415 no, that was it for which I cheefly strove
ST 733 but whereon doost thou *c*. meditate ?
Ard. 580 *c*. in case of murder, why, 'tis the way to
Ard. 644 a knave *c*. for bearing the other company
Ard. 1340 and thereon will I *c*. meditate

Chieftain.
SP 2021 hath beleagred Rhodes, whose chieftaine is a woman

Child.
HP 791 so that who so denieth the nursing of her *c*.
HP 801 the complexion of the *c*. becommeth strong and lustie
HP 1432 nourishment, which the Mother giveth to her Childe
HP 1674 arte depending upon Nature, shee is as it were her
   Chylde
Cor. 1175 (deere Brutus) thinke you Caesar such a chyld
ST Bal. 19 Horatio, my sweet onely childe

SP 275 a *c.* whose chin beares no impression of manhood
SP 342 to be dismounted by a Childe it vexeth me
JB 68 had lien with her and gotten her with *c.*
JB 125 and she and the childe fell also to eating of theirs
JB 132 she answered « 1 » ; so likewise said the childe
JB 161 she was knowne with *c.*, and safely delivered
JB 163 but that *c.* lived not long, but dyed
JB 181 at length he got her with *c.* againe
JB 217 into the countrey to be delivered of her childe
HP 209 heaven hath not graunted me a maiden *C.*

Child-bearing.
HP 601 a woman is more apt to *c.* in youth

Childhood.
SP 1547 even from my *c.* have I tendered thee

Childish.
STA 1945 growes lunaticke and *c.* for his Sonne

Childishness.
Ard. 439 'tis *c.* to stand upon an oath

Children.
HP Ind. 30 customs in bringing up of *C.*
HP Ind. 33 care of *C.*, how it is to bee
HP Ind. 61 education of *C.* as well appertaines to
HP Ind. 63 education of *C.*, and what it ought to be
HP Ind. 97 love of *C.*
HP Ind. 104 mothers ought to give their owne *C.* sucke
HP Ind. 105 mothers ought not to bee too tender to their *c.*
HP 216 getting *C.* before themselves were come unto their
HP 219 exceede their *c.* alwaies eyght and twenty or
HP 223 yet by example of their *c.* they might moderate
HP 225 used to them by their *C.* as is due to Parents
HP 231 their due, and nature bindeth *c.* unto
HP 233 by nature Chyldren are the fortresse and defences of
HP 779 now proceeding to the education of *C.*
HP 782 ought not to deny her milke to her owne *C.*
HP 793 commended by the bringing of her *c.* up
HP 804 to wash their newe borne *C.* in the Rivers
HP 817 if it shall please God to give thee *C.*
HP 844 bring up thy *C.* as they may become good
HP 848 neither shall thy *C.* be unfurnished of
HP 854 this part of education and bringing up of *C.*
HP 857 howe he is to educate and bring up his *C.*
HP 952 and may become discipline, as is that of *C.*
HP 955 considering it is no lesse needeful for them then *C.*
HP 1333 « and that her *c.* wel maintaine she mighte »
HP 1359 who beeing a fortunat mother of *C.*
HP 1509 forgets his house, his *C.*, and his Wife
HP 1562 devided and bequeathed amongst his *C.*
HP 1690 how to the *c.*, how to the servaunts
Cor. 1082 thy chyldren gainst thy *c.* thou hast arm'd
Cor. 1144 our Countries love then friends or chyldren are
Cor. 1305 raysing treasons in their Realmes by their chyldren
ST 2494 unhappy Mothers of such *c.* then
ST 2909 why hast thou butchered both my *c.* thus ?
SP 86 as doth the mother keepe her *c.* from
Ard. 222 bags of gold to make our *c.* rich
Ard. 1773 yet it will help my wife and *c.*
Ard. 1810 my *c.* shall be taught such prayers as these
SP 228 to put the men *c.* of that climate to the sword

Chill.
ST 879 and *c.* my throbbing hart with trembling feare

Chill-cold.
Cor. 729 a trembling horror, a chyl-cold shyvering

Chimaera's.
ST 3044 hang Balthazar about Chimeras neck

Chimney.
Ard. 1653 skull were opened to make more *c.* room

Chin.
SP 276 a child whose *c.* beares no impression of manhood
Ard. 693 his *c.* was bare

Chink.
Jer. 231 for gold and chinck makes the punck wanton

Chiomato.
HP 706 Non tosato o *c.*

Chiron.
Cor. 1371 nor hath Chyron powre or skill to recure them

Chisel.
HP 1332 in graving or cutting the Chizzel should not be so

Chivalry.
ST 112 we may reward thy blissfull chivalrie
ST 285 whome I admire and love for chivalrie
SP 264 myselfe will censure of your chivalrie
SP 767 thy name was conquerour, not my chivalrie
SP 1087 a disgrace to all my chivalrie to combate one so base
SP 1177 the flower of chivalrie and curtesie

Choice.
HP 450 who made choyse to die in Jerusalem
HP 616 made his choyse of a companion that shold helpe
HP 1081 and nourished with more choise and daintie meate
HP 1301 I speake of choyse wynes which get strength with age
Cor. 157 in vertues choyse, and vices needfull chace
Cor. 454 and choyce of streames the greatest River dryes
Jer. 320 welcom, worthy lord, Spaines choyse embassador
SP 187 and Jaques, Jaques, is the Spaniards choise
JB 65 hatred in her heart against her new made choyce

Choir.
ST 723 and, sitting safe, to sing in Cupids Quire

Choke.
Jer. 305 could *c.* bright honor in a skabard grave ?
Jer. 851 turne into chafe, and *c.* their insolence
Cor. 218 dyes, and choakes the good, which els we had enjoy'd

Choked.
Cor. 1735 and with a duskish yellow chokt the heavens
Cor. 1857 to see the passage choakt with bodies of the dead
ST 67 where usurers are choakt with melting golde
ST 1520 let not the earth be *c.* or infect with

Choler.
Cor. 1549 and to choller doth convart purest blood about the heart
Cor. 1555 and their choller then is rais'd, when
SP 250 rough wordes blowe my choller
SP 289 this fierie humor of choller is supprest by
Ard. 563 whenas I saw his *c.* thus to rise
Ard. 951 come, let's go drink : *c.* makes me as dry as a dog
Ard. 1208 your excuse hath somewhat mollifled my *c.*

Choose.
HP 600 to *c.* his wife rather yong then olde
Cor. 5 at least to chuse those forth that are in fault
Cor. 356 the sweetest season that the wise can chuse
Cor. 1123 and rather chuse (unarm'd) to serve with shame
Jer. 61 Ide rather *c.* Horatio were he not so young
Jer. 502 « not be murdred, and you can *c.* »
Jer. 522 « and you can *c.*, especially being warnd
Jer. 1125 Ile *c.* my Sister out her second love
ST 1405 I cannot *c.* but smile to thinke how
Ard. 332 I could not *c.*, her beauty fired my heart !

Choosing.
HP 526 care in *c.* of his wife

Chops.
Ard. 1514 his lordship *c.* me in, even when my

Chords.
ST 2268 talke not of cords, but let us now be gone, for with a cord

Chorus.

ST 91 and serve for *C.* in this Tragedie
SP 17 to serve for *C.* to this Tragedie
SP 24 Fortune is *c.* ; Love and Death be gone
SP 30 till in the *c.* place I make it knowne

Chose.
Jer. 67 I should have chose[n] Don Lorenzo
ST Bal. 33 she *c.* my sonne for her chiefe flower

Chosen.
HP Ind. 143 women, how to be *c.* in wedlock
Jer. 67 I should have chose[n] Don Lorenzo
SP 1617 in two extreames the least is to be *c.*

Christ.
SP 1131 and had he worshipt Mahomet for *C.*
SP 1346 and Guelpio, rather then denie his *C.*
SP 1507 O *C.*, receive my soule
SP 1508 harke, Brusor, she cals on *C.*
Ard. 2390 and let me meditate upon my saviour *C.*
Ard. 1775 needy and bare : for Christ's sake, let them have it !

Christendom.
SP 142 brave Knights of Christendome, and Turkish both
SP 352 take the braginst knave in *C.* with thee
SP 517 from the other skirts of Christendome call home
SP 522 till it have prickt the hart of Christendome
SP 1343 the Turkish armies did [oer-throw] in Christendome
SP 2078 thou hast betrayde the flower of Christendome
Ard. 229 the only cunning man of *C.*
Ard. 1812 it is the railingest knave in *C.*

Christian.
ST 2758 in reserving this faire *C.* Nimph
SP 1163 his habite argues him a *C.*
SP 1164 I, worthy Lord, a forlorne *C.*
SP 1205 I may have libertie to live a *C.*
SP 1445 but what two *C.* Virgins have we here ?
SP 1522 then let me live a *C.* Virgin still
SP 1716 I feare thou wilt never proove good *c.*
SP 1951 because I now am *C.* againe
SP 1957 to follow her, am now returnd a *C.*
SP 2061 and heere I promise thee on my *C.* faith
HP 404 Doctors of the Hebrues, and Christians of great account
SP 202 and made some Christians kneele to Mahomet
SP 508 how he hath borne him gainst the Christians
SP 1146 how did the Christians use our Knights ?
SP 1167 for, though you Christians account our Turkish race
SP 1649 alas, the Christians are but very shallow in

Christophil.
ST 1640 heere, take my Ring, and give it Christophill

Chronicles.
ST Bal. 121 from the *C.* of Spaine I did record Erastus life
ST 2584 the *C.* of Spaine record this

Church.
HP 349 under the shade of a Tree, or shroude of a *C.*
SP 54 when didst thou goe to *C.* on hollidaies
SP 1655 and in procession bare me to the *C.*
SP 1662 amidst their *C.* they bound me to a piller
Ard. 436 and given my hand unto him in the *c.* !
Ard. 1257 and holy *C.* rites makes us two but one

Church-yard.
Puck 40 Royden and some stationers in Paules churchyard

Churl.
Ard. 489 can the crabbed *c.* use you unkindly ?
Ard. 510 he looks so smoothly. Now, fie upon him, *c.* !
Ard. 514 and if the *c.* deny my interest
Ard. 521 indanger not yourself for such a *c.*
Ard. 560 and swore he would cry quittance with the *c.*
Ard. 568 by some device to make away the *c.*
Ard. 575 'twere cheerful news to hear the *c.* were dead

Churlish.
ST 20 but *c.* Charon, only boatman there

Churlishly.
JB 191 was nothing moved therewith, but *c.* answered

Chyro.
HP 837 or as Achylles of *C.* was

Cicero.
HP 965 commended so by *C.* in his Oration pro Milone
HP 1125 little things whereof *C.* was rather a dysprayser

Cinders.
Cor. 884 O sweet, deere, deplorable cynders
Cor. 2031 may trickling bathe your generous sweet cynders

Cinerem.
HP 1325 Impositum, *c.* et sopitos suscitat ignes

Cinna.
Cor. 360 against poore Sylla proud Cynna, Marius, and Carbo
Cor. 1161 against both Cynnas host and Marius

Circes.
HP Ind. 20 *C.* given to weaving
HP 1344 *C.*, which was not onely a woman and a Queene but a Goddesse
HP 1349 brought Penelope and *C.* in the number of
SP 817 what are thy teares but *C.* magike seas

Circle.
Jer. 198 and, madam, in this *c.* let your hart move
Jer. 1132 point at the rich *c.* of thy labouring hart
Jer. 84 your highnes cirkels me with honors boundes

Circumcised.
SP 1350 he shall be *c.* and have his rites
SP 1940 I am deceived but you were *c.*

Circumspect.
Ard. 2256 well, it behoves us to be *c.*

Circumstance.
ST 386 relate the *c.* of Don Andreas death
ST 1177 I therefore will by circumstances trie

'Cited.
ST 2701 hath scited me to heare Horatio plead with

Citeth.
HP 1643 cyteth a sentence put by Aristotle in

Cities.
HP 630 as we see the Cittizens in wel governed Citties obey
HP 633 as the orders of the Cittizens within their Citties
HP 833 they of some Cities in Lombardy are like
HP 1624 obtained in many famous Citties
Cor. 488 those great Citties, whose foundations reacht
Cor. 587 so peopled citties, that of yore were desert fields
Cor. 1331 the worthiest Citties of the conquered world

Citizen.
HP 1475 in other places where hee argueth like a Cittizen
HP 1547 and is not necessary or fitting for a Cittizen
HP 1554 so a Cittizen of any Cittie whatsoever
HP 1556 is no more a Cittizen, be hee what or who he will
Cor. 1537 a Cittizen so wrong'd of the honor him belong'd
HP 630 as we see the Cittizens in wel governed Citties obey
HP 633 as the orders of the Cittizens within their Citties
Cor. 372 growne great without the strife of Cittizens
Cor. 1108 Lybian Beares devoure the bodies of our Cittizens
Cor. 1414 I joy not in the death of Cittizens
Cor. 1458 if Cittizens my kindnes haue forgot
SP 1323 drum, sound a parle to the Citizens
Cor. 1289 that from their fellow cittizens did

Citrons.
HP 137 with fruits, as Mellons, Cytrons, and such like

City.
HP 20 the River that runneth before the Cittie
HP 48 Naples, a famous Cittie of Italie

HP 49 Bergamo, a Cittye situate in Lombardy
HP 100 to imitate the delicacy and neatness of the Cittie
HP 102 neither denie I him to be a Gentleman of the Cittie
HP 159 no neede to send for necessaries to the Cittie
HP 161 that I send to the Cittie for any thing necessarie
HP 844 good members of the Cittie where thy selfe inhabitest
HP 970 are not capable of any office within the Cittie
HP 1214 neere or far fro[m] any Cittie
HP 1222 transported easily in Carres or other carriages unto the Cittie
HP 1236 for the use of his house in the Cittie
HP 1500 the league and traffique that one Cittie hath with another
HP 1539 the Citty wher he liveth and inhabiteth
HP 1543 for a Prince or Ruler within the Cittie of Rome
HP 1554 so a Cittizen of any Cittie whatsoever
HP 1759ª Reggio a Cittie in Lomberdy
HP 1760ª Modone a Cittie in Greece
HP 1760ª Modona a Cittie in Italie
Cor. 146 against this Citty, ritch of violence?
Cor. 377 leaving our Cittie, where so long agoe Heavens did
Cor. 599 even so our cittie (in her prime
Cor. 1204 and hazarded our Cittie and our selves
Cor. 1384 yea, even this Cittie, that hath almost made an
Cor. 1641 marcht on the suddaine to the self-same Cittie
Cor. 1962 was never Citty where calamitie hath
SP 248 the ransome of a conquered citie
SP 982 thou knowest me for the Governour of the cittie
HP 857 that the Citties discipline may conforme and
Cor. 2 great Jupiter, our Citties sole Protector
Cor. 111 (exasperate at our up-rising) sought our Cities fall

Civet.
SP 362 he weres C., and, when it was askt him where

Civil.
HP Ind. 47 civill warres begun by Servants
HP 958 in the perill of some civill broyle or other troubles
HP 974 conflict amongst the Romains which they called Cyvill warre
HP 1108 some stretch further and extend to c. administration
HP 1111 who in theyr civill government doth seme
HP 1591 in our privat or c. life
HP 1751 Kingly, Lordly, Civill and Private
HP 1760 how the government of a civill and a
HP 1762 unlesse he call his government Civill that
HP 1768 those civill Governours or officers that
Cor. Arg. 6 upon the first fiers of the civill warres
Cor. 50 and civill furie, fiercer then thine hosts
Cor. 274 and doe with civill discord (furthering it)
Cor. 1135 or if (these civill discords now dissolv'd)
Cor. 1156 when he hath rooted civill warre from Rome
Cor. 1217 a fore-game fecht about for civill discord
Cor. 1501 free fro rage of civill strife
Ard. 509 who would have thought the c. sir so sullen?

Civilis.
HP 1752 Regia, Satrapicia, C. and privata

Civilly.
HP 629 but c. and in such sort as we see
HP 1562 to live well and c. with all

Clad.
Cor. 1705 me thinks I see poore Rome in horror c.
Jer. 625 at which I thundered words all c. in profe

Clamorous.
Ard. 1780 if with thy c. impeaching tongue

Clamours.
ST 120 both raising dreadfull clamors to the skie
ST 397 their harts were great, their c. menacing

Clang.
Cor. 1725 and every Eccho tooke the Trompets clange
HP 830 Where trumpets eccho clangs to those that of the custome skyll

Clap.
Jer. 602 c. a silver tongue within this pallat
ST 1665 and c. me up where none might come at me
Cor. 1659 and quickly claps his rustie Armour on

Claret-wine.
HP 332 I pledged him of a Cup of neate C. wine

Clarke.
Ard. 247 how! C.!
Ard. 262 C., here's my hand: my sister shall be thine
Ard. 287 as I am a gentlewoman, C., next day
Ard. 289 I'll make her dowry more than I'll talk of, C.
Ard. 421 but what a villain is that painter C.!
Ard. 542 will she have my neighbour C., or no?
Ard. 545 go to her, C.; she's all alone within
Ard. 592 how now, C.? have you found me false?
Ard. 601 what, sister, is it C. must be the man?
Ard. 605 ah, Master C., it resteth at my grant
Ard. 622 why, C., is it possible that you
Ard. 626 well questioned, Alice; C., how answer you that?
Ard. 1617 say, C., hast thou done the thing

Clashed.
Jer. 954 I long to heare the musick of c. swords

Clattering.
Cor. 1723 the clattring Armour, buskling as they paced

Clean.
HP Ind. 93 instruments of housholde to be kept cleane
HP 1044 maie bee pollished and kept so cleane
HP 1052 scowring and keeping cleane those tooles and instruments
HP 1093 serves to feede, apparrell, and keepe cleane the rest
Jer. 641 like a court hound that liks fat trenchers cleane
Ard. 844 I pray thee, Will, make c. thy bloody brow
Ard. 546 Michael my man is c. out of her books

Cleaner.
Jer. 456 no, Father, c. then Lorenzoes soule

Cleanliness.
HP Ind. 42 clenlines in housekeeping
HP 1045 cleanlines is not onelie pleasing or delightfull to beholde
HP 1049 cleanlines increaseth and preserveth the health
HP 1396 yet for the order and clenlines it deserves so much

Cleanly.
ST 1384 but, Sirra, see that this be cleanely done
Ard. 1262 and I will c. rid my hands of her

Cleanse.
HP 1036 the Horsekeeper rubbe the horses and clense the stable

Clear.
Cor. 622 that earst was cleere as heavens Queene
Cor. 1516 from our walls all woes to cleere
ST 235 these punishments may cleare his late offence
ST 2368 and cleare them up with those thy sunne bright eyes
SP 501 my innocence shall c. my negligence
Ard. 1353 be c. again, I'll ne'er more trouble thee
Ard. 1366 and c. a trespass with your sweet-set tongue!
Ard. 1470 then hemmed she out, to c. her voice should seem
Ard. 2276 my house is c., and now I fear them not
Puck 35 to cleere my self of being thought an Atheist

Cleared.
Cor. 1770 thryce did the Cornets of the souldiers (cleerd) turne to
Ard. 1726 see how the sun hath c. the foggy mist

Cleave.
Cor. 1745 they hewe their Armour, and they c. their casks

Cor. 1805 c., breake, and raging tempest-like o're turne
ST 576 in time small wedges c. the hardest Oake
Ard. 771 will c. as fast to your love as a plaster of pitch to
Ard. 2274 but c. to us as we will stick to you

Cleaveth.
Ard. 864 seest thou this gore that c. to my face?
Ard. 2173 the blood c. to the ground and will not out

Cleft.
Jer. 1057 else his unpitying sword had c. my hart

Clemency.
SP 1330 what, wilt thou yeeld, and trie our clemencie?

Cleopatra's.
SP 891 I, were it Cleopatraes union

Clerk.
HP 1112 mannedge some of their affaires, and him they call
    theyr Clerke
Ard. 1931 I made no more ado, but went to the c.
HP Ind. 25 Clerkes or Secretaries, who and what they ought to be

Clients.
SP 456 as the Lawyers use their rich Clyents, when

Clifford.
Ard. 32 yes, the Lord C., he that loves not me

Cliffs.
ST 1812 whose rockie cliffes when you have once behelde

Climate.
SP 229 to put the men children of that c. to the sword

Climbed.
Ard. 1234 but since I c. the top-bough of the tree

Cling.
Jer. 670 Andrea slaine? then, weapon, clyng my brest

Clippings.
HP 743 those prophane and superstitious cleppings

Cloak.
Cor. 888 under cloake of love did entertaine him
SP 1311 and cloake affection with hir modestie
Ard. 700 a livery c., but all the lace was off

Cloaked.
ST 2118 which under kindeship wilbe cloked best

Clock.
STA 2078 the Minutes jerring, and the Clocke striking twelve

Cloistered.
Cor. 759 that wont to haunt and trace by cloistred tombes

Close.
Cor. 703 gan c. the windowes of my watchfull eyes
ST 979 and ile c. up the glasses of his sight
SP 1195 perceive that any of their broode but c. their sight
Ard. 629 I fasten on my spectacles so c.
Ard. 2002 his sight, shall never c. till Arden's be shut up
ST 1180 harkening neere the Duke of Castiles house, c.
ST 1281 content your selfe, stand c., theres somewhat in 't
ST 1286 me thinks this corner is to c. with one
Ard. 797 stand c., and take you fittest standing
Ard. 1478 stand c., Will, I hear them coming
Ard. 1642 i' the broom, c. watching Arden's coming
Ard. 1782 I'll lay thee up so c. a twelve-month's day
Ard. 2186 keep thou it c., and 'tis unpossible
JB 226 for be it kept never so c., and done never so secret
Ard. 1581 in the broom c., too c. for you

Closed.
Cor. 877 and sadly cloz'd within an earthen Urne the
SP 339 and my Beaver closd for this encounter
Ard. 2060 I shall no more be c. in Arden's arms

Closely.
ST 1369 thou knowest the prison, c. give it him
ST 1568 so c. smootherd, and so long conceald
ST 2120 c. and safely fitting things to time

Closer.
Jer. 527 put his legs c., though it be painefull

Closet.
Jer. 422 this suit within my c. shall you weare
Ard. 192 remember, when I locked thee in my c.
Ard. 924 whose edge must search the c. of his breast

Closeth.
Cor. Arg. 38 c. the Catastrophe of this theyr Tragedie

Closure.
SP 752 and I must die by c. of my wound

Cloth.
Ard. 154 with a verse or two stolen from a painted c.
Ard. 239 ay, but we'll have it covered with a c.

Clothed.
ST 2470 c. in Sable and a Saffron robe

Clothes.
STA 937 I wonder how this fellow got his c.

Cloud.
HP 758 Lay doun with him upo[n] the grasse al covered with a
    clowde
HP 764 a Clowde shoulde bee sent to hide her
Cor. 575 no clowde but will be over-cast
Cor. 1728 where-with the dust, as with a darksome clowde
STA 2978 rowle all the world within thy pitchie c.
HP 6 environed on every side with clowdes ready to raine
Cor. 293 clowdes of adversitie will cover you
Cor. 347 but (like the Clowdes) continuallie doth range
Cor. 1721 whose swift shrill noyse did pierce into the clowdes
Cor. 1733 with pale, wanne clowdes discoloured the Sunne
Cor. 1994 sighes thicken the passage of the purest clowdes
Jer. 153 when two vext Clouds justle they strike out fire
ST 489 these clouds will overblow with litle winde
STA 2075 let the Clowdes scowle, make the Moone darke
ST 2367 disperce those cloudes and melanchollie lookes
Ard. 1235 and sought to build my nest among the clouds
Ard. 1539 have by their toil removed the darksome clouds
ST 816 to over-c. the brightnes of the Sunne

Cloud-compacted.
SP 748 ah, that my moyst and cloud compacted braine

Clouding.
SP 504 within forst furrowes of her clowding brow

Cloudy.
HP 360 and being short, colde, and cloudie it
ST 1148 the cloudie day my discontents records
Ard. 1082 and with the black fold of her c. robe

Cloven.
Cor. 1827 some should you see that had theyr heads halfe c.

Clowns.
HP 1063 weapo[n]s wherwithal the sturdy clownes ca[n] work
Cor. 475 both Clownes and Kings one self-same course must run
Cor. 1032 to Kings and Clownes doth equall ill

Club-man.
SP 2004 Hercules, the onely Club man of his time? dead

Clytie.
Cor. 634 while Clitie takes her progresse to the East

Coals.
Ard. 333 but time hath quenched these over-raging c.

Coarse.
Cor. 713 casting a thyn course lynsel ore hys shoulders

Coast.
Ard. 910 was never fostered in the c. of Kent
Cor. 330 doe c. the Earth with an eternall course
ST 1044 that howerly coastes the center of the earth
SP 199 along the coasts held by the Portingiuze
Cor. 1274 and fearles scowres in danger's coasts
Cor. 1399 upon the Coastes of Lybia, till he lost his

Cor. 1867 and casts him up neere to the Coasts of Hyppon
Coasting.
Cor. 1680 c. along and following by the foote
Coat.
HP 828 Your cote hath mittins, and your high Priests hats are
Jer. 1063 art thou true valliant? hast thou no cote of proofe
SP 768 thy lookes did arme me, not my coate of steele
JB 107 rising up from the fire her c. cast downe that
Cor. 1577 whose coates of steele base Death hath stolne into
SP 1714 O wicked turne c., that would have her stay
Cock.
Cor. 631 the cheerefull C. (the sad nights comforter)
SP 332 by C. and Pie, and Mouse foot, the
Cor. 1087 lyke cocks of Hay when July sheares the field
Cockatrice.
SP 821 what are thy lookes but like the C.
Cockshut.
Ard. 1126 nor prosper in the twilight, c. light
Cocytus.
Cor. 1469 can I too-soone goe taste C. flood?
Coelum.
SP 1708 O c., O terra, O maria, Neptune
Coffers.
HP 1041 in the house, Cortes, Tables, or C.
Coffin.
Cor. 873 I woave a Coffyn for his corse of Seggs
Coil.
ST 2139 how now, what noise? what coile is that you keepe?
Ard. 1389 zounds, here's a c.!
Coin.
HP 1626 transporting and conveighing Coyne from place to
  place
Jer. 33 tribute in words, my leedge, but not in coine
Jer. 36 tis not at his coine, but his slack homage
Jer. 93 let them keep coine, pay tribute with their blood
Jer. 141 forbeare a little coine, the Indies being so neere
ST 623 not with faire words, but store of golden coyne
ST 1253 they that for coine their soules endangered
ST 1254 to save my life, for coine shall venture theirs
SP 1831 a huge heape of our imperiall coyne
Coined.
HP 1183 that which is accounted (as gold or silver coyned)
Cold.
HP 304 that growe in colde Countries where
HP 343 and the Winter with extreame colde
HP 359 and being short, colde, and cloudie it
HP 799 in naturall heate, he accustome them to c.
HP 801a Antiperistasis, where heate expels c., or c. expulseth
  heate
HP 801a applied to well water, which is therefore c. in winter
HP 801a because, the hygh parts of the ayre being c.
HP 805 to indurat and harden them against the c.
HP 812 Like us to be inurd to c., and plundge them in the
  spring
HP 1257 some would be kept moyst and c., and some dry
Cor. 1646 that come to forrage when the c. begins
Jer. 268 to newe, before the first are thorougly c.
STA 967 drop all your stinges at once in my c. bosome
SP 1264 colde and comfortles for you
Ard. 361 husband, sit down; your breakfast will be c.
Ard. 1078 ay, by my faith; the air is very c.
JB 97 if he would have that colde morning a measse of
Cor. 410 my frightfull hart (stund in my stone-c. breast)
Cor. 729 a trembling horror, a chyl-c. shyvering
Collatine.
HP 1356 in this kinde of work was Lucretia often found, by

Collatyn
Collar.
Jer. 886 my hose will scarse make thee a standing coller
Collect.
HP 1779 c. enough, part out of Aristotles Bookes and
Collection.
HP 1608 Formall number is a c. of a summe, not applied to
HP 1609 Materiall number is a summarie c. of things numbred
Colligatum.
SP 1954 Quod eo modo c. est
Collop.
SP 1664 they lopt a c. of my tendrest member
Colo.
HP 1324 Qui tolerare c. vitam tenuique Minerva
Colonel.
ST 131 Don Pedro, their chiefe Horsemens Corlonell
Colour.
HP Ind. 19 colour of Wine, and what it ought to be
HP Ind. 82 grapes growing in Greece, of what colloour
HP 297 are white of colour, as are the Malmeseys
HP 329 hath yet a vermillion couller
HP 657 that no colloour better graceth or adornes
STA 2066 and let their beardes be of Judas his owne colloour
SP 409 but my Lucina, how she changed her c.
SP 709 what ailes you, madam, that your c. changes?
HP 692 embroidered the Peacocks taile with more variety of
  colloours
Jer. 420 I have a suit just of Andreas cullers
ST 118 both vaunting sundry colours of device
STA 2050 paint me [for] my Gallirie in your oile colours matted
SP 705 love makes him blinde, and blinde can judge no coulours
Ard. 597 the painter lays his colours to the life
Ard. 624 the colours being baleful and impoisoned
ST 354 counterfeits under the c. of a duteous friend
SP 1625 under couler of great consequence
Jer. 936 and to this crimson end our Coullers spred
ST 233 his colours ceaz'd, a blot unto his name
Coloured.
HP 665 to recover it with slime or artificiall coullered trash
ST 1041 that fained love had c. in his lookes
SP 360 he weares a c. lath in his scabberd
HP 301 white, or rather, gold-c.
ST 2242 suffered thy faire crimson c. spring with
SP 2006 that abraham-c. Troian? dead
Colt.
SP 434 why, then, thy Horse hath bin a C. in his time
STA 1761 a young Bacon, or a fine little smooth Horse-c.
Coltstaff.
Ard. 1934 and carried him about the fields on a c.
Combat.
ST 2410 graunt me the c. of them, if they dare
ST 2441 to combate, Acheron and Erebus
SP 89 and, when long c. makes my body faint
SP 243 endured some three or foure howers c.
SP 1462 cheekes, where the Rose and Lillie are in combate
SP 2056 and one that dares thee to the single combate
Cor. 87 can make no shift to c. with the Sea
ST 851 that it may combate with my ruder hand
ST 853 but first my lookes shall c. against thine
SP 1044 I seeke Erastus, and will c. him
SP 1050 I am in honor bound to c. him
SP 1078 with my single fist Ile c. thee
SP 1088 a disgrace to all my chivalrie to combate one so base
SP 1089 Ile send some Crane to combate with the Pigmew
SP 1703 whom I refused to c. for his minoritie?
SP 2059 then I will combate thee, what ere thou art

SP 2060 and in Erastus name ile *c.* thee
SP 2084 which to approove, Ile come to combate thee
Cor. 188 the former petty combats did displace

Combatants.

Jer. 888 Spanish *c.*, what, do you set
SP 101 each one of these approoved *c.*

Combated.

SP 172 I *c.* a Romane much renownd

Combating.

Cor. 1103 Juba and Petreus, fiercely combatting, have
Cor. 1662 and (combatting) had powre and wit to make

Combined.

ST Bal. 48 sayd with Horatio shee's combinde
SP 684 so both our hearts are still combind in one

Come.

HP 217 before themselves were *c.* unto their groweth
HP 236 have arived and *c.* unto their age
HP 459 of whom the crye is *c.* into our Countrey
HP 493 whose dignity doth *c.* so neere the Angels
HP 868 that we *c.* to the consideration of
HP 1140 I thinke it requisite to *c.* to that which
HP 1234 but to *c.* somewhat more perticulerly to the
HP 1276 there can not *c.* sufficient store of meate from
HP 1363 and *c.* into comparison with her good man
HP 1771 but for it may percase *c.* so to passe that
Cor. 20 yea, *c.* they are, and, fiery as before
Cor. 46 that we will *c.* thy borders to besiege
Cor. 338 will that day never *c.* that
Cor. 737 *c.* visite thee in the Elisian shades?
Cor. 931 and then *c.*, Murder; then *c.*, uglie Death
Cor. 1405 *c.* on, brave Caesar, and crowne thy head
Cor. 1506 thou of whom the Eneades are *c.*
Cor. 1646 that *c.* to forrage when the cold begins
Cor. 1682 for now (quoth he) is *c.* that happie day
Cor. 1830 to *c.* upon them with a fresh alarme
Cor. 1914 *c.*, wrathfull Furies, with your Ebon locks
Jer. 5 *c.* hether, boy Horatio; fould thy joynts
Jer. 201 *c.*, my soules spaniell, my lifes jetty substance
Jer. 271 *c.* then, how ere it hap, Andrea shall be crost
Jer. 274 *c.* hether, boy Horatio, didst thou here them?
Jer. 404 *c.*, son, *c.*, Lords
Jer. 442 *c.*, let us in; the next time you shall show
Jer. 444 *c.*, pull the table this way; so, tis well
Jer. 445 *c.*, write, Horatio, write
Jer. 483 *c.*, read then
Jer. 596 make it confused ere it *c.* to head
Jer. 630 tis all about the Court Andreas *c.*
Jer. 844 *c.*, valliant sperits, you Peeres of Portugale
Jer. 874 what, are you braving us before we *c.*?
Jer. 947 if brother-hood by strokes *c.* dewe
Jer. 968 *c.*, valliant sperits of Spaine
Jer. 976 *c.*, *c.*, I am wars tuter; strike a larum, drum
Jer. 1004 *c.*, meete me, Sir
Jer. 1039 but now (I am sorry, Prince) you *c.* to late
Jer. 1042 *c.*, *c.* lets see which of our strengths is stronger
Jer. 1059 *c.*, happy mortall, let me ranke by thee
Jer. 1066 *c.* lets meete, lets meete
Jer. 1126 *c.*, noble rib of honor, valliant carcasse
Jer. 1138 *c.* then, my friend, in purple I will
Jer. 1174 *c.*, Charon; *c.* hels Sculler, waft me ore
ST Bal. 43 who being *c.* into his sight, he
ST Bal. 78 my griefes are *c.*, my Joyes are gone
ST 177 and for some argument of more to *c.*
ST 195 *c.* marching on towards your royall seate
ST 462 but heere the Prince is *c.* to visite you
ST 510 now *c.* and sit with us, and taste our cheere

ST 563 *c.* we for this from depth of under ground
ST 814 if she give back, all this will *c.* to naught
ST 818 *c.*, Bel-imperia, let us to the bower
ST 877 *c.*, stop her mouth; away with her
STA 940 and bid my sonne Horatio to *c.* home
STA 943 *c.* hither; knowest thou who this is?
ST 994 *c.*, Isabell, now let us take him up
ST 1098 *c.*, my Lord, unbinde him
ST 1129 *c.*, Alexandro, keepe us companie
ST 1208 *c.* hither, Pedringano, seest thou this?
ST 1300 *c.* sir, you had bene better kept your bed
ST 1302 *c.* to the Marshals with the murderer
ST 1419 that I may *c.* (by justice of the heavens)
ST 1428 but *c.*, for that we came for: lets begin
ST 1431 gramercy, boy, but it was time to *c.*
ST 1436 *c.*, *c.*, *c.* on, when shall we to this geere?
ST 1434 *c.* on, sir, are you ready?
ST 1462 *c.*, sir
ST 1468 *c.*, are you ready? I pray, sir, dispatch
ST 1506 O sacred heavens, may it *c.* to passe
ST 1634 *c.*, Madam Bel-imperia, this may not be
ST 1665 and clap me up where none might *c.* at me
ST 1677 resolv'd to *c.* conferre with olde Hieronimo
ST 1826 *c.*, lets away to seek my Lord the Duke
ST 1827 now, Sir, perhaps I *c.* and see the King
ST 1869 in person, therefore, will he *c.* himselfe
STA 2009 bid him *c.* in, and paint some comfort
STA 2011 let him *c.* in
STA 2039 *c.*, let's talke wisely now
ST 2149 *c.* neere, you men, that thus importune me
ST 2153 *C.* on, sirs, whats the matter? — Sir, an Action
ST 2163 *c.* hether, father, let me know thy cause
ST 2211 *c.* on, olde Father, be my Orpheus
ST 2227 and art thou *c.*, Horatio, from the deapth
ST 2264 *c.* in, old man, thou shalt to Izabell
ST 2279 tis not unknowne to us, for why you *c.*
ST 2292 renowmed King, I *c.* not as thou thinkst
ST 2296 I *c.* to solemnize the marriage
ST 2305 *c.*, worthy Vice-roy, and accompany thy friend
ST 2364 *c.*, Bel-imperia, Balthazars content
ST 2434 *c.* on, Hieronimo, at my request
ST 2772 but let my friend, the Rhodian Knight, *c.* foorth
STA 2937 nay, then I care not; *c.*, and we shall be friends
STA 2968 hee might a *c.* to weare the crowne of Spaine
SP 16 and therefore *c.* I now as fittest person to
SP 103 are hither *c.* to try their force in armes
SP 151 for in thy honor hither are they *c.*
SP 207 O, if thou beest magnanimious, *c.* before me
SP 441 *c.*, sirra, let me see how finely youle cry this chaine
SP 405 *c.* therefore, gentle death, and ease my griefe
SP 578 shouldst *c.* about the person of a King
SP 618 *c.*, Janisaries, and helpe me to lament
SP 734 and *c.* an houre hence unto my lodging
SP 761 is *c.* to joyne both hearts in union
SP 848 desire Guelpio and signior Julio *c.* speake with me
SP 884 *C.*, sirs, lets go: — Drumsler, play for me
SP 888 I, marrie, this showes that Charleman is *c.*
SP 981 come bether, sirra; thou knowest me
SP 901 why, ile be heere as soone as ever I *c.* again
SP 1058 that once put by, I roughly *c.* upon him
SP 1082 why, wilt thou stay till I *c.* againe?
SP 1084 that shall be when I *c.* from Turkey
SP 1258 and now, Erastus, *c.* and follow me
SP 1271 *c.*, follow me, and I will heare the rest
SP 1319 if we be beaten backe, weele *c.* to you
SP 1325 we *c.* with mightie Solimans commaund

SP 1336 *c.*, fellow Souldiers ; let us to the breach
SP 1414 *c.*, Erastus, sit thee downe by me
SP 1529 *c.*, sit thee downe upon my right hand heere
SP 1533 Erastus and Perseda, *c.* you hether
SP 1564 *c.*, envie, then, and sit in friendships seate
SP 1631 *c.* thou againe ; but let the lady stay
SP 1636 Brusor, be gone ; for till thou *c.* I languish
SP 1763 although to me you never *c.* to soone ?
SP 1769 to *c.* your selfe in person and visit him
SP 1780 Lord Brusor, *c.* ; tis time that we were gon
SP 1787 *c.*, Lucina, lets in ; my heart is full
SP 1792 *c.*, fellowes, see when this matter comes in question
SP 1933 then, Brusor, *c.* ; and with some few men
SP 2063 but ere I *c.* to enter single fight
SP 2084 which to approove, Ile *c.* to combate thee
SP 2125 *c.* Brusor, helpe to lift her bodie up
Ard. 85 sweet Arden, *c.* again within a day or two
Ard. 110 is *c.* to town, and sends you word by me
Ard. 128 to *c.* this morning but along my door
Ard. 133 I know he loves me well, but dares not *c.*
Ard. 242 Arden, I know, will *c.* and show it me
Ard. 382 *c.*, Master Mosbie, will you sit with us ?
Ard. 397 leave this dallying, and let us away
Ard. 755 *c.*, let us be going, and we'll bait at
Ard. 789 *c.* I once at home, I'll rouse her
Ard. 792 *c.* but a turn or two, and then away
Ard. 817 is 't nothing else ? *c.*, Franklin, let's away
Ard. 901 *c.* to the purpose, Michael ; we hear
Ard. 940 this night *c.* to his house at Aldersgate
Ard. 941 the doors I'll leave unlocked against you *c.*
Ard. 951 *c.*, let's go drink ; choler makes me as dry as a dog
Ard. 1009 *c.*, Master Franklin, shall we go to bed ?
Ard. 1027 my master would desire you *c.* to bed
Ard. 1077 *c.*, Master Franklin, let us go to bed
Ard. 1090 and at some hour hence *c.* to us again
Ard. 1134 *c.*, let's go seek out Greene ; I know
Ard. 1145 *c.* in Paul's
Ard. 1147 *c.*, Master Franklin, you shall go with me
Ard. 1183 *c.*, Master Franklin ; we'll now walk in Paul's
Ard. 1383 *c.*, let us in to shun suspicion
Ard. 1385 *c.*, Will, see thy tools be in a readiness !
Ard. 1430 why, that thou shalt see, if he *c.* this way
Ard. 1440 o'ertake us ere we *c.* to Rainham Down
Ard. 1446 *c.*, Master Franklin, onwards with your tale
Ard. 1452 *c.*, Master Franklin, let us go on softly
Ard. 1475 *c.*, we are almost now at Rainham Down
Ard. 1486 *c.* you from London, and ne'er a man with you ?
Ard. 1491 you and your friend *c.* home and sup with me
Ard. 1496 will you *c.* to-morrow and dine with me
Ard. 1509 tainted for a penny-matter, and *c.* in question
Ard. 1510 *c.*, Master Arden, let us be going
Ard. 1532 therefore *c.*, Greene, and let us to Feversham
Ard. 1542 the season fits ; *c.*, Franklin, let's away
Ard. 1572 *c.*, Michael, are our horses ready ?
Ard. 1647 we have great haste ; I pray thee, *c.* away
Ard. 1677 stifled with this fog ; *c.*, let's away
Ard. 1702 *c.*, let us go on like a couple of blind pilgrims
Ard. 1880 *c.*, Franklin, let us strain to mend our pace
Ard. 1890 *c.* thou thyself, and go along with me
Ard. 1955 will *c.* and sup with you at our house this night
Ard. 1958 bid Mosbie steal from him and *c.* to me
Ard. 1974 now his way had been to have *c.* hand and feet
Ard. 1977 if the devil *c.*, and he have no more strength
Ard. 2014 that he may not *c.* home till supper-time
Ard. 2022 but *c.* not forth before in any case
Ard. 2025 *c.*, Master Greene, go you along with me

Ard. 2026 see all things ready, Alice, against we *c.*
Ard. 2029 *c.*, Black Will, that in mine eyes art fair
Ard. 2037 that I may *c.* behind him cunningly
Ard. 2085 when my husband is *c.* in, lock the street-door
Ard. 2086 he shall be murdered, or the guests *c.* in
Ard. 2139 *c.*, Alice, is our supper ready yet ?
Ard. 2141 *c.*, Master Mosbie, what shall be play for ?
Ard. 2202 fear you not, he'll *c.* anon ; meantime
Ard. 2244 go, Susan, and bid thy brother *c.*
Ard. 2245 but wherefore should he *c.* ?
Ard. 2251 *c.*, Susan, help to lift his body forth
Ard. 2254 sweet Mosbie, art thou *c.* ? Then weep that will
Ard. 2262 make the door fast ; let them not *c.* in
Ard. 2294 Master Franklin, what mean you *c.* so sad ?
Ard. 2302 ay, so they shall : *c.* you along with us
Ard. 2364 but wherefore stay we ? *C.* and bear me hence
Ard. 2370 that I can *c.* unto no sanctuary
Ard. 2381 *c.*, make haste and bring away the prisoners
Ard. 2383 I saw him *c.* into your house
JB 124 when he was *c.* she gave her husband
HP 1087 wherupon it comes to passe that good servants
Cor. 353 when Isie Winter's past, then comes the spring
Cor. 1491 that death that comes unsent for or unseene
Jer. 290 peace : who comes here ? newes
Jer. 616 but see, my Sister Bellimperia comes
Jer. 649 up, Lazarotto ; yonder comes thy prize
ST Bal. 109 sweete Bellimperia comes to me
ST 459 and heere he comes that murdred my delight
ST 1019 the Sickle comes not, till the corne be ripe
ST 1287 heere comes the bird that I must ceaze upon
ST 1658 but heere she comes
ST 1846 this way ile take, and this way comes the King
STA 1952 see where he comes
STA 2023 and there is none but what comes from him
STA 2042 is there no trickes that comes before thine eies ?
ST 2383 but, Balthazar, heere comes Hieronimo
ST 2775 here comes Lorenzo : looke upon the plot
SP 125 here comes a Messenger to haste me hence
SP 275 O heaven, she comes, accompanied with a child
SP 337 now comes in the infant that courts my mistresse
SP 687 but see, Ferdinando, where Perseda comes
SP 735 heere comes the Synon to my simple heart
SP 1002 see where Perseda comes, to save me a labour
SP 1535 see where he comes, my other best beloved
SP 1605 to one past cure good counsell comes too late
SP 1789 and when Erastus comes, our perjurd friend
SP 1792 see when this matter comes in question you stagger not
SP 1799 see where he comes, whome though I deerely love
Ard. 68 for being awake he comes not in my thoughts
Ard. 105 and here comes Adam of the Flower-de-luce
Ard. 138 and, Mosbie, thou that comes to me by stealth
Ard. 177 yonder comes Mosbie. Michael, get thee gone
Ard. 291 in good time see where my husband comes
Ard. 448 Alice, what's he that comes yonder ?
Ard. 449 one that comes to put in practice our
Ard. 641 see you them that comes yonder, Master Greene ?
Ard. 809 when the press comes forth of Paul's
Ard. 855 comes with a lowly curtsey to the earth
Ard. 879 see, yonder comes his man ; and wot you what ?
Ard. 911 how comes it then that such a knave
Ard. 1005 forget your griefs a while ; here comes your man
Ard. 1022 then comes his wife's dishonour in his thoughts
Ard. 1057 he comes, he comes ! ah, Master Franklin, help !
Ard. 1263 but here she comes, and I must flatter her
Ard. 1370 soft, Alice, here comes somebody
Ard. 1381 ah, would it were ! Then comes my happy hour

Ard. 1416 there comes a cur and stole it from them both
Ard. 1433 but, sirs, be sure to speed him when he comes
Ard. 1525 comes my Lord Cheiny to prevent his death
Ard. 1768 see where he comes to further my intent !
Ard. 1945 hence, Will ! here comes Mistress Arden
Ard. 1972 with that comes Franklin at him lustily
Ard. 1983 with that comes Arden with his arming sword
Ard. 1994 but here comes he that will
Ard. 2072 who comes with him ?

Come.

HP 1340 *C.* la nobil Greca ch' alle tele sue
HP 1648 Segue, *c.* 'l maestro fa il discente

Comedies.

HP 728 dauncings, *C.*, and other such assemblies
ST 2633 a Comedie ? fie, *C.* are fit for common wits
SP 2214 packe, Love and Fortune, play in Commedies

Comedy.

HP 1120 and such an one was Terence, the wryter of Comedie
HP 1744 to compose or wryte a Tragedie and Comedie bee
ST 2631 Hieronimo, methinkes a Comedie were better
ST 2632 a Comedie ? fie, Comedies are fit for common wits
SP 1928 and now begins my pleasant Comedie
SP 2039 least with thy woes thou spoile my commedie

Comeliness.

HP 906 if he chaunce to faile in action, co[m]lines, or utteraunce
HP 1382 grace and comlines in beautifying and adorning things

Comely.

HP 117 of countenance verie pleasant myxed with comelie gravitie
HP 715 and maintaine the same with *c.* ornaments
JB 23 which, for her favour and *c.* personage

Comest.

ST 2378 why commest thou so sadly to salute us thus ?

Comet.

SP 272 the reflecting eye of that admirable *c.* Perseda

Cometh.

HP 126 he *c.* from Novara
HP 614 it often commeth to passe that
HP 742 commeth not with those prophane and
HP 1212 it commeth into the consideration of Quallitie to

Comfort.

HP 230 expect and approve that ayde and *c.*
Cor. 1615 will haply *c.* this your discontent
Cor. 1789 both *c.* and encourage his to fight
Jer. 164 but be of *c.*, sweet ; Horatio knowes
Jer. 693 O, be of *c.*, sweet, call in thy sperits
Jer. 1148 my boy ads treble *c.* to my age
ST 531 that which may *c.* both your King and you
STA 1775 he was my *c.*, and his mothers joy
STA 1788 they doe not alwayes scape, that is some *c.*
STA 2009 bid him come in, and paint some *c.*
STA 2010 for surely there's none lives but painted *c.*
ST 2112 let this thy *c.* be, heaven covereth him that
ST 2796 yet liveth Solyman to *c.* thee
SP 1279 & 1280 for what was he but *c.* of my life ?
Ard. 20 *c.* thyself, sweet friend ; it is not strange
Ard. 996 yet let your *c.* be that others bear
JB 140 that whole night longe, without either *c.* or companie

Comforted.

HP 1086 that men and reasonable creatures are *c.* therwith ?

Comforter.

Cor. 631 the cheerefull Cock (the sad nights *c.*)

Comfortless.

SP 1264 colde and comfortles for you

Comic.

Jer. 196 the time being Commick will seeme short and

Coming.

HP 112 brought worde of his Father's comming
HP 1400 returning from Paris and comming by Beona
ST 493 the King, my Lords, is comming hither straight
ST 1465 yes, but there shalbe for my comming downe
SP 1226 before thy comming I vowd to conquer Rhodes
Ard. 226 we'll make him sure enough for *c.* there
Ard. 238 *c.* into the chamber where it hangs, may die
Ard. 378 a kiss at *c.* or departing from the town ?
Ard. 671 I see more company *c.* down the hill
Ard. 798 and at his *c.* forth speed him
Ard. 802 at his *c.* forth I'll run him through
Ard. 839 standing against a stall, watching Arden's *c.*
Ard. 1201 and *c.* down he found the doors unshut
Ard. 1478 stand close, Will, I hear them *c.*
Ard. 1487 my man's *c.* after, but
Ard. 1642 i' the broom, close watching Arden's *c.*
Ard. 1736 at their *c.* back meet with them once more
Ard. 1762 he is *c.* from Shorlow as I understand
Ard. 1770 my *c.* to you was about the plat
Ard. 2071 mistress, my master is *c.* hard by
Ard. 2146 I fear me he will spy me as I am *c.*
Ard. 2261 are *c.* towards our house with glaives and bills
JB 45 and upon a time comming unto her, requested that
JB 185 in the meane space Parker comming unto her, she
Ard. 1141 watch the out-*c.* of that prick-eared cur

Comings-in.

HP 1156 making that proportion with his comings in

Command.

HP 479 I beseech you commaund your Sons to sitte
HP 898 some are naturally borne to commande, and others to obey
HP 919 have such persons serve him as he might commaund
HP 1011 commaunde the rest, that are thy Hyndes and
HP 1075 commaund the negligent and unprofitable Servant to help
HP 1444 to serve those whom also she hath framed to commaund
Cor. 34 but faith continues not where men *c.*
Cor. 305 what holpe it thee that under thy commaund thou
Cor. 556 till heaven it selfe commaund it
Cor. 1383 have all been urg'd to yeeld to my commaund
Cor. 1449 yet Rome endures not the commaund of kings
Jer. 85 I will discharg the waight of your *c.*
Jer. 792 according [to] your gratious, dread Comand
ST 613 hath your Lordship any service to *c.* me ?
ST 792 wilt please your grace *c.* me ought beside ?
ST 1284 that thou by his *c.* shouldst meet with him
ST 2436 your Lordships to commaund. Pah : keepe your **way**
ST 2805 yet by thy power thou thinkest to commaund
SP 4 and I commaund you to forbeare this place
SP 581 your Highnesse knowes I spake at your *c.*
SP 1043 faire Love, according unto thy commaund
SP 1231 let not great Solimans *c.*
SP 1325 we come with mightie Solimans commaund
SP 1482 she is my vassaile, and I will commaund
SP 1577 commaund my shipping for to waft you over
SP 1592 what was it but abuse of Loves commaund ?
SP 1776 though loth, yet Solimans commaund prevailes
SP 2171 my last request, for I commaund no more
Ard. 264 you shall *c.* my life, my skill, and all
Ard. 549 you shall *c.* me to the uttermost
Ard. 1552 that honour's title nor a lord's *c.*
HP 480 obeying the gentle commaunds of their father
Cor. 249 alreadie wander under your commaunds
Cor. 1243 commaunds the world, and brideleth all the **earth**

Commanded.

HP 797 the Father is commau[n]ded to provide this reamedy
HP 925 in the absence of their Maisters record the things commaunded
HP 926 scarce performe even when they are commaunded
HP 934 whatsoever commaunded or required in him
HP 1682 as God commaunded the first man
Cor. Arg. 25 Spayne, where Pompeys Faction commaunded
Ard. 1548 for so his honour late c. me

Commander.
SP 194 have I been chiefe commaunder of an hoast
SP 527 and earths c. under Mahomet
SP 1031 thou great c. of the swift wingd winds
ST 2276 Kings and commanders of the westerne Indies

Commandeth.
ST 2790 why, let him die ; so love commaundeth me

Commanding.
Cor. 156 but in commaunding our affections

Commandment.
HP 1005 controld, and at commaundment of those higher officers
ST 1242 upon precise commandement of the King
ST 1278 tis by commandement in the Kings own name
JB 177 so that he had her at commandement
HP 921 that they may be capable of his commaundements
HP 1738 as the forme of their commaundements is distinguished, so are

Commandress.
JB 41 esteeming her the mistris and commaundres of his life

Commend.
HP 215 c. this custome of marrying yong me[n] so soone
HP 393 he cannot commende his Supper with
HP 604 wherewith it shall content her Husband to c. her
HP 815 which custome as I commende not, because
HP 994 I cannot c. those that are neither fitte
Jer. 1163 to thank Horatio, and c. his hart
ST 793 c. me to the king, and so farewell
SP 1268 your friends c. them to you
SP 1926 that you c. him to Erastus soule
ST 1087 humbly commends him to your Majestie
ST 1089 with these, the letters of the Kings commends

Commendable.
HP Ind. 75 feare not c. in a man
HP 294 conditions, me thinks, are not very c.
HP 653 the other two are indeede most c.
HP 863 most c. practises of mind and body
JB 24 her good behaviour and other c. qualities

Commendation.
HP 1355 weave, and that not without great c.
HP 295 that he should give Wine commendations of that sort
HP 1402 me thought, was worthy commendations
SP 1003 after my most hearty commendations

Commended.
HP 792 and c. by the bringing of her children up
HP 964 not without cause were Mylos servaunts c.
HP 1001 should the housholde care bee c.

Commender.
HP 464 whereof you are too courteous a c.

Commendeth.
HP 1475 hee c. and defendeth merchaunts

Commission.
ST 1544 the fellow had a faire c. to the contrary

Commissioners.
Puck 46 geven some instance to the late comission[rs]

Commit.
Cor. 161 revenge the crymes thy fathers did c.
Cor. 368 c. more murther then Rome ever made
JB 17 committe most haynous and grievous offences

Committed.
HP 1004 to whom the Toun affaires belong and are c.
Cor. 1924 say, freatfull heavens, what fault have I c.
ST 1301 then have c. this misdeed so late
JB (Title) c. by his owne wife, through the provocation of
JB (Title) two yeares after the murther was c.
JB 224 two yeares and a halfe after the murder was c.

Commixt.
ST 2891 an Easterne winde, c. with noisome aires

Commodious.
HP 83 large and most c. steps
HP 1593 it is thought both necessary and c.

Commodiously.
HP 448 c. consorted with perswasions
HP 1202 c. fitting and making equall things exchanged

Commodities.
HP Ind. 21 comodities of the Spring and of Autumn
HP Ind. 56 see **Discommodities**
HP 1221 the c. raised thereupon may be transported
HP 1468 where is want and scarcity of those comodities
HP 1481 trafflque their c. to Countreys where
HP 1483 bargained for the c. of a Countrey

Commodity.
HP 750 taste no lesse c. of the meats then the most

Common.
HP 459 upon some c. fault are fallen into
HP 530 to be c. and indifferently sustained
HP 1148 it is proper to the Maister, and the other c.
HP 1225 neere to any high way or c. street
Cor. 191 made thundring Mars (Dissentions c. friend)
Cor. 437 but who sorrowes not ? the griefe is c.
Cor. 725 farre from the c. hazard of the warrs
Cor. 763 it seeks the c. passage of the dead
Jer. 183 tis as c. to weepe at parting as to be a woman
Jer. 269 for this is c. ; the more she weepes
ST 335 that were a breach to c. law of armes
ST 2282 the troth and more then c. love you lend to us
ST 2330 the c. love and kindnes that Hieronimo hath wone
ST 2462 and slumbring is a c. wordly wile
ST 2633 a Comedie ? fie, Comedies are fit for c. wits
ST 2637 containing matter, and not c. things
SP 533 a c. presse of base superfluous Turkes
Ard. 345 make c. table-talk of her and thee
Ard. 974 if fear of God or c. speech of man

Commonly.
HP Ind. 107 nurses c. ordinary persons
HP 187 which most c. being unpossible
HP 283 Beasts that c. are stald and foddered
HP 1464 trade or science is at this day commonlie called Merchandize
Cor. 1318 for no Tyrant c., lyving ill, can kindly die
JB 30 but as the truest lovers are c. least regarded

Commonwealth.
HP 1118 in those good worldes of the Romaine Common wealth
HP 1478 the whole revenewes of the Common weath
HP 1635 a corrupter of a Common wealth, a disobeyer of
HP 1763 employed in office for the honours of C.
Cor. 370 return'd due honors to our Common-wealth
Cor. 661 our Common-wealth, our Empyre, and our honors
Cor. 1110 doth ryde tryumphing o're our Common-wealth
Cor. 1970 did topside turvey turne their Common-wealth

Commorants.
HP 62 told me by the Countreymen c. there that

Communicates.
HP 531 the soule communicats her operations

Community.

HP 537 the like communitie shoulde be in all offices
Compact.
HP 1439 flocks, Heards, and droves c.
Ard. 1632 yet neither with good mortar well c.
Compacted.
SP 748 ah, that my moyst and cloud c. braine
Companable.
HP 1438 for of Beastes some are tame and compynable
Companies.
Ard. 1710 what c. have passed your ferry
Companion.
HP 545 L'errante mia Consorte. « My wandering C. »
HP 587 not only to account her his c. in love
HP 597 for a fellow and c. of his life
HP 616 choyse of a c. that shold helpe
HP 751 the most incontinent and surfeiting co[m]panion
ST 1480 I, that c.
Ard. 306 she's no c. for so base a groom
Ard. 826 I had a glimpse of him and his c.
Ard. 1697 'twas Arden and his c.
Ard. 1650 like to a good companion's smoky brain
HP 226 for many times they are companions
HP 265 the companions of Ulisses bare not so many mishaps
HP 529 the Husband and the wyfe ought indeed to be companions
Cor. 2003 O deere companions, shall I, O, shall I
ST 1255 and better its that base companions dye
Ard. 687 thou art acquainted with such companions
Ard. 2090 Black Will and Greene are his companions
Ard. 2336 she will not know her old companions
Company.
HP 204 are more abasht with the c. of women
HP 211 for want of one to beare her c.
Cor. 740 and blesse me with my Pompeys c. ?
Cor. 861 that I have kept my Maister c.
Cor. 1558 feasts, nor friendly c.
Jer. 618 for c. hinders loves conference
ST 284 that Don Horatio beare us c.
ST 461 that for a while I wish no c.
ST 1129 come, Alexandro, keepe us companie
ST 1213 and since he hath not left my c.
ST 1497 I prethee, request this good c. to pray with me
ST 1662 and with extreames abuse my c.
ST 2235 Hieronimo will beare thee c.
ST 2435 let us entreat your c. to day
SP 77 let in my hart to keep thine c.
SP 440 and Ile beare you c.
Ard. 305 villain, what makes thou in her c. ?
Ard. 363 I cannot eat, but I'll sit for c.
Ard. 554 let's hear them that I may laugh for c.
Ard. 644 a knave chiefly for bearing the other c.
Ard. 671 I see more c. coming down the hill
Ard. 724 shall we have your c. to London ?
Ard. 755 I warrant I should be warden of the c. !
Ard. 947 now it were good we parted c.
Ard. 1188 I'll bear you c.
Ard. 1219 so you will except of my c.
Ard. 1220 disturbed thoughts drives me from c.
Ard. 1311 and wrapt my credit in thy c.
Ard. 1556 I merit still to have thy c.
Ard. 1933 I and my c. have taken the constable from his watch
Ard. 2100 his c. hath purchased me ill friends
Ard. 2127 your c. hath purchased me ill friends
Ard. 2171 Mosbie, go thou and bear them c.
JB 140 that whole night longe, without either comfort or companie
Puck 41 accuse nor will excuse by reson of his companie

Compare.
HP 381 will co[m]pare Autumn and the Spring togeather
HP 748 c. the embracings of the Husbande and the Wife
ST 1574 now may I make c. twixt hers and this
ST 1719 too pollitick for me, past all c.
SP 124 and then Erastus lives without c.
SP 1389 kinde, past all c., and more then my desart
Compared.
HP 341 me thinks no time may be c. to Autumn
HP 1414 c. it to some higher matter then an Armorie
Comparing.
HP 1392 co[m]paring little things with great we may
SP 50 c. it to twenty gratious things ?
Comparison.
HP 488 no proportion of c. with privat men
HP 622 as is desire in c. of understanding
HP 1363 and come into c. with her good man
HP 1740 that, in c. of number, the houshold of
Compass.
HP 61 the compasse whereunto it was accustomed
HP 514 did hardly compasse with much sparing
ST 1417 for all our wrongs, can compasse no redresse
Ard. 2063 Mosbie's arms shall c. me
Compassed.
ST 859 thus Elmes by vines are compast till they fall
Ard. 531 and never rest till I have c. it
Compasses.
HP 1164 those c. which gave begining to Geometry in Egypt
Compassing.
SP 1668 c. me with goodly ceremonies
Compassion.
Cor. 1951 t'will move c. in thee of my paines
ST 2677 mooves the King to justice or compasion
Compeers.
ST Bal. 55 Prince Baltazer with his compeeres
Compel.
HP 633 compell affections to be subject unto reason
ST 2760 whose eies compell, like powrefull Adamant
Compelled.
ST Bal. 47 compell'd therefore to unfold his mind
Competitors.
HP 227 they are ryvalls and c. in love
Complain.
HP 380 the one hath little cause to complaine of the other
ST 476 yes, to your gratious selfe must I complaine
ST 2232 goe backe, my sonne, complaine to Eacus
Ard. 395 I know it, sweet Alice ; cease to c.
Complaining.
ST 320 O yes, c. makes my greefe seeme lesse
SP 1874 what bootes c. wheres no remedy ?
Complaint.
ST 475 what bootes c., when thers no remedy ?
SP 1169 yet have we eares to heare a just c.
Cor. 343 nor can they (should they pittie my complaints)
ST 1339 with your complaintes unto my L[ord] the King
Complete.
HP 882 but compleat and uttered with more austeritie and
Ard. 1087 till in the watch our purpose be c.
Completed.
Ard. 1380 well, were his date c. and expired
Complexion.
HP Ind. 22 c. of servants, and
HP 664 will in no wise marre her naturall co[m]plexion
HP 801 the c. of the child becommeth strong and lustie
HP 850 not werish and of a womanish, effeminate c.
HP 996 such as are of strong c., fit for labor

Jer. 112 for such complexions best appease my pride
'Complices.
Ard. 2326 thy *c.* which have conspired and
Complot.
ST 1240 now to confirme the *c.* thou hast cast
ST 2687 this garden Plot — accursed *c.* of my miserie
Ard. 917 we have devised a complat under hand
Ard. 2009 will you two perform the *c.* that I have laid ?
Compose.
HP 1744 to *c.* or wryte a Tragedie and Comedie bee bothe
Composed.
HP 994 whereof a house or familie in deede should be *c.*
Jer. 195 then, Madam, be composd, as you weare wont
Jer. 254 deny his gifts, be all composd of hate
Composedly.
HP 1371 reserve not things *c.* but seperat and placd in sonder
Composition.
Ard. 566 grew to *c.* for my husband's death
Compound.
Ard. 611 you could *c.* by art a crucifix impoisoned
Comprehend.
Cor. 149 or that our hands the Earth can *c.*
Comprehended.
HP 79 it *c.* divers roomes and stories
HP 1525 is not *c.* in our understanding
Compression.
SP 630 an humor knit together by *c.*
Conceal.
HP 50 my name and surname I conceale
HP 56 that I desired to conceale some part of mine estate
HP 1447 not conceale what Theucidides hath observed
ST 645 and will conceale what ere proceeds from thee
ST 659 and that thou wilt conceale what thou hast tolde
ST 2520 and will conceale my resolution
ST 2523 I will consent, conceale, and ought that
Ard. 1282 and then — *c.* the rest, for 'tis too bad
ST 640 thy death shall bury what thy life conceales
Concealed.
ST 666 be still conceald from Bel-imperia
ST 1568 so closely smootherd, and so long conceald
ST 1637 are things concealde that els would breed unrest
ST 1701 but whats the cause that you concealde me since ?
Concealment.
ST 1655 as for her sweet hart, and *c.* so
Conceit.
HP 466 or superfluous *c.* of mine opinions
HP 1729 though I were swift of *c.* at first, yet now
Cor. Ded. 12 your true *c.* and entertainment of these
Cor. 1712 and conceite that we may rest the Maisters of
Jer. 161 shape frightful *c.* beyond the intent of act
ST 465 your prison then, belike, is your *c.*
ST 466 I, by *c.* my freedome is enthralde
ST 467 then with conceite enlarge your selfe againe
ST 468 what, if conceite have laid my hart to gage ?
ST 1728 in my conceipt, are things of more import
JB 8 so that in his owne *c.* hee might
ST 696 which pleasing wordes doe harbour sweet conceits
ST 697 which sweet conceits are lim'de with slie deceits
ST 1541 he that was so full of merrie conceits
Conceited.
ST 2610 for I have already *c.* that
Conceived.
Cor. 854 the rage, the hatred that they have conceiv'd
ST 1912 pride *c.* of yong Horatio his Sonne
JB 77 had she *c.* such deadly hatred against him
JB 158 ignorance rather then to any malice conceaved against

Conceives.
Jer. 1169 your friend *c.* in signes how you rejoyce
Concent.
HP 1387 altogeather consent, or musically aunswer crosse
Concern.
HP Ind. 48 how farre it dooth concerne a
Cor. 1445 O, but theyr Countries good concerns them more
ST 1814 if ought concernes our honour and your owne ?
ST 1550 and yet, though somewhat neerer me concernes
Ard. 1745 let me alone ; it most concerns my state
Concerned.
Puck 14 suspected for that libell that concern'd the state
Concerneth.
ST 1433 a neerer matter that *c.* him
Concerning.
HP Ind. 33 *c.* thinges that are
HP Ind. 112 opinions of some *c.* the soule
HP 1563 to say conserning this naturall gaine
HP 1688 *c.* Husbandry and Keeping of a house
HP 1774 said *c.* that so necessary care of
ST 1678 *c.* certaine matters of estate
SP 1688 then here my opinion *c.* that point
Puck 7 that yor Lp holds me in *c.* Atheisme
Conclude.
HP 896 therefore I *c.* that Autumn is
Cor. 925 *c.* with Caesars death to end our servitude
Cor. 1220 to fight for that, that did theyr deaths *c.*
Cor. 1856 and (to *c.*) his men dismayd to see the
ST 2114 and to *c.*, I will revenge his death
ST 2817 and thus *c.* I in our vulgar tung
ST 2891 and will as resolute *c.* his parte
SP 2018 to *c.* in a word : to be captious, vertuous
Ard. 439 I *c.*, 'tis childishness to stand upon an oath
Ard. 565 and, to *c.*, Mosbie, at last we grew to
Ard. 929 how and what way we may *c.* his death
Ard. 1942 to *c.*, what have I not done ?
Ard. 1952 and, to *c.*, sent me to bring you word
Concluded.
HP 606 conscribd and ordinarily *c.* in lesser tyme
HP 1687 may be *c.* and determined
ST 2664 and all shalbe *c.* in one Scene
JB 51 so astonished and dismayed that she *c.*
Conclusion.
ST 2658 the *c.* shall prove the intention
SP 646 for, in *c.* of his happines
Condemn.
SP 2123 yet justly how can I condemne my selfe
Jer. 540 your wife condemns you of a uncurtesie
Ard. 2330 this blood condemns me, and in gushing forth
Condemned.
HP 670 can not bee condemnd as arguments of much
HP 1640 hauving not onely beene *c.* by Aristotle
ST 1031 that, as he is *c.*, he may dye
ST 1453 and by our law he is condemnd to die
SP 83 or newes of pardon to a wretch condemnd
SP 1790 see [that] he be condemd by marshall law
SP 1919 by whom Erastus was condemnd to die
SP 1959 for my maister is condemnd and executed
SP 1967 but say, wherefore was he condemnd to die ?
SP 1969 what treason, or by whom was he condemnd ?
Ard. 746 dead as if he had been *c.* by
Ard. 2383 and I am by the law *c.* to die
JB 219 both araigned and *c.* for the murder at the
Condescent.
ST 2286 by appointment and our condiscent to morrow are
   they to be married

Condition.	Ard. 2347 *c.* this foul fault and be penitent
HP 29 (judging him to be of no base or meane condicion)	JB 214 neither would the woman confesse anything till
HP 913 not onely servile in *c.* and of fortune	**Confessed.**
HP 1539 his estate, *c.* of time, and customes of the Citty	ST 1432 dispatch : the faults approved and confest
HP 1549 ought not to exceede the rest in any such *c.*	Ard. 1902 a fault *c.* is more than half amends
Jer. 411 O entire is the *c.* of my hot desire	JB 162 although she since *c.* it was not
ST 1022 infortunate *c.* of Kings	JB 216 she co[n]fessed the fact in order, as I have declared
SP 261 I will suppresse my *c.*	**Confines.**
Ard. 148 on that *c.*, Michael, here's my hand	HP 21 that devideth the *c.* of Piemount from
Ard. 2137 and, on that *c.*, Mosbie, pledge me here	Cor. 1692 we fight not, we, t'enlarge our skant *c.*
JB 52 she concluded, on *c.* he would let his Action fal	**Confirm.**
ST 1214 his conditions such, as feare or flattering words may	HP 648 much confirme the womans chastitie
HP Ind. 23 conditions in Servants	Cor. 1936 whose resolutions did confirme the rest
HP Ind. 24 consideration in condicions of possessions	ST 1178 what I can gather, to confirme this writ
HP 103 unexperienced in Courte or on the worldes conditions	ST 1240 now to confirme the complot thou hast cast
HP 288 tha[n] of the good conditions of your Sonne	ST 2314 and to confirme their promised marriage
HP 293 which two conditions, me thinks, are not	Ard. 353 were to *c.* the rumour that is grown
HP 603 all formes of customes and conditions	**Confirmed.**
HP 612 that the Husband take a wife with these conditions	HP 73 thus more and more he *c.* mine opinion
HP 785 with the milke sucketh the conditions of the Nursse	Cor. 1596 Be more *c.* And, Madam, let not griefe
HP 841 yet was not Achilles such an one in his conditions	Jer. 1 thou art now confirmd Marshall of Spaine
HP 902 judge none otherwise of the conditions of men	Jer. 899 yet, O prince, be not *c.* in blud
HP 1230 all which conditions, as they much increase and	ST 179 but tell me now, hast thou confirmd a peace ?
SP 1051 he knowing your fierce conditions, hath	ST 2295 *c.* thy motion, and contented me
Puck 23 when he had heard of his conditions	Ard. 460 *c.* by letters patent from the king
Puck 32 nombred amongst the best conditions of men	ST 775 for strengthening of our late *c.* league
Conditional.	**Conflict.**
ST 180 no peace, my Liege, but peace conditionall	HP 973 *c.* amongst the Romains which they called Cyvill warre
Conduct.	Cor. 1873 the little while this naval *c.* lasted)
HP 36 doth favour mee with too noble a *c.*	ST 15 for in the late *c.* with Portingale
ST 1811 it will *c.* you to dispaire and death	ST 162 and in that *c.* was Andrea slaine
SP 193 under the *c.* of great Soliman	Ard. 991 worse than the *c.* at the hour of death
Conductors.	HP 982 many cruell conflicts and daungerous warres are caused
ST 2102 for evils unto ils *c.* be	SP 224 I keep no table to character my fore-passed conflicts
Confection.	**Conflicting.**
Ard. 424 some fine *c.* that might have given the broth	Ard. 1030 *c.* thoughts, encamped in my breast
JB 93 swelling of the body, or other signe of outward *c.*	**Conform.**
Confederate.	HP 240 shall happily conforme him selfe thereunto
ST 1558 « and was *c.* with the Prince and you »	HP 857 discipline may conforme and be agreeable therewith
ST 1317 that by those base confederates in our fault	HP 625 a woman that conformes her selfe to her Husband
ST 1664 amidst a crue of thy confederates	**Confound.**
ST 2917 but who were thy confederates in this ?	Cor. 1907 *c.* me quick, or let me sinck to hell
STA 2949 speake, who were thy confederates in this ?	Jer. 593 for confidence confounds the stratagem
Confer.	**Confused.**
ST 213 that, staying them, we may conferre and talke	HP 7 I heard a *c.* cry of dogs
ST 1677 resolv'd to come conferre with olde Hieronimo	Jer. 596 make it *c.* ere it come to head
Ard. 136 hinder our meetings when we would *c.*	ST 1133 confusde and filde with murder and misdeeds
Conference.	**Confusion.**
Jer. 618 for company hinders loves *c.*	Cor. 1816 the field was fild with all *c.*
Conferring.	STA 966 *c.*, mischiefe, torment, death and hell
Ard. 1197 were very late *c.* in the porch	STA 1793 and so doth bring *c.* to them all
Confess.	ST 2656 but this will be a meere *c.*
Jer. 30 confesse, Beard, thou art fifty full, not a haire lesse	ST 2672 wrought by the heavens in this *c.*
Jer. 532 I must confes, my Lord, it treats of love	**Conjecture.**
STA 1200 y'fayth, my Lord, tis an idle thing I must confesse	HP 953 they speake without sence and *c.* unreasonablie
ST 1297 sirra, confesse, and therein play the Priest	HP 1246 own *c.*, opinion of Prognostications, or speech of
ST 1439 confesse thy folly, and repent thy fault	Puck 6 hath movde me to *c.* some suspicion
ST 1442 first I confesse, nor feare I death therfore	**Conjecturing.**
SP 318 I injoy my life at thy hands, I confesse it	SP 239 I, *c.* the cause to be want of water, dismounted
SP 1388 I must confesse that Solyman is kinde	**Conjoined.**
SP 1868 wherein thou shalt confesse ile favour thee	HP 531 that the soule can bee conjoynd with any other **body**
SP 2043 I am my selfe strong, but I confesse death to be stronger	**Conjugis.**
Ard. 166 why, say I should be took, I'll ne'er *c.*	HP 1328 *C.*, et possit parvos educere natos
Ard. 357 at last *c.* how causeless they have injured her	**Conjunction.**
Ard. 934 I cannot but *c.*, sith you have urged me	HP Ind. 26 *c.* of man and wife like that of
Ard. 2272 and see you *c.* nothing in any case	HP 538 *c.* that the man hath with the Wife

HP 575 the straighter the *c.* is of the husbande and the Wife
Conjuratae.
ST 104 et *c.* curvato poplite gentes
Conjured.
Cor. 1261 practized, conspierd, conjur'd a thousand wnies and
Cor. 1883 and Heaven it selfe conjur'd to injure him)
Conjur.
HP 1346 Arguto *c.* percurrit pectine telas
Conquer.
Cor. 787 for thou, that wont'st to tame and *c.* all
Cor. 1689 I'le eyther *c.*, or this sword you see
ST 834 thou hast prevailde ; ile *c.* my misdoubt
SP 1224 by curtesie let Soliman *c.* thee
SP 1226 before thy comming I vowd to *c.* Rhodes
SP 1253 prepare a fleet to assault and *c.* Rhodes
SP 1553 that I *c.* both by my deserts
SP 2200 by wasting all I *c.* all the world
ST 1722 tis of thy beauty, then, that conquers Kings
Conquered.
Cor. 660 now we have lost our *c.* libertie
Cor. 788 art conquer'd now with an eternall fall
Cor. 1113 leades the *c.* honor of the people yok't
Cor. 1331 the worthiest Citties of the *c.* world
Cor. 1372 and all they scarcely *c.* a nooke
Cor. 1395 did (*c.*) flie, his troopes discomfited
Cor. 1443 in *c.* foes what credite can there be ?
Cor. 1525 he his foes hath *c.*
Cor. 1787 tyll, tyer'd or conquer'd, one submits or flyes
Cor. 1965 people stood so careles of their *c.* libertie
Cor. 1979 which (*c.*) perisht by the Romaine swords
ST 255 he wan my love, this other *c.* me
ST 553 since English warriours likewise *c.* Spaine
ST 863 so shalt thou yeeld, and yet have conquerd me
ST 977 faire worthy sonne, not conquerd, but betraid
ST 1585 thy cursed father, and thy *c.* selfe
SP 140 as with thy vertue thou hast *c.* me
SP 248 the ransome of a *c.* citie
SP 1223 it is enough that thou hast *c.* Soliman by strength
Conquering.
Cor. 109 did favour us with *c.* our foes
Cor. 184 t'enlarge the bounds of *c.* Thessalie
Cor. 497 faire Ilium, razed by the *c.* Greekes
Cor. 601 is now subdu'de by *c.* Time
Cor. 708 in tryumph borne amongst the *c.* Romans
Cor. 779 didst extend thy *c.* armes beyond the Ocean
Cor. 1109 the *c.* Tyrant, high in Fortunes grace
Cor. 1171 (backt with wintered souldiers us'd to *c.*)
Cor. 1394 when hee (to *c.* accustomed)
ST 2757 but thy desert in *c.* Rhodes is lesse then in
Conqueror.
Cor. 1410 made *C.* and Emperor at last
SP 196 [and] marcht [a] conquerour through Asia
SP 539 till Persea stoope, and thou be conquerour
SP 767 thy name was conquerour, not my chivalrie
Jer. 974 ride [home] all Conquerours, when the fight is done
SP 2011 where is tipsie Alexander, that great cup conquerour
Conquest.
Cor. 683 the self-same style by *c.* may continue
Cor. 848 Caesar, thou shalt not vaunt thy *c.* long
Cor. 1385 made an universall *c.* of the world
SP 247 my mercy in *c.* is equall with my manhood
SP 545 without a *c.*, or a mean revenge
SP 766 to win late *c.* from many victors hands
SP 1378 but had I slept, his *c.* had been small
Ard. 200 and boast not of thy *c.* over me
Cor. 330 by whom the glorie of thy conquests got might

Cor. 780 and throngdst thy conquests from the Lybian shores
Cor. 1349 to bruite the prayses of our conquests past ?
Cor. 1413 nor thirsted I for conquests bought with blood
Cor. 1504 brings conquests whereof Europe rings
Conscribed.
HP 605 conscribd and ordinarily concluded in lesser tyme
Conscience.
ST 1267 and he that would not straine his *c.* for
ST 1321 a guiltie *c.*, urged with the thought of former evils
ST 1806 that leadeth from a guiltie *C.* unto
Ard. 1760 his *c.* is too liberal, and he too niggardly to
Puck 11 as also in the feare of god, and freedom of my *c.*
Consent.
HP 728 give *c.* that she may goe apparelled as others
HP 1173 or by *c.* of Marketfolks
ST Bal. 107 whereto I straightway gave *c.*
ST 788 doe so, my Lord, and if he give *c.*
STA 1970 doth give *c.* to that is done in darkenesse
ST 2519 and heere I vow — so you but give *c.*
ST 2523 I will *c.*, conceale, and ought that
SP 15 twas I that made their harts *c.* to love
SP 634 I couple minds together by *c.*
SP 1832 all this is yours, quoth he, if you *c.*
SP 1843 will you *c.*, quoth he, to fire the fleete
Ard. 830 but, were my *c.* to give again, we
Ard. 2405 I had ne'er given *c.* to this foul deed
Puck 42 of whose *c.* if I had been, no question but
SP 370 brave Gentlemen, by all your free consents
Consented.
JB 72 she *c.* by his direction to poyson Brewen
Consenting.
HP 666 in no sort to be *c.* to such follies
SP 1728 and first I stinge them with *c.* love
Puck 64 I was neither agent nor *c.* therunto
Consequence.
HP 1675 her Chylde, and per *c.* Gods Neipce
SP 1625 under couler of great *c.*
SP 2197 your deedes are trifles, mine of *c.*
Ard. 727 and in a matter of great *c.*
Ard. 912 dare swear a matter of such *c.* ?
Consequently.
HP 786 the bodies and *c.* the manners of yong sucklings
HP 1036 and *c.* every other otherwise be occupied
HP 1746 it should consequentlie be as true that
Conservation.
HP Ind. 28 *c.* of things, howe it
HP 521 two purposes are proposed, *C.* and Encrease
HP 1144 is imployed to *C.* and Encrease
Conserve.
HP 1232 and teach thee to *c.* and multiply thy Revenewes
HP Ind. 46 conserves necessary in houses
HP 1274 without some kinde of liquor or conserves
Consider.
HP 591 to *c.* that no distinction of nobilitie
HP 1283 if (like a good husband) thou advise thee and *c.* it
HP 1723 that we *c.* whether they be discrepant in forme
SP 1616 *c.* in two extreames the least is to be chosen
Consideration.
HP Ind. 24 *c.* in condicions of possessions
HP 868 that we come to the *c.* of the third person
HP 1212 it commeth into the *c.* of Quallitie to know
HP 1375 purpose worthie of *c.*
HP 1725 the *c.* of the forme of a Princes Pallace
SP 463 what lighter paiment can there be then *c.* ?
Considered.
HP Ind. 124 riches, howe to be *c.*

HP Ind. 136 times of the yeere to bee *c.* of
HP 578 is in two speciall things to be *c.*
HP 1184 no quantity is more to be *c.* then that of money
HP 1425 now it rests to be *c.*, whether
HP 1556 for riches are to be *c.* alwaies in respect of
HP 1605 is not *c.* to be otherwise applied
HP 1616 this devision being thus *c.*, much
STA 1771 and what a losse were this, *c.* truly?
SP 464 well, sir, youle see me *c.*, will you not?
Ard. 1043 a dreadful thing to be *c.* of

Considereth.
HP 435 that diligently *c.* what was said
HP 1147 to him that perticulerly *c.* the care
HP 1642 the olde and new Law, who so *c.* not, let him

Considering.
HP 460 worthy to be pardoned (co[n]sidering your offence)
HP 685 *c.* that by nature shee is so desirous to
HP 955 *c.* it is no lesse needeful for them
HP 1113 *c.* that for the most part they are
HP 1260 a good huswife well *c.*, shold cause
HP 1365 *c.* that those benefits are small
HP 1433 *c.* that the Earth is the naturall
ST 2407 *c.* how I think of you my selfe

Consist.
HP Ind. 66 equallitie in marriage, wherein it doth *c.*
HP 1616 much more may riches multiply that *c.* in bare money
Cor. 155 our blysse consists not in possessions

Consisteth.
HP 1617 which *c.* in thinges measured and numbred

Consisting.
HP Ind. 87 huswifry *c.* much in spinning

Consitiri.
SP 958 a plain case : Qui tacet *c.* videtur

Consort.
HP 528 is termed by a tytle more effectuall, *C.*
HP 540 the name of *C.* or Felow is to be attributed to
Cor. 651 teares, that thus *c.* me in my myserie?
ST 3023 I may *c.* ny freends in pleasing sort
SP 127 and desires you to *c.* her to the triumphes
Puck 43 no question but I also shold have been of their *c.*
HP 529 companions and consorts of one selfe fortune

Consorte.
HP 544 L'errante mia *C.*

Consorted.
HP 75 to be *c.* with so well accomplished an Hoste
HP 448 commodiously *c.* with perswasions
HP 582 cannot be *c.* well under the bands of wedlock
HP 1638 and *c.* with so many perilous evils as are
ST 1042 when he in Campe *c.* Balthazar
ST 1684 I came, *c.* with the Prince, and

Conspiracies.
Cor. 835 or why from Catlins lewde *c.* preserv'd

Conspire.
Cor. 1442 will those *c.* my death that live by mee?
SP 921 for all these three *c.* my tragedie

Conspired.
Cor. 1261 practized, conspierd, conjur'd a thousand waies
Ard. 2327 *c.* and wrought his death shall rue it

Conspiring.
ST 1526 the blustring winds, *c.* with my words

Constable.
Ard. 1933 have taken the *c.* from his watch
Ard. 2378 the *c.* had twenty warrants to apprehend me

Constancy.
SP (Title) Loves *c.*, Fortunes inconstancy, and Deaths triumphs
SP 61 the meaning of my true harts constancie

SP 1411 perhaps thou doubts my friendships constancie
Ard. 210 to try thy *c.* have I been strange
Ard. 1630 why, what is love without true *c.*?

Constant.
Cor. 357 Heavens influence was nere so *c.* yet
SP 2128 was she not *c.*?

Constantinople.
SP 940 I will be in *C.*
SP 1021 to *C.*, whether I must follow him
SP 1719 farewell, *C.*; I will to Rhodes
SP 2020 the great Turque, whose seat is *C.*

Constitution.
HP 12 tough sinewed, and of a strong *c.*
HP 851 but of a strong and manlie *c.*

Constrain.
HP 409 which I will thus constraine my selfe to proove
ST 1631 well, force perforce, I must constraine my selfe

Constrained.
HP 347 *c.* to retyre them from the heate
Cor. 1416 and Romains wrong was I constraind to fight
ST 1582 woe to the cause of these *c.* warres

Constraint.
Cor. 1236 nor yeeld unto the yoke but by *c.*

Consul.
Cor. 1687 (being an auncient Senator, an Emperor and *C.*)

Consume.
Eng. Parn. 3 Under a tyrant, to *c.* ones age
Ard. 1268 till by the force thereof my part *c.*
Cor. 427 sorrow consumes mee, and, in steed of rest
Cor. 805 consumes the more, the more you seeke to quench it
Ard. 209 which even in bursting forth consumes itself

Consumed.
Cor. 876 which, when it was consum'd, I kindly tooke, and

Consumeth.
HP 855 *c.* that which the labour of
ST 1421 this toyles my body, this *c.* age

Consumpsit.
ST 304 In me *c.* vires fortuna nocendo

Contagions.
HP 369 resolved with the exceeding heate and *c.* of the day

Contagious.
HP 258 a necessarie meate for this *c.* weather

Contain.
HP 1381 the memory it selfe coulde scarce containe them
Cor. 1190 though they containe dead bodies numberles
SP 2174 and let one Epitaph containe us all
SP 1188 know thou that Rhodes, and all that Rhodes containes

Contained.
HP (Title) the notable thinges therein *c.*
HP (Title) *c.* in this Booke
HP 60 *c.* in the compasse whereunto it was accustomed
HP 419 all thinges *c.* in thys our variable and
Cor. 865 one self-same shyp containd us, when I saw
ST 62 but either sort containd within his bounds

Containeth.
Cor. 883 bones which (in extreames) an earthen Urne *c.*

Containing.
HP 83 *c.* five and twentie large and
ST Bal. (Title) The Spanish Tragedy *c.* the
ST (Title) *c.* the lamentable end of Don Horatio, and
ST 2637 *c.* matter, and not common things

Contemner.
HP 672 shewing himselfe a hater, *c.*, and carelesse of

Contemns.
ST 1521 that which heaven contemnes, and men neglect

Contemplate.

HP 361 convenient time to worke or to *c.*
HP 1115 capable of fashions, or apt to studie or contemplat
SP 2145 and on thy beautie [Ile] still *c.*

Contemplation.
HP 483 to *c.* and a quiet life
Ard. 1238 but whither doth *c.* carry me?
HP 361 our operations and contemplations are enclozed with
    darknes

Contemptible.
SP 269 I have rejected with contemptable frownes the

Contend.
HP 340 they contende of the woorthines betwixt
HP 722 thou shouldest *c.* not to discontent her
ST 2104 thinks with patience to *c.* to quiet life

Content.
HP 74 *c.* to be consorted with so well
HP 534 grieveth us the mind can hardly be *c.*
HP 604 wherewith it shall *c.* her Husband to commend her
HP 676 honest women desirous to *c.* their Husbands
HP 721 how much the more she shall *c.* thee, so much the more
HP 885 of one that better may *c.* him
HP 890 so governe hys familie as they shall rest *c.* of him
Cor. 1326 can live *c.*, although unknowne
Cor. 1978 *c.* to count the ghosts of those great Captains
Jer. 756 for not *c.* to stay the time of murder
Jer. 1002 *c.* : this is [a] joy mixed with spight
Jer. 1121 *c.* thee, boy ; thou shalt sustaine no wrong
ST 27 then was the Feriman of Hell *c.* to
ST 264 *c.* thee, Marshall, thou shalt have no wrong
ST 584 my feature is not to *c.* her sight
ST 592 yet might she love me to *c.* her sire
ST 1281 *c.* your selfe, stand close, theres somewhat in 't
ST 1720 but *c.* your selfe : the Prince is
ST 1934 your highnes highly shall *c.* his Majestie
ST 2157 *c.* you, sirs ; are you determined that
ST 2176 but mine, or thine, Bazulto, be *c.*
ST 2364 come, Bel-imperia, Balthazars *c.*
ST 2379 *c.* thy selfe, for I am satisfied
ST 2449 *c.* thy selfe, and doe not trouble me
ST 2456 *c.* thy selfe, Andrea ; though I sleepe, yet
ST 2543 assure your selfe, it would *c.* them well
SP 889 what, shall we play heere ? *c.*
SP 937 how say you, sir, are you *c.* ?
SP 1215 to trie thy valour : say, art thou *c.* ?
SP 1216 I, if my Soveraigne say *c.*, I yeeld
SP 1416 newes to our honour, and to thy *c.*
SP 1838 but seemd *c.* to flie with him to Rhodes
Ard. 216 I am *c.* for to be reconciled
Ard. 497 and though I might *c.* as good a man
Ard. 539 such as will *c.* thee well, sweetheart
Ard. 608 I am *c.* my sister shall be yours
Ard. 1560 *c.* ; sirrah, saddle your mistress' nag
Ard. 1864 for with that name I never shall *c.* thee
Ard. 1887 *c.* thee, sweet Alice, thou shalt have thy will
Ard. 2124 I am *c.* to drink to him for this once
Ard. 2143 *C.*
Ard. 2205 I pray you, be *c.*, I'll have my will
HP 153 « Like to those Jayes whose flight contents the world
Cor. 75 sith it contents not thy posteritie
ST 521 Hieronimo, this maske contentes mine eye
ST 711 (two chiefe contents, where more cannot be had)
SP 307 & 308 by the contents of this blade
Ard. 2388 but I dare swear thou knewest not the contents

Contented.
ST 2295 confirmed thy motion, and *c.* me

Contenteth.

HP 312 which also most *c.* me
ST 2345 and no man lives that long *c.* all
Ard. 1074 this negligence not half *c.* me

Continual.
Cor. 1995 and presse the ayre with your continuall plaints
SP 1112 perhaps my greefe and long continuall moane
SP 1219 but ever after thy continuall friend
Ard. 503 thus live I daily in *c.* fear
Ard. 1222 *c.* trouble of my moody brain
JB 165 being a continuall resorter to her house

Continually.
HP 705 call him Phoebus with these Epythetons almost co[n]ti-
    nually
HP 863 that they be *c.* exercised in those
HP 1047 as continuallie beastlines and filth corrupt
HP 1403 which, as it was not usd *c.*
Cor. 347 but (like the Clowdes) continuallie doth range
JB 69 but *c.* urged her to make him away

Continuance.
SP 64 my love is of a long *c.*, and merites

Continue.
HP 795 doo yet *c.* in their Mothers custodie
Cor. 104 or, standing now, she would *c.* thus
Cor. 172 that we *c.* our offence begunne
Cor. 358 in good or bad as to *c.* it
Cor. 683 the self-same style by conquest may *c.*
Cor. 690 the more unlike she should *c.* ever
ST 1739 weele goe *c.* this discourse at Court
ST 2472 as discontent that things *c.* so
JB 149 « for I am not long to *c.* in this world »
Cor. 34 but faith continues not where men command

Continued.
HP 557 *c.* her unwillingnes of having a second husbande
HP 983 are caused and *c.* by such as these
Ard. 428 then had he died and our love *c.*

Continueth.
HP 627 wherof by being obstinat she *c.* unfurnished

Contradict.
Cor. 1450 who dares to *c.* our Emporie ?

Contraries.
HP 753 Judges of theyr opposites and indigested *c.*
Puck 30 the verie *c.* to w^ch^, my greatest enemies will

Contrarily.
HP 581 or, *c.*, a Gentleman with a Begger

Contrary.
HP 214 much disliked and intreated to the contrarie
HP 406 one of them that hold the *c.*
HP 1293 (if occasion of resort of straungers be not to the *c.*)
HP 1746 differ not in form, but are opposit and contrarie
ST 1405 I would have sworne it, had I not seene the *c.*
ST 1544 the fellow had a faire commission to the *c.*

Contrived.
Ard. 537 to let thee know all that I have *c.*

Control.
Cor. 71 what helps it thee that under thy controll the
Cor. 124 a note of Chaunce that may the proude controle
Ard. 275 might I without *c.* enjoy thee still
Cor. 1244 and like a Prince controls the Romulists
ST 821 although my fainting hart controles my soule
Cor. 23 endure a million of base controls

Controlled.
HP 1005 controld, and at commaundment of those higher officers
ST 230 is now controlde by fortune of the warres

Controversy.
SP 1116 in controversie touching the Ile of Rhodes

Convectare.

HP 1454 C. juvat praedas et vivere rapto
Convenient.
HP 85 four square and of c. greatnes
HP 360 it giveth not men c. time to worke
HP 637 it is c. also that their vertues should be divers
HP 681 her bodie with c. ornaments should be
HP 714 so much the more c. it is that they account of it
HP 764 it was c. that, beeing ashamed of her selfe
HP 866 spoken so much as hath beene c.
HP 887 which was not c. for slaves
HP 1240 at such c. time as things are deerest
HP 1378 could not utter them in time c.
HP 1563 conserning this naturall gaine c. for a Housekeeper
ST 802 and shall be sent with all c. speed
SP 1934 lets saile to Rhodes with all c. speede
Conveniently.
HP 634 it hath beene c. ordeined of Nature
HP 1500 carryed or recarried most c.
ST 2876 that I might kill him more c.
Conversation.
HP 226 companions and brothers in their c.
Conversed.
Puck 38 to enquire of such as he conversd w^thall
Convert.
Cor. 594 those fountaines doe to floods convart?
Cor. 1549 and to choller doth convart purest blood about the
   heart
Converted.
Cor. 644 tyme past with me that am to teares c.
Ard. 1336 the holy word that had c. me
Converting.
HP 1691 and howe to the c. and imploying
Convey.
ST Bal. 50 did straight convaye them to the place
ST 41 why then, said Eacus, convay him hence
ST 1368 boy, goe, convay this purse to Pedringano
ST 1392 the winde convay our words amongst unfreendly eares
ST 1518 so, Executioner; convay him hence
Ard. 2270 but first c. the body to the fields
Ard. 2393 c. me from the presence of that strumpet
Conveyance.
ST 618 for thy conveiance in Andreas love
Conveyed.
SP 1976 to heere and see the matter well convaid
Conveying.
HP 1626 transporting and conveighing Coyne from place to
   place
Conviene.
HP 1651 Lo Genesi, dal principio, c.
Convinced.
Ard. 374 now will be c. or purge myself
Convivio.
HP 1743 approved by Socrates to Aristophanes in C. Platonis
Cook.
HP 395 drest by the most excellent Cooke the Duke hath
Ard. 1831 and take her unawares playing the c.
Ard. 1961 and as thou goest, tell John c. of our guests
Cooke.
Ard. 680 saying he served Sir Antony C.
Cookery.
HP 1354 the Kitchin C. and such like
Cool.
SP 662 to coole affection with our woords and lookes
Cooled.
SP 246 my Palfray cold his thirst
Copesmate.

Ard. 1323 go, get thee gone, a c. for thy hinds
Copious.
HP Ind. 7 Autumn more c. of fruites
Copper.
Ard. 1320 thy worthless c. shows thee counterfeit
Copy.
ST 2718 to give the King the coppie of the plaie
Coral.
SP 1461 lips of pure Corall, breathing Ambrosie
Cord.
ST 2269 talke not of cords, but let us now be gone, for with a
   c. Horatio was slaine
SP 1794 see that your strangling cords be ready
Core.
HP 939 M' impresse al c. e fece 'l suo simile
Coricius.
HP 140 the good old man, C., the Gardener
Corn.
VPJ 23 my crop of corne is but a field of tares
VPJ 41 thy crop of corne is tares availing naughts
HP 90 prettie lodgings for servaunts, and houses for Corne
HP 389 deceived by his servaunts in gathering of his Corne
HP 1067 « to fetch the watrie, rotten Corne »
HP 1281 all her houshold corne be some ground for bread
Cor. 199 falling as thick (through warlike crueltie) as eares of
   Corne
Cor. 903 and let faire Nylus (wont to nurse your Corne)
Cor. 1854 lyke eares of Corne with rage of windie showres
Jer. 222 from farmers that crack barns with stuffing corne
ST 1017 thou talkest of harvest, when the corne is greene
ST 1019 the Sickle comes not, till the corne be ripe
SP 1603 that thrust his sickle in my harvest corne
Ard. 1244 to make my harvest nothing but pure c.
Ard. 1622 why should he thrust his sickle in our c.
Cornelia.
Cor. Ded. 22 the passing of a Winters weeke with desolate C.
Cor. Arg. 1 C., the daughter of Metellus Scipio
Cor. 252 thou shouldst, C., have broke the
Cor. 463 no, no, C., Caron takes not paine to
Cor. 655 O poore C., have not wee good cause
Cor. 718 sleep'st thou, C.? sleepst thou, gentle wife
Cor. 880 I bring to faire C. to interr
Cor. 886 O poore C., borne to be distrest
Cor. 1589 yet must I report to sad C.
Cor. 1603 passions have we endurde, C., for your sake?
Cor. 1947 venge not thy wrong upon C.
Cor. 2017 dye, rather die, C.: and (to spare
Cor. 2028 C. must live (though life she hateth)
Cor. (Title) Pompey the Great, his faire Corneliaes Tragedie
Cor. 681 title be not expired in Cornelias blood
SP 1120 married C., daughter to the Governour?
Corner.
ST 124 each c. strongly fenst with wings of shot
ST 1286 me thinks this c. is to close with one
Ard. 498 yet doth he keep in every c. trulls
Cor. 320 that even in all the corners of the earth thy
SP 102 assembled from severall corners of the world
Cornet.
ST 132 did with his C. bravely make attempt
Cor. 1770 thryce did the Cornets of the souldiers (cleerd) turne to
Corn-grounds.
Cor. 216 and for faire Corne-ground are our fields surcloid with
Cornu.
HP 810 Flectere ludus equos, et spicula tendere c.
Coronae.
VPJ 61 Successere rogi regno, coruique c.

Coronation.
SP 1123 what, greater then at our *c.*?
Coronet.
Cor. 1520 new set with many a fresh-flowrd *C.*
Cor. 312 thy Helmet deckt with coronets of Bayes ?
Corporal.
Ard. 659 where I was a *c.*, and thou but a
Ard. 664 « one snatch good *c.* », when I stole the
Corpse.
ST 898 and left thy bloudie corpes dishonoured heere
Cor. 770 and ne're returneth to the Corse interd
Cor. 873 I woave a Coffyn for his corse of Seggs
Cor. 928 to see his tired corse lye toyling in his blood
Jer. 1140 honord Funerall for thy melting corse
Cor. 1579 beheld theyr corses scattred on the plaines
Cor. 1984 now (loaden) groane to feele the Romaine corses
Correct.
Jer. 360 allas, that Spaine should *c.* Portugal
Jer. 361 *c.*? O in that one word such
Jer. 1097 *c.* thy rascals, Prince ; thou *c.* him ?
Corrected.
ST (Title) newly *c.*, amended, and enlarged with new Additions
Correction.
Jer. 1096 my sword shall give *c.* to thy toong
Corregidor.
ST 2152 to plead in causes as Corrigidor
Correspondent.
HP 1755 are as *c.* for proportion to
Corrival.
Ard. 1584 the painter, my *c.*, that would needs
Corrupt.
HP 1048 beastlines and filth *c.*, disgrace, and spoile thinges
HP 1263 fish and fowle, which will bee suddainly *c.*
Cor. 175 which with their noisome fall *c.* the ayre
SP 788 yes, heavens are just, but thou art so *c.*
Corruptam.
HP 1065 Tum Cererem *c.* undis
Corrupted.
HP 431 things are first ingendred and afterward *c.*
Corrupter.
HP 1685 a *c.* of the Common wealth, a disobeyer of
Corruptible.
HP 420 in thys our variable and *c.* world
Corruption.
HP 421 the cause of generation and of *c.*
HP 429 beginneth with generation, not with *c.*
HP 1262 that will not keepe without *c.*
HP 1270 theyr moysture (that is cause of theyr *c.*)
HP 1679 beget or bring forth money without *c.*
HP 1680 that the *c.* of one bee the generation of another
Corse, *see* **Corpse.**
Corsic.
ST 2166 and melt the Corsicke rockes with ruthfull teares
Corsive.
ST 234 his Sonne distrest, a *c.* to his hart
Coruique.
VPJ 61 Successere rogi regno, *c.* coronae
Cosmographical.
HP 451 according to the Cosmographicall dyscription of some
Cost.
Jer. 121 hee loves my sister : that shall *c.* his life
ST 588 my presents are not of sufficient *c.*
ST 2221 alas, my lease, it *c.* me ten pound, and
ST 2496 whom they with care and *c.* have tendred so
SP 1011 I rather thinke it *c.* him very deare
SP 1012 I, so it did, for it *c.* Ferdinando his life

SP 1155 or *c.* me more brave Souldiers then all that Ile
Ard. 1608 such another word will *c.* you a cuff or
Ard. 1962 and bid him lay it on, spare for no *c.*
Costard.
Ard. 1975 hand and feet, one and two round, at his *c.*
Costly.
SP 1395 of rich imbroderie, or *c.* ornaments
Cothurnata.
ST 2636 Tragedia cothurnata, fitting Kings
Cottage.
HP 24 I have a little *C.* where you may repose
HP 1726 the forme of a Princes Pallace and a poore mans *C.*
Couch.
Ard. 976 and *c.* dishonour as dishonour buds
Couched.
SP 324 their Launces were coucht too hie, and
SP 1364 I coucht my selfe in poore Erastus eyes
Coucheth.
Ard. 1426 dog that *c.* till the fowling-piece be off
Council.
ST 562 I think our councell is already set
ST 1128 we with our Councell will deliberate
SP 1208 and in our Counsell shalt thou sit with us
Ard. 2287 I have the Council's warrant to apprehend him
Ard. 2366 and get the Council's warrant to apprehend them
Counsel.
HP 860 advise and counsell that thou bring them upp in
Jer. 42 thy counsell Ile imbrace as I do thee
ST 787 and worke it if my counsaile may prevaile
ST 835 and in thy love and councell drowne my feare
SP 121 counsell me not, for my intent is sworne
SP 528 so counsell I, as thou thyselfe hast said
SP 609 harts counsell bridle the fond intemperance of thy
    tongue ?
SP 1225 and now from armes to counsell sit thee downe
SP 1605 to one past cure good counsell comes too late
SP 1738 to counsell Soliman to slay his friend
Ard. 982 good *c.* is to her as rain to weeds
Ard. 2246 stay, Susan, stay, and help to *c.* me
Ard. 2247 alas, I *c.*! fear frights away my wits
Ard. 502 as counsels him to make away his wife
Ard. 1906 I know my wife counsels me for the best
Counselled.
Ard. 520 then, Master Greene, be *c.* by me
Counsellor.
SP 2138 how durst thou then, ungratious counseller
Count.
Cor. 1978 content to *c.* the ghosts of those great Captains
Ard. 528 or *c.* me false and perjured whilst I live
Countenance.
HP 28 in his very countenaunce a kind of gentilitie and
HP 116 of *c.* verie pleasant myxed with comelie gravitie
HP 123 turning to his elder Sonne with a pleasant *c.*
ST 95 but what portends thy cheerful *c.*
ST 1039 and theres no credit in the *c.*
SP 780 to check thy fraudfull *c.* with a blush ?
Ard. 258 that makes him frame a speaking *c.*
Ard. 769 « with a frowning look of your crabbed *c.* »
JB 95 with a mery pleasaunt *c.*, and very kindly
HP 699 the countenaunces of youthes, uppon whose faces hayre
    never came
Ard. 31 no nobleman will *c.* such a peasant
Ard. 202 for what hast thou to *c.* my love
Counter.
Ard. 821 you shall be well beaten and sent to the *C.*
Counterbuff.

Cor. 1765 and then it riseth with a counterbuffe

Counter-cambio.

SP 1015 and lost our box in counter cambio

Countercheck.

ST 744 give me a kisse, ile counterchecke thy kisse

SP 1371 to c. his hart by turning Turke

Counterfeit.

Cor. 762 they counterfet the dead in voyce and figure

ST 2210 the Thracian Poet thou shalt counterfeite

ST 2819 that this is fabulously c.

SP 364 is not this a counterfet foole?

SP 980 now it fits my wisdome to c. the foole

SP 1720 farewell, c. foole

Ard. 1320 thy worthless copper shows thee c.

ST 353 counterfeits under the colour of a duteous friend

ST 844 no, Cupid counterfeits the Nightingale

ST 2479 is this the kindnes that thou counterfeits?

Jer. 696 that was Alcario, my shapes counterfet

Ard. 234 sweet Alice, he shall draw thy c.

Counterfeiting.

Jer. 658 no, conterfeiting villaine

Countermured.

ST 1537 where, countermurde with walles of diamond

Countervail.

SP 548 whose skin will countervaile the hunters toile

Countess.

Cor. Ded. and rightly honoured Lady, The Countesse of Sussex

Countest.

Cor. 93 but vainely count'st thine owne victorious deeds

Counting-house.

Ard. 2018 locked within the c. shall

Ard. 2050 give me the key : which is the c.?

Ard. 2075 stand before the c. door

Ard. 2166 first lay the body in the c.

Countries.

HP 171 after the manner of our petit C.

HP 304 colde C. where the Sunne hath not

HP 1166 though they be divers according to the variety of Countreys

HP 1481 traffique their commodities to Countreys where

HP 1509 and travails into forren Countreys

Cor. 114 and tyerd our neighbour C. so with charge

SP 150 welcome these worthies by their severall c.

SP 639 I made those knights, of severall sect and c.

Country.

VPJ 18 health of thy Countrey, helpe to all our harmes

HP Ind. 45 country provision unbought

HP 41 said I was never till nowe in this Countrey

HP 43 for the Countrey is very pleasant, and

HP 98 amongst the woods and in a Countrey Towne

HP 156 remember you are in a C. Town

HP 203 the custome of our Countrey, carieth a certain priviledge

HP 459 of whom the crye is come into our Countrey

HP 996 labor, countrey busines, and household exercise

HP 1173 within the Countrey where he dwelleth

HP 1220 the bancks to any navigable water, or in a champant Countrey

HP 1237 be brought from his Ferme or Mannor in the Countrey

HP 1254 eyther from the Countrey, or bought about in Markets

HP 1483 bargained for the commodities of a Countrey

HP 1495 also in what Province, Shyre or Countrey

HP 1501 one Province or Countrey with another

HP 1630 the value of mony of some C. coyne beeing variable

Cor. 1142 the love that men theyr C. and theyr birth-right beare

Cor. 1265 bravely to doe his c. good

Cor. 1473 but for thy friends and C. all too-short

Cor. 1645 Campe of creeping Emmets in a Countrey Farme

Cor. 1683 day, wherein our C. shall approve our love

ST 2582 if, as it is our C. maner, you will but

SP 154 graced by thy c., but ten times more by

SP 219 but whats the word that glories your Countrey?

SP 220 sooth to say, the earth is my Countrey

SP 234 than the ruine of that whole countrey

SP 252 I have no word, because no countrey

SP 941 farewell, my c., dearer then my life

SP 942 farewell, sweete friends, dearer then countrey soyle

SP 1244 tis not my countrey, but Phylippos wrath

SP 1648 where a man lives well, there is his countrie

JB 217 carried into the countrey to be delivered of her childe

VPJ 83 the only life of countries state

Cor. 384 not die a better death then for his Countries weale

Cor. 966 not heavens feare, nor Countries sacred love

Cor. 1144 our Countries love then friends or chyldren are

Cor. 1251 that there is one that curbs their Countries weale

Cor. 1275 t'enlarge his countries liberty

Cor. 1445 O, but theyr Countries good concerns them more

Cor. 1446 what, thinke they mee to be their Countries foe?

Jer. 856 honor, your countries reputation, your lives freedome

ST 498 and learne my Father and my Countries health

SP 159 where for my countries cause I chargde my Launce

SP 254 therefore each countries word mine to pronounce

Country-fashion.

HP 230 drest, after our Countrey fashion, with Larde

Countryman.

HP 46 what are you, what Countreyman

Countrymen.

HP 62 told me by the Countreymen commorants there that

HP 1061 weapons, which the Countreymen did use

SP 1234 blade in the deare bowels of my countrimen

SP 1242 why favourst thou thy countrimen so much?

SP 1249 nor shalt thou war against thy Countrimen

Country-swain.

Cor. 816 lyke morall Esops mysled Country swaine

Country-wench.

Cor. 638 the C. unto her worke awakes

Couple.

Cor. 1785 and makes them c., when they see theyr prize

SP 634 I c. minds together by consent

SP 787 would never c. Woolves and Lambes together

Ard. 1702 come, let us go on like a c. of blind pilgrims

Ard. 1712 none but a c. of gentlemen, that went

Ard. 2193 a c. of ruffians threatened him yesternight

Coupled.

HP 580 cannot be c. under one selfe yoake

Courage.

Cor. 538 of certaine c. gainst incertaine chaunce

Cor. 1712 and let us fight with c., and conceite that

Cor. 1767 with self-same c., worth, and weapons to

Jer. 307 have c., boy : I shall prevent their plots

Jer. 358 not bate an inch of c. nor a haire of fate

Jer. 898 I know your curage to be trid and good

Jer. 1016 the glory of our foe, the hart of c.

Jer. 1037 had I not knowne my strength and c.

Jer. 1100 so strong a c. of so greene a set

SP 91 and add fresh c. to my fainting limmes

SP 164 our word of c. all the world hath heard

SP 179 what is thy word of c., brave man of Spaine?

Ard. 2055 will add unwonted c. to my thought

Jer. 937 our courages are new borne, our vallors bred

Ard. 1009 when bugs and fears shall kill our courages

Courageous.

HP 835 many of the Phrygians also were couragious

Cor. 47 nor feare the darts of our couragious troopes
Cor. 793 thy bravest Captaines, whose coragious harts
Jer. 1007 this fierce, couragious Prince, a noble worthy
Course.
HP 1531 no lesse then may suffise to direct hys *c.*
Cor. 328 by whom the former *c.* of thy faire deeds
Cor. 350 doe coast the Earth with an eternall *c.*
Cor. 475 both Clownes and Kings one self-same *c.* must run
Cor. 1869 did hourely keepe their ordinary *c.*
ST 43 and spend the *c.* of everlasting time
ST 2198 ore turnest then the upper billowes *c.* of waves to keep
SP 323 now sir, how likes thou this *C.?*
SP 326 now, sir, how like you this *c.?*
SP 402 though over-borne, and foyled in my *c.*
SP 419 beyond the *c.* of Titans burning raies
SP 1251 but, that our oath may have his currant *c.*
ST 481 alas, my Lord, these are but words of *c.*
Courser.
ST 246 this hand first tooke his *c.* by the raines
SP 426 but wheres your coursers taile?
Cor. 308 or watereth his Coursers in the West)
Court.
HP 81 before the house there was a little *C.*
HP 89 descended by as manie other steps into a little *C.*
HP 1733 private house (I meane not a little *C.*)
Ard. 943 over the threshold to the inner *c.*
HP 103 unexperienced in Courte or on the worldes conditions
HP 1774 endevour and apply themselves to serve in *C.*
HP 1780 and the rest by his owne experience in *C.*
Cor. 1921 then all the Captives in th' infernall *C.*
Jer. 59 shake the Kings hie *c.* three handfuls downe
Jer. 79 Ile wake the *C.*, or startle out some bloud
Jer. 101 Ambitions plumes, that florisht in our *c.*
Jer. 224 [one] from dicing houses: but from the *c.*, none, none
Jer. 329 is welcome to his friend, thou to our *c.*
Jer. 389 the valiant spirit ere trod the Spanish courte
Jer. 519 to say, knavery in the *C.* and honesty in a cheese house
Jer. 559 Jeronimo lives much absent from the *C.*
Jer. 584 tis all about the *c.* in every eare
Jer. 630 tis all about the *C.* Andreas come
Jer. 869 makes thy *c.* melt in Luxuriousnes
Jer. 1032 you braved me, Don, within my Fathers *c.*
ST Bal. 91 then to the *C.* forthwith I went
ST 4 I was a Courtier in the Spanish *C.*
ST 55 in keeping on my way to Plutos *C.*
ST 507 wrapt every houre in pleasures of the *C.*
ST 731 the *C.* were dangerous, that place is safe
ST 812 with greatest pleasure that our *C.* affords
ST 1086 and, well intreated in the *C.* of Spaine
ST 1430 bring forth the Prisoner, for the *C.* is set
ST 1591 and cry aloud for justice through the *C.*
ST 1621 why am I thus sequestred from the *C.?*
ST 1739 weele goe continue this discourse at *C.*
ST 1871 and in the presence of the *C.* of Spaine
ST 2204 knock at the dismall gates of Plutos *C.*
ST 2277 welcome, brave Vice-roy, to the *C.* of Spaine
ST 2332 wone by his deserts within the *C.* of Spaine?
ST 2341 whence growes the ground of this report in *C.?*
ST 2750 these be our pastimes in the *C.* of Spaine
SP 433 for neighing in the Emperours *c.*
Eng. Parn. 5 Whose cursed Courts with bloud and incest swell
HP 1041 in the house, Cortes, Tables, or Coffers
HP 1568 and mightie men in Princes Courts
HP 1717 the government of private houses and of Princes
   Courtes are different
Jer. 242 in her private gallery you shall place, to *c.* her

SP 1527 yet give me leave in honest sort to *c.* thee
SP 337 now comes in the infant that courts my mistresse
Courteous.
HP 44 and inhabited of people passing *c.*
HP 463 whereof you are too *c.* a commender
HP 719 modest, discreet, *c.*, and brought up in good discipline
ST 2351 I helde him thence with kind and curteous wordes
SP 895 for this so *c.* and unlookt for sport
SP 1150 *c.* in peace, in battell dangerous
SP 2134 faire spoken, wise, *c.*, and liberall
JB 96 giving him the good morrow in most *c.* manner
Courtesy.
HP 17 said: «Tell me, sir, of courtesie, whither is your journey?»
HP 68 necessity now bound me to accept his courtesie
HP 131 I, thanking him for his courtesie, praid
HP 1074 and when entercourse of love and courtesie entreats
ST 252 to him in curtesie, to this perforce
ST 2137 thy Cappe to curtesie, and thy knee to bow
SP 1054 in Knightly curtesie, I thanke thee
SP 1177 the flower of chivalrie and curtesie
SP 1224 by curtesie let Soliman conquer thee
SP 1585 the one so renownd for armes and curtesie
SP 1768 or have regard unto his curtesie
Ard. 263 then, brother, to requite this *c.*
Court-hound.
Jer. 641 leane like a court hound that liks fat trenchers cleane
Courtier.
HP 105 a Brother that hath long beene a *C.*
Jer. 114 a melancholy, discontented *c.*
Jer. 507 bending in the hams like an old *C.*
Jer. 736 hath his fame as well as a great *c.*
Jer. 776 is not this a monstrous *c.?*
ST 4 I was a *C.* in the Spanish Court
Jer. 433 cannot give a letter the right Courtiers crest?
Jer. 119 (for Courtiers wil doe any thing for gould)
Jer. 203 my names an honest name, a Courtiers name
ST 2580 and now it shall be plaide by Princes and Courtiers
Jer. 698 O, good words, my Lords, for those are courtiers vailes
Courting.
ST 2530 how now, Hieronimo? what, *c.* Bel-imperia?
ST 2531 such *c.* as, I promise you, she hath my hart
Courtly.
ST 2654 in *c.* French shall all her phraises be
Court-toad.
Jer. 777 he is the court tode, father
Cousin.
SP 964 ah, loving cousen, how art thou misdone by
Coutelace.
Cor. 193 arm'd with his blood-besmeard keene *C.*
Cor. 1678 and in the other graspt his Coutelas
Cover.
Cor. 293 clowdes of adversitie will *c.* you
Cor. 567 that *c.* all this earthly round
Cor. 904 *c.* your Land with Toades and Crocadils
Cor. 1648 *c.* the earth so thicke, as scarce we tread but
Jer. 586 and which the more to *c.*, I tooke a boule
ST 901 O heavens, why made you night to *c.* sinne?
STA 2977 fall, heaven, and *c.* us with thy sad ruines
Ard. 2279 peace, fool, the snow will *c.* them again
Ard. 1338 in this golden *c.* shall thy sweet phrases
Covered.
HP 94 in the midst thereof was a Table *c.*
HP 758 «Lay doun with him upo[n] the grasse al *c.* with a clowde»
Cor. 716 jawes, (which slyghtly cover'd with a scarce-seene skyn)
SP 1500 her face is coverd over quite, my Lord
SP 1505 now she is all *c.*, my Lord

Ard. 14 the earth hung over my head and *c.* me
Ard. 239 ay, but we'll have it *c.* with a cloth
Ard. 2375 and had not I with my buckler *c.* my head
Coverer.
ST 2843 but night, the *c.* of accursed crimes
Covereth.
ST 2113 heaven *c.* him that hath no buriall
Covering.
SP 431 for presumption, for *c.* the Emperors Mare
Covert.
SP 1466 where under *c.* lyes the fount of pleasure
Covet.
SP 853 nor do I *c.* but what is mine owne
Covetise.
Cor. 26 thy mortall covetize perverts our lawes
Covetous.
HP 1621 and so by *c.* desire to become infinit
ST 1913 and *c.* of having to himselfe the ransome
Cow.
SP 1666 even as a *C.* for tickling in the horne
Coward.
Cor. 1321 surprizd, doth *c.* poison quaile their breath, or
Cor. 1440 have in theyr *c.* soules devised snares
SP 727 I alwayes told you that such *c.* knights
Jer. 918 O vertuous *c.*
Jer. 919 to terme him *c.* for his vertuous merit
Jer. 920 *c.*? nay then, relentles rib of steele
SP 222 I repute myself no *c.*; for humilitie shall mount
SP 740 unlesse, forewarnd, the weakling *c.* flies
SP 741 thou foolish *c.*, flies? Erastus lives
SP 1686 came like a *c.* stealing after me
Ard. 909 a poorer *c.* than yourself was never
Ard. 1104 to let thee know I am no *c.*, I
Ard. 799 to the Nag's Head, there is this coward's haunt
Ard. 1132 cut not the nose from off the coward's face
Cor. 1627 and call our souldiers cowards to theyr face
Cowardice.
Cor. 535 tis not for frailtie or faint cowardize that
Cor. 1119 plaine in their Tombes of our base cowardise?
Jer. 900 not that I tast of feare or cowerdyse
ST 456 for what wast els but murderous cowardise
SP 1302 so dreadfull is our name to *c.*
Ard. 858 why, this would steel soft-mettled *c.*
Cowardly.
Jer. 1085 my foes are base, and slay me *c.*
Cowgomers.
HP 191 taste like Goords and *C.*
Coy.
ST 572 my Lord, though Bel-imperia seeme thus *c.*
SP 382 faire Ladies should be coye to showe their faces
SP 721 and thou misdoubts, perhaps, that ile prove coye
SP 1483 coye Virgin, knowest thou what offence it is to
ST 767 although she *c.* it as becomes her kinde
Coystril.
SP 1055 but hopes the coystrell to escape me so?
Ard. 1120 as dear as ever coistril bought so little sport
Ard. 1138 to be thus flouted of a coistril
Crabbed.
HP 615 exceeding waiward, *c.* and disobedient
Ard. 489 can the *c.* churl use you unkindly?
Ard. 769 « with a frowning look of your *c.* countenance »
Crack.
Jer. 221 from farmers that *c.* barns with stuffing corne
SP 2029 mans life is as a glasse, and a phillip may cracke it
Cracked.
Ard. 1921 I have *c.* as many blades as thou hast nuts

Craft.
Cor. 1622 in *c.* lamely they fought, to draw us
Crammed.
Ard. 1989 I would have *c.* in angels in thy fist
Crams.
Jer. 992 and *c.* his store house to the top with bloud
Crane.
SP 1089 Ile send some *C.* to combate with the Pigmew
Crannies.
Cor. 1647 leaving theyr crannyes to goe search about
Crassus.
HP 1540 Crassus sayd he was not rych that was not able to maintaine an Armie
Cor. Arg. 3 was first married to young Crassus
Cor. 254 when as thy husband Crassus (in his flowre) did
Cor. 280 for tis not heaven, nor Crassus (cause he sees
Cor. 1926 when (being but young) I lost my first love Crassus?
Cor. 45 now, Parthia, feare no more, for Crassus death
Crave.
ST Bal. 92 and of the King did Justice *c.*
ST 35 to *c.* a pasport for my wandring Ghost
ST 267 I *c.* no better then your grace awards
ST 439 Ile *c.* your pardon to goe seeke the Prince
SP 1203 then this, my gratious Lord, is all I *c.*
SP 1520 graunt [me] one boone that I shall *c.* of thee
Ard. 1068 I *c.* your pardons for disturbing you
Jer. 910 keepe your forfathers Othes; that vertue craves
ST 2397 Hieronimo, my father craves a word with you
SP 1324 what parle craves the Turkish at our hands?
Ard. 778 what haste my business craves to send to Kent?
Ard. 1777 that which he craves I dearly bought of him
Craving.
SP 1499 so *c.* pardon that I cannot strike
Crawl.
Ard. 318 instead of legs I'll make the *c.* on stumps
Crawled.
Cor. 1900 crawld to the Deck, and, lyfe with death to ease
Create.
Jer. 438 thinke, tis your love makes me *c.* this guise
Created.
HP 454 wherein at first he had *c.* it
ST 540 he after was *c.* Duke of Yorke
Creature.
HP 492 a reasonable *c.* whose dignity doth
HP 928 called Animal rationale, a Reasonable *C.*
Jer. 127 a most weeping *c.* — Thats a woman
SP 1468 a sweeter *c.* nature never made
Ard. 508 so fair a *c.* should be so abused
Ard. 1600 than from a serving *c.* like yourself?
HP 494 also in the industrie of other little creatures
HP 573 a desire most naturall in all reasonable creatures
HP 687 in other creatures hath effected that the bodies of the Male
HP 1086 that men and reasonable creatures are comforted therwith?
STA 1751 doth serve to ballace these light creatures we call Women
Ard. 1833 there's no better creatures in the world, than women
Credit.
HP 405 every manne may credite as he list
HP 726 where other honest women and those of *c.* doo assemble
HP 871 if we shall give credite to antiquities written of
HP 1154 and to maintaine his family with *c.*
HP 1306 necessary and fitt for the ability and credite of her house
HP 1396 albeit of it selfe it beare no great semblance of *c.*
Cor. 1443 in conquered foes what credite can there be?

ST 636 I have no *c.* with her as before
ST 1039 and theres no *c.* in the countenance
ST 2715 O sir, it is for the authors *c.*
SP 949 I may live upon *c.* all the while
Ard. 74 nay, love, there is no *c.* in a dream
Ard. 975 men, who mangle *c.* with their wounding words
Ard. 1301 let me repent the *c.* I have lost
Ard. 1311 and wrapt my *c.* in thy company
Ard. 1625 forsooth, for *c.* sake, I must leave thee !
JB 182 she was carefull for the saving of her *c.*
JB 187 and if you wil not for your owne *c.*, yet
Puck 55 servd almost theis iij. yeres nowe, in *c.* untill nowe
JB 188 yet for my credits sake, marrie me

Credulous.
Cor. 1487 t'is wisdom yet not to be *c.*
ST 1168 advise thee therefore, be not *c.*
SP 1025 that he was true, and you too *c.*

Creep.
SP 1192 thoughts should dare attempt, or but creepe neere my
    heart
Ard. 2147 to prevent that, *c.* betwixt my legs
STA 1752 and at nine moneths ende, creepes foorth to light

Creeping.
Cor. 1645 and as a houshold Campe of *c.* Emmets

Crept.
Jer. 436 which, once but *c.* into the vulger mouthes, is
Ard. 27 *c.* into service of a nobleman

Crest.
Jer. 453 cannot give a letter the right Courtiers *c.* ?
Jer. 834 that when it mounts up to thy warlick *c.*
SP 161 and gained the flower of Gallia in my *c.*

Crevice.
STA 1953 I prie through every *c.* of each wall

Crew.
VPJ 67 the traytrous *c.* late reapt reward
Cor. 1438 the hatefull crue that, wanting powre
ST 1664 amidst a crue of thy confederates
Ard. 785 a *c.* of harlots, all in love, forsooth

Cried.
Cor. 1831 here horse and man (o're-turnd) for mercy cryde
Jer. 623 at first they *c.* all war, as men
ST 883 no, no, it was some woman cride for helpe
Ard. 1885 and *c.* him mercy whom thou hast misdone
JB 10 the blood of the just Abel *c.* most shrill

Crier.
JB 227 for bloud is an unceassant *c.* in the eares of the Lord

Cries.
Cor. 144 whose mournfull cryes and shreekes to heaven ascend
Cor. 418 and thrice detaind, with dolefull shreeks and cryes
STA 1755 being borne, it poutes, cryes, and breeds teeth
STA 1949 cryes out : Horatio. Where is my Horatio ?
ST 2236 thy mother *c.* on righteous Rhadamant for
Ard. 1051 and pitiless Black Will *c.* : « Stab the slave ! »
Ard. 2368 but I am so pursued with hues and *c.*
ST 878 what out-*c.* pluck me from my naked bed

Crime.
Cor. 893 of the extreamest and most odious cryme
Cor. 161 revenge the crymes thy fathers did commit
ST 2843 but night, the coverer of accursed crimes

Crimson.
Jer. 92 Ile threaten *c.* wars
Jer. 407 up hether sayling in a *c.* fleete
Jer. 936 and to this *c.* end our Coullers spred
Jer. 1075 orewhelme thee in such *c.* streames
Jer. 1083 let them both meete in *c.* tinctures shine

Crimson-coloured.

ST 2242 faire crimson coloured spring with withered winter
    to be

Crispy.
Cor. 1344 turne not thy crispie tydes, like silver curle, backe

Croaking.
STA 2077 the Toades croking, the Minutes jerring

Croco.
HP 821 Vobis picta *c.* et fulgenti murice vestis

Crocodiles.
Cor. 904 cover your Land with Toades and Crocodils

Crop.
VPJ 23 my *c.* of corne is but a field of tares
VPJ 41 thy *c.* of corne is tares availing naughts
Cor. 641 Rose : whom (though she see) to *c.* she kindly feares

Cropped.
SP 798 soone cropt with age or with infirmities ?

Cross.
HP 1388 altogeather consent, or musically aunswer crosse
Cor. Arg. 35 these crosse events and haples newes of Affrique
Cor. 282 no, tis a secrete crosse, an unknowne thing
Cor. 1303 with huge cares doth crosse kings lives
Jer. 214 how might I crosse it, my sweet mischiefe ?
Jer. 228 but, Lazarotto, crosse my Sisters love
Jer. 234 how we may crose my Sisters loving hopes
ST 2325 still keepst him back, and seeks to crosse his sute
ST 2415 suspect Lorenzo would prevent or crosse my sute
SP 1 what, Death and Fortune crosse the way of Love ?
SP 917 to *c.* me with this haplesse accedent ?
SP 1106 and crosse him too, and sometimes flatter him
SP 1185 and *c.* the fulnes of my joyful passion
Ard. 1926 for a *c.* word of a tapster I have
SP 1771 were there no ships to crosse the Seas withall, my armes
SP 1772 my armes should frame mine oares to crosse the seas
Ard. 2345 I'll *c.* the water and take sanctuary
ST 741 speak thou faire words, ile crosse them with faire words
Ard. 1904 work crosses and debates 'twixt man and wife
Jer. 576 by my crosse I sweare, I could not think you but
ST 658 sweare on this crosse that what thou saiest is true
ST 2622 you, with a Crosse, like to a Knight of Rhodes

'Cross, *see* **Across.**

Cross-cast.
Cor. 583 the roundnes of two boules *c.*

Crossed.
Jer. 271 come, then, how ere it hap, Andrea shall be crost
Jer. 1173 Reveng, my passage now cannot be crost
SP 566 and for his highnesse vowe, I crost it not
ST 2280 or have so kingly crost the seas

Crowd.
Ard. 1993 and stab him in the *c.*, and steal away

Crown.
VPJ 65 crowne, scepter, roiall marriage bed
Cor. 608 the sun-bright crowne, that now the Tyrans head
Jer. 1137 in marble leaves that death is mortall crowne
ST 306 yes, Fortune may bereave me of my Crowne
ST 1875 there will he give his Crowne to Balthazar
ST 2300 heere take my Crowne, I give it her and thee
STA 2944 a prowder Monarch than ever sate under the Crowne
    of Spaine
STA 2968 hee might a come to weare the crowne of Spaine
SP 1525 what should he doe with crowne and Emperie that
SP 1567 Perseda, for my sake weare this crowne
SP 2115 the losse of halfe my Realmes, nay, crownes decay
VPJ 72 and crows for crownes they have
Cor. 316 Kings to lay their Crownes and Scepters at thy feete
Cor. 1329 while gazing eyes at crownes grow dim
ST 1874 league betwixt the Crownes of Spaine and Portingale

ST 724 that sweetest blisse is crowne of loves desire
ST 1018 the end is crowne of every worke well done
SP 1566 give me a cròwne, to crowne the bride withall
Cor. 1406 and crowne thy head, and mount thy Chariot
Jer. 1184 homeward with victory to crowne Spaines brow
Jer. 58 stout Don Andrea, mettle to the crowne
Jer. 385 but I stand even yet, jump crowne to crowne
Ard. 652 that for a *c.* he'll murder any man
Ard. 721 Will, there's a *c.* for thy good news
Ard. 833 I value every drop of my blood at a French *c.*
Ard. 1506 one of you give him a *c.*
Ard. 1516 I would his *c.* were molten down his throat
Ard. 2142 three games for a French *c.*, sir, and please you
SP 445 why, a hundred Crownes
SP 447 ten Crownes? And had but sixpence for
SP 849 and bid them bring some store of crownes with them
SP 872 what store of Crownes have you brought?
Ard. 673 once more, and share crowns with you too
Ard. 854 and sweet Alice Arden, with a làp of crowns

Crowned.
Cor. 792 thy rebell sonne, with *c.* front, tryumphing
Cor. 1035 and cares for *c.* Emperors shee doth reserve
Jer. 815 that I may see your Gray head crownd in white

Crows.
VPJ 72 and *c.* for crownes they have
Cor. 1428 and Crowes are feasted with theyr carcases
Cor. 1607 the earth, the sea, the vultures and the Crowes

Crucifix.
Ard. 612 you could compound by art a *c.* impoisoned
Ard. 616 I would have you make me such a *c.*

Cruel.
HP 982 cruell conflicts and daungerous warres are caused
Cor. 125 and shew Gods wrath against a cruell soule
Cor. 662 under thys cruell Tarquins tyrannie?
Cor. 1532 doth oppose himselfe agen bloody minded, cruell men
Cor. 1588 O cruell fortune
Cor. 1815 O cruell fortune
Cor. 1902 O cruell Gods, O heaven, O direfull Fates
Cor. 1954 that thou enflam'd'st so cruell a revenge
Jer. 842 Farwell. O cruell part
ST 2849 in black darke night, to pale dim *c.* death
SP 593 could satisfie thy *c.* destinie
SP 1007 makes me thinke that I have been to cruell
JB 12 a Lawe that the *c.* and unjust blood-sheader should
Puck 30 he was intemp[er]ate & of a *c.* hart

Cruellest.
Cor. 1456 good deeds the cruelst hart to kindnes bring

Cruelly.
Cor. 1893 scarce had he said, but, *c.* resolv'd

Cruelty.
Cor. 198 falling as thick (through warlike crueltie) as
Cor. 1202 the restfull Allmaynes with his crueltie he rashly styrd
SP 725 I will forget thy former crueltie
SP 1243 by whose crueltie thou art exylde?

Crushed.
Cor. 1825 a spunge, or a bunche of Grapes crusht in a

Cry.
HP 7 I heard a confused *c.* of dogs
HP 458 of whom the crye is come into our Countrey
Cor. 731 three times to *c.*, but could nor *c.*, nor speake
Cor. 1249 why *c.* you ayme, and see us used thus?
Jer. 479 O, I *c.* you mercy, Father, ment you so?
ST Bal. 100 and of my sonne did alwayes *c.*
ST 884 and heere within this garden did she crie
ST 1591 and *c.* aloud for justice through the Court
STA 1993 I doe not *c.* : aske Pedro, and aske Jaques

STA 2058 canst paint a dolefull crie?
STA 2060 nay, it should crie ; but all is one
STA 2085 make me curse, make me rave, make me *c.*
SP 186 the golden Fleece is that we *c.* upon
SP 203 him we adore, and in his name I crie, Mahomet
SP 441 come, sirra, let me see how finely youle *c.* this chaine
SP 458 crie the chayne for me Sub forma pauperis, for money
SP 469 a chaine, sir, a chaine, that your man bad me crie
SP 473 how durst thou be so bould to crie the chaine
Ard. 560 and swore he would *c.* quittance with the churl
Ard. 1060 what hath occasioned such a fearful *c.*?
Ard. 1069 so great a *c.* for nothing I ne'er heard
Ard. 1333 if thou *c.* war, there is no peace for me
Ard. 1859 didst thou not hear me *c.* ‹ they murder thee ? ›
Ard. 2221 what ails you, woman, to *c.* so suddenly?
ST 2851 I heare his dismall out-*c.* eccho in the aire

Cryest.
SP 461 he must not know that thou *c.* the Chaine

Crying.
HP 13 beating and *c.* out upon the doggs
Cor. 1719 thys sayd, his Army *c.* all at once
STA 2083 drawe me like old Priam of Troy, *c.*
SP 446 when, then, Ile have ten for the *c.* it
SP 447 sixpence for *c.* a little wench of thirty years old
SP 468 how now, sirra, what are you *c.*?
Ard. 1161 *c.* aloud, ‹ Thou art the game we seek ! ›

Crystal.
HP 1045 shine like Silver, or looke as bright as Christall
Cor. 1359 be't where the Sea is wrapt in Christall Ise
Cor. 1990 valing your Christall eyes to your faire bosoms

Cubile.
HP 1327 Exercet penso, castum ut servare *c.*

Cuckold's.
Jer. 434 state in every thing, save in a Cuckolds pate

Cucumbers, *see* **Cowgomers.**

Cudgel-stick.
Ard. 704 broke the tapster's head of the Lion with a *c.*

Cues.
Jer. 452 eate *C.*, drunk Cees, and cannot give a letter

Cuff.
Ard. 1608 such another word will cost you a *c.* or
SP 1069 a bout at cuffes, afore you and I part

Cuirasse.
HP 1420 the curasse and the Helmet to the Souldiour

Cunning.
Cor. Ded. 5 which both requireth *c.*, rest and oportunity
ST 2635 you meane to try my *c.* then, Hieronimo?
SP 1981 with *c.* wordes tempted my chastitie?
Ard. 229 the only *c.* man of Christendom

Cunningly.
ST 1632 then in your love beware ; deale *c.*
ST 1738 nay, and you argue things so *c.*, weele goe
SP 1788 Lord marshall, see you handle it *c.*
Ard. 165 but, Michael, see you do it *c.*
Ard. 420 ay, Alice, and it was *c.* performed
Ard. 2037 that I may come behind him *c.*
Ard. 2102 Oh, how *c.* she can dissemble !

Cup.
HP 330 I tasted of a *c.* of delicat white Wine
HP 332 I pledged him of a *C.* of neate Claret wine
ST 513 Signior Horatio, waite thou upon our *C.*
STA 934 did grace him with waiting on his *c.*
Ard. 1374 go in, Bradshaw; call for a *c.* of beer
Ard. 2117 sirrah, fetch me a *c.* of wine, I'll make them friends
Ard. 2218 sirrah Michael, give's a *c.* of beer
Ard. 2323 it is a *c.* of wine that Michael shed

Cupboard.
HP 95 the Cupboorde charged with curious plates of Candie
Cup-conqueror.
SP 2011 where is tipsie Alexander, that great cup conquerour
Cupid.
ST 844 no, *C.* counterfeits the Nightingale
ST 846 if *C.* sing, then Venus is not farre
SP 674 and *C.* bring me to thy nuptiall bed
SP 1497 for there sits Venus with *C.* on her knee
SP 1684 *C.*, God of love, not daring looke me in the
SP 1690 made their petition to *C.* to plague you
SP 1692 now sir, *C.*, seeing you alreadie hurt before
ST 723 and, sitting safe, to sing in Cupids Quire
Cur.
Cor. 847 vomit it, like to a Curre that Carrion hath devour'd
Ard. 1141 watch the out-coming of that prick-eared *c.*
Ard. 1416 there comes a *c.* and stole it from them both
Ard. 1234 make these curs pluck out each other's throat
Cur.
Puck 28 in ipsis inest causa *c.* diligantur
Curbed.
Cor. 58 and whose power, could never have been curb'd
Curbs.
Cor. 1251 that there is one that *c.* their Countries weale
Cure.
SP 1528 to ease, though not to *c.*, my maladie
SP 1605 to one past *c.* good counsell comes too late
Cured.
HP 1639 perilous evils as are hard or never to be *c.*
Curious.
HP 95 the Cupboorde charged with *c.* plates of Candie
HP 1353 greater and more *c.* observers of such things
Curl.
Cor. 1344 turne not thy crispie tydes, like silver curle
Curled.
HP 704 long *c.* locks trussed up in tresses
Ard. 692 long hair down his shoulders *c.*
Current.
SP 1251 but, that our oath may have his currant course
Currently.
Ard. 967 and should I not deal *c.* with them
Curriculo.
HP 1323 *C.* expulerat somnum, cum foemina primum
Curse.
STA 2085 make me *c.*, make me rave, make me cry
STA 2086 make me *c.* hell, invocate heaven, and
ST 2709 and as I *c.* this tree from further fruite
SP 1786 that for my carrying of Erastus hence, she *c.* me not
Ard. 1767 I'll *c.* the carle, and see what that will do
Ard. 1811 and thus I go, but leave my *c.* with thee
Ard. 1299 nay, if you ban, let me breathe curses forth
Ard. 1798 for curses are like arrows shot upright
Cursed.
Eng. Parn. 5 Whose *c.* Courts with bloud and incest swell
Jer. 684 O *c.* deed
ST Bal. 66 and curs'd and bann'd each thing was there
ST 922 for outrage fits our *c.* wretchednes
ST 995 and beare him in from out this *c.* place
ST 1385 thy *c.* father, and thy conquered selfe
ST 1817 built a habitation for their *c.* soules
·ST 2311 for vengeance on those *c.* murtherers
ST 2710 so shall my wombe be *c.* for his sake
SP 416 O cursed Fortune, enemy to Fame
SP 615 curst be that wrath that is the way to death
SP 616 if justice forst me on, curst be that justice
·Ard. 1796 or there run mad and end thy *c.* days !

JB 209 « woe is mee, it was for thy sake I did so *c.* a deede »
Curst.
Ard. 1635 'tis like to a *c.* wife in a little house
Curtain.
ST 2682 that I will have there behinde a curtaine
Curtal.
SP 387 hath overthrowne him and his Curtall both to the ground
Curtsey.
Ard. 663 and with a *c.* to the earth, « One snatch »
Ard. 855 comes with a lowly *c.* to the earth
Curvato.
ST 104 et conjuratae *c.* poplite gentes succumbunt
Cushion.
ST 2728 bring a chaire and *c.* for the King
Cuspide.
ST 146 Pede pes et *c.* cuspis
Cuspis.
ST 146 Pede pes et cuspide *c.*
Custody.
HP 795 doo yet continue in their Mothers custodie
Custom.
HP 202 not onely the Towne, but the custome of our Countrey
HP 215 this custome of marrying yong me[n] so soone
HP 271 regard to the conveniencie and custome of
HP 430 according to the custome of nature
HP 569 custome and the Lawes dyspence with them in this
HP 669 they are received and kept of custome
HP 712 an auncient custome, as we read of Hellen in Euripides
HP 805 which custome is by Virgil attributed to the Latins
HP 815 which custome as I commende not, because
HP 830 Where trumpets eccho clangs to those that of the custome skyll
HP 948 an use and custome dissonant and segregat from
HP 1288 which custome is not gueason in some houses
HP 1628 Exchange may be retained, not onely for the custome
HP 1756 that custome of the Dukes and other noble men
ST 676 goe and attend her, as thy custome is
STA 927 he had no custome to stay out so late
ST 1471 if you doo, I may chance to break your olde custome
HP Ind. 30 customs in bringing up of Children
HP 603 all formes of customes and conditions
HP 879 nothing requisite for our times or customes
HP 895 either by alteration of time or variety of customes
HP 1539 and customes of the Citty wher he liveth
Customary.
Jer. 3 by all the dewe and *c.* rights
Cut.
HP Ind. 89 hayre *c.* from Wemens heads, and why
HP 711 they use yet in some place of Italie to *c.* away theyr hayre
VPJ 31 my thred is *c.*, and yet it is not spunne
Cor. 592 *c.* from a spring by chaunce or arte
Jer. 746 Ile *c.* them downe, my words shall not be hong
ST 401 *c.* short his life to end his praise and woorth
STA 962 a youth, as I remember. I *c.* him downe
STA 1986 his weapon would have fall'n and *c.* the earth
STA 2080 and I with a trice to *c.* him downe
SP 432 marry, a foule fault; but why are his eares *c.*?
SP 1941 indeed I was a little *c.* in the porpuse
Ard. 463 so that all former grants are *c.* off
Ard. 522 but hire some cutter for to *c.* him short
Ard. 768 « that paltry painter, *c.* him off by the shins »
Ard. 1110 and if I do not, heaven *c.* me off !
Ard. 1132 *c.* not the nose from off the coward's face
Ard. 1537 and plat the news to *c.* him off to-morrow
Ard. 1544 that made you thus *c.* short the time of rest
Ard. 1931 went to the clerk and *c.* all the notches of his tallies

Ard. 2091 and they are cutters, and may *c.* you short
Ard. 2342 and broke her neck, and *c.* her tapster's throat
Cor. 1757 cuts, casts the ground, and madding makes a poole
Cutlass, *see* **Coutelace.**
Cutter.
Ard. 322 but hire some *c.* for to cut him short
Ard. 1755 I'll call those cutters forth your tenement
Ard. 2091 and they are cutters, and may cut you short
Cutteth.
Ard. 1023 and in the middle *c.* off his tale
Cutting.
HP 1532 in graving or *c.* the Chizzel should not be so
STA 1950 so that with extreame griefe and *c.* sorrow
Cybele's.
HP 831 « Cebiles Berecyntian pypes and Tymberils, you see, do »
Cygneam.
VPJ (Title) T. K. in *C.* Cantionem Chidiochi Tychborne
Cymbrian.
Cor. 1061 that did the Latin state defend from *C.* rage
Cynthia.
Cor. 633 doth sing to see how *C.* shrinks her horne
SP 2223 sparing none but sacred Cynthias friend
SP 2227 whose life is heavens delight, and Cynthias friend
Cypress-shades.
ST 44 under greene mirtle trees and Cipresse shades
Cyprian.
ST 779 heire unto our brother heere, Don Ciprian
ST 3040 and let Don Ciprian supply his roome
SP 635 who gave Rhodes Princes to the Ciprian Prince, but Love ?
ST 2421 house, the Duke of Castile, Ciprians ancient seat
Cyprus.
SP 149 brave Prince of Cipris, and our sonne in law
SP 1119 hath the young prince of Cipris married
SP 1314 brave prince of Cipris, and our sonne in law
SP 1419 the Prince of Cipris to is likewise slaine
SP 104 in honour of the Prince of Cipris nuptials
Cytherea.
Cor. 639 while Citherea sighing walkes to seeke her
D.
Dabis.
HP 1640ª Pecuniam tuam non *d.* fratri
Daemon, *see* **Demon.**
Dag.
Ard. 1393 or dare abide the noise the *d.* will make
Ard. 1515 even when my *d.* was levelled at his heart
Ard. 1424 at your dag's discharge make towards
Dagger.
SP 302 but swear upon my Dudgin *d.*
SP 1988 what, darest thou not ? give me the *d.* then
Ard. 153 but he hath sent a *d.* sticking in a heart
Ard. 161 and fling the *d.* at the painter's head
Ard. 1609 what, with a *d.* made of a pencil ?
Ard. 1928 pierced one barrel after another with my *d.*
JB 176 threaten to stabbe and thrust her through with his *d.*
Ard. 1046 in their ruthless hands their daggers drawn
Daily.
VPJ 12 admire, and *d.* hold thy name in reverence
HP 1085 as we may dailie see in dogs
Ard. 503 thus live I *d.* in continual fear
Ard. 1232 my *d.* toil begat me night's repose
JB 14 see it put in execution daylie before our eyes
Dainties.
ST 559 unless our *d.* were more delicate
Daintiest.
HP 246 the *d.* morsels of the Kid

Dainty.
HP 96 furnished with all sorts of daintie fruits
HP 695 the flesh of women, as it is more soft and daintie
HP 761 faire wordes, pleasing fashyons, and daintie whispering speech
HP 1082 and nourished with more choise and daintie meate
Jer. 230 oh Duckets, *d.* ducks : for, give me duckets
SP 1397 of musicke, viands, or of *d.* dames
Ard. 425 have given the broth some *d.* taste
Dale.
ST 1813 within a hugie *d.* of lasting night
ST 1833 downe by the *d.* that flowes with purple gore
Dalliance.
ST 758 tell our delight and mirthfull *d.*
Ard. 2259 we'll spend this night in *d.* and in sport
Dally.
Jer. 600 I beheld her *d.* with my shapes substance
ST 638 nay, if thou *d.*, then I am thy foe
ST 646 but if thou *d.* once againe, thou diest
ST 1048 nor shall I longer *d.* with the world
Dallying.
SP 485 in dalying war, I lost my chiefest peace
Ard. 397 come, leave this *d.*, and let us away
Dam.
Ard. 1267 but I will *d.* that fire in my breast
Dame.
HP 1342 « As did that noble Grecian *d.* that »
Cor. 260 if (like a royall *D.*) with faith fast kept
Jer. 547 name of any Lady, then no Spanish *d.*
ST 10 in secret I possest a worthy *d.*
ST 2587 to one Perseda, an Italian *D.*
SP 14 the historie of brave Erastus and his Rodian *D.* ?
SP 867 rather than ile seeke justice gainst the *D.*
Cor. 1701 thinke how this day the honorable Dames
Cor. 1989 weepe therefore, Roman Dames, and from henceforth
Jer. 542 love letters which you send to Spanish Dames
SP 1397 of musicke, viands, or of dainty dames
Damnable.
Puck 80 justlie accuse of that *d.* offence to
Damnation.
Jer. 116 upon whose eie browes hangs *d.*
Jer. 215 my sweet mischiefe ? hunny *d.*, how ?
Jer. 280 and shoved his soule out to *D.*
Damned.
Jer. 252 heeres no fine villainie, no damn[e]d brother
Jer. 239 hee dares bee damnd like thee
Jer. 288 unfould their hellish practise, damnd intent
Jer. 697 why speaks not this accursed, *d.* villaine ?
Jer. 741 this ominus mistake, this *d.* error
ST 1102 upon report of such a *d.* fact
ST 1210 this is that *d.* villain Serberine
ST 1344 for die he shall for this his *d.* deed
STA 1778 none but a *d.* murderer could hate him
ST 2905 speake, traitour ; *d.*, bloudy murderer, speake
STA 2940 O *d.* Devill, how secure he is
SP 1320 and heere, in spight of *d.* Turkes, weele
Damsel.
JB 50 the stout *d.*, that had never before
Dance.
SP 1639 and heere them play, and see my minions *d.*
Dancing.
ST 1613 dauncing about his newly healed wounds
HP 728 that she be forwarde with the first at all dauncings
Dane.
SP 98 the sudden Frenchman, and the bigbon'd *D.*
Danger.

Cor. 799 hath sav'd from *d.* in these furious broyles
ST 763 I, *d.* mixt with jealous dispite
ST 880 which never *d.* yet could daunt before?
SP 922 but *d.* waites uppon my words and steps
Ard. 754 a man might follow without *d.* of law
Ard. 1976 bears his sword-point half a yard out of *d.*
JB 51 that had never before been in the like daunger
Cor. 1274 and fearles scowres in danger's coasts
ST 16 my valour drew me into dangers mouth
Ard. 1241 but needs must on, although to danger's gate
Cor. 1409 to see theyr Caesar, after dangers past
ST 734 on dangers past, and pleasures to ensue
ST 735 on pleasures past, and dangers to ensue
ST 736 what dangers, and what pleasures doost thou mean?
ST 737 dangers of warre, and pleasures of our love
ST 738 dangers of death, but pleasures none at all
ST 739 let dangers goe, thy warre shall be with me

Dangerless.
Ard. 1168 and will not think his person *d.*

Dangerous.
HP 982 many cruell conflicts and daungerous warres are caused
ST 398 their strength alike, their strokes both *d.*
ST 692 and in that warre he gave me *d.* wounds
ST 751 the Court were *d.*, that place is safe
ST 762 *d.* suspition waits on our delight
ST 1808 a darkesome place and *d.* to passe
SP 1150 courteous in peace, in battell *d.*
SP 1238 or hide my head in time of *d.* stormes
SP 1757 when he hath past the *d.* time of stormes
Ard. 236 ay, but Mosbie, that is *d.*
Ard. 1900 *d.* to follow him whom he hath lately hurt

Dangerous-pointed.
Jer. 712 most doubtfull wars and dangerous pointed ends

Dangling.
Cor. 1999 tresses, now hang neglectly, *d.* downe your sholders

Dank.
Ard. 1386 is not thy powder *d.*, or will thy flint strike fire?

Dante.
HP 546 *D.*, who in his Canzonet of Noblesse said
HP 1642 read what verdict *D.* hath given of it in

Dapibus.
HP 142 Nocte domum *d.* mensas onerabat inemptis

Dare.
Cor. 64 once *d.* t'assault it, or attempt to lift theyr
Jer. 34 ha : *d.* he still procrastinate with Spaine?
Jer. 259 *d.* I? Ha, ha
Jer. 262 what *d.* not I enact, then? tush, he dies
Jer. 386 darst thou? — I *d.*
ST 1194 O no, my Lord; I *d.* not; it must not be
ST 2410 graunt me the combat of them, if they *d.*
SP 923 I *d.* not stay, for if the Governour
SP 1192 thoughts should *d.* attempt, or but creepe neere my
  heart
SP 1840 the rest I *d.* not speake, it is so bad
SP 1990 yet *d.* I beare her hence, to do thee good
Ard. 828 what, *d.* you not do it?
Ard. 830 yes, sir, we *d.* do it; but
Ard. 912 *d.* swear a matter of such consequence?
Ard. 915 sith thou hast sworn, we *d.* discover all
Ard. 1393 or *d.* abide the noise the dag will make
Ard. 1535 she'll think we *d.* not do it
Ard. 2388 but I *d.* swear thou knewest not the contents
Cor. 1246 dares to undertake the intercepting of his tyrannie
Cor. 1450 who dares to contradict our Emporie?
Jer. 258 what dares not hee do that neer hopes to inherit?
Jer. 259 hee dares bee damnd like thee

SP 2054 why, what art thou that dares resist my force?
SP 2056 and one that dares thee to the single combate
Ard. 133 I know he loves me well, but dares not come

Dared.
Puck 34 (wth yor L^ps favo^r) *d.* in the greatest cause

Darest.
Jer. 257 darst thou, sperit?
Jer. 386 darst thou? — I dare
SP 554 and *d.* thou infer a reason why
SP 1988 what, *d.* thou not? give me the dagger then
Ard. 1109 and afterwards attempt me when thou *d.*

Dareth.
Cor. 1255 he doth, deviseth, sees, nor *d.* ought

Daring.
Jer. 781 so *d.*, ha, so Peremptory?
Jer. 790 ha, soe peremptory, *d.*, stout?
Jer. 1030 are you remembred, Don, of a *d.* message
ST 117 both menacing alike with *d.* showes
ST 1059 why linger we? bring forth that *d.* feend
SP 182 what time a *d.* Rutter made a challenge
SP 1685 not *d.* looke me in the marshall face

Dark.
ST 899 amidst these darke and deathfull shades
STA 1960 what make you with your torches in the darke?
STA 2076 let the Clowdes scowle, make the Moone darke
ST 2849 in black darke night, to pale dim cruel death
Ard. 62 wished that *d.* night's purblind steeds would
Ard. 1731 saw you not how till now the sky was *d.*?
Ard. 1740 with making false footing in the *d.*
ST 143 and shivered Launces darke the troubled aire

Darkness.
HP 362 our operations and contemplations are enclozed with
  darknes
Cor. 1358 tyll heaven unlock the darknes of the night
ST 817 and that in darkenes pleasures may be done
ST 902 by day this deede of darkenes had not beene
STA 971 gird in my wast of griefe with thy large darkenesse
STA 1730 a lump bred up in darkenesse, and doth
STA 1970 doth give consent to that is done in darkenesse
STA 1974 doe sleepe in darkenes when they most should shine
Ard. 1081 and sheeting *d.* overhangs the earth

Darksome.
Cor. 234 but *d.* ugly Death with-holds his darte
Cor. 242 the *d.* mansions of pyning ghosts
Cor. 1728 where-with the dust, as with a *d.* clowde
ST 1808 a darkesome place and dangerous to passe
Ard. 1539 have by their toil removed the *d.* clouds

Dart.
Cor. 235 but darksome ugly Death with-holds his darte
Cor. 458 against th'inevitable *d.* of Death?
Cor. 502 with brandisht *d.* doth make the passage free
Cor. 504 would Death had steept his *d.* in Lernas blood
Cor. 530 twere more then base in us to dread his *d.*
Cor. 1541 for he saw that Envies *d.* (pricking still!
ST 855 thus I retort the *d.* thou threwst at me
SP 28 whose cheefest actor was my sable *d.*
SP 1687 and with his pointed *d.* prickt my posteriors?
Cor. 47 nor feare the darts of our couragious troopes
Cor. 1730 the Darts and Arrowes on theyr Armour glaunced
ST 854 then ward thy selfe : I *d.* this kisse at thee
SP 1474 how can mine eyes *d.* forth a pleasant looke

Darting.
Cor. 806 *d.* sparcles, till it finde a trayne to seaze upon
Cor. 1751 a fearfull Hagge, with fier-*d.* eyes

Dash.
Cor. 1738 and *d.* together like two lustie Bulls

Dashed.
Jer. 102 severe authority has dasht with justice
Date.
Jer. 432 the *d.* of his embassage nighe expired
Ard. 1380 well, were his *d.* completed and expired
Date.
HP 1640ᵃ *D.* mutuum nec inde sperantes
Daubings.
HP 680 artificiall Oyles and dawbings which they use
Daughter.
HP 656 and his *D.* very excellently approves that no
HP 1318 dwelling, either for her eldest sonne or *d.*
HP 1350 the *d.* of Alcinoe, the King of Phaeaces
Cor. Arg. 1 Cornelia, the *d.* of Metellus Scipio
Cor. 547 *d.*, beware how you provoke the heavens
Cor. 1601 me thinks, I heare my Maisters *d.* speake
Cor. 2021 that wert the wife to th' one, and th' others *d.*
ST Bal. 25 the Duke of Castyles *D.* then
ST 766 what saies your *d.* Bel-imperia?
ST 778 besides that she is *d.* and halfe heire
ST 1882 that bends his liking to my *d.* thus
ST 2918 that was thy *d.* Bel-imperia
STA 2980 that was thy *d.*, Bel-imperia
STA 2965 shuld ha'e been married to your *d.* : ha, wast not so?
SP 1120 married Cornelia, *d.* to the Governour?
ST 813 endeavour you to winne your daughters thought
Daunt.
ST 880 which never danger yet could *d.* before?
David.
HP 1640ᵃ *D.* : Qui habitabit, &c. qui pecuniam
Davus.
HP 912 though he be happily *D.*, Syrus, or Geta
Day.
VPJ 25 the *d.* is past, and yet I saw no sunne
HP 357 the difference betwixt the *d.* and night
HP 357 in Winter the daie, which is most unworthy
HP 363 in the Summer the daie becomes victor
HP 369 resolved with the exceeding heate and contagions of the *d.*
HP 379 formeth the *d.* and night of such equalitie
HP 833 at this *d.* they of some Citties in Lombardy are
HP 876 and are at this *d.* for the most part manumitted
HP 893 who for the greater number are at thys *d.* freemen
HP 976 and at this *d.* of those fearefull Hostes which
HP 1127 is (at this *d.*) utterly extinguished
HP 1343 bated in the night as much as she had woven by *d.*
HP 1464 trade or science is at this *d.* commonlie called Merchandize
Cor. Ded. 24 spend one howre of the *d.* in some kind service
Cor. 38 thys *d.*, we see, the father and the sonne have
Cor. 338 will that *d.* never come that your
Cor. 341 ne're shall I see that *d.*, for Heaven and Time have
Cor. 424 thus *d.* and night I toyle in discontent
Cor. 696 we dreame by night what we by *d.* have thought
Cor. 1137 Brutus thys *d.* beares the self-same Armes to be
Cor. 1223 no, Brutus, never looke to see that *d.*
Cor. 1357 or where his Chariot staies to stop the *d.*
Cor. 1561 *d.* or night they never rest
Cor. 1586 Scipio hath lost the *d.*
Cor. 1668 bravely to fight for honor of the *d.*
Cor. 1682 for now (quoth he) is come that happie *d.*
Cor. 1684 brave Romains, know this is the *d.* and houre
Cor. 1701 thinke how this *d.* the honorable Dames
Cor. 2018 thy worthles life that yet must one *d.* perish)
Jer. 22 O fortunate houre, blessed mynuit, happy *d.*
Jer. 25 this *d.* my years strike fiftie, and in Rome

Jer. 109 one peeres for *d.*, the other gappes for night
Jer. 367 twill keepe his *d.*, his houre, nay minute ; twill
Jer. 639 the evening to begins to slubber *d.*
Jer. 872 this must be the *d.* that all they have
Jer. 944 and he this *d.* gives me the deepest wound
Jer. 1185 the *d.* is ours and joy yeelds happy treasure
ST 359 had he lived, the *d.* had sure bene ours
ST 569 their love to mortall hate, their *d.* to night
ST 605 my sommers *d.* will turne to winters night
ST 831 and heavens have shut up *d.* to pleasure us
ST 902 by *d.* this deede of darkenes had not beene
STA 933 his Majestie the other *d.* did grace him with
ST 1148 the cloudie *d.* my discontents records
ST 1151 eies, life, world, heavens, hel, night and *d.*
ST 1418 but shall I never live to see the day
ST 1469 I pray, sir, dispatch ; the *d.* goes away
ST 1587 the *d.* and place where he did pittie thee
ST 2316 and this is the *d.* that I have longd so
ST 2336 which, long forgot, I found this other *d.*
ST 2902 life, which I this *d.* have offered to my Sonne
SP 92 this *d.* the eger Turke of Tripolis
SP 373 the prize and honor of the *d.* is his
SP 401 there spend we the remainder of the *d.*
SP 406 as he this *d.* hath matcht and mated too
SP 505 as stormes that fall amid a sun shine *d.*
SP 679 that same *d.*, whose warme and pleasant sight
SP 681 be our first *d.* of joy and perfect peace
SP 691 the fairest shine that shall this *d.* be seene
SP 1080 I tell thee, if Alcides lived this *d.*
SP 1125 at tilt, who woone the honor of the *d.*?
SP 1295 Ile serve the one by *d.*, the other by night
SP 1669 that *d.*, me thought, I sat in Pompeyes Chaire
SP 1823 that very *d.* Erastus went from hence
SP 1826 I never saw them, I, untill this *d.*
SP 2186 this *d.* shall be the peryod of my blisse
Ard. 58 summer-nights are short, and yet you rise ere *d.*
Ard. 86 come again within a *d.* or two, or else I die
Ard. 132 do, and one *d.* I'll make amends for all
Ard. 287 next *d.* thou and Susan shall be married
Ard. 406 nay, every *d.*, and stay no longer there
Ard. 406 I never live good *d.* with him alone
Ard. 505 as every *d.* I wish with hearty prayer
Ard. 511 and if he live a *d.*, he lives too long
Ard. 596 a match, i'faith, sir : ay, the *d.* is mine
Ard. 766 « one *d.* I fell asleep and lost my master's pantofles »
Ard. 1080 black night hath hid the pleasures of the *d.*
Ard. 1483 I have longed this fortnight's *d.* to speak with you
Ard. 1724 I hope to see him one *d.* hanged upon a hill
Ard. 1782 I'll lay thee up so close a twelve-month's *d.*
JB 53 to marrie him by a certain *d.*, and to make him
JB 185 upon one *d.* above the rest most earnest with him to
Cor. 494 in one daies space (to our eternall mones)
ST 1645 which, as a nine daies wonder, being ore-blowne
SP 644 I gave Erastus onely that dayes prize
VPJ 43 short were thy daies, and shadowed was thy sun
VPJ 81 raigne, live, and blisfull dayes enjoy
Cor. 574 that gouverneth and guides our dayes
Cor. 739 death dissolve the fatall trouble of my daies
Cor. 921 this is the hope that feeds my haples daies
Cor. 1064 and Pompey, whose dayes haply led so long
Cor. 1499 guilding these our gladsome daies with
Cor. 1533 for he short[e]neth their dayes
Cor. 1903 O radiant Sunne that slightly guildst our dayes
Jer. 429 besids, within these few daies heele returne
ST 1616 that dyde, I, dyde a mirrour in our daies
ST 3032 adding sweet pleasure to eternall daies

SP 82 then sunny daies to naked Savages
SP 114 yong slippes are never graft in windy daies
SP 598 and live in servile bondage all my dayes
SP 600 in blood hath shortned our sweet Halebs dayes
SP 1111 and waste his dayes in fruitlesse obsequies?
SP 1510 the self same musick that in auncient daies brought
SP 1742 Perseda, these dayes are our dayes of joy
Ard. 182 'tis yet but early days, thou needst not fear
Ard. 635 within this ten days
Ard. 667 ay, Will, those days are past with me
Ard. 1796 or there run mad and end thy cursed days!
Ard. 2334 the widow Chambly in her husband's days I kept
JB 75 not been maried to Brewen above three dayes, whe[n]
HP 1070 and another hath more d. then work
Cor. 72 the Morne and Mid-d. both by East and West
ST 2468 as brightly burning as the mid-daies sunne
ST 790 in celebration of the nuptiall d.
Ard. 18 which at our marriage-d. the priest put on

Day-bright.
Cor. 1788 Caesar, whose kinglike lookes, like day bright starres

Daylight.
Cor. 1149 why spend we day-light, and why dies he not
STA 1966 then we burn day light
Ard. 1233 my night's repose made d. fresh to me

Day-wages.
HP 1012 gyving every one hys sallary or day wages

Dazzle.
SP 904 dasell mine eyes, or ist Lucinas chaine?

Dead.
Cor. 49 wont to terrifie thee with their names, are d.
Cor. 197 where in the flowred Meades d. men were found
Cor. 399 but hee is d., (O heavens), not d. in fight
Cor. 440 besides the losse of good men d. and gone
Cor. 486 both warrs fierce lightning fiers — are they not d.?
Cor. 762 they counterfet the d. in voyce and figure
Cor. 765 it seeks the common passage of the d.
Cor. 864 honored with true devotion, both alive and d.
Cor. 887 why liv'st thou toyl'd, that (d.) mightst lye at rest?
Cor. 935 Pompey may not revive, and (Pompey d.)
Cor. 992 thrise happy were I d.
Cor. 1075 and till the time that they are d., is no man blest
Cor. 1187 are full of d. mens bones by Caesar slayne
Cor. 1190 though they containe d. bodies numberles
Cor. 1593 or wherefore am I not already d.?
Cor. 1649 but we shall see a thousand of them d.
Cor. 1741 till, d. or fled, the one forsake the field
Cor. 1857 the passage choakt with bodies of the d.
ST 263 so Hares may pull d. Lyons by the beard
ST 340 tell me no more of newes, for he is d.
ST 379 if Balthazar be d., he shall not live
ST 875 yet is he at the highest now he is d.
ST 1599 nor any phisick to recure the d.
ST 1636 thou art assurde that thou sawest him d.?
STA 2933 but are you sure they are d.?
STA 2936 I, all are d.; not one of them survive
SP 185 hit the haughtie challenger, and strooke him d.
SP 1889 ah, poore Erastus, art thou d. already?
SP 2004 Hercules, the onely Club man of his time? d.
SP 2006 that abraham-coloured Troian? d.
SP 2008 that well knit Accill[es]? d.
SP 2010 that fraudfull squire of Ithaca, iclipt Ulisses? d.
SP 2012 or Pompey that brave warriour? d.
Ard. 524 when he is d., you shall have twenty more
Ard. 569 when he is d., he should have twenty more
Ard. 575 'twere cheerful news to hear the churl were d.
Ard. 746 he's d. as if he had been condemned by

Ard. 749 here is ten pound, and when he is d.
Ard. 1058 call on the neighbours, or we are but d.!
Ard. 1639 house were a-fire, or some of his friends d.
Ard. 1729 what, is the deed done? is Arden d.?
Ard. 2044 and, when he is d., you shall have forty more
Ard. 2335 and now he's d., she is grown so stout
JB 160 within a small space after her husband was d.
JB 180 the space of two yeares after her husband was d.
Puck 33 to taxe or to opbraide the deade

Dead-grown.
Cor. 222 and wil ye needs bedew my d. joyes

Deadly.
Cor. 1457 but resolution is a d. thing
Jer. 276 my eares have sukt in poyson, d. Poyson
ST 1899 and bring my Sonne to shew his d. wounds
SP 2098 a kisse I graunt thee, though I hate thee deadlie
SP 2148 « Tyrant, my lips were sawst with d. poyson »
Ard. 340 the d. hatred of my heart's appeased
JB 78 conceived such d. hatred against him
JB 91 bought a strong d. poyson whose working
Puck 8 Atheisme, a deadlie thing wch I was undeserved chargd
    wth all

Dead-men.
Cor. 363 as there were none but d. to be seene

Dead-sad.
Cor. 241 Powers, that rule the silent deepes of d. Night

Deaf.
Cor. 466 and hell it selfe is deafe to my laments
ST 312 so is she deafe, and heares not my laments
ST 726 be deafe, my eares, heare not my discontent
STA 2976 he deafe, my senses, I can heare no more

Deafed.
SP 1936 my troubled cares are deft with loves alarmes

Deal.
ST 1140 if you unjustly deale with those, that in your justice
    trust?
ST 1346 and thus experience bids the wise to deale
ST 1652 then in your love beware, deale cunningly
Ard. 904 you d. too mildly with the peasant
Ard. 967 and should I not d. currently with them

Dealest.
Cor. 1923 that unprovoked deal'st so partiallie

Dealing.
Cor. 891 your disloyall d. hath defam'd your King
Ard. 518 God's my witness, I mean plain d.
ST 1139 how should we tearme your dealings to be just

Dealt.
ST 231 and cards once d., it bootes not aske, why so?
ST 1252 I know my secret fault, and so doe they; but I have d.
    for them
Ard. 541 how have you d. and tempered with my sister?

Dear.
Cor. Arg. 34 having over-mourn'd the death of her deere hus-
    band
Cor. 288 and let theyr double losse that held me deere
Cor. 884 O sweet, deere, deplorable cynders
Cor. 1175 (deere Brutus) thinke you Caesar such a chyld
Cor. 1177 he bought it deere, you know, and traveled too farre
Cor. 1224 for Caesar holdeth signiorie too deere
Cor. 1600 farewell, deere Father
Cor. 1933 thy death, deere Scipio, Romes eternall losse
Cor. 2003 O deere companions, shall I, O, shall I
Jer. 126 I faith, my deare bosome, to take solemne leave
Jer. 129 and what it is to love, and be loved deere
Jer. 133 O yes: but not a wandring honor, deere
Jer. 146 nay, heare me, deere

Jer. 155 O deere Andrea, pray, lets have no wars
Jer. 159 respective deere, O my lives happines
Jer. 179 be in my absence my deare selfe, chast selfe
Jer. 619 welcom, my lifes selfe forme, deere Don Andrea
Jer. 692 raise up my deere love, Bellimperia
Jer. 838 harke, the drum beckens me ; sweet deere, farwell
Jer. 896 shall pay deere trybute, even there lives and all
Jer. 904 the deere dropes of many a purple part that
Jer. 989 by all that thou holdst deere upon this earth
Jer. 1056 no, my deere selfe, for I was blest by thee
Jer. 1086 farewell deere, dearest Bellimperia
ST Bal. 73 then Isabella, my deare wyfe
ST Bal. 137 and sayd my sonne was as deare to me
STA 958 deare Hieronimo, cast a more serious eye
ST 1173 deare was the life of my beloved Sonne
STA 1990 deare Hieronimo, come in a doores
STA 2026 I, sir ; no man did hold a sonne so deere
ST 2594 one of his Bashawes whom he held full deere
ST 2788 deare is Erasto in our princly eye
ST 2847 upon my Sonne, my deere Horatio
ST 2910 as deare to me was my Horatio, as yours
STA 2953 as deare to me was my Horatio, as yours
SP 118 and they must winne it deere that winne it thence
SP 605 and I as deare to thee as unto Haleb
SP 669 but say, my deare, when shall the gates of heaven
SP 1011 I rather thinke it cost him very deare
SP 1234 blade in the deare bowels of my countrimen
SP 1513 no, my deare, Love would not let me kill thee
SP 1538 for thee, my deare Erastus, have I lived
SP 1927 heere ends my deere Erastus tragedie
SP 2105 for kissing her whom I do hould so deare
SP 2178 forgive me, deere Erastus, my unkindnes
Ard. 38 to violate my d. wife's chastity
Ard. 39 (for d. I hold her love, as d. as heaven)
Ard. 891 God's d. lady, how chance your face is so bloody?
Ard. 1119 and he shall buy his merriment as d. as

Dearer.

Cor. 556 we ought not to surrender that deerer part
Cor. 1143 exceeds all loves, and deerer is by farre
ST Bal. 75 and loving him d. then life
ST 2773 Erasto, d. then my life to me
SP 601 ah, what is d. bond then brotherhood?
SP 941 farewell, my country, d. then my life
SP 942 farewell, sweete friends, d. then countrey soyle
SP 944 d. to me then all the world besides
SP 1892 whose life to me was d. then mine owne?
Ard. 198 Arden to me was d. than my soul
Ard. 1568 but that I hold thee d. than my life

Dearest.

HP 208 all my deerest thinges
HP 1240 at such convenient time as things are deerest
HP 1497 where they are helde deerest, and where best cheape
Cor. 16 our fathers hazarded their derest blood
Cor. 302 Pompey, what holpe it thee, (say, deerest life)
Cor. 720 wake, deerest sweete, and (ore our Sepulchers)
Cor. 738 O deerest life, or when shall sweetest death
Cor. 868 earth, did homage to it with his deerest blood
Cor. 1509 rather cause thy deerest sonne, by his
Cor. 1583 Scipio (my deerest Maister) is deceas'd
Cor. 1845 would melt with nothing but theyr deerest blood
Cor. 1889 but thee my deerest, nere-deceiving sword?
Cor. 2027 no, lovely Father and my deerest husband
Jer. 1086 farewell deere, d. Bellimperia
ST Bal. 128 because he slew her d. friend
STA 974 O sweet Horatio, O my d. sonne
ST 1034 by hate deprived of his d. sonne

ST 1109 but even the slaughter of our deerest sonne
ST 1331 must look like fowlers to their d. freends
ST 1427 who, when he lived, deserved my d. blood
ST 2181 and when I dyde it in thy deerest blood
ST 2737 once his mother and thy deerest wife
SP 915 thou didst bereave me of my d. love
SP 943 farewell, Perseda, d. of them all
Ard. 417 hereafter think of me as of your d. friend
Ard. 794 the other is Franklin, Arden's d. friend
Ard. 1793 either there be butchered by thy d. friends

Dearly.

Cor. 1141 I love, I love him deerely. But the love that men
SP 1799 see where he comes, whome though I deerely love
SP 2099 I loved thee deerelie, and accept thy kisse
SP 2108 she loved me deerely, and I loved her
Ard. 1280 thou knowest how d. Arden loved me
Ard. 1777 that which he craves I d. bought of him
JB 170 price thereof, and have bought her merrement deerely

Dearth.

HP 1248 he heares or feareth any d. or scarcity
HP 1469 other things whereof there is some d.
Cor. 486 yes, and their death (our d.) hath hid them

Death.

Eng. Parn. 11 Honour indeede, and all things yeeld to d.
VPJ 33 I sought my d., and founde it in my wombe
VPJ 51 thou soughtst thy d., and found it in desert
VPJ 91 without thee, d. a second life, life
VPJ 92 life double d. should be
HP 470 a fewe yeeres before his d.
HP 555 divorced by d. from that first band of Matrimonie
HP 709 at the d. of theyr husbands spoyling and disrobing
    themselves
HP 876 (for that they were preservd from d.)
Cor. (Title) her Father and Husbandes downe-cast, d., and
    fortune
Cor. Arg. 34 having over-mourn'd the d. of her deere husband
Cor. 45 now, Parthia, feare no more, for Crassus d.
Cor. 78 as menaceth our d. and thy decay?
Cor. 201 O warre, if thou wert subject but to d.
Cor. 219 d. dwels within us, and if gentle Peace
Cor. 261 thou with thy former husbands d. hadst slept
Cor. 344 once ease my life, but with the pangs of d.
Cor. 384 Pompey could not die a better d.
Cor. 468 if over Pompey I should weepe to d.
Cor. 477 then wherefore mourne you for your husband's d.
Cor. 480 no more then wretched we their d. could scape
Cor. 486 yes, and their d. (our dearth) hath hid them
Cor. 520 no feare of d. should force us to doe ill
Cor. 521 if d. be such, why is your feare so rife?
Cor. 528 (to fright us) sette pale d. before our eyes
Cor. 536 that men (to shunne mischaunces) seeke for d.
Cor. 539 he that retyres not at the threats of d.
Cor. 546 for tis a d. to lyve a Tyrants slave
Cor. 738 d. dissolve the fatall trouble of my daies
Cor. 821 and stung to d. the foole that fostred her
Cor. 910 I doe but what I ought to mourne his d.
Cor. 926 with Caesars d. to end our servitude
Cor. 937 Caesar bewail'd his d.
Cor. 937 his d. hee mournd, whom, while hee lyv'd
Cor. 941 he murdred Pompey that pursu'd his d.
Cor. 949 what got he by his d.?
Cor. 957 he tooke no pleasure in his d., you see
Cor. 984 yes, newes of Caesars d. that medcyn beares
Cor. 992 yes, cause your d.
Cor. 996 there is no d. so hard torments mee so
Cor. 999 deprive me wholy of the hope of d.

Cor. 1008 that Caesars *d.* shall satisfie his wrong
Cor. 1077 he onely, that no *d.* doth dread, doth live at rest
Cor. 1150 that by his *d.* we wretches may revive?
Cor. 1154 made fight to *d.* with show of liberty
Cor. 1227 what reck I *d.* to doe so many good?
Cor. 1280 from obscure *d.* shall free his name
Cor. 1323 people have devis'd, or their guarde, to seeke their *d.*
Cor. 1414 I joy not in the *d.* of Cittizens
Cor. 1442 will those conspire my *d.* that live by mee?
Cor. 1452 I feare them not whose *d.* is but deferd
Cor. 1491 that *d.* that comes unsent for or unseene
Cor. 1575 that scornefull destinie denyes my *d.*
Cor. 1613 such a *d.* excels a servile life
Cor. 1671 them that already dream'd of *d.* or flight
Cor. 1754 encourageth the over-forward hands to bloode and *d.*
Cor. 1817 of murder, *d.*, and direfull massacres
Cor. 1859 losse, and souspirable *d.* of so brave souldiers
Cor. 1900 crawld to the Deck, and, lyfe with *d.* to ease
Cor. 1932 nought but my Fathers *d.* could expiate?
Cor. 1933 thy *d.*, deere Scipio, Romes eternall losse
Jer. (Title) and the life and *d.* of Don Andraea
Jer. 115 whose famisht jawes look like the chap of *d.*
Jer. 120 to be Andreas *d.* at his retourne
Jer. 306 what, harping still upon Andreas *d.*?
Jer. 571 that Don Andrea may prevent his *d.*
Jer. 667 sure, this pretends my *d.*; this
Jer. 694 Andrea lives : O let not *d.* beguile thee
Jer. 991 now *d.* doth heap his goods up all at once
Jer. 1024 drop doune as thick as if *d.* mowed them
Jer. 1074 multitudes that made thee stoope to *d.*
Jer. 1087 yet heerein joy is mingled with sad *d.*
Jer. 1137 in marble leaves that *d.* is mortall crowne
ST Bal. (Title) with the pittiful *d.* of old Hieronimo
ST Bal. 27 to relate the *d.* of her beloved friend
ST Bal. 76 her owne hand straight doth worke her *d.*
ST Bal. 164 which on Horatios *d.* depends
ST Bal. 165 whose *d.* I could anew bewayle
ST (Title) with the pittifull *d.* of Hieronimo
ST 17 till life to *d.* made passage through my wounds
ST 37 drew forth the manner of my life and *d.*
ST 87 where thou shalt see the author of thy *d.*
ST 173 and our Carbines pursued them to the *d.*
ST 194 such as warres fortune hath reserv'd from *d.*
ST 254 he promisde life, this other threatned *d.*
ST 261 he hunted well that was a Lyons *d.*
ST 330 my *d.* were naturall, but his was forced
ST 378 keepe him till we determine of his *d.*
ST 386 relate the circumstance of Don Andreas *d.*
ST 388 and in his *d.* hath buried my delights
ST 422 could win pale *d.* from his usurped right
ST 433 but for thy kindnes in his life and *d.*
ST 443 yet what availes to waile Andreas *d.*
ST 448 till I revenge the *d.* of my beloved?
ST 635 alas, my Lord, since Don Andreas *d.*
ST 640 thy *d.* shall bury what thy life conceales
ST 668 deserves my duteous service, even till *d.*
ST 738 dangers of *d.*, but pleasures none at all
ST 889 this place was made for pleasure, not for *d.*
STA 966 confusion, mischiefe, torment, *d.*, and hell
ST 1049 procrastinating Alexandros *d.*
ST 1061 not that I feare the extremitie of *d.*
ST 1072 my guiltles *d.* will be aveng'd on thee
ST 1099 let him unbinde thee that is bound to *d.*
ST 1118 which, villaine, shalbe ransomed with thy deeth
ST 1131 oh life, no life, but lively fourme of *d.*
ST 1144 solicite me for notice of his *d.*

ST 1159 « Hieronimo, revenge Horatios *d.* »
ST 1174 and of his *d.* behoves me be reveng'd
ST 1211 that hath, I feare, revealde Horatios *d.*
ST 1318 touching the *d.* of Don Horatio
ST 1411 a scurvie jest that a man should jest himselfe to *d.*?
ST 1426 so ist my duety to regarde his *d.*
ST 1442 first I confesse, nor feare I *d.* therfore
ST 1556 « and in my *d.* I shall reveale the troth »
ST 1703 your first favourite Don Andreas *d.*
ST 1811 it will conduct you to dispaire and *d.*
ST 1839 heele doe thee justice for Horatios *d.*
ST 1862 whose *d.* he had so solemnely bewailde
STA 1987 had he been framed of naught but blood and *d.*
STA 2080 O no, there is no end : the end is *d.* and madnesse
ST 2114 and to conclude, I will revenge his *d.*
ST 2183 that of thy *d.* revenged I should be
ST 2252 and seekes not vengeance for Horatioes *d.*
ST 2496 to forget so soone the *d.* of those, whom
ST 2500 nor shall his *d.* be unrevengd by me
ST 2506 that wrought his downfall with extreamest *d.*
ST 2518 to let his *d.* be unreveng'd at full
ST 2525 joyne with thee to revenge Horatioes *d.*
ST 2597 not otherwise to be wonne, but by her husbands *d.*
ST 2699 revenge on her that should revenge his *d.*
ST 2822 the *d.* of Ajax or some Romaine peere
ST 2849 in black darke night, to pale dim cruel *d.*
ST 2865 at Horatios *d.* I weeping dipt within
ST 2988 we will devise the 'xtremest kinde of *d.*
ST 2997 mourne the losse of our beloved brothers *d.*
ST 3017 both done to *d.* by olde Hieronimo
ST 3055 for heere, though *d.* hath end their miserie
SP 7 and what are Tragedies but acts of *d.*?
SP 23 and then from love deliver them to *d.*?
SP 84 that waiteth for the fearefull stroke of *d.*
SP 477 whose knowledge were to me a second *d.*?
SP 494 and losse of happines is worse than *d.*
SP 495 come therefore, gentle *d.*, and ease my griefe
SP 547 the ones a Lyon almost brought to *d.*
SP 615 curst be that wrath that is the way to *d.*
SP 685 which never can be parted but by *d.*
SP 827 hard doome of *d.*, before my case be knowne
SP 934 or suffer *d.* for Ferdinandos *d.*
SP 1034 for heere is nothing but revenge and *d.*
SP 1067 for her to give him doome of life or *d.*
SP 1245 Phylippos wrath (it must be tould), for Ferdinandos *d.*
SP 1285 His parting is my *d.* — His deaths my lives departing
SP 1321 weele gaine a glorious *d.* or famous victorie
SP 1332 for feare of servile *d.*, thats but a sport?
SP 1417 the Governour is slaine that sought thy *d.*
SP 1471 what can my tongue utter but griefe and *d.*?
SP 1492 and at my hands receive the stroake of *d.*
SP 1798 whose *d.* might save my poore Erastus life
SP 1860 foule *d.* betide me, if I sweare not true
SP 1862 mischiefe and *d.* shall light upon you both
SP 1867 now it resteth I appoint thy *d.*
SP 1895 let them receive the stroke of *d.*
SP 1963 but say, what *d.* dyed my poore Erastus?
SP 1964 nay, God be praisd, his *d.* was reasonable
SP 1966 but strangled? ah, double *d.* to me
SP 1992 nor shall her *d.* alone suffice for his
SP 2013 I am my selfe strong, but I confesse *d.* to be stronger
SP 2017 I am wise, but quiddits will not answer *d.*
SP 2019 are to be nothing when it pleaseth *d.* to be envious
SP 2042 where we at leasure will lament her *d.*
SP 2077 in that one mans *d.* thou hast betrayde the
SP 2092 but with thy hand first wounded to the *d.*

SP 2127 is she not faire ? — Even in the houre of *d*.
SP 2160 and I am weake even to the very *d*.
SP 2162 for that my *d*. was wrought by her devise
SP 2163 who, living, was my joy, whose *d*. my woe
SP 2179 I have revenged thy *d*. with many deaths
SP 2192 for even in *d*. their soules are knit
Ard. 566 grew to composition for my husband's *d*.
Ard. 572 to London, for to bring his *d*. about
Ard. 738 no revenge but *d*. will serve the turn
Ard. 740 and I will lay the platform of his *d*.
Ard. 748 if once Black Will and I swear his *d*.
Ard. 929 how and what way we may conclude his *d*.
Ard. 936 I have vowed my master Arden's *d*.
Ard. 991 worse than the conflict at the hour of '*d*.
Ard. 1042 have sworn my *d*., if I infringe my vow
Ard. 1055 my *d*. to him is but a merriment
Ard. 1091 where we will give you instance of his *d*.
Ard. 1130 and in that *d*. may die unpitied
Ard. 1384 ay, to the gates of *d*. to follow thee
Ard. 1525 comes my Lord Cheiny to prevent his *d*.
Ard. 1618 ay, here it is ; the very touch is *d*.
Ard. 1621 make him wise in *d*. that lived a fool
Ard. 1757 shall wound my husband Hornsby to the *d*.
Ard. 1877 for in thy discontent I find a *d*.
Ard. 1878 a *d*. tormenting more than *d*. itself
Ard. 2058 when this door opens next, look for his *d*.
Ard. 2177 because I blush not at my husband's *d*.
Ard. 2188 my husband's *d*. torments me at the heart
Ard. 2327 conspired and wrought his *d*. shall rue it
Ard. 2353 and, would my *d*. save thine, thou should'st not die
Ard. 2412 Michael and Bradshaw in Feversham must suffer *d*.
Ard. 2413 let my *d*. make amends for all my sins
Ard. 2420 thus have you seen the truth of Arden's *d*.
JB 66 it turned to Brewens *d*. and destruction
JB 71 and although she often refused to work his *d*.
ST 564 to see him feast that gave me my deaths wound ?
ST 2103 and death's the worst of resolution
ST 2240 sweet boy, how art thou chang'd in deaths black shade
SP 596 could ransome thee from fell deaths tirannie
SP 1285 His parting is my *d*. — His deaths my lives departing
Cor. 1220 to fight for that, that did theyr deaths conclude
Cor. 1232 no, let me rather dye a thousand deaths
ST Bal. 77 and now their deaths doth meet in one
ST 2499 so loved his life, as still I wish their deathes
ST 2521 I will ere long determine of their deathes
ST 2704 thy negligence in pursute of their deaths
ST 2706 ah nay, thou doest delay their deaths
ST 2931 pleasde with their deaths, and easde with their revenge
SP 1345 first Julio will die ten thousand deaths
SP 1621 better that Erastus die ten thousand deaths
SP 2179 I have revenged thy *d*. with many deaths
Cor. 234 but darksome ugly *D*. with-holds his darte
Cor. 238 and that, if *D*. upon my life should seaze
Cor. 458 against th'inevitable dart of *D*. ?
Cor. 501 *D*. (haply that our willingnes doth see)
Cor. 504 would *D*. had steept his dart in Lernas blood
Cor. 772 none but inevitable conquering *D*. descends to hell
Cor. 931 and then come, Murder ; then come, uglie *D*.
Cor. 1470 no, Anthony, *D*. cannot injure us
Cor. 1490 but *D*. it selfe doth sometime pleasure us
Cor. 1577 whose coates of steele base *D*. hath stolne into
Cor. 1584 and *D*., that sees the Nobles blood so rife
Cor. 1944 to whom sweet *D*. hath given blessed rest
STA 2961 I can not looke with scorne enough on *D*.
SP 1 what, *D*. and Fortune crosse the way of Love ?
SP 3 nay, what are you both, but subjects unto *D*. ?

SP 13 why, thinkes *D*. Love knows not the historie of
SP 24 Fortune is chorus ; Love and *D*. be gone.
SP 37 tush, Fortune can doo more then Love or *D*.
SP 497 but stay a while, good *D*., and let me live
SP 623 now, *D*. and Fortune, which of all us three
SP 654 I, and by *D*. had been surprisd, if Fates
SP 660 who is [the] greatest, Fortune, *D*., or Love
SP 920 and to acuse fell Fortune, Love, and *D*.
SP 1108 and heere and there in ambush *D*. will stand
SP 1376 nor rescue Rhodes from out the hands of *D*. ?
SP 1999 *D*., which the poets faine to be pale and meager
SP 2183 and now pale *D*. sits on my panting soule
SP 2202 in this last act note but the deedes of *D*.
SP 2213 and they must wait upon the Carre of *D*.
SP 2215 for powerfull *D*. best fitteth Tragedies
SP 2216 I go, yet Love shall never yeeld to *D*.
SP 2220 I, now will *D*., in his most haughtie pride
SP 2224 whom *D*. did feare before her life began
SP 2226 fates have graven it in their tables that *D*. shall die
Cor. 233 in Deaths sad kingdom hath my husband lodg'd
Cor. 474 all things are subject to Deaths tiranny
Cor. 509 Death's alwaies ready, and our time is knowne
Cor. 524 we aske Deaths ayde to end lifes wretchednes
ST 13 Deaths winter nipt the blossomes of my blisse
SP (Title) Loves constancy, Fortunes inconstancy, and Deaths Triumphs
SP 1372 and save his life, in spite of Deaths despight
Death-bed.
SP 72 my Grandame on her death bed gave it me
Deathful.
ST 899 amidst these darke and deathfull shades
Death-threatening.
Ard. 1053 the wrinkles in his foul death-threat'ning face
Debates.
Ard. 1904 work crosses and *d*. 'twixt man and wife
Debt.
ST 2154 Sir, an Action. — Of Batterie ? — Mine of *D*.
Decay.
Cor. 78 as menaceth our death and thy *d*. ?
Cor. 91 praie to th' Glauc's and Trytons, pleas'd with thy *d*.
ST 190 and soone *d*. unlesse he serve my liege
SP 506 I read her just desires, and my *d*.
SP 2115 the losse of halfe my Realmes, nay, crownes *d*.
SP 2218 then times and kingdomes fortunes shall *d*.
Ard. 984 grow as Hydra's head that plenished by *d*.
Ard. 1554 but my deserts or your desires *d*.
Decayed.
ST 2837 all fled, faild, died, yea, all decaide with this
Decease.
Cor. 553 at such a Kings departure or *d*.
ST 2192 that he delivereth for his Sonnes diceasse
ST 2995 hope that Spaine expected after my discease
Deceased.
Cor. 1583 Scipio (my deerest Maister) is deceas'd
Jer. 850 of all those captive Portugales *d*.
ST 94 some few that are deceast by fortune of the warre
ST 1525 with ceasles plaints for my *d*. sonne ?
Deceit.
HP 1579 through *d*., and unconsorted with some labor
SP 1181 this face of thine shuld harbour no *d*.
ST 697 which sweet conceits are lim'de with slie deceits
ST 698 which slie deceits smooth Bel-imperias eares
Deceitful.
ST 2484 O unkind father, O deceitfull world
Deceive.
Cor. 960 he never trusted him, but to *d*. him

Ard. 949 should you *d.* us, 'twould go wrong with you
Ard. 1418 Arden escapes us, and deceives us all
Deceived.
HP 389 for, if hee be *d.* by his servaunts in
HP 1176 he cannot be *d.* by his Bailieffe
Cor. 761 to pensive mindes (*d.* wyth theyr shadowes)
ST 382 *d.* the King, betraid mine enemy
STA 1962 no, no, you are deceiv'd — not I, you are deceiv'd
SP 279 you are *d.*, sir ; he swore not
SP 1940 I am *d.* but you were circumcised
SP 2082 ah. foolish man, therein thou art *d.*
Ard. 1114 the villain Michael hath *d.* us
Ard. 1722 this is no Hough-Monday ; you are *d.*
Ard. 2284 you are *d.* ; it was a Londoner
Ard. 2300 I am too sure : would God I were *d.*
Deceiving.
Cor. 1889 but thee my deerest, nere-*d.* sword ?
Decent.
HP 734 honest shame (a *d.* thing in honest wome[n])
Decide.
Ard. 299 Mosbie, that question we'll *d.* anon
Decii.
Cor. 1388 heere let the *D.* and theyr glory die
Deciphered.
HP 703 most fayre, were *d.* without beards
Deciphering.
HP 777 (taking a wife of our *d.*)
Deck.
Cor. 1900 crawld to the *D.*, and, lyfe with death to ease
Cor. 604 crowne, that now the Tyrans head doth *d.*
ST 839 the more will Flora decke it with her flowers
SP 673 with Rosie chaplets *d.* thy golden tresses
SP 803 why didst thou *d.* her with my ornament ?
HP 150 and then he decks his boord about with meats
Decked.
Cor. 312 thy Helmet deckt with coronets of Bayes ?
Cor. 1518 his warlike browes still be deckt with Lawrel boughes
Cor. 2002 our mournfull habits may be deckt no more
Declaration.
ST 2150 I, sir, and heeres my *d.*
ST 2218 oh, sir, my *d.*
Declare.
ST Bal. 144 unlesse I shuld it straight *d.*
Declared.
SP 1858 that all is true that heere you have declard
JB 216 co[n]fessed the fact in order, as I have *d.*
Decline.
Ard. 127 and bid him, if his love do not *d.*
Declining.
ST 63 the left hand path, *d.* fearefully
Decorum.
HP 1351 the Greekes observed not so much *d.*
Decrease.
HP 1193 dooth not only *d.* but perisheth
Decreaseth.
HP 661 *d.* and with draweth from them
Decree.
Ard. 194 *d.* to murder Arden in the night ?
Ard. 1242 then, Arden, perish thou by that *d.*
Decreed.
Cor. 403 and bitter chaunce *d.* to have me there
SP 1596 all three have *d.* that I shall love her still
SP 2158 I, fates, injurious fates, have so *d.*
Decrepit.
HP 229 theyr young desires, but (beeing *d.*)
Dederit.

HP 1640ᵃ qui pecuniam non *d.* ad usuram
Dedicate.
HP Ded. this worke I dedicat to your defence
Dedicated.
HP 1749 a pamphilet that is *d.* to Aristotle
Dedication.
Cor. Ded. 6 the *d.* of so rough, unpollished a worke to
Deed.
Cor. 404 decreed to have me there, to see this bloody *d.*
Jer. 285 O father, tis a charitable *d.* to
Jer. 684 O cursed *d.*
Jer. 737 wherefore didst thou this accursed *d.* ?
Jer. 762 O impious deede, to make the heire of honor
ST 455 reape long repentance for his murderous *d.*
ST 902 by day this deede of darkenes had not beene
STA 956 that such a blacke deede of mischiefe should be done
STA 970 and drop this deede of murder downe on me
ST 1060 and let him die for his accursed *d.*
ST 1113 rent with remembrance of so foule a *d.*
ST 1134 O sacred heavens, if this unhallowed *d.*
ST 1229 to meet the Prince and me, where thou must doe this *d.*
ST 1344 for die he shall for this his damned *d.*
ST 1567 that such a monstrous and detested *d.*
ST 2907 why hast thou done this undeserving *d.* ?
SP 389 Erastus, be thou honoured for this *d.*
SP 1734 and after make repentance of the *d.*
Ard. 274 yet nothing could inforce me to the *d.*
Ard. 534 and whosoever doth attempt the *d.*
Ard. 800 but now I'll leave you till the *d.* be done
Ard. 850 but wouldst thou charm me to effect this *d.*
Ard. 1459 witness produced that took her with the *d.*
Ard. 1729 what, is the deed done ? is Arden dead ?
Ard. 2057 tush, get you gone ; 'tis we must do the *d.*
Ard. 2078 Black Will is locked within to do the *d.*
Ard. 2250 my brother, you, and I shall rue this *d.*
Ard. 2360 witness sufficiently thou didst the *d.*
Ard. 2363 and they and I have done this murderous *d.*
Ard. 2400 I knew not of it till the *d.* was done
Ard. 2405 I had ne'er given consent to this foul *d.*
Ard. 2432 two years and more after the *d.* was done
JB 73 deede done, Parker promised to marrie her
JB 209 « woe is mee, it was for thy sake I did so cursed a deede »
HP 486 the deedes of greatest Kings, that turne the eyes
Cor. 93 but vainely count'st thine owne victorious deeds
Cor. 328 by whom the former course of thy faire deeds
Cor. 1389 and noble deeds were greater then his fortunes
Cor. 1420 theyr disgrace, that reckt not of his vertuous deeds
Cor. 1456 good deeds the cruelst hart to kindnes bring
Cor. 1466 ascend to heaven upon my winged deeds
ST 186 these words, these deeds, become thy person well
ST 2993 what age hath ever heard such monstrous deeds ?
SP 152 to grace thy nuptials with their deeds at armes
SP 265 and with impartiall eyes behold your deedes
SP 1152 and, all in all, their deedes heroicall
SP 1815 just, or in his deeds more loyall and upright
SP 2136 affable ; and, all in all, his deeds heroyacall
SP 2197 your deedes are trifles, mine of consequence
SP 2202 in this last act note but the deedes of Death
Ard. 6 here are the deeds, sealed and subscribed
Deem.
HP 183 because I deeme them scarce
SP 1157 their horse, I deeme them fiftie thousand strong
Deemed.
SP 1450 I should have deemd them Junoes goodly Swannes
Deep.
Jer. 1022 now wounds are wide, and bloud is very deepe

ST 2482 thy passions, thy protestations, and thy deepe lamentes
SP 778 and faine *d.* oathes to wound poor silly maides
Ard. 1270 such *d.* pathaires, like to a cannon's burst
JB 60 deepe intrest in the possession of her person, stormed
HP 566 « would with lightning drive me to the deepe »
Jer. 91 five marchants wealths into the deepe doth throw
ST 174 till, Phoebus waving to the western deepe
ST 2199 whilest lesser waters labour in the deepe
Cor. 240 Powers, that rule the silent deepes of dead-sad Night
Cor. 505 that I were drown'd in the Tartarean deepes
Cor. 1001 and slept with Pompey in the peacefull deepes
Cor. 1749 makes it a Quagmire, where (kneedeepe) they stand
Deeper.
ST 111 with *d.* wage and greater dignitie
SP 1494 strike, strike ; thy words pierce *d.* then thy blows
Deepest.
Cor. 489 reacht from *d.* hell, and with their tops tucht heaven
Jer. 944 gives me the *d.* wound, Ile call him brother
Jer. 946 to gaine that name, ile give the *d.* blowe
ST 64 was ready dounfall to the *d.* hell
ST 295 for *d.* cares break never into teares
ST 3035 this hand shall hale them downe to *d.* hell
SP 2221 fetch his imperiall Carre from *d.* hell
Deep-fetched.
Ard. 1012 what pity-moving words, what *d.* sighs
Deeply.
Ard. 988 is *d.* trenched in my blushing brow
Deep-ways.
SP 543 whose bones hath made their deep waies passable
Deer.
Ard. 1149 a toil was pitched to overthrow the *d.*
Ard. 1157 which late, methought, was pitched to cast the *d.*
Defaced.
Cor. 1997 your robes (defac'd and rent) be witnes of
Defacing.
HP 1575 which, not defiling or *d.* him, are
Defamed.
Cor. 891 your disloyall dealing hath defam'd your King
Cor. 1195 he with his souldiers hath himselfe defam'd
SP 2080 in slaughtering him thy vertues are *d.*
Default.
Cor. Ded. 18 that excellent Garnier hath lost by my defaulte
Defeat.
Cor. 1072 and will not see that Fortune can her hopes defeate
Defence.
HP Ded. this worke I dedicat to your *d.*
HP Ind. 130 servaunts, a *d.* to their Maister
Cor. 13 but we, disloiall to our owne *d.*
Cor. 145 importuning both vengeance and *d.* against
Cor. 389 hee gave his bodie (as a Barricade) for Romes *d.*
Cor. 571 fraile men, or mans more fraile *d.*
Cor. 628 bravely to fight in Romes *d.*
Cor. 1160 did arme himselfe (but in his owne *d.*)
SP 532 upon a paltrie Ile of small *d.*
HP 284 Chyldren are the fortresse and defences of their Parents
Defend.
HP 957 and strength as not only serveth to *d.* the[m]selves
Cor. 954 his owne from beeing broke he doth *d.*
Cor. 1060 that dyd the Latin state *d.*
Cor. 1268 what may the innocent *d.*
Cor. 1434 untill th' ill spyrit, that doth them *d.*
Cor. 1482 what more assurance may our state *d.*
Cor. 1539 to *d.* himselfe from harmes, was
Cor. 1841 so that, dispayring to *d.* themselves
SP 769 thy beauty did *d.* me, not my force
SP 1170 and justice to *d.* the innocent

SP 2089 Ile not *d.* Erastus innocence
Ard. 1855 marry, God *d.* me from such a jest !
Defended.
Cor. 667 and will the heavens, that have so oft *d.*
Cor. 837 to cast so soone a state, so long *d.*, into
Defendeth.
HP 1475 hee commendeth and *d.* merchaunts
Defending.
Cor. 401 upon a Forte besieg'd, *d.* of a breach
Defer.
Jer. 617 I will *d.* it till some other time
Deferimus.
HP 808 natos ad flumina primum *d.*
Deferred.
Cor. 1452 I feare them not whose death is but deferd
Jer. 643 that till tomorrow shall be now deferd
Defiance.
Jer. 793 I bad *d.* with a vengfull hand
Jer. 950 breath like your name, a Generall *d.*
Jer. 951 *d.* to the Portugales
Jer. 953 *d.* to the Spaniards
Defile.
Ard. 40 shall on the bed which he thinks to *d.*
Defiled.
Cor. 621 basely seen by shameles rape to be defilde
Defiling.
HP 647 violate the bandes by so *d.* of the marriage bedde
HP 1575 which, not *d.* or defacing him, are
Defined.
HP Ind. 6 Artificers *d.*
Deflowered.
SP 1424 and faire Perseda murthered or deflowerd
Deformed.
Cor. 712 hys hayre and beard deform'd with blood and sweat.
Defy.
ST 1307 and doe your worst, for I defie you all
Degree.
HP 1129 observed and maintained in more high *d.*
Dehiscat.
HP 560 Sed mihi vel tellus optem prius ima *d.*
Deign.
ST 542 that Portingale may daine to beare our yoake
ST 2749 at whose request they deine to doo't themselves
Deigned.
ST 2508 vowes such revenge as she hath daind to say ?
Delay.
ST 2706 ah nay, thou doest *d.* their deaths
Deliberate.
ST 1128 we with our Councell will *d.*
Delicacy.
HP 99 to imitate the *d.* and neatness of the Cittie
Delicate.
HP 330 I tasted of a cup of delicat white Wine
HP 743 cleppings as the *d.* and wanton Lover doth
HP 790 cannot be so gentle or *d.* as the Mothers
HP 1409 cast such a delicat reflection
ST 559 unless our dainties were more *d.*
HP 148 « Hyed home at night and fild his bord with delicats
unbought »
Ard. 1228 and he but pines amongst his delicates, whose
Delicately.
HP 797 as oftentimes they bring them up too delicatly
Delicious.
SP 1309 but I will after my delitious love
Delight.
HP 708 women, who *d.* in theyr hayre as Trees doo in theyr leaves.

Cor. 1388 are yee not styrred with a strange *d.*
Jer. 28 a yeare of joy, of pleasure, and *d.*
Jer. 196 be composd, as you weare wont, to musick and *d.*
ST 459 and heere he comes that murdred my *d.*
ST 585 my wordes are rude, and worke her no *d.*
ST 758 tell our *d.* and mirthfull dalliance
ST 762 dangerous suspition waits on our *d.*
ST 980 for once these eyes were onely my *d.*
ST 2564 and Kings and Emperours have tane *d.* to
SP 33 though Fortune have *d.* in change
SP 489 wherein was linkt the sum of my *d.*
SP 632 onely to feed mens eyes with vaine *d.?*
SP 909 whose neere alye he was and cheefe *d.*
SP 1046 for, till we meete, my hart shall want *d.*
SP 1180 mine eyes may view with pleasure and *d.*
SP 1296 and I will pay you both your sound *d.*
SP 1753 to worke each others blisse and hearts *d.*
SP 2227 whose life is heavens *d.*, and Cynthias friend
HP Ind. 53 delights of the Spring and of Autumne
HP 378 they are fraught with millions of delights
Cor. 126 for heaven delights not in us, when we doe
ST 388 and in his death hath buried my delights
ST 1505 solelie delights in interdicted things
Delighted.
SP 1130 a man whose presence more *d.* me
Delightful.
HP 1046 is not onelie pleasing or delightfull to beholde
ST 492 in some delightfull sports and revelling
ST 1867 the newes are more delightfull to his soule
Deliver.
HP 1287 there may be one to *d.* out such thinges
SP 23 and then from love *d.* them to death?
SP 946 to run away with this Chaine, or *d.* it
SP 947 if I deliver it, and follow my maister
Ard. 989 I will *d.* over to your hands
Puck 16 & wᶜʰ unaskt I did *d.* up
Jer. 208 I want a midwive to *d.* it
Delivered.
SP 490 when she *d.* me the Carkanet
SP 939 when thou hast *d.* it, take ship
SP 1023 he *d.* me the chaine, and bad me give it you
JB 161 she was knowne with child, and safely *d.*
JB 217 into the countrey to be *d.* of her childe
Delivereth.
ST 2192 laments that he *d.* for his Sonnes diceasse
Delivery.
ST 1373 bid him not doubt of his deliverie
ST 1554 « that you would labour my deliverie »
Della.
HP 1131 writte[n] by Signior Giovanni *d.* Casa
Deluded.
STA 948 that there are more *d.* then my selfe
STA 949 *D.* — I
Demand.
Jer. 45 to demaund his mind and the neglect of tribute
Jer. 139 but to *d.* the tribute, Ladie
ST 625 if thou but satisfie my just demaund
ST 627 what ere it be your Lordship shall demaund
ST 630 then, Pedringano, this is my demaund
Ard. 1085 pleads to me for life with just *d.*
JB 44 to demaund his golde and jewels againe
Demanded.
JB 131 then he demaunded if she were well
Demean.
ST 1910 I have not seene him to demeane him so
Demeaned.

SP 371 this knight unknowne hath best demeand himself
Demeanour.
SP 267 the faire demeanor of these warlike Knights
SP 1148 what thinkst thou of their valour and demeanor?
Ard. 1309 whose beauty and *d.* far exceeded thee
Demi-goddess.
Jer. 604 within the presence of this demy Goddesse
Demon.
Cor. 777 some false Daemon that beguild your sight
Demonstration.
ST 198 whereby by *d.* shall appeare
SP 35 showne by *d.* what intrest I have
Demophoon.
SP 1813 more then was Phillis with her Demophon
Den.
Cor. 995 fling mee alive into a Lyons denn
Ard. 1128 but lie and languish in a loathsome *d.*
Denayed.
Jer. 908 let not wonted fealty be *d.* to our desart
Denial.
JB 213 who stoode in the *d.* thereof very stoutly
Puck 5 the denyall of that favoʳ (to my thought resonable)
Denied.
Jer. 750 who replide in scorne, and his hot suite denide
Jer. 778 trybute denide us, ha?
Jer. 819 to be denide our honor, why, twere base
SP 381 nay, valiant sir, we may not be denide
JB 173 if she *d.* him either money or whatsoever else
Denies.
HP 791 in some sort *d.* to be the mother of it
Cor. 1575 that scornefull destinie denyes my death
SP 696 and who so else *d.* shall feele the rigour
Denieth.
HP 791 who so *d.* the nursing of her child
Denis.
Eng. Parn 4 A self-shaven Dennis, or an Nero fell
SP 175 Saint *D.* is for Fraunce, and that for me
Deny.
HP 102 neither denie I him to be a Gentleman of the Cittie
HP 311 I denie not that perhaps he loved
HP 698 yet can we not *d.* but that the countenaunces of youthes
HP 782 ought not to *d.* her milke to her owne Children
Jer. 253 but, say she should *d.* his gifts, be
Jer. 339 I not *d.* but tribute hath bin due to Spaine
Jer. 823 *d.* us tribute that so many yeeres
ST 1342 or els his Highnes hardly shall *d.*
ST 2110 if destinie denie thee life, Hieronimo, yet
ST 2209 denye my passage to the slimy strond
SP 957 for good luck sake, if he *d.* me not
SP 1213 denie not Soliman his owne request
SP 1346 and Guelpio, rather then denie his Christ
Ard. 321 why, canst thou *d.* thou wert a botcher once?
Ard. 514 and if the churl *d.*, my interest
Ard. 561 and, if he did *d.* his interest, stab him
JB 167 she durst not denie him anything he requested
Denying.
SP 1426 in not *d.* thy poore supplyant
Deo.
ST 103 O multum dilecte *D.*, tibi militat aether
Depainteth.
HP 658 then that which shamefastnes *d.*
Depart.
HP 884 the disobedient, stifnecked, and unprofitable servant
to *d.*
SP 893 and, Gentlemen, unmaske ere you *d.*
SP 1573 they must *d.*, or I shall not be quiet

379848

SP 1575 mervaile not that all in hast I wish you to *d.*
SP 2168 and when my soule from body shall *d.*
Ard. 400 loth am I to *d.*, yet I must go
Ard. 1629 and life shall end before my love *d.*
Jer. 331 I had in charge, at my *d.* from Spaine
ST 197 for so I gave in charge, at my *d.*
ST 290 two daies, my Liege, are past since his *d.*
ST 430 for twas my favour at his last *d.*
SP 1946 my weeping flouds of teares for your *d.*
Departed.
SP 1284 had I not askt it, my friend had not *d.*
Departing.
SP 1285 His parting is my death. — His deaths my lives *d.*
Ard. 378 a kiss at coming or *d.* from the town?
Departure.
Cor. 553 at such a Kings *d.* or decease
Cor. 943 hee that of his *d.* tooke the spoyle
Depend.
HP 420 chiefely depende upon the motion of the Sunne
HP 1672 of whom both heaven and Nature doe *d.*
Cor. 564 upon their motion doe *d.*
SP 1618 if so your life *d.* upon your love
SP 1619 and that her love depends upon his life
ST Bal 164 which on Horatios death depends
Depended.
SP 648 whereon *d.* all his hope and joy
Depending.
HP 1673 arte *d.* upon Nature, shee is as it were her Chylde
Deplorable.
Cor. 278 O *d.* Pompey; I am shee
Cor. 884 O sweet, deere, *d.* cynders
Deplored.
Cor. 471 great losses greatly are to be deplor'd
Deposed.
HP 496 hath thus *d.* and discharged him of
HP 910 hath beene *d.* or bereft of his dignitie
Deposing.
HP 760 taking upon her the person of a Lover, and *d.* the
    habit of a Wife
Deprive.
Cor. 999 *d.* me wholy of the hope of death
Deprived.
ST 89 depriv'd of life by Bel-imperia
ST 1034 by hate *d.* of his dearest sonne
SP 650 even for that Chaine shall be *d.* of life
SP 2001 hath *d.* Erastus trunke from breathing vitalitie
Depth.
ST 563 come we for this from *d.* of under ground
ST 2227 and art thou come, Horatio, from the deapth
Derision.
Jer. 299 for honesty, spoken in *d.*, points out knavery
Derived.
HP 464 is now deriv'd from my misfortunes
HP 1319 in so much as it was *d.* first from her
HP 1564 taken and *d.* from the Earth
SP 1543 and from whose absence I *d.* my sorrow
Derogate.
HP 907 they doe not yet derrogat from his olde title
Descant.
ST 1407 scorne the audience, and *d.* on the hangman
Descend.
Cor. 192 amongst the forward Souldiers first discend
Cor. 220 and if gentle Peace discend not soone
Cor. 773 descends to hell, with hope to rise againe
Descended.
HP 88 we *d.* by as manie other steps

ST 18 when I was slaine, my soule *d.* straight
Ard. 203 being *d.* of a noble house
Descent.
Cor. 1397 long'd to shew himselfe discent of Affrican
ST 5 my discent, though not ignoble, yet inferiour far
Described.
HP (Title) wherein is perfectly and profitably *d.*
SP 1178 is this the man that thou hast so describde?
Description.
HP 451 according to the Cosmographicall dyscription of some
Descry.
Jer. 674 Lords, cannot you yet discry who is the owner
Desert.
VPJ 51 thou soughtst thy death, and found it in *d.*
HP 1023 some respect to the estate and *d.* of every one
Cor. 202 and by *d.* mightst fall to Phlegiton
ST 280 and that just guerdon may befall *d.*
ST 908 how could thou strangle vertue and *d.* ?
ST 2757 but thy *d.* in conquering Rhodes is lesse then in
SP 407 but vertue should not envie good *d.*
SP 797 thats not my fault, nor her desart
SP 1210 the least of these surpasse my best desart
SP 1211 unlesse true loyaltie may seeme desart
SP 1389 kinde, past all compare, and more then my desart
SP 1651 a man of my *d.* and excellence
Ard. 1553 yet if true love may seem *d.*
ST 240 for in our hearing thy deserts were great
ST 311 Fortune is blinde, and sees not my deserts
ST 369 that thou couldst see no part of our deserts?
ST 2332 wone by his deserts within the Court of Spaine?
ST 2405 that one of your deserts should once have reason to
SP 1175 so his deserts binds me to speake for him
SP 1553 that I conquer both by my deserts
Ard. 938 doth challenge nought but good deserts of me
Ard. 1554 but my deserts or your desires decay
Cor. 588 *d.* fields where none would byde
Cor. 1775 like two fierce Lyons fighting in a Desart
SP 197 the *d.* plaines of Affricke have I staind
Cor. 1982 that made the fayre Thrasymene so dezart
Desertful.
Jer. 909 let not wonted fealty be denayed to our desart full
    kingdome.
Deserve.
HP 264 *d.* to have old Nestor at the[m]
HP 1013 wages, more or lesse as in theyr labours they *d.*
Cor. 130 we *d.* to have the self-same measure that we serve
ST 227 *d.* but evill measure at our hands
ST 242 and I shall studie to *d.* this grace
ST 270 you both *d.*, and both shall have reward
ST 826 in steed of watching, ile *d.* more golde
Ard. 1351 and I *d.* not Mosbie's muddy looks
HP 1397 yet for the order and clenlines it deserves so much
ST 299 and therefore better then my state deserves
ST 668 deserves my duteous service, even till death
ST 799 and well his forwardnes deserves reward
SP 122 and be my fortune as my love deserves
Ard. 1758 a fine device! why, this deserves a kiss
Deserved.
Cor. 168 for what the Father hath deserv'd, we know, is
Cor. 1316 they have caught *d.* skarrs
ST 432 for after him thou hast *d.* it best
ST 486 I reapt more grace then I deserv'd or hop'd
ST 514 for well thou hast *d.* to be honored
ST 1427 who, when he lived, *d.* my dearest blood
ST 1564 of whom my Sonne, my Sonne *d.* so well?
ST 1671 unlesse, by more discretion then diserv'd, I

JB 29 was better beloved, yet least *d.* it
Deservest.
ST 727 dye, hart : another joyes what thou *d.*
Deserving.
ST 9 by duteous service and *d.* love
Designs.
Cor. 375 but flattring Chaunce, that trayn'd his first designes
Cor. 1639 Scipio no sooner heard of his designes
Puck 73 sure to breake [thro] their lewde designes
Desire.
VPJ 68 reapt reward, not fitting their *d.*
HP Ind. 48 *d.* of ryches, and how farre it dooth
HP 40 so that I prevented his *d.*, and in
HP 266 for the *d.* of Feisants or Partrich
HP 572 a *d.* most naturall in all reasonable creatures
HP 572 especially if they doo it for *d.* of succession
HP 622 as is *d.* in comparison of understanding
HP 623 *d.* (which of it selfe is unreasonable)
HP 639 draweth as earnest love and *d.* of others to
HP 718 a wife, such an one as I *d.* thou maist have
HP 766 saith Jove had not the[n] so much *d.* towards her
HP 771 *d.* to rule theyr family wyth honest and
HP 1136 sufficiently spoken (though not so much as you *d.*)
HP 1621 and so by covetous *d.* to become infinit
HP 1694 *d.* that thou record effectually those things
Cor. 118 and, soly through *d.* of publique rule
Cor. 132 and can with reason chasten his *d.*
Cor. 967 nor auncient lawes, nor nuptiall chast *d.*
Cor. 1494 I could *d.* that I might die so well
Cor. 1620 and their *d.* to be approov'd in Armes
Cor. 1819 had more *d.* to sleepe then seeke for spoyle
Jer. 411 O entire is the condition of my hot *d.*
ST 593 I, but her reason masters his *d.*
ST 724 that sweetest blisse is crowne of loves *d.*
ST 2756 every excelence that Soliman can give, or thou *d.*
SP 677 full fraught with love and burning with *d.*
SP 737 *d.* perswades me on, feare puls me back
SP 848 *d.* Guelpio and signior Julio come speake with me
SP 1206 I, that, or any thing thou shalt *d.*
SP 1214 a vertuous envie pricks me with *d.* to
SP 1514 though Majestie would turne *d.* to wrath
SP 1589 repent that ere I gave away my hearts *d.*
SP 1640 for till that Brusor bring me my *d.*
SP 1743 what could I more *d.* then thee to wife ?
SP 1774 *d.* should frame me winges to flie to him
Ard. (Title) the unsatiable *d.* of filthy lust and the
Ard. 475 *d.* of wealth is endless in his mind
Ard. 1027 my master would *d.* you come to bed
JB 118 ‹ for I have an earnest *d.* to eat some ? ›
JB 166 whose welcome was answerable to his desier ?
HP 222 their desires are yet unaccomplished
HP 229 match them in theyr young desires
HP 620 our immoderate desires that in our minds so
HP 729 not to forbid her those honest recreations and desires
HP 1519 but the Housekeeper hath his desires of riches
Cor. 374 toyld to stoope the world and Rome to his desires
ST 3010 when blood and sorrow finnish my desires
SP 127 and desires you to consort her to the triumphes
SP 506 I read her just desires, and my decay
SP 1179 that what my heart desires, mine eyes may view
SP 1486 why, thats the period that my heart desires
Ard. 1554 but my deserts or your desires decay
Desired.
HP Ind. 15 beefe sought for and *d.* by
HP 45 he could no longer hide what he *d.*
HP 55 that I *d.* to conceale some part of mine estate

HP 136 who *d.* to doo me honor, beeing a straunger
HP 321 not because the Poet *d.* bitter Wyne
HP 696 so are they ordinarilie more *d.* to be gazed on
Cor. 934 mine eyes have seene what I in hart desir'd
Cor. 1165 and gave up rule, for he desier'd it not
Jer. 894 I have *d.* him peace, that we might war
ST Bal. 26 desir'd Horatio to relate the death of
Desiring.
Cor. 19 *d.* Armes to ayde our Capitoll
Desirous.
HP Ind. 37 *d.* to preserve his wealth
HP 39 as if he were *d.*, it seemd, to understande
HP 195 more *d.* of reasoning and talk
HP 674 women *d.* to seeme faire to please others
HP 676 honest women *d.* to content their Husbands
HP 686 by nature shee is so *d.* to adorne and beautifie her bodie
HP 1131 (for that thou art *d.* to peruse his workes)
HP 1151 that is *d.* to preserve his wealth
Desist.
HP 754 neither will I yet *d.* in this mine enterprise
ST 2801 tyrant, *d.* soliciting vaine sutes
Desolate.
Cor. Ded. 22 the passing of a Winters weeke with *d.* Cornelia
Cor. 215 all sad and *d.* our Citty lyes
Cor. 1910 O miserable, *d.*, distresful wretch
SP 1275 & 1276 my friend is gone, and I am *d.*
Despair.
ST 570 their hope into dispaire, their peace to warre
ST 1811 it will conduct you to dispaire and death
ST 2701 sorrow and dispaire hath scited me to
Cor. 691 my fearefull dreames doe my despairs redouble
Despairing.
Cor. 1841 so that, dispayring to defend themselves
Ard. 504 so *d.* of redress as every day I wish
Despatch.
Jer. 287 Ile dispatch letters to don Andrea
ST 867 quickly dispatch, my maisters
ST 1452 dispatch : the faults approved and confest
ST 1468 I pray, sir, dispatch ; the day goes away
ST 1510 *d.*, and see this execution done
ST 2732 dispatch, for shame ; are you so long ?
SP 1879 dispatch, for our time limited is past
Despatched.
Jer. 645 let that be first dispatcht
ST 289 is our embassadour dispatcht for Spaine ?
ST 561 now let us in, that you may be dispatcht
Ard. 529 then here's my hand, I'll have him so dispatched
Ard. 1521 what, is he down ? is he dispatched ?
Desperate.
ST 1555 ‹ if you neglect my life is *d.* ›
STA 1944 like a desperat man, growes lunaticke
SP 1085 is this little *d.* fellow gon ?
Ard. (Title) two *d.* ruffians, Black Will and Shakebag
Despise.
HP 1669 ‹ Nature and arte (her follower) they *d.* ›
Despised.
JB 42 his suite *d.*, and his goodwill nothing regarded
Despite.
Cor. 1415 but through my selfe-wild enemies despight
ST Bal. 147 and in *d.* did give it them
ST 568 Ile turne their freendship into fell despight
ST 763 I, danger mixt with jealous dispite
ST 2930 and therefore in despight of all thy threats
SP 1372 and save his life, in spite of Deaths despight
SP 2066 first let my tongue utter my hearts despight
Ard. 2131 I'll see your husband in *d.* of you

Despiteful.
ST 310 such is the folly of dispightfull chance
Despitefully.
SP 2035 butcherd dispightfullie without the walles
Despoiled.
HP 3 dispoiled of their fruite
Cor. 120 yet now we live despoild and robd by one of
Destined.
ST 689 I think Horatio be my destinde plague
Destinies.
Cor. 230 and let the *D.* admit me passage to
ST 703 but in his fall ile tempt the *d.*
Ard. 921 marked in my birth-hour by the *d.*
Destiny.
Cor. 326 since thy hard hap, since thy fierce destinie
Cor. 1417 t'eclipse thy fame, but destinie revers'd th' effect of
Cor. 1575 that scorneful destinie denyes my death
Cor. 1969 when thwarting Destinie at Affrique walls did
ST 2108 if destinie thy miseries do ease, then hast thou
ST 2110 if destinie denie thee life, Hieronimo, yet
ST 2465 imagine thou what tis to be subject to destinie
SP 593 could satisfie thy cruel destinie
Destroyed.
Cor. 221 Latium (alreadie quaild) will be destroyd
SP 1399 and Rhodes it selfe is lost, or els destroyde
SP 1400 if not destroide, yet bound and captivate
Destruction.
SP 347 I give thee leave : go to thy *d.*
JB 66 it turned to Brewens death and *d.*
JB 19 hazard of their soules and the destructions of their bodies
Detain.
Ard. 1771 the plat of ground which wrongfully you *d.*
Jer. 335 whether neglect, or will, detains it so
Ard. 1790 that plot of ground which thou detains from me
Detained.
Cor. 418 and thrice detaind, with dolefull shreeks and cryes
Jer. 334 these three years *d.* and kept back
Detect.
SP 1921 stab in the marshall, least he *d.* us unto the world
Ard. 1052 « the peasant will *d.* the tragedy »
Detecting.
Ard. 1252 or fright me by *d.* of his end
Deteriorated.
HP 507 hath not beene *d.* since by mee
Determinate.
HP 1520 hath his desires of riches certaine and determinat
HP 1599 worketh to a certaine set and determinat ende
Determination.
HP 1598 said to have no end or absolute *d.*
Determine.
HP 423 that the motion of the Sunne *d.* the differences
Cor. 1133 if he determyn but to raigne in Rome
ST 378 keepe him tell we *d.* of his death
ST 791 and let himselfe *d.* of the time
ST 2521 I will ere long *d.* of their deathes
ST 2885 did otherwise *d.* of her end
Determined.
HP 68 I had not yet *d.* to refuse
HP 1687 may be concluded and *d.*
Cor. 948 they had determin'd once of Caesars end
ST 1679 that by the Vice-roy was *d.*
ST 2157 are you *d.* that I should plead your
ST 2577 it was *d.* to have been acted by
JB 43 he *d.* that, seeing his suite took no effect
Detested.
ST 1567 that such a monstrous and *d.* deed

ST 1815 dost cast up filthy and *d.* fumes
Ard. 1988 for every drop of his *d.* blood
Detests.
Cor. 1230 *d.* to learne what tasts of servitude
Detur.
ST 998 Misceat, & nostro *d.* medicina dolori
Deus.
VPJ 78 det spirare tibi saecula multa *D.*
Device.
HP 401 and eloquent devise more then meanelie learned
HP 1721 of swifter understanding and more eloquent devise
ST 51 made this *d.* to end the difference
ST 118 both vaunting sundry colours of *d.*
ST 282 how likes Don Balthazar of this *d.* ?
ST 555 I drinke to thee for this devise
ST 2386 what new *d.* have they devised, tro ?
ST 3013 false Pedringano hangd by quaint *d.*
SP 869 by game, or change, by one devise or other
SP 1630 O fine devise ; Brusor, get thee gone
SP 2162 for that my death was wrought by her devise
Ard. 568 by some *d.* to make away the churl
Ard. 1749 first tell me how you like my new *d.*
Ard. 1758 a fine *d.* ! why, this deserves a kiss
Ard. 1882 his skin was pierced only through my *d.*
Ard. 2034 ay, and that bravely, too. Mark my *d.*
Ard. 2043 a fine *d.* ! you shall have twenty pound
Devil.
Jer. 310 to hooke the divell from his flaming cell
Jer. 500 « if you be, thank the divell and Lorenzo »
Jer. 508 say, gainst Lorenzo and the divell
Jer. 521 « if you be, thanke the divell and Lorenzo »
Jer. 529 « Thy assured friend gainst Lorenzo and the divell »
Jer. 537 your the last man I thought on, save the divell
Jer. 568 he should have hard his name yokt with the divell
Jer. 660 I, Don Andrea, or else Don the devill
Jer. 744 faith, by my selfe, my short sword, and the devill
Ard. 919 to send thee roundly to the *d.* of hell
Ard. 1512 the *d.* break all your necks at four miles' end !
Ard. 1523 the *d.* he is ! why, sirs, how escaped he ?
Ard. 1909 he whom the *d.* drives must go perforce
Ard. 1977 if the *d.* come, and he have no more strength
JB 3 how busie the divell hath beene to provoke
JB 15 yet doth the Divell so worke in the hearts of a number
Jer. 799 hell : tho he blab there, the diveles will not tell
ST 1908 needes must he goe that the divels drive
Devise.
Cor. 970 all these, nor anything we can *d.*
ST 482 and but *d.* to drive me from this place
ST 491 meanewhile let us *d.* to spend the time in
ST 2504 and give it over, and *d.* no more
ST 2526 whatsoever I *d.*, let me entreat you
ST 2988 we will *d.* the 'xtremest kinde of death
SP 1260 sportes my Minions and my Euenukes can *d.*
Ard. 928 here *d.* with us how and what way
Devised.
HP 1140 to come to that which we *d.* and
Cor. 1322 or their people have devis'd, or their guarde, to
Cor. 1440 have in theyr coward soules *d.* snares
ST 1120 not so meane a torment as we heere devisde for him
ST 1169 this is *d.* to endanger thee
ST 1221 and harken to me, thus it is devisde
ST 2386 what new device have they *d.*, tro?
Ard. 816 fray, *d.* to pick men's pockets in the throng
Ard. 917 we have *d.* a complat under hand
Ard. 1853 and me unhappy that *d.* the jest
JB 120 this sly shift she *d.* to have his absence

Deviseth.
Cor. 1255 he doth, *d.*, sees, nor dareth ought
Devoting.
Cor. Ded. 26 perpetually thus *d.* my poore selfe
Devotion.
Cor. Arg. 26 a Towne in Affrique at the *d.* of Caesar
Cor. 864 honored with true *d.*, both alive and dead
Ard. 588 a man, I guesse, of great *d.*?
Ard. 1341 and hold no other sect but such *d.*
Devour.
Cor. 905 that may infect, devoure, and murder you
Cor. 1108 Lybian Beares devoure the bodies of our Cittizens
ST 903 O earth, why didst thou not in time devoure
Devoured.
Cor. 847 vomit it, like to a Curre that Carrion hath devour'd
Devourer.
Jer. 885 *d.* of apparell, thou huge swallower
Devoutly.
Ard. 847 remember how *d.* thou hast sworn
Dew.
Cor. 635 where, wringing wet with drops of silver *d.*
Cor. 1992 and dewe your selves with springtides of your teares
Cor. 642 but (kissing) sighes, and dewes hym with her teares
Jer. 906 before the evening deawes quench the sunnes rage
Dewed.
Cor. 784 Rome, thou art tam'd, and th' earth, dewd with thy bloode
ST 419 there laid him downe, and dewd him with my teares
Dewy.
SP 244 my body distilled such *d.* showers of swet
Dexterity.
SP 49 marking thy lilly hands dexteritie
Diadem.
ST 371 thou hadst some hope to weere this Diadome
ST 536 when English Richard wore the *D.*
Cor. 1302 to revenge proud Diadems, with huge cares
Cor. 1337 grac'd with a thousand kingly diadems
Diadema.
VPJ 58 en, *d.* tibi, sceptraque, pactus Hymen
Diamond.
ST 1537 where, countermurde with walles of *d.*
Diana.
Ard. 2066 had chaste *D.* kissed him, she like me
SP 2131 Was she not chaste?—As is Pandora or Dianaes thoughts
Dice.
SP 879 go without the chaine, unlesse you carrie false *d.*
SP 881 nay, I use not to go without a paire of false *D.*
SP 902 but is there no reward for my false *d.*?
SP 1009 faith, in a mummery, and a pair of false *d.*
SP 1096 Erastus usde such *d.*, as, being false
Ard. 123 bear him from me these pair of silver *d.*
Dicendum.
HP 1062 *D.* et quae sint duris agrestibus arma
Dicing-houses.
Jer. 224 [one] from dicing houses
Dick.
Ard. 555 this morning, Master Greene, *D.* Greene I mean
Ard. 1964 *D.* Greene and I do mean to sup with you
Ard. 1759 faith, *D.* Reed, it is to little end
Dictator.
Cor. 1180 no, but *D.*, in effect as much
Dido.
HP 557 nor without great admiration should Dydo have
ST Bal. (Title) to the tune of Queene *D.*
ST 3048 my Bel-imperia falne as *D.* fell
Die.

VPJ 36 and now I *d.*, and now I was but made
VPJ 89 to *d.* for thee were sweete, to live were
HP 450 who made choyce to *d.* in Jerusalem
HP 452 moreover it was his will to dye in the Spring
Cor. 8 be pour'd on me, that one may *d.* for all
Cor. 212 or fast enough doe foolish men not *d.*
Cor. 225 your ceaselesse springs) not suffer me to *d.*?
Cor. 230 Heavens, let me dye, and let the Destinies admit
Cor. 234 fayne would I *d.*, but darksome ugly Death
Cor. 331 might *d.* disgrac'd with mine unhappines
Cor. 383 Pompey could not *d.* a better death
Cor. 476 and what-soever lives is sure to *d.*
Cor. 478 sith, being a man, he was ordain'd to *d.*?
Cor. 519 then must I dye
Cor. 545 then let me *d.*, my libertie to save
Cor. 579 the formes of things doe never *d.*
Cor. 1232 no, let me rather dye a thousand deaths
Cor. 1319 no Tyrant commonly, lyving ill, can kindly *d.*
Cor. 1368 heere let the Decii and theyr glory *d.*
Cor. 1437 and keepe theyr state in Spaine, in Spaine to *d.*
Cor. 1464 but so to *d.*, as dying I may live
Cor. 1486 better it is to *d.* then be suspitious
Cor. 1494 I could desire that I might *d.* so well
Cor. 1685 that we must all live free, or friendly *d.*
Cor. 1879 dye bravely, with their fauchins in their fists
Cor. 1892 that, being free borne, I shall not *d.* a slave
Cor. 2017 dye, rather *d.*, Cornelia : and (to spare thy
Cor. 2022 but if I *d.*, before I have entomb'd my
Jer. 220 from rich that *d.* and build no hospitals
Jer. 690 O, tis Andrea : O, I swound, I *d.*
Jer. 862 to live like captives, or as free borne *d.*?
Jer. 864 to *d.* with honor, scorne captivity
Jer. 1128 that I could *d.*, wert but to bleed with thee
Jer. 1135 betweene the stroke, but now alack must *d.*
ST 194 nor thou nor he shall dye without reward
ST 470 I *d.*, if it returne from whence it lyes
ST 687 yet must I take revenge, or dye my selfe
ST 727 dye, hart : another joyes what thou deservest
ST 862 O stay a while, and I will *d.* with thee
ST 870 O, save his life, and let me dye for him
ST 1051 that, as he is condemned, he may dye
ST 1060 and let him *d.* for his accursed deed
ST 1065 that thus I *d.* suspected of a sinne
ST 1226 for dye he must, if we do meane to live
ST 1255 and better its that base companions dye
ST 1259 for dye they shall, slaves are ordeind to no other end
ST 1341 assure thee, Don Lorenzo, he shall dye
ST 1344 for *d.* he shall for this his damned deed
ST 1453 and by our law he is condemnd to *d.*
ST 2789 but if he be your rivall, let him *d.*
ST 2790 why, let him *d.*; so love commaundeth me
ST 2791 yet greeve I that Erasto should so *d.*
ST 2797 faire Queene of beautie, let not favour *d.*
ST 2821 to *d.* to day for fashioning our Scene
ST 2904 why staiest thou him that was resolvd to *d.*?
SP 587 O Soliman, for loving thee I *d.*
SP 752 and I must *d.* by closure of my wound
SP 924 if the Governour surprise me heere, I *d.* by marshall law
SP 1198 that on the earth it may untimely *d.*
SP 1269 Perseda hath the chaine, and is like to *d.* for sorrow
SP 1277 returne him back, faire starres, or let me *d.*
SP 1278 returne him backe, fair heavens, or let me *d.*
SP 1345 first Julio will *d.* ten thousand deaths
SP 1487 and *d.* thou shalt, unlesse thou change thy minde
SP 1572 remoove the cause, and then the effect will *d.*
SP 1620 is it not better that Erastus *d.*

SP 1623 but by what means shall poore Erastus *d.* ?
SP 1900 thus *d.*, and thus ; for thus you murtherd him
SP 1919 by whom Erastus was condemnd to *d.*
SP 1967 but say, wherefore was he condemnd to *d.* ?
SP 1997 and first Perseda shall with this hand *d.*
SP 2090 but [*d.*] maintaining of Persedas beautie
SP 2097 yet kisse me, gentle love, before thou *d.*
SP 2103 ah, let me kisse thee too, before I dye
SP 2104 nay, *d.* thou shalt for thy presumption
SP 2151 let me see Rhodes recoverd ere I *d.*
SP 2157 before I *d.*, for doubtlesse *d.* I must
SP 2161 yet some thing more contentedly I *d.*
SP 2226 fates have graven it in their tables that Death shall *d.*
Ard. 86 come again within a day or two, or else I *d.*
Ard. 140 as surely shall he *d.* as I abhor him
Ard. 171 but, mistresse, tell her, whether I live or *d.*
Ard. 238 coming into the chamber where it hangs, may *d.*
Ard. 272 venture life, and *d.* with him you love
Ard. 276 enjoy thee still, then Arden should not *d.*
Ard. 277 but seeing I cannot, therefore let him *d.*
Ard. 286 and he shall *d.* within an hour after
Ard. 407 than thou must needs, lest that I *d.* for sorrow
Ard. 519 for I had rather *d.* than lose my land
Ard. 615 he should *d.* poisoned that did view it well
Ard. 971 I am resolved, and Arden needs must *d.*
Ard. 994 or else she'll *d.*, and so your sorrows end
Ard. 1130 and in that death may *d.* unpitied
Ard. 1520 for by this bullet Arden might not *d.*
Ard. 1869 thus am I still, and shall be while I *d.*
Ard. 2079 what, shall he *d.* to-night ?
Ard. 2099 but I had rather *d.* than bid him welcome
Ard. 2353 and, would my death save thine, thou should'st not *d.*
Ard. 2383 and I am by the law condemned to *d.*
Ard. 2399 ah, gentle brother, wherefore should I *d.* ?
Ard. 2417 faith, I care not, seeing I *d.* with Susan
Cor. 217 worthles Gorse, that yerely fruitles dyes
Cor. 981 my passion neither dyes, nor dryes the heate
Cor. 1149 why spend we day-light, and why dies he not
Cor. 1471 for he lives long that dyes victorious
Jer. 262 what dare not I enact, then ? tush, he dies
Jer. 650 now lives Andrea, now Andrea dies
Jer. 1147 just at this instant her hart sincks and dies
ST 861 now maist thou read that life in passion dies
ST 2460 nor dies Revenge, although he sleepe awhile
SP 739 I go ; make reconing that Erastus dyes
SP 1506 why now at last she dyes
SP 2164 ah, Janisaries, now dyes your Emperour
Ard. 1004 that will not out till wretched Arden dies

Died.

HP 9 in so much as it there *d.* at my feete
Cor. Arg. 4 who *d.* with his Father in the disconfiture of the
Cor. Arg. 30 leapt over boord into the Sea, and there dyed
Cor. 390 bravely he *d.*, and (haplie) takes it ill that
Cor. 393 if he had *d.*, his fauchin in his fist
Cor. 933 Ile downe with joy : because, before I *d.*, mine eyes
Cor. 1104 Affranius and Faustus murdred dyed
Cor. 1118 or shall theyr ghosts, that dide to doe us good
Cor. 1612 assure your selfe, that Scipio bravely dyed
ST Bal. 11 would I had dyed in tender yeares
ST Bal. 131 then dyed my foes by dint of knife
ST 38 this Knight (quoth he) both liv'd and *d.* in love
ST 47 he *d.* in warre, and must to Martiall fields
ST 828 the cause was mine ; I might have *d.* for both
ST 1616 that dyde, I, dyde a mirrour in our daies
STA 1942 much distraught, since his Horatio dyed
STA 1997 where my Horatio dyed, where he was murdered ?

ST 2514 and in that Letter how Horatio *d.*
ST 2696 « There, murdred, dide the sonne of Isabell »
ST 2697 I, heere he dide, and heere I him imbrace
ST 2837 all fled, faild, *d.*, yea, all decaide with this
ST 2883 for though the story saith she should have *d.*
SP 18 had I not beene, they had not dyed so soone
SP 231 the men *d.*, the women wept, and the grasse grew
SP 1117 in controversie touching the Ile of Rhodes my brothers dyde
SP 1301 her love Fernando *d.* at the same
SP 1904 by whose treacherie Erastus dyed
SP 1963 but say, what death dyed my poore Erastus ?
SP 2079 dyed he because his worth obscured thine ?
Ard. 428 then had he *d.* and our love continued
Ard. 2427 the painter fled and how he *d.* we know not
JB 153 immediatly after he had eaten it, he dyed
JB 163 but that child lived not long, but dyed

Diest.

ST 641 thou dyest for more esteeming her then me
ST 646 but if thou daily once againe, thou *d.*
SP 588 no, Amurath, for murthering him thou dyest

Diet.

HP 271 the conveniencie and custome of Noblemens dyet
HP 1551 *see* **Disdiet**

Dieted.

HP 749 the temperate suppers of well *d.* men

Differ.

HP 922 they *d.* from Horses, Mules, and other Beastes
HP 1113 but these doo farre *d.* from the other
HP 1745 albeit they onely *d.* not in form, but are
HP 1753 albeit wee *d.* farre from those of elder times
HP 1761 how the government of a civill and a private house doo *d.*
Cor. 1182 and wherein *d.* they whose powre is such ?

Difference.

HP Ind. 50 *d.* betwixt Exchaunge and Usury
HP Ind. 51 *d.* of Servaunt and soveraigne or Maister
HP Ind. 55 *d.* betwixt the instruction of
HP Ind. 59 *d.* in merchandize
HP 357 the *d.* betwixt the day and night
HP 1167 is (notwithstanding) no occasion of substantiall *d.*
HP 1622 yet betwixt Exchange and Usury there is some *d.*
HP 1722 but since wee found that there is *d.*
Jer. 1115 untill my leedge shall end the *d.*
ST 51 made this device to end the *d.*
ST 258 and might seeme partiall in this *d.*
SP 2201 and now, to end our *d.* at last
HP Ind. 100 matrimonie maketh equall many differences
HP 417 these six differences of place ought
HP 423 motion of the Sunne determine the differences of the place
HP 596 Matrimonie maketh equall many differences
HP 894 as the Lawes and dyfferences of Nature are not chaunged

Different.

HP Ind. 131 Servaunts *d.* from slaves
HP 1101 and is also *d.* fro[m] Artificers
HP 1717 the government of private houses and of Princes Courtes are *d.*
Jer. 108 which are as *d.* as heaven and hell

Differeth.

HP 946 *d.* much from that wherwith we governe Beasts
HP 1096 wherin he *d.* from all the other instruments
HP 1099 and heerein *d.* from the hand
HP 1734 onely *d.* from the other in the pompe and

Difficulties.

HP 1498 the fashions, sleights, and *d.* of transporting

Dig.
Cor. 1636 the selfe-same day to *d.* and cast new Trenches
Digest.
Cor. 1552 suffreth nothing to *d.*
Digested.
HP Ded. Worth more then this, *d.* thus in haste
HP 278 that are so easilie *d.*
Digni.
Puck 27 when Tullie saith *D.* sunt amicitia
Dignified.
HP 449 *d.* with the presence of the true Sonne of God
Dignities.
ST 624 and lands and living joynd with *d.*
Dignity.
HP 119 his *d.* was much augmented
HP 492 whose *d.* doth come so neere the Angels
HP 910 hath beene deposed or bereft of his dignitie
ST 111 with deeper wage and greater dignitie
Dilecte.
ST 103 O multum *d.* Deo, tibi militat aether
Diligantur.
Puck 28 in ipsis inest causa cur *d.*
Diligence.
HP 1190 judgment, experience, and dilligence
JB 179 yet could she scant please him with her *d.*
Diligent.
HP 1124 a most *d.* observer of some little things
HP 1370 ought above all things to be *d.* heerein
Diligently.
HP 435 that *d.* considereth what was said
Dim.
ST 2849 in black darke night, to pale *d.* cruel death
SP 304 O, thou seekst thereby to *d.* my glory
Dimmed.
ST 2231 whose lights are dimd with over-long laments?
Diminish.
HP 1230 as they much increase and deminish the price
Dindyma.
HP 824 ite per alta *D.*
Dine.
Ard. 1184 and *d.* together at the ordinary
Ard. 1496 will you come to-morrow and *d.* with me
Ard. 1547 to *d.* with my Lord Cheiny
Ard. 1579 to my Lord Cheiny's, where we mean to *d.*
Ard. 1693 should never *d.* nor sup without candle-light
Ard. 1713 that went to *d.* at my Lord Cheiny's
Dinged.
ST 405 which pauncht his horse and dingd him to the ground
Dinner.
Ard. 1454 meat you ate at *d.* cannot brook with you
Dint.
ST Bal. 131 then dyed my foes by *d.* of knife
Dio.
HP 1649 Si che vostr' arte a *D.* quasi e' Nipote
Dip.
Cor. 1792 who nicely did but dyp his speare in blood
Dipped.
Jer. 457 thats dipt in inck made of an envious gall
ST Bal. 68 I dipt a napkin in his blood
ST 2865 I weeping dipt within the river of his bleeding wounds
Dire.
ST Bal. 3 feeding on nought but *d.* annoyes
ST 2740 the plot is laide of *d.* revenge
Direct.
HP 1531 no lesse then may suffise to *d.* hys course
ST Bal. 42 to fetch her man he doth *d.*

Directed.
HP 1512 object *d.* unto household government
HP 1594 not *d.* and imployed to some other use
irectio n.
Ard. 1185 and by my man's *d.* draw to the quay
JB 73 she consented by his *d.* to poyson Brewen
JB 90 as Parker had before given *d.*
JB 207 poyson, and after thy *d.* I did minister it unto him
Directly.
HP 87 *d.* against the Gate whereby wee entred
Ard. 945 leads *d.* to my master's chamber
Direful.
Cor. 1578 and in thys *d.* warre before mine eyes
Cor. 1817 of murder, death, and direfull massacres
Cor. 1902 O cruell Gods, O heaven, O direfull Fates
ST 1142 with direfull visions wake my vexed soule
SP 1910 I doome you to ten thousand direfull torments
Dirge.
ST 996 Ile say his *d.*, singing fits not this case
Disarm.
SP 384 Ile be your Page this once, for to disarme you
Disastrous.
Cor. 339 that your desastrous griefes shall turne to joy
Cor. 649 but what *d.* or hard accident
Cor. 1617 and what *d.* accident did breake
Disburdened.
Ard. 933 and thou *d.* of the oath thou made
Discente.
HP 1648 Segue, come 'l maestro fa il *d.*
Discern.
Ard. 1540 that Sol may well *d.* the trampled path
Discerned.
Ard. 1732 that neither horse nor man could be *d.* ?
Discharge.
HP 979 and *d.* the greatest doubt thou canst imagine
Cor. 1157 will there-withall *d.* the powre he hath
Jer. 85 I will discharg the waight of your command
Jer. 238 discharg, discharg, good Lazarotto, how we
SP 563 and did *d.* a faithfull subjects love
SP 1052 ready to *d.* it uppon you, when you go by
Ard. 1424 at your dag's *d.* make towards
Ard. 1519 well, I'll *d.* my pistol at the sky
Discharged.
HP 496 deposed and *d.* him of the weight of
ST 355 *d.* his Pistoll at the Princes back
ST 1449 be satisfied, and the law dischargde
Ard. 1271 *d.* against a ruinated wall
Discipline.
HP 719 brought up in good *d.* under the education of
HP 818 bring them up under so soft and easie *d.*
HP 857 *d.* may conforme and be agreeable therewith
HP 947 teaching Beastes is not *d.*
HP 952 is accompanied with reason, and may become *d.*
SP 167 well famed thou art for *d.* in warre
Discoloured.
Cor. 1733 with pale, wanne clowdes *d.* the Sunne
Discomfiture.
Cor. Arg. 4 in the disconfiture of the Romains
Discomfited.
Cor. 745 and followed him, be so *d.* ?
Cor. 1162 whom when he had *d.* and chas'd
Cor. 1395 did (conquered) flie, his troopes *d.*
Cor. 1427 well, Caesar, now they are *d.*, and
Cor. 1847 his people so *d.* and scorn'd
Discomfort.
ST 532 and make your late *d.* seeme the lesse

Discommodities.
HP Ind. 56 discomodities of Sommer and Winter
HP 375 inconveniences and discomodities of the Winter and Sommer
Discommodity.
HP 390 feeles some losse and discommoditie
HP 1627 without great discomoditie and perill
Discontent.
HP 722 thou shouldest contend not to d. her
Cor. 237 hels horror is mylder then mine endles d.
Cor. 424 thus day and night I toyle in d.
Cor. 1615 will haply comfort this your d.
ST 726 be deafe, my eares, heare not my d.
ST 985 then will I joy amidst my d.
ST 2472 as d. that things continue so
SP 1384 peace, foole, a sable weed fits d.
Ard. 513 shall set you free from all this d.
Ard. 1229 whose troubled mind is stuffed with d.
Ard. 1877 for in thy d. I find a death
JB 83 and to shew the d. she had of his dwelling
ST 1054 nor discontents it me to leave the world
ST 1148 the cloudie day my discontents records
Discontented.
Jer. 114 a melancholy, d. courtier
ST 1063 doo I (O King) thus d. live
Discord.
Cor. 185 through murder, d., wrath, and enmitie
Cor. 274 and doe with civill d. (furthering it)
Cor. 1217 for civill d., wrought by Caesars sleights
Cor. 1135 or if (these civill discords now dissolv'd)
ST 2267 a song, three parts in one, but all of discords fram'd
Cor. 1750 blood-thirstie D., with her snakie hayre
Discourse.
HP 290 the d. that you have made of Wine
HP 476 the dyscourse your Father made unto you
HP 1141 devised and devided for the second part of our d.
HP 1686 our d. of naturall and not naturall gaine
HP 1701 my Father's d., gathered by him into a little Booke
HP 1704 that my d. should not be made in vaine
HP 1716 and heerein onely fayled his d.
Cor. 972 I feare your griefes increase with thys d.
Cor. 1616 d. the manner of his hard mishap
Cor. 1706 and aged Senators in sad d.
ST 107 unfolde in breefe d. your forme of battell
ST 1739 weele goe continue this d. at Court
SP 6 Melpomene is wholy bent to tragedies d.
SP 1163 least with the d. thou shouldst
SP 1842 the rest, and worst will I d. in briefe
Ard. 455 full d. and flat resolve me of the thing I seek
Discoursed.
HP 134 these things thus d., the
Discover.
Ard. 913 sith thou hast sworn, we dare d. all
Discovered.
HP 186 and not d. on al sides to the Sunne
Cor. 1782 theyr tongues discover'd, and theyr tailes long trailing
Discreet.
HP 719 modest, d., courteous, and brought up in good discipline
Cor. 530 as d. Princes sett theyr Garrisons in
Discreeter.
Puck 3 hath yet in his d. judgmᵗ feared to offende
Discreetly.
HP 1406 so d. ordered and with such proportion
Discrepant.
HP 1723 consider whether they be d. in forme or greatnes

Discretion.
HP Ded. let others carpe, tis your d. that must
HP 663 as a woman of d. will in no wise marre
HP 1038 therefore (wyth dyscretion) dispose the works
ST 1671 unlesse, by more d. then deserv'd, I
ST 1924 and given to one of more d.
ST 2625 which to your d. shall seeme best
Ard. 246 I pray thee leave it to my d.
Disdain.
HP 1016 dysdayne not nowe and than to see such grosse
HP 1082 nor should the Maister of the house dysdaine, or
HP 1309 to dysdaine or scorne to set her hand
HP 1360 the lesse she may dysdaine to busie herselfe
HP 1397 seene it without disdayne and diverslie admiring it
Cor. 127 when we doe that to another, which our selves dysdaine
Cor. 235 with-holds his darte, and in disdaine doth flye me
Cor. 1687 I disdaine the world should see me to become a slave
ST 454 he shall, in rigour of my just disdaine
ST 578 and she in time will fall from her disdaine
SP 1193 honour should force disdaine to roote it out
Cor. 1585 full-gorged triumphes, and disdaines my lyfe
Disdained.
Cor. 858 dragd through the streets, d. to bee borne
JB 34 was still d. and cast off, albeit he had
Disdaineth.
Cor. 515 a noble minde d. servitude
Disdainfully.
JB 46 to whom d. she made answere that
Disdiet.
HP 1551 growing by disorder or disdyet more then Nature made it
Disease.
ST 1598 no, thers no medicine left for my d.
Ard. 1590 sick? of what d.?
HP 25 repose yourselfe with less d. then in any other place
HP 478 to harken thereunto with the dysease of those that are about us
Disfurnish.
ST 1458 thou wouldst faine furnish me with a halter, to d. me of my habit
Disgaged.
Cor. 764 for when our soule the body hath d.
Disgorge.
Cor. 1382 where seav' nfold Nilus doth d. it selfe
Disgrace.
HP 1048 beastlines and filth corrupt, d., and spoile thinges
Cor. 534 so fond we are to feare the worlds d.
Cor. 1259 his owne d., and Caesars violence
Cor. 1419 and Caesars prayse increasd by theyr d.
Cor. 1626 nay, even our Trenches, to our great d.
ST 1187 hath upon some d. a while remoov'd her hence
ST 1192 and her d. makes me unfortunate
ST 1688 remembring that olde d. which you
ST 1705 and better wast for you, being in d.
SP 417 thus to d. thy honored name
SP 1087 a d. to all my chivalrie to combate one so base
Disgraced.
Cor. 331 might die disgrac'd with mine unhappines
Disgracious.
SP 803 if I were so disgratious in thine eye
Disgrade.
HP 497 to d. me of this petit government of houshold
Disguise.
Cor. 953 by which d. (what ere he doth pretend)
Jer. 426 in this d. I may both wed, bed, and
Cor. 760 which eaths appeare in sadde and strange disguises

Disguised.
Jer. 423 and so disguisd, woe, sue, and then at last
Jer. 758 and in all parts d., as there you see
ST 402 she, she her selfe, disguisde in armours maske
Dish.
VPJ 22 my feast of joy is but a d. of paine
Dishes.
HP 249 with the Kidde was served (in severall dyshes) some
HP 251 and in two other dyshes two payre of Pygeons
Dishonest.
HP 1489 seeme not either inconvenient or d.
Dishonour.
ST 1171 and he, for thy d. done, should draw thy
ST 2486 with what d. and the hate of men
ST 2487 from this d. and the hate of men ?
SP 1360 the most d. that could ere befall
Ard. 338 if I d. her or injure thee
Ard. 976 and couch d. as d. buds
Ard. 1022 then comes his wife's d. in his thoughts
Dishonourable.
SP 1191 if any ignoble or d. thoughts
Dishonoured.
Cor. 616 (because her name dishonored stood)
Jer. 338 and find it much dishonord by base homage
ST 898 and left thy bloudie corpes d. heere
Ard. 1893 will you follow him that hath d. you ?
Disjoin.
HP 839 will lay a part this argument, or at least dysjoyne it
from the rest
Disjoined.
HP 1100 united to the bodie, but he seperate and disjoyned from
HP 1426 or utterly disjoyned and estraunged from it
ST 728 watch still, mine eyes, to see this love disjoynd
SP 2193 their soules are knit, though bodyes be disjoynd
Dislike.
HP 1770 d. of manie things which neverthelesse are
Ard. 279 your trick of poisoned pictures we d.
Disliked.
HP 213 much d. and intreated to the contrarie
HP 1472 if great, not much to be dislyked
Dislodge.
Cor. 246 d. my soule, and keepe it with your selves
Disloyal.
Cor. 13 but we, disloiall to our owne defence
Cor. 891 thys your disloyall dealing hath defam'd your King
Ard. (Title) murdered, by the means of his d. and wanton wife
Ard. 1894 why, canst thou prove I have been d. ?
Disloyalty.
SP 783 for this thy perjurde false d.
Dismal.
ST 2204 knock at the dismall gates of Plutos Court
ST 2851 I heare his dismall out-cry eccho in the aire
SP 9 and lowd laments, to tell a dismall tale
SP 584 what dismall Planets guides this fatall hower ?
Ard. 1059 what dismal outcry calls me from my rest ?
Dismayed.
Cor. 1856 and (to conclude) his men dismayd to see the
ST 158 that, halfe dismaid, the multitude retirde
ST 487 my Lord, be not dismaid for what is past
JB 51 so astonished and d. that she concluded
Dismembered.
Cor. 857 and thy dismembred body (stab'd and torne)
Cor. 1822 dismembred bodies drowning in theyr blood
Dismiss.
SP 1562 by this thou shalt dismisse my garison
Dismissed.

ST 219 the rest martch on, but ere they be dismist
Dismount.
SP 487 least he d. me while my wounds are greene
Dismounted.
HP 31 a hyreling that came with me, I d.
HP 115 who, d., immediately came up
SP 239 I, conjecturing the cause to be want of water, d.
SP 342 to be d. by a Childe it vexeth me
Disobedience.
HP Ind. 57 d. of Wives, whence it riseth
Disobedient.
HP 615 exceeding waiward, crabbed and d.
HP 884 the d., stifnecked, and unprofitable servant
Disobeyer.
HP 1635 a d. of the Lawes of God, a Rebell and
Disorder.
HP 1551 for as the nose uppon some mans face, growing by d.
Disordered.
Cor. 1670 not feare them that they had so oft d.
Disparagement.
ST 1670 for I have done you no d.
ST 2563 why, Nero thought it no d.
Dispensations.
HP 1750 governments or d. of a house are devided into
Dispense.
HP 569 custome and the Lawes dyspence with them in this
Cor. 918 that heaven doth with wicked men dispence
Cor. 1476 Heaven sets our time ; with heaven may nought
dispence
Jer. 1114 with my bloud dispence, untill my leedge shall
Disperse.
ST 2367 disperce those cloudes and melanchollie lookes
Dispersed.
SP 2176 the poison is disperst through everie vaine
Displace.
Cor. 188 the former petty combats did d.
Displease.
SP 819 if words and teares d., then view my lookes
Displeased.
Cor. 171 they are the more d., when they see
Cor. 229 as my d. soule may shunne my hart
Cor. 273 are now displeas'd with Pompey and my selfe
Ard. 114 but tell me, is he angry or d. ?
Ard. 2104 I pray you be not angry or d.
Displeasure.
SP 654 he was overthrowne by Fortunes high d.
SP 1069 I am bound, in paine of my maisters d.
Dispose.
HP 1038 d. the works that are or cannot be devided
HP 1379 and d. them to the tongue and penne
Cor. 510 to be at heavens d., and not our owne
Ard. 606 you see my sister's yet at my d.
Ard. 946 there take him and d. him as ye please
Puck 65 for want or of his owne d. to lewdnes
Disposed.
HP 92 verie orderlie and artificially d.
HP 481 that time that Charles the fift desposed his Monarchie
HP 1239 when he shall bee d. to sojourne there
HP 1293 may be sparingly d., for thrift or liberalitie is
HP 1369 as things preserved may the better be d.
HP 1412 disposd the household of his glorious Sig. Capitano
Cor. 1049 and many times (dispos'd to jest)
ST 1285 how fit a place, if one were so disposde
HP 632 as in our soules, wherein as wel the well dysposed
powers
HP 1386 wel d. Epythetons and significa[n]t termes

Disposeth.
HP 949 the right hande holdeth and *d.* any sort of
Cor. 702 a dulnes, that *d.* us to rest

Disposition.
HP 70 from your owne *d.* then from Fortune
Cor. Ded. 8 your noble and heroick dispositions

Dispossessed.
JB 38 and tryumphant in the teares of the *d.*

Dispraise.
HP 466 *d.* of others, or superfluous conceit
Cor. 1534 their dayes, or prolongs them with *d.*

Dispraised.
HP 1767 profit of those things which are despised and dispraysed

Dispraiser.
HP 1126 little things whereof Cicero was rather a dysprayser

Dispregia.
HP 1655 *D.*, poichè in altro pon la spene

Disputation.
Puck 16 fragments of a *d.*, toching that opinion

Disrobed.
HP 1569 *d.* of their Purple, returned to the Plough
ST 1528 disroabde the medowes of their flowred greene

Disrobing.
HP 710 at the death of theyr husbands spoyling and *d.* themselves

Dissemble.
ST 768 and yet *d.* that she loves the Prince
ST 991 or, at the least, *d.* them awhile
SP 1310 for well I wot, though she desemble thus
Ard. 2102 oh, how cunningly she can *d.* !

Dissembling.
ST 2124 *d.* quiet in unquietnes
SP 756 Ile frame my selfe to his *d.* art

Dissention.
ST 1340 this their *d.* breeds a greater doubt
Cor. 191 made thundring Mars (Dissentions common friend)

Dissevered.
HP 550 that tyes the body and the soule togeather is *d.*
Ard. 41 see his *d.* joints and sinews torn

Dissimilem.
VPJ 59 *D.* votis mercedem nacta, sed ausis

Dissimulation.
Ard. (Title) malice and *d.* of a wicked woman

Dissolutely.
Cor. 1116 but, Brutus, shall we dissolutelie sitte, and see

Dissolution.
Ard. 979 and sorrow for her *d.*

Dissolve.
Ard. 218 thine overthrow? first let the world *d.*

Dissolved.
Cor. 1135 or if (these civill discords now dissolv'd)

Dissonant.
HP 948 custome *d.* and segregat from reason

Dissuade.
HP 671 he can practise no way better to dyswade her
ST 1323 I am perswaded, and diswade me not

Distaff.
HP 1332 « Hard at their distaffe doth she hold her maids »

Distained.
ST 321 my late ambition hath distaind my faith

Distilled.
SP 244 my body *d.* such dewy showers of swet

Distinction.
HP Ind. 58 *d.* of nobilitie betwixt man and wife
HP 591 to consider that no *d.* of nobilitie
HP 897 this *d.* of Soveraigne, Ruler, Governour, or Maister, is

HP 978 record and bring to mind our plain *d.*
HP 1437 distinguished according to the *d.* of Beastes
HP 1752 which *d.* I reproove not
HP 1765 and that this is his *d.* may wee gather

Distinguished.
HP Ind. 4 Action *d.*
HP Ind. 78 gaine unnaturall, how it is *d.*
HP Ind. 110 offices, how and when to be *d.*
HP 735 a kind of feare *d.* from servile base feare
HP 1008 houses so *d.* and multiplyed with offycers
HP 1104 which also is *d.* from workmanship
HP 1437 *d.* according to the distinction of Beastes
HP 1737 a Prince is still to be *d.* from a private man
HP 1738 as the forme of their commaundements is *d.*, so are
HP 1739 so are the governments of Princes and of private men *d.*

Distract.
ST 1915 *d.*, and in a manner lunatick
ST 1922 but if he be thus helplessly *d.*
ST 2356 but whats a silly man, *d.* in minde to thinke

Distracted.
STA 2074 still with a *d.* countenance going a long

Distraught.
STA 1942 our Maisters minde is much *d.*

Distress.
Cor. 448 if all the world were in the like distresse
Cor. 523 you will not that (in our distresse) we aske Deaths ayde
Cor. 647 and whose first fortunes (fild with all distresse)
Cor. 1263 represse, or kill out-right, this cause of our distresse
Cor. 1888 what refuge now remaines for my distresse
ST 314 and therefore will not pittie my distresse
ST 407 taking advantage of his foes distresse
ST 1363 « To stand good L[ord] and help him in distres »
ST 2350 and, for I pittied him in his distresse
SP 1104 and give him aide and succour in distresse

Distressed.
Cor. 886 O poore Cornelia, borne to be distrest
ST 284 his Sonne distrest, a corsive to his hart

Distressful.
Cor. 1910 O miserable, desolate, distresful wretch
ST 753 that summons home distressfull travellers
ST 1143 and with the wounds of my distressfull sonne
ST 2169 give way unto my most distressfull words
Ard. 1275 'tis thy policy to forge *d.* looks
Ard. 1809 this charge I'll leave with my *d.* wife

Distribute.
HP 1282 and so *d.* it indifferentlie

Distributed.
HP 1039 works that are or cannot be devided or *d.*

Distrust.
ST 1245 thus must we worke that will avoide *d.*
ST 1807 a forrest of *d.* and feare
Ard. 351 the world shall see that I *d.* her not

Disturbed.
Jer. 903 firmely move without *d.* spleenes
Ard. 1220 *d.* thoughts drives me from company

Disturbing.
Ard. 1068 I crave your pardons for *d.* you

Ditch.
Ard. 1686 I shall fall into some *d.* or other
Ard. 1707 why, how now? who is this that's in the *d.*?

Ditty.
SP 52 but I have framde a dittie to the tune

Dive.
ST 699 and through her eares *d.* downe into her hart
STA 1956 *d.* in the water, and stare up to heaven
SP 956 Ile be so bolde as to *d.* into this Gentlemans pocket

Divers.
HP Ind. 31 care of housekeeping of *d.* sortes
HP 80 *d.* roomes and stories, one above another
HP 588 (in dyvers actions of publique aparance)
ST 2428 for *d.* causes it is fit for us that we
Ard. 1498 I have *d.* matters to talk with you about
Ard. 1919 *d.* with silver noses for saying « There goes
Ard. 1954 with *d.* of his neighbours and his friends
JB 25 was beloved of *d.* young men, especially of
JB 70 *d.* and sundry times had they talke together
Diverse.
HP 636 the offices and dueties should be divers
HP 638 it is convenient also that their vertues should be divers
HP 892 the Lawes and usages of men are variable and divers
HP 1165 though they be divers according to the variety of Countreys
Diversely.
HP 1398 seene it without disdayne and diverslie admiring it
HP 1742 yet are they to be governed diversly
Divide.
HP 997 these would I devide into two formes
HP 1584 this wee devide into two formes or kindes
Divided.
HP Ind. 33 how it is to bee devided twixt
HP Ind. 39 is devided into two parts
HP 164 the which I have devided into foure parts
HP 178 « you have well devided your lands » (quoth I)
HP 518 the care of a good housholder is devided into two thinges
HP 780 be devided so betweene the Father and the Mother
HP 1039 works that are or cannot be devided or distributed
HP 1140 which we devised and *d.* for the second part
HP 1144 and is devided betwixt the Master and Mistresse
HP 1347 « Upon a wel devided loome thy wife doth weave apace »
HP 1561 devided and bequeathed amongst his Children
HP 1613 that cannot be devided are of number certaine
HP 1750 dispensations of a house are devided into foure parts
Cor. 36 a state devided cannot firmely stand
Ard. 1266 fire *d.* burns with lesser force
Divideth.
HP 20 that devideth the confines of Piemount from
Divine.
Cor. 846 for I *d.* that thou must vomit it
Jer. 1054 for by this act I hold thy arm devine
STA 1973 and those that should be powerfull and *d.*
Puck 24 nor wold indeed the forme of devyne praiers used
Divinely.
HP 1098 he is Animatus, and divinelie is enriched with a soule
Divining.
Cor. 763 devining of our future miseries
Divinity.
Jer. 836 O what devinity proceeds from love
Division.
HP Ind. 54 devision of lande Quadrupartite
HP 1611 albeit in respect of the partition or devision it seeme
HP 1613 this devision being thus considered, much
Divorce.
ST 14 forcing *d.* betwixt my love and me
Divorced.
HP 555 that woman or man, that have beene *d.* by death
Doctors.
HP 403 the opinion of some *D.* of the Hebrues
Dog.
SP 322 better a *D.* fawne on me, then barke
Ard. 833 I have had ten pound to steal a *d.*

Ard. 952 come, let's go drink : choler makes me as dry as a *d.*
HP 7 I heard a confused cry of dogs
HP 13 beating and crying out upon the doggs
HP 1085 as we may dailie see in dogs
Ard. 1415 whilst two stout dogs were striving for a bone
Ard. 1425 like the longing water-*d.* that coucheth till
Ard. 1992 Greene and we two will *d.* him through the fair
Doings.
HP 1122 there is somewhat of theyr dooings in his works
Doleful.
Cor. 418 and thrice detaind, with dolefull shreeks and cryes
Cor. 975 my dolefull spyrits endles myseries
ST 390 I nill refuse this heavie dolefull charge
STA 2058 canst paint a dolefull crie ?
Dolori.
ST 998 Misceat, & nostro detur medicina *d.*
Domineer.
SP 950 or dominere with the money when I have sold it
Domineered.
Ard. 665 and domineer'd with it amongst good fellows
Domino.
Cor. 2038 Non prosunt *D.*, quae prosunt omnibus, Artes. Tho. Kyd
Domum.
HP 142 Nocte *d.* dapibus mensas onerabat inemptis
Don.
Jer. 357 *D.*, Ile not bate an inch of courage nor
Jer. 1030 are you remembred, *D.*, of a daring message
Jer. 1032 you braved me, *D.*, within my Fathers court
Jer. 1171 I prethee, rest ; it shall be done, sweet *D.*
Jer. (Title) and the life and death of *D.* Andraea
Jer. 57 Oh, heeres a Lad of mettle, stout *D.* Andrea
Jer. 70 pray, king, pray, peeres, let it be *D.* Andrea
Jer. 82 then, *D.* Andrea —
Jer. 94 farwell then, *D.* Andrea ; to thy chargde
Jer. 257 at his returne to Spaine, Ile murder *D.* Andrea
Jer. 287 Ile dispatch letters to *d.* Andrea
Jer. 365 meete, *D.* Andrea ? yes, in the battles Bowels
Jer. 373 meet, *D.* Andrea ? I tell thee, noble spirit
Jer. 406 remember, *D.* Andrea, that we meet
Jer. 443 shall show all *D.* Andrea, not Alcario
Jer. 448 to *D.* Andrea, Spaines embassador ?
Jer. 571 that *D.* Andrea may prevent his death
Jer. 581 worthy embassador, brave *D.* Andrea
Jer. 619 welcom, my lifes selfe forme, deere *D.* Andrea
Jer. 657 why *D.*, *D.* Andrea
Jer. 660 I, *D.* Andrea, or else *D.* the devill
Jer. 672 lives *D.* Andrea ?
Jer. 752 firmly planted in *D.* Andreas bosome
Jer. 926 I bind thee, *D.* Andrea, by thy honer
Jer. 983 can you not find [me] *D.* Andrea forth ?
Jer. 1155 *D.* Andreas ghoast salutes me, see, embraces me
Jer. 17 my leedge, how like you *D.* Horatios spirit ?
Jer. 480 art thou a scholler, *D.* Horatio
Jer. 67 I should have chose[n] *D.* Lorenzo
Jer. 924 and thou, *D.* Pedro, mine
Jer. 965 *D.* Pedro
Jer. 967 I, I, *D.* Pedro, my boy shall meete thee
Jer. 1069 O my sad fates, *D.* Pedro weltring in his gore
Jer. 1072 valliant *D.* Pedro
Jer. 68 I, *D.* Rogero
Jer. 1078 I, in valliant bloud of *D.* Rogeroes sheding
ST 5 my name was *D.* Andrea ; my discent
ST 156 till *D.* Andrea with his brave Launciers
ST 386 relate the circumstance of *D.* Andreas death
ST 414 but then was *D.* Andreas carkasse lost ?

ST 635 alas, my Lord, since *D.* Andreas death
ST 1689 disgrace which you for *D.* Andrea had indurde
ST 1703 your first favourite *D.* Andreas death
ST 2173 supplication of *D.* Bazulto for his murdred Sonne »
ST 88 *D.* Balthazar, the Prince of Portingale
ST 223 welcome *D.* Balthazar ; welcome Nephew
ST 282 how likes *D.* Balthazar of this device ?
ST 349 *D.* Balthazar, amidst the thickest troupes
ST 357 and therewithall *D.* Balthazar fell doune
ST 406 then yong *D.* Balthazar with ruthles rage
ST 452 and where *D.* Balthazar that slew my love
ST 508 supposing that *D.* Balthazar is slaine
ST 779 heire unto our brother heere, *D.* Ciprian
ST 3040 and let *D.* Ciprian supply his roome
ST (Title) containing the lamentable end of *D.* Horatio, and
ST 25 by *D.* Horatio, our Knight Marshals sonne
ST 284 that *D.* Horatio beare us company
ST 435 she will be *D.* Horatios thankfull freend
ST 436 and (Madame) *D.* Horatio will not slacke
ST 650 what, *D.* Horatio, our Knight Marshals sonne ?
ST 1318 touching the death of *D.* Horatio
ST 1560 « I holpe to murder *D.* Horatio too »
ST 1885 his ransome due to *D.* Horatio
ST 827 by fetching *D.* Lorenzo to this match
ST 1283 for heere did *D.* Lorenzos Page appoint that
ST 1313 why tell me, *D.* Lorenzo, tell me, man, if
ST 1341 assure thee, *D.* Lorenzo, he shall dye
ST 1382 he shall not want while *D.* Lorenzo lives
ST 2207 to torture *D.* Lorenzo and the rest
ST 2272 go forth, *D.* Pedro, for thy Nephews sake
ST 2746 my Nephew *D.* Lorenzo, and my Neece ?
ST 3041 place *D.* Lorenzo on Ixions Wheele
ST 131 *D.* Pedro, their chiefe Horsemens Corlonell
ST 3000 and thou, *D.* Pedro, do the like for us
ST 134 *D.* Rogero, worthy man of warre

Doom.
Cor. 209 for the fatall dombe the Fates make hast enough
ST 53 to dome him as best seemes his Majestie
ST 79 and begd that onely she might give my doome
ST 266 will both abide the censure of my doome ?
ST 1114 my guiltie soule submits me to thy doome
ST 3022 that, by the vertue of her Princely doome
ST 3038 let me be judge, and doome them to unrest
SP 827 hard doome of death, before my case be knowne
SP 1067 for her to give him doome of life or death
SP 1910 I doome you to ten thousand direfull torments

Doomed.
SP 1493 domde to thy selfe by thine owne wilfulnes
SP 1629 and then he shall be doomd by marshall law

Door.
SP 1052 hath planted a double cannon in the doore
Ard. 128 to come this morning but along my *d.*
Ard. 1113 this is the *d.*; but soft, methinks 'tis shut
Ard. 1916 though we be hanged at his *d.* for our labour
Ard. 2058 when this *d.* opens next, look for his death
Ard. 2076 stand before the counting-house *d.*
Ard. 2262 make the *d.* fast ; let them not come in
Jer. 217 from userers doores there goes one pathe
Jer. 1167 secrets in hell are lockt with doores of brasse
ST 2898 breake ope the doores ; runne, save Hieronimo
Ard. 941 the doors I'll leave unlocked against you come
Ard. 1070 are the doors fast locked and all things safe ?
Ard. 1071 I cannot tell ; I think I locked the doors
Ard. 1073 ne'er trust me but the doors were all unlocked
Ard. 1195 and left the doors unbolted and unlocked
Ard. 1201 and coming down he found the doors unshut

Ard. 1657 driven him out at doors with a wet pair of eyes
Ard. 1950 no sooner came the surgeon in at doors
Ard. 2115 the doors are open, sir, you may be gone
Ard. 2116 nay, that's a lie, for I have locked the doors
Ard. 2169 mistress, the guests are at the doors
Ard. 2242 bring them to the doors, but do not stay
Ard. 2339 and she was ready to thrust me out at doors
JB 183 she would not goe forth of her doores for feare
ST 1498 that ere gronde at my office doore
SP 1694 wish you to have an eye to the back dore
Ard. 2264 out at the back-*d.*, over the pile of wood
SP 1827 his Cabine doore fast shut, he first began
Ard. 2085 when my husband is come in, lock the street-*d.*
STA 1990 deare Hieronimo, come in a doores
STA 2034 Pedro, Jaques, goe in a doores ; Isabella, goe
STA 2038 goe in a doores, I say

Dopo.
HP 1646 Tu troverai non *d.* molte carte

Dote.
STA 1754 to make a father *d.*, rave, or runne mad ?
ST 1825 imperfection of his age doth make him *d.*
Ard. 22 ay, but to *d.* on such a one as he
Jer. 240 dotes on your Sister, Bellimperia

Doted.
ST 1015 on whom I *d.* more then all the world

Doter.
Jer. 748 was a huge dotar on Bellimperias beautye

Doth.
Jer. 47 kind words which *d.* oft besiedge the eares

Double.
VPJ 92 life *d.* death should be
HP 82 and there they ascended by *d.* staires
Cor. 288 and let theyr *d.* losse that held me deere
ST 214 talke with our brave prisoner and his *d.* guard
SP 900 your gould shall be repaide with *d.* thankes
SP 1052 hath planted a *d.* cannon in the doore
SP 1966 but strangled ? ah, *d.* death to me

Doubled.
Ard. 997 your woes, twice *d.* all, with patience

Doublet.
ST 1482 live till his olde *d.* will make thee a new trusse ?
Ard. 696 a watchet satin *d.* all-to torn

Doubt.
HP 72 no neede to *d.* of your abode
HP 434 which without *d.* he shall see
HP 980 and discharge the greatest *d.* thou canst imagine
HP 1729 yet now (I *d.*) I shall not be so prompt
Jer. 19 I, and no *d.* his merit will purchase more
Jer. 949 father, I *d.* it not
ST 243 but tell me (for their holding makes me *d.*)
ST 331 no *d.*, my Liege, but still the Prince survives
ST 601 and *d.* not but weele finde some remedie
ST 769 I *d.* not, I, but she will stoope in time
ST 822 why, make you *d.* of Pedriganos faith ?
ST 1028 as we both *d.* and dread our overthrow
ST 1340 this their dissention breeds a greater *d.*
ST 1373 bid him not *d.* of his deliverie
ST 1804 then list to me, and Ile resolve your *d.*
ST 1878 no *d.*, my Lord, it is an argument of
ST 2608 O, that will I, my Lords, make no *d.* of it
SP 772 but wherefore makes Perseda such a *d.*
SP 1105 and *d.* not to, but Fortune will be there
Ard. 1171 I stood in *d.* whether I waked or no
ST 1023 seated amidst so many helpeles doubts
ST 1386 and now or never ends Lorenzos doubts
SP 1411 perhaps thou doubts my friendships constancie

Ard. 379 you wrong yourself and me to cast these doubts
Doubted.
HP 416 it may bee *d.* whether these sixe
HP 1417 it may be *d.* whether this arte of
Doubtful.
Cor. 677 to whom in doubtfull things we seeke accesse
Jer. 712 most doubtfull wars and dangerous pointed ends
ST 607 to sound the bottome of this doubtfull theame
ST 2293 with doubtfull followers, unresolved men
SP 945 now am I growing into a *d.* agony
Ard. 1803 the pilot quaking at the *d.* storm
Puck 3 though I thinke he rest not doubtfull of myne inocence
Doubtless.
HP 648 he shall doubtles much confirme the womans chastitie
ST 1824 doubtles this man is passing lunaticke
SP 1086 doubtlesse he is a very tall fellow
SP 2157 before I die, for doubtlesse die I must
Ard. 1943 *d.*, he is preserved by miracle
Puck 72 ffor doubtles even then yor L^ps shalbe sure
Dove.
Ard. 1316 that showed my heart a raven for a *d.*
SP 1451 or Venus milke white Doves, so milde they are
Dove-house.
HP 255 the Pigeons, them I have from my owne Dovehouse
Down.
HP 205 come and sat her *d.*
HP 374 that she blushing held downe her head
HP 758 ‹ Lay doun with him upo[n] the grasse al covered with a clowde ›
HP 989 other meane or policy to pacifie or put the[m] *d.*
HP 1223 or whether it lie steepeward downe the hyls
Cor. 174 that breaths her heavie poisons downe to hell
Cor. 613 shall keepe the Romaine valure downe
Cor. 766 downe by the fearefull gates of Acheron
Cor. 781 downe to the Scithian swift-foote feareles Porters
Cor. 790 thy head hung downe, thy cheeks with teares besprent
Cor. 1026 over night lye calmely downe
Cor. 1634 downe to the Sea-side ; where before faire Tapsus
Cor. 1756 fiered with a quenchles rage, runnes up and downe
Cor. 1852 to beate them downe as fierce as thundring flints
Cor. 1973 when (fierd) their golden Pallaces fell downe
Cor. 1999 tresses, now hang neglectly, dangling downe your sholders
Jer. 59 shake the Kings hie court three handfuls downe
Jer. 384 I, when you get me downe
Jer. 588 when it would scarce go downe for extreame laughter
Jer. 746 Ile cut them downe, my words shall not be hong
Jer. 761 I tooke him for Andrea, downe he fell
Jer. 880 thaile throw thee downe, little Jeronimo
Jer. 929 where ile set downe, in caractors on thy flesh
Jer. 1024 drop doune thick as if death mowed them
Jer. 1067 and break our haughty sculs downe to our feete
Jer. 1107 tis easie to seize those were first laid downe
Jer. 1117 I could whip al these, were there hose downe
Jer. 1136 have writ it downe in marble leaves
ST 90 heere sit we downe to see the misterie
ST 249 but first I forc'd him lay his weapons downe
ST 357 and therewithall Don Balthazar fell doune
ST 419 there laid him downe, and dewd him with my teares
ST 511 sit downe, young Prince, you are our second guest
ST 512 Brother, sit downe ; and, Nephew, take your place
ST 699 and through her eares dive downe into her hart
STA 962 a youth, as I remember. I cut him downe
STA 970 and drop this deede of murder downe on me
ST 1465 yes, but there shalbe for my comming downe
ST 1833 downe by the dale that flowes with purple gore

ST 1840 turne downe this path : thou shalt be with him straite
STA 2036 will range this hidious orchard up and downe
STA 2080 and I with a trice to cut him downe
STA 2094 thus would I teare and drage him up and downe
ST 2132 will beare me downe with their nobilitie
ST 2680 doune with these branches and these loathsome bowes
ST 2682 downe with them, Isabella ; rent them up
ST 2725 you would vouchsafe to throw me downe the key
ST 2752 set downe in English, more largely, for the easier
ST 3035 this hand shall hale them downe to deepest hell
ST 3053 then haste we doune to meet thy freends and foes
SP 332 and the silver knight are both downe
SP 478 would you have me runne up and downe the towne
SP 536 as withered leaves with Autume throwen downe
SP 905 false treacher, lay downe the chaine
SP 907 that lye my weapon shall put *d.* thy throate
SP 1040 and then and there fall downe amid his armes
SP 1061 then fals he downe, poore wretch, upon his knee
SP 1107 and lift him up, and throw him downe againe
SP 1221 nay, nay, Erastus, throw not downe thy weapons
SP 1225 and now from armes to counsell sit thee downe
SP 1307 informd him that I sought him up and downe
SP 1414 come, Erastus, sit thee downe by me
SP 1491 then kneele thou downe
SP 1529 come, sit thee downe upon my right hand heere
SP 1897 helpe to send them *d.* to everlasting night
SP 1906 and throw them headlong downe into the valley
SP 2144 and now Perseda, heere I lay me downe
Ard. 254 and lay their ears *d.* to the lowly earth
Ard. 361 husband, sit *d.* ; your breakfast will be cold
Ard. 671 I see more company coming *d.* the hill
Ard. 692 long hair *d.* his shoulders curled
Ard. 739 will you kill him ? here's the angels *d.*
Ard. 766 ‹ do walk up and *d.* Paul's till one day I fell asleep ›
Ard. 822 look to your signs, for I'll pull them *d.* all
Ard. 839 a boy let *d.* his shop-window and broke his head
Ard. 1186 and with the tide go *d.* to Feversham
Ard. 1201 and coming *d.* he found the doors unshut
Ard. 1308 whose dowry would have weighed *d.* all thy wealth
Ard. 1466 first did she cast her eyes *d.* to the earth
Ard. 1516 I would his crown were molten *d.* his throat
Ard. 1521 what, is he *d.* ? is he dispatched ?
Ard. 1799 which falling *d.* light on the shooter's head
Ard. 1805 even in that fearful time would I fall *d.*
Ard. 1941 sure to have had his sign pulled *d.* and
Ard. 2068 from her watery bower fling *d.* Endymion
Ard. 2106 you are welcome, Master Mosbie ; will you sit *d.* ?
Ard. 2203 you may do well to bid his guests sit *d.*
Ard. 2208 or, an thou sayest the word, let us sit *d.* too
Ard. 2341 and as she followed me, I spurned her *d.* the stairs
Ard. 2358 study not for an answer ; look not *d.*
JB 106 having set the porringer doune beside her
JB 108 her coat cast downe that measse which
Ard. 1208 where you may front him well on Rainham *D.*
Ard. 1216 because they two may be in Rainham *D.*
Ard. 1440 o'ertake us ere we come to Rainham *D.*
Ard. 1475 come, we are almost now at Rainham *D.*
Ard. 953 thus feeds the lamb securely on the *d.*
Ard. 1306 that I have took more purses in this *d.*
Ard. 1443 thou shalt never go further than that *d.*
Cor. 1746 till streames of blood like Rivers fill the downes
Cor. 933 Ile downe with joy : because, before I died, mine eyes
ST 2203 Ile downe to hell, and in this passion knock at
SP 26 I will not downe to everlasting night till
SP 1318 I with the rest will downe unto the strand
Ard. 176 when he may have it for a right *d.* blow ?

Down-cast.
Cor. (Title) her Father and Husbandes downe-cast, death, and fortune

Downfall.
ST 64 was ready dounfall to the deepest hell
ST 2506 that wrought his d. with extreamest death
SP 237 from Titans Easterne uprise to his Western downefall
Ard. 1237 and makes me dread my d. to the earth

Downright.
Ard. 1436 back to Rochester : the horse halts d.

Downward.
Jer. 877 thou man, from thy hose downe ward, scarse so much

Dowry.
ST 777 her d. shall be large and liberall
Ard. 289 I'll make her d. more than I'll talk of, Clarke
Ard. 1308 whose d. would have weighed down all thy wealth

Dozen.
SP 131 bid my men bring my horse, and a dosen staves
SP 132 you shall have your horses and two dosen of staves
SP 425 beside two dossen small inferior bones

Drag.
ST 363 I saw them d. it to the Spanish tents
STA 2094 thus would I teare and drage him up and downe

Dragged.
Cor. 858 dragd through the streets, disdained to bee borne
ST 3050 let him be dragde through boyling Acheron

Dram.
Ard. 284 put but a d. of this into his drink

Draught.
Jer. 124 Andreas Himens d. shall be in bloud
Ard. 253 make heavenly gods break off their nectar draughts

Drave.
Cor. Arg. 26 tempest tooke him on the Sea, that d. him backe

Draw.
VPJ 86 through thee we d. our breath of joy
Cor. 453 anothers teares d. teares fro forth our eyes
Cor. 1623 lamely they fought, to d. us further on
Cor. 1629 could d. our Captaines to endanger us
ST 1171 for thy dishonour done, should d. thy life in question
SP 1115 then, farewell, sorrow ; and now, revenge, d. neere
Ard. 841 zounds, d., Shakebag, I am almost killed
Ard. 1125 and never let me d. a sword again
Ard. 1185 and by my man's direction d. to the quay
Ard. 1189 d., Shakebag, for here's that villain Michael
Ard. 1841 O monstrous ! nay, then it is time to d.
STA 2050 and d. me five yeeres yonger then I am
STA 2062 canst thou d. a murderer ?
STA 2083 drawe me like old Priam of Troy
Ard. 234 sweet Alice, he shall d. thy counterfeit
Ard. 623 that you should paint and d. it out yourself
Ard. 231 that whoso looks upon the work he draws
Ard. 598 his pencil draws no shadows in his love
HP 1269 drawes away theyr moysture
Cor. 814 the sword which murdrer-like against thy selfe he drawes
Cor. 1865 but as one mischiefe drawes another on, a
Ard. 1468 then softy draws she forth her handkercher

Draweth.
HP 659 increaseth and d. as earnest love and

Drawn.
Cor. 855 and many a Romaine sword already drawne
ST 1661 first, to affright me with thy weapons drawne
ST 2771 drawne by the influence of her lights, I yield
Ard. 1046 in their ruthless hands their daggers d.
Ard. 1160 with falchion d., and bent it at my breast
Ard. 1553 could once have d. you from these arms of mine

Down-cast.
ST 54 to this effect my pasport straight was drawne
ST 2617 and heere, my Lords, are severall abstracts drawne
Ard. 241 it may not be, for when the picture's d.

Dread.
HP 731 the d. wherewith base slaves or servaunts are
Cor. 530 twere more then base in us to d. his dart
Cor. 991 he can doe mee no mischiefe that I d.
Cor. 1077 he onely, that no death doth d., doth live at rest
ST 1028 as we both doubt and d. our overthrow
SP 285 what, saunce d. of our indignation ?
Ard. 1237 and makes me d. my downfall to the earth
Jer. 65 right pleasing, our d. Soveraigne
Jer. 81 right pleasing, our d. Soveraigne
Jer. 727 wars, my d. leedge
Jer. 792 according [to] your gratious, d. Comand
ST 376 vouchsafe, d. Soveraigne, to heare me speake
ST 1101 d. Lord, in kindnes you could do no lesse
ST 1883 now last (d. Lord) heere hath his highnes sent
SP 529 pardon me, d. Soveraigne, I hold it not
Jer. 1023 tis now about the heavy d. of battaile

Dreadful.
ST 56 through dreadfull shades of ever glooming night
ST 120 both raising dreadfull clamors to the skie
SP 1032 dreadfull Neptune, bring him backe againe
SP 1302 so dreadfull is our name to cowardice
Ard. 1043 a d. thing to be considered of
Ard. 1165 and, when the d. forest-king is gone
Ard. 1802 and saw a d. southern flaw at hand

Dream.
Cor. 696 we dreame by night what we by day have thought
Cor. 749 my feare proceeds not of an idle dreame
ST 882 I did not slumber ; therefore twas no dreame
STA 954 were not, Isabella ? doest thou dreame it is ?
ST 1265 it is no dreame that I adventure for
Ard. 74 nay, love, there is no credit in a d.
Ard. 1064 I had a fearful d. that troubled me
Ard. 1079 Michael, farewell ; I pray thee d. no more
Ard. 1177 and this, I warrant you, procured your d.
Cor. 646 whose sweeter sleepes are turnd to fearefull dreames
Cor. 691 my fearefull dreames doe my despairs redouble
Cor. 692 why suffer you vayne dreames your heade to trouble ?
Cor. 695 God graunt these dreames to good effect bee brought
ST 83 where dreames have passage in the silent night
ST 364 I, I, my nightly dreames have tolde me this
STA 941 I and his mother have had strange dreames to night
ST 1149 early begins to register my dreames
SP 1961 ah no ; my nightly dreames foretould me this
Ard. 1179 but oftentimes my dreams presage too true

Dreamed.
Cor. 1671 them that already dream'd of death or flight
ST 2455 thus wordlings ground, what they have dreamd, upon

Dreams'-effects.
Cor. 430 the fearefull dreames effects that trouble mee

Dreamt.
Jer. 98 Lorenzo is not drempt on in this age
Ard. 1148 this night I d. that, being in a park

Dregs.
Ard. 771 « who, drunk with the d. of your favour, will cleave »

Dressed.
HP 250 drest, after our Countrey fashion, with Larde
HP 395 that might be drest by the most excellent Cooke
Ard. 1884 thou wouldst have followed him, and seen him d.
Ard. 1907 I'll seek out Mosbie where his wound is d.

Drew.
ST 16 my valour d. me into dangers mouth
ST 37 d. forth the manner of my life and death

SP 1019 with that they *d*., and there Ferdinando had the
JB 136 now, when it *d*. some what late, she tould
Drewest.
Ard. 1849 thou drew'st thy sword, enraged with jealousy
Dried.
HP 1272 which (beeing dryed) wold become both hard and
Dries.
Cor. 454 and choyce of streames the greatest River dryes
Cor. 982 my passion neither dyes, nor dryes the heate
Ard. 1221 and *d*. my marrow with their watchfulness
Drift.
Jer. 591 is the villaine Lazarotto acquainted with our *d*.?
ST 2509 why then I see that heaven applies our *d*.
Ard. 590 I have a *d*. will quiet all
Ard. 178 and let not him nor any know thy drifts
Ard. 450 to put in practice our intended drifts
Ard. 579 what! to acquaint each stranger with our drifts
Drink.
HP 1282 and othersome made fit for *d*.
HP 1288 and to bid a stranger drinke
Cor. 1374 dyd live to see my souldiers drinke at Loyre
ST 535 I drinke to thee for this devise
Ard. 284 put but a dram of this into his *d*.
Ard. 722 I'll *d*. no water for thy sake whilst this lasts
Ard. 951 come, let's go *d*.; choler makes me as dry as a dog
Ard. 1223 feebles my body by excess of *d*.
Ard. 1939 saying, « Will it please your worship *d*.? »
Ard. 2124 I am content to *d*. to him for this once
Drinking-schools.
Jer. 223 from drinking schooles one
Drive.
HP 566 with lightning *d*. me to the deepe
Cor. 73 the golden Sunne, where ere he *d*. his glittring Chariot
Jer. 1094 *d*. them hence while I make war
ST 482 and but devise to *d*. me from this place
ST 1150 and *d*. me forthe to seeke the murtherer
ST 1908 needes must he goe that the divels *d*.
SP 1261 to *d*. away this melancholly moode
Ard. 1220 disturbed thoughts drives me from company
Ard. 1909 he whom the devil drives must go perforce
Driven.
HP 1277 suddainly are *d*. to entertaine a straunger
Ard. 1657 *d*. him out at doors with a wet pair of eyes
JB 48 having been thus *d*. off longer than hee thought good
Puck 49 lesse by farr hath dryven so manye imo extra caulas
Dronk *see* **Drunk.**
Droop.
Ard. 1 Arden, cheer up thy spirits, and *d*. no more!
Drop.
Cor. 842 if yet our harts retaine one *d*. of blood
Cor. 1225 but know, while Cassius hath one *d*. of blood
Jer. 1079 and each *d*. worth a thousand Portugales
ST 2224 shew me one *d*. of bloud fall from the same
Ard. 832 I value every *d*. of my blood at a French crown
Ard. 1988 for every *d*. of his detested blood I
Cor. 635 where, wringing wet with drops of silver dew
Jer. 15 Ile speake in drops, when I do faile in words
Jer. 904 the deere dropes of many a purple part
SP 779 are there no honest drops in all thy cheekes
Ard. 1467 watching the drops that fell amain from thence
Jer. 681 why then rot off, and *d*. upon the ground
Jer. 1024 *d*. doune as thick as if death mowed them
ST 148 on every side *d*. Captaines to the ground
ST 587 such as doe *d*. from Pan and Marsias quill
STA 967 *d*. all your stinges at once in my cold bosome
STA 970 and *d*. this deede of murder downe on me

SP 1841 heavens, heer you this, and drops not vengeance on
them?
Drought.
SP 225 there happened a sore *d*. in some part of Belgia
Drove.
Cor. 699 softly *d*. his slow-pac'd Teeme
HP 1439 flocks, Heards, and droves compact
Drown.
Cor. 414 (enlarg'd) to drowne the payne it did abide
Jer. 182 you drowne my honores in those flowing watters
ST 835 and in thy love and councell drowne my feare
ST 900 to drowne thee with an ocean of my teares?
Drowned.
Cor. 505 that I were drown'd in the Tartarean deepes
Cor. 2023 before I have entomb'd my *d*. Father
Ard. 1651 half *d*. with new ale overnight
Ard. 1703 help, Will, help, I am almost *d*.
Drowning.
Cor. 1822 dismembred bodies *d*. in theyr blood
Drowsiness.
Ard. 1096 this *d*. in me bodes little good
Drowsy.
Cor. 753 when drousy sleep, that wak'd mee at unwares
Drudge.
Ard. 323 why, what art thou now but a velvet *d*.?
Drugs.
Jer. 55 and be as bitter as physitions *d*.
SP 1848 but that we lackt such *d*. to mixe with powder
Ard. 628 how I do work of these impoisoned *d*.
Drum.
Jer. 838 harke, the *d*. beckens me; sweet deere, farwell
Jer. 840 The *d*. agen. — Hath that more power then I?
Jer. 871 hark, Portugales: I heare their Spanish *d*.
Jer. 875 weele be as shrill as you: strike a larum, *d*.
Jer. 977 I am wars tuter; strike a larum, *d*.
SP 850 four Visards, foure Gownes, a boxe, and a Drumme
SP 1323 *d*., sound a parle to the Citizens
SP 2045 *d*., sound a parle
Jer. 893 wherefore meete our drums but [for] to
ST 119 both cheerly sounding trumpets, drums, and fifes
Drumsler.
SP 884 *D*., play for me, and ile reward thee
SP 901 and, fellow *D*., ile reward you well
Drunk.
HP 1303 should be first dronk or sold if thou have any quantitie
Cor. 1953 (if thy hart be not of flynt, or drunck with rigor)
Jer. 378 when we have drunke hot bloud together
Jer. 452 eate Cues, *d*. Cees, and cannot give a letter
Ard. 770 who, *d*. with the dregs of your favour, will cleave
Dry.
HP 1257 some would be kept moyst and cold, and some *d*.
Cor. 224 (cause I cannot *d*. your ceaselesse springs)
Cor. 456 my teares shall *d*., and I my griefe forget
Jer. 250 his bounty amongst souldiers sokes him *d*.
Ard. 871 when she is *d*. sucked of her eager young
Ard. 951 come, let's go drink: choler makes me as *d*. as a dog
Dry-shod.
SP 1948 parted the seas, and we came over drie-shod
Duck.
Jer. 231 for, give me duckets, Ile fetch you *d*. inough
Jer. 230 oh Duckets, dainty ducks: for, give me duckets
Duckets.
Jer. 229 and ile raine showers of *D*. in thy palme
Jer. 230 oh *D*., dainty ducks: for, give me *d*.
ST 221 on every souldier two *d*. and on every leader ten
SP 996 shall have three thousand *D*. for his paines

Dudgeon.
SP 301 but swear upon my Dudgin dagger
Due.
HP 225 by their Children as is *d.* to Parents
HP 231 which is their *d.*, and nature bindeth children unto
Cor. 370 return'd *d.* honors to our Common-wealth
Cor. 915 *d.* punishment succeeds not alwaies after an offence
Cor. 1700 the Romaine state (*d.* to the victor) thereon ruminate
Jer. 2 by all the dewe and customary rights
Jer. 332 of tribute *d.* unto our masters kingdome
Jer. 339 I not deny but tribute hath bin *d.* to Spaine
Jer. 635 I had my hier, and thou shalt have thy *d.*
Jer. 947 nay, then, if brother-hood by strokes come dewe
Jer. 1046 your a prince ; I know youle pay your dew
ST 424 I saw him honoured with *d.* funerall
ST 1885 his ransome *d.* to Don Horatio
ST 1919 the Princes raunsome ; let him have his *d.*
SP 894 that I may know to whom my thankes is *d.*
Ard. 1086 as loth to give *d.* audit to the hour
Puck 58 holdes yo* hono** & the state in that dewe reverence
Due.
HP 1650 Da questi *d.*, se tu ti rechi a mente
Duke.
HP 396 the most excellent Cooke the *D.* hath
Jer. 490 ‹ But not the honest son of a *D.* ›
Jer. 516 but not the honest son of a *D.*
ST Bal. 141 the *D.*, the Viceroy, and the King
ST Bal. 158 I kill'd the *D.*, then standing by
ST 440 for so the *D.*, your father, gave me charge
ST 1186 the *D.*, my father, hath upon some disgrace
ST 1280 so neare the *D.* his brothers house
ST 1647 my Lord the *D.*, you heard, enquired for her
ST 1826 come, lets away to seek my Lord the *D.*
ST 2385 and wheres the *D.* ?
Jer. 488 ‹ Yet hees an honest dukes son ›
Jer. 515 yet hees an honest Dukes sonne
STA 926 he would goe visit Balthazar at the Dukes Palace
ST 1796 pray you, which is the next way to my L[ord] the Dukes ?
HP 1756 that custome of the Dukes and other noble men
ST Bal. 25 the *D.* of Castyles Daughter then
ST Bal. 86 the streets, hard by the *D.* of Castiles house
ST Bal. 103 the *D.* of Castyle, hearing then how I
ST 506 I frolike with the *D.* of Castiles Sonne
STA 939 Jaques, runne to the *D.* of Castiles presently
ST 1179 and harkening neere the *D.* of Castiles house
ST 2270 go, Brother, it is the *D.* of Castiles cause
ST 2273 and greet the *D.* of Castile
ST 2421 my homely house, the *D.* of Castile, Ciprians ancient seat
ST 3016 the *D.* of Castile and his wicked Sonne both done to death
ST 547 brave John of Gaunt, the *D.* of Lancaster
Jer. 239 Alcario, the *D.* Medinas sonne
Jer. 677 it is Alcario, *D.* Medinas son
Jer. 731 my leedge, Alcario, *D.* Medinas son
HP 1758 houses of the Dukes of Savoy, Ferrara
Ard. 2 my gracious Lord, the *D.* of Somerset
ST 540 he after was created *D.* of Yorke
Dulce.
VPJ 79 Pro te *d.* mori, nisi pro te vivere durum
HP 293 praysing Wine called it Nigrum et *d.*
Dull.
Cor. 645 whose mournfull passions *d.* the mornings joyes
Jer. 210 this *d.*, leaden, and tormenting elfe
SP 544 to sound a homeward, *d.*, and harsh retreate
Dulness.

Cor. 702 a dulnes, that disposeth us to rest
Duly.
STA 2002 *d.* twice a morning would I be sprinkling it
Puck 24 devyne praiers used duelie in his L** house
Dumps.
SP 1405 why, how now, Erastus, alwaies in thy dumpes ?
Duramus.
HP 808 saevoque gelu *d.* et undis
During.
ST 184 *d.* life. his tribute shal be truly paide
Duris.
HP 1062 Dicendum et quae sint *d.* agrestibus arma
Durst.
Cor. Ded. 4 how I durst undertake a matter of this moment
Cor. 1398 he *d.* affront me and my warlike bands
ST 1570 now see I what I *d.* not then suspect
SP 472 how *d.* thou be so bould to crie the chaine
SP 1819 my selfe would be his witnesse, if I *d.*
SP 1836 we said not I, nor *d.* we say him nay
SP 1890 what bould presumer *d.* be so resolved
SP 2138 how *d.* thou then, ungratious counseller
Ard. 1137 that ne'er *d.* say before but ‹ yea › or ‹ no ›
Ard. 1924 there *d.* not a whore set up, unless she
JB 167 that she *d.* not denie him anything he requested
Durum.
VPJ 79 Pro te dulce mori, nisi pro te vivere *d.*
HP 807 *D.* a stirpe genus, natos ad flumina primum
Duskish.
Cor. 1735 and with a *d.* yellow chokt the heavens
Dust.
Cor. 1728 where-with the *d.*, as with a darksome clowde
Jer. 913 for heaven can be revenged on their *d.*
Jer. 1182 spent upon the Funerall of Andreas *d.*
Ard. 1453 the annoyance of the *d.* or else
Ard. 1636 and buries all his haughty pride in *d.*
Dutch.
Cor. 59 for neither could the flaxen-hair'd high *D.*
Duteous.
ST 9 by *d.* service and deserving love
ST 354 counterfeits under the colour of a *d.* friend
ST 668 deserves my *d.* service, even till death
SP 580 your Highnesse knowes I speake in dutious love
Duties.
HP 636 the offices and dueties should be divers
Jer. 1181 these honord rights and worthy *d.* spent
Puck 84 Yo* L** most humble in all *d.*, Th. Kydde
Dutiful.
SP 398 Erastus will be dutifull in all
Duty.
HP 1029 thy cheefe care and the duetie of thy Steward shall be thys
HP 1142 make mention of the duetie of a Huswife
ST 628 my bounden duety bids me tell the truth
ST 1426 so ist my duety to regarde his death
SP 575 Ile hazard dutie in my Soveraignes presence
SP 1853 and, as our *d.* and aleageance bound us
Ard. 761 ‹ My *d.* remembered, Mistress Susan ›
Puck 9 aswell in duetie to yo* L* and the lawes
Puck 66 have w** pretext of duetie or religion
Dwell.
HP 845 where thy selfe inhabitest, or they shall dwel
Jer. 971 O let me *d.* a little on that name
ST 3036 where none but furies, bugs, and tortures *d.*
SP 75 should finde a harbour for my hart to *d.*
SP 762 and till I came whereas my love did *d.*
Ard. 1339 shall thy sweet phrases and thy letters *d.*

Cor. 219 death dwels within us, and if gentle Peace
Ard. 1239 the way I seek to find, where pleasure dwells
Ard. 2161 in Southwark dwells a bonny northern lass
Dwelleth.
HP 1173 within the Countrey where he d.
Dwelling.
HP 1317 any sufficie[n]t house or d.
JB 22 of late d. in London a proper young woman
JB 84 to shew the discontent she had of his d.
Dwelt.
JB 86 neere to the place where this graceles Parker d.
Dye.
HP 678 tricking up their selves with Die and suche like filth
Cor. 1055 that with Ausonian blood did die our warlike field
Dyed.
HP 827 Your robes are d. with Saffron and with glistring purple
    buds
Cor. 1780 theyr jawbones dy'd with foming froth and blood
Cor. 1885 looking upon his weapon, dide with blood
Cor. 1974 when through the slaughter the Afrique seas were
    dide
ST 2181 and when I dyde it in thy deerest blood
Dying.
Cor. 29 and humbled to theyr of-spring left thee d.
Cor. 519 yet d. thinke this stil
Cor. 885 O myserable woman, lyving, d.
Cor. 1464 but so to die, as d. I may live
Cor. 1829 here one new wounded helps another d.
ST 2179 the lively portraict of my d. selfe
ST 3031 and there live, d. still in endles flames
SP 1288 For whom weepe you ? — Ah, for Fernandos d.
ST 3026 where never d. warres are still inurde
E.
Each.
HP 1593 measuring the worth and value of e. thing
Cor. 1106 have e. done other equall violence
Cor. 1737 doe at the halfe pyke freely charge e. other
Cor. 1766 so did the Armies presse and charge e. other
Cor. 1769 with burning hate let e. at other flie
Cor. 1778 and proov'd e. others force sufficient
Jer. 151 eatch imperious over others spleen
Jer. 1079 and e. drop worth a thousand Portugales
ST Bal. 66 and cur'sd and bann'd e. thing was there
ST Bal. 83 I rent and tore e. thing I got
ST Bal. 113 but when wee knew e. others mind
ST 3 ech in their function serving others need
ST 114 their frontiers, leaning on e. others bound
ST 124 e. corner strongly fenst with wings of shot
ST 721 e. howre doth wish and long to make resort
ST 759 till then e. houre will seeme a yeere and more
STA 1953 I prie through every crevice of e. wall
STA 1954 looke on e. tree, and search through every brake
ST 2424 embrace e. other, and be perfect freends
ST 2559 I meane, e. one of you to play a part
ST 2618 for e. of you to note your partes
ST 2648 e. one of us must act his parte in
SP 101 e. one of these approoved combatants
SP 213 perdie, e. female is the weaker vessell
SP 253 e. place is my habitation
SP 254 therefore e. countries word mine to pronounce
SP 637 for, till by Fortune persons meete e. other
SP 640 e. one by armes to honor his beloved
SP 898 gentlemen, e. thing hath sorted to our wish
SP 1255 strive by mutuall kindnes to excell e. other
SP 1293 then take e. one halfe of me, and cease to weepe
SP 1552 they love e. other best : what then should follow

SP 1753 to worke e. others blisse and hearts delight
Ard. 579 what ! to acquaint e. stranger with our drifts
Ard. 1236 e. gentle stirry gale doth shake my bed
Ard. 1254 make these curs pluck out e. other's throat
Ard. 2406 leave to accuse e. other now
Cor. 1727 they ranne at ever-e. other hand and foote
Eacus.
ST 33 *see* **Aeacus.**
Eager.
SP 92 this day the eger Turke of Tripolis
SP 2182 follow thee, with e. moode, thorow eternall night
Ard. 871 when she is dry sucked of her e. young
Ard. 1427 then seizeth on the prey with e. mood
Eagerly.
ST 161 heere-hence the fight was e. renewd
Eagle.
Cor. 1917 and th' *E.* tyering on Prometheus
Ard. 1345 thou hast been sighted as the e. is
SP 1071 eagles are chalenged by paltry flyes
SP 1194 as ayre bred Eagles, if they once perceive that
Ear.
HP 1389 pleasant to the eare, is painfull to the memorie
Jer. 584 tis all about the court in every eare
Jer. 773 speech ; tis able to infect a vertuous eare
ST 81 forthwith, Revenge, she rounded thee in th' eare
ST 344 mine eare is readie to receive ill newes
SP 813 that please the eare but seeke to spoile the heart ?
Ard. 694 a mutchado, which he wound about his e.
Ard. 2435 to make it gracious to the e. or eye
Cor. 1833 that stopt theyr eares, and would not heare a word
Jer. 48 besiedge the eares of rough heawn tyrants more
Jer. 49 Oh, a polyticke speech beguiles the eares of foes
Jer. 276 my eares have sukt in poyson, deadly Poyson
Jer. 537 nor fits it newes so soone kisse subjects [ears]
Jer. 985 shriller then all the trumpets, to pierce Andreas ears
ST 698 which slie deceits smooth Bel-imperias eares
ST 699 and through her eares dive downe into her hart
ST 726 be deafe, my eares, heare not my discontent
ST 729 heare still, mine eares, to heare them both lament
ST 1392 convay our words amongst unfreendly eares
ST 2802 relentless are mine eares to thy laments
SP 432 marry, a foule fault ; but why are his eares cut ?
SP 1169 yet have we eares to heare a just complaint
SP 1936 my troubled eares are deft with loves alarmes
Ard. 254 and lay their ears down to the lowly earth
Ard. 1343 wilt thou not hear ? what malice stops thine ears ?
Ard. 1412 when he that gave it him holloed in his ear
Ard. 1861 no, ears and all were witched ; ah me
Ard. 1928 held him by the ears till all his beer hath run out
JB 10 cried most shrill in the eares of the righteous God
JB 228 for bloud is an unceassant crier in the eares of the Lord
Cor. 199 falling as thick (through warlike crueltie) as eares of
    Corne
Cor. 1954 lyke eares of Corne with rage of windie showres
Ard. 1243 doth e. the iand and weed thee up to make
Eared.
Ard. 1141 watch the out-coming of that prick-e. cur
Earl.
ST 524 was English Robert, Earle of Gloster
ST 535 was Edmund, Earle of Kent in Albion
Early.
Cor. 1356 beames doth e. light the Pearled Indians
ST 1149 e. begins to regester my dreames
Ard. 57 husband, what mean you to get up so e. ?
Ard. 182 'tis yet but e. days, thou needst not fear
Ard. 654 how now, fellow Bradshaw ? whither away so e. ?

Ard. 1545 it was no chase that made me rise so *e.*

Earnest.

HP 659 which increaseth and draweth as *e.* love
ST 2568 in faith, Hieronimo, and you be in *e.*
ST 2812 were this in *e.*, Bel-imperia, you
JB 33 not withstanding his long and *e.* suite
JB 118 for I have an *e.* desire to eat some ? ›

Earnestly.

HP 455 beganne earnestlie to looke upon me, and said

Earth.

VPJ 35 I trod the *e.*, and knew it was my tombe
VPJ 53 thou trodst the *e.*, and now on *e.* thou art
VPJ 82 thou shining lampe of th' *e.*
HP Ind. 60 *E.*, universall nurse of all thinges
HP Ind. 74 fruites of the *e.* are naturall gaines
HP 185 hanging alwaies on the *e.* and
HP 187 they soke up the superfluous humours of the *e.*
HP 192 which also hang upon the *e.* unripened
HP 565 that the parched *e.* did rive and raught me in
HP 1169 the *e.* restoreth that which it receiveth
HP 1483 had and raised of the fruits of the *e.*
HP 1484 the *E.* is the naturall and universall Mother of us all
HP 1565 taken and derived from the *E.*
Cor. 41 while th' *e.*, that gron'd to beare theyr carkasses
Cor. 119 Rome and the *e.* are waxen all as one
Cor. 149 or that our hands the *E.* can comprehend
Cor. 306 thou saw'st the trembling *e.* with horror mazed ?
Cor. 320 that éven in all the corners of the *e.* thy
Cor. 350 doe coast the *E.* with an eternall course
Cor. 462 and wandreth in the Center of the *e.* ?
Cor. 487 hath hid them both embowel'd in the *e.*
Cor. 559 what e're the massie *E.* hath fraight
Cor. 784 Rome, thou art tam'd, and th' *e.*, dewd with thy bloode
Cor. 867 and when the man that had afright the *e.*
Cor. 906 els *e.* make way, and hell receive them quicke
Cor. 1024 the Sunne, that lends the *e.* his light
Cor. 1093 yet are there Gods, yet is there heaven and *e.*
Cor. 1184 he hath unpeopled most part of the *e.*
Cor. 1243 commaunds the world, and brideleth all the *e.*
Cor. 1354 the sea, the *e.*, and all is almost ours
Cor. 1360 or where the Sommer doth but warme the *e.*
Cor. 1380 th' *e.* that the Euxine sea makes somtymes marsh
Cor. 1607 the *e.*, the sea, the vultures and the Crowes
Cor. 1611 O *e.*, why op'st thou not ?
Cor. 1648 cover the *e.*, so thicke, as scarce we tread but
Cor. 1731 and with theyr fall the trembling *e.* was shaken
Cor. 1764 one while the top doth almost touch the *e.*
Cor. 1828 and on the *e.* theyr braines lye trembling
Cor. 1853 and lay them levell with the charged *e.*
Cor. 1882 his people put to sword, Sea, *E.*, and Hell
Cor. 1985 theyr *e.* we purple ore, and on theyr Tombes we heape
Jer. 343 our fathers fawltes in heaven ; why then on *e.* ?
Jer. 933 our Fathers faultes in heaven, why then on *e.* ?
Jer. 989 by all that thou holdst deere upon this *e.*
ST 300 I, I, this *e.*, Image of mellancholly
ST 903 O *e.*, why didst thou not in time devoure the
ST 1044 that howerly coastes the centre of the *e.*
ST 1057 as for the *e.*, it is too much infect to
ST 1520 let not the *e.* be choked or infect with
ST 1523 my woes, whose weight hath wearied the *e.* ?
ST 1897 away, Ile rip the bowels of the *e.*
STA 1948 then starting in a rage, falles on the *e.*
STA 1955 beate at the bushes, stampe on our grandam *e.*
STA 1986 his weapon would have fall'n and cut the *e.*
STA 2028 that's a lie as massie as the *e.*
ST 2202 though on this *e.* justice will not be found

ST 2228 to aske for justice in this upper *e.*
ST 2234 for justice is exiled from the *e.*
ST 2502 for heere I sweare, in sight of heaven and *e.*
ST 2689 barren the *e.*, and bliselesse whosoever
ST 2693 the *e.* with Serpents shall be pestered
ST 2767 what ever joy *e.* yields, betide your Majestie
ST 2768 *e.* yields no joy without Persedaes love
SP 220 sooth to say, the *e.* is my Countrey
SP 230 that the mothers teares might releeve the pearched *e.*
SP 542 whose bloud hath bin manured to their *e.*
SP 629 why, what is jewels, or what is gould but *e.*
SP 1198 that on the *e.* it may untimely die
SP 2189 but I, that have power in *e.* and heaven above
Ard. 14 the *e.* hung over my head and covered me
Ard. 254 and lay their ears down to the lowly *e.*
Ard. 646 so vile a rogue as he, lives not again upon the *e.*
Ard. 663 and with a curtsey to the *e.*, ‹ One snatch
Ard. 855 comes with a lowly curtsey to the *e.*
Ard. 878 whose *e.* may swallow up this Arden's blood
Ard. 922 to give an end to Arden's life on *e.*
Ard. 1016 then fix his sad eyes on the sullen *e.*
Ard. 1081 and sheeting darkness overhangs the *e.*
Ard. 1198 for here I swear, by heaven and *e.* and all
Ard. 1237 and makes me dread my downfall to the *e.*
Ard. 1466 first did she cast her eyes down to the *e.*
Ard. 1635 and, being touched, straight falls unto the *e.*
Ard. 2356 in heaven I'll love thee, though on *e.* I did not
Ard. 2416 seeing no hope on *e.*, in heaven is my hope
JB 19 soules and the destructions of their bodies on *e.*
Cor. 355 to whom mylde Autumne doth earths treasure bring
Cor. 1364 Caesar is now earthes fame, and Fortunes terror
Cor. 2036 and (when my soule Earths pryson shall forgoe)
SP 527 and earths commander under Mahomet

Earthen.

Cor. 877 and sadly cloz'd within an *e.* Urne the
Cor. 883 bones which (in extreames) an *e.* Urne containeth

Earthly.

Eng. Parn. 13 And living toyleth in an earthlie gaile
Cor. 568 cover all this *e.* round with Majestie
Cor. 1465 and leaving off this *e.* Tombe of myne

Ease.

HP Ind. 2 for the helpe and *e.* of one another
HP Ind. 92 idlenes and *e.* make some servants evill
HP 1025 may with idlenes and *e.* become pestilent
HP 1073 we can *e.* it wyth the left
HP 1076 to help and *e.* the weary and the well imployed
HP 1576 Idleness and superfluous *e.* are enemies profest
HP 1778 time and *e.* to learne and to collect enough
Cor. 239 the payne supposed would procure mine *e.*
Cor. 344 once *e.* my life, but with the pangs of death
Cor. 445 O, but men beare mis-fortunes with more *e.*
Cor. 979 for when, to *e.* th' oppression of my hart
Cor. 1653 to *e.* our Army, if it should retyre
Cor. 1900 crawld to the Deck, and, lyfe with death to *e.*
ST Bal. 82 found out the murtherers, to *e.* my mones
ST 715 where riding all at *e.* she may repaire
ST 837 why sit we not ? for pleasure asketh *e.*
ST 917 to know the author were some *e.* of greife
ST 1551 I will, to *e.* the greefe that I sustaine
ST 2108 if destinie thy miseries doe *e.*, then hast thou health
ST 2365 my sorrowes *e.* and soveraigne of my blisse
ST 3043 (Juno forgets olde wrath, and graunts him *e.*)
ST 3054 to place thy freends in *e.*, the rest in woes
SP 495 come therefore, gentle death, and *e.* my griefe
SP 919 great *e.* it were for me to purge my selfe
SP 1528 to *e.*, though not to cure, my maladie

SP 1637 and now, to *e*. my troubled thoughts at last
Ard. 43 to *e*. thy grief and save her chastity
Eased.
ST 2931 pleasde with their deaths, and easde with their revenge
Ard. 1886 ne'er shall my heart be *e*. till this be done
Easier.
Cor. 1453 a man may *e*. make his friend his foe
ST 2752 in English, more largely, for the *e*. understanding
Easily.
HP 79 we might *e*. perceive it comprehended
HP 278 that are so easilie digested
HP 513 have easely accomplist what he (being
HP 612 *e*. exercise in her that superioritie that
HP 732 nor yet to be so *e*. induced to watch or follow her
HP 736 and is as *e*. accompanied with love
HP 1221 may be transported *e*. in Carres or other carriages
HP 1244 all which he may *e*. doo, if, in
HP 1384 with the use of Poetry very easilie perceiveth
HP 1619 *e*. may a great quantity of mony be heaped up
ST 1322 urged with the thought of former evils, *e*. cannot erre
ST 2103 to quiet life, his life shall *e*. end
SP 1847 we said the taske might easilie be performd
Ard. 627 very *e*. : I'll tell you straight
East.
Cor. 72 the Morne and Mid-day both by *E*. and West
Cor. 148 or over-runne the world from *E*. to West
Cor. 634 while Clitie takes her progresse to the *E*.
SP 1327 from *E*. to West, from South to Septenrion
Cor. 1762 as on the Alpes the sharpe Nor-North-*e*. wind
Ard. 1224 and nips me as the bitter north-*e*. wind
Eastern.
ST 2691 an Easterne winde, commixt with noisome aires
SP 237 from Titans Easterne uprise to his Western downefall
Easy.
HP 680 much more easie to be entreated
HP 818 bring them up under so soft and easie discipline
HP 1204 made the entercourse of buying and selling very easie
Cor. 1342 with thine easie streames that glide as smothly as
Jer. 1037 it had bin easie then to have me borne
Jer. 1107 tis easie to seize those were first laid downe
ST 2358 alas, how easie is it for him to erre
Eat.
HP 182 eate of them and tarry not for me
HP 259 to eate of two kinds of wilde flesh
HP 274 did eate such kinde of flesh?
HP 1273 become both hard and naught to eate without some
HP 1688 in the sweate of thy face thou shalt eate thy bread
Jer. 452 eate Cues, drunk Cees, and cannot give a letter
Ard. 160 as she shall *e*. the heart he sent with salt
Ard. 285 or any kind of broth that he shall *e*.
Ard. 363 I cannot *e*., but I'll sit for company
Ard. 365 husband, why pause ye? why *e*. you not?
Ard. 387 give me a spoon, I'll *e*. of it myself
Ard. 956 and takes advantage for to *e*. him up
JB 119 for I have an earnest desire to *e*. some? »
Eaten.
HP 182 for if I have *e*. but a little, it hath
HP 261 none other flesh *e*. then Beefe, Porke
HP 1261 those that wyll not keepe to be first *e*.
Ard. 427 but had he *e*. but three spoonfuls more
JB 126 within a pretty while after hee had *e*. his
JB 153 immediatly after he had *e*. it, he dyed
Eaths.
Cor. 760 which *e*. appeare in sadde and strange disguises
Eating.
HP 355 slothfull and sleepie betwixt idlenes and *e*.

JB (2nd Title) was poysoned of his owne wife in eating
JB 126 and she and the childe fell also to *e*. of theirs
Ebon.
Cor. 1914 come, wrathfull Furies, with your *E*. locks
Echo.
HP 830 Where trumpets eccho clangs to those that of the
   custome skyll
Cor. 1725 and every Eccho tooke the Trompets clange
ST 2851 I heare his dismall out-cry eccho in the aire
Ard. 1031 awake me with the *e*. of their strokes
Eclipse.
Cor. 1417 they sought t'*e*. thy fame, but destinie
SP 537 fog not thy glory with so fowle *e*.
Ard. 1671 ay, and it hath influences and eclipses
Economy.
HP (Title) *see* **Oeconomia**
Ecstasy.
ST 600 my Lord, for my sake leave this extasie
Edge.
SP 1503 twill breake the *e*. of my keene Semitor
Ard. 924 knife whose *e*. must search the
Edicate.
SP 282 O harsh, un-*e*., illiterate pesant
Edified.
Cor. 590 forsaken as before, yet after are re-*e*.
Edmund.
ST 535 was *E*., Earle of Kent in Albion
Educat.
ST 997 O aliquis mihi quas pulchrum ver *e*. herbas
Educate.
HP 856 howe he is to *e*. and bring up his Children
Education.
HP Ind. 61 *e*. of Children as well appertaines to
HP Ind. 63 *e*. of Children, and what it ought to be
HP 720 under the *e*. of a grave Matron and wise mother
HP 779 now proceeding to the *e*. of Children
HP 839 for such an *e*. makes the[m] rather wilde
HP 853 this part of *e*. and bringing up of Children
Educere.
HP 1328 Conjugis, et possit parvos *e*. natos
Effect.
HP 1612 it seeme that it may multiply in *e*.
Cor. 695 God graunt these dreames to good *e*. bee brought
Cor. 1134 or follow'd Pompey but to thys *e*.
Cor. 1180 no, but Dictator, in *e*. as much
Cor. 1418 but destinie rever'sd th' *e*. of theyr ambition
Jer. 87 cannot *e*. the vertue of your charge
ST Bal. 41 which for to bring well to *e*.
ST 54 to this *e*. my pasport straight was drawne
ST 1176 but live t'*e*. thy resolution
ST 1743 incertain to *e*. his Pilgrimage
ST 2524 and ought that may *e*. for thine availe
SP 70 I have forgot the rest, but thats the *e*.
SP 71 thats the *e*. ; which to *e*., accept this
SP 141 heavens heare my harty praier, and it *e*.
SP 1560 and now, to turne late promises to good *e*.
SP 1572 remoove the cause, and then the *e*. will die
SP 1634 and if this take *e*., thou shalt be Viceroy
Ard. 830 but wouldst thou charm me to *e*. this deed
JB 44 seeing his suite took no *e*., to demaund
JB 89 wickedly went to *e*. it, even according
HP 382 inferior to Autumn as hope is to effects
Cor. 430 the fearefull dreames effects that trouble mee
ST 2193 if loves effects so strives in lesser things
ST 3009 I, now my hopes have end in their effects
Effected.

HP 688 hath *e.* that the bodies of the Male be more adorned

Cor. (Title) *e.* by her Father and Husbandes downe-cast, death, and fortune

Cor. 291 and all your hopes with hap may be *e.*

Effectual.

HP 528 is termed by a tytle more effectuall, Consort

Effectually.

HP 1142 we wil *e.* make mention of the duetie of

HP 1694 record *e.* those things whereof I have

Puck 75 shalbe examined & rypped up *e.*

Effeminate.

HP 850 not werish, and of a womanish, *e.* complexion

Jer. 111 tis she I hug as mine *e.* bride

Effert.

ST 1001 Gramina Sol pulchras *e.* in luminis oras

Efficacy.

HP 1381 of so great efficacye and force is order

Eftsoons.

HP 53 I am eftsoones shrowded under the estate of Savoy

HP 112 who eftsoones was returned from surveighing

HP 237 whereunto your selfe being eftsoones nigh

HP 867 eftsoones it remaineth that we come to the consideration of the

Cor. 1840 but there had Caesar eftsoones tyranniz'd

Egypt.

HP 1165 those compasses which gave begining to Geometry in *E.*

Cor. Arg. 10 and carrie her with him into Egipt

Cor. Arg. 19 after he had ordred the affayres of Egipt

Cor. 800 for which misdeed be Egipt pestered with

Cor. 1186 *E.,* Emathia, Italy and Spayne

Egyptians.

Cor. 806 when I saw the murdring Egiptians bereave his lyfe

Eight.

HP 1137 as four to *e ,* or sixe at least

ST 1238 but, sirra, let the houre be *e.* a clocke

Eight-and-twenty.

HP 219 eyght and twenty or thirty yeares at the least

Eighteen.

HP 11 a youth of eighteene or twenty yeeres of age

Ard. 889 at the Nag's Head, at the *e.* pence ordinary

Either.

HP 83 eyther of them containing five and twentie large

HP 168 necessarie *e.* for fire, the use of

HP 309 *e.* pleasing to the sences or acceptable to

HP 893 *e.* by alteration of time or variety of customes

HP 1253 eyther from the Countrey, or bought about in Markets

HP 1317 house or dwelling, *e.* for her eldest sonne or daughter

HP 1489 seeme not *e.* inconvenient or dishonest

HP 1523 are not infinit *e.* in number or in greatnes

HP 1555 *e.* miserably gotten or encreased by wrong

HP 1606 Number is reputed *e.* according to the formall or materiall beeing

HP 1640 every or *e.* of which hauving not onely beene

HP 1727 so shoulde the care of *e.* houskeeping be one

HP 1748 the manner and facultie of eyther is alike

Cor. 768 it eyther turneth to the Stygian Lake, or

Cor. 1320 but eyther trayterously surprizd, doth

Cor. 1366 Rome, speake no more of eyther Scipio, nor of

Cor. 1393 with eyther Armies murdred souldiers gore

Cor. 1689 I'le eyther conquer, or this sword you see

ST 62 but *e.* sort containd within his bounds

ST 129 meane-while, our Ordinance plaied on *e.* side

ST 680 but golde doth more then *e.* of them both

ST 704 and *e.* loose my life, or winne my love

ST 1485 to trusse up many an honester man then *e.* thou or he

ST 1593 and *e.* purchase justice by intreats, or

SP 619 and beare my joyes on *e.* side of me

SP 622 bearing in *e.* hand his hearts decay

SP 1154 for eyther Rhodes shall be brave Solymans, or

SP 1161 it eyther shall be mine, or burie me

SP 1984 I, more then I love *e.* life or soule

Ard. 550 as far as *e.* goods or life may stretch

Ard. 1082 and I, a judge to censure *e.* side

Ard. 1402 then *e.* thou or all thy kin are worth

Ard. 1793 *e.* there be butchered by thy dearest friends

JB 16 without respect *e.* of the feare of God, or

JB 140 that whole night longe, without *e.* comfort or companie

Ejectione.

ST 2156 mine an *E.* firmae by a Lease

Eke.

ST Bal. 130 and *e.* his soule to hell did send

ST Bal. 136 and *e.* the murtherers did impart ; and sayd

ST Bal. 159 and *e.* my selfe bereav'd of life

Elder.

HP 122 turning to his *e.* Sonne

HP 501 thou art his *e.* as also more enclind to

HP 886 forgotten of those men of *e.* times

HP 1753 albeit wee differ farre from those of *e.* times

Ard. 173 for I will rid mine *e.* brother away

Cor. 881 to interr within his Elders Tombe that honoured her

Eldest.

HP 213 to have married myne *e.* Sonne

HP 1317 house or dwelling, either for her *e.* sonne or daughter

SP 2003 where is the *e.* sonne of Pryam

Elect.

SP 76 even in thy brest doo I *e.* my rest

Elected.

Ard. 328 to live with God and his *e.* saints

Election.

Jer. 64 how stand ye, Lords, to this *e.* ?

Jer. 80 how stand you, Lords, to this *e.* ?

Elegy.

VPJ (Title) Tychbornes Elegie written with his owne hand

Element.

SP 227 grasse was seared with the Sunne Gods *E.*

SP 240 in which place there was no such *E.*

Elf.

Jer. 210 this dull, leaden, and tormenting elfe

Jer. 754 then hired me with gold — O fate, thou elfe

Elizabeth.

VPJ 17 Live, Soveraigne Ladie, Live, *E.*

Elizabetham.

VPJ (Title) Ad serenissimam reginam *E.,* Apostrophe

Elms.

ST 859 thus Elmes by vines are compast till they fall

Eloquent.

HP 401 and *e.* devise more then meanelie learned

HP 1721 of swifter understanding and more *e.* devise

Else.

HP 1171 of all whatsoever els belongeth to husbandry

HP 1290 of houshold necessaries as all things els

HP 1687 but whatsoever els we purposed at first

Cor. 7 els let the mischiefe that should them befall

Cor. 218 and choakes the good, which els we had enjoy'd

Cor. 276 els onely I am cause of both theyr wraths

Cor. 906 els earth make way, and hell receive them quicke

Cor. 922 els had my life beene long agoe expired

Cor. 927 els (god to fore) my selfe way live to see his

Cor. 1461 els cannot Caesars Emporie endure

Cor. 1943 what have I els to wreak your wrath upon ?

Jer. 458 elce had my pen no cause to write at all

Jer. 532 our foes will stride *e.* over me and you

Jer. 660 I, Don Andrea, or *e*. Don the devill
Jer. 766 whers the pardon ? S foot, ile peach *e*.
Jer. 893 trybute, ha, ha ; what elles ?
Jer. 1057 *e*. his unpitying sword had cleft my hart
ST 456 for what wast els but murderous cowardise
ST 1108 him, whom thou knowest that no unkindnes els
ST 1342 or els his Highnes hardly shall deny
ST 1637 or els, my Lord, I live not
ST 1657 concealde that els would breed unrest
ST 1660 els wouldst thou not have used thy Sister so
ST 1694 and carry you obscurely some where els
ST 2433 what els ? it were a shame it should not be so
SP 232 *e*. had my Frize-land horse perished
SP 574 I charge thee, say wherein ; or *e*., by Mahomet
SP 696 and who so *e*. denies shall feele the rigour
SP 1399 and Rhodes it selfe is lost, or els destroyde
SP 1539 and I for thee, or els I had not lived
SP 1812 why then to thee, or unto any *e*., I heere protest
Ard. 86 come again within a day or two, or *e*. I die
Ard. 237 for thou. or I, or any other *e*.
Ard. 775 « Yours, Michael, or *e*. not Michael »
Ard. 817 is't nothing *e*. ? come, Franklin, let's away
Ard. 994 or *e*. she'll die, and so your sorrows end
Ard. 1286 our harvest *e*. will yield but loathsome weeds
Ard. 1453 the dust or *e*. some meat you ate at dinner
Ard. 1493 the occasion is great, or *e*. would I wait on you
Ard. 1563 our house would run away, or *e*. be stolen
Ard. 1794 or *e*. be brought for men to wonder at
Ard. 2010 ay, or *e*. think me a villain
Ard. 2148 one ace, or *e*. I lose the game
Ard. 2152 nothing but take you up, sir, nothing *e*.
Ard. 2195 is't nothing *e*. ? tush, he'll be here anon
Ard. 2225 or *e*. I should have heard of him ere now
Ard. 2268 and cause suspicion, where *e*. would be none
JB 174 if she denied him either money or whatsoever *e*.
JB 197 thou and no man *e*. that can triumph in my spoyle
Elsewhere.
HP 124 « for I have never seene him hereabouts or elswhere »
HP 156 not such as you are used to taste *e*.
SP 1239 imploy me else where in thy forraine wars
Elysian.
Cor. 508 then I and Pompey in th' Elisian shade
Cor. 737 come visite thee in the Elisian shades ?
Cor. 769 or staies for ever in th' Elisian fields
ST 73 which brought me to the faire Elizian greene
ST 1603 he sleepes in quiet in the Elizian fields
ST 1808 and Ferrie over to th' Elizian plaines
SP 1465 twixt which a vale leads to the Elisian shades
Emathia.
Cor. 1186 Egypt, *E*., Italy and Spayne
Embarks.
Cor. 77 embarques us in so perilous a way
Embased.
Cor. 782 thou art embas'd ; and at this instant yeeld'st thy
Embassador, *see* **Ambassador.**
Embassage.
Jer. 44 I hold it meete, by way of *E*., to
Jer. 331 this embasage, to put your brest in mind of
Jer. 432 the date of his *e*. nighe expired
Embassy.
Jer. 642 but has the King pertooke your *e*. ?
Embers.
HP 1330 and she gins the ymbers up to rake
Embossed.
Cor. 491 whose Temples, Pallaces, and walls embost
Cor. 1677 in one hand held his Targe of steele embost

Embowelled.
Cor. 487 hath hid them both embowel'd in the earth
Embrace.
Cor. 317 t'*e*. thy knees, and, humbled by theyr fate
Cor. 752 and, thinking to *e*. him, opte mine armes
Jer. 42 thy counsell Ile imbrace as I do thee
Jer. 976 so now kisse and imbrace : come, come
Jer. 1190 imbrace them, and take friendly leave
ST 2424 *e*. each other, and be perfect freends
ST 2697 I, heere he dide, and heere I him imbrace
Jer. 1155 Don Andreas ghoast salutes me, see, embraces me
Embraced.
Cor. 1897 and I stept to him to have embrac'd him
ST 68 and wantons are imbraste with ouglie Snakes
Embracements.
Cor. 734 but his airie spirit beguiled mine embrasements
Embracing.
Cor. 735 left me *e*. nothing but the wind
HP Ind. 96 lovers wanton embracings different from
HP 742 in her entertainment and embracings
HP 748 compare the embracings of the Husbande and the Wife to
Ard. 2062 snakes of black Tisiphone sting me with their embracings !
Embroidered.
HP 691 *e*. the Peacocks taile with more variety of collours
Embroidery.
Cor. Ded. 11 spoyling paper with the others Pharisaical embroiderie
SP 1395 I have little minde of rich imbroderie, or costly
Emmets.
Cor. 1645 Campe of creeping *E*. in a Countrey Farme
Emonye, *see* **Haemonia.**
Emoriar.
ST 1008 *E*. tecum : sic, sic juvat ire sub umbras
Emperor.
HP 495 Charles the fift, that thrise renowmd *E*.
Cor. 1410 made Conqueror and *E*. at last
Cor. 1524 when their *E*. they meete
Cor. 1604 Where is thine *E*. ? — Where our Captaines are
Cor. 1674 meane-while our *E*. (at all poynts arm'd)
Cor. 1687 (being an auncient Senator, an *E*. and Consul)
ST 2612 great Soliman, the Turkish Emperour
ST 2744 the Tragedie of Soliman, the Turkish Emperour
ST 2768 your sonne, that represents the Emperour Solyman
SP 1272 for now I must attend the Emperour
SP 1326 Monarch and mightie *E*. of the world
SP 1368 of Solyman, the Turkish Emperour
SP 1382 and the gilded gowne the Emperour gave you
SP 1726 of Soliman, the Turkish Emperour
SP 1985 what, shall I stab the Emperour for thy sake ?
SP 2164 ah, Janisaries, now dyes your Emperour
SP 2166 and if you ever loved your Emperour
SP 431 for presumption, for covering the Emperors Mare
SP 433 for neighing in the Emperours court
Cor. 710 great Emperors fast bound in chaynes of brasse
Cor. 1035 and cares for crowned Emperors shee doth reserve
ST 2564 and Kings and Emperours have tane delight to
Empery.
Cor. 244 do exercise your mirthlesse Empory
Cor. 1450 who dares to contradict our Emporie ?
Cor. 1481 els cannot Caesars Emporie endure
SP 1525 what should he doe with crowne and Emperie that
Empire.
HP 499 is no lesse then is his *E*. to his Majestie
Cor. 154 and is with others Empyre set on fire
Cor. 661 our Common-wealth, our Empyre, and our honors

Cor. 675 upon theyr helmes, the Empyre that is stole
Cor. 1136 he render not the Empyre back to Rome
Cor. 1198 he hath enricht the *E.* with newe states
Cor. 1340 and how your *E.* and your praise begins
Cor. 1699 as for the *E.*, and the Romaine state

Employ.
SP 1239 imploy me else where in thy forraine wars

Employed.
HP 212 absent and imployed otherwise
HP 776 he may be happily *e.* better in some other action
HP 1144 is imployed to Conservation and Encrease
HP 1594 not directed and imployed to some other use
HP 1762 busied and *e.* in office for the
ST 2575 for I must needes be imployed in your play
ST 2794 will, which is, thou shouldest be thus imploid
SP 737 I, thus should men of valour be imployd
SP 1752 let our studies wholie be imploid to worke
HP 1077 to help and ease the weary and the well imployed

Employest.
Cor. 1090 *e.* our lives, and lavishest our blood

Employing.
HP 1691 and howe to the converting and imploying

Employments.
Jer. 206 this lazy age, that yeelds me no imployments

Empress.
SP 693 shame to loves Queene, and Empresse of my thoughts

Empty.
HP 206 purposelie left *e.* for her
Jer. 13 Ile *e.* all my vaines to serve your wars
ST 1401 heeres nothing but the bare emptie box
ST 2248 sent from the emptie Kingdome of blacke night

Empyreal.
ST 1536 but they are plac't in those *e.* heights

Enact.
Jer. 262 what dare not I *e.*, then ? tush, he dies

Enamoured.
HP 1357 when they were enamored of her

Encamp.
Cor. 1433 and (joyned with the Exiles there) *e.*

Encamped.
Cor. 1637 where he (encampt) resolv'd by force to
Cor. 1839 they gan retyre, where Juba was encampt
Ard. 1030 conflicting thoughts, *e.* in my breast

Enchained.
Cor. 67 like Captives lyv'd eternally enchaynd

Enchanted.
Jer. 833 prove inchaunted armour being charmed by love
Ard. 1298 and all the causes that *e.* me !
Ard. 1313 and thou unhallowed has *e.* me

Enclose.
Cor. 2084 the happie vessels that *e.* your bones

Enclosed.
HP 362 our operations and contemplations are enclozed with darknes

Encounter.
Cor. 304 t'*e.* with the least of my mishaps?
Cor. 1621 sought nothing more then to *e.* us
ST 128 they brought another wing to incounter us
SP 168 upon the incounter of thine enemy
SP 178 upon thy first *e.* of thy foe
SP 208 upon the first *e.* of your foe
SP 339 and my Beaver closd for this *e.*
SP 410 when at the *e.* I did loose a stirrop
SP 795 yet mine sufficient to *e.* thine
Ard. 1472 to *e.* all their accusations
Cor. Arg. 20 and there (after many light encounters) was

Ard. 872 shows to the prey that next encounters her

Encountered.
ST 396 by yong Don Balthazar encountred hand to hand
SP 1139 all the Knights that there incountred him

Encountering.
Cor. 299 (according to th' encountring passages)

Encourage.
Cor. 672 will they not once againe *e.* them
Cor. 1789 both comfort and *e.* his to fight
Ard. 2051 here would I stay and still *e.* you

Encouraged.
Cor. 1935 whose silver haires *e.* the weake
ST 160 brought rescue and encouragde them to stay

Encourageth.
Cor. 1753 and with her murdring whip *e.* the

Encouraging.
Cor. 1849 to seeke by new *e.* his men to come

Encroachest.
SP 1699 that thus incrochest upon my familiaritie

End.
HP 87 and as manie in the upper *e.*
HP 138 which, at the *e.* of Supper, were
HP 206 sat her down at the upper *e.* of the Table
HP 412 there can bee perceived neither beginning nor ende
HP 857 to the ende that the Citties discipline may
HP 1019 to the ende that they, seeing thyselfe somtimes
HP 1515 every arte dooth infinitly seeke the *e.* it purposeth
HP 1598 have no *e.* or absolute determination as Usurie
HP 1599 worketh to a certaine set and determinat ende
HP 1600 and to a certaine ende doo all those meanes and
HP 1699 practise is in the *e.* imposed to all instructions of humaine life
HP 1704 to the ende that my discourse should not be made in vaine
Cor. Arg. 19 in the *e.* of Winter marched
Cor. Arg. 86 the pitteous manner of her Fathers ende
Cor. 337 what *e.* (O race of Scipio) will the Fates afford
Cor. 386 but (wishing) could not find so faire an *e.*
Cor. 500 but whatsoe're hath been begun, must *e.*
Cor. 524 we aske Deaths ayde to *e.* lifes wretchednes
Cor. 566 both their beginning and their *e.*
Cor. 926 with Caesars death to *e.* our servitude
Cor. 948 they had determin'd once of Caesars *e.*
Cor. 1062 did prove thy furie in the *e.*
Cor. 1266 and liveth to no other *e.*
Cor. 1435 doe bring their treasons to a bloody *e.*
Cor. 1614 the manner of his end will haply comfort this
Cor. 1690 (which brightly shone) shall make an end of me
Cor. 1937 whose ende, sith it hath ended all my joyes
Jer. 936 and to this crimson *e.* our Coullers spred
Jer. 1113 untill my leedge shall *e.* the difference
ST Bal. 88 which show'd Horatios wofull *e.*
ST (Title) containing the lamentable *e.* of Don Horatio, and
ST 51 made this device to *e.* the difference
ST 269 then by my judgement thus your strife shall *e.*
ST 401 cut short his life to *e.* his praise and woorth
ST 451 the more to spight the Prince that wrought his *e.*
ST 595 I, but her hopes aime at some other *e.*
ST 1018 the *e.* is crowne of every worke well done
ST 1122 that may yet be invented for thine *e.*
ST 1126 to *e.* those thinges articulated heere by
ST 1259 dye they shall, slaves are ordeind to no other *e.*
ST 1389 but to what *e.* ?
ST 1638 as for his resolution in his *e.*, leave that
STA 1752 and at nine moneths ende, creepes foorth to light
STA 2087 and in the ende leave me in a traunce

STA 2088 and is this the *e.*?
STA 2089 O no, there is no *e.* : the *e.* is death and madnesse
ST 2105 to quiet life, his life shall easily *e.*
ST 2708 and none but I bestirre me — to no ende
ST 2832 heere lay my hope, and heere my hope hath ende
ST 2872 and to this *e.* the Bashaw I became
ST 2885 did otherwise determine of her *e.*
ST 2893 and, Gentles, thus I *e.* my play
ST 3009 I, now my hopes have *e.* in their effects
ST 3055 for heere, though death hath *e.* their miserie
SP 135 or *e.* the period of my youth in blood
SP 1413 which hath no measure, and shall never *e.*
SP 1907 so let their treasons with their lives have *e.*
SP 1978 Lucina, came thy husband to this *e.*
SP 2201 and now, to *e.* our difference at last
SP 2226 that Death shall die, if he attempt her *e.*
Ard. (Title) and the shameful *e.* of all murderers
Ard. 186 is this the *e.* of all thy solemn oaths ?
Ard. 389 then should my cares and troubles have an *e.*
Ard. 775 « I *e.*, Yours, Michael, or else not Michael »
Ard. 922 to give an *e.* to Arden's life on earth
Ard. 994 or else she'll die, and so your sorrows *e.*
Ard. 1252 or fright me by detecting of his *e.*
Ard. 1419 Why, he begun. — And thou shalt find I'll *e.*
Ard. 1512 the devil break all your necks at four miles' *e.*!
Ard. 1614 stayed you behind your master to this *e.*?
Ard. 1629 and life shall *e.* before my love depart
Ard. 1759 faith, Dick Reede, it is to little *e.*
Ard. 1796 or there run mad and *e.* thy cursed days !
JB 166 and so bould in the *e.* he grew with her that
JB 200 « marry me to the *e.* thou mightest poyson me »
JB 214 till in the ende shee was made to beleeve that
Cor. 1576 oft have I seene the ends of mightier men
Jer. 712 most doubtfull wars and dangerous pointed ends
ST Bal. 132 but Bellimperia ends her life
ST Bal. 166 but that in it the murtherers ends
ST 1386 and now or never ends Lorenzos doubts
SP 1927 heere ends my deere Erastus tragedie
Ard. 1854 though begun in sport, yet ends in blood !

Endanger.
Cor. 1629 could draw our Captaines to *e.* us
ST 1169 this is devised to *e.* thee
Ard. 521 indanger not yourself for such a churl

Endangered.
ST 1253 they that for coine their soules *e.*
Ard. 2122 whose life I have *e.* without cause ?

Endeavour.
HP 1773 may endevour and apply themselves to serve in
Jer. 319 father, my best indevour shall obay you
ST 813 *e.* you to winne your daughters thought
Cor. Ded. 13 conceit and entertainement of these small ende-
vours

Ended.
HP 333 we *e.* our merry Supper
HP 1329 « The first sleepe *e.*, after midnight did the »
Cor. 1221 the warrs once *e.*, we shall quickly know
Cor. 1876 *e.* the lives of his best fighting men
Cor. 1937 whose ende, sith it hath *e.* all my joyes
SP 2212 their loves and fortunes *e.* with their lives

Endless.
Cor. 189 and Campe to Campe did endlesse battailes wage
Cor. 237 hels horror is mylder then mine endles discontent
Cor. 975 my dolefull spyrits endles myseries
Cor. 983 can nothing then recure these endlesse teares ?
Cor. 1281 to live in endles memorie
Cor. 1580 and endles numbers falling by my side

ST 66 and poore Ixion turnes an endles wheele
ST 297 this better fits a wretches endles moane
ST 916 O, wheres the author of this endles woe ?
ST 3042 and let the lovers endles paines surcease
ST 3048 and take from Siciphus his endles mone
ST 3051 and there live, dying still in endles flames
ST 3056 Ile there begin their endles Tragedie
Ard. 475 desire of wealth is *e.* in his mind

Endure.
Cor. 23 our shamefull soules *e.* a million of base controls
Cor. 1681 and to *e.* what ere betyded them
Cor. 1920 I suffer more, more sorrowes I *e.*
Puck 22 ffor never cold my L. *e.* his name or sight
Cor. 1449 yet Rome endures not the commaund of kings
ST 434 be sure, while Bel-imperias life endures

Endured.
Cor. Ded. 20 privie broken passions that I *e.* in the writing it
Cor. 1260 the wrong is great, and over-long endur'd
Cor. 1271 hath waters force and fire endur'd
Cor. 1603 what plaints, what passions have we endurde
ST 169 not long betweene these twaine the fight indurde
ST 1689 disgrace which you for Don Andrea had indurde
SP 243 *e.* some three or foure howers combat

Endureth.
HP 385 *e.* even untill then

Endymion.
Ard. 2068 from her watery bower fling down *E.*
Ard. 2070 not half so lovely as *E.*

Enemies.
HP 1577 Idlenes and superfluous ease are *e.* profest
Cor. 318 so many *e.* in battaile ranged
Cor. 673 to fill our fields with blood of *e.*
Ard. 356 until our *e.* have talked their fill
Puck 30 my greatest *e.* will saie by me
Cor. 398 his noble Roman blood mixt with his *e.*
Cor. 1415 but through my selfe-wild *e.* despight

Enemy.
HP 619 fallen into the handes of a perpetuall enemie
Cor. Arg. 29 fall alive into the hands of his so mightie Enemie
Cor. 800 forbeare to tempt the *e.* againe
Cor. 1159 Sylla (assaulted by the enemie) did arme
Cor. 1837 the murdring Enemie pesle-mesle pursued them
Cor. 1843 offred to yeeld unto the *e.*
Cor. 2014 adorne and grace his graceles *E.*?
Jer. 572 and know his *e.* by his envious breath
ST 382 deceived the King, betrayd mine *e.*
ST 1659 thou art no brother, but an *e.*
SP 156 upon the onset of the *e.*
SP 168 upon the incounter of thine *e.*
SP 190 upon the first brave of thine *e.*
SP 209 what is your brave upon the *e.*?
SP 416 O cursed Fortune, *e.* to Fame
SP 420 Page, set aside the jesture of my *e.*
SP 483 ah, treacherous Fortune, *e.* to Love
SP 573 as thou art *e.* to thy Soveraigne
SP 1218 and now, Erastus, thinke me thine enemie
SP 2055 a Gentleman, and thy mortall enemie
Ard. 583 who threats his *e.*, lends him a sword
Cor. 1851 and when he saw the enemies pursuite to

Enfold.
Jer. 440 Lorenzoes bounty I do more enfould then

Enforce.
ST 2194 if love *e.* such moodes in meaner wits
SP 1233 inforce me sheath my slaughtering blade in
Ard. 274 yet nothing could inforce me to the deed
Ard. 2098 you may *e.* me to it, if you will

Enforced.
HP 348 in the Winter is e. to keepe the Haven
Cor. 1540 was enforc'd to take up Armes
ST 259 inforct by nature and by law of armes
ST 528 and by successe of warre e. the King
SP 631 besides Love hath inforst a foole
Enforcing.
Cor. 1309 (hate e. them thereto)
Enfranchised.
HP 877 for the most part manumitted and enfranchized
Engender.
HP 984 servile fortune can e. servile evils in a gentle mind
HP 1028 putrifie the good and e. naughtie Fish
Cor. 1308 feare that doth e. hate
Engendered.
HP 431 things are first ingendred and afterward corrupted
HP 1442 that Nature hath engendred not onely bruite Beasts
Cor. 1783 till jealous rage (e. with rest)
Puck 48 wold have ingendred more impatience when
Engendereth.
Cor. 593 engendreth fountaines, whence againe those
Engendering.
HP 433 the generation and e. of thinges
Engines.
Ard. 46 sweet words are fittest e. to
England.
ST 343 when it by little E. hath been yoakt
SP 165 Saint George for E., and Saint George for me
Ard. 2380 farewell, E. ; I'll to Flushing now
English.
Jer. 884 full as tall as an E. gallows
ST 524 was E. Robert, Earle of Gloster
ST 529 to beare the yoake of the E. Monarchie
ST 536 when E. Richard wore the Diadem
ST 553 since E. warriours likewise conquered Spaine
ST 2752 set downe in E., more largely, for the easier
SP 99 and E. Archers, hardy men at armes
Englishman.
ST 546 was, as the rest, a valiant E.
SP 153 first, welcome, thrise renowned E.
SP 333 the English man is a fine knight
Engraven.
Ard. 1295 even in my forehead is thy name ingraven
ST 36 see **Graven**
Engrossed.
STA 2022 God hath e. all justice in his hands
Enjoin.
ST 2133 thou must enjoyne thine eies to observation
Enjoined.
ST 392 when both our Armies were enjoynd in fight
Enjoy.
VPJ 81 raigne, live, and blisfull dayes e.
ST 517 tribute is paid, and we e. our right
ST 780 and shall e. the moitie of his land
ST 785 he shall e. the kingdome after us
SP 317 injoy thy life and live ; I give it thee
SP 318 I injoy my life at thy hands, I confesse it
SP 804 that she must needes injoy my interest
SP 1294 or if you gladly would injoy me both
Ard. 219 nay, Mosbie, let me still e. thy love
Ard. 276 might I without control e. thee still
Ard. 336 mayest thou e. her long
Ard. 2354 rise up, sweet Arden, and e. thy love
SP 1565 how can I love him that injoyes my right?
Enjoyed.
Cor. 218 and choakes the good, which els we had enjoy'd

Cor. 2007 and of the joyes mine auncestors enjoy'd
Cor. 2008 when they enjoy'd their lives and libertie?
ST 248 I ceaz'd his weapon and enjoyde it first
Enjoyeth.
HP 352 neither e. it the third part of
Enlarge.
Cor. 115 as with their losse we did our bounds e.
Cor. 184 t'e. the bounds of conquering Thessalie
Cor. 856 t'e. the libertie that thou usurpst
Cor. 1275 t'e. his countries liberty
Cor. 1692 we fight not, we, t'e. our skant confines
ST 467 then with conceite e. your selfe againe
ST 1646 my gentle Sister will I now inlarge
Enlarged.
Cor. 414 (enlarg'd) to drowne the payne it did abide
ST 1641 and bid him let my Sister be enlarg'd
Enmity.
Cor. 185 through murder, discord, wrath, and enmitie
Ennobled.
Cor. 1229 a generous or true enobled spirit detests to
Enough.
HP 91 past into a Garden large e., and
HP 241 ten or twelve yeeres hence, and time inough
HP 1779 collect e., part out of Aristotles Bookes and
Cor. 147 tis not e. (alas) our power t'extend
Cor. 210 for the fatall dombe the Fates make hast e.
Cor. 212 or fast e. doe foolish men not die
Cor. 1467 and shall I not have lived long e.
Cor. 1472 thy prayses show thy life is long e.
Jer. 281 for, give me duckets, Ile fetch you duck inough
Jer. 525 bending in the hams e., like a Gentleman usher?
Jer. 807 thers time e. to let out blood e.
Jer. 825 twere e. to make [the] tranquile saints of angry stuffe
ST 1046 no more, Villuppo, thou hast said e.
ST 1637 thats e.
STA 2961 I can not looke with scorne e. on Death
SP 66 e., Erastus, thy Perseda knowes
SP 914 wast not e. when I had lost the Chaine
SP 1223 it is e. that thou hast conquered Soliman by strength
Ard. 226 we'll make him sure e. for coming there
Ard. 278 e., sweet Alice ; thy kind words makes me melt
Ard. 386 my life for yours, ye shall do well e.
Ard. 813 zounds, I am tame e. already
Ard. 1708 you are well e. served to go without a guide
Ard. 2112 we shall have guests e., though you go hence
Ard. 2217 tush, Michael ; fear not her, she's wise e.
Ard. 2227 fear not, Mistress Arden, he's well e.
Ard. 2436 for simple truth is gracious e.
Enow.
Jer. 217 as there are paths to hell, and thats e., ifaith
Enquire.
HP 128 that hee would e. no further of my state
Puck 38 Lett it but please yo' Lp to e.
Enquired.
HP 56 he e. no further of me
ST 1648 the Duke, you heard, e. for her yester-night
ST 1710 hath not my Father then enquirde for me?
Enquiry.
ST 1248 this slie inquiry of Hieronimo
SP 463 that am to make inquirie after it
SP 475 bid thee onely underhand make privie inquirie
SP 1770 without inquirie what should be the cause
Enraged.
Cor. 195 the troopes e. with the Trumpets sound
SP 241 e. therefore, with this Semitor. [I]
Ard. 1849 thou drew'st thy sword, e. with jealousy

Enriched.
BP 1098 he is Animatus, and divinelie is e. with a soule
Cor. 1198 he hath enricht the Empire with newe states
ST 200 are safe returnd, and by their foes inricht
Enrolled.
SP 144 e. in the brass leaved booke of
Ensign.
Jer. 1144 Ile kisse this little ensigne, this soft banner
Cor. 74 where ere he drive his glittring Chariot, findes our Ensignes spred
Cor. 1376 beheld the swift Rheyn under-run mine Ensignes
Cor. 1855 their battailes scattred, and their Ensignes taken
Ensue.
ST 644 and shield thee from what ever can e.
ST 734 on dangers past, and pleasures to e.
ST 735 on pleasures past, and dangers to e.
Ensuing.
Cor. 531 but when, for feare of an e. ill, we
ST 1278 will stand betweene me and e. harmes
Enter.
HP 189 which cannot e. into every part
Cor. 134 to e. Asia? What, were they the heires to
Cor. 1215 and (ere they e.) use some exercise
ST 2144 why, let them e., and let me see them
SP 2065 but ere I come to e. single fight
Ard. 942 no sooner shall ye e. through the latch
ST Bal. 56 enters my bower all in the night
ST Bal. 115 when Bloody Baltazar enters in
SP 1162 whats he that thus bouldly enters in?
Entered.
HP 84 we entred into a faire Hall
HP 87 directly against the Gate whereby wee entred
HP 1400 I entred the Hospitall, wherein, though
Jer. 567 heard the letter read, just as he e.
SP 115 yong schollers never e. with the rod
SP 395 hath entred such a youngling in the warre
Enterprize.
HP 754 neither will I yet desist in this mine enterprise
ST 1217 repent that ere I usde him in this enterprise
Entertain.
HP 1278 suddainly are driven to entertaine a straunger
Cor. 452 I, when himselfe will entertaine none such
Cor. 733 and flonge abroad mine armes to entertaine him
Cor. 889 that under cloake of love did entertaine him
ST 811 therefore, whiles I doe entertaine the Prince
STA 955 can thy soft bosome intertaine a thought, that
ST 2288 to this intent we entertaine thy selfe
ST 2541 to entertaine my father with the like
VPJ 16 thy Princely mind most Princely Enterteignes
Entertained.
HP 457 I have e. a greater guest then I expected
HP 1770 things which neverthelesse are entertaind and praised
Jer. 794 he intertained it?
ST 1861 to heare his Sonne so princelie entertainde
Entertaineth.
HP 1291 the appetites of those he e.
Entertainment.
HP Ind. 102 meate wanting upon sudden e. of guests
HP 744 in her e. and embracings
Cor. Ded. 12 conceit and entertainment of these small endevours
ST 2310 seest thou this entertainement of these Kings?
ST 2537 at the entertainment of the Embassadour
Enthral.
Cor. 14 faint-harted do those liberties enthrall
Enthralled.

Cor. 838 into the bondage where (enthrald) we pine?
ST 466 I, by conceit my freedome is enthralde
Enthronized.
Cor. 709 when he (enthroniz'd) at his feete beheld great
Enticed.
HP 756 e. hym with love and lovely termes and amorous games
Enticement.
JB (2nd Title) through the entisement of John Parker, was poysoned
Enticing.
Ard. 197 'fore I was tangled with thy 'ticing speech
Entire.
Cor. 1818 the feeble bands that yet were left entyre
Jer. 410 O e. is the condition of my hot desire
Entirely.
HP 364 cannot so e. exercise their office in the night
Jer. 1127 I loved thee so e., when thou breathedst
Entitled.
Ard. 462 all the lands of the Abbey of Feversham, generally intitled
Ard. 526 lands whereof my husband is possessed shall be intitled
Entomb.
ST 984 Ile not intombe them, till I have reveng'd
Entombed.
Cor. 2022 if I die, before I have entomb'd my
ST 2998 that he may bee entomb'd, what ere befall
SP 2173 interd, where my Erastus lyes intombd
Entrails.
Cor. 187 whose e. fyerd with rancor, wrath and rage
Cor. 1103 undaunted Cato tore his e. out
JB 142 vomiting till his intrailes were all shrunke and broken
Entrance.
Cor. 1625 he would attempt the e. on our barrs
ST 1082 what news hath urg'd this sodain e.?
Entrap.
Cor. 336 none others hopes with mischiefe may e.?
ST 1167 and to intrap thy life this traine is laide
Entrapped.
SP 1805 hast thou intrapt me to this tretcherie
Entreat.
HP 1693 to speake and to entreate perticulerly
ST 385 wherein I must intreat thee to relate
ST 1123 intreate me not; go, take the traytor hence
ST 1337 my Lord, let me e. you to take the paines to
ST 2435 let us e. your company to day
ST 2527 let me e. you, grace my practises
ST 2534 wee are to entreate your helpe. — My helpe?
ST 2571 could you e. your sister Bel-imperia to make one?
ST 2717 let me entreate your grace to give the King
ST 2723 let me e. your grace that, when the
SP 1230 if poore Erastus may once more intreate
SP 1517 intreate a pardon for my rash misdeede
Ard. 46 intreat her fair; sweet words are fittest engines to
Ard. 717 let me intreat you to carry this letter to
JB 117 shall I intreate you to fetch mee a penny worth of
Puck 1 at my last being wth yor Lp to entreate
HP 1074 and when entercourse of love and courtesie entreats
ST 499 how Spaine intreats their prisoner Balthazar
ST 1593 and either purchase justice by intreats, or
SP 1408 nor all my faire intreats and blandishments?
SP 1545 for whom I thwarted Solimans intreats
Entreated.
HP 213 much disliked and intreated to the contrarie
HP 680 easie to be e. should the husbande be in graunting
ST 1086 and, well intreated in the Court of Spaine
Entreateth.

ST 1697 Witnesse, that this is true which he *e*. of?
SP 1766 his highnes by me intreateth you, as
Entreaties.
Ard. 1765 if prayers and fair *e*. will not serve
Entreating.
ST Bal. 116 *e*. me to show some sport
Entreaty.
Cor. 1808 and neither prayers, intreatie, nor example
ST 2574 little intreaty shall serve me, Hieronimo
SP 2047 at whose intreatie is this parle sounded?
SP 2048 at our intreatie; therefore yield the towne
Entrench.
Cor. 1652 one while at Tapsus we begin t'*e*.
Entries.
HP 1184 in the quadering and making even of the enteries
Envenomed.
Cor. 1131 but if (envenom'd with ambitious thoughts)
ST 1037 had been envenomde with such extreame hate
Envies.
ST 809 O no, she *e*. none but pleasant things
Envious.
Cor. 327 thy fierce destinie (*e*. of all thine honors)
Cor. 391 that (*e*.) we repine at heavens will
Cor. 1421 but thus we see it fareth with the *e*.
Cor. 1544 made his *e*. foe so hote
Cor. 1946 O *e*. Julia, in thy jealous hart
Jer. 457 thats dipt in inck made of an *e*. gall
Jer. 572 and know his enemy by his *e*. breath
ST 381 with an *e*., forged tale deceived the King
SP 1737 subornd Brusor with *e*. rage to
SP 2019 nothing when it pleaseth death to be *e*.
Ard. 1797 fie, bitter knave, bridle thine *e*. tongue
Environed.
HP 5 *e*. on every side with clowdes ready to raine
HP 81 a little Court *e*. with Trees
HP 1218 or whether they be guirt or *e*. with hylles
Envy.
Cor. 1545 wicked Envie, feeding still foolish those
SP 407 but vertue should not envie good desert
SP 689 all the world loves, none hates but envie
SP 1214 a vertuous envie pricks me with desire to
SP 1564 come, envie, then, and sit in friendships seate
Cor. 1541 for he saw that Envies dart (pricking still
Envying.
ST 400 *e*. at Andreas praise and worth
Epitaph.
SP 2174 and let one *E*. containe us all
Epitheton.
SP 218 may very well beare a feminine *E*.
HP 705 the Poets call him Phoebus with these Epythetons
HP 1386 wel disposed Epythetons and significa[n]t termes
Epoi.
HP 146 *E*. la mensa ingombra
Equal.
HP Ind. 100 matrimonie maketh equall many differences
HP 586 more honor and esteeme of her then of his equall
HP 593 matrimonie maketh equall many differences
HP 718 fayre, yong, equall in estate with thee
HP 1202 commodiously fitting and making equall things exchanged
HP 1282 distribute it indifferentlie with equall measure
HP 1587 to make equall the inequality of things exchangd
Cor. 507 a match more equall never could be made
Cor. 584 (so they with equall pace be aim'd)
Cor. 1032 to Kings and Clownes doth equall ill
Cor. 1106 have each done other equall violence

Cor. 1293 their glorie equall with the best
Jer. 860 let thers be equall to quit yours againe
SP 79 accept this ring to equall it
SP 247 my mercy in conquest is equall with my manhood
SP 793 to her whose worth will never equall mine?
Cor. 35 equals are ever bandying for the best
Equality.
HP Ind. 65 equallitie in marriage to be respected
HP Ind. 66 equallitie in marriage, wherein it doth consist
HP 379 formeth the day and night of such equalitie
HP 577 this equallity of marriage is in two speciall things to be
Equalling.
Cor. 1986 we heape our bodies, *e*. theyr ruine
Equally.
HP 188 equallie ripened by the vertue of the Sunne
Equinoctial.
HP 443 the world began in the Autumnal aequinoctial
Equity.
Cor. 1099 for equitie and right have neither helpe nor grace
ST 2148 halfe the paine that he will in pursuit of equitie
Equos.
HP 810 Flectere ludus *e*., et spicula tendere cornu
Erasto.
ST 2773 *E*., dearer than my life to me
ST 2777 ah, my *E*., welcome to Perseda
ST 2778 thrice happie is *E*., that thou livest
ST 2781 love betwixt *E*. and faire Perseda
ST 2783 remoove *E*., mighty Solyman
ST 2785 *E*. is my friend; and while he lives
ST 2787 let not *E*. live to grieve great Soliman
ST 2788 deare is *E*. in our princly eye
ST 2791 yet greeve I that *E*. should so die
ST 2792 *E*., Solyman saluteth thee
ST 2804 which seazd on my *E*., harmelesse Knight
ST 2795 ay me, *E*.; see, Solyman, Erastoes slaine
ST 2779 Rhodes losse is nothing to Erastoes joy
Erastus.
ST 2614 *E*., the Knight of Rhodes
SP 14 the historie of brave *E*. and his Rodian Dame?
SP 46 but her *E*. over-eied her sporte?
SP 66 enough, *E*., thy Perseda knowes
SP 67 she whom thou wouldst have thine, *E*., knowes
SP 116 ah, my *E*., there are Europes Knights
SP 124 and then *E*. lives without compare
SP 138 I wish *E*. in his maiden warres
SP 388 what, young *E*.? is it possible?
SP 389 *E*., be thou honoured for this deed
SP 398 *E*. will be dutifull in all
SP 408 therefore, *E*., happy laude thy fortune
SP 625 have not I taught *E*. and Perseda by
SP 644 I gave *E*. onely that dayes prize
SP 708 ah, false *E*., how am I betraid
SP 726 ah, false *E*., full of treacherie
SP 739 I go; make reconing that *E*. dyes
SP 741 *E*. lives, the fairest shaped
SP 753 ah, false *E*., how had I misdoone
SP 760 well, now *E*., my hearts onely joy
SP 764 what love meanes, my *E*., pray thee tell
SP 773 as if *E*. could forget himselfe?
SP 791 ah, false *E*., how had I misdone
SP 839 that she hath wrongd *E*. and her frend
SP 861 how now, *E*., wherein may we pleasure thee?
SP 908 flie, *E*., ere the Governour have any newes
SP 965 how art thou misdone by false *E*.
SP 976 I, sir, very well; it was my maister *E*.
SP 987 learne where *E*. is, and bring me word

SP 1020 and whether fled my poore *E.* then?
SP 1030 ah, poore *E.*, how thy starres malign
SP 1039 untill I meete *E.*, my sweete friend
SP 1044 I seeke *E.*, and will combat him
SP 1096 *E.* usde such dice, as, being false
SP 1101 and forst *E.* into banishment
SP 1127 his name *E.*, not twentie yeares of age
SP 1176 this is *E.*, the Rhodian worthie
SP 1182 *E.*, ile not yet urge to know the cause
SP 1200 *E.*, to make thee well assurde
SP 1212 *E.*, now thou hast obtaind thy boone
SP 1218 and now, *E.*, thinke me thine enemie
SP 1221 nay, nay, *E.*, throw not downe thy weapons
SP 1230 if poore *E.* may once more intreate
SP 1241 *E.* will be formost in the battaile
SP 1254 meane time *E.* and I will strive by
SP 1258 and now, *E.*, come and follow me
SP 1300 because that, when *E.* spake my name
SP 1305 I brought not bound unto her *E.*
SP 1362 I plast *E.* in the favour of Solyman
SP 1405 why, how now, *E.*, alwaies in thy dumpes?
SP 1414 come, *E.*, sit thee downe by me
SP 1434 well, well, *E.*, Rhodes may blesse thy birth
SP 1538 for thee, my deare *E.*, have I lived
SP 1555 *E.* and Perseda, come you hether
SP 1557 *E.*, none but thou couldst win Perseda
SP 1558 Perseda. none but thou couldst win *E.*
SP 1561 be thou, *E.*, Governour of Rhodes
SP 1574 *E.* and Perseda, mervaile not that
SP 1578 whe[n] *E.* doth forget this favor
SP 1583 farewell, *E.* ; Perseda, farewell to
SP 1620 is it not better that *E.* die
SP 1623 but by what means shall poore *E.* dye?
SP 1704 where is *E.* ?
SP 1705 all friends, and *E.* maryed to Perseda
SP 1706 and *E.* made governour of Rhodes
SP 1779 till he bring backe *E.* unto you
SP 1785 that for my carrying of *E.* hence she curse me not
SP 1789 and when *E.* comes, our perjurd friend
SP 1802 *E.*, Lord Governour of Rhodes, I arrest you
SP 1823 that very day *E.* went from hence
SP 1863 *E.*, thou seest what witnes hath
SP 1884 unfortunate *E.* ; no more but that for me
SP 1889 ah, poore *E.*, art thou dead already?
SP 1904 witnesses by whose treacherie *E.* dyed
SP 1911 see *E.* be interd with honour in a kingly sepulcher
SP 1919 by whom *E.* was condemnd to die
SP 1963 but say, what death dyed my poore *E.* ?
SP 2073 against the spotlesse life of poore *E.* ?
SP 2094 that Soliman slew *E.* in hope to win Perseda
SP 2100 why didst thou love *E.* more then me ?
SP 2133 what was *E.* in thy opinion ?
SP 2173 interd, where my *E.* lyes intombd
SP 2178 forgive me, deere *E.*, my unkindnes
SP 2187 I gave *E.* woe and miserie
SP 2203 where is *E.* now, but in my triumph ?
ST Bal. 122 from the Chronicles of Spaine I did record *E.* life
SP 1289 For whom mourne you ? — Ah, for *E.* flying
SP 1365 I coucht my selfe in poore *E.* eyes
SP 1418 a worthy man, though not *E.* friend
SP 1701 do you not know me ? I am *E.* man
SP 1733 and give Perseda to *E.* hands
SP 1735 I fild *E.* sailes with winde
SP 1798 whose death might save my poore *E.* life
SP 1891 for to bereave *E.* life from him
SP 1894 and at *E.* hand let them receive the

SP 1917 why, now *E.* ghost is satisfied
SP 1926 that you commend him to *E.* soule
SP 1927 heere ends my deere *E.* tragedie
SP 2001 hath deprived *E.* trunke from breathing vitalitie
SP 2060 and in *E.* name ile combat thee
SP 2089 Ile not defend *E.* innocence
SP 2120 even for *E.* death the heavens have plagued me

Ere.
Cor. 1002 I lyve in hope to see *e.* long that Caesars death
Cor. 1215 and (*e.* they enter) use some exercise
Jer. 157 in the last battaile, *e.* more wretches fall
Jer. 596 make it confused *e.* it come to head
Jer. 895 which, eare Sunne fall, shall pay
ST 23 *e.* Sol had slept three nights in Thetis lap
ST 125 but *e.* we joynd and came to push of Pike
ST 567 *e.* we go from hence, Ile turne their
ST 756 shall carroll us asleepe, *e.* we be ware
ST 906 to leese thy life *e.* life was new begun ?
ST 1020 be still ; and *e.* I lead thee from this place
ST 1493 that *e.* gronde at my office doore
ST 2521 I will *e.* long determine of their deaths
SP 113 thy beauty yet shall make me knowne *e.* night
SP 134 such glory as no time shall *e.* race out
SP 704 not Mars himselfe had eare so faire a Buckler
SP 743 that *e.* sunne saw within our hemyspheare
SP 893 and, Gentlemen, unmaske *e.* you depart
SP 908 flie, Erastus, *e.* the Governour have any newes
SP 1022 but *e.* he went, with many sighes and teares
SP 1304 takes it unkindly that, *e.* he went, I brought not
SP 1855 but *e.* we could summon him a land
SP 1873 I see this traine was plotted *e.* I came
SP 2046 I would sacke the towne, *e.* I would sound a parle
SP 2065 but *e.* I come to enter single fight
SP 2102 not give Soliman a kisse *e.* this unhappy time ?
SP 2151 let me see Rhodes recoverd *e.* I die
Ard. 58 summer-nights are short, and yet you rise *e.* day
Ard. 92 for yet *e.* noon we'll take horse and away
Ard. 93 *e.* noon he means to take horse and away !
Ard. 614 that *e.* long be should die poisoned
Ard. 1429 as I have seen them beat their wings *e.* now !
Ard. 1440 see ye o'ertake us *e.* we come to Rainham Down
Ard. 1570 and that shall be *e.* night, and if I live
Ard. 2212 I care not though I be hanged *e.* night
Ard. 2225 or else I should have heard of him *e.* now
JB 67 he *e.* then had lien with her and gotten her with child

Erebus.
ST 2441 to combate, Acheron and *E.*

Erect.
HP 1517 *e.* and builde with as much exelency
Cor. 608 and by a shephards hands *e.*

Ergo.
ST 1006 *E.* tuos oculos nunquam (mea vita) videbo

Erichtho.
ST 2439 awake, *E.* ; Cerberus, awake

Err.
ST 1322 urged with the thought of former evils, easily cannot erre
ST 2320 heavens will not let Lorenzo erre so much
ST 2358 alas, how easie is it for him to erre

Errant.
SP 1136 under the habit of some *e.* knight

Errante.
HP 544 L'*e.* mia Consorte

Error.
Jer. 482 I pray you, pardon me ; twas but youths hasty *e.*
Jer. 741 this ominus mistake, this damned *e.*

Cor. 25 'tis thou that train'st us into all these errors
ST 2828 not to excuse grosse errors in the play

Erst.
Cor. 622 that earst was cleere as heavens Queene
Cor. 1084 bloode, that earst was shed to save thy libertie
Cor. 1967 O Gods, that earst of Carthage tooke some care

Erunt.
HP 1785 Me mea, sic tua te ; caetera mortis e.

Escape.
ST 2601 and, to e. the Bashawes tirannie, did stab
SP 968 the murtherer will e. without revenge
SP 1000 ever see wise man e. as I have done ?
SP 1035 but hopes the coystrell to e. me so ?
SP 2153 spoile all, kill all ; let none e. your furie
Ard. 806 stay, Michael, you may not e. us so
Ard. 1518 did ever man e. as thou hast done ?
Ard. 2263 tell me, sweet Alice, how shall I e. ?
Ard. 2365 those ruffians shall not e. ; I will up to London
Ard. 1418 Arden escapes us, and deceives us all
Cor. 480 no more then wretched we their death could scape
Cor. 513 to scape the feares that followes Fortunes glaunces
Cor. 1835 he that had hap to scape, doth helpe a fresh to
ST 1509 God forbid a fault so foule should scape unpunished
STA 1788 they doe not alwayes scape, that is some comfort
SP 818 where none scape wrackt but blindfould Marriners ?
SP 992 but for Assurance that he may not scape

Escaped.
Cor. 325 escapt not free fro thy victorious hands ?
Ard. 825 as by this means Arden hath e.
Ard. 841 Arden e. us and passed by unthought on
Ard. 1523 the devil he is ! why, sirs, how e. he ?
Ard. 1784 have they e. you, then, and passed the ferry ?
Cor. 879 which, having scapt the rage of wind and Sea

Eschew.
HP 776 which to e. (taking a wyfe of our deciphering) he
Ard. 347 then, Mosbie, to e. the speech of men

Especial.
HP 386 one especiall is Grape-gathering for the wine-presse
HP 1460 have knowledge of, but especiall of Husbandrie
HP 1692 five e. points whereof we promised to speake

Especially.
HP 571 e. if they doo it for desire of succession
HP 802 some nations, and e. those of Aquitan and
HP 1079 is especiallie to be usd and shewn
HP 1130 that Treatise of under officers (e.) writte[n] by
Cor. 1981 e. that proudest Hanniball
Jer. 504 ‹ e. being warned before hand ›
Jer. 505 ‹ e. ›
Jer. 523 ‹ e. being warnd beforehand ›
Jer. 975 e. ride thee home so, my son
ST 2589 e. the soule of Soliman, who
JB 25 beloved of divers young men, e. of two Goldsmithes
JB 102 (e. being so lately married)
ST 2427 specially with you, my lovely Lord

Espied.
SP 1945 when he espyde my weeping flouds of teares

Espoused.
HP 547 said that the soule was e. to the bodie

Espy.
ST Bal. 87 as then a Letter there I did e.

Esquire.
HP Ded. Maister Thomas Reade Esquier

Estate.
HP 53 shrowded under the e. of Savoy
HP 56 that I desired to conceale some part of mine e.
HP 578 in two speciall things to be considered — E. and Age

HP 581 a noble woman matching with a man of base e.
HP 598 and thus touching the e. of man and wife
HP 718 fayre, yong, equall in e. with thee
HP 843 thy private e. requires that so thou teach and
HP 865 better their e. with praise and honesty
HP 1023 some respect to the e. and desert of every one
HP 1360 the further off she is from nobles[se] or e.
HP 1539 living well, according to his e.
HP 1770 usd and exercised in affaires of more e.
Cor. 956 his owne e. more firmely he assures
ST 277 for thine e. best fitteth such a guest
ST 810 she both will wrong her owne e. and ours
ST 1678 concerning certaine matters of e.
JB 67 although he was not as then in e. to marrie
ST 2195 if love expresse such power in poore estates

Esteem.
HP 151 ‹ With meats of meane esteeme
HP 585 more honor and esteeme of her then of his equall

Esteemed.
HP 1207 more e. then the matter or the thing made
JB 155 but e. her a very honest woman
JB 27 and well e. for fine workmanship in their trade

Esteeming.
ST 641 thou dyest for more e. her then me
JB 41 e. her the mistris and commaundres of his life

Estimate.
HP 1588 and to estimat and measure prices

Estimation.
HP 463 happily blazon mine e. or sufficiencie

Estranged.
HP 1427 or utterly disjoyned and estraunged from it

Eternal.
Cor. 223 and nourish sorrow with eternall teares ?
Cor. 350 doe coast the Earth with an eternall course
Cor. 494 in one daies space (to our eternall mones)
Cor. 788 art conquer'd now with an eternall fall
Cor. 1918 be my eternall tasks, that th' extreame fire
Cor. 1933 thy death, deere Scipio, Romes eternall losse
ST 1 when this eternall substance of my soule did
ST 3032 adding sweet pleasure to eternall daies
ST 764 shall send thy soule into eternall night
SP 586 to wander with them through eternall night
SP 2110 then wait on her thorough e. night
SP 2182 follow thee, with eager moode, thorow eternall night
SP 1898 to waite upon thee through eternall shade
JB 2 before the sight of the eternall God

Eternally.
Cor. 67 like Captives lyv'd e. enchaynd

Eternity.
Eng. Parn. 1 Time is a bondslave to eternitie

Eternized.
Cor. 1475 yet Rome may wish his life e.

Etheocles.
HP 905 represents the person of Agamemnon, Atreus, or E.

Etna, see Aetna.

Eunuchs.
SP 1260 sportes my Minions and my Euenukes can devise
SP 1638 I will go sit among my learned Euenukes

Euphrates.
Cor. 1352 more fam'd then Tyger or fayre E. ?

Euripides.
HP 713 an aunicent custome, as we read of Hellen in E.

Europe.
HP 108 ‹ and in what part of E. and of Italie › (quoth I)
Cor. 1504 brings conquests whereof E. rings
SP 116 ah, my Erastus, there are Europes Knights

Euxine.
Cor. 1380 th' earth that the *E.* sea makes somtymes marsh
Even.
HP 371 who *e.* then that shee woulde
HP 385 endureth *e.* untill then
HP 515 with exceeding toyle *e.* of his owne person
HP 549 and *e.* as after that the bande that tyes the
HP 623 and *e.* as desire (which of it selfe is unreasonable)
HP 926 scarce performe *e.* when they are commaunded
HP 928 *e.* as the Moone and the Starres receive light by
HP 1513 *e.* as every arte dooth infinitly seeke the end it
HP 1535 *e.* so should riches be proportioned and limitted
HP 1662 « In Genesis *e.* God himselfe doth say »
HP 1724 then *e.* as the consideration of the forme
Cor. 122 and *e.* that yoke, that wont to tame all others
Cor. 186 *e.* to the peacefull Indians pearled seate
Cor. 320 that *e.* in all the corners of the earth thy
Cor. 599 *e.* so our cittie (in her prime
Cor. 1147 why hast we not, *e.* while these words are uttred
Cor. 1384 yea, *e.* this Cittie, that hath almost made an
Cor. 1390 proov'd to his losse, but *e.* in one assault
Cor. 1626 nay, *e.* our Trenches, to our great disgrace
Cor. 1630 *e.* so our battails, scattred on the sands
Cor. 1983 for *e.* those fields that mourn'd to beare their bodies
Jer. 23 able to ravish *e.* my sence away
Jer. 377 woot thou, prince ? why *e.* for that I love [thee]
Jer. 553 love to Andrea, I, *e.* to his very bosome
Jer. 821 is *e.* as necessary as our bloud
Jer. 896 shall pay deere trybute, *e.* there lives and all
Jer. 1129 and wish me wounds, *e.* for society
ST Bal 146 *e.* with my teeth I bit my tongue
ST 651 *e.* him, my Lord
ST 668 deserves my duteous service, *e.* till death
ST 1109 but *e.* the slaughter of our deerest sonne
ST 1492 wel, thou art *e.* the meriest peece of mans flesh that
ST 1696 *e.* so, my Lord ? and you are witnesse
STA 2012 but *e.* so Masters ungratefull servants reare
ST 2385 *e.* so : — what new device have
SP 73 and there, *e.* there, I vow'd unto myselfe to
SP 76 *e.* in thy brest doo I elect my rest
SP 200 *e.* to the verge of golde abounding Spaine
SP 650 *e.* for that Chaine shall be deprived of life
SP 1140 *e.* for his vertues sake, I wish that fortune
SP 1547 *e.* from my childhood have I tendered thee
SP 1580 nor will Perseda slacke *e.* in her praiers
SP 1666 *e.* as a Cow for tickling in the horne
SP 2120 *e.* for Erastus death the heavens have plagued me
SP 2127 Is she not faire ? — *E.* in the houre of death
SP 2133 kinde, *e.* to his foes, gentle and affable
SP 2160 and I am weake *e.* to the very death
SP 2192 of life, but not of love ; for *e.* in death their
Ard. 209 which *e.* in bursting forth consumes itself
Ard. 1152 *e.* there, methoughts, a gentle slumber took me
Ard. 1295 *e.* in my forehead is thy name ingraven
Ard. 1515 *e.* in that fearful time would I fall down
Ard. 1805 *e.* in that fearful time would I fall down
Ard. 1948 when Mosbie bled, he *e.* wept for sorrow
Ard. 2164 I'll make booty of the quean *e.* to her smock
Ard. 2198 I saw him walking behind the Abbey *e.* now
JB 89 *e.* according as Parker had before given direction
Puck 72 doubtles *e.* then yor Lrs shalbe sure
HP 1183 in the quadering and making *e.* of the enteries
HP 1592 in respect of making eve[n] inequalities
Jer. 385 but I stand *e.* yet, jump crowne to crowne
Evening.
HP 18 « I would to Vercellis » (quoth I) « this *e.*

HP 23 to lodge with me this *e.*
Jer. 639 the *e.* to begins to slubber day
Jer. 906 before the *e.* deawes quentch the sunnes rage
ST 1237 at S. Luigis Parke, behinde the house ; this *e.*, boy
Ard. 1481 or will this black-faced *e.* have a shower ?
Events.
Cor. Arg. 35 these crosse *e.* and haples newes of Affrique
ST 2899 Hieronimo, doe but enforme the King of these *e.*
Ever.
HP 195 were *e.* more desirous of reasoning and talk
Cor. Ded. 23 and *e.* spend one howre of the day in some kind
  service
Cor. Arg. 3 and the vertues of the minde as *e.* any was
Cor. 35 equals are *e.* bandying for the best
Cor. 368 commit more murther then Rome *e.* made
Cor. 690 the more unlike she should continue *e.*
Cor. 769 or staies for *e.* in th' Elisian fields
Cor. 898 and injur'd him that *e.* us'd you kindly
Cor. 902 Tygers and Lyons, breed with you for *e.*
Cor. 1063 because thou *e.* hatedst Monarchie
Cor. 1292 no Sepulcher shall ere exclude their glorie
Jer. 12 if *e.* you have foes, or red field scars
Jer. 389 the valiant spirit ere trod the Spanish courte
Jer. 671 live, truest friend, for *e.* loved and blest
Jer. 770 the most notorious rogue that *e.* breathd
ST 1026 but *e.* subject to the wheele of chance
STA 2064 the most notorious villaines that *e.* lived in all Spaine
ST 2688 fruitlesse for *e.* may this garden be
ST 2980 that *e.* was invented for a wretch
ST 2993 what age hath *e.* heard such monstrous deeds ?
SP 991 why, ile be heere as soone as *e.* I come again
SP 1005 yours for *e.*, and *e.*, and *e.*
SP 1029 to wrong my friend whose thoughts were *e.* true
SP 1122 the greatest pompe that ere I saw
SP 1219 but *e.* after thy continuall friend
SP 1360 the most dishonour that could ere befall
SP 1402 if forst from faith, for *e.* miserable
SP 1767 intreateth you, as *e.* you respect his future love
SP 2141 be this, therefore, the last that ere thou speake
SP 2166 and if you *e.* loved your Emperour
Ard. 207 see that which I *e.* feared, and find too true
Ard. 390 was *e.* silly woman so tormented ?
Ard. 1120 as dear as *e.* coistril bought so little sport
Ard. 1209 why now, Greene, 'tis better now nor e'er it was
Ard. 1322 but mads me that *e.* I thought thee fair
Ard. 1397 than e'er thou handledst pistols in thy life
Ard. 1518 did *e.* man escape as thou hast done ?
Ard. 1688 didst thou *e.* see better weather to
Ard. 1718 did you *e.* see such a mist as this ?
Ard. 1778 although the rent of it was *e.* mine
Ard. 2028 and if he e'er go forth again, blame me
Ard. 2386 was I *e.* privy to your intent or no
JB 52 and not to think *e.* the worse of her afterward, to
JB 58 the worst bargain that *e.* he made in his life
JB 110 « as good sugur sops as *e.* I made in my life »
JB 196 « and wo worth thee » (quoth shee) that *e.* I knewe thee
Puck 12 the first and most (thoughe insufficient) surmize that *e.*
Ever-each.
Cor. 1727 they ranne at *e.* other hand and foote
Ever-glooming.
ST 56 through dreadfull shades of ever glooming night
Everlasting.
VPJ 9 good fortune and an *e.* fame attend on thee
Jer. 260 I have no hope of *e.* height
Jer. 380 woundes will tie an *e.* setled amity
Jer. 742 breeds in my soule an *e.* terror

ST 43 and spend the course of *e.* time
ST 921 blow sighes, and raise an *e.* storme
ST 1873 of kingly love and *e.* league
SP 26 I will not downe to *e.* night till
SP 1897 helpe to send them down to *e.* night
Ard. 1088 and Arden sent to *e.* night
Evermore.
HP 292 who *e.* in praysing Wine called it
HP 619 who *e.* none otherwise impugneth and
HP 1373 and *e.* know what she hath and what shee wants
HP 1455 « liking *e.* to live upo[n] the spoile »
Cor. Ded. 4 such as *e.* is traveld with th' afflictions of the minde
Cor. 1277 now shall they love him ever-more
Ever-thirsting.
SP 1598 like ever thirsting, wretched Tantalus
Ever-turning.
SP 853 ah, vertuous Lampes of ever turning heavens
Every.
HP 5 environed on *e.* side with clowdes
HP 93 hangings and *e.* other ornament beseeming
HP 189 which cannot enter into *e.* part
HP 286 « And they are filled *e.* one with olde wine
HP 405 *e.* manne may credite as he list
HP 521 touching *e.* of which I will particularly reason
HP 1012 gyving *e.* one hys sallary or day wages
HP 1024 some respect to the estate and desert of *e.* one
HP 1029 to keepe evrie one pertlculerlie exercised
HP 1036 and consequently *e.* other otherwise be occupied
HP 1051 *e.* servant should perticulerlie have such care
HP 1055 for such are, is, or should be *e.* toole
HP 1401 wherein, though *e.* Roome I sawe
HP 1458 *e.* of which naturall gaines it seemeth
HP 1515 *e.* arte dooth infinitly seeke the end it purposeth
HP 1528 in *e.* arte the instruments should be proportioned and
HP 1640 *e.* or either of which hauving not onely beene
Cor. 362 and spilt such store of blood in *e.* street
Cor. 411 faintlie redoubled ev'ry feeble stroke
Cor. 804 and, ceaseles lanching out on everie side
Cor. 1034 mischaunce, that *e.* man abhors
Cor. 1521 so, in *e.* place let be Feasts, and Masks
Cor. 1548 poure sundry passions *e.* houre
Cor. 1667 and *e.* Regiment warn'd with a worde
Cor. 1725 and *e.* Eccho tooke the Trompets clange
Cor. 1794 who (staggering) fell with *e.* feeble wound
Jer. 584 tis all about the court in *e.* eare
Jer. 607 have *e.* sillable a musick stop
ST 148 on *e.* side drop Captaines to the ground
ST 220 we will bestow on *e.* souldier two duckets
ST 221 on *e.* souldier two duckets, and on *e.* leader ten
ST 507 wrapt *e.* houre in pleasures of the Court
ST 1018 the end is crowne of *e.* worke well done
ST 1409 an odde jest for me to stand and grace *e.* jest he makes
ST 1575 of everie accident I neere could finde till now
STA 1953 I prie through *e.* crevice of each wall
STA 1954 looke on each tree, and search through *e.* brake
ST 2096 I, heaven wil be revenged of *e.* ill
ST 2752 for the easier understanding to *e.* publique Reader
ST 2755 and be thou grac't with *e.* excelence that
SP 42 goe *e.* way, and not the way I would ?
SP 1064 and thus I beare him thorough *e.* streete
SP 2132 souldiers, assault the towne on *e.* side
SP 2176 the poison is disperst through euerie vaine
Ard. 405 but write from London to me *e.* week
Ard. 406 nay, *e.* day, and stay no longer there
Ard. 408 I'll write unto thee *e.* other tide
Ard. 498 yet doth he keep in *e.* corner trulls

Ard. 505 as *e.* day I wish with hearty prayer
Ard. 578 to make recount of it to *e.* groom
Ard. 832 I value *e.* drop of my blood at a French crown
Ard. 986 for *e.* searching eye to overread
Ard. 1162 with this I woke and trembled *e.* joint
Ard. 1634 but that it shakes with *e.* blast of wind
Ard. 1937 stand *e.* morning with a quart-pot in their hand
Ard. 1988 for *e.* drop of his detested blood
Ard. 2129 been ill spoken of in *e.* place
Ard. 2292 ay, search, and spare you not, through *e.* room
JB 161 *e.* neighbour thinking it had been her husbands
Everyone.
HP 576 so much the more ought every one provide to be
Everything.
HP 163 I have aboundaunce of every thing
HP 1082 for everie thing that belongs to the
Cor. 600 (in her prime prescribing Princes every thing)
Jer. 454 O thers a kind of state in every thing
Everywhere.
VPJ 8 and *e.* aboundeth godly love
Cor. 1307 feareth all men every where
Cor. 1820 every where lay Armed men, ore-troden with theyr horses
SP 1647 my valour every where shall purchase friends
Evidently.
JB 3 we may *e.* see how busie the divell
JB 20 as by this example following may *e.* be proved
Evil.
HP Ind. 92 idlenes and ease make some servants evill
HP 530 all the good and all the evill incidênt to life
HP 1025 breeding evill thoughts, and bringing forth worse works
Cor. 1496 feare of evill doth afflict us more then th' evill it selfe
Jer. 567 though it had happend evill, he should have
Jer. 743 say, slave, how came this accursed evill ?
ST 227 deserve but evill measure at our hands
ST 839 nay, evill newes flie faster still than good
JB 116 though the well meaning man thought on no evill
JB 154 no person as then suspecting any manner of *e.*
HP 984 sevile fortune can engender servile evils in a gentle mind
HP 1689 and consorted with so many perilous evils
Cor. 3 that if (provok'd against us by our evils) you
Cor. 167 is slow in punishing the evils we have done
ST 1322 a guiltie conscience, urged with the thought of former evils
ST 2102 for evils unto ils conductors be
Evil-sounding.
Ard. 1158 with that he blew an *e.* horn
Examined.
Puck 75 shalbe *e.* & rypped up effectually
JB 212 carried before Alderman Howard to be *e.*
Example.
HP 223 yet by *e.* of their children they might moderate
HP 497 I also thinke by his *e.* to
HP 842 propose him or his behaviour for theyr *e.*
HP 985 an *e.* of the Scythians worth while the noting
HP 1250 remembring that *e.* of Thales, who
HP 1348 in which *e.* he followed Homer, who
HP 1772 your sonnes, following the *e.* of theyr Uncle
Cor. 1808 and neither prayers, intreatie, nor *e.*
JB 20 as by this *e.* following may evidently be proved
IB 225 the Lord give all men grace by their *e.* to
HP 490 with the authority of theyr examples
HP 967 whose examples, if I should but practise to recount
Exasperate.

Cor. 110 jealous Italie (*e.* with our up-rising)
Cor. 986 his wrath against you t'will *e.*
ST 1338 to *e.* and hasten his revenge
ST 1704 my Fathers olde wrath hath *e.*
Excedere.
HP 1665 Et unum alium *e.* per artem et naturam
Exceed.
HP 219 ought to exceede their children alwaies
HP 608 the man ought to exceede the woman so many yeeres
HP 1548 ought not to exceede the rest in any such condition
Cor. 596 that oft exceede their wonted bounds
ST Bal. 4 thinking your griefes all griefes exceede
Cor. 786 the force of heaven exceeds thy former strength
Cor. 1143 exceeds all loves, and deerer is by farre
Exceeded.
HP 228 where, if they *e.* more in yeres
Cor. 1301 my hand, my hap, my hart *e.* his
Ard. 1309 whose beauty and demeanour far *e.* thee
Exceedeth.
HP 593 betwixt men and women farre *e.* it
Exceeding.
HP 369 our bodies resolved with the *e.* heate
HP 515 and with *e.* toyle even of his owne person
HP 615 *e.* waiward, crabbed and disobedient
HP 1554 *e.* others in his riches
ST 1025 and oft supplanted with *e.* hate
ST 2599 she, stirde with an *e.* hate therefore
SP 794 what, is Lucinaes wealth *e.* mine?
Exceedingly.
JB 133 immediatlie after he began to vomet *e.*
Excel.
SP 1255 strive by mutuall kindnes to excell each other
Cor. 1613 such a death excels a servile life
Excellence.
ST 2755 and be thou grac't with every excelence that
ST 2759 Perseda, blisfull lampe of *E.*
SP 692 except Persedas beautious *e.*
SP 1129 I never saw, except your *e.*, a man
SP 1651 a man of my desert and *e.*
Excellency.
HP 1517 with as much exelency and perfection as he can
Excellent.
HP (Title) that *e.* Orator and Poet
HP 395 drest by the most *e.* Cooke the Duke hath
HP 1124 who beeing an *e.* Grammarian, was also
Cor. Ded. 17 what grace that *e.* Garnier hath lost by
Jer. 353 an *e.* foe; we shall have scuffling good
Jer. 735 an *e.* villaine hath his fame as well as a
STA 2048 Bazardo, afore-god, an *e.* fellow
ST 2603 O, *e.*!
SP 329 by my faith, me thought it was *e.*
Excellently.
HP 656 *e.* approves that no collour better graceth
Except.
HP 879 (*e.* percase in those partes where slaves yet serve)
Cor. 925 *e.* some man (resolved) shall conclude
Cor. 1665 *e.* some fewe that stayd to guard the Trench
ST Bal. 45 *e.* straightwayes he should recite his
ST 93 all wel, my soveraigne Liege, *e.* some few
ST 199 that all (*e.* three hundred or few more)
SP 692 *e.* Persedas beautious excellence
SP 1129 I never saw, *e.* your excellence, a man
SP 1422 *e.* some few that turne to Mahomet
Ard. 1219 so you will *e.* of my company
Excepted.
Eng. Parn. 12 (Vertue *e.*) which alone survives

Excess.
Ard. 1223 feebles my body by *e.* of drink
Excessive.
HP 1597 multiply or accumulat infinite and *e.* profits
Exchange.
HP Ind. 50 difference betwixt Exchaunge and Usury
HP 1199 exchaunge of things was made with out returne of money
HP 1205 more certaine then when they onely used exchaunge
HP 1228 or such as use to bartre or *e.*
HP 1508 which is doone by traffique and exchaunge
HP 1512 reape his profite of exchaunge by a second object
HP 1585 the one is called Exchaunge, the other Usurie
HP 1596 in which *e.* Nature is not imitated
HP 1596 exchaunge that doth multiply or accumulat
HP 1602 *E.* may multiply in profits infinitly
HP 1604 and in *e.* is not considered to be otherwise
HP 1622 yet betwixt *E.* and Usury there is some difference
HP 1623 *E.* may be retained, not only for the custome
HP 1625 for *e.* is used in steede of our
HP 1632 the Reall *e.* of mony might bee in some sort reduced
Exchanged.
HP 1203 commodiously fitting and making equall things *e.*
HP 1493 all things that are used to be exchaunged
HP 1588 to make equall the inequality of things exchangd
HP 1589 not for that it ought to be exchangd
Exchangeth.
HP 1461 mingleth and exchaungeth the profit of all those
HP 1628 the party that exchaungeth may have some
Exchanging.
HP 1308 the buying, selling, or *e.* other things
Excite.
Cor. 104 to *e.* to Armes the troopes enraged with
Exclaim.
Cor. 419 I gan exclaime and bellow forth against
ST 2836 and he exclaime against thee to the King
ST 2839 to heare Hieronimo exclaime on thee?
ST 1524 or mine exclaimes, that have surcharged the aire
Exclude.
Cor. 516 can bondage true nobility *e.*?
Cor. 1292 no Sepulcher shall ere *e.* their glorie
Excrement.
SP 277 not an hayre, not an *e.*
Excuse.
ST 2828 not to *e.* grosse errors in the play
Ard. 1192 for God's sake, sirs, let me *e.* myself
Ard. 1208 your *e.* hath somewhat mollified my choler
Ard. 1533 ay, and *e.* ourselves to Mistress Arden
JB 81 and to *e.* her from his bed, she sayd
Puck 41 I in no sort can accuse nor will *e.* by reson of
ST 2485 with what excuses canst thou shew thy selfe
Ard. 1549 ay, such kind husbands seldom want excuses
Excused.
ST 1711 sister, he hath, and thus excusde I thee
ST 2703 to holde excusde thy negligence in
Execrations.
ST 1586 and band with bitter *e.* be the day
Execute.
HP 921 capable of his commaundements, and *e.* them willingly
Executed.
SP 1959 for my maister is condemnd and *e.*
Ard. 2409 where they in Smithfield must be *e.*
JB 222 and they were *e.* on Wednesday last, being the
Execution.
VPJ (Title) after the apprehension and *e.* of Babington
VPJ (Title) in the Tower before his *E.*

Jer. 764 beare him away to *e*.
ST 1440 for ther's thy place of *e*.
ST 1510 dispatch, and see this *e*. done
Ard. 2419 to speedy *e*. with them all !
JB 14 see it put in *e*. daylie before our eyes
Executioner.
ST 1388 and thats to see the *E*.
ST 1518 so, *E*.; convay him hence
Exempt.
ST 1927 till when, our selfe will *e*. [him] the place
Exercet.
HP 1327 *e*. penso, castum ut servare cubile
Exercise.
HP Ind. 64 *e*. of Housekeepers for health
HP Ind. 67 *e*. a Husbandmans phisicke
HP 364 *e*. their office in the night
HP 519 in his personne he is to *e*. three offices
HP 612 easily *e*. in her that superioritie that
HP 851 *e*. themselves in practise of the mind and body
HP 997 labor, countrey busines, and household *e*.
HP 1056 every toole to him that hath the *e*. thereof
HP 1574 wherein he shall also *e*. himselfe
HP 1681 it doth not *e*. the arte according as God
Cor. 244 do *e*. your mirthlesse Empory
Cor. 1215 and (ere they enter) use some *e*.
SP 148 that *e*. their war with friendly blowes
HP 1575 busied in those exercises of the bodie
Exercised.
HP 276 *e*. themselves with much labour)
HP 280 because they be much *e*. and stirring
HP 863 *e*. in those most commendable practises of
HP 873 and to keepe them *e*. in obedience
HP 1030 particulerlie *e*. in his perticuler office
HP 1479 those things whereof they exercized trafique
HP 1710 you (it seemes) have *e*. them as industriously
HP 1769 being usd and *e*. in affaires of more estate
SP 1158 their footemen more, well *e*. in war
Exhalation.
HP 1215 by the *e*. of whose evill vapours the ayre becommeth filthy
Exhorting.
Cor. 1680 *e*. them to charge, and fight like men
Exiges.
HP 1640ᵃ frugum superabundantia[m] non *e*.
Exile.
SP 1546 and for whose *e*. I lamented thus
Cor. 1433 and (joyned with the Exiles there) encamp
Jer. 103 and pollicy and pride walke like two exiles
Exiled.
Cor. 665 they runne by Land and Sea (lyke exil'd us) from
ST 2234 for justice is *e*. from the earth
SP 1243 by whose crueltie thou art exylde ?
Exonerate.
HP 617 to lighten and exonerat that ponderous and heavie loade
Exorcisms.
Ard. 1814 but I will break thy spells and *e*.
Expect.
HP 230 *e*. and approve that ayde and comfort
HP 1008 *e*. to have our houses so distinguished and
Cor. 512 what good *e*. wee in a fiery gap ?
SP 1328 if you resist, *e*. what warre affordes
Expected.
HP 457 I have entertained a greater guest then I *e*.
HP 1721 and more eloquent devise then I *e*.
ST 316 what helpe can be *e*. at her hands
ST 2995 hope that Spaine *e*. after my disease

Expediunt.
HP 1066 cerealiaque arma, *e*. fessi rerum
Expel.
Cor. 1511 to expell fro forth the Land firce warrs
HP 801ᵃ Antiperistasis, where heate expels cold, or cold
Expense.
HP 513 with little more expence have easely accomplisht
HP 1155 so to live as his expence may proove the least
HP 1161 nor supply the necessity of some expence which
HP 1244 in sparing that expence he used at first
HP 1153 the quallitie and quantity of his revenues and expences
HP 1184 making even of the enteries with the expences
HP 1232 so may they be occasion of sparing in expences
Experience.
HP 470 (loaden both with age and with *e*.)
HP 1190 judgment, *e*., and dilligence
HP 1247 Prognostications, or speech of other mens *e*.
HP 1780 and the rest by his owne *e*. in Court
ST 1346 and thus *e*. bids the wise to deale
ST 1718 I know not, I, by what *e*.
ST 2565 to make *e*. of their wits in plaies
Ard. 1660 speaks thou this of thine own *e*. ?
Experimented.
HP 514 (being unlettered and not *e*. in the world)
Expert.
Cor. 743 regiments, made of so many *e*. Souldiours
Expiate.
Cor. 1932 nought but my Fathers death could *e*. ?
Expired.
Cor. 681 title be not *e*. in Cornelias blood
Cor. 922 els had my life beene long agoe *e*.
Cor. 1976 now is our haples time of hopes *e*.
Jer. 432 the date of his embassage nighe *e*.
Ard. 1380 well, were his date completed and *e*.
Exploit.
ST 217 by vertue of thy worthy sonnes *e*.
Express.
ST 2195 if love expresse such power in poore estates
STA 2981 now to expresse the rupture of my part
SP 1821 why face to face expresse you not the treasons
Expressly.
ST 1277 that we are thus *e*. chargde to watch
Expugnation.
SP 1642 since the *e*. of the Rhodian Ile
Expulerat.
HP 1323 Curriculo *e*. somnum, cum foemina primum
Expulse.
ST 1247 and thus one ill another must *e*.
Expulseth.
HP 801ᵃ where heate expels cold, or cold *e*. heate
Extant.
HP 339 two Letters that are *e*. to be reade
HP 1123 (of whom are many Letters *e*.
Extasy, *see* **Ecstasy.**
Extempore.
SP 281 Jester : O *e*., O flores
Extend.
HP 1108 some stretch further and *e*. to civil administration
HP 1298 neyther ought her care only *e*. to the spending
Cor. 147 tis not enough (alas) our power t'*e*.
Cor. 482 that Romes high worth to Affrique did *e*.
Cor. 778 didst *e*. thy conquering armes beyond the Ocean
STA 2053 *e*. to this, or some such like purpose [?]
Extended.
Cor. 1832 cryde, with hands *e*. to the merciles
Exterior.

HP 901 the people that onely have regarde to *e*. things
Exterminate.
Cor. 1172 bent to *e*. who ever sought to
Extinct.
STA 2076 the Starres *e*., the Windes blowing
Extincto.
ST 1005 Noster in *e*. moriatur pectore sensus
Extinguished.
HP 1127 utterly *e*. betwixt Maisters and Servants
Extirp.
Cor. 1256 that may exstirpe or raze these tyrannies
Extirpen.
Ard. 1260 and will *e*. me to plant another
Extolled.
Eng. Parn. 14 at last to be extol'd in heavens high joyes
Extortioner.
SP 336 fie upon thee, *e*.
Extra.
Puck 49 when lesse by farr hath dryven so manye imo *e*. caulas
Extreme.
HP 342 the Sommer with extreame heate, and the
HP 343 and the Winter with extreame colde
HP 866 raigneth not like a Lord, but like an extreame Tirant
HP 816 to us that have not used it it seemes extreame
Cor. 741 but may my father (O extreame mishap)
Cor. 859 amongst the rest of mine extreame mishaps
Cor. 997 as his extreame tryumphing in our woe
Cor. 1858 incessantly lamenting th' extreame losse
Cor. 1918 that th' extreame fire within my hart may
Jer. 588 when it would scarce go downe for extreame laughter
ST 1037 had beene envenomde with such extreame hate
ST 1911 with extreame pride conceived of yong Horatio
STA 1950 so that with extreame griefe and cutting sorrow
JB 16 the feare of God, or extreame punishment in this world
JB 141 all that night was he extreame sicke
Cor. 883 bones which (in extreames) an earthen Urne containeth
ST 1052 in such extreames will nought but patience serve
ST 1053 but in extreames what patience shall I use?
ST 1121 but with the bitterest torments and extreames
ST 1414 thus must we toyle in other mens extreames
ST 1553 my Lord, I write as mine extreames requirde
ST 1662 and with extreames abuse my company
ST 2121 but in extreames advantage hath no time
SP 1617 in two extreames the least is to be chosen
Extremely.
ST 1860 then and as a man extreamely over-joyd to heare
Extremest.
Cor. 898 of the extreamest and most odious cryme
ST 1024 first we are plast upon extreamest height
ST 2506 that wrought his downfall with extreamest death
ST 2088 we will devise the 'xtremest kinde of death
Extremities.
Cor. 1595 th' undaunted hart that is required in *e*.?
ST 2186 for all as one are our extremeties
ST 2306 accompany thy friend with thine *e*.
Extremity.
ST 1061 not that I feare the extremitie of death
SP 1329 mischiefe, murther, bloud, and extremitie
Eye.
HP 1089 at a winck of the *e*., or bent of the brow
Jer. 251 and therefore great gifts may bewitch her eie
ST 521 Hieronimo, this maske contentes mine *e*.
ST 841 her jealous *e*. will thinke I sit too neere
STA 959 cast a more serious *e*. upon thy griefe
ST 1595 so that you say, this hearbe will purge the *e*.

ST 2788 deare is Erasto in our princly *e*.
ST 2798 but with a gratious *e*. behold his griefe
SP 74 untill my wandring *e*. should finde a harbour
SP 271 the reflecting *e*. of that admirable comet Perseda
SP 380 I, in the *e*. of an infant a Peacocks taile is glorious
SP 803 if I were so disgratious in thine *e*.
SP 1391 what pleaseth the *e*., when the sence is altered?
SP 1694 wish you to have an *e*. to the back dore
Ard. 259 a weeping *e*. that witnesses heart's grief
Ard. 371 I cannot speak or cast aside my *e*.
Ard. 986 for every searching *e*. to overread
Ard. 1397 go to, you carry an *e*. over Mistress Susan
Ard. 1868 if homely, I seem sluttish in thine *e*.
Ard. 2435 to make it gracious to the ear or *e*.
HP 486 turne the eyes of all the world upon theyr actions
HP 678 suche like filth pleaseth not their husbands eyes
Cor. Arg. 13 before her eyes, and in the presence of his young Sonne
Cor. 224 O eyes, and will yee (cause I cannot dry your
Cor. 277 and of the sinne that ceeleth up thine eyes
Cor. 426 that rydes upon the mysts, scarce moysteneth mine eyes
Cor. 453 anothers teares draw teares fro forth our eyes
Cor. 528 (to fright us) sette pale death before our eyes
Cor. 650 hath bath'd your blubbred eyes in bitter teares
Cor. 703 gan close the windowes of my watchfull eyes
Cor. 711 but all amaz'd, with fearefull, hollow eyes
Cor. 754 dyd with hys flight unclose my feareful eyes
Cor. 934 mine eyes have seene what I in hart desir'd
Cor. 977 fresh springs of water at my weeping eyes
Cor. 982 nor dryes the heate the moysture of mine eyes
Cor. 1022 that (blynd herselfe) can bleare our eyes
Cor. 1329 while gazing eyes at crownes grow dim
Cor. 1578 and in thys direful warre before mine eyes
Cor. 1702 with blubbred eyes and handes to heaven uprear'd
Cor. 1709 theyr harts and eyes lye hovering over us
Cor. 1751 a fearfull Hagge, with fier-darting eyes
Cor. 1786 with bristled backs, and fire-sparkling eyes
Cor. 1990 valing your Christall eyes to your faire bosoms
Jer. 21 rise higher and greater in thy Soveraines eies
Jer. 186 be woman in all partes, save in thy eies
Jer. 263 I will make way to Bellimperias eies
Jer. 710 the first object mine eies met was
Jer. 753 unwise he still pursued it with blind lovers eies
Jer. 1146 alas, I pitty Bellimperias eies
ST Bal. 134 with weeping eyes and mournefull hart
ST 210 he never pleasd his fathers eyes till now
ST 347 then heare that truth which these mine eyes have seene
ST 368 wast Spanish gold that bleared so thine eyes
ST 479 on whose aspect mine eyes finde beauties bowre
ST 725 O sleepe, mine eyes, see not my love prophande
ST 728 watch still, mine eyes, to see this love disjoynd
ST 860 for in my troubled eyes now maist thou read
ST 980 for once these eyes were onely my delight
ST 1088 these eies beheld, and these my followers
ST 1130 Oh eies, no eies, but fountains fraught with teares
ST 1151 eies, life, world, heavens, hel, night and day
ST 1565 what have I heard, what have mine eies behelde?
STA 2042 is there no trickes that comes before thine eies?
ST 2134 thou must enjoyne thine eies to observation
ST 2162 with mournefull eyes and hands to heaven upreard?
ST 2177 heere, take my handkercher, and wipe thine eies
ST 2230 to wring more teares from Isabellas eies
ST 2258 thy eies are gum'd with teares, thy cheekes are wan
ST 2368 and cleare them up with those thy sunne bright eyes
ST 2760 whose eies compell, like powrefull Adamant
SP 265 and with impartiall eyes behold your deedes

SP 603 if wilfull folly did not blind mine eyes
SP 632 onely to feed mens eyes with vaine delight?
SP 638 thou canst not teach their eyes to wound their hearts
SP 777 ah, how thine eyes can forge alluring lookes
SP 904 dasell mine eyes, or ist Lucinas chaine?
SP 1180 that what my heart desires, mine eyes may view
SP 1365 I coucht my selfe in poore Erastus eyes
SP 1460 quick lampelike eyes, like heavens two brightest orbes
SP 1474 how can mine eyes dart forth a pleasant looke
SP 1476 if tongue with griefe, and eyes with teares be fild
SP 2146 contemplate, until mine eyes shall surfet by my gasing
Ard. 12 and those foul objects that offend mine eyes!
Ard. 1016 then fix his sad eyes on the sullen earth
Ard. 1018 now will he cast his eyes up towards the heavens
Ard. 1315 and put another sight upon these eyes
Ard. 1466 first did she cast her eyes down to the earth
Ard. 1657 driven him out at doors with a wet pair of eyes
Ard. 1687 unless my feet see better than my eyes
Ard. 2001 these mine eyes, offended with his sight, shall never close
Ard. 2029 come, Black Will, that in mine eyes art fair
JB 15 we see it put in execution daylie before our eyes
JB 221 the man to be hanged in the same place before her eyes
ST 85 heere, I wot not how, in twinkling of an e.
SP 1308 but he was gone in twinckling of an e.
Cor. 1357 neither Phoebus fairest e., feasts
SP 631 and by the world's bright e. first brought to light
SP 1199 for looking but a scue at heavens bright e.

Eyebrows.

Jer. 116 upon whose eie browes hangs damnation
STA 2067 and let their eie-browes juttie over
SP 1459 small pensild eye browes, like two glorious rainbowes

Eyed.

SP 46 but her Erastus over-eied her sporte?
SP 1943 the mightie pinky-ey'd, brand bearing God
Ard. 690 hawk-nosed and very hollow-e.

Eyesight.

Ard. 1083 obscures us from the e. of the world

F.

Fabii.

Cor. 1367 nor of the F., or Fabritians

Fabritians.

Cor. 1367 nor of the Fabii, or F.

Fabulously.

ST 2819 that this is f. counterfeit

Face.

HP 672 dyswade her from such muddy making faire her f.
HP 1351 as the nose uppon some mans f., growing by disorder
HP 1683 in the sweate of thy f. thou shalt eate thy bread
Cor. 158 farre from our harts, for stayning of our f.
Cor. 1627 and call our souldiers cowards to theyr f.
Jer. 382 why should my f., thats placed above my mind
Jer. 665 his garments, ha, like mine ; his f. made like
ST Bal. 52 joying in sight of others f.
STA 1071 and all those Starres that gaze upon her f.
STA 1984 in my boyes f. there was a kind of grace
ST 2150 now must I beare a f. of gravitie
ST 2237 within thy f. my sorrowes I may see
ST 2411 Ile meet him f. to f., to tell me so
SP 96 bearing in his f. the empresse of a noble warriour
SP 334 now, by the marble f. of the Welkin
SP 376 charactered with ages print upon thy warlike f.
SP 378 and let me see the f. that vanquished me
SP 380 I long to see thy f., brave warriour
SP 1181 this f. of thine shuld harbour no deceit
SP 1500 her f. is coverd over quite, my Lord

SP 1685 not daring looke me in the marshall f.
SP 1821 why f. to f. expresse you not the treasons
Ard. 864 seest thou this gore that cleaveth to my f.?
Ard. 892 how chance your f. is so bloody?
Ard. 985 her faults, methink, are painted in my f.
Ard. 1045 staring and grinning in thy gentle f.
Ard. 1053 the wrinkles in his foul death-threat'ning f.
Ard. 1132 cut not the nose from off the coward's f.
Ard. 1387 then ask me if my nose be on my f.
Ard. 1469 and modestly she wipes her tear-stained f.
Ard. 1675 scratch you by the f. with my bramble-bush
HP 697 neyther are their faces shadowed with beards
HP 699 youthes, uppon whose faces hayre never came
Cor. 1715 may perrish in the presse before our faces
SP 382 faire Ladies should be coye to showe their faces

Faced.

Jer. 577 Andreas selfe, so legd, so facst, so speecht
STA 1969 and yonder pale f. Hee-cat there, the Moone
Ard. 689 A lean-f. writhen knave
Ard. 1039 that grim-f. fellow, pitiless Black Will
Ard. 1481 or will this black-f. evening have a shower?

Faciei.

HP 662ª Ovid De med. f. Certus amor moru[m] est

Faciunt.

ST 999 Aut si qui f. annorum oblivia

Fact.

ST 1102 upon report of such a damned f.
ST 1331 he that is apprehended for the f.
Ard. 1458 she being reprehended for the f.
JB (Title) for which f. she was burned, and he hanged in
JB 8 to accuse Caine for so fowle a f.
JB 216 she co[n]fessed the f. in order, as I have declared

Faction.

Cor. Arg. 24 Spayne, where Pompeys F. commaunded

Factor.

HP 1177 or abused by his F., beeing a Merchaunt
HP Ind. 70 factors and surveighors and overseers
HP 1510 leaving the care of them to Factors

Faculty.

HP 1427 the facultie of getting may be Natural
HP 1748 for the manner and facultie of eyther is alike

Fade.

VPJ 52 thou look'dst for life, yet lewdlie forc'd it f.
Cor. 576 and what now florisheth, must f.
Cor. 577 and that that fades, revive at last

Fail.

HP 906 if he chaunce to faile in action, co[m]lines, or utteraunce
Jer. 15 Ile speake in drops, when I do faile in words
ST 675 be therefore wise, and faile me not
ST 1239 Bid him not faile. — I fly, my Lord
SP 1222 throw not downe thy weapons, as if thy force did faile
Ard. 1619 if all the rest do f., will catch Master Arden
SP 415 when valour failes, then gould must make the way

Failed.

HP 1716 and heerein onely fayled his discourse
Cor. 342 for Heaven and Time have faild in power to
Cor. 689 Fortune is fickle. — But hath fayld him never
ST 2837 all fled, faild, died, yea, all decaide with this

Failing.

Ard. 2149 marry, sir, there's two for f.
Jer. 366 here is my gage, a never fayling pawne
SP 512 lay my never f. siege to win that plot
SP 2190 stung them both with never f. love

Fain.

Cor. 234 fayne would I die, but darksome ugly Death
Cor. 1772 and thrice the best of both was faine to breathe

ST 1457 thou wouldst faine furnish me with a halter
ST 1828 the King sees me, and faine would heare my sute
SP 984 thou art a bondman, and wouldst faine be free?
Ard. 269 and *f.* would have your husband made away
Ard. 1029 he is, and *f.* would have the light away
Ard. 2372 at last be *f.* to go on board some hoy

Faint.

Cor. 535 tis not for frailtie or *f.* cowardize that
SP 89 and, when long combat makes my body *f.*
SP 238 insomuch that my Steed began to *f.*
SP 366 by the faith of a squire, he is a very *f.* knight
Ard. 1982 Mosbie, perceiving this, began to *f.*

Faint-hearted.

Cor. 14 faint-harted do those liberties enthrall
SP 1305 Erastus, that faint hearted run away
Ard. 2053 tush, you are too *f.*; we must do it

Fainting.

ST 821 although my *f.* hart controles my soule
SP 91 and add fresh courage to my *f.* limmes

Faintly.

Cor. 411 faintlie redoubled ev'ry feeble stroke
Cor. 1622 and therefore (*f.* skyrmishing) in craft

Fair.

VPJ 15 these foure faire giftes (O Prince, of right renound)
HP 84 we entred into a faire Hall
HP 96 ‹ faire and passing well placed › (quoth I) ‹ is this
HP 153 contents the world, cause faire they seeme
HP 625 beautified with many faire and necessary vertues
HP 671 dyswade her from such muddy making faire her face
HP 673 those that are faire with that filthy spunging
HP 675 desirous to seeme faire to please others
HP 689 the Hart with his fayre and bushie braunched hornes
HP 703 who of all the other Gods were most fayre
HP 718 fayre, yong, equall in estate with thee
HP 761 faire wordes, pleasing fashyons, and daintie whispering speech
Cor. (Title) Pompey the Great, his faire Corneliaes Tragedie
Cor. Ded. 16 this faire president of honour
Cor. Arg. 33 where this most faire and miserable Ladie, having
Cor. 216 and for faire Corne-ground are our fields surcloid
Cor. 328 by the former course of thy faire deeds
Cor. 386 but (wishing) could not find so faire an end
Cor. 497 faire Ilium, razed by the conquering Greekes
Cor. 880 I bring to faire Cornelia to interr
Cor. 903 and let fayre Nylus (wont to nurse your Corne)
Cor. 1352 more fam'd then Tyger or swift Euphrates?
Cor. 1497 O Faire Sunne, that gentlie smiles from
Cor. 1505 and faire Venus, thou of whom the Eneades are come
Cor. 1634 where before faire Tapsus, he made his
Cor. 1776 to winne the love of some faire Lyonesse
Cor. 1811 as in the faire Calabrian fields when Wolves
Cor. 1982 that made the fayre Thrasymene so dezart
Cor. 1990 vaiing your Christall eyes to your faire bosoms
Jer. 18 what, doth it not promise faire?
Jer. 558 as the faire cheeke of high authority
Jer. 580 welcome, faire Lord, worthy embassador
Jer. 813 O, be as fortunate as thou art faire
Jer. 1009 he promised to meete faire, and single me out
ST 73 which brought me to the faire Elizian greene
ST 78 whereat faire Proserpine began to smile
ST 102 from whose faire influence such justice flowes
ST 253 he spake me faire, this other gave me strokes
ST 437 humbly to serve faire Bel-imperia
ST 477 in whose faire answere lyes my remedy
ST 610 by force, or faire meanes will I cast about
ST 623 reward, not with faire words, but store of golden coyne

ST 712 thus in the midst of loves faire blandishments
ST 741 speak thou faire words, ile crosse them with faire words
ST 806 to winne faire Bel-imperia from her will
ST 830 sweet, say not so; faire fortune is our freend
ST 977 faire worthy sonne, not conquerd, but betraid
ST 1014 and they abuse *f.* Bel-imperia
ST 1484 I, and many a faire yeere after
ST 1544 the fellow had a faire commission to the contrary
ST 1734 then, faire, let Balthazar your keeper be
ST 1842 this way, or that way : — soft and faire, not so
ST 1907 nay, soft and faire; you shall not neede to strive
ST 1975 provoke them not, faire sir, with tempting words
ST 2242 thy faire crimson coloured spring with withered winter to be
ST 2298 faire Bel-imperia, with my Balthazar
ST 2369 wherein my hope and heavens faire beautie lies
ST 2758 in reserving this faire Christian Nimph
ST 2782 love betwixt Erasto and faire Perseda
ST 2797 faire Queene of beautie, let not favour die
ST 3014 faire Isabella by her selfe misdone
ST 3027 Ile lead faire Isabella to that traine
ST 3030 joyes that vestall Virgins and faire Queenes possesse
SP 166 like welcome unto thee, faire Knight of Fraunce
SP 267 the faire demeanor of these warlike Knights
SP 290 faire Ladie
SP 382 faire Ladies should be coye to showe their faces
SP 391 thrive, faire beginner, as this time doth promise
SP 643 came short in reaching of faire honors marke
SP 667 O holy oath, faire hand, and sugred kisse
SP 704 not Mars himselfe had eare so faire a Buckler
SP 796 is she more faire then I? Thats not my fault
SP 1043 faire Love, according unto thy commaund
SP 1179 stand up, faire Knight, that what my heart desires
SP 1277 returne him back, faire starres, or let me die
SP 1278 returne him backe, *f.* heavens, or let me die
SP 1406 nor all my faire intreats and blandishments?
SP 1420 faire blossome, likely to have proved good fruite
SP 1424 and faire Perseda murthered or deflowerd
SP 1457 faire lockes, resembling Phoebus radiant beames
SP 1470 now, faire Virgin, let me heare thee speake
SP 1635 and faire Lucina Queene of Tripolie
SP 1730 humble himselfe at faire Persedas feete
SP 1795 ah that Perseda were not half so faire
SP 1886 this is a faire warning for me to get me gon
SP 2126 Is she not faire? — Even in the houre of death
SP 2207 wheres faire Perseda, but in my triumph?
Ard. 46 intreat her *f.*; sweet words are fittest engines
Ard. 508 so *f.* a creature should be so abused
Ard. 544 think you that maids look not for *f.* words?
Ard. 548 and if *f.* Susan and I can make a gree
Ard. 1317 which thou art not *f.*, I viewed thee not till now
Ard. 1322 but mads me that ever I thought thee *f.*
Ard. 1580 so, *f.* weather after you
Ard. 1765 if prayers and *f.* entreaties will not serve
Ard. 1822 seeks by *f.* means to redeem old faults
Ard. 2029 come, Black Will, that in mine eyes art *f.*
Ard. 2031 instead of *f.* words and large promises
Ard. 1957 and, when my husband walks into the *f.*
Ard. 1992 Greene and we two will dog him through the *f.*
HP 1503 which for the most part are called Fayres or Marts

Fairer.

HP 700 are fayrer and farre more lovely then those of bearded men
ST 847 I, thou art Venus, or some *f.* starre
SP 701 that I was fairest, and yet Perseda *f.*
SP 1566 now is she *f.* then she was before

Fairest.
Cor. 1285 shall bring the *f.* flowers that grow in Rome
Cor. 1557 neither Phoebus *f.* eye, feasts
ST 394 for glorious cause still aiming at the *f.*
SP 691 the *f.* shine that shall this day be seene
SP 701 that I was *f.*, and yet Perseda fairer
Fairest-shaped.
SP 742 the fairest shaped but fowlest minded man
Fair-spoken.
SP 2134 faire spoken, wise, courteous, and liberall
Fair-springing.
SP 2112 faire springing Rose, ill pluckt before thy time
Faith.
Eng. Parn. 10 who neither fayth, honour, nor right respects
VPJ 46 thy *f.* bare fruit as thou hadst faithles beene
HP 651 from breaking of her *f.* unto her Husbande
Cor. 34 but *f.* continues not where men command
Cor. 260 if (like a royall Dame) with *f.* fast kept
Cor. 272 those powers, those spirits (mov'd with my light *f.*)
Cor. 554 to leave the place and falsefie his *f.*
Jer. 988 by thy worthy bloud, thy honored *f.*
ST 321 my late ambition hath distaind my *f.*
ST 322 my breach of *f.* occasiond bloudie warres
ST 822 why, make you doubt of Pedringanos *f.*?
ST 1257 nor shall they live, for me to feare their *f.*
SP 366 now, by the *f.* of a squire, he is a very
SP 1401 if captivate, then forst from holy *f.*
SP 1402 if forst from *f.*, for ever miserable
SP 1404 and God is lost, if *f.* be overthrowne
SP 2061 and heere I promise thee on my Christian *f.*
Jer. 126 I *f.*, my deare bosome, to take solemne leave
Jer. 217 as there are paths to hell, and thats enow, ifaith
Jer. 744 *f.*, by my selfe, my short sword, and the devill
Jer. 1040 that were proud steele, yfaith, that should
STA 1200 y'fayth my Lord, tis an idle thing I must confesse
ST 1472 *f.*, you have reason
ST 1487 *f.*, I cannot tell, nor I care not greatly
ST 2538 you have given me cause ; I, by my *f.*, have you
ST 2568 in *f.*, Hieronimo, and you be in earnest
SP 329 by my *f.*, me thought it was excellent
SP 426 a shrewd losse, by my *f.*, sir
SP 971 *f.*, sir, for pure good will
SP 1009 *f.*, in a mummery, and a pair of false dice
SP 1076 no, by my *f.*, sir
SP 1353 I *f.*, sir, no
SP 1381 *f.*, maister, me thinkes you are unwise that you
SP 1672 *f.*, I am wearie of the office alreadie
SP 1970 *f.*, two great Knights of the post swore
SP 2027 *f.*, he can doe little that cannot speake
Ard. 354 by my *f.*, sir, you say true
Ard. 596 a match, i'*f.*, sir : ay, the day is mine
Ard. 779 *f.*, friend Michael, this is very ill
Ard. 900 but say, i'*f.*, what, if I should?
Ard. 1078 ay, by my *f.*; the air is very cold
Ard. 1395 yes, *f.*, and of a lordaine, too, as big as
Ard. 1598 i'*f.*, to keep her from the painter
Ard. 1609 *f.*, 'tis too weak, and therefore
Ard. 1759 *f.*, Dick Reede, it is to little end
Ard. 1923 *f.*, in a manner I have
Ard. 1986 *f.*, I was so amazed, I could not strike
Ard. 2007 *f.*, Alice, no longer than this night
Ard. 2240 *f.*, friend Michael, and thou sayest true
Ard. 2417 *f.*, I care not, seeing I die with Susan
Jer. 845 that owe your lives, your faiths, and services
Faithful.
Cor. 2030 where (languishing) my fumous, *f.* teares

SP 563 and did discharge a faithfull subjects love
SP 2209 wheres faithfull Piston, but in my triumph?
Faithless.
VPJ 46 thy faith bare fruit as thou hadst faithles beene
Cor. 267 from my first husband stole my faithles griefe
Cor. 888 O faithles hands, that under cloake of love did
Cor. 1379 the faithles Moore, the fierce Numidian
SP 728 were faithlesse swaines and worthie no respect
Falchion.
Cor. 393 if he had died, his fauchin in his fist
Cor. 1879 dye bravely, with their fauchins in their fists
ST 2621 a black mustacio, and a Fauchion
Ard. 1160 with *f.* drawn, and bent it at my breast
Falcons.
SP 56 marking my times as Faulcons watch their flight?
Fall.
VPJ 40 thy feast of joy is finisht with thy *f.*
HP 1188 their price and profits rise and *f.*
Cor. Arg. 28 and for hee woulde not *f.* alive into the hands of
Cor. 111 (exasperate with our up-rising) sought our Citties *f.*
Cor. 173 which with their noisome *f.* corrupt the ayre
Cor. 202 and by desert mightst *f.* to Phlegiton
Cor. 446 with more ease, the more indifferently that they *f.*
Cor. 569 have both theyr rising and theyr *f.*
Cor. 788 art conquer'd now with an eternall *f.*
Cor. 1000 for I had died before the *f.* of Rome
Cor. 1301 when he lets his just wrath *f.*
Cor. 1731 and with theyr *f.* the trembling earth was shaken
Jer. 157 ere more wretches *f.*, or walke on stilts
Jer. 383 my face, thats placed above my mind, *f.* under it?
Jer. 612 then *f.* into your former vaine of termes
Jer. 1026 so fast they *f.*, so fast to fate life yeelds
ST 138 both battailes joyne and *f.* to handie blowes
ST 515 now, Lordings, *f.* too ; Spaine is Portugall
ST 578 and she in time will *f.* from her disdaine
ST 703 but in his *f.* ile tempt the destinies
ST 730 live, hart, to joy at fond Horatios *f.*
ST 859 thus Elmes by vines are compast till they *f.*
ST 2224 shew me one drop of bloud *f.* from the same
ST 2671 now shall I see the *f.* of Babylon
STA 2977 *f.*, heaven, and cover us with thy sad ruines
SP 484 didst thou advance me for my greater *f.*?
SP 505 as stormes that *f.* amid a sun shine day
SP 1040 and then and there *f.* downe amid his armes
SP 1512 and made him *f.* from skirmishing to kissing
Ard. 995 if neither of these two do haply *f.*
Ard. 1686 I shall *f.* into some ditch or other
Ard. 1747 in case we *f.* into a second fog
Ard. 1805 even in that fearful time would I *f.* down
Ard. 1999 I could have took the weapon thou let'st *f.*
Ard. 2182 this wench doth nothing : *f.* unto the work
JB 52 she concluded, on condition he would let his Action **fal**
Jer. 426 this fals out rare ; in this disguise I may
Jer. 431 all fals out for the purpose : all hits jumpe
Jer. 979 his sword so fals upon the Portugales, as he
ST 150 heere falles a body scindred from his head
STA 1948 then starting in a rage, falles on the earth
SP 1061 then fals he downe, poore wretch, upon his knee
Ard. 1635 and, being touched, straight falls unto the earth
Ard. 2351 speaks as it falls, and asks me why I did it
Jer. 895 eare Sunne *f.*, shall pay deere trybute
Fallen.
VPJ 28 my fruite is falne, and yet my leaves are greene
HP 459 upon some common fault are *f.* into mis-fortunes
HP 618 *f.* into the handes of a perpetuall enemie
STA 1966 his weapon would have fall'n and cut the earth

ST 3018 my Bel-imperia falne as Dido fell
Cor. 707 with a ghastly looke, all pale and brawne-falne

Falling.

Cor. 198 *f.* as thick (through warlike crueltie) as eares of Corne
Cor. 1580 and endles numbers *f.* by my side
SP 87 from water pits, or *f.* in the fire
SP 751 hinder my teares from *f.* on the ground
Ard. 1799 which *f.* down light on the shooter's head

Fallunt.

Puck 71 qui tum cum maximé *f.*

False.

Cor. 777 some *f.* Daemon that beguild your sight
Cor. 833 why from Molossus and *f.* Hanibal have yee
Cor. 946 Photis and *f.* Achillas he beheaded
Jer. 648 it must not be ; I play to falce a part
Jer. 709 belike twas *f.* Andrea, for
ST Bal. 97 but *f.* Lorenzo put mee out
ST 365 *f.*, unkinde, unthankfull, traiterous beast
ST 1106 say, *f.* Villuppo, wherefore didst thou thus falsly
ST 1215 feare or flattering words may make him *f.*
ST 1578 O *f.* Lorenzo, are these thy flattering lookes ?
ST 3013 *f.* Pedringano hangd by quaint device
ST 3049 *f.* Pedringano, for his trecherie, let him be
SP 708 ah, *f.* Erastus, how am I betraid
SP 726 ah, *f.* Erastus, full of treacherie
SP 753 ah, *f.* Erastus, how had I misdoone
SP 783 for this thy perjurde *f.* disloyalty
SP 791 ah, *f.* Erastus, how had I misdone
SP 826 and they are all as *f.* as thou thy selfe
SP 879 go without the chaine, unlesse you carrie *f.* dice
SP 881 nay, I use not to go without a paire of *f.* Dice
SP 902 but is there no reward for my *f.* dice ?
SP 905 *f.* treacher, lay downe the chaine
SP 965 how art thou misdone by *f.* Erastus
SP 1009 faith, in a mummery, and a pair of *f.* dice
SP 1098 Erastus usde such dice, as, being *f.*
SP 1861 and mischiefe light on me, if I sweare *f.*
SP 2206 wheres falce Lucina, but in my triumph ?
Ard. 21 not strange that women will be *f.* and wavering
Ard. 212 try me whom thou ne'er found *f.* ?
Ard. 528 or count me *f.* and perjured whilst I live
Ard. 592 how now, Clarke ? have you found me *f.* ?
Ard. 1740 with making *f.* footing in the dark
Ard. 2238 and there are many *f.* knaves abroad

Falsehood.

HP 391 they practise never so little falshood
Ard. 196 before I saw that *f.* look of thine

Falsely.

ST 1074 or for thy meed hast *f.* me accusde
ST 1107 thus falsly betray Lord Alexandros life ?
ST 1572 though falsly they have wrongd both her, my selfe

Falsify.

Cor. 554 to leave the place, and falsefie his faith

Fame.

VPJ 9 good fortune and an everlasting *f.* attend on thee
Cor. 180 warre, that hath sought Th' Ausonian *f.* to reare
Cor. 265 Pompey, the *f.* that ranne of thy frayle honors
Cor. 1124 then (arm'd) to save their freedom and their *f.* ?
Cor. 1278 his glory, spred abroade by *F.* on wings of
Cor. 1341 through *f.*, which hee of stranger Nations wins ?
Cor. 1364 Caesar is now earthes *f.*, and Fortunes terror
Cor. 1417 they sought t'eclipse thy *f.*, but destinie
Cor. 1693 to purchase *f.* to our posterities
Jer. 735 villaine hath his *f.* as well as a great courtier
Jer. 938 therefore, Andrea, as thou tenderst *f.*
SP 177 for *f.* doth sound thy valour with the rest

SP 416 O cursed Fortune, enemy to *F.*
SP 1166 thy vertuous *f.* and mine owne miserie
Ard. 1300 and if you stand so nicely at your *f.*
ST Bal. 20 prickt forth by fames aspiring wings

Famed.

Cor. 309 made thy name be farre more fam'd and feard
Cor. 1352 more fam'd then Tyger or fayre Euphrates ?
Cor. 1397 discent of Affrican (so fam'd for Armes)
Cor. 1468 that in so short a time am so much fam'd ?
SP 167 well *f.* thou art for discipline in warre
SP 1144 we may ourselves be famd for vertues

Familiar.

HP 1121 who was so *f.* with Lelius and Scipio
HP 1521 that appertaine unto *f.* or publique cares
Ard. 1835 who is that ? Mosbie ? what, so *f.* ?
Puck 26 that I shold love or be familer frend, wth one so

Familiarity.

SP 1700 incrochest upon my familiaritie without speciall admittance ?

Families.

HP Ind. 68 *f.* or housholdes, of what sorte
HP 872 of housekeeping and government of *f.*
HP 1107 some are placed in care of *f.* and

Family.

HP 472 government of his house and care of his familie
HP 771 to rule theyr *f.* wyth honest and
HP 890 the Housekeeper shall so governe hys familie
HP 993 whereof a house or familie in deede should be
HP 1024 a *f.* well fedde and truely paid
HP 1154 and to maintaine his *f.* with credit
HP 1239 so much as may suffise him and his *f.*
HP 1394 the reformation of the house or familie none other then
HP 1536 the Housekeeper and the *f.* that he is charged withall
HP 1572 not as a Phisition but as a father of a familie
HP 1574 and see his familie and servaunts busied
HP 1741 is as little as a rich mans familie
HP 1748 to governe a Princes houshold as a private familie
Cor. 678 by whom our *f.* hath bene adorn'd

Famine.

Cor. 176 maigre famin, which the weake foretell
Cor. 900 pestered with battaile, *f.*, and perpetuall plagues
Cor. 1188 th' infectious plague, and Famins bitternes

Famish.

Cor. 994 torture mee, pull me in peeces, *f.*, fire mee up

Famished.

Jer. 115 whose famisht jawes look like the chap of death

Famous.

HP 48 Naples, a *f.* Cittie of Italie
HP 496 the weight of his so *f.* Monarchie
HP 1624 obtained in many *f.* Citties
Cor. 1332 whose honor, got by *f.* victories, hath
SP 327 prettie, prettie, but not *f.*
SP 1321 weele gaine a glorious death or *f.* victorie

Famulasque.

HP 1326 noctem addens operi, *f.* ad lumina longo

Fancy.

SP 63 to hasty lovers whose *f.* soone is fled
Ard. 1099 bugs and fears shall kill our courages with their fancy's work

Fantasies.

Ard. 1180 to such as note their nightly *f.*

Fantasy.

HP 685 neyther should a womans fantasie so sharplie be offended
Ard. 1174 this *f.* doth rise from Michael's fear

Far.

HP Ind. 48 and how farre it dooth concerne a

HP 23 not *f.* hence, neere that River
HP 60 it farre surpast the wonted limmits
HP 78 not *f.* situate from the Riverside
HP 280 and theyr fatte is farre more naturall
HP 382 the springe so farre inferior to Autumn
HP 593 ordeined betwixt men and women farre exceedeth it
HP 700 fayrer and farre more lovely then those of bearded men
HP 1113 but these doo farre differ from the other
HP 1213 whether the Landes or possessions lye neere or *f.*
HP 1227 or *f.* from frequence or resort of Passengers
HP 1733 should farre surpasse that Pallace for a Prince
Cor. 158 farre from our harts, for stayning of our face
Cor. 309 made thy name be farre more fam'd and feard
Cor. 725 farre from the common hazard of the warrs
Cor. 1143 exceeds all loves, and deerer is by farre
Cor. 1178 and traveled too farre to leave it so
Cor. 1325 lives most happilie that, free and farre from majestie
Jer. 309 Lorenzo has a reach as *f.* as hell
ST 6 yet inferiour *f.* to gratious fortunes of my
ST 32 not farre from hence, amidst then thousand soules
ST 846 if Cupid sing, then Venus is not farre
ST 1043 farre more inconstant had you thought the Sunne
ST 1801 oh, forbeare, for other talke for us *f.* fitter were
ST 1816 not *f.* from thence, where murderers have
ST 2916 avenged with greater *f.* than these afflictions
STA 2959 revenged with greater *f.* then these afflictions
SP 81 and *f.* more welcome is this change to me
SP 418 by overthrowing him that *f.* hath spred thy praise
SP 562 and, *f.* from flattery, I spoke my minde
SP 582 and to the purpose, *f.* from flattery
SP 716 no, no ; her beautie *f.* surpasseth mine
SP 722 tis *f.* from noble thoughts to tyrannise over a
SP 1709 did I turne Turke to follow her so *f.?*
Ard. 280 some other poison would do better *f.*
Ard. 550 as *f.* as either goods or life may stretch
Ard. 1309 whose beauty and demeanour *f.* exceeded thee
Puck 48 when lesse by farr hath dryven so manye
Ard. 73 Arden, leave to urge her over-*f.*

Fare.
HP 1017 to see such grosse or homely kind of *f.*
HP 1022 those relicts and fragme[n]ts of that finer *f.*
ST 1160 and better *f.* then Bel-imperia doth
Ard. 874 so should it *f.* with men of firm resolve
ST 92 now say, L[ord] Generall, how fares our Campe?
SP 759 how fares Perseda, my sweete second selfe?
Ard. 1226 well fares the man, howe'er his cates do taste
Jer. 1180 I never want a *f.* to passe to hell

Fareth.
Cor. 1421 but thus we see it *f.* with the envious

Farewell.
Cor. 1600 *f.*, deere Father
Jer. 94 farwel then, Don Andrea ; to thy chargde
Jer. 187 farewell, my Lord : be mindfull of my love, and
Jer. 273 farwell, true brace of villaynes
Jer. 561 farwell, Jeronimo
Jer. 810 farwell, brave Lords ; my wishes are bequeathd
Jer. 838 harke, the drum beckens me ; sweet deere, farwell
Jer. 842 doot quickly then : farwell
Jer. 842 farwell. O cruell part
Jer. 1086 *f.* deere, dearest Bellimperia
ST 793 commend me to the king, and so *f.*
ST 803 then once againe *f.*, my Lord
ST 804 *f.*, my Lord of Castile, and the rest
ST 1206 why then, *f.*
ST 1823 Why, ha, ha, ha. *F.*, good ha, ha, ha
ST 2669 on, then, Hieronimo ; *f.* till soone

SP 712 why then, *f.* : Fernando, lets away
SP 897 well, then ile looke for you ; till then, *f.*
SP 941 *f.*, my country, dearer then my life
SP 942 *f.*, sweete friends, dearer then countrey soyle
SP 943 *f.*, Perseda, dearest of them all
SP 1115 then, *f.*, sorrow ; and now, revenge, draw neere
SP 1583 *f.*, Erastus : Perseda, *f.* to
SP 1719 *f.*, Constantinople ; I will to Rhodes
SP 1720 *f.*, counterfeit foole
SP 1781 Perseda, *f.* ; be not angrie
SP 1786 she curse me not ; and so *f.* to both
SP 1882 *f.*, Perseda ; no more but that for her
Ard. 131 I'll tell him what you say, and so *f.*
Ard. 205 whose servant thou may'st be ! — and so *f.*
Ard. 409 and so *f.*, sweet Alice, till we meet next
Ard. 410 *f.*, husband, seeing you'll have it so
Ard. 414 Mosbie, *f.*, and see you keep your oath
Ard. 417 your dearest friend, and so *f.*
Ard. 532 till then *f.*
Ard. 535 a happy hand I wish, and so *f.*
Ard. 720 that will I, Master Greene, and so *f.*
Ard. 722 *f.*, Bradshaw ; I'll drink no water
Ard. 1079 Michael, *f.* ; I pray thee dream no more
Ard. 1571 *f.*, sweet Alice, we mind to sup with thee
Ard. 2168 Mosbie, *f.*, and Michael, *f.* too
Ard. 2271 until to-morrow, sweet Alice, now *f.*
Ard. 2380 *f.*, England ; I'll to Flushing now

Farm.
HP 1237 be brought from his Ferme or Mannor in the Countrey
Cor. 1645 Campe of creeping Emmets in a Countrey Farme
Ard. 174 and then the *f.* of Bolton is mine own

Farmers.
Jer. 221 from *f.* that crack barns with stuffing corne

Farther.
ST 1095 these are his highnes *f.* articles

Fashion.
HP 154 if, I, after their *f.*, fill your Table with
HP 250 drest, after our Countrey *f.*, with Larde
HP 784 infancie, apt to be molded of any *f.*
HP 1391 the forme or *f.* of the World is none other then an order
ST 2501 although I beare it out for fashions sake
HP 761 faire wordes, pleasing fashyons, and daintie whispering speech
HP 1115 capable of fashions, or apt to studie or contemplat
HP 1496 the fashions, sleights, and difficulties of transporting

Fashioned.
Jer. 243 let his protestations be fashoned with rich Jewels

Fashioning.
ST 2821 to die to day for *f.* our Scene

Fast.
Cor. 212 or *f.* enough doe foolish men not die
Cor. 260 if (like a royall Dame) with faith *f.* kept
Cor. 710 great Emperors *f.* bound in chaynes of brasse
Cor. 789 now shalt thou march (thy hands *f.* bound behind thee)
Cor. 1761 and nowe better then we retyre as *f.*
Cor. 1802 theyr warlike Armies (*f.* lockt foote to foote)
Cor. 1825 crusht in a Wine-presse, gusheth out so *f.*, as
Jer. 246 not spare an oath without a jewell to bind it *f.*
Jer. 1026 so *f.* they fall, so *f.* to fate life yeelds
ST 2373 but not too *f.*, least heate and all be done
ST 2469 but after them doth Himen hie as *f.*
SP 1827 his Cabine doore *f.* shut, he first began
SP 1881 whose tongue is *f.* tide with galling sorrow
Ard. 771 will cleave as *f.* to your love as a plaster of pitch to
Ard. 1070 are the doors *f.* locked and all things safe ?
Ard. 2262 make the door *f.* ; let them not come in

Fasten.
Ard. 629 I *f.* on my spectacles so close
Ard. 1633 nor with cement to *f.* it in the joints
Fastened.
HP 1100 for that the hand is fastned and united to the bodie
Faster.
ST 839 nay, evill newes flie *f.* still than good
Fast-guarded.
Cor. 775 gates, *f.* by a fell remorceles Monster
Fasting.
Ard. 1666 bargain, and you shall not have it fresh and *f.*
Fat.
HP 280 and theyr fatte is farre more naturall
HP 287 with olde wine and *f.* venison
Jer. 641 like a court hound that liks *f.* trenchers cleane
Fata.
ST 2106 *F.* si miseros juvant, habes salutem
ST 2107 *F.* si vitam negant, habes sepulchrum
Fatal.
Cor. 209 for the fatall dombe the Fates make hast enough
Cor. 739 death dissolve the fatall trouble of my daies
Cor. 1922 O troubled Fate, O fatall misery
ST 2681 bowes of this unfortunate and fatall Pine
ST 2839 they murdred me that made these fatall markes
ST 3047 let Serberine goe roule the fatall stone
SP 584 what dismall Planets guides this fatall hower?
SP 1915 was sooner tumbled from the fatall tower
Ard. 1792 be ruinous and *f.* unto thee!
Fatal-pointed.
Jer. 668 aymes at some fatall pointed tragedy
Fatch.
ST 1353 and no man knowes it was my reaching *f.*
Fate.
Cor. 232 rest where powerfull *f.* in Deaths sad kingdom
Cor. 317 t'embrace thy knees, and, humbled by theyr *f.*
Cor. 1922 O troubled *F.*, O fatall misery
Jer. 99 hard *f.*, when villaines sit not in the highest state
Jer. 163 and fears ill *f.* which heaven hath yet withstood
Jer. 358 not bate an inch of courage nor a haire of *f.*
Jer. 754 then hired he me with gold — O *f.*, thou elfe
Jer. 1026 so fast they fall, so fast to *f.* life yeelds
ST Bal. 28 her love Andreas wofull *f.*
ST 2245 ah, ruthlesse *f.*, that favour thus transformes
Cor. 210 for the fatall dombe the Fates make hast enough
Cor. 262 but partiall Fortune, and the powerful Fates
Cor. 837 what end (O race of Scipio) will the Fates afford
Cor. 1902 O cruell Gods, O heaven, O direfull Fates
Jer. 1069 O my sad fates, Don Pedro weltring in his gore
ST 301 seeks him whome fates adjuge to miserie
SP 655 by Death had been surprisd, if Fates had given me leave
SP 2158 I, fates, injurious fates, have so decreed
SP 2225 for holy fates have graven it in their tables
Father.
HP Ind. 33 devided twixt *F.* and the Mother
HP Ind. 62 appertaines to the Mother as the *F.*
HP 49 my mother a Neapolitan, my *f.* of Bergamo
HP 101 my *F.* is, whom God graunt a long life
HP 113 anon there came the *F.* on horsebacke
HP 127 making neerer to his *F.*, he whisperd to him
HP 243 more acceptable to the Sonne than the *f.*
HP 399 I remember I have hearde my *F.* saie
HP 422 and is indeede the *f.* of all living things
HP 436 of God the *F.* to those inferior Gods
HP 469 my *F.* (loaden both with age and with experience)
HP 476 the dyscourse your *F.* made unto you
HP 480 obeying the gentle commaunds of their *f.*

HP 483 my good *F.*, beeing then threescore and tenne
HP 504 as I was taught not long since of my *F.*
HP 508 twice as much encreased since my *f.* left it
HP 519 a *F.*, a Husband, and a Maister
HP 770 (as a *F.* or Mother, Maister or Maistres of a house)
HP 780 devided so betweene the *F.* and the Mother
HP 797 the *F.* is commau[n]ded to provide this reamedy
HP 854 is, or ought to be, in a manner the care of a *F.*
HP 856 that should prescribe an order to the *F.*
HP 867 to doo in the person of a Husband and a *F.*
HP 882 as is used by the *F.* to the son
HP 1571 not as a Phisition but as a *f.* of a familie
HP 1708 your *f.* hath not onely well and
Cor. (Title) her *F.* and Husbandes downe-cast, death, and fortune
Cor. Arg. 4 died with his *F.* in the disconfiture of the Romains
Cor. Arg. 15 but Scipio her *F.* (beeing made Generall
Cor. 38 the *f.* and the sonne have fought like foes
Cor. 168 for what the *F.* hath deserv'd, we know, is
Cor. 682 and that my *F.* now (in th' Affrique wars)
Cor. 741 but may my *f.* (O extreame mishap)
Cor. 827 *f.* to good Quirinus, our first founder
Cor. 1600 farewell, déere *F.*
Cor. 1846 and Scipio, my *F.*?
Cor. 1942 for, both my husbands and my *F.* gone
Cor. 2006 and last, not least, bereft of my best *F.*
Cor. 2023 entomb'd my drowned *F.* in some Sepulcher
Cor. 2027 no, lovely *F.* and my deerest husband
Jer. 40 Marshall, our kingdome calles thee *f.*
Jer. 275 O my true brested *f.*
Jer. 285 O *f.*, tis a charitable deed to
Jer. 311 O. sprightly *f.*, heele out rech you then
Jer. 319 *f.*, my best indevour shall obay you
Jer. 456 no, *F.*, cleaner then Lorenzoes soule
Jer. 470 'S foot, *F.* ile not write him « honest Lord »
Jer. 479 O, I cry you mercy, *F.*, ment you so?
Jer. 777 he is the court tode, *f.*
Jer. 949 *f.*, I doubt it not
Jer. 982 never had *f.* a more happier boy
ST Bal. 117 unto his *F.* and the King
ST 229 the trespasse that my *f.* made in peace
ST 440 for so the Duke, your *f.*, gave me charge
ST 895 I am thy *F.*; who hath slaine my sonne?
ST 1186 the Duke, my *f.*, hath upon some disgrace
ST 1585 thy cursed *f.*, and thy conquered selfe
ST 1676 his highnes and my *f.* were resolv'd
ST 1710 hath not my *F.* then enquirde for me?
STA 1754 to make a *f.* dote, rave, or runne mad?
ST 2163 come hether, *f.*, let me know thy cause
ST 2167 say, *F.*, tell me what's thy sute?
ST 2190 see heere a loving *F.* to his sonne
ST 2211 come on, olde *F.*, be my Orpheus
ST 2229 to tell thy *f.* thou art unreveng'd
ST 2244 Horatio, thou art older then thy *F.*
ST 2355 my gracious *f.*, beleeve me, so he doth
ST 2374 I see my Lord, my *f.*
ST 2397 Hieronimo, my *f.* craves a word with you
ST 2484 O unkind *f.*, O deceitfull world
ST 2541 to entertaine my *f.* with the like
ST 2826 the hopeles *f.* of a hapless Sonne
Ard. 732 if thou'lt have thy own *f.* slain
Ard. 1363 so, whatsoe'er my Mosbie's *f.* was
HP 112 brought worde of his Father's comming
HP 1701 this was my Father's discourse, gathered
Cor. Arg. 36 the pitteous manner of her Fathers ende
Cor. 719 and seest thy Fathers misery and mine?

Jer. 6 kneele by thy fathers loynes, and thank my leedge
Jer. 16 well spoke, my boy ; and on thy fathers side
Jer. 930 foure precious lines, spoke by our fathers mouth
Jer. 1082 you braved me, Don, within my Fathers court
ST 210 he never pleasd his fathers eyes till now
ST 225 young prince, although thy fathers hard misdeedes
ST 334 then they have slaine him for his fathers fault
ST 498 and learne my F. and my Countries health
ST 617 since I did shield thee from my fathers wrath
ST 749 then be thy fathers pleasant bower the field
ST 761 returne we now into your fathers sight
ST 1698 to thrust Horatio forth my fathers way
ST 1704 my Fathers olde wrath hath exasperate
STA 2973 a youth, one that they hanged up in his father's garden
ST 3011 Horatio murdered in his Fathers bower
SP 557 were it not [that] thou art my fathers sonne
SP 2026 my fathers sonne, my mothers solace, my proper selfe
HP Ind. 40 to the Fathers and Maisters thereof
HP 218 the fathers ought to exceede their children alwaies
HP 228 their Fathers could not match them in
Cor. 16 our fathers hazarded their derest blood
Cor. 28 our fathers found thee at their former walls
Cor. 161 revenge the crymes thy fathers did commit
Cor. 1932 nought but my Fathers death could expiate ?
Cor. 1968 which by our Fathers (pittiles) was spoyl'd
ST 1917 this is the love that Fathers beare their Sonnes
ST 2495 but monstrous Fathers to forget so soone
Jer. 343 answer at next birth our fathers fawltes in heaven
Jer. 847 O, let our fathers scandall nere be seene
Jer. 933 answere at next birth our Fathers faults in heaven

Father-in-law.
HP 739 O my beloued father in law whom I have hourely
    feard

Fatigant.
HP 809 Venatu invigilant pueri, sylvasque f.

Fattened.
HP 282 not so soone puft up and f. as

Fatteneth.
HP 281 Swine, or other Beastes that fatneth by the hande

Fatter.
SP 948 have thanks, but they will make me never the f.

Fatto.
HP 937 Si che son f. uom ligio

Fauchin, see **Falchion.**

Fault.
HP 459 uppon some common f. are fallen into mis-fortunes
Cor. 5 at least to chuse those forth that are in f.
Cor. 1924 say, freatfull heavens, what f. have I committed
Jer. 686 S foot, twas yur f., my lord ; you
ST 334 then they have slaine him for his fathers f.
ST 583 it is my f., not she that merites blame
ST 1251 as for my selfe, I know my secret f.
ST 1317 that by those base confederates in our f.
ST 1439 confesse thy folly, and repent thy f.
ST 1509 God forbid a f. so foule should scape unpunished
ST 2318 thou wouldst be loath that any f. of thine should
SP 432 marry, a foule f. ; but why are his eares cut ?
SP 796 thats not my f., nor her desart
SP 802 but what talke I of her ? the f. is thine
SP 809 whose greatest f. was over loving thee ?
SP 830 myselfe in f., and yet not worthie blame
SP 831 because that Fortune made the f., not Love
Ard. 413 and if he stay, the f. shall not be mine
Ard. 486 God knows 'tis not my f. ; but wonder not
Ard. 1350 weigh all thy good turns with this little f.
Ard. 1874 pardon me, sweet Alice, and forgive this f. !

Ard. 1883 and if sad sorrow taint thee for this f.
Ard. 1902 a f. confessed is more than half amends
Ard. 2347 confess this foul f. and be penitent
JB 198 refusest to make amends for thy f.
ST 1452 dispatch : the faults approved and confest
VPJ 39 thy prime of youth is frozen with thy faults
Jer. 343 answer at next birth our fathers fawltes in heaven
Jer. 933 answere at next birth our Fathers faults in heaven
Ard. 985 her faults, methink, are painted in my face
Ard. 1822 and seeks by fair means to redeem old faults

Faustus.
Cor. 1104 Affranius and F. murdred dyed

Favour.
HP 36 doth f. mee with too noble a conduct
HP 70 I had rather acknowledge this f.
HP 76 that I receive the f. to be lodged
HP 132 as I willingly received thys f. of him
Cor. 109 did f. us with conquering our foes
Jer. 1088 I keepe her faver longer then my breath
ST 430 for twas my f. at his last depart
ST 453 himselfe now pleades for f. at my hands
ST 707 her f. must be wonne by his remoove
ST 708 now, Madame, since by f. of your love
STA 1197 I reserve your f. for a greater honor
ST 1261 and holde on, Fortune, once more f. me
ST 1269 unworthy such a f. may he faile
ST 2245 ah, ruthlesse fate, that f. thus transformes
ST 2557 now would your Lordships f. me so much
ST 2797 faire Queene of beautie, let not f. die
SP 719 by f. and by justice of the heavens
SP 1362 I plast Erastus in the f. of Solyman
SP 1578 whe[n] Erastus doth forget this f., then let him
SP 1868 wherein thou shalt confesse ile f. thee
SP 1872 such f. send all Turkes, I pray God
Ard. 33 but through his f. let him not grow proud
Ard. 377 what f. hast thou had more than a kiss
Ard. 771 who, drunk with the dregs of your f., will cleave
Ard. 1075 get you to bed, and if you love my f.
Ard. 1561 no, begged f. merits little thanks
Ard. 1997 ay, Mistress Arden, this is your f.
JB 23 which, for her f. and comely personage
JB 35 the good will and f. of al her friends and kinsfolk
JB 43 and seeing no hope of her good will and f.
Puck 2 some speaches from you in my favor to my Lorde
Puck 6 the denyall of that favor (to my thought resonable)
Puck 34 thus muche have I (wth yor L^p^e favor)
Cor. Ded. 9 assur'd of your honourable favours past
Cor. 102 for we are proude, when Fortune favours us
Cor. 378 Heavens did theyr favors lavishly bestow
ST 508 and graste with favours of his Majestie
ST 622 now to these favours will I adde reward
STA 984 these be favours which doe assure me he cannot
SP 770 thy favours bore me, not my light foote Steed
Ard. 188 have I for this given thee so many favours
JB 33 earnest suite, the gifts and favours which she received
JB 36 he had her favours whosoever had her frowns
Puck 54 as I maie still reteyne the favors of my Lord

Favourable.
SP 394 whose f. hand hath entred

Favoured.
HP 106 highlie f. of the good Cardinall Vercellis
Cor. 1063 so long thou seem'dst t'have f.
ST 621 thou knowest how I have f. thee

Favourer.
Ard. 932 so shall thy mistress be thy f.

Favourest.

SP 1242 why favourst thou thy countrimen so much
Favourite.
ST 1703 your first *f.* Don Andreas death
Ard. 1324 I am too good to be thy *f.*
Ard. 256 we that are the poets' favourites must have a love
Fawn.
SP 322 better a Dog fawne on me, then barke
Fawning.
Ard. 28 and by his servile flattery and *f.*
Fealty.
Jer. 908 let not wonted *f.* be denayed to our desart
Fear.
HP Ind. 75 feare not commendable in a man
HP 650 onely by shame, love, or feare
HP 652 Feare is as worthy of praise as blame
HP 734 hate or feare thee with the dread wherewith base slaves
HP 735 a kind of feare distinguished from servile base feare
HP 736 as easily accompanied with love as servile feare with hate
HP 737 this feare, which more properly is tearmed shamefast-ness
HP 861 bring them upp in the feare and love of God
Cor. 45 now, Parthia, feare no more, for Crassus death
Cor. 47 nor feare the darts of our couragious troopes
Cor. 53 of whom so many Nations stood in feare
Cor. 289 byd you beware for feare you be beguild
Cor. 429 and if I winck, it is for feare to see the
Cor. 514 a noble minde doth never feare mischaunces
Cor. 520 no feare of death should force us to doe ill
Cor. 521 if death be such, why is your feare so rife ?
Cor. 531 but when, for feare of an ensuing ill, we
Cor. 533 then tis (for feare) that we our selves doe kill
Cor. 534 so fond we are to feare the worlds disgrace
Cor. 543 and (sooth to say) why feare we, when we see
Cor. 544 see the thing we feare lesse then the feare to be ?
Cor. 657 O, but I feare that Fortune seekes new flawes
Cor. 684 but wretched that I am, alas, I feare
Cor. 685 what feare you, Madam ?
Cor. 746 Madam, never feare
Cor. 748 encrease a more then needfull feare in you
Cor. 749 my feare proceeds not of an idle dreame
Cor. 801 for feare you feele a third calamitie
Cor. 913 I feare the heavens will not heare our prayer
Cor. 966 not heavens feare, nor Countries sacred love
Cor. 972 I feare your griefes increase with thys discourse
Cor. 987 I neither stand in feare of him nor his
Cor. 988 t'is pollicie to feare a powrefull hate
Cor. 1094 that seeme to feare a certaine Thunderer
Cor. 1306 therefore he, whom all men feare, feareth all men
Cor. 1308 feare that doth engender hate
Cor. 1313 live in feare of petty things
Cor. 1429 and yet I feare you have too kindly sav'd those that
Cor. 1436 I feare not those that to theyr weapons flye
Cor. 1452 I feare them not whose death is but deferd
Cor. 1453 I feare my foe, untill he be interd
Cor. 1459 whom shall I then not feare
Cor. 1495 the feare of evill doth afflict us more then
Cor. 1658 runnes to the tent, for feare we should be gone
Cor. 1669 he showes that auncient souldiers need not feare
Cor. 1696 for Rome we fight, and those that fled for feare
Jer. 154 and you, I feare me, war, which peace forfend
Jer. 264 to weepe, I feare, but not to tender love
Jer. 313 boy, feare not, I will out stretch them al
Jer. 711 I much feare me, by all signes pretends
Jer. 724 nay, then I feare Spaines inevitable ill
Jer. 900 not that I tast of feare or cowerdyse

ST 116 both furnisht well, both full of hope and feare
ST 391 yet teares and sighes, I feare, will hinder me
ST 558 my Lord, I feare we sit but over long
ST 599 I, but I feare she cannot love at all
ST 639 and feare shall force what freendship cannot winne
ST 684 sad, that I feare she hates me whome I love
ST 835 and in thy love and councell drowne my feare
ST 836 I feare no more ; love now is all my thoughts
ST 879 and chill my throbbing hart with trembling feare
ST 1031 that would be feard, yet feare to be beloved
ST 1061 not that I feare the extremitie of death
ST 1062 (for Nobles cannot stoop to servile feare)
ST 1147 and feare my hart with fierce inflamed thoughts
ST 1211 that hath, I feare, revealde Horatios death
ST 1215 feare or flattering words may make him false
ST 1257 nor shall they live, for me to feare their faith
ST 1271 as for the feare of apprehension, I know
ST 1309 feare of preventing our mishaps too late
ST 1391 for feare the privie whispring of the winde convay
ST 1434 for feare his Lordship had forgotten me
ST 1442 first I confesse, nor feare I death therfore
ST 1727 to love and feare, and both at once, my Lord
ST 1731 but I that feare. — Whome ? — Bel-imperia
ST 1732 feare your selfe ? — I, Brother. — How ?
ST 1733 as those, that what they love, are loath, and feare to loose
ST 1735 no, Balthazar doth feare as well as we
ST 1807 a forrest of distrust and feare
ST 2516 my feare and care in not beleeving it
ST 2694 and passengers, for feare to be infect, shall
SP 724 therefore be blithe, sweet love, abandon feare
SP 757 desire perswades me on, feare puls me back
SP 873 feare not for money, man, ile beare the Boxe
SP 1090 not that I feare, but that I scorne to fight
SP 1287 I speake not this to shrinke away for feare
SP 1352 for feare of servile death, thats but a sport ?
SP 1716 and I feare thou wilt never proove good christian
SP 1931 feare not, my Lord ; Lucina plaies her part
SP 2224 whom Death did feare before her life began
Ard. 130 this may he do without suspect or *f.*
Ard. 139 shalt neither *f.* the biting speech of men
Ard. 182 'tis yet but early days, thou needst not *f.*
Ard. 243 *f.* not ; we'll have that shall serve the turn
Ard. 266 *f.* him not ; leave ; I have talked sufficient
Ard. 508 thus live I daily in continual *f.*
Ard. 972 if *f.* or stormy threats, if love of me
Ard. 974 if *f.* of God or common speech of men
Ard. 1067 my trembling joints witness my inward *f.*
Ard. 1101 and wrongs me too in telling me of *f.*
Ard. 1106 thy speech bewrayed an inly kind of *f.*
Ard. 1174 this fantasy doth rise from Michael's *f.*
Ard. 1592 a *f.* of what ?
Ard. 2089 'twas more for *f.* of you than love of him
Ard. 2146 I *f.* he will spy me as I am coming
Ard. 2159 tush, *f.* him not ; he will be secret
Ard. 2202 *f.* you not, he'll come anon ; meantime
Ard. 2210 I *f.* me, Michael, all will be bewrayed
Ard. 2216 no, but my mistress, for I *f.* she'll tell
Ard. 2217 tush, Michael ; *f.* not her, she's wise enough
Ard. 2227 *f.* not, Mistress Arden, he's well enough
Ard. 2232 and tell him what a *f.* he hath put me in
Ard. 2245 but wherefore should he come ? Here is nought but *f.*
Ard. 2247 alas. I counsel ! *f.* frights away my wits
Ard. 2276 my house is clear, and now I *f.* them not
Ard. 2278 which makes me *f.* our footsteps will be spied
Ard. 2311 I *f.* me you'll prove one of them yourself

Ard. 2313 I *f.* me he was murdered in this house
JB 16 without respect either of the feare of God, or
JB 184 for feare her neighbours should perceave her great bellie
Puck 10 as also in the feare of god, and freedom of my conscience
Puck 68 in all humillitie & in the feare of god
Puck 78 and thus (for nowe I feare me I growe teadious)
Cor. 513 to scape the feares that followes Fortunes glaunces
Cor. 641 Rose : whom (though she see) to crop she kindly feares
Jer. 163 and fears ill fate which heaven hath yet withstood
ST 720 my hart, with feares and hopes long tost
Ard. 1098 sleep, when bugs and fears shall kill our courages

Feared.
HP 739 O my beloved father in law whom I have hourely feard
Cor. 309 made thy name be farre more fam'd and feard
Cor. 522 my works will shew I never feard my life
ST 1031 that would be feard, yet feare to be beloved
SP 1678 nay, if thou hadst, I had not feard thee, I
Ard. 207 that which I ever *f.*, and find too true
Ard. 650 all the camp *f.* him for his villainy
Puck 4 hath yet in his discreeter judgm^t *f.* to offende

Fearest.
Cor. 1438 whom fear'st thou then, Mark Anthony ?

Feareth.
HP 1248 he heares or *f.* any dearth or scarcity
Cor. 1307 therefore he, whom all men feare, *f.* all men

Fearful.
HP 976 those fearefull Hostes which the great Turke mustereth
Cor. 430 the fearefull dreames effects that trouble mee
Cor. 484 fought, before the fearefull Carthagenian walls)
Cor. 646 whose sweeter sleepes are turnd to fearefull dreames
Cor. 691 my fearefull dreames doe my despairs redouble
Cor. 711 but all amaz'd, with fearefull, hollow eyes
Cor. 754 dyd with hys flight unclose my feareful eyes
Cor. 766 downe by the fearefull gates of Acheron
Cor. 1751 a fearfull Hagge, with fier-darting eyes
ST 2444 such fearefull sights, as poore Andrea sees
SP 84 that waiteth for the fearefull stroke of death
Ard. 1060 what hath occasioned such a *f.* cry ?
Ard. 1064 I had a *f.* dream that troubled me
Ard. 1261 'tis *f.* sleeping in a serpent's bed
Ard. 1346 and heard as quickly as the *f.* hare
Ard. 1805 even in that *f.* time would I fall down

Fearfully.
ST 63 the left hand path, declining fearefully

Fearing.
Cor. 1327 he *f.* none, none *f.* him
SP 1657 I, *f.* they would adore me for a God

Fearless.
Cor. 671 with feareles harts do guard our Romaine hopes ?
Cor. 781 downe to the Scithian swift-foote feareles Porters
Cor. 823 and feareles kept us from th' assault of foes
Cor. 1274 and fearles scowres in danger's coasts
ST 654 stand up, I say, and feareles tell the truth

Feast.
VPJ 22 my *f.* of joy is but a dish of paine
VPJ 40 thy *f.* of joy is finisht with thy fall
Jer. 96 lets in to celebrate our second *f.*
ST 288 and *f.* our prisoner as our friendly guest
ST 494 to *f.* the Portingall Embassadour
ST 509 put off your greetings, till our *f.* be done
ST 564 to see him *f.* that gave me my deaths wound ?
Ard. 1213 your penance, to *f.* us all at the Salutation
Ard. 1528 and bids him to a *f.* to his house at Shorlow
HP Ind. 14 beefe at feasts

HP Ind. 71 feasts not forbidden to Women
HP 724 not restraining her from going to feasts
Cor. 1522 Feasts, and Masks, and mirthfull glee
Cor. 1558 feasts, nor friendly company

Feasted.
Cor. 1428 and Crowes are *f.* with theyr carcases

Feathered.
Ard. 1355 my wings are *f.* for a lowly flight

Feats.
ST 350 to winne renowne did wondrous *f.* of armes

Feature.
ST 584 my *f.* is not to content her sight
SP 123 so be thy fortune as thy features serves

Fed.
HP 288 they fedde therof at will without any
HP 1024 a family well fedde and truely paid
Cor. 978 still *f.* by thoughts, lyke floods with winters rayne
STA 1756 he must be *f.*, be taught to goe, and speake

Fee.
ST 274 his ransome therefore is thy valours *f.*
SP 421 give him a Fidlers *f.*, and send him packing
Ard. 851 tell me of gold, my resolution's *f.*
Jer. 69 I am wars Champion, and my fees are swords

Feeble.
Cor. 411 faintlie redoubled ev'ry *f.* stroke
Cor. 1794 who (staggering) fell with every *f.* wound
Cor. 1818 the *f.* bands that yet were left entyre
Ard. 970 let pity lodge where *f.* women lie
Ard. 1223 feebles my body by excess of drink

Feed.
HP 267 desire of Feisants or Partrich, but to feede uppon Beefe
HP 1015 howbeit yet thou art to feede thy Servaunts
HP 1092 being it (indeede) that serves to feede
Cor. 795 now murdred lye for Foule to feede upon
Cor. 1226 blood, to feede this worthles body that you see
Cor. 1915 and feede your selves with mine enflamed blood
ST 294 and *f.* our sorrowes with some inward sighes
ST 710 and that with lookes and words we *f.* our thoughts
SP 632 onely to *f.* mens eyes with vaine delight ?
Cor. 300 nor spareth it what purely feeds the hart
Cor. 921 this is the hope that feeds my haples daies
Jer. 556 the Badger feeds not till the Lyons served
Ard. 953 thus feeds the lamb securely on the down

Fee'd.
Ard. 447 they shall be soundly *f.* to pay him home

Feeding.
Cor. 1543 *f.* still foolish those that doe thy will
ST Bal. 3 *f.* on nought but dire annoyes

Feel.
Cor. 81 when foming billowes feele the Northern blasts
Cor. 801 for feare you feele a third calamitie
Cor. 1984 now (loaden) groane to feele the Romaine corses
Jer. 362 O in that one word such torments do I feele
Jer. 921 what vertue cannot, thou shalt make him feele
ST 2263 and selfe same sorrow feele I for my Sonne
SP 697 shall feele the rigour of my Sword and Launce
SP 2159 for now I feele the poyson gins to worke
SP 2175 ah, now I feele the paper tould me true
JB 132 now I feele my selfe sicke at the very heart
HP 390 onely feeles some losse and discommoditie
Cor. 1250 but Brutus lives, and sees, and knowes, and feeles that

Feeleth.
ST 3028 where pittie weepes, but never *f.* paine

Feeling.
JB 127 *f.* also a grievous griping of his inward partes

Feelingly.

ST 1576 and now I /. perceive they did what

Feet.

HP 9 in so much as it there died at my feete
Cor. 316 Kings to lay their Crownes and Scepters at thy feete
Cor. 709 at his feete beheld great Emperors fast bound
Cor. 1009 her feete, more swift then is the winde
Jer. 1062 this haughtie prince, and wound him at our feete
Jer. 1067 and break our haughty sculs downe to our feete
ST 1592 wearing the flints with these my withered /.
SP 1066 that done, I lay him at my mistres feete
SP 1515 there lyes my sword, humbled at thy feete
SP 1730 humble himselfe at faire Persedas feete
SP 1818 since first I set my /. on Turkish land
SP 2091 I, now I lay Perseda at thy feete
Ard. 1687 unless my /. see better than my eyes
Ard. 1974 now his way had been to have come hand and /.
Ard. 2316 the print of many /. within the snow

Feign.

HP 273 the Poets faigne that Noble men of their time
SP 778 and faine deep oathes to wound poor silly maides
SP 2000 Death, which the poets faine to be pale and meager

Feigned.

HP 271 he faigned or forgat that which properlie
HP 755 Homer faigned that Juno, taking away Venus garter
ST Bal. 155 then fained I my pen was naught
ST 1041 that fained love had coloured in his lookes
ST 1571 that Bel-imperias Letter was not fainde
ST 1572 nor fained she, though falsly they have
ST 1656 under fained jest are things concealde that els would
ST 2461 for in unquiet quietnes is faind

Felicities.

Cor. 563 all fortunes, all /., upon their motion doe

Felicity.

SP 2119 and with her love my hearts felicitie

Fell.

Cor. 406 he almost felt the poygnard when he /.
Cor. 1794 who (staggering) /. with every feeble wound
Cor. 1973 when (fierd) their golden Pallaces /. downe
Jer. 761 I tooke him for Andrea, downe he /.
ST 357 and therewithall Don Balthazar /. doune
ST 358 and when he /., then we began to flie
ST 3018 my Bel-imperia falne as Dido /.
Ard. 766 one day I /. asleep and lost my master's pantofles
Ard. 1062 as I /. asleep, upon the threshold
Ard. 1467 watching the drops that /. amain from thence
JB 125 and she and the childe /. also to eating of theirs
Eng. Parn. 4 a selfe-shaven Dennis, or an Nero /.
Cor. 773 gates, fast-guarded by a /. remorceles Monster
Cor. 944 whose /. ambition (founded first in blood)
ST 29 that leades to /. Avernus ougly waves
ST 136 and stopt the malice of his /. approch
ST 568 Ile turne their freendship into /. despight
ST 1819 fixt by Jove, in his /. wrath
SP 596 could ransome thee from /. deaths tirannie
SP 920 and to acuse /. Fortune, Love, and Death
HP 1422 Tymber of him that fells and seazoneth the wood

Fellow.

HP 540 the name of Consort or Felow is to be attributed to
HP 597 a slave or servaunt, but for a /. and companion
STA 937 I wonder how this /. got his clothes
ST 1366 /., be gone ; my boy shall follow thee
ST 1499 my maisters, you see heers a good /.
ST 1548 the /. had a faire commission to the contrary
STA 2017 what wouldst thou have, good /.? — Justice, Madame
STA 2035 this good /. heere and I will range this
STA 2048 Bazardo, afore-god, an excellent /.

STA 2091 when I am mad : then methinkes I am a brave /.
SP 310 Basilisco — Knight, good /., Knight, Knight
SP 311 Knave, good /., Knave, Knave
SP 901 and, /. Drumsler, ile reward you well
SP 1047 my petty /., where hast thou hid thy maister ?
SP 1085 is this little desperate /. gon ?
SP 1086 doubtlesse he is a very tall /.
Ard. 156 a /. that can both write and read and
Ard. 654 how now, /. Bradshaw ? Whither away so early ?
Ard. 663 you were glad to call me « /. Will »
Ard. 670 you are too proud to be my /.
Ard. 686 going to London upon hope to find the /.
Ard. 730 give my /. George Shakebag and me
Ard. 1039 that grim-faced /., pitiless Black Will
Ard. 1776 Franklin, hearest thou this /. speak ?
HP 1079 love of Servants to their fellowes in their sicknes
Cor. 1710 on then, brave men, my fellowes and Romes friends·
ST 2713 how now, Hieronimo, where's your fellows
SP 1792 come, fellowes, see when this matter comes in question
Ard. 655 O Will, times are changed : no fellows now
Ard. 660 no fellows now ! because you are a goldsmith
Ard. 666 domineer'd with it amongst good fellows
Ard. 672 I would be fellows with you once more, and

Fellow-citizens.

Cor. 1289 that from their fellow cittizens did

Fellowship.

HP 511 and /. of the worlde more then he
HP 635 needful that in the felowship of ma[n] and wife

Fellow-soldiers.

SP 1336 come, fellow Souldiers ; let us to the breach
Ard. 648 at Boulogne he and I were /.
Ard. 638 was not thou and I /. at Boulogne

Felt.

Cor. 406 in mine armes he almost /. the poygnard
JB 128 he tould his wife he /. himselfe not well
Puck 47 my paines and undeserved tortures /. by some
Puck 51 but whatsoever I have /. R[ight] Ho[nourable]

Feltered.

HP 690 the princely Lyon with his proude and feltred locks

Female.

HP 694 more regard to the beauty of the F. then the Male
Jer. 248 gifts and giving will melt the chastest seeming /. living
SP 213 perdie, each /. is the weaker vessell
HP 689 the bodies of the Male be more adorned then the Females
HP 691 feltred locks which the Females never have)

Feminine.

SP 218 may very well beare a /. Epitheton

Fence.

Ard. 1352 a /. of trouble is not thickened still
Ard. 1978 no more strength than I have /.

Fenced.

ST 124 each corner strongly fenst with wings of shot
SP 511 to be well assured by him how Rhodes is fenc'd
SP 1153 then tell me, Brusor, how is Rhodes fenst ?
SP 1160 how ever Rhodes be fencd by sea or land
SP 1695 sooth thou sayest, I must be fencd behinde

Ferdinand.

SP 890 since Signior F. will have it so
SP 962 ah, F., the stay of my old age

Ferdinando.

SP 665 F. is Lucinaes onely joy
SP 668 O never may F. lack such blisse
SP 687 but see, F., where Perseda comes
SP 1012 I, so it did, for it cost F. his life
SP 1017 then F. met us on the way
SP 1019 and there F. had the prickado

SP 1268 *F.* is buried ; your friends commend them to you
SP 934 or suffer death for Ferdinandos death
SP 1245 Phylippos wrath (it must be tould),for Ferdinandos death
Feres.
SP 48 sit sowing with thy *f.*, but I was by
Ferinae.
HP 285 Implentur veteris Bacchi pinguisque *f.*
Fernando.
SP 712 why then, farewell : *F.*, lets away
SP 892 Signior *F.*, I am sure tis you
SP 899 shee tooke me for *F.*, markt you that ?
SP 1091 Fortune, thou madest *F.* finde the chaine
SP 1096 meane time, I brought *F.* on the way
SP 1301 her love *F.* died at the same
SP 1288 for whom weepe you ? — Ah, for Fernandos dying
Ferrara.
HP 1758 the houses of the Dukes of Savoy, *F.*
Ferried.
ST 2443 o'er-*f.* Caron to the flerie lakes
Ferro.
HP 826 Idaeae ; sinite arma viris, et cedite *f.*
Ferry.
Cor. 464 to *f.* those that must be fetcht againe
ST 1896 and Ferrie over to th' Elizian plaines
Ard. 1710 what companies hath passed your *f.*
Ard. 1734 they escaped you, then, and passed the *f.*?
Ferryman.
ST 27 then was the Feriman of Hell content to
Ard. 1644 oh, *f.*, where art thou ?
Ard. 1667 yes, I pray thee, good *f.*
Ferrymen.
Ard. 1582 they'll be your *f.* to long home
Fertile.
Cor. 665 from fertill Italy to proudest Spayne
Fessi.
HP 1066 cerealiaque arma expediunt *f.* rerum
Festivall.
SP 1122 greatest pompe that ere I saw at such a festivall
Fetch.
HP 1067 to *f.* the watrie, rotten Corne
Jer. 231 for, give me duckets, Ile *f.* you duck inough
Jer. 1093 and *f.* Andreas ransome fourth thy vaines
ST Bal. 42 to *f.* her man he doth direct
ST 1050 goe, some of you, and *f.* the traitor forth
ST 2924 *f.* forth the tortures
SP 978 to *f.* the Sexten to bury him, I thinke
SP 1077 then *f.* thy weapons ; and with my single fist
SP 1624 Ill *f.* him backe againe, under couler of
SP 1674 O take me not unprovided, let me *f.* my weapons
SP 1721 Brusor is sent to *f.* my maister back againe
SP 1739 Brusor is sent to *f.* him back againe
SP 2221 *f.* his imperiall Carre from deepest hell
Ard. 88 whilst Michael *f.* our horses from the field
Ard. 143 to *f.* my master's nag
Ard. 2015 I'll *f.* Master Arden home, and we like friends
Ard. 2074 *f.* in the tables, and when thou hast done
Ard. 2083 that's brave. I'll go *f.* the tables
Ard. 2117 sirrah, *f.* me a cup of wine, I'll make them friends
Ard. 2172 and, Susan, *f.* water and wash away this blood
JB 117 to *f.* mee a penny worth of red herrings
ST Bal. 154 the authors of this bloody *f.*
ST 1353 and no man knowes it was my reaching fatch
Fetched.
Cor. 464 to ferry those that must be fetcht againe
Cor. 1216 a fore-game fecht about for civill discord
Ard. 1012 what pity-moving words, what deep-*f.* sighs

Fetching.
ST 827 by *f.* Don Lorenzo to this match
Fever.
Ard. 1591 of a great *f.*
Ard. 1593 a great *f.*
Ard. 1594 a *f.*? God forbid !
Feversham.
Ard. (Title) Master Arden of *F.* in Kent
Ard. 5 all the lands of the Abbey of *F.*
Ard. 461 of all the lands of the Abbey of *F.*
Ard. 718 carry this letter to Mistress Arden of *F.*
Ard. 786 Arden of *F.* hath highly wronged me
Ard. 902 we hear you have a pretty love in *F.*
Ard. 1186 and with the tide go down to *F.*
Ard. 1410 why, so can Jack of *F.*
Ard. 1437 he travelled in such pain to *F.*
Ard. 1522 ay, in health towards *F.*, to shame us all
Ard. 1532 therefore come, Greene, and let us to *F.*
Ard. 1743 get you to *F.* to the Flower-de-luce
Ard. 1774 leave in *F.*, God knows, needy and bare
Ard. 2412 Michael and Bradshaw in *F.* must suffer death
Few.
HP 190 there are *f.* good mellons to be found
HP 255 with these fewe have we furnished a poore Supper
HP 470 a fewe yeeres before his death
Cor. 1642 where *f.* men might doe much, which
Cor. 1665 except some fewe that stayd to guard the Trench
Jer. 429 besids, within these *f.* daies heele returne
ST 93 except some *f.* that are deceast by
ST 199 that all (except three hundred or *f.* more)
SP 1422 except some *f.* that turne to Mahomet
SP 1933 come ; and with some *f.* men lets saile to Rhodes
Fewer.
Jer. 594 the *f.* in a plot of jealousie build a
Fickle.
Cor. 689 Fortune is *f.* — But hath fayld him never
Cor. 1019 *f.* in our adversities
Cor. 1020 and *f.* when our fortunes rise
Cor. 1479 Fortune is *f.*, Heaven imperious
ST 318 and minde more mutable then *f.* windes?
SP 912 ah, *f.* and blind guidresse of the world
Fidler's.
SP 421 give him a Fidlers fee, and send him packing
Fie.
Jer. 449 *f.*: I am a shamed to see it
Jer. 455 *f.*, *f.*, Horatio : what, is your pen foule ?
ST 1845 no, no ; *f.*, no : pardon me, ile none of that
ST 2033 a Comedie ? *f.*, Comedies are fit for common wits
SP 396 *f.* upon thee, extortioner
SP 341 now *f.* upon the Turke
Ard. 510 he looks so smoothly. Now, *f.* upon him, churl !
Ard. 1356 Mosbie ? *f.*! no, not for a thousand pound
Ard. 1648 *f.*, what a mist is here !
Ard. 1797 *f.*, bitter knave, bridle thine envious tongue
Ard. 2414 *f.* upon women ! this shall be my song
Field.
VPJ 23 my crop of corne is but a *f.* of tares
HP 989 they advidse to carry with them to the *f.*
Cor. 1056 with Ausonian blood did die our warlike *f.*
Cor. 1067 when the Pharsalian *f.* he led
Cor. 1087 lyke cocks of Hay when July sheares the *f.*)
Cor. 1169 and lyke rude Brennus brought his men to *f.*
Cor. 1439 that, wanting powre in fielde to conquer you
Cor. 1664 well, forth to *f.* they marched all at once
Cor. 1713 that we may rest the Maisters of the *f.*
Cor. 1741 till, dead or fled, the one forsake the *f.*

Cor. 1816 the *f.* was fild with all confusion
Cor. 1864 to raise newe forces, and returne to *f.*
Jer. 12 if ever you have foes, or red *f.* scars
ST Bal. 14 and wonne great honour in the fielde
ST Bal. 21 did so behave him in the fielde that
ST 746 but, gratious Madame, then appoint the *f.*
ST 749 then be thy fathers pleasant bower the *f.*
ST 856 nay then, to gaine the glory of the *f.*
SP 155 by thy approoved valour in the *f.*
SP 181 when twenty thousand Spaniards were in *f.*
Ard. 88 whilst Michael fetch our horses from the *f.*
Ard. 656 though we were once together in the *f.*
Jer. 905 that must be acted on the feeldes greene stage
HP 1180 (as are Fields, Meadowes, Woods)
Cor. 216 our fields surcloid with worthles Gorse
Cor. 588 were desert fields where none would byde
Cor. 670 that from the Lybique playnes and Spanish fields
Cor. 673 to fill our fields with blood of enemies
Cor. 769 or staies for ever in th' Elisian fields
Cor. 1392 when the Thessalian fields were purpled ore
Cor. 1644 the fields are spred, and as a houshold Campe
Cor. 1811 as in the faire Calabrian fields when Wolves
Cor. 1983 for even those fields that mourn'd to beare their bodies
Jer. 806 trample the fields before you?
Jer. 1025 as sithmen trim the long haird Ruffian fields
ST 42 to walke with lovers in our fieldes of love
ST 47 he died in warre, and must to Martiall fields
ST 60 was ready way unto the foresaid fields
ST 1603 he sleepes in quiet in the Elizian fields
ST 3025 Ile lead my freend Horatio through those feeldes
SP 192 against the Sophy in three pitched fields
Ard. 1934 and carried him about the fields on a coltstaff
Ard. 2270 but first convey the body to the fields
Ard. 2314 murdered in this house and carried to the fields
Fiend.
ST 1059 why linger ye? bring forth that daring feend
ST 1145 the ougly feends do sally forth of hell
ST 1903 for Ile goe marshall up the feendes in hell
SP 2069 for whome hell gapes, and all the ugly feendes do waite
Fierce.
Cor. Arg. 20 was a *f.* and furious battaile given amongst them
Cor. 61 nor yet the *f.* and fiery humor'd French
Cor. 326 since thy hard hap, since thy *f.* destinie
Cor. 385 for oft he search't amongst the *f.* allarms
Cor. 485 both brothers, and both warrs *f.* lightning fiers
Cor. 527 perhaps some *f.*, offended King (to fright us)
Cor. 668 defended our Romaine walls from fury of *f.* kings
Cor. 830 against the Samnites, Sabins, and *f.* Latins?
Cor. 1379 the faithles Moore, the *f.* Numidian
Cor. 1512 firce warrs quenchles fire-brand
Cor. 1775 like two *f.* Lyons fighting in a Desart
Cor. 1852 to beate them downe as *f.* as thundring flints
Jer. 1007 this *f.*, couragious Prince, a noble worthy
ST 1147 and feare my hart with *f.* inflamed thoughts
SP 1051 he knowing your *f.* conditions, hath
Ard. 1451 so *f.* a qualm yet ne'er assailed me
Fiercely.
HP 838 that thou shouldest bring the[m] up so *f.*
Cor. 803 blaze that *f.* burnes a house already fired
Cor. 1105 Juba and Petreus, *f.* combatting, have
Cor. 1804 they *f.* open both Battalions
Cor. 1874 behold, his owne was *f.* set upon
Cor. 1971 when forcefull weapons *f.* tooke away their
ST 691 and with that sword he *f.* waged warre
Fierceness.

Cor. 492 in power and force, and fiercenes, seem'd to threat
Fiercer.
Cor. 50 and civill furie, *f.* then thine hosts
Fiery.
Cor. 20 yea, come they are, and, *f.* as before
Cor. 206 nor all the plagues that fierie Pluto hath
Cor. 512 what good expect wee in a *f.* gap?
Cor. 774 for ghosts of men are lockt in *f.* gates
Cor. 980 I breathe an Autumne forth of *f.* sighes
Cor. 1333 hath fild heavens fierie vaults with fright-full horror
Cor. 1564 with her *f.* poysoned tongues
ST 1612 backt with a troup of *f.* Cherubins
ST 1834 by the dale that flowes with purple gore, standeth a firie Tower
ST 2443 o'er-ferried Caron to the fierie lakes
SP 96 the *f.* Spaniard bearing in his face the
SP 289 this fierie humor of choller is supprest by
Fiery-humoured.
Cor. 61 nor yet the fierce and fiery humor'd French
Fifes.
ST 119 both cheerly sounding trumpets, drums, and *f.*
Fifth.
HP 481 that time that Charles the fift desposed his Monarchie
HP 495 Charles the fift, that thrise renowmed Emperor
Fifty.
HP 116 of midle age, yet neerer threescore then fiftie
Jer. 25 this day my years strike fiftie, and in Rome
Jer. 31 confesse, beard, thou art *f.* full, not a haire lesse
Jer. 26 in Rome they call the *f.* year the year of Jubily
Jer. 29 this shalbe my yeare of Jubily, for tis my *f.*
SP 1157 their horse, I deeme them fiftie thousand strong
Fig.
Ard. 1527 preserved a *f.*! The Lord Cheiny hath preserved him
Fight.
Cor. 399 not dead in *f.*, with pike in hand
Cor. 628 bravely to *f.* in Romes defence
Cor. 1154 made *f.* to death with show of liberty
Cor. 1220 to *f.* for that, that did theyr deaths conclude
Cor. 1347 tell the foming Seas the honour of our *f.*?
Cor. 1416 and Romains wrong was I constraind to *f.*
Cor. 1618 so many people bent so much to *f.*
Cor. 1668 bravely to *f.* for honor of the day
Cor. 1680 exhorting them to charge, and *f.* like men
Cor. 1691 we *f.* not, we, like thieves, for others wealth
Cor. 1692 we *f.* not, we, t'enlarge our skant confines
Cor. 1695 but t'is for publique freedom that we *f.*
Cor. 1696 for Rome we *f.*, and those that fled for feare
Cor. 1697 nay more, we *f.* for safetie of our lyves
Cor. 1712 and let us *f.* with courage, and conceite that
Cor. 1744 when with theyr swords (flesht with the former *f.*)
Cor. 1789 both comfort and encourage his to *f.*
Jer. 797 grew Violent, and wished the *f.* begune
Jer. 814 and heaven blesse you, my father, in this *f.*
Jer. 974 ride [home] all Conquerours, when the *f.* is done
Jer. 993 might I now and Andrea in one *f.*
Jer. 1003 to misse a Lord, and meete a prince in *f.*
ST 127 from out our rearward to begin the *f.*
ST 161 heere-hence the *f.* was eagerly renewd
ST 168 to challenge forth that Prince in single *f.*
ST 169 not long betweene these twaine the *f.* indurde
ST 352 in single *f.* with their Lord Generall
ST 392 when both our Armies were enjoynd in *f.*
ST 396 their *f.* was long, their harts were great
ST 458 without respect of honour in the *f.*?
ST 538 and tooke the King of Portingale in *f.*
SP 210 I *f.* not with my tongue; this is my oratrix

Fighting. (continued)

SP 247 my mercy in conquest is equall with my manhood in *f.*
SP 1090 not that I feare, but that I scorne to *f.*
SP 2063 but ere I come to enter single *f.*
SP 2087 I, but heere you, are you so foolish to *f.* with him ?
Fighting.
Cor. 1775 like two fierce Lyons *f.* in a Desart
Ard. 1474 this *f.* at my heart makes short my wind
Fighting-men.
Cor. 1876 ended the lives of his best fighting men
Figurative.
Jer. 481 and canst not aime at *F.* speech ?
Figure.
Cor. 762 they counterfet the dead in voyce and *f.*
ST 1070 *see* **Prefigure.**
HP 701 and Love by the judiciall figures of antiquitie hath
Figured.
HP Ind. 95 Love *f.* without a bearde
SP 293 he saw my anger *f.* in my brow
Figuring.
SP 53 *f.* Perseda twenty kinde of wayes?
Filching.
Ard. 809 here will be old *f.*, when the press comes
Filed.
Ard. 2434 no *f.* points are foisted in to make it gracious
Fill.
HP 154 *f.* your Table with unbought viands
HP 319 pray *f.* with bitter wines
Cor. 673 to *f.* our fields with blood of enemies
Cor. 1746 till streames of blood like Rivers *f.* the downes
Ard. 356 until our enemies have talked their *f.*
Ard. 2114 I pray thee, Mosbie, let her prate her *f.*
Filled.
HP 91 a Garden large enough, and *f.* with fruitfull Trees
HP 143 hyed home at night and fild his bord with delicats unbought
HP 288 they are *f.* every one with olde wine
Cor. 647 and whose first fortunes (fild with all distresse)
Cor. 1333 hath fild heavens fierie vaults with fright-full horror
Cor. 1796 him he enflam'd, and spur'd, and fild with horror
Cor. 1816 the field was fild with all confusion
ST 211 nor fild my hart with overcloying joyes
ST 1133 confusde and filde with murder and misdeeds
SP 1476 if tongue with griefe, and eyes with teares be fild
SP 1735 I fild Erastus sailes with winde
Filling.
ST Bal. 80 *f.* the ayre with mournefull groanes
Fillip.
SP 2029 mans life is as a glasse, and a phillip may cracke it
Ard. 1411 that sounded for a *f.* on the nose
Filth.
HP 678 tricking up their selves with Die and suche like *f.*
HP 1041 be no uncleanes, *f.*, or Rubbishe
HP 1048 beastlines and *f.* corrupt, disgrace, and spoile thinges
Filthiest.
Cor. 301 more then the most infected *f.* part
Filthiness.
HP 1314 that without noysomnes or filthines she may be bolde to touch
Filthy.
HP 673 *f.* spunging, proigning, painting, and pollishing themselves
HP 1047 bettereth things by Nature base and filthie
HP 1215 the ayre becommeth *f.* and infected
ST 1815 doth cast up *f.* and detested fumes
SP 1878 where filthie lust must murther honest love
Ard. (Title) the unsatiable desire of filthie lust and the

Ard. 501 there, forsooth, he revels it among such *f.* ones
Ard. 2249 smeared in blood and *f.* gore
Find.
HP 239 cannot yet *f.* in his hart to be married
HP 349 whether they first *f.*
HP 381 soone finde the springe so farre inferior to
HP 614 that he shal *f.* her so exceeding waiward
HP 1403 so did I *f.* it passing neat and queintly tricked up
HP 1657 not turning many leaves thou there shalt finde
HP 1730 prompt to *f.*, or so judicial as to censure
Cor. Ded. 16 I could not finde then this faire president of honour
Cor. Arg. 9 returnd to *f.* her out, and carrie her with him
Cor. 386 but (wishing) could not *f.* so faire an end
Cor. 806 darting sparcles, till it finde a trayne to seaze upon
Cor. 860 I finde my fortune not the least in this
Jer. 338 and *f.* it much dishonord by base homage
Jer. 983 can you not finde [me] Don Andrea forth ?
Jer. 990 sweat now to *f.* me in the hight of bloud
Jer. 1006 where might I *f.* this vallorous Balthezer ?
Jer. 1021 pray sweat to *f.* him out
Jer. 1027 I have sweat much, yet cannot *f.* him
ST Bal. 37 Lorenzo then, to finde the cause why
ST Bal. 62 the murtherers I sought to finde
ST 447 but how can love *f.* harbour in my brest
ST 479 on whose aspect mine eyes finde beauties bowre
ST 601 and doubt not but weele finde some remedie
ST 611 to finde the truth of all this question out
ST 653 and thou shalt finde me kinde and liberall
ST 673 then shalt thou finde that I am liberall
ST 918 for in revenge my hart would *f.* releife
ST 992 so shall we sooner finde the practise out
ST 1447 peace, impudent, for thou shalt finde it so
ST 1538 I finde the place impregnable ; and they
ST 1575 of everie accident I neere could finde till now
ST 1617 but say, where shall I finde the men, the murderers
ST 1619 to finde them out that murdered my Sonne ?
ST 1803 the way to him, and where to finde him out
ST 1820 your selves shall finde Lorenzo bathing him in
STA 2081 finde it to be my sonne Horatio
ST 2400 I hear you *f.* your selfe agrieved at my Sonne
ST 2512 Madame, tis true, and now I *f.* it so
SP 75 should finde a harbour for my hart to dwell
SP 482 Ile doe the best I can to finde your chaine
SP 521 through which our passage cannot finde a stop
SP 732 now must I *f.* the meanes to rid him hence
SP 989 I shall finde you at the Castle, shall I not ?
SP 1045 seeke him, finde him, bring him to my sight
SP 1091 Fortune, thou madest Fernando finde the chaine
SP 1190 if we but finde thee well inclind to us
Ard. 156 I shall *f.* a fellow that can
Ard. 207 that which I ever feared, and *f.* too true
Ard. 686 I am going to London upon hope to *f.* the fellow
Ard. 1239 the way I seek to *f.*, where pleasure dwells
Ard. 1325 ay, now I see, and too soon *f.* it true
Ard. 1419 why, he begun. — And thou shalt *f.* I'll end
Ard. 1877 for in thy discontent I *f.* a death
Ard. 2041 that those that *f.* him murdered may suppose
Ard. 2231 and if you *f.* him, send him home to me
Ard. 2234 I'll seek him out, and *f.* him if I can
Ard. 2301 *f.* out the murderers, let them be known
Ard. 2310 but wherefore stay you ? *f.* out the murderers
Ard. 2318 and you shall *f.* part of his guiltless blood
Ard. 2319 for in his slipshoe did I *f.* some rushes
Ard. 2398 but now I *f.* it and repent too late
JB 101 if I could not *f.* in my heart to doe so
HP 618 he findes he is nowe matcht and fallen into the

Cor. 74 where ere he drive his glittring Chariot, findes our
Ensignes spred
Cor. 1861 trots to the Haven, where his ships he finds
SP 444 but what must he have that findes it?

Finding.
ST Bal. 61 and *f.* then his senslesse form
ST Bal. 74 *f.* her sonne bereav'd of breath
ST 76 heere *f.* Pluto with his Proserpine

Fine.
HP 708 nor so soft and *f.* as uppon women
Jer. 252 heeres no *f.* villainie, no damn[e]d brother
ST 1455 to doo what, my *f.* officious knave?
STA 1761 a young Bacon, or a *f.* little smooth Horse-colt
SP 333 the English man is a *f.* knight
SP 1630 O *f.* devise; Brusor, get thee gone
Ard. 424 some *f.* confection that might have
Ard. 1691 this were a *f.* world for chandlers, if
Ard. 1758 a *f.* device! why, this deserves a kiss
Ard. 2043 a *f.* device! you shall have twenty pound
JB 27 well esteemed for *f.* workmanship in their trade

Finely.
SP 441 come, sirra, let me see how *f.* youle cry this chaine

Fineness.
HP 1632 worth, weight, and *f.* of the Golde and Sylver

Finer.
HP 1022 those relicts and fragme[n]ts of that *f.* fare

Finger.
ST 1409 pointing my *f.* at this boxe
ST 1479 what, he that points to it with his *f.*?
Ard. 17 nay, on his *f.* did I spy the ring
JB 173 to appoint her, held hee up but his *f.* at any time
SP 1063 thus do I take him on my fingers point
Ard. 751 my fingers itches to be at the peasant
JB 202 meane to keepe me as long out of thy fingers as I can
Ard. 1690 or play with a wench at pot-*f.*?

Finish.
Cor. 1939 that I may *f.* the Catastrophe
ST 408 did *f.* what his Halberdiers begun
ST 3010 when blood and sorrow finnish my desires
Ard. 863 as I to *f.* Arden's tragedie

Finished.
VPJ 40 thy feast of joy is finisht with thy fall
Cor. Arg. 31 Caesar (having *f.* these warres, and
Cor. 32 and hongst (O Hell) upon a Forte halfe finisht thy

Fire.
HP 168 necessarie either for *f.*, the use of
Cor. 154 and is with others Empyre set on *f.*
Cor. 819 and kindly layd it by his houshold *f.*
Cor. 1271 hath waters force and *f.* endur'd
Cor. 1734 the *f.* in sparks fro forth theyr Armour flew
Cor. 1881 and by the foe fulfild with *f.* and blood
Cor. 1918 that th' extreame *f.* within my hart may
Jer. 153 when two vext Clouds justle they strike out *f.*
Jer. 958 I am all *f.*, Andrea
ST 1708 that were to adde more fewell to your *f.*
STA 1792 violence leapes foorth like thunder wrapt in a ball of *f.*
SP 87 from water pits, or falling in the *f.*
SP 1569 as the *f.*, that lay with honours hand rackt up in ashes
SP 1641 I may asswage, but never quench loves *f.*
SP 1843 will you consent, quoth he, to *f.* the fleete
Ard. 1266 *f.* divided burns with lesser force
Ard. 1267 but I will dam that *f.* in my breast
Ard. 1386 is not thy powder dank, or will thy flint strike *f.*?
Ard. 1394 or will not wink at flashing of the *f.*
Ard. 1742 here's to pay for a *f.* and good cheer
JB 107 while she put the posnet on the *f.* againe

JB 107 rising up from the *f.* her coat cast downe
Puck 77 live & shake the vyper of my hand into the fier
HP 1159 (as by fires, tempests, inundations, and other such)
Cor. Arg. 6 upon the first fiers of the civill warres
Cor. 485 both brothers, and both warrs fierce lightning fiers
ST 1070 that shall prefigure those unquenched fiers
Cor. 924 will *f.* his shamefull bodie with their flames
Cor. 994 torture mee, pull me in peeces, famish, *f.* mee up
STA 2084 « the house is a *f.*, the house is a *f.*
Ard. 1658 then looks he as if his house were a-*f.*
Ard. 337 hell-*f.* and wrathful vengeance light on me

Fire-brand.
Cor. 1512 firce warrs quenchles *f.*
ST 1836 and twixt his teeth he holdes a *f.*
SP 1947 he with his fier brand parted the seas
Cor. 1565 fire-brands in their brests they beare

Fired.
Cor. 187 whose entrails fyerd with rancor, wrath and rage
Cor. 803 blaze that fiercely burnes a house already *f.*
Cor. 1755 Bellona, fiered with a quenchles rage, runnes
Cor. 1978 when (fierd) their golden Pallaces fell downe
SP 1971 that he would have firde the Turkes Fleete
Ard. 332 I could not choose, her beauty *f.* my heart!

Fire-darting.
Cor. 1751 a fearfull Hagge, with fier-darting eyes

Fire-sparkling.
Cor. 1786 with bristled backs, and *f.* eyes

Fireworks.
SP 1828 began to question us of all sorts of fire-workes

Firm.
Jer. 38 if my opinion might stand firme within your
Jer. 867 now, Spaine, sit firme; ile make thy towers shake
SP 2120 as firme as are the poles whereon heaven lies
Ard. 874 so should it fare with men of *f.* resolve

Firmae.
ST 2156 mine an Ejectione *f.* by a Lease

Firmest.
Cor. 1890 yea, thee, my latest fortunes *f.* hope

Firmly.
Cor. 36 a state devided cannot firmely stand
Cor. 956 his owne estate more firmely he assures
Cor. 964 there is nothing in the soule of man so firmely grounded
Jer. 751 were all *f.* planted in Don Andreas bosome
Jer. 828 by that argument you *f.* prove honor to
Jer. 902 firmely move without disturbed spleenes

First.
HP (Title) *f.* written in Italian by
HP Ind. 51 founded *f.* by Nature
HP Ind. 142 weaving, how *f.* found out
HP 165 the *f.* and greatest part I plow
HP 216 should *f.* be getting Children before
HP 349 whether they *f.* find
HP 430 things are *f.* ingendred and afterward corrupted
HP 447 but the *f.* opinion, as by naturall reason
HP 454 wherein at *f.* he had created it
HP 499 but *f.*, before I shall surrender this that
HP 522 and *f.* of hys body rather then hys goods
HP 555 divorced by death from that *f.* band of Matrimonie
HP 565 *f.* wold I that the parched earth did rive
HP 568 he hath my love that *f.* had me
HP 647 if hee himselfe doo not *f.* violate the bandes
HP 727 that she be forwarde with the *f.* at all dauncings
HP 766 when he *f.* tooke her to his Wife
HP 788 that *f.* and tender age of infancie
HP 789 the *f.* nourishment which the little ones receive
HP 794 but that *f.* age past over

HP 798 that *f.* age aboundeth in naturall heate
HP 811 a painful people by our byrth, for *f.* our babes we bring
HP 897 is *f.* founded upon Nature
HP 999 the *f.* shall be the stewarde
HP 1150 that is not *f.* and wholy kept togeather
HP 1197 and money which was *f.* found out by mans appointment
HP 1244 in sparing that expence he used at *f.*
HP 1260 those that wyll not keepe to be *f.* eaten
HP 1303 should be *f.* dronk or sold if thou have any quantitie
HP 1318 was this arte *f.* attributed to Minerva
HP 1320 in so much as it was derived *f.* from her
HP 1329 the *f.* sleepe ended, after midnight did the
HP 1682 as God commaunded the *f.* man
HP 1688 but whatsoever els we purposed at *f.*
HP 1729 though I were swift of conceit at *f.*, yet now
Cor. Arg. 3 was *f.* married to young Crassus
Cor. Arg. 6 upon the *f.* fiers of the civill warres
Cor. 135 heires to Persia or the Medes, *f.* Monarchies ?
Cor. 192 amongst the forward Souldiers *f.* discend
Cor. 194 who *f.* attempted to excite to Armes the troopes
Cor. 255 did *f.* beare Armes, and bare away my love
Cor. 267 from my *f.* husband stole my faithles griefe
Cor. 375 but flattring Chaunce, that trayn'd his *f.* designes
Cor. 578 to florish as it *f.* was made
Cor. 647 and whose *f.* fortunes (fild with all distresse)
Cor. 827 father to good Quirinus, our *f.* founder
Cor. 944 whose fell ambition (founded *f.* in blood)
Cor. 1660 brought at *f.* an hoste of men to Affrique
Cor. 1673 that they o're-layd them in the *f.* assault
Cor. 1774 and fought as freshly as they *f.* beganne
Cor. 1784 returnes them sharper set then at the *f.*
Cor. 1926 when (being but young) I lost my *f.* love Crassus ?
Jer.(Title) The *F.* Part of Jeronimo, With the Warres of Portugall
Jer. 156 *f.* let them pay the souldiers that were maimde
Jer. 266 weepe a while, as widdowes use, till their *f.* sleepe
Jer. 268 sould to newe, before the *f.* are thoroughly cold
Jer. 388 but thou wilt yeeld *f.* — No
Jer. 623 at *f.* they cried all war, as men
Jer. 645 let that be *f.* dispatcht
Jer. 709 for the *f.* object mine eies met
Jer. 720 a bad guest, when the *f.* object is a bleeding brest
Jer. 840 O, let me kisse thee *f.*
Jer. 931 when *f.* thou camst embassador ; these they are
Jer. 1105 hees my prisoner ; I seizd his weapons *f.*
Jer. 1107 tis easie to seize those were *f.* laid downe
Jer. 1108 my lance *f.* threw him from his warlicke steede
Jer. 1119 the vanquisht yeilds to both, to you [the] *f.*
ST (Title) such grosse faults as passed in the *f.* impression
ST 246 this hand *f.* tooke his courser by the raines
ST 247 but *f.* my launce did put him from his horse
ST 248 I ceaz'd his weapon and enjoyde it *f.*
ST 249 but *f.* I forc'd him lay his weapons downe
ST 273 Horatio, thou didst force him *f.* to yeeld
ST 372 if *f.* my Sonne and then my selfe were slaine
ST 523 the *f.* arm'd knight that hung his Scutchin up
ST 603 *f.* that must needs be knowne, and then removed
ST 690 *f.*, in his hand he brandished a sword
ST 747 where triall of this warre shall *f.* be made
ST 750 where *f.* we vowd a mutuall amitie
ST 853 but *f.* my lookes shall combat against thine
ST 1024 *f.* we are plast upon extreamest height
ST 1296 who *f.* laies hand on me, ile be his Priest
ST 1442 *f.* I confesse, nor feare I death therfore
ST 1661 *f.*, to affright me with thy weapons drawne
ST 1703 your *f.* favourite Don Andreas death

ST 1865 *f.*, for the marriage of his Princely Sonne
ST 1926 tis best that we see further in it *f.*
ST 2467 the two *f.* the nuptiall torches boare
ST 2540 as for the passing of the *f.* nights sport
ST 2639 as fitting for the *f.* nights revelling
ST 2932 *f.* take my tung, and afterwards my hart
STA 2982 *f.* take my tongue, and afterward my hart
SP 153 *f.*, welcome, thrise renowned Englishman
SP 178 upon thy *f.* encounter of thy foe
SP 190 upon the *f.* brave of thine enemy
SP 208 upon the *f.* encounter of your foe
SP 631 and by the world's bright eye *f.* brought to light
SP 636 Fortune, that *f.* by chance brought them together
SP 681 be our *f.* day of joy and perfect peace
SP 1345 *f.* Julio will die ten thousand deaths
SP 1442 *f.*, thanks to heaven ; and next to Brusors valour
SP 1601 well governd friends do *f.* regard themselves
SP 1728 and *f.* I stunge them with consenting love
SP 1818 since *f.* I set my feet on Turkish land
SP 1827 his Cabine doore fast shut, he *f.* began
SP 1997 and *f.* Perseda shall with this hand die
SP 2057 *f.* tell me, doth Perseda live or no ?
SP 2066 *f.* let my tongue utter my hearts despight
SP 2092 but with thy hand *f.* wounded to the death
SP 2139 *f.* cause me murther such a worthy man
Ard. 25 a botcher, and no better at the *f.*
Ard. 218 thine overthrow ? *f.* let the world dissolve
Ard. 793 the *f.* is Arden, and that's his man
Ard. 1145 *f.* go make the bed, and afterwards
Ard. 1190 *f.*, Will, let's hear what he can say
Ard. 1466 *f.* did she cast her eyes down to the earth
Ard. 1749 *f.* tell me how you like my new device
Ard. 1925 unless she have agreed with me *f.*
Ard. 2056 make me the *f.* that shall adventure on him
Ard. 2166 *f.* lay the body in the counting-house
Ard. 2270 but *f.* convey the body to the fields
JB 6 the onelye sonnes of the *f.* man, Adam
JB 79 lay not with him after the *f.* night of her marriage
JB 84 lodged never a night but the *f.* in his house
Puck 12 the *f.* and most (thoughe insufficient) surmize
Puck 14 when I was *f.* suspected for that libell
Puck 20 my *f.* acquaintance wth this Marlowe, rose upon

Fish.
HP 1028 putrifie the good and engender naughtie *F.*
HP 1264 *f.* and fowle, which will bee suddainly corrupt
HP 1268 baking of some kinds of flesh or *f.*
SP 222 or the marine moisture to the red guild *f.*
SP 284 by gods *f.*, friend, take you the Latins part ?

Fisica.
HP 1645 E se tu ben la tua *f.* note

Fist.
Cor. 393 if he had died, his fauchin in his *f.*
Cor. 1793 and who more roughly smear'd it to his fiste
ST 2890 bearing his latest fortune in his *f.*
SP 1077 with my single *f.* Ile combat thee
Ard. 1989 I would have crammed in angels in thy *f.*
Cor. 1879 dye bravely, with their fauchins in their fists

Fit.
HP Ind. 127 salary or wages *f.* for Servaunts
HP 162 necessarie or *f.* for the life of a poore Gentlema[n]
HP 469 an indifferent and *f.* Judge of a matter
HP 814 to frame their horses *f.* for service, and their
HP 995 neither fitte for warre in mind nor body
HP 996 *f.* for labor, countrey busines, and
HP 1282 and othersome made *f.* for drink
HP 1305 necessary and fitt for the ability and credite of her house

HP 1529 the instruments should be proportioned and *f.*
Cor. 506 I am an offring *f.* for Acheron
Cor. 1214 annoynt theyr sinewes *f.* for wrestling
Cor. 1640 but, being afeard to loose so *f.* a place
ST 1285 how *f.* a place, if one were so disposde
ST 2122 and therefore all times *f.* not for revenge
ST 2428 it is *f.* for us that we be freends
ST 2546 why then, ile *f.* you ; say no more
ST 2633 a Comedie ? fie, Comedies are *f.* for common wits
Jer. 557 nor fits it newes so soone kisse subjects [ears]
ST 297 this better fits a wretches endles moane
ST 442 for sollitude best fits my cheereles mood
ST 496 then heere it fits us to attend the King
ST 922 for outrage fits our cursed wretchednes
ST 998 Ile say his dirge, singing fits not this case
ST 1345 why so, this fits our former pollicie
ST 2307 a place more private fits this princely mood
SP 661 as fits the time, so now well fits the place to
SP 980 now it fits my wisdome to counterfeit the foole
SP 1384 peace, foole, a sable weed fits discontent
Ard. 1542 the season fits ; come, Franklin, let's away
Fitten.
Ard. 710 why, 'twas one Jack *F.*
Ard. 713 let Lord Cheiny seek Jack *F.* forth
Fitter.
HP 682 *f.* for vizards, pageants, and poppets then wholesome
HP 683 for albeit superfluous pompe be *f.* for a stage
Cor. Ded. 15 a *f.* present for a Patronesse so well accomplished
ST 1801 oh, forbeare, for other talke for us far *f.* were
Ard. 653 the *f.* is he for my purpose, marry !
Fittest.
SP 16 as *f.* person to serve for Chorus to
Ard. 46 sweet words are *f.* engines to
Ard. 797 stand close, and take you *f.* standing
Ard. 1422 well, take your *f.* standings, and
Fitteth.
ST 277 for thine estate best *f.* such a guest
SP 2215 for powerfull Death best *f.* Tragedies
Fitting.
VPJ 68 reapt reward, not *f.* their desire
HP 121 reverence which I thought *f.* both his yeres and
HP 840 the Lacedemonians reputed *f.* for a noble man
HP 887 not onely *f.*, but most needfull for freemen
HP 1202 commodiously *f.* and making equall things exchanged
HP 1547 and is not necessary or *f.* for a Cittizen
ST 2120 closely and safely *f.* things to time
ST 2370 my lookes, my Lord, are *f.* for my love
ST 2636 Tragedia cothurnata, *f.* Kings
ST 2639 as *f.* for the first nights revelling
SP 1406 still in black habite *f.* funerall ?
Ard. 1207 a place well-*f.* such a stratagem
Five.
HP 1692 those *F.* especial points whereof we
Jer. 91 *f.* marchants wealths into the deepe doth throw
STA 2050 and draw me *f.* yeeres yonger then I am
SP 258 I am his, for some *f.* launces
Ard. 849 tush, I have broken *f.* hundred oaths !
Five-and-twenty.
HP 83 five and twentie large and most
ST 526 arrived with five and twenty thousand men
Fix.
Ard. 1016 then *f.* his sad eyes on the sullen earth
Fixed.
Jer. 189 tis *f.* upon my hart ; adew, soules friend
ST 1818 there, in a brazen Caldron fixt by Jove
Flame.

ST 709 our hidden smoke is turned to open *f.*
ST 1819 fixt by Jove, in his fell wrath, upon a sulpher *f.*
Cor. 807 finde a trayne to seaze upon, and then it flames amaine
Cor. 924 will fire his shamefull bodie with their flames
ST 1069 binde him, and burne his body in those flames
ST 2372 new kindled flames should burne as morning sun
ST 3051 and there live, dying still in endles flames
SP 1571 rackt up in ashes, revives againe to flames
Cor. 1716 and that his troopes (as tucht wyth lightning flames)
Ard. 208 a woman's love is as the lightning-*f.*
Flaming.
Cor. 802 Caesar is like a brightlie *f.* blaze that
Jer. 310 to hooke the divell from his *f.* cell
Flashing.
Ard. 1394 or will not wink at *f.* of the fire
Flat.
ST 1461 Ile not change without boot, thats *f.*
ST 1847 and heere Ile have a fling at him thats *f.*
SP 1073 I must have a bout with you, sir, thats *f.*
Ard. 456 full discourse and *f.* resolve me of the thing I seek
Ard. 1681 nay, by my troth, sir, but *f.* knavery
Flatly.
ST 2291 if I, say so ; if not, say *f.* no
Flatter.
SP 564 thou, Aristippus like, didst *f.* him
SP 583 thinks thou I *f.* ? Now I *f.* not
SP 1106 and crosse him too, and sometimes *f.* him
Ard. 1263 but here she comes, and I must *f.* her
Flattering.
Cor. 112 but we, soone tickled with such flattring hopes
Cor. 375 but flattring Chaunce, that trayn'd his first designes
ST Bal. 9 and now her *f.* smiles I blame
ST Bal. 10 her *f.* smiles hath done me wrong
ST 1215 feare or *f.* words may make him false
ST 1578 O false Lorenzo, are these thy *f.* lookes ?
Flattery.
ST 1082 sith feare or love to Kings is flatterie
SP 562 and, far from *f.*, I spoke my minde
SP 582 and to the purpose, far from *f.*
SP 928 for love, or gaine, or flatterie
Ard. 28 and by his servile *f.* and fawning
Flaw.
Ard. 1802 and saw a dreadfull southern *f.* at hand
Cor. 657 O, but I feare that Fortune seekes new flawes
Flaxen-haired.
Cor. 59 for neither could the flaxen-hair'd high Dutch
Flectere.
HP 810 *F.* ludus equos, et spicula tendere cornu
Fled.
Cor. 1526 never leaving till they *f.*
Cor. 1696 for Rome we fight, and those that *f.* for feare
Cor. 1741 till, dead or *f.*, the one forsake the field
ST 172 when he was taken, all the rest they *f.*
ST 2837 all *f.*, faild, died, yea, all decaide with this
SP 63 to hasty lovers whose fancy soone is *f.*
SP 1020 and whether *f.* my poore Erastus then ?
Ard. 2427 the painter *f.* and how he died we know not
Fleece.
SP 186 the golden *F.* is that we cry upon
Ard. 1127 when I would *f.* the wealthy passenger
Fleers.
Cor. 1017 she fleres againe, I know not how, still to beguile
Fleet.
Cor. Arg. 28 he was assailed, beaten and assaulted by the
    adverse Fleete
SP 1156 their fleete is weake

SP 1258 prepare a *f.* to assault and conquer Rhodes
SP 1843 will you consent, quoth he, to fire the fleete
SP 1971 that he would have firde the Turkes Fleete
Jer. 407 up hether sayling in a crimson fleete

Flesh.

HP 259 to eate of two kinds of wilde *f.*
HP 261 none other *f.* eaten then Beefe, Porke
HP 274 did eate such kinde of *f.?*
HP 278 but the *f.* of wild Beasts, although
HP 646 he cannot abstaine from pleasures of the *f.*
HP 695 the *f.* of women, as it is more soft and daintie
HP 1264 Salt and Vineger doo not onely keep *f.*
HP 1268 baking of some kinds of *f.* or fish
Jer. 929 where ile set downe, in caractors on thy *f.*
ST 2 soule did live imprisond in my wanton *f.*
ST 1492 the meriest peece of mans *f.* that ere gronde at my office doore
SP 2194 thou didst but wound their *f.*, their minds are free
Ard. 2089 then stab him till his *f.* be as a sieve

Fleshed.

Cor. 360 flesh'd so long, till they gan tiranize the Towne
Cor. 1744 when with theyr swords (flesht with the former fight)

Flew.

Cor. 1734 the fire in sparks fro forth theyr Armour *f.*

Flies.

Eng. Parn. 6 an Owle that flyes the light of Parliaments
Cor. 1008 when shee hath heap't her gifts on us, away shee *f.*
Cor. 1787 tyll, tyer'd or conquer'd, one submits or flyes
Cor. 1813 make forth amongst the flock, that scattered flyes
SP 740 unlesse, forewarnd, the weakling coward *f.*
SP 741 thou foolish coward, *f.?* Erastus lives
Cor. 314 beat backe like flyes before a storme of hayle?
SP 1071 eagles are chalenged by paltry flyes

Flight.

HP 152 like to those Jayes whose *f.* contents the world
HP 992 put them presently to *f.*
Cor. 754 dyd with hys *f.* unclose my fearefull eyes
Cor. 1671 them that already dream'd of death or *f.*
Jer. 1150 the Portugales are slaine and put to *f.*
ST 1716 thy hate, his love; thy *f.*, his following thee
SP 34 Ile stay my *f.*, and cease to turne my wheele
SP 56 marking my times as Faulcons watch their *f.?*
Ard. 1355 my wings are feathered for a lowly *f.*
SP 183 to change a bullet with our swift *f.* shot

Fling.

Cor. 995 *f.* mee alive into a Lyons denn
Ard. 161 and *f.* the dagger at the painter's head
Ard. 2068 from her watery bower *f.* down Endymion
Ard. 2343 and now I am going to *f.* them in the Thames
ST 1847 and heere Ile have a *f.* at him, thats flat

Flint.

Cor. 1952 and urge thee (if thy hart be not of flynt
ST 577 in time the *F.* is pearst with softest shower
Ard. 47 to race the *f.* walls of a woman's breast
Ard. 1386 is not thy powder dank, or will thy *f.* strike fire?
Cor. 1852 to beate them downe as fierce as thundring flints
ST 1592 wearing the flints with these my withered feet

Flint-heart.

SP 195 and put the flint heart Perseans to the sword

Flinty.

Ard. 1766 or make no battery in his *f.* breast

Floatest.

Cor. 83 doth topside-turvey tosse thee as thou flotest

Flock.

Cor. 1813 make forth amongst the *f.*, that scattered flyes
HP 172 whereon the Heards and little flocks

HP 1182 numbred by Algorisme (as Flocks and Heards)
HP 1210 and some with life, as Flocks and Heards
HP 1439 flocks, Heards, and droves compact
HP 1488 his flocks, heards, and such like
HP 1565 from the Earth, Heards, and Flocks

Flood.

Cor. 1469 can I too-soone goe taste Cocytus *f.?*
ST 24 and slakte his smoaking charriot in her floud
Ard. 1146 and afterwards go hearken for the *f.*
Ard. 1204 but now I am going to see what *f.* it is
Cor. 594 those fountaines doe to floods convart?
Cor. 595 those floods to waves, those waves to seas
Cor. 978 still fed by thoughts, lyke floods with winters rayne
ST 920 O, gush out teares, fountaines and flouds of teares
SP 1475 when they are stopt with flouds of flowing teares?
SP 1945 when he espyde my weeping flouds of teares

Flora.

ST 839 the more will *F.* decke it with her flowers
ST 840 I, but if *F.* spie Horatio heere
ST 2624 attire your selfe like Phoebe, *F.*, or the huntresse

Flores.

SP 281 Jester : O extempore, O *f.*

Flourish.

HP 221 when the youth of their sonnes begin to *f.*
Cor. 578 to florish as it first was made

Flourished.

Jer. 101 Ambitions plumes, that florisht in our court
Ard. 984 as Hydra's head that flourish'd by decay (Delius, and Bullen)
Ard. 1971 he in a bravery *f.* o'er his head

Flourisheth.

Cor. 576 and what now florisheth, must fade

Flout.

ST 1406 *f.* the gallowes, scorne the audience, and

Flouted.

Ard. 1138 to be thus *f.* of a coistril

Flow.

Jer. 808 tribute shall *f.* out of their bowels
ST 102 from whose faire influence such justice flowes
ST 1833 downe by the dale that flowes with purple gore

Flower.

Cor. 254 when as thy husband Crassus (in his flowre) did
ST Bal. 33 she chose my sonne for her chiefe *f.*
ST 387 who, living, was my garlands sweetest *f.*
SP 161 and gained the *f.* of Gallia in my crest
SP 1177 the *f.* of chivalrie and curtesie
SP 2078 thou hast betrayde the *f.* of Christendome
HP 173 reserved for hearbes, flowers, and rootes
HP 383 as hope is to effects, and floures to fruits
HP 730 as incident to youth as flowrs to the Spring time
Cor. 1285 the fairest flowers that grow in Rome
ST 839 the more will Flora decke it with her flowers
SP 680 brings in the spring with many gladsome flowers
Ard. 1361 flowers do sometimes spring in fallow lands

Flower-de-luce.

Ard. 105 and here comes Adam of the *F.*
Ard. 1743 get you to Feversham to the *F.*
Ard. 2265 and for one night lie at the *F.*
Ard. 2332 and one of you go to the *F.*

Flowered.

Cor. 197 where in the flowred Meades dead men were found
ST 1528 disroabde the medowes of their flowred greene
Cor. 1520 new set with many a fresh-flowrd Coronet

Flowing.

Jer. 182 you drowne my honores in those *f.* watters
ST 19 to passe the *f.* streame of Acheron

SP 1475 when they are stopt with flouds of *f.* teares ?
Flumina.
HP 807 natos ad *f.* primum deferimus
Flung.
Cor. 732 I mov'd mine head, and flonge abroade mine armes
ST Bal. 89 had *f.* from prison where they kept her strong
Flushing.
Ard. 2373 go on board some hoy, and so to *F.*
Ard. 2380 farewell, England ; I'll to *F.* now
Ard. 2425 Black Will was burned in *F.* on a stage
Fly.
Cor. 1395 did (conquered) flie, his troopes discomfited
Cor. 1436 I feare not those that to theyr weapons flye
Cor. 1743 *f.* forth as thicke as moates about the Sunne
Cor. 1769 with burning hate let each at other flie
Cor. 1807 our men at Armes (in briefe) begin to flye
Cor. 1912 what shall I doe, or whether shall I flye
ST 339 nay, evill newes flie faster still than good
ST 358 and when he fell, then we began to flie
ST 1239 bid him not faile. — I *f.*, my Lord
SP 859 no more can flie then iron can Adamant
SP 908 flie, Erastus, ere the Governour have any newes
SP 1774 desire should frame me winges to flie to him
SP 1838 but seemd content to flie with him to Rhodes
Cor. 235 with-holds his darte, and in disdaine doth flye me
ST 686 sad, that sheele flie me, if I take revenge
SP 910 nay, Gentlemen, flye you and save your selves
SP 2180 and, sweet Perseda, flie not Soliman
Flying.
SP 1289 for whom mourne you ? — Ah, for Erastus *f.*
SP 1504 and peeces *f.* backe will wound my selfe
Foaming.
Cor. 81 when foming billowes feele the Northern blasts
Cor. 1347 tell the foming Seas the honour of our fight ?
Cor. 1780 theyr jawbones dy'd with foming froth and blood
Foddered.
HP 283 Beasts that commonly are stald and *f.*
Foe.
Cor. 723 the selfe-same *f.* and fortune following them
Cor. 1446 what, thinke they mee to be their Countries *f.* ?
Cor. 1453 I feare my *f.*, untill he be interd
Cor. 1454 a man may make his *f.* his friend, you know
Cor. 1455 a man may easier make his friend his *f.*
Cor. 1536 gives them over to their *f.*
Cor. 1544 made his envious *f.* so hote
Cor. 1651 dyd scoure the plaines in pursuite of the *f.*
Cor. 1878 before the *f.* and in theyr Captaines presence
Cor. 1881 and by the *f.* fulfild with fire and blood
Cor. 1898 t'attend the mercy of his murdring *f.*
Jer. 352 was thy full friend, is now returned thy *f.*
Jer. 353 an excellent *f.* ; we shall have scuffling good
Jer. 1016 the glory of our *f.*, the hart of courage
Jer. 1130 heaven and this arme once saved thee from thy *f.*
ST 171 and forcst to yeelde him prisoner to his *f.*
ST 688 nay, if thou dally, then I am thy *f.*
SP 178 upon thy first encounter of thy *f.*
SP 208 upon the first encounter of your *f.*
SP 723 to tyrannise over a yeelding *f.*
SP 932 ah, hard attempt, to tempt a *f.* for ayde
SP 1711 and is she linkt in liking with my *f.* ?
ST 407 taking advantage of his foes distresse
VPJ 11 this makes thy friends, this makes thy foes admire
Cor. 39 have fought like foes Pharsalias miserie
Cor. 109 did favour us with conquering our foes
Cor. 823 and feareles kept us from th' assault of foes
Cor. 1276 were all the world his foes before

Cor. 1443 in conquered foes what credite can there be ?
Cor. 1525 he his foes hath conquered
Jer. 12 if ever you have foes, or red field scars
Jer. 49 Oh, a polyticke speech beguiles the eares of foes
Jer. 165 I go to knit friends, not to kindle foes
Jer. 355 trybute for trybute, then : and foes for foes
Jer. 532 our foes will stride else over me and you
Jer. 839 this scarfe shall be my charme gainst foes and hell
Jer. 942 can we be foes, and all so well agreed ?
Jer. 1085 my foes are base, and slay me cowardly
ST Bal. 53 and to their foes they did impart the place
ST Bal. 111 to see me with his foes agree
ST Bal. 131 then dyed my foes by dint of knife
ST 200 are safe returnd, and by their foes inricht
ST 367 that thou shouldst thus betray him to our foes ?
ST 3024 and on my foes worke just and sharp revenge
ST 3053 then haste we doune to meet thy freends and foes
SP 535 whose name hath shakt thy foes
SP 595 or twenty thousand millions of our foes
SP 707 still friends ? still foes ; she weares my Carcanet
SP 1151 kinde to their foes, and liberall to their friends
SP 2135 kinde, even to his foes, gentle and affable
Ard. 962 and buckler thee from ill-intending foes
Jer. 1145 this soft banner, smeard with foes bloud
Foeman.
SP 2002 a brave Cavelere, but my aprooved *f.*
Foemina.
HP 1323 Curriculo expulerat somnum, cum *f.* primum
Fog.
SP 537 *f.* not thy glory with so fowle eclipse
Ard. 1677 I am almost stifled with this *f.*
Ard. 1747 in case we fall into a second *f.*
Foggy.
Ard. 1726 see how the sun hath cleared the *f.* mist
Foil.
SP 1138 seene him foile and overthrow all the Knights
Foiled.
SP 402 though over-borne, and foyled in my course
Foisted.
Ard. 2484 no filed points are *f.* in to make it gracious
Fold.
Jer. 5 come hether, boy Horatio ; fould thy joynts
Jer. 447 what, *f.* paper that way to a noble man ?
SP 1935 for till I fould Perseda in mine armes, my
Ard. 1082 and with the black *f.* of her cloudy robe
Folded.
Cor. 428 with *f.* armes I sadly sitte and weepe
Folk.
HP Ind. 96 different from those of married folke
Follies.
HP 666 in no sort to be consenting to such *f.*
Follow.
HP 438 it must followe that the Pole Antartick is
HP 444 it would *f.* that it began in the Spring
HP 733 nor yet to be so easily induced to watch or *f.* her
Jer. 728 doth presage what shall hereafter *f.*
ST 380 Villuppo, *f.* us for thy reward
ST 706 doe you but *f.* me, and gaine your love
ST 771 yet heerein shall she *f.* my advice
ST 820 I *f.* thee, my love, and will not backe
ST 1366 fellow, be gone ; my boy shall *f.* thee
SP 295 but I will *f.* for revenge
SP 939 when thou hast delivered it, take ship and *f.* me
SP 947 or deliver it, and *f.* my maister
SP 947 if I deliver it, and *f.* my maister
SP 1021 to Constantinople, whether I must *f.* him

SP 1035 then let him go ; ile shortly *f.* him
SP 1103 but with my goulden wings ile *f.* him
SP 1258 and now, Erastus, come and *f.* me
SP 1271 come, *f.* me, and I will heare the rest
SP 1355 that I would *f.* her, though she went to hell
SP 1552 they love each other best : what then should *f.*
SP 1709 did I turne Turke to *f* her so far ?
SP 1946 teares for your depart, he bad me *f.* him
SP 1956 so I became a Turke to *f.* her
SP 1957 to *f.* her, am now returnd a Christian
SP 2181 when as my gliding ghost shall *f.* thee
Ard. 533 good fortune *f.* all your forward thoughts
Ard. 754 a man might *f.* without danger of law
Ard. 1010 I pray you, go before : I'll *f.* you
Ard. 1384 ay, to the gates of death to *f.* thee
Ard. 1578 see you *f.* us to the Isle of Sheppy
Ard. 1646 go before to the boat, and I will *f.* you
Ard. 1741 he needs would *f.* them without a guide
Ard. 1893 will you *f.* him that hath dishonoured you ?
Ard. 1901 dangerous to *f.* him whom he hath lately hurt
HP 534 the malcontentment of the minde followes
HP 789 it followes that the first nourishment which the
Cor. 513 to scape the feares that followes Fortunes glaunces
Cor. 792 thy rebell sonne, with crowned front, tryumphing followes thee
ST 718 that pleasure followes paine, and blisse annoy
ST 2814 but now what followes for Hieronimo ?
ST 2815 marrie, this followes for Hieronimo
SP 1740 mark well what followes, for the historie prooves

Followed.
HP 38 I folowed him, but he regarded oft, and
HP 491 providence of our almighty God *f.* by Nature
HP 1348 in which example he *f.* Homer, who
HP 1578 gaines which are gotte and *f.* with paine and sweat
Cor. 744 that lov'd our liberty and follow'd him
Cor. 940 but hee that followd Pompey with the sword ?
Cor. 1134 or follow'd Pompey but to thys effect
SP 1947 he bad me follow him : I *f.* him
Ard. 1884 thou would'st have *f.* him, and seen him dressed
Ard. 2341 and as she *f.* me, I spurned her down the stairs

Followers.
ST 1088 these eies beheld, and these my *f.*
ST 2289 thy *f.*, their pleasure, and our peace
ST 2293 with doubtfull *f.*, unresolved men

Following.
HP 1772 your sonnes, *f.* the example of theyr Uncle
Cor. 723 the selfe-same foe and fortune *f.* them
Cor. 1027 but, in the morrow *f.*, might perceive
Cor. 1630 coasting along and *f.* by the foote
Jer. 267 who in the morrow *f.* will be sould
ST 1716 thy hate, his love ; thy flight, his *f.* thee
Ard. 1738 in *f.* so slight a task as this
JB 20 as by this example *f.* may evidently be proved

Folly.
Cor. 43 that as much blood in wilfull follie spent
ST 310 such is the *f.* of dispightfull chance
ST 1439 confesse thy *f.*, and repent thy fault
SP 603 if wilfull *f.* did not blind mine eyes
SP 1072 thy *f.* gives thee priviledge ; begon, begon
SP 1298 my heart is full ; I cannot laugh at follie
Ard. 1843 ah, Arden, what *f.* blinded thee ?

Fond.
Cor. 534 so *f.* we are to feare the worlds disgrace
ST Bal. 8 on whom *f.* fortune smiled long
ST 730 live, hart, to joy at *f.* Horatios fall
SP 610 bridle the *f.* intemperance of thy tongue ?

SP 652 the *f.* Bragardo, to presume to armes
SP 1526 that cannot governe private *f.* affections ?
SP 1796 or that Soliman were not so *f.*
Ard. 1172 such great impression took this *f.* surprise

Fondly.
SP 1962 which, foolish woman, *f.* I neglected

Food.
HP Ind. 14 more used for fashion then foode
HP 1435 nourishments and foode that we receive of Beastes

Fool.
Cor. 821 and stung to death the foole that fostred her
SP 354 it is a world to heere the foole prate and brag
SP 364 is not this a counterfet foole ?
SP 631 besides Love hath inforst a foole
SP 875 was not he a foole that went to shoote, and
SP 880 mas, the foole sayes true ; lets have some got
SP 980 now it fits my wisdome to counterfeit the foole
SP 1384 peace, foole, a sable weed fits discontent
SP 1720 farewell, counterfeit foole
SP 1960 be patient, sweete Perseda, the foole but jests
Ard. 1621 make him wise in death that lived a *f.*
Ard. 1719 such a *f.* as will rather be hought than
Ard. 1975 like a *f.* bears his sword-point half a yard
Ard. 2279 peace, *f.*, the snow will cover them again
Cor. 105 O fooles, looke back and see the roling stone
STA 1767 reccons his parents among the rancke of fooles
SP 999 God sends fortune to fooles

Foolery.
SP 886 sirra Piston, mar not our sport with your *f.*

Foolish.
HP 551 *f.* is that opinion of some that imagined
Cor. 212 or fast enough doe *f.* men not die
Cor. 818 and full of *f.* pitty tooke it up
Cor. 1546 feeding still *f.* those that doe thy will
SP 741 thou *f.* coward, flies ? Erastus lives
SP 1599 *f.* Soliman, why did I strive to
SP 1962 which, *f.* woman, fondly I neglected
SP 2082 ah, *f.* man, therein thou art deceived
SP 2087 I, but heere you, are you so *f.* to fight with him ?
SP 2196 hence *f.* Fortune, and thou wanton Love
Ard. 880 the *f.* knave's in love with Mosbie's sister

Foolishness.
Ard. 2226 she will undo us through her *f.*

Foot.
HP 30 seeing him a foote, giving my
Cor. 1630 coasting along and following by the foote
Cor. 106 whereon she blindly lighting sets her foote
Cor. 1727 they ranne at ever-each other hand and foote
Cor. 1802 theyr warlike Armies (fast lockt foote to foote)
ST 317 whose foote [is] standing on a rowling stone
ST 852 set forth thy *f.* to try the push of mine
ST 1476 alas, sir, you are a *f.* too low to reach it
SP 242 [I], all on foote, like an Herculian offspring
Cor. 781 downe to the Scithian swift-foote feareles Porters
SP 333 by Cock and Pie, and Mouse *f.*, the
SP 162 against the light foote Irish have I served
SP 770 thy favours bore me, not my light foote Steed

Footing.
Cor. 831 from once *f.* in our Fortresses have yee repeld the
Ard. 1740 with making false *f.* in the dark

Footman.
HP 114 on horsebacke, attended with a footeman

Footmen.
SP 1158 their footemen more, well exercised in war

Footsteps.
Ard. 2278 which makes me fear our *f.* will be spied

For.

HP 50 I conceale, *f.* they are so obscure, as if I shoulde
HP 1694 but *f.* it is my chiefe desire that thou record
HP 1771 but *f.* it may percase come so to passe that some
Cor. Arg. 28 and *f.* hee woulde not fall alive into the hands of
ST 1040 no ; *f.*, my Lord, had you behelde the traine
ST 1115 *f.* not *f.* Alexandros injuries, but *f.* reward
ST 2350 and, *f.* I pittied him in his distresse
ST 483 but *f.* thy kindnes in his life and death
HP 1013 *f.* as they may rather have too much then want
ST 2652 and, *f.* because I know that Bel-imperia hath
HP 668 which, *f.* that they are received and kept of custome, can not bee
HP 875 (*f.* that they were preservd from death)
HP 1099 differeth from the hand *f.* that the hand is fastned
HP 1131 which (*f.* that thou art desirous to peruse his workes)
HP 1136 *f.* that our speeche hath reference as well to
HP 1589 not *f.* that it ought to be exchangd
HP 1589 *f.* of mony (as touching the mettall) we have no neede
SP 1782 be not angrie *f.* I carry thy beloved from thee
SP 1869 ile favour thee, *f.* that thou wert beloved of Soliman
SP 2162 *f.* that my death was wrought by her devise
Ard. 1888 *f.* that I injured thee, and wronged my friend, shame
Jer. 700 why should I make two tailes, *f.* to be found in two ?
Jer. 894 but [*f.*] to tender and receive the somes of
ST Bal. 41 which *f.* to bring well to effect
ST Bal. 44 he threatneth *f.* to rid his life
ST Bal. 125 then *f.* to act this Tragedy, I gave
ST Bal. 133 then *f.* to specifie my wronges
SP 384 Ile be your Page this once, *f.* to disarme you
SP 1577 commaund my shipping *f.* to waft you over
SP 1713 O wicked Turque, *f.* to steale her hence
SP 1852 we came aland, not minding *f.* to returne
SP 1891 so resolved *f.* to bereave Erastus life
SP 2070 do waite *f.* to receive thee in their jawes
Ard. 216 I am content *f.* to be reconciled
Ard. 480 as careless as he is careful *f.* to get
Ard. 522 but hire some cutter *f.* to cut him short
Ard. 557 came hither, railing, *f.* to know the truth
Ard. 567 I gave him ten pound *f.* to hire knaves
Ard. 572 to London, *f.* to bring his death about
Ard. 956 and takes advantage *f.* to eat him up
Ard. 2229 he was not wont *f.* to stay thus late
Cor. 397 *f.* why, t'have seene his noble Roman blood mixt
ST 2446 awake ? *f.* why ?
ST 2528 *f.* why the plots already in mine head
SP 895 this so courteous and unlookt *f.* sport

Forage.

Cor. 1646 that come to forrage when the cold begins

Foraging.

Ard. 1164 that sees a lion *f.* about

Forasmuch.

HP 419 *f.* as all thinges contained in thys our
HP 542 *f.* as Petrarch, reasoning of the soule
HP 569 *f.* as custome and the Lawes dyspence
HP 783 *f.* as that first and tender age of
HP 798 that, *f.* as that first age
HP 874 but *f.* as theyr Servaunts in olde times
HP 894 yet *f.* as the Lawes and
HP 1007 but for asmuch as our fortune hath not gyven
HP 1107 but *f.* as of actions, some are placed in
HP 1149 but *f.* as nothing can be encreased that
HP 1177 but *f.* as I have said that he ought to be
HP 1368 but *f.* as things preserved may
HP 1430 and *f.* as nothing is more naturall
HP 1524 for as much as this word infinit, as touching

HP 1586 *f.* as money was founde out and
HP 1724 *f.* as if they onely differ in the greatnes, then even

Forbad.

HP 1353 *f.* the Mistres of the house all other works

Forbear.

HP 679 of modestie and love will suddainly forbeare it
Cor. 287 hence-forth forbeare to seeke my murdring love
Cor. 800 forbeare to tempt the enemy againe
Jer. 140 alas, that Spaine cannot of peace forbeare
ST 1800 oh, forbeare, for other talke for us far fitter were
SP 4 and I commaund you to forbeare this place
SP 1349 forbeare to hurt him : when we land in Turkie
Ard. 349 *f.* his house
Ard. 350 *f.* it ! nay, rather frequent it more
Ard. 398 *f.* to wound me with that bitter word

Forbearance.

Ard. 842 but *f.* is no acquittance

Forbid.

HP 729 to *f.* her those honest recreations and desires
HP 767 not forbidde for a little while to represent the
HP 787 be so narrowly forbidde the often use of wynes
ST 1508 God *f.* a fault so foule should scape unpunished
Ard. 1594 a fever ? God *f.* !
JB 150 « Now, God *f.* » (quoth she), and with that she

Forbidden.

HP Ind. 71 feasts not *f.* to Women
HP 783 unlesse she be prevented or *f.* by infirmitie
ST 1396 my Maister hath *f.* me to looke in this box
ST 1399 that, they are most *f.*, they will soonest attempt

Force.

HP 305 where the Sunne hath not so much *f.*
HP 1381 of so great efficacye and *f.* is order
HP 1624 the *f.* of reason that it seemes to beare
Cor. 143 whom we by *f.* have held in servitude
Cor. 492 in power and *f.*, and fiercenes, seem'd to threat the
Cor. 520 no feare of death should *f.* us to doe ill
Cor. 529 to *f.* us doe that goes against our hart
Cor. 786 the *f.* of heaven exceeds thy former strength
Cor. 1234 nor meekely beare the rider but by *f.*
Cor. 1271 hath waters *f.* and fire endur'd
Cor. 1638 resolv'd by *f.* to hold us hard at work
Cor. 1778 and proov'd each others *f.* sufficient
Jer. 1151 by Spaniards *f.*, most by Horatioes might
ST 273 Horatio, thou didst *f.* him first to yeeld
ST 610 by *f.*, or faire meanes will I cast about
ST 639 feare shall *f.* what freendship cannot winne
ST 701 thus hath he tane my body by his *f.*
ST 1631 well, *f.* perforce, I must constraine my selfe
ST 2205 getting by *f.*, as once Alcides did
ST 2264 by *f.* of windie sighes thy spirit breathes
ST 2928 but never shalt thou *f.* me to reveale
STA 2974 one that did *f.* your valiant Sonne to yeeld
SP 103 are hither come to try their *f.* in armes
SP 109 takes the Sun-beames burning with his *f.*
SP 769 thy beauty did defend me, not my *f.*
SP 1193 honour should *f.* disdaine to roote it out
SP 1222 throw not downe thy weapons, as if thy *f.* did faile
SP 1571 revives againe to flames, the *f.* is such
SP 1773 and should the seas turne tide to *f.* me backe
SP 1801 such is the *f.* of marrow burning love
SP 2054 why, what art thou that dares resist my *f.* ?
Ard. 117 were thy house of *f.*, these hands of mine
Ard. 1266 fire divided burns with lesser *f.*
Ard. 1268 till by the *f.* thereof my part consume
Ard. 2430 which he by *f.* and violence held from Reede
Cor. Arg. 16 assembled new forces, and occupied the

Cor. 1864 to raise newe forces, and returne to field
ST 182 the fury of your forces wil be staide
SP 530 not good pollicie to call your forces home
Forced.
VPJ 52 thou look'dst for life, yet lewdlie forc'd it fade
HP Ind. 13 beauty f. by painting insupportable
Cor. 433 must I my selfe be forc'd to ope the way whereat
ST 171 and forcst to yeelde him prisoner to his foe
ST 249 but first I forc'd him lay his weapons downe
ST 330 my death were naturall, but his was f.
ST 693 and by those wounds he f. me to yeeld
SP 504 within forst furrowes of her clowding brow
SP 614 if love of Haleb forst me on to wrath
SP 616 if justice forst me on, curst be that justice
SP 985 whom honors title forst me to misdoe
SP 1101 and forst Erastus into banishment
SP 1401 if captivate, then forst from holy faith
SP 1402 if forst from faith, for ever miserable
Ard. 1036 my mistress she hath f. me with an oath
Forceful.
Cor. 1971 when forcefull weapons fiercely tooke away their
Forceth.
SP 786 if heavens were just, that power that f. love
Forcing.
ST 14 f. divorce betwixt my love and me
'Fore.
Ard. 197 see **Before**
Jer. 1187 foregod, I have just mist them : ha
Forearmed.
Ard. 583 forewarned, f.; who threats his enemy
Forefathers.
Jer. 340 by our forfathers base captivitie
Jer. 910 Portugales, keepe your forfathers Othes
Fore-game.
Cor. 1216 a f. fecht about for civill discord
Forego.
Cor. 2036 and (when my soule Earths pryson shall forgoe)
ST 772 advice, which is to love him, or forgoe my love
ST 809 if she neglect him and forgoe his love
HP 428 removing foregoes not, but aprocheth us
Forehead.
ST 2259 thy f. troubled, and thy muttring lips murmure
SP 1458 smooth forhead, like the table of high Jove
Ard. 1295 even in my f. is thy name ingraven
Fore-heard.
SP 1633 having forehard of Basiliscoes worth
Foreign.
HP 1509 and travails into forren Countreys
Cor. 724 send Sextus over to some forraine Nation
SP 1239 imploy me else where in thy forraine wars
Foremost.
ST 31 1 past the perils of the formost porch
SP 1241 Erastus will be formost in the battaile
Fore-passed.
SP 224 I keep no table to character my f. conflicts
SP 1755 when as we call to minde forepassed greefes
Forerunner.
Jer. 723 ha, Andrea, the foore runner of these newes ?
'Foresaid, see Aforesaid.
Forest.
ST 1807 from a guiltie Conscience unto a forrest of distrust and
    feare
Cor. 1724 ronge through the Forrests with a frightfull noyse
Forest-king.
Ard. 1165 and, when the dreadful f. is gone
Foretell.

Cor. 176 maigre famin, which the weake f.
ST 829 and yet my hart foretels me some mischaunce
Foretold.
SP 1961 ah no ; my nightly dreames foretould me this
Forewarned.
SP 740 unlesse, forewarnd, the weakling coward flies
Ard. 583 f., forearmed ; who threats his enemy
Forfend.
Jer. 154 and you, I feare me, war, which peace f.
Jer. 714 angels of heaven forefend it
Forgat.
HP 271 he faigned or f. that which properlie
Forge.
SP 777 ah, how thine eyes can f. alluring lookes
Ard. 1275 'tis thy policy to f. distressful looks to
Forged.
Jer. 673 to see so strang a likenes f. and wrought
ST 881 with an envious, f. tale deceived the King
ST 1698 you (gentle brother) f. this for my sake
Forgery.
ST 360 O wicked forgerie : O traiterous miscreant
Forget.
HP 968 to recount, I should soone f. my purpose
HP 1696 in so precise a sort as thou heereafter not f. them
Cor. 456 my teares shall dry, and I my griefe f.
Jer. 387 I shall f. the Law. — Do, do
Jer. 695 doe not f. that was Alcario
ST Bal. 71 and that I would not it f.
ST 2439 Hieronimo cannot f. his sonne Horatio
ST 2495 but monstrous Fathers to f. so soone
ST 2647 whats that, Hieronimo ? f. not any thing
SP 725 I will f. thy former crueltie
SP 773 as if Erastus could f. himselfe ?
SP 1578 whe[n] Erastus doth f. this favor, then let him
SP 1751 and now, Perseda, lets f. oulde greefes
Ard. 343 the base terms I gave thee late, f. them
Ard. 1005 f. your griefs a while ; here comes your man
Ard. 1287 f., I pray thee, what hath passed betwixt us
Ard. 1367 I will f. this quarrel, gentle Alice
Ard. 1421 but, if I do f.
Ard. 1875 f. but this and never see the like
HP 1508 forgets his house, his Children, and his Wife
ST 3043 (Juno forgets olde wrath, and graunts him ease)
Forgetful.
Ard. 577 so f. of our state to make recount of it
Forgetting.
HP 585 hee ought (not f. that he is her husband)
Forgive.
Cor. 170 but to f. the apter that they be
SP 2178 f. me, deere Erastus, my unkindnes
Ard. 1874 pardon me, sweet Alice, and f. this fault !
Ard. 2382 f. me, Arden : I repent me now
ST 2707 forgives the murderers of thy noble sonne
Forgiven.
ST 2381 we have forgotten and f. that
Forgot.
Cor. 1122 and say : see where they goe that have theyr race f.
Cor. 1458 if Cittizens my kindnes have f.
ST Bal. 110 thinking my sonne I had f.
ST 797 the Princes raunsome must not be f.
ST 2482 and that, I hope, olde grudges are f.
ST 2536 which, long f., I found this other day
SP 70 I have f. the rest, but thats the effect
SP 686 and, if I live, this shall not be f.
SP 1758 if my Love will have olde greefes f.
Forgotten.

HP 886 one thing hath beene *f.* of those men of elder times
ST 1434 for feare his Lordship had *f.* me
ST 2381 we have *f.* and forgiven that
Forlorn.
ST Bal. 63 but missing them I stood forlorne
SP 1164 I, worthy Lord, a forlorne Christian
SP 1579 then let him live abandond and forlorne
Ard. 860 the *f.* traveller, whose lips are glued with
Form.
HP (Title) the true Oeconomia and forme of Housekeeping
HP Ind. 32 whether they varie in forme onely or
HP Ind. 76 forme of getting, what
HP 232 that apt forme of speech used by Lucretius
HP 931 receyve within themselves the forme of that vertue
HP 933 so doth the servaunt reserve the forme of those impressions
HP 1391 the forme or fashion of the World is none other then an order
HP 1393 we may well report that the forme of a house is the order
HP 1426 whether to get be a forme or part of housekeeping
HP 1480 that forme of merchandize is just and honest
HP 1723 consider whether they be discrepant in forme or greatnes
HP 1725 the forme of a Princes Pallace and a poore mans Cottage
HP 1737 to be distinguished from a private man, by forme
HP 1737 as the forme of their commaundements is distinguished, so
HP 1745 albeit they onely differ not in *f.*, but are
Jer. 619 welcom, my lifes selfe forme, deere Don Andrea
ST Bal. 61 and finding then his senslesse *f.*
ST 108 unfolde in breefe discourse your forme of battell
ST 123 our battels both were pitcht in squadron forme
ST 1131 oh life, no life, but lively fourme of death
Puck 24 nor wold indeed the forme of devyne praiers used
HP 165 the which I have devided into foure parts or formes
HP 603 receive and retaine all formes of customes
HP 907 these would I devide into two formes
HP 1377 the Images and formes of visible and intelligible things
HP 1584 this wee devide into two formes or kindes
Cor. 579 the formes of things doe never die
Cor. 581 reformes another thing thereby
Forma.
SP 457 when they let the poore goe under *F.* pauperis
SP 458 crie the chayne for me Sub *f.* pauperis, for money
Formal.
HP 1607 Number is reputed either according to the formall or materiall beeing
HP 1607 Formall number is a collection of a summe, not applied to
HP 1609 Formall number may infinitly encrease
HP 1619 for albeit the number of mony bee not formall
Formam.
HP 662ᵃ *f.* populabitur aetas
Formed.
HP 624 *f.* and beautified with many faire and
Former.
Cor. 28 our fathers found thee at their *f.* walls
Cor. 69 what helps it that thou ty'dst the *f.* World
Cor. 188 the *f.* petty combats did displace
Cor. 261 thou with thy *f.* husbands death hadst slept
Cor. 328 by whom the *f.* course of thy faire deeds
Cor. 380 may give poore Rome her *f.* libertie
Cor. 582 that still the *f.* shape retaines
Cor. 656 cause for *f.* wrongs to furnish us with teares?
Cor. 786 the force of heaven exceeds thy *f.* strength

Cor. 959 nay, he was mov'd with *f.* amitie
Cor. 1591 will agravate my *f.* misery
Cor. 1744 when with theyr swords (flesht with the *f.* fight)
Cor. 1800 a fresh remembrance of our *f.* sins
Jer. 612 then fall into your *f.* vaine of termes
Jer. 629 and talke of *f.* suites and quests of love
ST Bal. 1 you that have lost your *f.* joyes
ST 110 unto the height of *f.* happines
ST 1322 a guiltie conscience, urged with the thought of *f.* evils
ST 1345 why so, this fits our *f.* pollicie
ST 2734 recompt thy *f.* wrongs thou hast received
SP 725 I will forget thy *f.* crueltie
SP 812 and all my *f.* love is turnd to hate
Ard. 462 so that all *f.* grants are cut off
Ard. 483 had rested still within their *f.* state
Ard. 570 and repossess his *f.* lands again
Ard. 1290 ay, to my *f.* happy life again
Puck 4 reteyning me wᵗʰout yoʳ honoʳˢ *f.* pryvitie
Puck 77 suspect me guiltie of the *f.* shipwrack
Formeth.
HP 379 *f.* the day and night of such equalitie
Forsake.
Cor. 1741 till, dead or fled, the one *f.* the field
Ard. 434 what? shall an oath make thee *f.* my love?
Cor. 307 or (where the sunne forsakes the Ocean sea
Forsaken.
HP 372 is by him *f.* and awaked
Cor. 589 become *f.* as before, yet after
Cor. 1958 did revive the lights of thy *f.* bed
Forslowed.
Ard. 1304 *f.* advantages, and spurned at time
Forsook.
Ard. 1305 ay, Fortune's right hand Mosbie hath *f.*
Forsooth.
SP 983 I, *f.*, sir
SP 985 I, *f.*, sir
Ard. 500 there, *f.*, he revels it among such filthy ones
Ard. 785 a crew of harlots, all in love, *f.*
Ard. 1625 *f.*, for credit sake, I must leave thee!
Forsworn.
Jer. 173 then ile be sure you shall not be forsworne
Jer. 911 let them not ly forsworne now in their graves
Ard. 1464 having *f.* it with such vehement oaths
Ard. 2134 I'll go to Rome rather than be *f.*
JB 147 she asked him if he would have her forsworne
Fort.
Cor. 32 and hongst (O Hell) upon a Forte halfe finisht thy
Cor. 400 with pike in hand upon a Forte besieg'd
Forte.
HP 961 Ch' innanzi a buon signor fa servo *f.*
Forthwith.
HP 137 *f.* was the Table furnished with fruits
ST Bal. 91 then to the Court *f.* I went
ST 81 *f.*, Revenge, she rounded thee in th' eare
ST 1235 and bid him *f.* meet the Prince and me
SP 733 goe thou foorthwith, arme thee from top to toe
SP 1870 thou shalt foorthwith be bound unto that post
Fortified.
Cor. 549 have plac'd our soules, and forteflde the same
Fortify.
SP 1994 weele fortifie our walles, and keepe the towne
Fortitude.
HP 639 to man are Wisedome, *F.*, and Liberalitie: To woman, Modestie and Chastitie
Jer. 1008 made of the ribs of Mars and *f.*?
Fortnight's.

Ard. 1422 I have longed this *f.* day to speak with you

Fortress.

HP 233 Chyldren are the fortresse and defences of their Parents

Cor. 831 from once footing in our Fortresses have yee repeld the

Fortuna.

ST 304 In me consumpsit vires *f.* nocendo

Fortunate.

HP 1359 who beeing a fortunat mother of Children

Jer. 22 O *f.* houre, blessed mynuit, happy day

Jer. 813 O, be as *f.* as thou art faire

Jer. 969 valliant Andrea, *f.* Lorenzo

Jer. 972 be all as *f.* as heavens blest host

Fortune.

VPJ 9 good *f.* and an everlasting fame attend on thee

HP Ind. 72 *f.* maketh many men servile

HP 35 « *F.* » (quoth I) « doth favour mee with

HP 47 and what good *f.* ledde you into these parts?

HP 52 the wrath of *F.* and of mightie me[n] I shun

HP 70 from your owne disposition then from *F.*

HP 529 companions and consorts of one selfe *f.*

HP 583 by some accident of *F.*, a man marrieth

HP 914 not onely servile in condition and of *f.*

HP 981 manie are servaunts by *F.* that are free by Nature

HP 984 servile *f.* can engender servile evils in a gentle mind

HP 1007 as our *f.* hath not gyven us that wealth

HP 1159 losses which by chaunce or *F.* may betide him

Cor. (Title) her Father and Husbandes downe-cast, death, and *f.*

Cor. 99 the more that *F.* hath with others stood

Cor. 102 for we are proude, when *F.* favours us

Cor. 262 but partiall *F.*, and the powerful Fates

Cor. 346 and tickle *F.* staies not in a place

Cor. 364 within a while, I saw how *F.* plaid

Cor. 606 if *f.* chaunce but once to check

Cor. 657 O, but I feare that *F.* seekes new flawes

Cor. 659 wherein can *F.* further injure us

Cor. 689 *F.* is fickle. — But hath fayld him never

Cor. 723 the self-same foe and *f.* following them

Cor. 860 I finde my *f.* not the least in this

Cor. 1004 *F.* in powre imperious

Cor. 1072 and will not see that *F.* can her hopes defeate

Cor. 1099 t'is *F.* rules, for equitie and right have

Cor. 1478 but *F.* and the heavens have care of us

Cor. 1479 *F.* is fickle, Heaven imperious

Cor. 1588 O cruell *f.*

Cor. 1815 O crnel *f.*

Cor. 2013 (which both the world and *F.* heapt on him)

Jer. 704 Horatio, twas well, as *f.* stands

Jer. 837 what happier *f.*, then, my selfe can move?

ST Bal. 8 on whom fond *f.* smiled long

ST 39 and for his love tried *f.* of the warres

ST 40 and, by warres *f.*, lost both love and life

ST 94 some few that are deceast by *f.* of the warre

ST 97 speak, man, hath *f.* given us victorie?

ST 194 such as warres *f.* hath reserv'd from death

ST 230 is now controlde by *f.* of the warres

ST 306 yes, *F.* may bereave me of my Crowne

ST 307 heere, take it now; let *F.* doe her worst

ST 311 *F.* is blinde, and sees not my deserts

ST 342 and Ile bewray the *f.* of thy Sonne

ST 830 sweet, say not so; faire *f.* is our freend

ST 1030 as *F.* toyleth in the affaires of Kings

ST 1261 and holde on, *F.*, once more favour me

ST 1385 now stands our *f.* on a tickle point

ST 2890 bearing his latest *f.* in his fist

SP 1 what, Death and *F.* crosse the way of Love?

SP 24 *F.* is chorus; Love and Death be gone

SP 25 I tell thee, *F.*, and thee, wanton Love

SP 33 though *F.* have delight in change

SP 37 tush, *F.* can doo more then Love or Death

SP 354 I go, and *F.* guide my Launce

SP 416 O cursed *F.*, enemy to Fame

SP 483 ah, treacherous *F.*, enemy to Love

SP 496 cut short what malice *F.* misintends

SP 498 time may restore what *F.* tooke from me

SP 623 now, Death and *F.*, which of all us three

SP 636 *F.*, that first by chance brought them together

SP 637 for, till by *F.* persons meete each other

SP 660 who is [the] greatest, *F.*, Death, or Love

SP 831 because that *F.* made the fault, not Love

SP 866 *F.* may make me maister of mine owne

SP 920 and to acuse fell *F.*, Love, and Death

SP 1091 *F.*, thou madest Fernando finde the chaine

SP 1094 but *F.* would not let her keepe it long

SP 1097 ran not by *F.*, but necessitie

SP 1105 and doubt not to, but *F.* will be there

SP 1109 to mar what Love or *F.* takes in hand

SP 1359 the greatest honor *F.* could affoord

SP 1361 now, *F.*, what hast thou done in this later passage?

SP 1591 and therefore *F.* now will be revengde

SP 1596 Heavens, Love, and *F.*, all three have decreed

SP 1724 now, *F.*, what hast thou done in this latter act?

SP 2196 hence foolish *F.*, and thou wanton Love

SP 2214 packe, Love and *F.*, play in Commedies

SP 2217 but *F.* shall; for when I waste the world

SP 2219 meane time will *F.* governe as she may

SP 122 and be my *f.* as my love deserves

SP 123 so be thy *f.* as thy features serves

SP 136 such *f.* as the good Andromache wisht

SP 408 therefore, Erastus, happy laude thy *f.*

SP 414 which by good *f.* I have found to day

SP 911 least you pertake the hardness of my *f.*

SP 999 God sends *f.* to fooles

SP 1141 I wish that *f.* of our holy wars would

Ard. 533 good *f.* follow all your forward thoughts

Cor. 290 ye may be ritch and great in Fortunes grace

Cor. 513 to scape the feares that followes Fortunes glaunces

Cor. 1109 the conquering Tyrant, high in Fortunes grace

Cor. 1364 Caesar is now earthes fame, and Fortunes terror

Cor. 1890 yea, thee, my latest fortunes firmest hope

SP (Title) Loves constancy, Fortunes inconstancy, and Deaths Triumphs

SP 2 why, what is Love but Fortunes tenis-ball?

SP 628 the Ring and Carkanet were Fortunes gifts

SP 654 he was overthrowne by Fortunes high displeasure

SP 1373 that Love and Fortunes power could neither save

SP 1377 why, Brusors victorie was Fortunes gift

SP 1590 what was it but abuse of Fortunes gift?

ST 298 yet this is higher then my fortunes reach

Ard. 1305 ay, Fortune's right hand Mosbie hath forsook

Cor. 563 all fortunes, all felicities, upon their motion doe

Cor. 647 and whose first fortunes (fild with all distresse)

Cor. 688 O no, our losse lyfts Caesars fortunes hyer

Cor. 798 nowe you, whom both the gods and Fortunes grace

Cor. 1020 and fickle when our fortunes rise

Cor. 1389 and noble deeds were greater then his fortunes

ST 7 to gratious fortunes of my tender youth

SP 2212 their loves and fortunes ended with their lives

Forty.

Ard. 806 how can I miss him, when I think on the *f.* angels

Ard. 2044 and, when he is dead, you shall have *f.* more

Forward.

HP 727 that she be forwarde with the first at all dauncings

Cor. 192 amongst the *f.* Souldiers first discend
Jer. 1170 see, see, he points to have us goe *f.* on
ST 782 in case the match goe *f.*, the tribute
ST 1457 O sir, you are to *f.*
SP 266 *f.*, brave Ladies, place you to behold the
Ard. 533 good fortune follow all your *f.* thoughts
Ard. 1108 go *f.* now in that we have begun
Cor. 1754 encourageth the over-*f.* hands to bloode and death
SP 263 mount, ye brave Lordings, forwards to the tilt
Ard. 2315 backwards and forwards may you see the print

Forwardness.
Jer. 866 I am assured of your forwardnes
ST 799 and well his forwardnes deserves reward

Foster.
Ard. 1155 an ill-thewed *f.* had removed the toil

Fostered.
HP 171 whereupon the Vines, after the manner of our petit
　Countries, are laid and *f.*
Cor. 821 and stung to death the foole that fostred her
Ard. 910 a poorer coward than yourself was never *f.*

Fought.
Cor. 39 have *f.* like foes Pharsalias miserie
Cor. 483 and those two Scipios (that in person *f.*
Cor. 1370 and *f.* more battailes then the best of them
Cor. 1623 lamely they *f.*, to draw us further on
Cor. 1774 and *f.* as freshly as they first beganne
SP 198 and there in three set battles *f.*
SP 235 I *f.* on horseback with an hundred Kernes
Ard. 1103 it should be slipt till I had *f.* with thee

Foul.
Cor. 334 what foule infernall, or what stranger hell
Jer. 455 fie, fie, Horatio : what, is your pen foule?
ST 71 and all foule sinnes with torments overwhelmd
ST 337 his ransomes worth will stay from foule revenge
ST 1112 rent with remembrance of so foule a deed
ST 1509 God forbid a fault so foule should scape unpunished
SP 432 marry, a foule fault ; but why are his eares cut?
SP 537 fog not thy glory with so fowle eclipse
SP 1860 foule death betide me, if I sweare not true
Ard. 12 and those *f.* objects that offend mine eyes !
Ard. 1053 the wrinkles in his *f.* death-threat'ning face
Ard. 1227 that tables not with *f.* suspicion
Ard. 1321 it grieves me not to see how *f.* thou art
Ard. 2347 confess this *f.* fault and be penitent
Ard. 2405 I had ne'er given consent to this *f.* deed
JB 8 to accuse Caine of so fowle a fact

Foulest-minded.
SP 742 the fairest shaped but fowlest minded man

Foul-mouthed.
SP 2085 injurious, foule mouthd knight, my wrathfull arme

Found.
VPJ 33 I sought my death, and founde it in my wombe
VPJ 51 thou soughtst thy death, and *f.* it in desert
HP Ind. 99 money, why and how founde out and used
HP Ind. 142 weaving, how first *f.* out
HP 190 there are few good mellons to be *f.*
HP 913 when it happeneth that some one is *f.*
HP 1197 money which was first *f.* out by mans appointment
HP 1356 in this kinde of work was Lucretia often *f.*
HP 1587 money was founde out and used (a while) to make
HP 1721 but since wee *f.* that there is difference
HP 1757 which proportion also may be *f.* amongst
Cor. 28 our fathers *f.* thee at their former walls
Cor. 197 where in the flowred Meades dead men were *f.*
Cor. 817 that fownd a Serpent pyning in the snowe
Jer. 492 « O, that villainy should be *f.* in the great Chamber »

Jer. 516 « O that villainy should be *f.* in the great chamber »
Jer. 700 why should I make two tailes, for to be *f.* in two?
Jer. 1012 and could he not be *f.*?
ST Bal. 39 at last he *f.*, within a pause, howe he
ST Bal. 81 not yet *f.* out the murtherers, to ease my mones
ST 606 I have already *f.* a stratageme
ST 1686 *f.* Bel-imperia with Horatio
ST 1691 by being *f.* so meanely accompanied
ST 1695 least that his highnes should have *f.* you there
ST 2202 though on this earth justice will not be *f.*
ST 2513 I *f.* a letter, written in your name
ST 2556 which, long forgot, I *f.* this other day
ST 2853 where hanging on a tree I *f.* my sonne
SP 361 and when twas *f.* upon him, he said
SP 414 which by good fortune I have *f.* to day
SP 649 and more then so ; for he that *f.* the chaine
Ard. 212 try me whom thou ne'er *f.* false?
Ard. 282 and yet in taste not to be *f.* at all
Ard. 592 how now, Clarke? have you *f.* me false?
Ard. 681 a search was made, the plate was *f.* with me
Ard. 1201 and coming down he *f.* the doors unshut
Ard. 1858 hast thou not lately *f.* me over-kind?
JB 199 although I never *f.* any by thee
Puck 16 were founde some fragments of a disputation

Foundation.
Jer. 595 build a *f.* surest, when multitudes
Cor. 488 whose foundations reacht from deepest hell

Founded.
HP Ind. 51 *f.* first by Nature
HP 898 is first *f.* upon Nature
Cor. 944 whose fell ambition (*f.* first in blood)

Fount.
SP 1466 where under covert lyes the *f.* of pleasure

Fountain.
Jer. 196 melt it selfe into thy vaines, and thou the fountaine
Cor. 593 engendreth fountaines, whence againe those
Cor. 594 those fountaines doe to floods convart?
ST 920 O, gush out teares, fountaines and flouds of teares
ST 1130 Oh eies, no eies, but fountains fraught with teares
SP 1464 brests, like two overflowing Fountaines

Fountain-water.
STA 2003 sprinkling it with fountaine water

Four.
VPJ 15 these foure faire giftes (O Prince, of right renound)
HP 165 the which I have devided into foure parts or formes
HP 1157 as *f.* to eight, or sixe at least
HP 1751 are devided into foure parts
Jer. 930 foure precious lines, spoke by our fathers mouth
SP 243 endured some three or foure howers combat
SP 850 and, sirra, provide me foure Visards
SP 851 foure Visards, foure Gownes, a boxe, and a Drumme
Ard. 1511 your way and mine lies *f.* miles together
Ard. 1512 the devil break all your necks at *f.* miles' end !

Four-square.
HP 85 four square and of convenient greatnes

Fourteen.
SP 180 at foureteene yeeres of age was I made Knight

Fourth.
HP 173 the *f.* I have reserved for hearbes

Fowl.
HP 1264 fish and fowle, which will bee suddainly corrupt
Cor. 795 now murdred lye for Foule to feede upon
SP 221 as the aire to the fowle, or the marine moisture to

Fowle.
Ard. 1933 Mosbie, Franklin, Bradshaw, Adam *F.*, with divers

Fowlers.

ST 1351 must look like *f.* to their dearest freends
Fowling-piece.
Ard. 1426 water-dog that coucheth till the *f.* be off
Fox.
SP 369 it will be better then the *F.* in the hole for me
Fragments.
HP 1021 those relicts and fragme[n]ts of that finer fare
Puck 16 *f.* of a disputation, toching that opinion
Fraight, *see* **Freight.**
Frail.
Cor. 265 Pompey, the fame that ranne of thy frayle honors
Cor. 571 fraile men, or mans more fraile defence
Frailty.
Cor. 535 tis not for frailtie or faint cowardize that
Frame.
HP 813 ‹ to *f.* their horses fit for service and ›
ST 845 to *f.* sweet musick to Horatios tale
ST 1146 and *f.* my steps to unfrequented paths
SP 756 Ile *f.* my selfe to his dissembling art
SP 1772 my armes should *f.* mine oares to crosse the seas
SP 1774 desire should *f.* me winges to flie to him
Ard. 258 that makes him *f.* a speaking countenance
Ard. 1178 it may be so, God *f.* it to the best
Framed.
HP 923 Beastes whom Nature hath also *f.* apt to learne
HP 1443 but hath *f.* men, that are apt to obey
HP 1444 to serve those whom also she hath *f.* to commaund
STA 1987 had he been *f.* of naught but blood and death
ST 2267 a song, three parts in one, but all of discords fram'd
SP 52 but I have framde a dittie to the tune
Cor. 586 which by old nature is new-*f.*
Framing.
HP 119 I, *f.* my passage towardes the good man
France.
HP 42 going into Fraunce I past by Pyemount
HP 1226 Travailers, Italian Merchants, or those of Germany or Fraunce
SP 160 in *F.* I tooke the Standard from the King
SP 166 like welcome unto thee, faire Knight of Fraunce
SP 169 what is thy mot, renowned Knight of Fraunce?
SP 175 Saint Denis is for Fraunce, and that for me
Franchised.
Cor. 27 and teares our freedom from our franchiz'd harts
Cor. 1074 from chaunce is nothing franchized
Frank.
Cor. 1146 or if so franck a will your soule possesse
SP 842 it must be so; Lucinas a franke Gaimster
SP 845 shees a franke gaimster, and inclinde to play
Franklin.
Ard. 9 *F.,* thy love prolongs my weary life
Ard. 23 is monstrous, *F.,* and intolerable
Ard. 89 *F.* and I will down unto the quay
Ard. 224 and he and *F.* will to London straight
Ard. 383 *F.,* thou hast a box of mithridate
Ard. 411 and, Master *F.,* seeing you take him hence
Ard. 783 see, Master *F.,* here's proper stuff
Ard. 791 now, Master *F.,* let us go walk in Paul's
Ard. 794 the other is *F.,* Arden's dearest friend
Ard. 817 is't nothing else? come, *F.,* let's away
Ard. 828 met him and *F.* going merrily to the
Ard. 972 no, *F.,* no : if fear or stormy threats
Ard. 989 Ah, *F., F.,* when I think on this
Ard. 1003 here, here it lies, ah *F.,* here it lies
Ard. 1009 come, Master *F.,* shall we go to bed?
Ard. 1057 he comes, he comes ! ah, Master *F.,* help !
Ard. 1077 come, Master *F.,* let us go to bed

Ard. 1147 come, Master *F.,* you shall go with me
Ard. 1170 so, trust me, *F.,* when I did awake
Ard. 1183 come, Master *F.,* we'll now walk in Paul's
Ard. 1187 say, Master *F.,* shall it not be so?
Ard. 1196 *F.* and my master were very late
Ard. 1198 and *F.* left his napkin where he sat
Ard. 1446 come, Master *F.,* onwards with your tale
Ard. 1452 come, Master *F.,* let us go on softly
Ard. 1542 the season fits ; come, *F.,* let's away
Ard. 1776 *F.,* hearest thou this fellow speak?
Ard. 1830 come, *F.,* let us strain to mend our pace
Ard. 1905 I pray thee, gentle *F.,* hold thy peace
Ard. 1949 and railed on *F.* that was cause of all
Ard. 1953 Mosbie, *F.,* Bradshaw, Adam Fowle, with divers
Ard. 1972 with that comes *F.* at him lustily
Ard. 2012 you, Master Greene shall single *F.* forth
Ard. 2200 Master *F.,* where did you leave my husband?
Ard. 2230 good Master *F.,* go and seek him forth
Ard. 2257 ay, for *F.* thinks that we have murdered him
Ard. 2294 Master *F.,* what mean you come so sad?
Ard. 2296 ah, by whom? Master *F.,* can you tell?
Ard. 2299 but, Master *F.,* are you sure 'tis he?
Ard. 2328 ah, Master *F.,* God and heaven can tell
Frantic.
Ard. 1862 accursed to link in liking with a *f.* man !
Franticly.
ST Bal. 79 then frantickly I ran about
ST Bal. 99 that frantickly I ran about
Fratri.
HP 1640ᵃ Pecuniam tuam non dabis *f.*
Fraudful.
SP 780 to cheek thy fraudfull countenance with a blush?
SP 2010 or that fraudfull squire of Ithaca, iclipt Ulisses?
Ard. 963 do lead thee with a wicked *f.* smile
Fraught.
HP 877 they are *f.* with millions of delights
Cor. 294 so (pestilently) *f.* with change of plagues is
Cor. 387 till, *f.* with yeeres and honor both at once
ST 656 full *f.* with lines and arguments of love
ST 1130 Oh eies, no eies, but fountains *f.* with teares
SP 677 full *f.* with love and burning with desire
Fray.
SP 1698 beare of some blowes when you run away in a fraye
Ard. 814 what troublesome *f.* or mutiny is this?
Ard. 815 'tis nothing but some brabling paltry *f.*
Ard. 1756 who, in a manner to take up the *f.*
Frayed.
Cor. 540 is not, as are the vulgar, slightly fraied
Free.
HP 981 manie are servaunts by Fortune that are *f.* by Nature
HP 1550 is requisit and meet in the uniting of *f.* men
Cor. 325 escapt not *f.* fro thy victorious hands?
Cor. 502 with brandisht dart doth make the passage *f.*
Cor. 629 to *f.* our Towne from tyrannie
Cor. 809 all powreles give proud Caesars wrath *f.* passage
Cor. 1228 in spite of Caesar, Cassius will be *f.*
Cor. 1273 to *f.* the truth from tyrannie
Cor. 1280 from obscure death shall *f.* his name
Cor. 1297 that to *f.* them fro the hands of a Tyrant
Cor. 1325 he onely lives most happilie that, *f.* and
Cor. 1501 *f.* fro rage of civill strife
Cor. 1685 that we must all live *f.,* or friendly die
Cor. 1758 a poole, which in her rage *f.* passage doth afford
Cor. 1820 no place was *f.* from sorrow ; every where lay
Jer. 846 to seet you *f.* from base captivity
ST 239 yet *f.* from bearing any servile yoake

ST 1067 so am I f. from this suggestion
ST 1274 besides, this place is f. from all suspect
ST 1633 till heaven, as I have hope, shall set me f.
ST 2352 curteous wordes, as f. from malice to Hieronimo as
SP 370 brave Gentlemen, by all your f. consents
SP 811 heere, give her this ; Perseda now is f.
SP 984 thou art a bondman, and wouldst fain be f.?
SP 986 then do but this, and I will make thee f.
SP 2194 thou didst but wound their flesh, their minds are f.
Ard. 513 shall set you f. from all this discontent
Ard. 1850 hurt thy friend whose thoughts were f. from harm
Ard. 1860 called I not help to set my husband f.?
JB 86 had f. accesse to practise with her about the

Free-born.
Cor. 1892 that, being free borne, I shall not die a slave
Jer. 848 as a base blush upon your free borne cheeks
Jer. 862 to live like captives, or as free borne die?

Freedom.
Cor. 27 and teares our f. from our franchiz'd harts
Cor. 121 of th' ancient f. wherein we were borne
Cor. 1124 then (arm'd) to save their f. and their fame?
Cor. 1695 but t'is for publique f. that we fight
Jer. 856 honor, your countries reputation, your lives freedome
ST 466 I, by conceit my freedome is enthralde
Puck 10 as also in the feare of god, and f. of my conscience

Freely.
Cor. 1129 I f. marcht with Caesar in hys warrs
Cor. 1290 did f. chase vile servitude
Cor. 1737 doe at the halfe pyke f. charge each other
Ard. 3 hath f. given to thee and to thy heirs

Freemen.
HP 888 not onely fitting, but most needful for f.
HP 893 who for the greater number are at thys day f.

Freight.
Cor. 559 what e're the massie earth hath fraight

Freight, *see* **Fraught.**

French.
HP 65 to waft over some F. Gentlemen
Cor. 61 nor yet the fierce and fiery humor'd F.
ST 2644 seene the like in Paris, mongst the F. Tragedians
ST 2653 I know that Bel-imperia hath practised the F.
ST 2654 in courtly F. shall all her phraises be
Ard. 832 I value every drop of my blood at a F. crown
Ard. 2142 three games for a F. crown, sir, and please you

Frenchman.
Jer. 526 made him straddle too much like a F.
SP 98 the sudden F., and the bigbon'd Dane
SP 343 O, well run, Maister. He hath overthrowne the F.

Frenzy.
Cor. 840 one that with blind frenzie buildeth up his throne?

Frequence.
HP 1227 or far from f. or resort of Passengers

Frequent.
ST 2420 Hieronimo, f. my homely house
Ard. 384 and, Arden, though I now f. thy house
Ard. 350 nay, rather f. it more
Ard. 2101 and therefore will I ne'er f. it more
Ard. 2130 henceforth f. my house no more
Jer. 599 this is the gallery where she most frequents

Fresh.
Cor. 977 f. springs of water at my weeping eyes
Cor. 1800 a f. remembrance of our former sins
Cor. 1850 to come upon them with a f. alarme
Jer. 400 we have f. sperits that can renew it againe
Jer. 789 we have f. spirites that can renew it againe
ST 404 brought in a f. supply of Halberdiers

ST 983 seest thou those wounds that yet are bleeding f.?
SP 91 and add f. courage to my fainting limmes
Ard. 1024 pouring f. sorrow on his weary limbs
Ard. 1233 my night's repose made daylight f. to me
Ard. 1666 a bargain, and you shall not have it f. and fasting
Cor. 1835 he that had hap to scape, doth helpe a f. to

Fresh-flowered.
Cor. 1520 new set with many a fresh-flowrd Coronet

Freshly.
Cor. 1774 and fought as f. as they first beganne

Fretful.
Cor. 1924 say, freatfull heavens, what fault have I committed
Cor. 1959 unworthely opposing of thy freatfull jelosie
Ard. 1011 ah, what a hell is f. jealousy!

Friars.
Jer. 218 from friers that nurse whores there goes another path

Friday.
JB 153 and on the F. he was buried, no person

Friend.
HP 253 a Gentleman, a friende and neighbor of ours
Cor. 191 made thundring Mars (Dissentions common f.)
Cor. 947 that was because that, Pompey being theyr freend
Cor. 1059 so noble Marius, Arpins f.
Cor. 1454 a man may make his foe his f., you know
Cor. 1455 a may may easier make his f. his foe
Jer. 189 tis fixed upon my hart ; adew, soules f.
Jer. 282 I like thy true hart, boy ; thou lovest thy f.
Jer. 329 is welcome to his f., thou to our court
Jer. 352 was thy full f., is now returned thy foe
Jer. 507 « Thy assured f. », say, « gainst Lorenzo and
Jer. 528 « Thy assured f. gainst Lorenzo and
Jer. 671 live, truest f., for ever loved and blest
Jer. 1051 thou art a wondrous f., a happy sperit
Jer. 1089 my other soule, my bosome, my harts f.
Jer. 1138 come then, my f., in purple I will beare thee
Jer. 1158 O my pale friende, wert thou anything but a ghoast
Jer. 1169 your f. conceives in signes how you rejoyce
ST Bal. 27 to relate the death of her beloved f.
ST Bal. 32 because he slewe her chiefest f.
ST Bal. 128 because he slew her dearest f.
ST 354 counterfeits under the colour of a duteous f.
ST 420 and sighed and sorrowed as became a freend
ST 426 and weare it in remembrance of my freend
ST 435 she will be Don Horatios thankfull freend
ST 450 Ile love Horatio, my Andreas freend
ST 594 yet might she love me as her brother's freend
ST 626 tell truth, and have me for thy lasting freend
ST 714 my hart (sweet freend) is like a ship at sea
ST 830 sweet, say not so ; faire fortune is our freend
ST 1013 but tis my freend Horatio that is slaine
ST 1258 Ile trust my selfe, my selfe shall be my freend
ST 1335 injurious villaine, murderer of his freend
ST 1629 me for thy freend Horatio handled thus
ST 1879 an argument of honorable care to keepe his freend
ST 2306 accompany thy f. with thine extremities
ST 2409 the hope of Spaine, mine honorable freend?
ST 2593 then gan he break his passions to a freend
ST 2772 but let my f., the Rhodian Knight, come foorth
ST 2785 Erasto is my f. ; and while he lives
ST 3025 Ile lead my freend Horatio through those feeldes
SP 284 by gods fish, f., take you the Latins part?
SP 393 give me thy hand, I vowe myselfe thy f.
SP 571 I take it, Haleb, thou art f. to Rhodes
SP 572 not halfe so much am I a f. to Rhodes
SP 676 a blisful war with me, thy chiefest f.?
SP 839 that she hath wrongd Erastus and her frend

SP 1029 to wrong my f. whose thoughts were ever true
SP 1039 untill I meete Erastus, my sweete f.
SP 1209 and be great Solimans adopted f.
SP 1219 but ever after thy continuall f.
SP 1275 & 1276 my f. is gone, and I am desolate
SP 1283 had I not lost it, my f. had not been slaine
SP 1284 had I not askt it, my f. had not departed
SP 1409 wert thou my f., thy mind would jumpe with mine
SP 1418 a worthy man, though not Erastus f.
SP 1530 this seat I keep voide for another f.
SP 1738 to counsell Soliman to slay his f.
SP 1789 and when Erastus comes, our perjurd f.
SP 1876 to moane Perseda, and accuse my f.
SP 2223 sparing none but sacred Cynthias f.
SP 2227 whose life is heavens delight, and Cynthias f.
Ard. 20 comfort thyself, sweet f.; it is not strange
Ard. 44 be patient, gentle f., and learn of me to
Ard. 121 stay, Adam, stay; thou wert wont to be my f.
Ard. 417 hereafter think of me as of your dearest f.
Ard. 657 yet thy f. to do thee any good I can
Ard. 779 faith, f. Michael, this is very ill
Ard. 794 the other is Franklin, Arden's dearest f.
Ard. 930 so shalt thou purchase Mosbie for thy f.
Ard. 1488 my honest f. that came along with me
Ard. 1491 you and your f. come home and sup with me
Ard. 1494 a gentleman, my honest f.
Ard. 1497 and bring your honest f. along with you?
Ard. 1649 this mist, my f., is mystical
Ard. 1654 f., what's thy opinion of this mist?
Ard. 1850 and hurt thy f. whose thoughts were free from harm
Ard. 1880 thou wouldst have marked the speeches of thy f.
Ard. 1889 for that I injured thee, and wronged my f.
Ard. 2240 faith, f. Michael, and thou sayest true
Ard. 2295 Arden, thy husband and my f., is slain
Puck 26 that I shold love or be familer frend, wᵗʰ one so
VPJ 11 this makes thy friends, this makes thy foes admire
HP 1510 leaving the care of them to Factors, Friends, and Servaunts
Cor. Arg. 14 and some other Senators his friends
Cor. 1144 our Countries love then friends or chyldren are
Cor. 1207 to render him, and reconcile old frends
Cor. 1305 by their chyldren, friends, or wives
Cor. 1473 but for thy friends and Country all too-short
Cor. 1710 on then, brave men, my fellowes and Romes friends
Jer. 165 I go to knit friends, not to kindle foes
Jer. 1188 thou hast more friends to take thy leave of
ST Bal. 105 did send for me to make us friends
ST 516 we both are freends; tribute is paid
ST 776 I know no better meanes to make us freends
ST 807 yong virgins must be ruled by their freends
ST 1351 must look like fowlers to their dearest freends
ST 2424 embrace each other, and be perfect freends
ST 2426 freends, quoth he? see, Ile be freends with you all
ST 2429 it is fit for us that we be freends
STA 2937 nay, then I care not; come, and we shall be friends
ST 3023 I may consort my freends in pleasing sort
ST 3053 then haste we doune to meet thy freends and foes
ST 3054 to place thy freends in ease, the rest in woes
SP 699 heres none but friends; yet let me challenge you
SP 706 why then the mends is made, and we still friends
SP 707 still friends? still foes; she weares my Carcanet
SP 942 farewell, sweet friends, dearer then countrey soyle
SP 1151 kinde to their foes, and liberall to their friends
SP 1268 your friends commend them to you
SP 1410 for what are friends but one minde in two bodies?
SP 1423 I, there it is: now all my friends are slaine

SP 1532 so shall I joy betweene two captive friends
SP 1584 me thinks I should not part with two such friends
SP 1601 well governd friends do first regard themselves
SP 1646 or for my friends that there were murthered
SP 1647 my valour every where shall purchase friends
SP 1705 do you not know that they are all friends
Ard. 341 and thou and I'll be friends, if this prove true
Ard. 491 your honourable friends, nor what you brought?
Ard. 1326 often hath been told me by my friends
Ard. 1639 house were a-fire, or some of his friends dead
Ard. 1752 marching arm in arm, like loving friends
Ard. 1798 either there be butchered by thy dearest friends
Ard. 1912 his friends must not be lavish in their speech
Ard. 1946 ah, gentle Michael, art thou sure they're friends?
Ard. 1954 with divers of his neighbours and his friends
Ard. 2015 and we like friends will play a game or two
Ard. 2092 therefore I thought it good to make you friends
Ard. 2097 Alice, bid him welcome; he and I are friends
Ard. 2100 his company hath purchased me ill friends
Ard. 2117 sirrah, fetch me a cup of wine, I'll make them friends
Ard. 2127 your company hath purchased me ill friends
JB 26 of good friends, and well esteemed for fine
JB 35 the good will and favour of al her friends and kinsfolk
Cor. 449 our friendes mis-fortune doth increase our owne
Friendly.
Cor. 1558 feasts, nor f. company
Cor. 1685 that we must all live free, or f. die
Jer. 51 if f. phraises, honied speech, bewitching accent
Jer. 1190 imbrace them, and take f. leave
ST 288 and feast our prisoner as our f. guest
ST 421 but neither freendly sorrow, sighes, nor teares
ST 579 and rue the sufferance of your freendly paine
ST 2431 why, this is f. done, Hieronimo
SP 148 that exercise their war with f. blowes
SP 1149 brave men at armes, and f. out of armes
Ard. 1856 couldst thou not see us f. smile on thee
Friendly-tempered.
Jer. 86 if friendly tempred phraise cannot effect
Friendship.
HP 1117 f. which by Aristotle is applied in the highest
HP 1128 those lawes of f. ought to be observed
ST 166 f. and hardie valour, joynd in one
ST 568 Ile turne their freendship into fell despight
ST 633 speake, man, and gaine both freendship and reward
ST 689 feare shall force what freendship cannot winne
Ard. 931 and by his f. gain his sister's love
SP 1411 perhaps thou doubts my friendships constancie
SP 1534 if friendships yoake were not at libertie
SP 1564 come, envie, then, and sit in friendships seate
Frigescit.
HP 394 good Wines, without which Non solum f. Venus
Fright.
Cor. 528 (to f. us) sette pale death before our eyes
Ard. 1252 or f. me by detecting of his end
Ard. 2247 alas, I counsel! fear frights away my wits
Frighted.
ST 122 and heaven it selfe was f. with the sound
Frightful.
Cor. 410 my frightfull hart (stund in my stone-cold breast)
Cor. 1833 have fild heavens fierie vaults with fright-full horror
Cor. 1724 ronge through the Forrests with a frightfull noyse
Jer. 161 shape f. conceit beyond the intent of act
Jer. 655 what frightfull villaines this, his sword unsthethed?
Frisking.
STA 1759 or melt in passion ore a f. Kid
Frizeland.

Fro.

HP 14 tooke the poor Kidde *f.* forth their mouthes
HP 59 arrowe *f.* forth the strongest bow of Parthia
HP 176 is somewhat seperat fro[m] my possessions
Cor. Arg. 7 sent her *f.* thence to Mitilen
Cor. 226 then make the blood *f.* forth my branch-like vaines
Cor. 325 escapt not free *f.* thy victorious hands ?
Cor. 453 anothers teares draw teares *f.* forth our eyes
Cor. 1297 that to free them *f.* the hands of a Tyrant
Cor. 1501 free *f.* rage of civill strife
Cor. 1511 to expell *f.* forth the Land fierce warrs
Cor. 1631 he thought to tyre and wearie as *f.* thence
Cor. 1734 the fire in sparks *f.* forth theyr Armour flew
Cor. 1812 when Wolves, for hunger ranging *f.* the wood
Cor. 1895 that *f.* the wound the smoky blood ran bubling
Cor. 1908 thrust me *f.* forth the world, that mongst the
ST 137 while they maintaine hot skirmish too and *f.*
SP 55 but I have waited on thee too and *f.*

Frolic.

Jer. 1 frolick, Jeronimo ; thou art now confirmd Marshall
ST 187 but now, Knight Marshall, frolicke with thy King
ST 506 I frolike with the Duke of Castiles Sonne
STA 924 he supt with us to-night, frolicke and mery
Ard. 512 but *f.*, woman ! I shall be the man

Front.

Cor. 792 thy rebell sonne, with crowned *f.*, tryumphing
Cor. 1675 whose silver hayres and honorable *f.* were
ST 1725 of that thine ivorie *f.*, my sorrowes map
SP 245 that from the warlike wrinckles of my *f.*
Ard. 1206 where you may *f.* him well on Rainham Down

Frontiers.

ST 114 knit their *f.*, leaning on each others bound

Frost.

VPJ 21 my prime of youth is but a *f.* of cares

Froth.

Cor. 1780 theyr jawbones dy'd with foming *f.* and blood

Froward.

ST 770 and were she *f.*, which she will not be
Ard. 495 when he's at home, then have I *f.* looks

Frowardness.

Ard. 1821 the old humour of her wonted forwardness

Frown.

Cor. 611 and once more unjust Tarquins frowne
Cor. 1028 might perceive her frowne
Ard. 2119 *f.* not, I'll have it so
Ard. 2355 and *f.* not on me when me meet in heaven
SP 269 I have rejected with contemptable frownes the
JB 37 he had her favours whosoever had her frowns

Frowned.

ST Bal. 95 then, vexed more, I stamp'd and frown'd

Frowning.

Cor. 685 that the *f.* heavens oppose themselves against
Ard. 769 ‹ cut him off by the shins with a *f.* look ›

Frozen.

VPJ 39 thy prime of youth is *f.* with thy faults
Ard. 1388 or whether my tongue be *f.* in my mouth

Frugum.

HP 1640ª usuram et *f.* superabundantia[m]

Fruit.

VPJ 28 my fruite is falne, and yet my leaves are greene
VPJ 46 thy faith bare *f.* as thou hadst faithles beene
HP 8 dispoiled of their fruite
HP 334 all sorts of fruite in great aboundance
HP 353 fruite it bringeth forth for spoile of weather
HP 384 whatsoever fruite Sommer hath brought forth

STA 2007 it bore thy *f.* and mine : O wicked, wicked plant
ST 2709 and as I curse this tree from further fruite
SP 1420 faire blossome, likely to have proved good fruite
Ard. 187 is this the *f.* thy reconcilement buds ?
HP Ind. 7 Autumn more copious of fruites
HP Ind. 73 fruites preserved in Vineger
HP Ind. 74 fruites of the earth are naturall gaines
HP 96 furnished with all sorts of daintie fruits
HP 137 forthwith was the Table furnished with fruits
HP 344 we can neither temperate the one with fruits, nor
HP 383 as hope is to effects, and floures to fruits
HP 1265 many sorts of fruits that will quickly putrifie
HP 1269 some kinds of flesh or fish and divers sorts of fruits
HP 1433 had and raised of the fruits of the earth
ST 869 these are the fruits of love. (they stab him)
ST 2480 are these the fruits of thine incessant teares ?

Fruitful.

HP 91 a Garden large enough, and filled with fruitfull Trees
HP 175 gryft so many fruitfull Plants

Fruitfulness.

HP 1249 great aboundaunce of the yere and fruitfulnes of
seasons

Fruitless.

Cor. 217 worthles Gorse, that yerely fruitles dyes
ST 2548 and 'plide my selfe to fruitles Poetrie
ST 2688 fruitlesse for euer may this garden be
SP 968 and spend the time in fruitlesse plaints
SP 1111 and waste his dayes in fruitlesse obsequies ?

Frying.

SP 2177 and boyles, like Etna, in my *f.* guts

Fuel.

ST 1708 that were to adde more fewell to your fire

Fuggendo.

HP 149 Le quai *f.* tutt' il mondo onora

Fulfilled.

Cor. 1881 and by the foe fulfild with fire and blood

Fulfilling.

Cor. 2033 *f.* with my latest sighes and gasps the happie vessels

Fulgenti.

HP 821 Vobis picta croco et *f.* murice vestis

Full.

VPJ 37 my glasse is *f.*, and now my glasse is runne
HP 352 is *f.* of labour and of sweat
Cor. 818 and *f.* of foolish pitty tooke it up
Cor. 869 o're whom I shed *f.* many a bitter teare
Cor. 1187 are *f.* of dead mens bones by Caesar slayne
Cor. 1904 O night starrs, *f.* of infelicities
Jer. 80 confesse, Beard, thou art fifty *f.*, not a haire lesse
Jer. 143 to *f.* of spleene for an imbassador
Jer. 352 was thy *f.* friend, is now returned thy foe
Jer. 883 *f.* as tall as an English gallows
Jer. 909 fealty be denayed to our desart *f.* kingdome
Jer. 1143 and *f.* as often as I thinke one thee
ST 116 both furnish well, both *f.* of hope and feare
ST 656 *f.* fraught with lines and arguments of love
ST 1541 he that was so *f.* of merrie conceits
STA 1781 and his great minde, too ful of Honour
ST 2518 to let his death be unreveng'd at *f.*
ST 2594 one of his Bashawes whom he held *f.* deere
SP 677 *f.* fraught with love and burning with desire
SP 726 ah, false Erastus, *f.* of treacherie
SP 1298 my heart is *f.* ; I cannot laugh at follie
SP 1398 no, no ; my hope *f.* long agoe was lost
SP 1787 come, Lucina, lets in ; my heart is *f.*
SP 2149 ‹ To plague thy hart that is so *f.* of poyson ›
Ard. 388 would it were *f.* of poison to the brim

Ard. 4585 you can f. discourse and flat resolve me of
Ard. 2376 and run f. blank at all adventures
Full-gorged.
Cor. 1585 f. triumphes, and disdaines my lyfe
Fully.
SP 1829 when he had f. resolved him what might be
Fulmine.
HP 561 Vel pater omnipotens adigat me f. ad umbras
Fulness.
HP 289 without any noisome or superfluous fulness
SP 1185 and cross the fulnes of my joyful passion
Fumes.
ST 1815 dost cast up filthy and detested f.
Fumous.
Cor. 2030 (languishing) my f., faithful teares may
Function.
ST 3 ech in their f. serving others need
Funeral.
Jer. 158 or walke on stilts to timelesse Funerall
Jer. 1140 for honord Funerall for thy melting corne
Jer. 1161 as if he did rejoyce at funerall
Jer. 1176 my Funerall rights are made, my herse hung rich
Jer. 1182 spent upon the Funerall of Andreas dust
ST 424 I saw him honoured with due funerall
SP 998 and honored with Balme and funerall
SP 1406 still in blacke habite fitting funerall?
ST 26 my funerals and obsequies were done
Furies.
Cor. 1914 come, wrathfull F., with your Ebon locks
ST 65 where bloudie f. shakes their whips of steele
STA 1785 and there is Nemesis, and F., and things called whippes
ST 2206 a troupe of f. and tormenting hagges
ST 3036 where none but f., bugs, and tortures dwell
Furious.
Cor. Arg. 20 was a fierce and f. battaile given amongst them
Cor. 799 hath sav'd from danger in these f. broyles
SP 2009 where is that f. Ajax, the sonne of Telamon
Furnish.
HP 919 may well f. his house, seeking no
HP 1278 f. her messe with those junckets
HP 1316 may f. any sufficie[n]t house or dwelling
Cor. 656 cause for former wrongs to f. us with teares?
ST 1457 thou wouldst faine f. me with a halter, to disfurnish me of my habit
ST 2628 so f. and performe this Tragedie
Furnished.
HP 92 the Hall was f. with hangings
HP 95 f. with all sorts of daintie fruits
HP 137 forthwith was the Table f. with fruits
HP 255 with these fewe have we f. a poore Supper
HP 265 were not f. with other viands
HP 994 in deede should be composed or f.
HP 1238 and to leave his house there f. of so
ST 116 both furnish well, both full of hope and feare
ST 2530 now, were your studie so well f.
Furrows.
SP 504 within forst furrowes of her clowding brow
Ard. 691 with mighty f. in his stormy brows
Further.
HP 56 he enquired no f. of me
HP 128 that hee would enquire no f. of my state
HP 506 and, f., that he hath not taken her for a slave
HP 920 seeking no f. vertue in them
HP 1108 some stretch f. and extend to civil administration
HP 1212 f. it commeth into the consideration of

HP 1359 the f. off she is from nobles[se] or estate
Cor. 113 wag'd f. warre with an insatiate hart
Cor. 138 within the bounds of f. Brittanie?
Cor. 162 but if (their f. furie to withstand
Cor. 165 a f. plague will pester all the land
Cor. 659 wherein can Fortune f. injure us
Cor. 1941 I cannot looke for f. happines
ST 449 yes, second love shall f. my revenge
ST 1220 heere, for thy f. satisfaction, take thou this
ST 1250 and this suspition boads a f. ill
ST 1635 boy, talke no f.; thus farre things goe well
ST 1863 this for thy f. satisfaction
ST 1926 tis best that we see f. in it first
ST 2709 and as I curse this tree from f. fruite
SP 1228 and f. us in manage of these wars?
Ard. 907 to f. Mosbie to your mistress' bed
Ard. 1443 thou shalt never go f. than that down
Ard. 1768 see where he comes to f. my intent!
Ard. 2377 I am sure I had ne'er gone f. than that place
Furthering.
Cor. 274 and doe with civill discord (f. it)
Furthermore.
HP 612 he shall f. easily exercise
HP 1162 f. (to be certified of his substance and the
Fury.
Eng. Parn. 9 sets his Peeres at oddes, and on their furie whets
Cor. 50 and civill furie, fiercer then thine hosts
Cor. 162 but if (their further furie to withstand
Cor. 668 defended our Romaine walls from f. of fierce kings
Cor. 1062 did prove thy furie in the end
Jer. 149 stampt with the marke of f., and you too
ST 182 the f. of your forces wil be staide
ST 1667 what madding furie did possesse thy wits?
ST 1706 to absent your selfe, and give his f. place
ST 1906 will none of you restraine his f.?
ST 2247 what, not my Sonne? thou then a furie art
SP 344 it is the f. of his horse, not the strength of his arme
SP 1909 least in my wrathfull furie I doome you to
SP 2153 spoile all, kill all; let none escape your furie
SP 2156 yet that alayes the furie of my paine
Future.
Cor. 648 afford no hope of f. happinesse
Cor. 763 devining of our f. miseries
SP 1767 intreateth you, as ever you respect his f. love
G.
Gadding.
Ard. 1867 if well attired, thou thinks I will be g.
Gadshill.
Ard. 2379 I robbed him and his man once at G.
Gage.
Jer. 366 here is my g., a never fayling pawne
ST 468 what, if conceite have laid my hart to g.?
Gain.
VPJ 24 and al my good is but vaine hope of gaine
HP Ind. 77 gaine in war[r]e naturall
HP Ind. 78 gaine unnaturall, how it is distinguished
HP Ind. 79 gaine purchased with sweat or sweete
HP Ind. 80 gaine honestly made by the Mistrese of the house
HP Ind. 108 naturall gayne, how to be raysed
HP 1306 but honestly gaine, which is as requisite in her as
HP 1432 above the rest must that gayne needes be
HP 1436 of the gayne that may be made of them
HP 1440 these they make their gaine to hunt
HP 1446 may also bee tearmed naturall gayne
HP 1457 and that may well be called Naturall gayne
HP 1490 naturall gayne necessary for a houskeeper

HP 1563 to say concerning this naturall gaine
HP 1573 that kind of gayne which most preserveth health
HP 1581 we have reasoned of that manner of gayne
HP 1629 may have some sufficient gaine allowed
HP 1635 an arteficiall gayne, a corrupter of the Common wealth
HP 1686 our discourse of naturall and not naturall gaine
Cor. 1039 the Merchant, that for private gaine
Jer. 946 to gaine that name, ile give the deepest blowe
Jer. 948 I hope, boy, thou wilt gaine a brother too
ST Bal. 49 the Villaine then, for hope of freendship
ST 633 speake, man, and gaine both freendship and reward
ST 706 doe you but follow me, and gaine your love
ST 836 nay then, to gaine the glory of the field
ST 2214 till we do gaine that Proserpine may grant
ST 2592 Persedas love, and could not gaine the same
SP 928 for love, or gaine, or flatterie
SP 1320 weele gaine a glorious death or famous victorie
SP 1396 of honors titles, or of wealth, or gaine
Ard. 476 and he is greedy-gaping still for g.
Ard. 931 and by his friendship g. his sister's love
HP Ind. 74 fruites of the earth are naturall gaines
HP 1459 every of which naturall gaines it seemeth
HP 1578 and to make more reckoning of those gaines
Gained.
Cor. 2015 or see the wealth that Pompey gain'd in warre
SP 161 and g. the flower of Gallia in my crest
'Gainst, see Against.
Gale.
Eng. Parn. 13 And living toyleth in an earthlie gaile
Ard. 1236 each gentle stirry g. doth shake my bed
Galea.
HP 1453 Caniciem g. premimus, semperque recentes
Gall.
Jer. 54 then let him raise his g. up to his toong
Jer. 457 thats dipt in inck made of an envious g.
ST Bal. 36 to turne my sweete to bitter g.
SP 1472 the sound is hunnie, but the sence is g.
Ard. 1382 till then my bliss is mixed with bitter g.
Gallant.
Jer. 74 noble spyrits, g. bloods
Galled.
Ard. 772 « as a plaster of pitch to a g. horse-back »
Cor. 1880 then Scipio (that saw his ships through-g.
Galleries.
Jer. 682 strew all the g. with gobbits round
Gallery.
Jer. 241 him in her private g. you shall place
Jer. 599 this is the g. where she most frequents
Jer. 637 this g. leads to Bellimperias lodging
STA 2049 I'de have you paint me [for] my Gallirie
ST 2724 when the traine are past into the gallerie
Galleys.
SP 1316 the Turkes have past our Gallies, and are landed
SP 1837 because we were alreadie in his gallyes
SP 1849 as were not in his gallyes to be got
Gallia.
SP 161 and gained the flower of G. in my crest
Galling.
SP 1881 whose tongue is fast tide with g. sorrow
Gallon.
Ard. 757 a g. of sack to handsel the match withal
Gallop.
Ard. 96 g. with Arden 'cross the Ocean
Gallows.
Jer. 884 full as tall as an English g.
ST 1406 flout the gallowes, scorne the audience, and

ST 1547 you will stand between the gallowes and me?
STA 2006 till at the length it grew a gallowes
Ard. 168 may beg me from the g. of the sheriff
Game.
HP 10 the unexpected pleasure of which g. stayed me
Cor. 1213 to grace themselves with honor of the g.)
SP 869 by g., or change, by one devise or other
Ard. 1161 crying aloud, « Thou art the g. we seek »
Ard. 2016 will play a g. or two at tables here
Ard. 2140 it will by then you have played a g. at tables
Ard. 2148 one ace, or else I lose the g.
HP 757 with love and lovely termes and amorous games
Ard. 2142 three games for a French crown, and please you
Cor. 1216 a fore-g. fecht about for civill discord
Gamester.
SP 842 it must be so ; Lucinas a franke Gaimster
SP 843 shees a franke gaimster, and inclinde to play
'Gan, see Began.
Gap.
Cor. 512 what good expect wee in a fiery g.?
Gaped.
Cor. 1174 now, having got what he hath g. for
Gapes.
Jer. 109 one peeres for day, the other gappes for night
ST 142 and g. to swallow neighbour bounding landes
SP 2069 accursed homicide, for whome hell g.
Ard. 1054 g. open wide, like graves to swallow men
Gaping.
Ard. 476 and he is greedy-g. still for gain
Gardant.
Ard. 1538 see how the hours, the g. of heaven's gate
HP 133 I might show myselfe mindful and regardant
Cor. 1779 passant regardant softly they retyre
Garden.
HP 91 and thence we past into a G.
HP 177 an other g. full of all sorts of sallet hearbes
ST 884 and heere within this g. did she crie
ST 885 and in this g. must I rescue her
ST 2688 fruitlesse for ever may this g. be
STA 2973 a youth, one that they hanged up in his father's g.
Ard. 1362 weeds in gardens, roses grow on thorns
Gardener.
HP 140 the good old man, Coricius, the G.
Garden-plot.
ST 2686 no, not an herb within this garden Plot
ST 2846 to take advantage in my Garden plot upon
Garland's.
ST 387 who, living, was my garlands sweetest flower
Garment.
ST 262 not he that in a g. wore his skin
HP 1311 soyled places which may spoile or ray her garments
Jer. 665 his garments, ha, like mine ; his face made like
ST 890 those garments that he weares I oft have seen
STA 952 my soone Horatio : his garments are so like
SP 1390 but what helps gay garments, when the minds oprest?
SP 1449 and were their garments turned from black to white
Garnier.
Cor. (Title) by that excellent Poet Ro : G.
Cor. Ded. 17 what grace that excellent G. hath lost by
Garrison.
SP 1562 by this thou shalt dismisse my garison
Cor. 550 sette theyr Garrisons in strongest places
Garter.
HP 755 Homer faigned that Juno, taking away Venus g.
HP 762 that she had taken wyth the g. from Venus
Gasp.

Jer. 402 many a new wound must gaspe through an old scar
Cor. 2033 fulfilling with my latest sighes and gasps

Gasping.
Jer. 876 to single thee out of the *g.* armye

Gat.
HP 45 at a beck of the youth *g.* him swiftly on before

Gate.
HP 82 double staires which were without the *G.*
HP 87 directly against the *G.*
HP 88 another *G.*, and thereby we descended
Cor. 1481 maintaine a watchfull guard about your *g.*
ST 824 goe, Pedringano, watch without the *g.*
Ard. 1241 but needs must on, although to danger's *g.*
Ard. 1538 see how the hours, the gardant of heaven's *g.*
Cor. 766 downe by the fearefull gates of Acheron
Cor. 774 for ghosts of men are lockt in fiery gates
Cor. 1408 and in a route against thy gates they rushe
ST 75 the walles of brasse, the gates of adamant
ST 82 and bad thee lead me through the gates of Horn
ST 1530 and broken through the brazen gates of hell
ST 2204 knock at the dismall gates of Plutos Court
SP 520 that Key will serve to open all the gates
SP 669 when shall the gates of heaven stand all wide ope[n]
SP 2032 the gates are shut; which prooves that Rhodes revolts
Ard. 1202 he locked the gates, and brought away the keys
Ard. 1384 ay, to the gates of death to follow thee

Gather.
HP 1217 may *g.* vertue to refine and purge the ayre
HP 1765 *g.* by the wordes that he hath written
ST 1178 what I can *g.*, to confirme this writ
SP 216 and thereby *g.* that this blade, being

Gathered.
HP Ind. 81 grapes *g.* out of season
HP Ind. 84 grapes *g.* in Autumn
HP 975 Armies which the Soldane *g.* of slaves
HP 1185 money which may bee *g.* and received of
HP 1307 profit *g.* by the buying, selling, or exchanging
HP 1620 quantity of mony be heaped up and *g.* togeather
HP 1701 discourse, *g.* by him into a little Booke
Ard. 1448 a heavy blood is *g.* at my heart

Gatherers.
HP 1 that the Grape-*g.* were wont to presse their Wines

Gathereth.
HP 1364 for she not onely *g.* but encreaseth
HP 1482 all those things togeather which he *g.*
HP 1487 and what he *g.* of his owne Revenewes

Gathering.
HP 306 the time of Grape-*g.*
HP 386 especiall is Grape-*g.* for the wine-presse
HP 389 deceived by his servaunts in *g.* of his Corne

Gaul.
Cor. 137 what interest had they to Afferique? to Gaule or Spaine?
Cor. 1185 both Gaule and Affrique perrish by his warres
Cor. 832 have yee repeld the lustie warlike Gaules?
Cor. 1216 the Gaules were but a fore-game fecht about for
Cor. 1373 the Gauls, that came to Tiber to carouse
Cor. 1200 he hath reveng'd the Gaules old injurie

Gaunt.
ST 547 brave John of *G.*, the Duke of Lancaster

Gave.
HP Ind. 86 Homer, what properties he *g.* to Wine
HP 14 and *g.* it to a pesaunt attending on him
HP 1164 those compasses which *g.* begining to Geometry in Egypt
Cor. 327 destinie (envious of all thine honors) *g.* thee mee

Cor. 388 hee *g.* his bodie (as a Barricade) for Romes defence
Cor. 1165 and *g.* up rule, for he desier'd it not
ST Bal. 18 and *g.* my honour to my sonne
ST Bal. 107 whereto I straightway *g.* consent
ST Bal. 126 I *g.* their parts Immediatly
ST Bal. 157 but when to me they *g.* the knife
ST 197 for so I *g.* in charge at my depart
ST 253 he spake me faire, this other *g.* me strokes
ST 440 for so the Duke, your father, *g.* me charge
ST 564 to see him feast that *g.* me my deaths wound?
ST 692 and in that warre he *g.* me dangerous wounds
ST 2223 that can not be, I *g.* it never a wound
ST 2417 Hieronimo, I never *g.* you cause
ST 2547 I *g.* my minde and plide my selfe to
ST 2712 the haplesse brest, that *g.* Horatio suck
ST 2838 from forth these wounds came breath that *g.* me life
SP 72 my Grandame on her death bed *g.* it me
SP 561 his highnes *g.* me leave to speake my will
SP 567 but *g.* my censure, as his highnesse bad
SP 635 who *g.* Rhodes Princes to the Ciprian Prince, but Love?
SP 644 I *g.* Erastus onely that dayes prize
SP 715 praise I *g.* Lucina with my glosing stile?
SP 765 matchlesse Perseda, she that *g.* me strength
SP 807 which, as my life, I *g.* to thee in charge?
SP 833 I lost the pretious Carcanet she *g.* me
SP 1383 and the gilded gowne the Emperour *g.* you
SP 1589 repent that ere I *g.* away my hearts desire
SP 1594 what was it but abuse of heavens that *g.* her me?
SP 1727 and *g.* Lucina into Brusors hands
SP 1839 with that he purst the gould, and *g.* it us
SP 2187 I *g.* Erastus woe and miserie
Ard. 342 as for the base terms I *g.* thee late
Ard. 422 was it not a goodly poison that he *g.*?
Ard. 567 I *g.* him ten pound for to hire knaves
Ard. 1412 when he that *g.* it him holloed in his ear
Ard. 1951 my master took to his purse and *g.* him money
Ard. 2418 my blood be on his head that *g.* the sentence
JB 125 when he was come she *g.* her husband

Gavest.
Cor. 813 tis thou (O Rome) that gav'st him first the sword
JB 207 thou *g.* me the poyson, and after thy direction I

Gay.
SP 1390 but what helps *g.* garments, when the minds oprest?

Gaze.
STA 1971 and all those Starres that *g.* upon her face
SP 671 with gladsome lookes to gase at Hymens robes?
SP 1196 when they should gase against the glorious Sunne
Ard. 1017 ashamed to *g.* upon the open world

Gazed.
HP 696 so are they ordinarilie more desired to be *g.* on

Gazing.
Cor. 1329 while *g.* eyes at crownes grow dim
SP 2146 until mine eyes shall surfet by my gasing
Ard. 235 that Arden may, by *g.* on it, perish

Gear.
ST 1436 come, come, come on, when shall we to this geere?
ST 1445 where we shall satisfie you for this geare?
ST 1456 to goe to this geere
ST 1459 so I should goe out of this geere, my raiment, into that geere, the rope
ST 2670 Youle ply this geere? — I warrant you

Geason.
HP 1288 which custome is not gueason in some houses

Geldings.
Ard. 2046 Michael shall saddle you two lusty *g.*

Gelu.

HP 808 saevoque *g.* duramus et undis

General.

Jer. 803 wheres our lord generall, Lorenzo, stout Andrea
Jer. 949 Lord *G.*, breath like your name
Jer. 1094 Lord Generall, drive them hence
ST 92 now say, L[ord] Generall, how fares our Campe?
ST 176 thanks, good L[ord] Generall for these good newes
ST 352 in single fight with their Lord Generall
Cor. Arg. 15 made Generall of those that survived
ST 107 but, Generall, unfolde in breefe discourse
ST 356 as though he would have slaine their Generall
Jer. 950 breath like your name, a Generall defiance
Ard. 348 upon whose *g.* bruit all honour hangs

Generally.

HP 1030 and generallie all, in such busines as
STA 932 besides, he is so *g.* beloved
Ard. 462 *g.* intitled, so that all former grants

Generation.

HP 421 the Sunne, which is the cause of *g.* and
HP 429 beginneth with *g.*, not with corruption
HP 433 to the *g.* and engendering of thinges
HP 441 beginneth *g.* in those parts of the
HP 453 to redeeme our humaine *g.* in that time
HP 611 become unable and unfit for *g.*
HP 1680 that the corruption of one bee the *g.* of another

Generous.

Cor. 1229 a *g.* or true enobled spirit detests to
Cor. 2031 may trickling bathe your *g.* sweet cynders

Genesi.

HP 1651 Lo *G.*, dal principio, conviene

Genesis.

HP 1662 « In *G.* even God himselfe doth say »

Gente.

HP 1652 Prender sua vita & avanzar la *g.*

Gentes.

ST 104 et conjuratae curvato poplite *g.*

Gentility.

HP 28 a kind of gentilitie and grace

Gentle.

HP 111 of lesse yeeres, but no lesse *g.* spirit
HP 480 obeying the *g.* commaunds of their father
HP 790 cannot be so *g.* or so delicate as the Mothers
HP 965 servile fortune can engender servile evils in a *g.* mind
Cor. 219 and if *g.* Peace discend not soone
Cor. 653 say, *g.* sisters, tell me, and believe
Cor. 718 sleep'st thou, Cornelia? sleepst thou, *g.* wife
Cor. 1346 and with a *g.* murmure hast to tell the
Jer. 130 I have hard of your honor, *g.* brest
Jer. 302 in, *g.* soule; Ile not bee long away
ST 755 the *g.* Nightingale shall carroll us asleepe
ST 1646 my *g.* Sister will I now inlarge
ST 1698 you (*g.* brother) forged this for my sake
ST 1712 but, Bel-imperia, see the *g.* Prince
ST 1889 justice, O, justice, justice, *g.* King
ST 1918 but *g.* brother, goe give to him this golde
ST 2233 *g.* boy, be gone, for justice is exiled
ST 2440 solicite Pluto, *g.* Proserpine
SP 495 come therefore, *g.* death, and ease my griefe
SP 2038 nay, *g.* Brusor, stay thy teares a while
SP 2097 yet kisse me, *g.* love, before thou die
SP 2135 kinde, even to his foes, *g.* and affable
Ard. 44 be patient, *g.* friend, and learn of me to
Ard. 87 I cannot long be from thee, *g.* Alice
Ard. 91 meanwhile prepare our breakfast, *g.* Alice
Ard. 381 why, *g.* Mistress Alice, cannot I be ill
Ard. 402 ah, if thou love me, *g.* Arden, stay

Ard. 958 that thus thy *g.* life is levelled at?
Ard. 992 *g.* Arden, leave this sad lament
Ard. 1014 woes aecompanies this *g.* gentleman!
Ard. 1043 staring and grinning in thy *g.* face
Ard. 1152 even there, methoughts, a *g.* slumber took me
Ard. 1238 each *g.* stirry gale doth shake my bed
Ard. 1359 sweet Mosbie is as *g.* as a King
Ard. 1364 himself is valued *g.* by his worth
Ard. 1367 I will forget this quarrel, *g.* Alice
Ard. 1905 I pray thee, *g.* Franklin, hold thy peace
Ard. 1946 ah, *g.* Michael, art thou sure they're friends?
Ard. 1956 ah, *g.* Michael, run thou back again
Ard. 2118 and, *g.* Mistress Alice, seeing you are so stout
Ard. 2189 it shall not long torment thee, *g.* Alice
Ard. 2399 ah, *g.* brother, wherefore should I die?
Jer. 1194 so good night, kind gentles
ST 2893 and, Gentles, thus I end my play
Ard. 1358 we beggars must not breathe where gentles are

Gentleman.

HP Ded. To the Worshipfull and Vertuous *G.*
HP 94 other ornament beseeming the lodging of a *G.*
HP 98 can not be possest but of some noble *G.*
HP 102 neither denie I him to be a *G.* of the Cittie
HP 136 as it pleased the good old *G.*
HP 162 necessarie or fit for the life of a poore Gentlema[n]
HP 232 a *G.*, a friende and neighbor of ours
HP 581 or, contrarily, a *G.* with a Begger
HP 909 that represents the person of a nobleman, or *G.*
HP 911 be called the Noble or the *G.* stil
HP 1242 and yet are necessary for a *G.*
HP 1781 the *G.* seeming to be satisfied
Jer. 1192 your welcome, all, as I am a *G.*
ST 2188 this gentlenes shewes him a *G.*
SP 2055 a *G.*, and thy mortall enemie
Ard. 36 I am by birth a *g.* of blood
Ard. 204 and matched already with a *g.*
Ard. 484 alas, poor *g.*, I pity you
Ard. 564 I whetted on the *g.* with words
Ard. 723 now, *g.*, shall we have your company
Ard. 1014 woes accompanies this gentle *g.*!
Ard. 1457 ay, where the *g.* did check his wife
Ard. 1910 poor *g.*, how soon he is bewitched!
SP 956 Ile be so bolde as to dive into this Gentlemans pocket

Gentleman-like.

ST 1403 I would say it were a peece of *g.* knavery

Gentleman-usher.

Jer. 525 bending in the hams enough, like a Gentleman usher?

Gentlemen.

HP 65 to waft over some French *G.*
HP 1109 there are some *G.* (amongst who[m] I wish
ST 1293 harke, *G.*, this is a Pistol shot
ST 2578 acted by *G.* and schollers too
ST 2752 *G.*, this Play of Hieronimo, in sundrie languages
SP 129 the Prince and all the outlandish *G.* are ready
SP 370 brave *G.*, by all your free consents
SP 893 and, *G.*, unmaske ere you depart
SP 898 *G.*, each thing hath sorted to our wish
SP 910 nay, *G.*, flye you and save your selves
Ard. 344 the knights and *g.* of Kent make
Ard. 477 nor cares he though young *g.* do beg
Ard. 934 well, *g.*, I cannot but confess
Ard. 1493 I have made a promise to a gentleman
Ard. 1712 none but a couple of *g.*, that went
Ard. 1965 ah, *g.*, how missed you of your
Ard. 2433 *g.*, we hope you'll pardon this naked tragedy

Gentleness.

ST 2188 this gentlenes shewes him a Gentleman
Gentlewoman.
HP 473 the auncient G., giving thanks, arose
SP 453 should have ten shillings for horsing a G.
Ard. 287 as I am a g., Clarke, next day
SP 857 last night he was bidden to a gentlewomans to supper
Gently.
Cor. 1497 O Faire Sunne, that gentlie smiles from
Jer. 167 the phraise he useth must be g. stylde
ST 1656 jest with her g.; under fained jest are
Genus.
HP 807 Durum a stirpe g., natos ad flumina primum
HP 1664 Humanum g. vitam sumere
Geometry.
HP 1165 those compasses which gave begining to G. in Egypt
HP 1180 Quantitie which is measured by Geometrie
George.
SP 165 Saint G. for England, and Saint G. for me
Ard. 730 give my fellow G. Shakebag and me
Germans.
Cor. 1375 and those brave Germains, true borne Martialists
Germany.
HP 303 that are of the Rheyne of Germanie
HP 1226 Travailers, Italian Merchants, or those of G. or Fraunce
SP 207 you are a Rutter borne in Germanie
Gesture.
SP 420 Page, set aside the jesture of my enemy
Get.
HP 19 ‹ you might happily g. thither › (quoth he)
HP 1301 I speake of choyse wynes which g. strength with age
HP 1425 whether to g. be a forme or part of housekeeping
Jer. 384 I, when you g. me downe
Jer. 687 peace; no words; ile g. thy pardon
Jer. 767 peace, Lazarotto, ile g. it of the King
SP 298 if thou beest a right warrior, g. from under me
SP 470 g. you away, sirra. I advise you
SP 711 no, I shall soone g. home
SP 837 if I can but g. the Chaine againe
SP 887 they g. not one wise word of me
SP 1630 O fine devise; Brusor, g. thee gone
SP 1886 this is a faire warning for me to g. me gon
Ard. 57 husband, what mean you to g. up so early?
Ard. 177 yonder comes Mosbie. Michael, g. thee gone
Ard. 199 base peasant, g. thee gone, and boast
Ard. 480 as careless as he is careful for to g.
Ard. 819 marry, this 'mends, that if you g. not away
Ard. 881 and for her sake, whose love he cannot g.
Ard. 1075 g. you to bed, and if you love my favour
Ard. 1089 Greene, g. you gone, and linger here about
Ard. 1143 sirrah, g. you back to Billingsgate
Ard. 1439 well, g. you back to Rochester; but
Ard. 1441 for 'twill be very late ere we g. home
Ard. 1717 no, sir; g. you gone
Ard. 1720 a fool as will rather be hought than g. his way
Ard. 1743 g. you to Feversham to the Flower-de-luce
Ard. 2057 tush, g. you gone; 'tis we must do the deed
Ard. 2366 and g. the Council's warrant to apprehend them
Geta.
HP 912 though he be happily Davus, Syrus, or G.
Getteth.
HP 1428 which g. the living out of those thinges that
Getting.
HP Ind. 76 forme of g., what
HP 216 g. Children before themselves were come unto
HP 1423 the art of housekeeping and g. is not all one
HP 1427 the facultie of g. may be Natural

ST 2205 g. by force, as once Alcides did
Ard. 26 by base brokage g. some small stock
HP Ind. 32 whether they varie in forme onely or in gettings
Getulie.
Cor. 666 to proudest Spayne, or poorest G.
Ghastly.
Cor. 460 Persiphone, or Plutos gastlie spirits
Cor. 706 the ghost of Pompey, with a g. looke
Ghiande.
HP 148 Simili a quelle g.
Ghost.
Cor. 232 that my poore g. may rest where powerfull fate
Cor. 706 came glyding by my bed the g. of Pompey
Cor. 1152 to see this massacre, and send his g. to theyrs
Cor. 1568 pierc'd as sore as Prometheus g.
Cor. 1948 but, sacred g., appease thine ire, and see
Jer. 272 let mee alone; Ile turne him to a ghoast
Jer. 1155 see, Don Andreas ghoast salutes me, see, embraces me
Jer. 1159 O my pale friende, wert thou anything but a ghoast
Jer. 1172 I am a happy G.
ST 35 to crave a pasport for my wandring G.
ST 2253 I am a greeved man, and not a G.
ST 2698 his Ghoast solicites with his wounds revenge on
SP 1917 why, now Erastus g. is satisfied
SP 2181 when as my gliding g. shall follow thee
Cor. 243 the darksome mansions of pyning ghosts
Cor. 774 for ghosts of men are lockt in fiery gates
Cor. 1118 or shall theyr ghosts, that dide to doe us good
Cor. 1978 content to count the ghosts of those great Captains
Cor. 2037 encrease the number of the ghosts be-low
SP 1113 ads but a trouble to my brothers ghoasts
Giant.
Jer. 314 my minds a g., though my bulke be small
Jer. 978 O valiant boy; stroake with a Giants arme
Giddy.
SP 2016 a giddie goddesse that now giveth and anon taketh
Gift.
ST 781 Ile grace her marriage with an unckles g.
SP 1377 why, Brusors victorie was Fortunes g.
SP 1590 what was it but abuse of Fortunes g.
VPJ 15 these foure faire giftes (O Prince, of right renound)
Cor. 1007 when shee hath heap't her gifts on us
Jer. 52 well tuned mellody, and all sweet guifts of nature
Jer. 214 great gifts and gold have the best toong to move
Jer. 247 gifts and giving will melt the chastest seeming female living
Jer. 251 and therefore great gifts may bewitch her eie
Jer. 253 but, say she should deny his gifts, be
SP 628 the Ring and Carkanet were Fortunes gifts
SP 1607 with secret letters woe her, and with gifts
SP 1608 my lines and gifts will but returne my shame
SP 2015 I am adorned with natures gifts
JB 33 earnest suite, the gifts and favours which she received
JB 46 requested that he might have his gifts againe
Giglot.
Ard. 1306 to take a wanton g. by the left
Gilded.
SP 1382 and the g. gowne the Emperour gave you
Gilding.
Cor. 1499 guilding these our gladsome dayes
Gilled.
SP 222 or the marine moisture to the red guild fish
Gilt.
Ard. 1319 and now the rain hath beaten off thy g.
'Gin, see **Begin.**
Giorno.

HP 1341 Scemò la notte, quanto il *g.* accrebbe
Giovanni.
HP 1131 writte[n] by Signior *G.* della Casa
Gird.
STA 971 *g.* in my wast of griefe with thy large darkenesse
Girdle.
SP 1682 his skin is but pistol profe from the *g.* upward
Ard. 2359 his purse and *g.* found at thy bed's head
Girl.
ST 2377 and welcome, Bel-imperia. How now, girle?
SP 270 glances of many amorous girles, or rather ladies
Girt.
HP 1218 and whether they be guirt or environed with hylles
Jer. 1064 hast thou no cote of proofe *g.* to thy loines?
ST 2834 through *g.* with wounds, and slaughtred as you see
Give.
HP Ind. 104 mothers ought to *g.* their owne Children sucke
HP 19 this evening, if the time would *g.* me leave
HP 295 that he should *g.* Wine commendations of that sort
HP 723 *g.* consent that she may goe apparelled as others
HP 726 nor on the other side to *g.* the bridle of libertie
HP 817 if it shall please God to *g.* thee Children
HP 870 and if we shall *g.* credite to antiquities written of
HP 880 the Maister to *g.* them admonition
HP 1731 if my heart or happe would *g.* me leave
HP 1777 time and good manners will hardly *g.* us leave
Cor. Arg. 11 a newe Armie, and *g.* a second assault to Caesar
Cor. 376 may change her lookes, and *g.* the Tyrant over
Cor. 380 may *g.* poore Rome her former libertie
Cor. 381 I know they cannot *g.* a second life to Pompey
Cor. 809 all powreles *g.* proud Caesars wrath free passage
Jer. 230 Oh Duckets, dainty ducks : for, *g.* me duckets
Jer. 381 what, *g.* no place?
Jer. 452 *g.* a letter the right Courtiers crest?
Jer. 946 to gaine that name, ile *g.* the deepest blowe
Jer. 1050 and *g.* you acquittance with a wound or two
Jer. 1096 my sword shall *g.* correction to thy toong
Jer. 1133 *g.* him my blessing, and then all is done
Jer. 1162 Reveng, *g.* my toong freedom to paint her part
ST Bal. 147 and in despite did *g.* it them
ST 79 and begd that onely she might *g.* my doome
ST 671 and *g.* me notice in some secret sort
ST 744 *g.* me a kisse, ile counterchecke thy kisse
ST 788 doe so, my Lord, and if he *g.* consent
ST 814 if she *g.* back, all this will come to naught
ST 1202 *g.* but successe to mine attempting spirit
ST 1369 thou knowest the prison, closely *g.* it him
ST 1539 they resist my woes, and *g.* my words no way
ST 1546 I warrant thee, *g.* it me
ST 1604 why, did I not *g.* you gownes and goodly things
ST 1640 heere, take my Ring, and *g.* it Christophill
ST 1683 to *g.* him notice that they were so nigh
ST 1706 to absent your selfe, and *g.* his fury place
ST 1875 there will he *g.* his Crowne to Balthazar
ST 1896 *g.* me my sonne; you shall not ransome him
ST 1918 but gentle brother, goe *g.* to him this golde
STA 1970 doth *g.* consent to that is done in darkenesse
ST 2154 *g.* place
ST 2169 way unto my most distressfull words
ST 2300 heere take my Crowne, I *g.* it her and thee
ST 2354 and *g.* it over, and devise no more
ST 2319 and heere I vow — so you but *g.* consent
ST 2635 *g.* me a stately written Tragedie
ST 2718 to *g.* the King the coppie of the plaie
ST 2756 every excelence that Soliman can *g.*, or thou desire
STA 2947 Ide *g.* them all, I, and my soule to boote

SP 38 Why stay we then? Lets *g.* the Actors leave
SP 206 and therefore *g.* not you a strangers welcome
SP 302 not to go till I *g.* thee leave
SP 317 injoy thy life and live ; I *g.* it thee
SP 347 I *g.* thee leave : go to thy destruction
SP 393 *g.* me thy hand, I vowe myselfe thy friend
SP 421 *g.* him a Fidlers fee, and send him packing
SP 480 what you want in shooes, ile *g.* ye in blowes
SP 488 take thou the honour, and *g.* me the chaine
SP 579 must I *g.* aime to this presumption?
SP 811 heere, *g.* her this ; Perseda now is free
SP 918 ah, if but time and place would *g.* me leave
SP 937 take this chaine, and *g.* it to Perseda
SP 1023 delivered me the chaine, and bad me *g.* it you
SP 1067 for her to *g.* him doome of life or death
SP 1104 and *g.* him aide and succour in distresse
SP 1217 then *g.* us swordes and Targets
SP 1527 yet *g.* me leave in honest sort to court thee
SP 1556 and both *g.* me your hands
SP 1566 *g.* me a crowne, to crowne the bride withall
SP 1676 didst thou not meane to *g.* me the privie stab?
SP 1733 and *g.* Perseda to Erastus hands
SP 1775 I go, Perseda ; thou must *g.* me leave
SP 1875 yet *g.* me leave, before my life shall end
SP 1988 what, darest thou not? *g.* me the dagger then
SP 2101 or why didst not *g.* Soliman a kisse ere
SP 2106 but *g.* me leave to weepe over hir
SP 2198 I *g.* worlds happines and woes increase
Ard. 387 *g.* me a spoon, I'll eat of it myself
Ard. 412 in hope you'll hasten him home, I'll *g.* you this
Ard. 638 you'll *g.* me l. to play your husband's part
Ard. 707 what wilt thou *g.* him that can tell thee
Ard. 729 I'll *g.* you twenty angels for your pains
Ard. 730 *g.* my fellow George Shakebag and me
Ard. 741 *g.* me the money, and I'll stab him
Ard. 757 I'll *g.* thee a gallon of sack to
Ard. 831 but were my consent to *g.* again, we
Ard. 869 but, *g.* me place and opportunity
Ard. 914 tush, *g.* me leave, there's no more but this
Ard. 922 to *g.* an end to Arden's life on earth
Ard. 1033 can *g.* to neither wished victory
Ard. 1086 as loth to *g.* due audit to the hour
Ard. 1091 where we will *g.* you instance of his death
Ard. 1373 that Master Greene importuned me to *g.* you
Ard. 1506 one of you *g.* him a crown
Ard. 1748 these knaves will never do it, let us *g.* it over
Ard. 1914 I think we shall never do it ; let us *g.* it over
Ard. 2050 *g.* me the key : which is the counting-house?
Ard. 2153 what! groans thou? nay, then *g.* me the weapon!
Ard. 2163 and if she will not *g.* me harborough
Ard. 2407 and listen to the sentence I shall *g.*
JB 224 the Lord *g.* all men grace by their example to
Puck 61 when tyme shall serve I shall geve greater instance
Cor. 1538 gives them over to their foe
Jer. 254 as my mind gives me that she wooll
Jer. 433 gives strength unto our plot
Jer. 620 my words iterated gives thee as much
Jer. 944 and he this day gives me the deepest wound
STA 960 weake apprehension gives but weake beleife
SP 628 were Fortunes gifts ; Love gives no gould or jewels
SP 1072 thy folly gives thee priviledge ; begon, begon
Ard. 2218 sirrah Michael, give's a cup of beer
Given.
HP Ind. 20 Circes *g.* to weaving
HP 63 would have gyven more then ordinary for their passage
HP 1002 busines of the stable and of horses should be gyven

HP 1007 as our fortune hath not gyven us that wealth
HP 1842 read what verdict Dante hath g. of it in
Cor. Arg. 21 was a fierce and furious battaile g. amongst them
Cor. 1205 against a harmeles Nation, kindly g.
Cor. 1945 sweet Death hath g. blessed rest
Jer. 583 what, have you g. it out Andrea is returnd ?
ST 97 speak, man, hath fortune g. us victorie ?
ST 1888 heere, see it g. to Horatio
ST 1924 and g. to one of more discretion
ST 2536 assure your selves of me ; for you have g. me cause
SP 655 had been surprisd, if Fates had g. me leave
Ard. 3 hath freely g. to thee and to thy heirs
Ard. 188 have I for this g. thee so many favours
Ard. 250 provided, as you have g. your word
Ard. 425 that might have g. the broth some dainty taste
Ard. 436 and g. my hand unto him in the church !
Ard. 2019 shall at a certain watchword g. rush forth
Ard. 2094 you have g. me my supper with his sight
Ard. 2405 I had ne'er g. consent to this foul deed
JB 90 as Parker had before g. direction
Puck 39 that is (as I am geven to understand) wᵗʰ
Puck 45 of my religion & life I have alredie geven some
    instance
Givest.
Cor. 1053 to him that ne're put speare in rest giv'st victory
Giveth.
HP 360 it g. not men convenient time to worke
HP 432 and there g. beginning to the
HP 767 it g. us to understand that married women
HP 1431 nourishment, which the Mother g. to her Childe
SP 2016 a giddie goddesse that now g. and anon taketh
Giving.
HP 30 g. my Horse to a hyreling
HP 471 g. up the government of his house
HP 473 the auncient Gentlewoman, g. thanks, arose
HP 1012 gyving every one hys sallary or day wages
Jer. 104 g. attendance, that were once attended
Jer. 247 gifts and g. will melt the chastest seeming female living
SP 1650 in g. judgement of a man at armes
JB 96 g. him the good morrow in most courteous manner
Glad.
ST 682 both well and ill : it makes me g. and sad
ST 683 g., that I know the hinderer of my love
ST 685 g., that I know on whom to be reveng'd
Ard. 418 I am g. he is gone ; he was about to stay
Ard. 662 you were g. to call me ‹ fellow Will ›
Ard. 2288 I am g. it is no worse
JB 56 being not a little g. of his good successe
Gladly.
ST Bal. 119 which g. I prepar'd to show
SP 1294 or if you g. would injoy me both
Gladness.
Cor. 1657 doth leape for gladnes, and (to murder vow'd)
Gladsome.
Cor. 1499 guilding these our g. daies with
ST 201 a g. sight : I long to see them heere
SP 671 for celestiall Gods with g. lookes to gase
SP 680 brings in the spring with many g. flowers
Glaives.
Ard. 2261 are coming towards our house with g. and bills
Glanced.
Cor. 1730 the Darts and Arrowes on theyr Armour glaunced
Glances.
Cor. 513 to scape the feares that followes Fortunes glaunces
SP 270 the sweet g. of many amorous girles, or
Glass.

VPJ 37 my glasse is full, and now my glasse is runne
VPJ 55 thy glorie and thy glasse are timeles runne
SP 108 as the glasse that takes the Sun-beames burning
SP 110 Ile be the glasse and thou that heavenly Sun
SP 2029 mans life is as a glasse, and a phillip may cracke it
Glasses.
ST 979 and Ile close up the g. of his sight
Glauc's.
Cor. 91 and a sportfull praie to th' G. and Trytons
Glee.
Cor. 1522 Feasts, and Masks, and mirthfull g.
Glide.
Cor. 1343 g. as smothly as a Parthian shaft
Cor. 757 he slides more swiftly from mee then the Ocean glydes
Gliding.
Cor. 703 came glyding by my bed the ghost of Pompey
SP 2181 when as my g. ghost shall follow thee
Glimpse.
Ard. 826 I had a g. of him and his companion
Glistering.
HP 827 ‹ your robes are dyed with Saffron and with glistring
    purple buds ›
HP 904 in Purple and g. all in Golde and precious stones
Glittering.
Cor. 74 the golden Sunne, where ere he drive his glittring
    Chariot
Jer. 802 are up in armes, g. in steel
Jer. 1102 and let revenge hang on our g. swords
Glooming.
ST 56 through dreadfull shades of ever g. night
Gloria.
VPJ 76 splendida, sola, vigens, g., vita, salus
Glories.
SP 219 but whats the word that g. your Countrey ?
Glorious.
HP 1412 Gnato, that disposd the household of his g. Sig. Capitano
Cor. 1335 O g. temples, O proude Pallaces
ST 394 for g. cause still aiming at the fairest
SP 330 I, in the eye of an infant a Peacocks taile is g.
SP 1196 when they should gase against the g. Sunne
SP 1321 weele gaine a g. death or famous victorie
Glory.
VPJ 55 thy glorie and thy glasse are timeles runne
Cor. 321 thy wandring g. was so greatly knowne ?
Cor. 330 by whom the glorie of thy conquests got might
Cor. 1278 his g., spred abroade by Fame on wings of
Cor. 1293 no Sepulcher shall ere exclude their glorie
Cor. 1368 heere let the Decii and theyr g. die
Cor. 1387 that (ill-advis'd) repined at my g.
Cor. 1404 for brideling those that dyd maligne our g.
Cor. 1543 for his suddaine g. got)
Jer. 1016 the g. of our foe, the hart of courage
ST 856 nay then, to gaine the g. of the field
STA 1965 when as the Sun-God rides in all his glorie
SP 134 such g. as no time shall ere race out
SP 304 O, thou seekst thereby to dim my g.
SP 537 fog not thy g. with so fowle eclipse
SP 1670 and viewd the Capitoll, and was Romes greatest glorie
Gloster.
ST 524 was English Robert, Earle of G.
Glove.
ST 483 Madam, your G.
Ard. 1460 her g. brought in which there she left behind
Glozes.
Cor. Ded. 10 neyther making needles g. of the one, nor
Glozing.

SP 715 praise I gave Lucina with my glosing stile?
Ard. 2437 and needs no other points of glosing stuff

Glued.

Ard. 861 whose lips are *g.* with summer's parching heat

Glutted.

ST 897 beene *g.* with thy harmeles blood

Gnashing.

Cor. 715 and (*g.* of his teeth) unlockt his jawes

Gnat.

SP 106 though like a *G.* amongst a hive of Bees
SP 570 the humming of a *g.* in Summers night

Gnato.

HP 1412 *G.*, that disposd the household of his glorious Sig.
  Capitano

Go.

HP 33 and thether will I goe before
HP 723 give consent that she may goe apparelled as others
Cor. 256 goe break the bands by calling Hymen once more
Cor. 1403 and rendring thanks to heaven, as we goe
Cor. 1469 can I too-soone goe taste Cocytus flood?
Jer. 137 if thou wouldst remaine heere with me, and not *g.*
Jer. 165 I *g.* to knit friends, not to kindle foes
Jer. 194 it is for honor; prethee let him goe
Jer. 294 *g.*, tell it Abrod now; but see you put no new
Jer. 317 son Balthezer, we pray, do you goe meet him
Jer. 588 when it would scare *g.* downe for extreame laughter
Jer. 986 *g.*, search agen; bring him, or neare returne
Jer. 1019 *g.*, Captaine, passe the leaft wing squadron; hie
Jer. 1170 see, see, he points to have us goe forward on
ST 212 goe, let them march once more about these walles
ST 250 let goe his arme, upon our priviledge
ST 439 Ile crave your pardon to goe seeke the Prince
ST 441 I, goe, Horatio, leave me heere alone
ST 473 tush, tush, my Lord, let goe these ambages
ST 567 be still, Andrea; ere we *g.* from hence
ST 676 goe and attend her, as thy custome is
ST 705 lets goe, my Lord; your staying staies revenge
ST 739 let dangers goe, thy warre shall be with me
ST 782 in case the match goe forward, the tribute
ST 824 goe, Pedringano, watch without the gate
ST 860 O let me goe, for in my troubled eyes
STA 925 and said he would goe visit Balthazar
STA 928 he may be in his chamber; some *g.* see
ST 1050 goe, some of you, and fetch the traitor forth
ST 1123 intreate me not; *g.*, take the traytor hence
ST 1231 and ile goe arme my selfe to meet him there
ST 1234 goe, sirra, to Serberine, and bid him
ST 1237 this evening, boy. — I goe, my Lord
ST 1368 boy, goe, convay this purse to Pedringano
ST 1383 Away. — I goe, my Lord, I runne
ST 1403 I must *g.* to Pedringano, and tell him
ST 1456 to goe to this geere
ST 1459 so I should goe out of this geere, my raiment
ST 1590 I will *g.* plaine me to my Lord the King
ST 1635 boy, talke no further; thus farre things goe well
ST 1739 weele goe continue this discourse at Court
STA 1757 he must be fed, be taught to goe, and speake
ST 1794 good leave have you: nay, I pray you goe
ST 1831 goe too, I see their shifts, and say no more
ST 1857 Hieronimo beware; goe by, goe by
ST 1903 for Ile goe marshall up the feendes in hell
ST 1908 needes must he goe that the divels drive
ST 1918 but gentle brother, goe give to him this golde
STA 2034 Pedro, Jaques, goe in a doores; Isabella, goe
STA 2038 goe in a doores, I say
STA 2051 let five yeeres goe, let them goe like

ST 2232 goe backe, my sonne, complaine to Eacus
ST 2270 *g.*, Brother, it is the Duke of Castiles cause
ST 2271 I *g.*
ST 2272 *g.* forth, Don Pedro, for thy Nephews sake
ST 2363 goe, one of you, and call Hieronimo
ST 2375 Truce, my love; I will goe salute him
ST 2396 nay, stay, Hieronimo — goe, call him, sonne
STA 2946 as many Heavens to *g.* to, as those lives
ST 2996 *g.*, beare his body hence, that we may mourne
ST 3047 let Serberine goe roule the fatall stone
SP 42 goe every way, and not the way I would?
SP 54 when didst thou goe to Church on hollidaies
SP 129 the outlandish Gentlemen are ready to goe to the
  triumphs
SP 131 goe sirra, bid my men bring my horse, and
SP 259 although it *g.* against my starres to jest, yet
SP 296 I must talke with you before you goe
SP 302 not to *g.* till I give thee leave, but stay with me
SP 311, 313 will not offer to *g.* from the side of Piston
SP 347 I give the leave: *g.* to thy destruction
SP 350 well, goe; mount thee, goe
SP 351 I *g.*, and Fortune guide my Launce
SP 412 therefore will I now goe visit her
SP 457 when they let the poore goe under Forma pauperis
SP 733 goe thou foorthwith, arme thee from top to toe
SP 739 I *g.*; make reconing that Erastus dyes
SP 851 for I intend to *g.* in mummery
SP 878 loose your money, and *g.* without the chaine
SP 881 nay, I use not to *g.* without a paire of false Dice
SP 925 therefore I *g.*: but whether shall I *g.*?
SP 929 to Turkie must I goe; the passage short
SP 1033 but, Eolus and Neptune, let him *g.*
SP 1035 then let him *g.*; ile shortly follow him
SP 1049 where you had not best *g.* to him
SP 1053 ready to discharge it uppon you, when you *g.* by
SP 1252 Brusor, goe levie men
SP 1386 Ile *g.* provide your supper
SP 1431 *g.*, then, *g.* spend thy mournings all at once
SP 1531 goe, Janisaries, call in your Governour
SP 1609 here me, my Lord: let me *g.* over to Rhodes
SP 1638 I will *g.* sit among my learned Euenukes
SP 1775 I *g.*, Perseda; thou must give me leave
SP 1899 thy soule shall not *g.* mourning hence alone
SP 2041 *g.*, Brusor, beare her to thy private tent
SP 2216 I *g.*, yet Love shall never yeeld to Death
Ard. 315 for this shall *g.* with me
Ard. 399 Arden shall *g.* to London in my arms
Ard. 400 loth am I to depart, yet I must *g.*
Ard. 404 *g.*, if thou wilt, I'll bear it as I may
Ard. 545 *g.* to her, Clarke; she's all alone within
Ard. 674 let that pass, and tell me whither you *g.*
Ard. 717 before you *g.*, let me intreat you
Ard. 791 now, Master Franklin, let us *g.* walk in Paul's
Ard. 893 *g.* to, sirrah, there is a chance in it
Ard. 949 should you deceive us, 'twould go wrong with you
Ard. 999 then stay with me in London; *g.* not home
Ard. 1009 come, Master Franklin, shall we *g.* to bed?
Ard. 1010 I pray you, *g.* before; I'll follow you
Ard. 1072 I like not this, but I'll *g.* see myself
Ard. 1077 come, Master Franklin, let us *g.* to bed
Ard. 1095 I am so heavy that I can scarce *g.*
Ard. 1098 nay, then let's *g.* sleep, when bugs and fears shall
Ard. 1102 were 't not a serious thing we *g.* about
Ard. 1108 *g.* forward now in that we have begun
Ard. 1134 come, let's *g.* seek out Greene; I know
Ard. 1145 first *g.* make the bed, and afterwards

Ard. 1146 and afterwards g. hearken for the flood
Ard. 1147 come, Master Franklin, you shall g. with me
Ard. 1186 and with the tide g. down to Feversham
Ard. 1323 g., get thee gone, a copesmate for thy hinds
Ard. 1374 g. in, Bradshaw ; call for a cup of beer
Ard. 1443 thou shalt never g. further than that down
Ard. 1432 come, Master Franklin, let us g. on softly
Ard. 1536 why, then let us g., and tell her all the matter
Ard. 1546 to g. to the Isle of Sheppy
Ard. 1557 let her g. along with us
Ard. 1562 if I should g., our house would run away
Ard. 1564 nay, see how mistaking you are ! I pray thee, g.
Ard. 1576 why, I pray you, let us g. before
Ard. 1578 g. to, sirrah, see you follow us to the
Ard. 1596 g. to, you carry an eye over Mistress Susan
Ard. 1645 here, here, g. before to the boat, and
Ard. 1679 as we g., let us have some more of your
Ard. 1702 come, let us g. on like a couple of blind pilgrims
Ard. 1708 to g. without a guide such weather as this
Ard. 1811 and thus I g., but leave my curse with thee
Ard. 1890 come thou thyself, and g. along with me
Ard. 1909 he whom the devil drives must g. perforce
Ard. 1918 I have made some g. upon wooden legs
Ard. 1960 I'll g. tell him
Ard. 2025 come, Master Greene, g. you along with me
Ard. 2028 and if he e'er g. forth again, blame me
Ard. 2083 that's brave. I'll g. fetch the tables
Ard. 2112 we shall have guests enough, though you g. hence
Ard. 2113 I pray you, Master Arden, let me g.
Ard. 2134 I'll g. to Rome rather than be forsworn
Ard. 2171 Mosbie, g. thou and bear them company
Ard. 2230 good Master Franklin, g. and seek him forth
Ard. 2244 g., Susan, and bid thy brother come
Ard. 2281 hark, hark, they knock ! g., Michael, let them in
Ard. 2332 and one of you g. to the Flower-de-luce
Ard. 2372 at last be fain to g. on board some hoy
JB 114 vex not at the matter, your ill lucke goe with them
JB 137 tould her husband she must needs goe home to her
JB 172 she must runne or goe wheresoever he pleased to
JB 183 in so much that she would not goe forth of her doores

Goads.
Cor. 1801 for then (as if provokt with pricking goades)

Gobbets.
Jer. 682 strew all the galleries with gobbits round

God.
VPJ 6 it happ'ly pleasd our highest G. in safety to preserve
VPJ 42 thy good G. knowes thy hope, thy hap and all
VPJ 48 and G. that saw thee hath preservde our Queene
VPJ 87 G. graunt thee long amongst us breathe
VPJ 88 G. shield thee from annoy
HP 36 G. graunt in other things she shewe
HP 101 my Father is, whom G. graunt a long life
HP 163 for (G. be praised) I have aboundance of
HP 436 of G. the Father to those inferior Gods
HP 450 with the presence of the true Sonne of G.
HP 491 the providence of our almighty G.
HP 817 if it shall please G. to give thee Children
HP 861 bring them upp in the feare and love of G.
HP 1636 a disobeyer of the Lawes of G., a Rebell
HP 1660 « So that our arte is Neipce to G. by kind »
HP 1668 « Without regard of G. or Godly lawes »
HP 1671 that G. is animal sempiternum et optimum
HP 1676 offending Nature we immediatly offende G.
HP 1676 he that offendeth arte offendeth G.
HP 1681 it offendeth G. because it doth not exercise the
HP 1681 as G. commaunded the first man

Cor. 695 G. graunt these dreames to good effect bee brought
Cor. 815 and violates both G. and Natures lawes
Jer. 498 « if you be not, thanke G. and Jeronimo »
Jer. 521 « if you be not, thanke G. and Jeronimo »
Jer. 535 G. save you, good knight Marshall
ST Bal. 167 for murther G. will bring to light
STA 953 O would to G. it were not so
STA 965 O G., confusion, mischiefe, torment, death, and hell
ST 1474 pray G., I be not preserved to breake your knaves pate
ST 1508 G. forbid a fault so foule should scape unpunished
ST 1540 O Lord, sir : G. bless you, sir : the man, sir
STA 2015 G. bless you, sir
STA 2022 G. hath engrossed all justice in his hands
STA 2024 O then I see that G. must right me
STA 2054 « G. bless thee, my sweet sonne »
ST 2862 with G. amende that mad Hieronimo
SP 422 ho, G. save you, sir
SP 999 G. sends fortune to fooles
SP 1333 and that great G., which we do truly worship
SP 1403 for what is misery but want of G. ?
SP 1404 and G. is lost, if faith be overthrowne
SP 1581 but still solicite G. for Soliman
SP 1720 G. send him good shipping
SP 1872 such favour send all Turkes, I pray G.
SP 1964 nay, G. be praisd, his death was reasonable
Ard. 320 I do appeal to G. and to the world
Ard. 328 as I intend to live with G. and his elected saints
Ard. 392 G. will revenge it, Arden, if thou dost
Ard. 486 G. knows 'tis not my fault ; but wonder not
Ard. 488 ah, Master Greene, G. knows how I am used
Ard. 761 « hoping in G. you be in good health »
Ard. 974 if fear of G. or common speech of men
Ard. 1173 G. grant this vision bedeem me any good
Ard. 1178 it may be so, G. frame it to the best
Ard. 1442 ay, G. he knows, and so doth Will and Shakebag
Ard. 1503 not hanged, G. save your honour
Ard. 1531 the time hath been, — would G. it were not past
Ard. 1594 a fever ? G. forbid !
Ard. 1774 leave in Feversham, G. knows, needy and bare
Ard. 1788 G., I beseech thee, show some miracle
Ard. 1806 and ask of G., whate'er betide of me
Ard. 1819 G. knows she is grown passing kind of late
Ard. 1855 marry, G. defend me from such a jest !
Ard. 2128 I for you, G. knows, have undeserved been
Ard. 2233 I like not this ; I pray G. all be well
Ard. 2300 I am too sure ; would G. I were deceived
Ard. 2328 G. and heaven can tell I loved him
Ard. 2382 Mistress Arden, you are now going to G.
JB 2 before the sight of the eternall G.
JB 10 cried most shrill in the eares of the righteous G.
JB 16 without respect either of the feare of G., or
JB 72 yet at length, the grace of G. being taken from her
JB 115 speaking, G. knowes, with a wicked thought
JB 150 « Now, G. forbid » (quoth she), and with that she
Puck. 10 as also in the feare of g., and freedom of my conscience
Puck. 69 in all humillitie and in the feare of g.
Puck. 80 that damnable offence to the awefull Matie of g.
HP 1675 her Chylde, and per consequence Gods Neipce
Cor. 125 and shew Gods wrath against a cruell soule
STA 2012 Gods will that I should set this tree
Ard. 518 ay, God's my witness, I mean plain dealing
Ard. 891 God's dear lady, how chance your face is so bloody ?
Ard. 1192 for God's sake, sirs, let me excuse myself
Cor. 927 els (g. to fore) my selfe may live to see his
STA 2048 Bazardo, afore-g., an excellent fellow
Jer. 1187 foregod, I have just mist them

ST Bal. 112 the which I never meant, *G.* wot
SP 1657 I, fearing they would adore me for a *G.*
SP 1681 O shoote no more ; great *G.*, I yield to thee
SP 1684 Cupid, *G.* of love, not daring looke me in the
SP 1943 the mightie pinky-ey'd, brand bearing *G.*
Ard. 101 Love is a *G.*, and marriage is but words
STA 1965 when as the Sun-*G.* rides in all his glorie
SP 227 grasse was seared with the Sunne Gods Element
HP 436 of *G.* the Father to those inferior Gods
HP 703 so Bacchus, so Apollo, who of all the other Gods were
  most fayre
Cor. 95 now we are hated both of Gods and men ?
Cor. 245 yee gods (at whose arbitrament all stand)
Cor. 420 and bellow forth against the Gods themselves
Cor. 676 then, home-borne houshold gods, and ye good spirits
Cor. 798 nowe you, whom both the gods and Fortunes grace
Cor. 822 O gods, that once had care of these our walls
Cor. 923 I trust the gods, that see our hourely wrongs
Cor. 1093 yet are there Gods, yet is there heaven and earth
Cor. 1095 no, no, there are no Gods ; or, if there be, they
Cor. 1708 sit invocating for us to the Gods
Cor. 1887 since all our hopes are by the Gods beguil'd
Cor. 1902 O cruell Gods, O heaven, O direfull Fates
Cor. 1967 O Gods, that earst of Carthage tooke some care
ST 1423 and neither Gods nor men be just to me
ST 3052 blaspheming Gods and all their holy names
SP 670 for celestiall Gods with gladsome lookes to gase
Ard. 253 make heavenly gods break off their nectar draughts
SP 284 by gods fish, friend, take you the Latins part ?

Goddess.
HP 1319 first attributed to Minerva, goddesse of wysedome
HP 1345 not onely a woman and a Queene but a Goddesse
Cor. 1905 O triple titled Heccat, Queene and Goddesse
SP 2016 a giddie goddesse that now giveth and anon taketh
Jer. 604 within the presence of this demy Goddesse

Godhead.
SP 1660 aspire to purchase *G.*, as did Hercules

Godly.
VPJ 8 and everywhere aboundeth *g.* love
HP 1668 Without regard of God or *G.* lawes

God-morrow.
SP 690 All haile, brave Cavelere. God morrow, Madam

Goers-by.
Ard. 1129 hated and spit at by the *g.*

Goes.
HP 415 the Sunne *g.* against the *Primum mobile*
Cor. 529 to force us doe that *g.* against our hart
Jer. 218 from userers doores there *g.* one pathe
Jer. 219 from friers that nurse whores there *g.* another path
ST 1469 I pray, sir, dispatch ; the day *g.* away
ST 1850 and heere, I heere — there *g.* the hare away
SP 355 he *g.* many times supperles to bed, and yet
SP 459 for money *g.* very low with me at this time
SP 951 hetherto all *g.* well ; but, if I be taken
Ard. 536 all this *g.* well ; Mosbie, I long for thee
Ard. 1920 silver noses for saying, « There *g.* Black Will ! »

Goest.
Ard. 1961 and as thou *g.*, tell John cook of our guests

Going.
HP 41 but heretofore *g.* into Fraunce I
HP 724 not restraining her from *g.* to feasts
STA 2074 still with a distracted countenance *g.* a long
SP 971 seeing he was *g.* towards heaven
Ard. 142 how now, Michael, whither are you *g.* ?
Ard. 685 now I am *g.* to London upon hope to
Ard. 756 come, let us be *g.*, and we'll bait at

Ard. 828 *g.* merrily to the ordinary
Ard. 885 how now, Michael, whither are you *g.* ?
Ard. 887 and I am *g.* to prepare his chamber
Ard. 1204 but now I am going to see what flood it is
Ard. 1510 come, Master Arden, let us be *g.*
Ard. 1881 who *g.* wounded from the place, he said
Ard. 2343 and now I am *g.* to fling them in the Thames
Ard. 2382 Mistress Arden, you are now *g.* to God

Gold.
HP 904 in Purple and glistering all in Golde and precious stones
HP 1183 that which is accounted (as *g.* or silver coyned)
HP 1619 as that which is applyed to *G.* and Silver
HP 1632 worth, weight, and fineness of the *G.* and Sylver
HP 1670 « For in their *G.* their hope beguiled lies »
Cor. 2001 that with the *g.* and pearle we us'd before
Jer. 119 (for Courtiers wil doe any thing for gould)
Jer. 231 for *g.* and chinck makes the punck wanton
Jer. 244 great gifts and *g.* have the best toong to move
Jer. 441 then the greatest mine of Indians brightest *g.*
Jer. 754 then hired he me with *g.* — O fate, thou elfe
Jer. 868 and all that *g.* thou hadst from Portugale
ST 67 where usurers are choakt with melting golde
ST 368 wast Spanish *g.* that bleared so thine eyes
ST 680 but golde doth more then either of them both
ST 826 in steed of watching, ile deserve more golde
ST 1264 heere is the golde, this is the golde proposde
ST 1918 but gentle brother, goe give to him this golde
SP 415 when valour failes, then gould must make the way
SP 450 I, that was a wench, and this is Golde
SP 628 were Fortunes gifts ; Love gives no gould or jewels
SP 629 why, what is jewels, or what is gould but earth
SP 900 your gould shall be repaide with double thankes
SP 1839 with that he purst the gould, and gave it us
Ard. 221 my saving husband hoards up bags of *g.*
Ard. 446 which, as I hear, will murder men for *g.*
Ard. 851 tell me of *g.*, my resolution's fee
Ard. 1199 with certain *g.* knit in it, as he said
Ard. 1230 my golden time was when I had no *g.*
Ard. 2042 some slave or other killed him for his *g.*
Ard. 2167 we have our *g.* ; Mistress Alice, adieu
Ard. 2344 I have the *g.* ; what care I though it be known !
JB 40 receaved of Brewen both golde and jewels
JB 44 to demaund his golde and jewels againe
Jer. 634 *G.*, I am true ; I had my hier, and thou shalt have thy due

Gold-abounding.
SP 200 even to the verge of golde abounding Spaine (Qq. golde,
  aboording etc)

Gold-coloured.
HP 301 white, or rather, *g.*

Golden.
VPJ 64 doth *g.* proffers make
Cor. 73 and that the *g.* Sunne, where ere he drive
Cor. 1973 when (fierd) their *g.* Pallaces fell downe
Jer. 118 him with a goulden baite will I allure
ST 623 not with faire words, but store of *g.* coyne
SP 94 and he thats titled by the *g.* spurre
SP 186 the *g.* Fleece is that we cry upon
SP 673 with Rosie chaplets deck thy *g.* tresses
SP 1036 not with slow sailes, but with loves goulden wings
SP 1103 but with my goulden wings ile follow him
Ard. 1154 but in the pleasure of this *g.* rest
Ard. 1230 my *g.* time was when I had no gold
Ard. 1338 and in this *g.* cover shall thy sweet phrases
Ard. 1541 path wherein he wont to guide his *g.* car
Ard. 2032 my hands shall play you *g.* harmony

Goldsmith.

Ard. 664 a *g.* and have a little plate in your shop !
JB (Title) John Brewen, *G.* of London, committed by
JB (2nd Title) the murder of John Brewen, *G.* of London
JB 26 two Goldsmithes, which were Batchelers, of good friends, and

Gone.

Cor. 251 (yet once both theyrs) survive, now they are *g.*?
Cor. 440 besides the losse of good men dead and *g.*
Cor. 1658 runnes to the tent, for feare we should be *g.*
Cor. 1942 for, both my husbands and my Father *g.*
Jer. 97 Andreas *g.* embassador
Jer. 236 thou knowest Andreas *g.* embassador
Jer. 413 you know Andreas *g.* embassador
ST Bal. 78 my griefes are come, my Joyes are *g.*
ST 291 and tribute paiment *g.* along with him?
ST 887 a man hangd up and all the murderers *g.*
ST 919 then is he *g.*? and is my sonne *g.* too?
STA 942 well sir, begon
ST 1366 fellow, be *g.*; my boy shall follow thee
ST 1429 for heere lyes that which bids me to be *g.*
ST 1838 away, Hieronimo ; to him be *g.*
ST 2233 gentle boy, be *g.*, for justice is exiled
ST 2268 talke not of cords, but let us now be *g.*
ST 2395 what, so short? then Ile be *g.*
ST 2892 as any of the Actors *g.* before
SP 24 Fortune is chorus ; Love and Death be *g.*
SP 291 now, by my troth, she is gon
SP 977 thy maister? and whether is he *g.* now?
SP 1072 thy folly gives thee priviledge ; begon, begon
SP 1085 is this little desperate fellow gon?
SP 1256 Brusor, be gon : and see not Soliman till thou
SP 1275 & 1276 my friend is *g.*, and I am desolate
SP 1308 but he was *g.* in twinckling of an eye
SP 1385 away, begone
SP 1630 O fine devise ; Brusor, get thee *g.*
SP 1636 Brusor, be *g.*: for till thou come I languish
SP 1780 Lord Brusor, come ; tis time that we were gon
SP 1886 this is a faire warning for me to get me gon
Ard. 120 nay, and you be so impatient, I'll be *g.*
Ard. 177 yonder comes Mosbie. Michael, get thee *g.*
Ard. 199 base peasant, get thee *g.*, and boast
Ard. 223 and now is he *g.* to unload the goods
Ard. 290 yonder's your husband. Mosbie, I'll be *g.*
Ard. 418 I am glad he is *g.*; he was about to stay
Ard. 449 Mosbie, be *g.* : I hope 'tis one that comes to
Ard. 822 well, I'll be *g.*, but look to your signs
Ard. 895 nay, an you be offended, I'll be *g.*
Ard. 1089 Greene, get you *g.*, and linger here about
Ard. 1118 the white-livered peasant is *g.* to bed
Ard. 1165 and when the dreadful forest-king is *g.*
Ard. 1169 but quakes and shivers, though the cause be *g.*
Ard. 1323 go, get thee *g.*, a copesmate for thy hinds
Ard. 1432 brawl not when I am *g.* in any case
Ard. 1717 no, sir ; get you *g.*
Ard. 1817 now that our horses are *g.* home before
Ard. 2057 tush, get you *g.* ; 'tis we must do the deed
Ard. 2095 methinks your wife would have me *g.*
Ard. 2115 the doors are open, sir, you may be *g.*
Ard. 2377 I am sure I had ne'er *g.* further than that place
SP 1312 with love of me her thoughts are over *g.*

Good.

VPJ 9 *g.* fortune and an everlasting fame attend on thee
VPJ 13 honour'd art, Princely behaviour, zeale to *g.*
VPJ 24 and al my *g.* is but vaine hope of gaine
VPJ 42 thy *g.* God knowes thy hope, thy hap and all
HP Ind. 28 howe it should bee used by a *g.* huswife

HP Ind. 137 to bee considered of a housholder and *g.* husbands
HP 11 tall of stature, of a *g.* aspect
HP 47 and what *g.* fortune ledde you into these parts?
HP 106 highlie favoured of the *g.* Cardinall Vercellis
HP 108 of Italie « (quoth I) » is that *g.* Cardinall knowne
HP 135 as it pleased the *g.* old Gentleman
HP 139 the *g.* old man, Coricius, the Gardener
HP 159 to the Cittie for the supply of *g.* manners
HP 190 there are few *g.* mellons to be found
HP 212 thought *g.* to have married myne
HP 238 tha[n] of the *g.* conditions of your Sonne
HP 393 commende his Supper with *g.* Wines
HP 480 the *g.* olde man began thus
HP 483 my *g.* Father, beeing then threescore and tenne
HP 503 touching things belonging to *g.* government
HP 506 with industrie, sparing, and *g.* husbandry
HP 517 the care of a *g.* householder is devided into two thinges
HP 525 the *g.* Housekeeper, then, ought principally to
HP 529 all the *g.* and all the evill incident to life
HP 643 a *g.* Husband to offend the league of
HP 719 brought up in *g.* discipline under the education of
HP 816 so yet I thinke *g.* to advise thee that
HP 844 *g.* members of the Cittie where thy selfe inhabitest
HP 843 *g.* servitors and subjects to their Prince
HP 847 in *g.* letters if they bee learned
HP 855 the care of a Father and *g.* Housekeeper
HP 918 the *g.* Housekeeper (that woulde have such
HP 1028 putrifie the *g.* and engender naughtie Fish
HP 1087 wherupon it comes to passe that *g.* servants
HP 1118 in those *g.* worldes of the Roman Common wealth
HP 1189 a *g.* Husbands judgment, experience
HP 1211 whereof the *g.* Housekeeper (oftentime) receiveth profit
HP 1233 if (like a *g.* husband) thou advise thee and
HP 1259 a *g.* huswife well considering, shold cause
HP 1274 a *g.* Huswife makying store for her provision
HP 1279 in such *g.* sort as there shalbe no misse
HP 1291 a *g.* Huswife should so provide that
HP 1308 neither ought a *g.* Huswife to dysdaine or scorne to
HP 1316 wherewith a *g.* Huswife may furnish
HP 1370 the *g.* Huswife ought above all things to be
HP 1463 unworthye or against the title of *g.* Husbandry
HP 1549 interrupt or spoyle that *g.* proportion
HP 1747 a *g.* Steward knoweth as well how to governe
HP 1776 time and *g.* manners will hardly give us leave
Cor. 97 for one man grieveth at anothers *g.*
Cor. 108 heaven heretofore (enclinde to do us *g.*)
Cor. 179 and nere did *g.*, where ever it befell
Cor. 218 and choakes the *g.*, which els we had enjoy'd
Cor. 358 in *g.* or bad as to continue it
Cor. 398 blood mixt with his enemies, had done him *g.*
Cor. 440 besides the losse of *g.* men dead and gone
Cor. 511 can wee be over-hastie to *g.* hap?
Cor. 512 what *g.* expect wee in a fiery gap?
Cor. 655 O poore Cornelia, have not wee *g.* cause
Cor. 676 then, home-borne houshold gods, and ye *g.* spirits
Cor. 695 God graunt these dreames to *g.* effect bee brought
Cor. 827 father to *g.* Quirinus, our first founder
Cor. 1118 or shall theyr ghosts, that dide to doe us *g.*
Cor. 1227 what reck I death to doe so many *g.*?
Cor. 1265 bravely to doe his country *g.*
Cor. 1295 repay *g.* with ingratitude
Cor. 1445 O, but theyr Countries *g.* concerns them more
Cor. 1456 *g.* deeds the cruelst hart to kindnes bring
Cor. 1844 whose stony hart, that nere dyd Romaine *g.*
Jer. 78 Lorenzo is not thought upon : *g.*

Jer. 92 I, I, thats *g.*
Jer. 123 O sweete, sweete pollicie, I hugg thee ; *g.*
Jer. 177 they are, my *g.* Lord
Jer. 193 O, *g.* Horatio, no
Jer. 233 discharg, discharg, *g.* Lazarotto, how we
Jer. 357 sudden blowes, and thats as *g.* as warres
Jer. 535 God save you, *g.* knight Marshall
Jer. 698 O, *g.* words, my Lords, for those are courtiers vailes
Jer. 898 I know your curage to be trid and *g.*
Jer. 959 art thou ? *g.* : why, then, ile quench thee
Jer. 1194 so *g.* night, kind gentles
ST Bal. 70 that so had spoyl'd my chiefest *g.*
ST Bal. 101 and say'd 'twere *g.* I should resigne
ST 176 thanks, *g.* L[ord] Generall for these *g.* newes
ST 292 I, my *g.* Lord.
ST 339 nay, evill newes flie faster still than *g.*
ST 438 but now, if your *g* liking stand thereto
ST 484 thanks, *g.* Horatio, take it for thy paines
ST 795 that is perfourmd alreadie, my *g.* Lord
ST 990 meane while, *g.* Isabella, cease thy plaints
ST 1256 then by their life to hazard our *g.* haps
ST 1361 I, my *g.* Lord
ST 1363 « To stand *g.* L[ord] and help him in distres »
ST 1489 that that is *g.* for the body is likewise *g.* for the soule
ST 1497 I prethee, request this *g* company to pray with me
ST 1498 I, mary, sir, this is a *g.* motion
ST 1499 my maisters, you see heers a *g.* fellow
ST 1601 *g.* Madam, affright not thus yourselfe
STA 1764 in very little time, will grow to some *g.* use
ST 1794 *g.* leave have you ; nay, I pray you goe
ST 1823 Why, ha, ha, ha. Farewell. good ha, ha, ha
STA 2017 what wouldst thou have, *g.* fellow? — Justice, Madame
STA 2033 this *g.* fellow heere and I will range this
ST 2246 ah, my *g.* Lord, I am not your yong Sonne
ST 2308 or heere, or where your highnes thinks it *g.*
ST 2360 twere *g.*, my L[ord], that Hieronimo and I were reconcilde
ST 2418 my *g.* Lord, I know you did not
ST 2535 why, my *g.* Lords, assure your selves of me
ST 2551 marrie, my *g.* Lord, thus
ST 2566 nay, be not angrie, *g.* Hieronimo
ST 2571 now, my *g.* Lord, could you entreat your
ST 2659 shall prove the intention, and all was *g.*
ST 2717 but, *g.* my Lord, let me entreate your grace to
ST 2721 one thing more, my *g.* Lord
ST 2752 was thought *g.* to be set downe in English, more largely
ST 2910 O, *g.* words : as deare to me was my Horatio
STA 2953 O, *g.* words : as deare to me was my Horatio
ST 3019 and *g.* Hieronimo slaine by himselfe
SP 133 wish me *g.* hap, Perseda, and Ile winne
SP 136 such fortune as the *g.* Andromache wisht
SP 310 Basilisco — Knight, *g.* fellow, Knight, Knight
SP 311 Knave, *g.* fellow, Knave, Knave
SP 390 so yong, and of such *g.* accomplishment
SP 397 impose me taske, how I may do you *g.*
SP 407 but vertue should not envie *g.* desert
SP 414 which by *g.* fortune I have found to day
SP 455 why, and reason *g.* : let them paie that best may
SP 497 but stay a while, *g.* Death, and let me live
SP 580 not *g.* pollicie to call your forces home
SP 738 this is *g.* argument of thy true love
SP 790 as in the Spider *g.* things turne to poison
SP 956 dive into this Gentlemans pocket, for *g.* luck sake
SP 971 faith, sir, for pure *g.* will
SP 1004 my maister was in *g.* health at the sending
SP 1053 I tell you, for pure *g.* will

SP 1420 faire blossome, likely to have proved *g.* fruite
SP 1560 and now, to turne late promises to *g.* effect
SP 1582 whose minde hath proved so *g.* and gratious
SP 1605 to one' past cure *g.* counsell comes too late
SP 1716 I feare thou wilt never proove *g.* christian
SP 1720 God send him *g.* shipping
SP 1990 yet dare I beare her hence, to do thee *g.*
Ard. 291 in *g.* time see where my husband comes
Ard. 494 I never live *g.* day with him alone
Ard. 497 and though I might content as *g.* a man
Ard. 533 *g.* fortune follow all your forward thoughts
Ard 552 they be so *g.* that I must laugh for joy
Ard. 573 but call you this *g.* news ?
Ard. 657 yet thy friend to do thee any *g.* I can
Ard. 664 « one snatch, *g.* corporal », when I stole the
Ard. 666 domineer'd with it amongst *g.* fellows
Ard. 669 *g.* neighbour Bradshaw, you are too proud
Ard. 709 who, I pray thee, *g.* Will ?
Ard. 721 Will, there's a crown for thy *g.* news
Ard. 762 « hoping in God you be in *g.* health »
Ard. 938 doth challenge nought but *g.* deserts of me
Ard. 947 now it were *g.* we parted company
Ard. 959 the many *g.* turns that thou hast
Ard. 982 *g.* counsel is to her as rain to weeds
Ard. 1096 this drowsiness in me bodes little *g.*
Ard. 1173 God grant this vision bedeem me any *g.*
Ard. 1188 at your *g.* pleasure, sir ; I'll bear you company
Ard. 1310 this certain *g.* I lost for changing bad
Ard. 1324 I am too *g.* to be thy favourite
Ard. 1350 weigh all thy *g.* turns with this little fault
Ard. 1436 it were not *g.* he travelled in such pain
Ard. 1490 ay, my *g.* lord, and highly bound to you
Ard. 1632 yet neither with *g.* mortar well compact
Ard. 1650 like to a *g.* companion's smoky brain
Ard. 1667 yes, I pray thee, *g.* ferryman
Ard. 1742 here's to pay for a fire and *g.* cheer
Ard. 1761 to part from any thing may do thee *g.*
Ard. 1834 than women are when they are in *g.* humours
Ard. 2092 therefore I thought it *g.* to make you friends
Ard. 2096 no, *g.* Master Mosbie ; women will be prating
Ard. 2111 no, *g.* Master Mosbie
Ard. 2230 *g.* Master Franklin, go and seek him forth
JB 24 her *g.* behaviour and other commendable qualities
JB 26 of *g.* friends, and well esteemed for fine
JB 34 the *g.* will and favour of al her friends and kinsfolk
JB 42 his suite despised, and his goodwill nothing regarded
JB 43 and seeing no hope of her *g.* will and favour
JB 48 driven off longer than hee thought *g.* of
JB 54 and this before *g.* witnes she vowed to performe
JB 56 being not a little glad of his *g.* successe
JB 99 « I, mary, with a *g.* will, wife, » (quoth he)
JB 109 « I have spilt a measse of as *g.* sugur sops as ever »
JB 111 « yes » quoth she, « that there is, two as *g.* as they »
JB 112 « two as *g.* as they, or I will make them as *g.* »
JB 113 « but it greeves me that any *g.* thing should so »
JB 119 « that I will » quoth he, « with a *g.* will
Puck 79 assuring yor *g.* L[or]s that if I knewe eny
Jer. 953 an excellent foe ; we shall have scuffling *g.*
SP 690 All haile, brave Cavelere. God morrow, Madam
JB 96 giving him the *g.* morrow in most courteous manner
HP 518 two thinges, that is his body and hys goods
HP 520 in his goods two purposes are proposed
HP 522 and first of hys body rather then hys goods
Cor. 663 under his outrage now are all our goods
Cor. 1444 besides theyr lives, I did theyr goods restore
Cor. 1698 our goods, our honors, and our auncient lawes

Jer. 991 now death doth heap his goods np all at once
Ard. 90 for I have certain goods there to unload
Ard. 223 and now is he gone to unload the goods
Ard. 550 as far as either goods or life may stretch
Cor. 15 which to preserve (unto our after g.) our fathers

Goodly.

HP 97 « well placed » (quoth I) « is this goodlie house
ST 1604 why, did I not give you gownes and g. things
STA 2939 see, here's a g. nowse will hold them all
SP 1450 I should have deemd them Junoes g. Swannes
SP 1668 compassing me with g. ceremonies
Ard. 422 was it not a g. poison that he gave ?

Goodman.

HP 120 the good man and maister of the house
HP 207 and the good man of the house beganne againe
HP 252 « this wilde boare » (quoth the good man) « was taken
HP 1364 and come into comparison with her good man
Ard. 316 and mark my words, you g. botcher

Goodness.

HP 1492 the nature, goodnes, and value of all things

Goodwife.

HP 871 but the g. of the house also

Goose.

SP 355 he will jet as if it were a G. on a greene

Gore.

Cor. 1393 purpled ore with eyther Armies murdred souldiers g.
Jer. 1069 O my sad fates, Don Pedro weltring in his g.
ST 1833 downe by the dale that flowes with purple g.
Ard. 864 seest thou this g. that cleaveth to my face ?
Ard. 2249 smeared in blood and filthy g.

Gored.

Cor. 929 gor'd with a thousand stabs, and round about

Gorged.

Cor. 1585 full-g. triumphes, and disdaines my lyfe

Gorse.

Cor. 217 our fields surcloid with worthles G.

Gossip.

Jer. 296 as thus — « shal I tell you, g. ?

Got.

HP 1578 gaines which are gotte and followed with paine and
sweat
Cor. 330 by whom the glorie of thy conquests g. might
Cor. 949 what g. he by his death ?
Cor. 1057 to one that ne're g. victorie was urg'd to yeelde
Cor. 1164 he layd apart the powre that he had g.
Cor. 1174 now, having g. what he hath gaped for
Cor. 1332 whose honor, g. by famous victories, hath
Cor. 1543 for his suddaine glory g.
Cor. 1632 and g. hys willing hosts to march by night
ST Bal. 83 I rent and tore each thing I g.
STA 937 I wonder how this fellow g. his clothes
SP 835 but how she g. it, heaven knows, not I
SP 880 mas, the foole sayes true ; lets have some g.
SP 1008 how g. he this from of Lucinas arme ?
SP 1014 after we had g. the chaine in mummery
SP 1849 as were not in his gallyes to be g.
Ard. 2340 but whether she would or no, I g. me up
JB 181 at length he g. her with child againe

Gotten.

HP 1445 whatsoever is g. or obtained in the warres
HP 1555 either miserably g. or encreased by wrong
HP 1580 have beene and yet are used to be g.
Ard. 201 g. by witchcraft and mere sorcery !
Ard. 759 I have g. such a letter as will touch the painter
JB 68 had lien with her and g. her with child
JB 82 till he had g. her a better house

JB 148 « stay in the house one night, till you had g. another ? »

Gourds.

HP 191 taste like Goords and Cowgomers

Govern.

HP 890 the Housekeeper shall so governe hys familie
HP 946 differeth much from that wherwith we governe Beasts
HP 1747 a good Steward knoweth as well how to governe
SP 1516 and I myselfe, that governe many kings
SP 1526 that cannot governe private fond affections ?
SP 1744 or then to governe Rhodes ? and that I doe
SP 2219 meane time will Fortune governe as she may
Ard. 1624 or g. me that am to rule myself ?

Governed.

HP 946 the manner wherwith servaunts are g.
HP 1742 yet are they to be g. diversly
Ard. 1662 women are, that is to say, g. by the moon
HP 630 as we see the Cittizens in wel g. Citties obey
SP 1601 well governd friends do first regard themselves

Governeth.

Cor. 574 that gouverneth and guides our dayes

Governing.

HP 1775 care of g. a Princes house

Government.

HP 471 giving up the g. of his house and
HP 498 to disgrade me of this petit g. of houshold
HP 503 touching things belonging to good g.
HP 871 housekeeping and g. of families
HP 1111 who in theyr civill g. doth seme to
HP 1512 object directed unto household g.
HP 1713 whether houshold care or housholde g. be all one
HP 1716 the g. of private houses and of Princes Courtes are
different
HP 1760 how the g. of a civill and a
HP 1761 unlesse he call his g, Civill
HP 1766 that private g. is the least, and yet
HP 1722 found that there is difference in houshold governments
HP 1738 so are the governments of Princes and
HP 1750 governments or dispensations of a house are devided
into
HP 1754 the governments of those houses of the

Governor.

HP 379 the Sun (like a most indifferent Governour)
HP 869 a Governour or Maister, terme it as you list
HP 897 this distinction of Soveraigne, Ruler, Governour, or
Maister, is
HP 1755 Viceroyes of Naples, Sicilie, and the Governour of Mylain
SP 908 flie, Erastus, ere the Governour have any newes
SP 923 if the Governour surprise me heere, I die
SP 982 thou knowest me for the Governour of the cittie
SP 1120 married Cornelia, daughter to the Governour ?
SP 1267 the Governour will hang you, and he catch you
SP 1339 there lies the Governour, and there his Sonne
SP 1417 the Governour is slaine that sought thy death
SP 1531 goe, Janisaries, call in your Governour
SP 1561 be thou, Erastus, Governour of Rhodes
SP 1706 and Erastus made governour of Rhodes
HP 1759 and those Governours of Asti, Vercellis
HP 1769 those civill Governours or officers that
SP 1761 Thankes, Lord Governour. — And thankes to you,
Madame
SP 1802 Erastus, Lord Governour of Rhodes, I arrest you

Gown.

STA 2068 in my shirt, and my gowne under myne arme
SP 1382 and the gilded gowne the Emperour gave you
Ard. 30 and bravely jets it in his silken g.
Jer. 450 hast thou worne gownes in the University

ST 1604 why, did I not give you gownes and goodly things
SP 850 foure Visards, foure Gownes, a boxe, and a Drumme
Grace.
HP 28 a kind of gentilitie and *g.*
HP 1382 *g.* and comlines in beautifying and adorning things
Cor. Ded. 17 what *g.* that excellent Garnier hath lost by
Cor. 290 ye may be ritch and great in Fortunes *g.*
Cor. 798 nowe you, whom both the gods and Fortunes *g.*
Cor. 1100 have neither helpe nor *g.* in heavens sight
Cor. 1109 the conquering Tyrant, high in Fortunes *g.*
Cor. 1507 henceforth vary not thy *g.* from
ST 242 and I shall studie to deserve this *g.*
ST 486 I reapt more *g.* then I deserv'd or hop'd
STA 1984 in my boyes face there was a kind of *g.*
SP 1586 the other so adorned with *g.* and modestie
JB 72 yet at length, the *g.* of God being taken from her
JB 224 the Lord give all men *g.* by their example to
Cor. 1213 to *g.* themselves with honor of the game
Cor. 2014 adorne and *g.* his graceles Enemy?
Jer. 538 much doth your presence *g.* our homely roofe
ST 520 to *g.* our banquet with some pompous jest
ST 781 Ile grace her marriage with an unckles gift
STA 933 did *g.* him with waiting on his cup
ST 1409 an odde jest for me to stand and *g.* every jest he makes
ST 2527 let me entreat you, *g.* my practises
ST 2538 to *g.* the King so much as with a shew
ST 2558 as but to *g.* me with your acting it
SP 152 to *g.* thy nuptials with their deeds at armes
Cor. Arg. 2 as much accomplisht with the graces of the bodie
Jer. 535 who, I? before your *g.* it must not be
ST 257 but that I know your *g.* for just and wise
ST 267 I crave no better then your *g.* awards
ST 792 wilt please your *g.* command me ought beside?
ST 1881 nor am I least indebted to his *g.*
ST 2717 let me entreate your *g.* to give the King
ST 2723 let me ehtreat your *g.* that, when the
ST 2769 let then Perseda on your *g.* attend
ST 193 this tels me that your graces men of warre
SP 672 when shall the graces, or Lucinas hand
SP 1498 and all the Graces smiling round about her
Graced.
HP Ded. of that which Tassos pen so highly gracde
Cor. 679 and *g.* with the name of Affrican
Cor. 1337 grac'd with a thousand kingly diadems
ST 508 and graste with favours of his Majestie
ST 2382 and thou art *g.* with a happier Love
ST 2755 and be thou grac't with every excelence that
SP 154 thrise renowned Englishman, graced by thy country
Graceless.
Cor. 2014 adorne and grace his graceles Enemy?
SP 775 aye me, how gracelesse are these wicked men
JB 86 neere to the place where this graceles Parker dwelt
Graceth.
HP 657 better *g.* or adornes a womans cheekes then that
Gracing.
ST 2630 Hieronimo was liberall in *g.* of it so
SP 700 challenge you for *g.* me with a malignant stile
Gracious.
HP 54 a magnanimous, just, and gratious Prince
Jer. 43 then, my *G.* leedge, I hold it meete
Jer. 783 word for word, my gratious soveraine
Jer. 792 according [to] your gratious, dread Comand
ST 7 yet inferiour far to gratious fortunes of my
ST 207 that was my sonne, my gratious soveraigne
ST 241 and in our sight thy selfe art gratious
ST 476 yes, to your gratious selfe must I complaine

ST 746 but, gratious Madame, then appoint the field
STA 969 be *g.* to me, thou infective night
ST 1911 my gratious Lord, he is with extreame pride
STA 1976 the heavens are *g.*, and your miseries and
ST 2316 I, my *g.* Lord, and this is the day that
ST 2385 my *g.* father, beleeve me, so he doth
ST 2798 but with a gratious eye behold his griefe
SP 50 comparing it to twenty gratious things?
SP 1178 my gratious Soveraigne, as this Knight seemes
SP 1203 then this, my gratious Lord, is all I crave
SP 1229 my *g.* Soveraigne, without presumption
SP 1425 ah, gratious Soliman, now showe thy love
SP 1440 my gratious Lord, rejoyce in happinesse
SP 1578 my gratious Lord, whe[n] Erastus doth forget this favor
SP 1582 whose minde hath proved so good and gratious
SP 1746 and thanks to gratious heavens, that so
SP 1817 innocent, than I have bene to gratious Soliman
Ard. 2 my *g.* Lord, the Duke of Somerset
Ard. 2435 to make it *g.* to the ear or eye
Ard. 2436 for simple truth is *g.* enough
Graft.
SP 114 yong slippes are never *g.* in windy daies
HP 175 I have gryft so many fruitfull Plants
Grain.
HP 166 with wheate and all kind of graine
Cor. 200 that (wastfull) shed their graine uppon the ground
Gramercy.
ST 1431 *G.*, boy, but it was time to come
Gramina.
ST 1001 *G.* Sol pulchras effert in luminis oras
Grammarian.
HP 1124 who beeing an excellent *G.*, was also
Grandam.
STA 1955 beate at the bushes, stampe our *g.* earth
SP 72 my Grandame on her death bed gave it me
Grandfather.
Cor. 1253 the sonne, of noble Brutus, hys great *G.*
Grant.
VPJ 87 God graunt thee long amongst as breathe
HP 36 God graunt in other things she shewe
HP 101 my Father is, whom God graunt a long life
Cor. 625 so *g.* your plagues (which they provoke)
Cor. 695 God graunt these dreames to good effect bee brought
Jer. 1198 for my sons sake, greant me a man at least
ST 2214 that Prosperine may *g.* revenge on
ST 2410 graunt me the combat of them, if they dare
SP 1520 graunt [me] one boone that I shall crave of thee
SP 1521 what ere it be, Perseda, I graunt it thee
SP 2098 a kisse I graunt thee, though I hate thee deadlie
Ard. 459 I heard your husband hath the *g.* of late
Ard. 469 he hath the *g.* under the Chancery seal
Ard. 558 whether my husband had the lands by *g.*
Ard. 602 it resteth in your *g.*; some words are past
Ard. 605 ah, Master Clarke, it resteth at my *g.*
Ard. 607 but, so you'll *g.* me one thing I shall ask
Ard. 617 and then I'll *g.* my sister shall be yours
Ard. 1035 with just demand, and I must *g.* it him
Ard. 1173 God *g.* this vision bedeem me any good
ST 3043 (Juno forgets olde wrath, and graunts him ease)
Ard. 462 so that all former grants are cut off
Granted.
HP 209 heaven hath not graunted me a maiden Child
HP 613 that superioritie that hath been graunted unto man
HP 1354 Cookery and such like, but graunted they might weave
SP 316 licensed, obtayned, and *g.*
SP 1202 aske what thou wilt; it shall be graunted thee

Granteth.

HP 442 Which who so graunteth, it would seeme

Granting.

HP 680 easie to be entreated should the husbande be in graunting

Grape.

HP 328 though it bee prest from one selfe same G.

HP Ind. 81 grapes gathered out of season

HP Ind. 82 grapes growing in Greece, of what collour

HP Ind. 84 grapes gathered in Autumn

HP 300 made of the Grapes that grow in Greece

HP 305 not so much force as it can rypen Grapes

Cor. 1824 whose blood, as from a spunge, or bunche of Grapes crusht

Grape-gatherers.

HP 1 that the G. were wont to presse their Wines

Grape-gathering.

HP 306 before the time of G.

HP 386 especiall is G. for the wine-presse

Grasp.

Jer. 372 for all Spaines wealth Ide not graspe hands

Grasped.

Cor. 1678 and in the other graspt his Coutelas

Grass.

HP 758 « Lay doun with him upo[n] the grasse al covered with a clowde »

ST 151 there legs and armes lye bleeding on the grasse

SP 226 the jucie grasse was seared with

SP 231 the men died, the women wept, and the grasse grew

Ard. 2431 and in the g. his body's print was seen two years

Grass-green.

Cor. 1345 backe to thy grass-greene bancks to welcom us

Gratefully.

Jer. 10 and that shall answere g. for me

Gratulate.

SP 260 yet to g. this benigne Prince

Grave.

HP 720 under the education of a g. Matron and wise mother

Cor. 1120 shall lamed Souldiours and g. gray-haird men

VPJ 74 their bed become their g.

Jer. 305 could choke bright honor in a skabard g.?

Jer. 853 whose servile acts live in their graves

Jer. 911 let them not ly forsworne now in their graves

Ard. 1054 gapes open wide, like graves to swallow men

Graven.

ST 36 Minos, in g. leaves of Lotterie, drew forth the

SP 117 that carry honour g. in their helmes

SP 2225 for holy fates have g. it in their tables

Graving.

HP 1532 in g. or cutting the Chizzel should not be so

Gravity.

HP 117 of countenance verie pleasant myxed with comelie gravitie

ST 2150 now must I beare a face of gravitie

Graze.

HP 173 and little flocks I have are wont to g.

Grazing.

HP 1171 whatsoever els belongeth to husbandry or g.

Great.

HP Ind. 40 care of housekeeping as g. to

HP Ind. 58 nobilitie betwixt man and wife, how g.

HP Ind. 88 hayre a g. ornament of nature

HP 275 they are of g. nourishment, and they

HP 277 had neede of g. nourishment

HP 279 although they be of g. nourishment, yet

HP 334 all sorts of fruite in g. aboundance

HP 404 Doctors of the Hebrues, and Christians of g. account

HP 509 looked to my husbandry with so g. care

HP 557 nor without g. admiration should Dydo have

HP 591 no distinction of nobilitie can be so g.

HP 654 not without g. reason was it said of Aristotle

HP 706 but hayre (which is a g. orname[n]t of Nature)

HP 977 those feareful Hostes which the g. Turke mustereth

HP 1002 as in g. houses it hath beene accustomed

HP 1249 g. aboundance of the yere and fruitfulnes of seasons

HP 1355 weave, and that not without g. commendation

HP 1381 of so g. efficacye and force is order

HP 1392 co[m]paring little things with g. we may well report

HP 1472 if g., not much to be dislyked

HP 1576 are g. helps to health

HP 1620 easily may a g. quantity of mony be heaped up

HP 1627 without g. discomoditie and perill

HP 1732 leave to keepe a g., yet private house

Cor. (Title) Pompey the G., his faire Corneliaes Tragedie

Cor. Arg. 5 she tooke to second husbande Pompey the g.

Cor. 863 Pompey the g., whom I have honored

Cor. 2 g. Jupiter, our Citties sole Protector

Cor. 51 hath in a manner this g. Towne oreturn'd

Cor. 181 (now growne so g. with Souldiers bodies that

Cor. 290 ye may be ritch and g. in Fortunes grace

Cor. 372 growne g. without the strife of Cittizens·

Cor. 471 g. losses greatly are to be deplor'd

Cor. 472 the losse is g. that cannot be restor'd

Cor. 488 and those g. Cities, whose foundations

Cor. 710 g. Emperors fast bound in chaynes of brasse

Cor. 751 I saw g. Pompey, and I heard hym speake

Cor. 824 g. Jupiter, to whom our Capitol

Cor. 1176 a chyld, slightly to part with so g. signiorie ?

Cor. 1260 the wrong is g., and over-long endur'd

Cor. 1362 there lyves no King (how g. so e're he be)

Cor. 1411 I call to witnes heavens g. Thunderer, that

Cor. 1626 nay, even our Trenches, to our g. disgrace

Cor. 1978 content to count the ghosts of those g. Captains

Cor. 2009 and must I live to see g. Pompeys house

Jer. 244 g. gifts and gold have the best toong to move

Jer. 251 and therefore g. gifts may bewitch her eie

Jer. 301 hees a g. man, therefore we must not

Jer. 492 « O, that villainy should be found in the g. Chamber »

Jer. 517 « O, that villainy should be found in the g. chamber »

Jer. 736 hath his fame as well as a g. courtier

Jer. 927 thy valiansie, and all that thou holdst g.

ST Bal. 14 and wonne g. honour in the fielde

ST Bal. 23 and with g. honour did present him to

ST 157 in their maine battell made so g. a breach

ST 240 for in our hearing thy deserts were g.

ST 397 their harts were g., their clamours menacing

STA 952 ha, are they not g. perswasions ?

ST 1127 by our g. L[ord] the mightie King of Spaine

ST 1316 for I suspect, and the presumptions g.

ST 1501 till some other time ; for now I have no g. need

STA 1781 and his g. minde, too ful of Honour

ST 2612 g. Soliman, the Turkish Emperour

ST 2787 let not Erasto live to grieve g. Soliman

SP 193 under the conduct of g. Soliman

SP 499 ah no, g. losses sildome are restord

SP 526 g. Soliman, heavens onely substitute

SP 658 the worthy brethren of g. Soliman

SP 919 g. ease it were for me to purge my selfe

SP 1031 thou g. commander of the swift wingd winds

SP 1209 and be g. Solimans adopted friend

SP 1231 let not g. Solimans command

SP 1333 and that g. God, which we do truly worship

SP 1358 preserved to be presented to *g.* Soliman
SP 1478 the pure affection of *g.* Soliman?
SP 1541 ah, pardon me, *g.* Soliman, for this is she
SP 1559 couldst win Erastus, from *g.* Soliman
SP 1615 why lives he then to greeve *g.* Soliman?
SP 1625 under couler of *g.* consequence
SP 1681 O shoote no more ; *g.* God, I yield to thee
SP 1729 and made *g.* Soliman, sweete beauties thrall
SP 1745 and that I doe, thankes to *g.* Soliman
SP 1764 so it is, my Lord, that upon *g.* affaires
SP 1807 without the leave or licence of my Lord, *g.* Soliman?
SP 1833 to leave *g.* Soliman and serve in Rhodes
SP 1854 we made all knowne unto *g.* Soliman
SP 1913 *g.* Hectors sonne, although his age did
SP 1970 faith, two *g.* Knights of the post swore
SP 2011 where is tipsie Alexander, that *g.* cup conquerour
SP 2020 the *g.* Turque, whose seat is Constantinople
SP 2050 *g.* Soliman, Lord of all the world
SP 2211 and wheres *g.* Soliman, but in my triumph?
Ard. (Title) the *g.* malice and dissimulation of a wicked woman
Ard. 19 can any grief be half so *g.* as this?
Ard. 403 yet, if thy business be of *g.* import
Ard. 588 a man, I guess, of *g.* devotion?
Ard. 727 and in a matter of *g.* consequence
Ard. 1069 so *g.* a cry for nothing I ne'er heard
Ard. 1172 such *g.* impression took this fond surprise
Ard. 1495 the occasion is *g.*, or else would I wait on you
Ard. 1591 of a *g.* fever
Ard. 1593 a *g.* fever
Ard. 1647 we have *g.* haste ; I pray thee, come away
JB 18 to the *g.* hazard of their soules and the destructions
JB 151 made a shewe of *g.* heavines and sorrow
JB 184 for feare her neighbours should perceave her *g.* bellie

Greater.
HP 103 spent the *g.* part of his time in
HP 457 I have entertained a *g.* guest then I expected
HP 575 the *g.* then and straighter the conjunction
HP 746 never *g.* sweet in love then that which
HP 893 servaunts, who for the *g.* number are
HP 916 as the *g.* number are
HP 1352 *g.* and more curious observers of such things
HP 1531 nor *g.* then the Mariner can guide
Cor. Ded. 8 then which the world affoords no *g.* misery
Cor. Arg. 17 and occupied the *g.* part of Afrique
Cor. 1389 and noble deeds were *g.* then his fortunes
Cor. 1535 or (his *g.* wrath to show) gives them
Jer. 21 rise higher and *g.* in thy Soveraines eies
Jer. 881 words *g.* then thy selfe, it must not [be]
ST Bal. 6 loe, here a sight of *g.* woe
ST Bal. 58 the more to worke my *g.* spight
ST 111 with deeper wage and *g.* dignitie
STA 1197 I reserve your favour for a *g.* honor
ST 1340 this their dissention breeds a *g.* doubt
ST 2916 avenged with *g.* far than these afflictions
STA 2939 revenged with *g.* far then these afflictions
SP 484 didst thou advance me for my *g.* fall?
SP 1123 what, *g.* then at our coronation?
SP 1693 a *g.* punishment to hurt you behind
SP 1754 our present joyes will be so much the *g.*
Ard. 697 the inner side did bear the *g.* show
Ard. 1401 would mount to a *g.* sum of money
Puck 61 I shall geve *g.* instance wᶜʰ I have observd

Greatest.
HP 166 the first and *g.* part I plow
HP 486 the deedes of *g.* Kings, that turne the eyes of
HP 980 and discharge the *g.* doubt thou canst imagine

HP 1385 with the *g.* arte and industrie
Cor. 454 and choyce of streames the *g.* River dryes
Cor. 1763 wind, shaking a Pynetree with theyr *g.* powre
Jer. 283 it is the *g.* argument and sign that I
Jer. 441 then the *g.* mine of Indians brightest gold
Jer. 1149 his share is *g.* in this victory
ST 812 with *g.* pleasure that our Court affords
ST 1311 our *g.* ils we least mistrust, my Lord
SP 624 hath in the Actors showne the *g.* power?
SP 660 who is [the] *g.*, Fortune, Death, or Love
SP 809 whost *g.* fault was over loving thee?
SP 1121 with the *g.* pompe that ere I saw
SP 1359 the *g.* honor Fortune could affoord
SP 1670 and viewd the Capitoll, and was Romes *g.* glorie
SP 2188 miserie amidst his *g.* joy and jollitie
Puck 30 my *g.* enemies will saie by me
Puck 34 dared in the *g.* cause, wᶜʰ is to cleere my self of

Great-grandfather.
Cor. 1253 the sonne, of noble Brutus, hys great Grandfather

Greatly.
Cor. 321 thy wandring glory was so *g.* knowne?
Cor. 471 great losses *g.* are to be deplor'd
ST 215 it *g.* pleaseth us that in our victorie
ST 1487 faith, I cannot tell, nor I care not *g.*
SP 262 he is beholding to you *g.*, sir
Ard. 1814 it *g.* matters not what he says
Ard. 1820 *g.* changed from the old humour of

Greatness.
HP 85 four square and of convenient greatnes
HP 487 their greatnes and magnificence
HP 1523 are not infinit either in number or in greatnes
HP 1527 cannot well be handled, managed, or lifted for their greatnes
HP 1723 consider whether they be discrepant in forme or greatnes
HP 1724 forasmuch if they onely differ in greatnes, then even
HP 1735 differeth from the other in the pompe and greatnes
Cor. 1423 howbeit I never meant my greatnes should by

Greca.
HP 1340 Come la nobil *G.* ch' alle tele sue

Grecian.
HP 300 are called *G.* wines, because they
HP 1342 ‹ As did that noble *G.* dame that bated

Gree.
Ard. 548 and if fair Susan and I can make a *g.*

Greece.
HP Ind. 82 grapes growing in *G.*, of what collour
HP Ind. 134 Thales one of the seaven wise men of *G.*
HP 301 made of the Grapes that grow in *G.*
HP 329 from one selfe same Grape as the Wine of *G.* is
HP 1760ᵃ Modone a Cittie in *G.*

'Greed, *see* **Agreed.**

Greedy-gaping.
Ard. 476 and he is *g.* still for gain

Greek.
HP 314 the Malmesey [and] Greeke and Romaine Wines
HP 1201 which (by the Greeke interpretation) signifieth Law
Cor. 63 The *G.*, Th' Arabian, Macedons or Medes
ST 2651 you, my Lord, in Latin ; I in Greeke ; you in
HP 1351 the Greekes observed not so much decorum
Cor. 497 faire Ilium, razed by the conquering Greekes
SP 137 valiant Hector wounded with the Greekes

Green.
VPJ 28 my fruite is falne, and yet my leaves are greene
Jer. 905 that must be acted on the feeldes greene stage
Jer. 1100 so strong a courage of so greene a set

ST 44 under greene mirtle trees and Cipresse shades
ST 829 my yeeres were mellow, his but young and greene
ST 1017 thou talkest of harvest, when the corne is greene
ST 1528 disroabde the medowes of their flowred greene
SP 437 least he dismount me while my wounds are greene
ST 73 which brought me to the faire Elizian greene
SP 355 he will jet as if it were a Goose on a greene
Cor. 1345 backe to thy grass-greene bancks to welcom us

Greene.
Ard. 296 G., one of Sir Antony Ager's men
Ard. 587 you know this G.; is he not religious?
Ard. 880 I tell thee, G., the forlorn traveller
Ard. 1089 G., get you gone, and linger here about
Ard. 1134 come, let's go seek out G.; I know
Ard. 1139 Shakebag, let's seek out G., and
Ard. 1209 why now, G., 'tis better now nor e'er it was
Ard. 1243 G. doth ear the land and weed thee up to
Ard. 1406 O G., intolerable!
Ard. 1532 therefore come, G., and let us to Feversham
Ard. 1913 sirrah G., when was I so long in killing a man?
Ard. 1917 thou knowest, G., that I have lived in
Ard. 1992 G. and we two will dog him through the fair
Ard. 2090 Black Will and G. are his companions
Ard. 2426 G. was hanged at Osbridge in Kent
Ard. 1378 ‹ We thank our neighbour Bradshaw. — Yours,
     Richard G. ›
Ard. 1964 Dick G. and I do mean to sup with you
Ard. 555 this morning, Master G., Dick G. I mean
Ard. 457 what is it Master G.? if that I may
Ard. 466 true, Master G.; the lands are his in state
Ard. 488 ah, Master G., God knows how I am used
Ard. 493 ah, Master G., be it spoken in secret here
Ard. 520 then, Master G., be counselled by me
Ard. 641 see you them that comes yonder, Master G.?
Ard. 647 I tell you, Master G., at Boulogne
Ard. 715 Master G., I'll leave you
Ard. 720 that will I, Master G., and so farewell
Ard. 1373 that Master G. importuned me to give you
Ard. 2012 you, Master G., shall single Franklin forth
Ard. 2025 come, Master G., go you along with me
Ard. 2197 ah, Master G., did you see my husband lately?
Ard. 2384 about a letter I brought from Master G.

Greenwich.
Ard. 2423 murdered in Southwark as he passed to G.

Greet.
Jer. 631 Andreas come: would I might greete him
ST 1615 rare hermonie to g. his innocence
ST 2273 and g. the Duke of Castile

Greetings.
ST 509 put off your g., till our feast be done

Grew.
Cor. 408 mine haire g. bristled, like a thornie grove
Cor. 423 my woes waxt stronger, and my selfe g. weake
Jer. 797 Baltheser, his son, g. violent
STA 1772 Horatio g. out of reach of these insatiate humours
STA 2004 at last it grewe, and bore, and bore
STA 2006 till at the length it g. a gallowes
ST 2840 the cause was love, whence g. this mortall hate
STA 2960 mee thinkes, since I g. inward with Revenge
SP 44 and still increased as I g. my selfe
SP 59 thus in my youth: now, since I g. a man
SP 231 the men died, the women wept, and the grasse g.
Ard. 565 we g. to composition for my husband's death
JB 167 and so bould in the end he g. with her that
Puck 13 [as] therein might be raisde of me, grewe thus

Grey.

HP 1455 ‹ We hide our gray haires with our helmets ›
Jer. 815 that I may see your Gray head crownd in white

Grey-haired.
Cor. 1120 and grave gray-haird men poynt at us

Greyhounds.
HP 9 overtaken by two swift Grey-hounds

Grief.
Cor. 267 from my first husband stole my faithles griefe
Cor. 422 till (griefe to heare, and hell for me to speake)
Cor. 437 but who sorrowes not? the griefe is common
Cor. 456 my teares shall dry, and I my griefe forget
Cor. 853 the shame, the griefe, the rage, the hatred that
Cor. 976 my griefe is lyke a Rock, whence (ceaseles) strayne
Cor. 1590 whose ceaseles griefe (which I am sorry for)
Cor. 1596 and, Madam, let not griefe abuse your wisdom
Cor. 1799 till out-ward rage with inward griefe begins a
Cor. 1991 raine showres of greefe upon your Rose-like cheeks
ST 820 O yes, complaining makes my greefe seeme lesse
ST 913 what world of griefe; my sonne Horatio!
ST 917 to know the author were some ease of greife
STA 959 cast a more serious eye upon thy greefe
STA 971 gird in my wast of griefe with thy large darkenesse
STA 975 how strangly had I lost my way to griefe
ST 1207 my griefe no hart, my thoughts no tung can tell
ST 1531 I will, to ease the greefe that I sustaine
STA 1950 so that with extreame griefe and cutting sorrow
ST 2213 sound the burden of thy sore harts greife
ST 2256 thou art the lively image of my griefe
ST 2798 but with a gratious eye behold his griefe
ST 2800 if by Perseda his g. be not releast
SP 495 come therefore, gentle death, and ease my griefe
SP 746 but inward cares are most pent in with greefe
SP 1112 perhaps my greefe and long continuall moane
SP 1174 as this Knight seemes by greefe tyed to silence
SP 1270 I, thats the greefe, that we are parted thus
SP 1286 and here my tongue dooth stay with swolne **hearts**
     greefe
SP 1287 and here my swolne harts greef doth stay my tongue
SP 1471 what can my tongue utter but griefe and death?
SP 1476 if tongue with griefe, and eyes with teares be fild
Ard. 19 can any g. be half so great as this?
Ard. 45 to ease thy g. and save her chastity
Ard. 259 a weeping eye that witnesses heart's g.
Ard. 990 my heart's g. rends my other powers
Ard. 1020 sometimes he seeketh to beguile his g.
Ard. 2392 how long shall I live in this hell of g.?
Cor. 339 that your desastrous griefes shall turne to joy
Cor. 972 I feare your griefes increase with thys discourse
Cor. 973 my griefes are such, as hardly can be worse
ST Bal. 4 thinking your griefes all griefes exceede
ST Bal. 78 my griefes are come, my Joyes are gone
ST Bal. 161 the Kinges, that scorn'd my griefes before
SP 1751 and now, Perseda, lets forget oulde greefes
SP 1755 when as we call to minde forepassed greefes
SP 1758 if my Love will have olde greefes forgot
Ard. 993 she will amend, and so your griefs will cease
Ard. 1005 forget your griefs a while; here comes your man

Grieve.
Cor. 654 it grieves me that I know not why you g.
ST 2787 let not Erasto live to g. great Soliman
ST 2791 yet greeve I that Erasto should so die
SP 1613 why lives he then to greeve great Soliman?
Cor. 654 it grieves me that I know not why you g.
Ard. 824 my broken head grieves me not so much as
Ard. 1321 it grieves me not to see how foul thou art
JB 112 ‹ but it greeves me that any good thing should so ›

Grieved.
ST Bal. 102 resigne my Marshallship, which griev'd my mind
ST 2253 I am a greeved man, and not a Ghost
ST 2855 and greeved I (think you) at this spectacle?
SP 233 whose losse would have more g. me than
Ard. 1829 for sure she g. that she was left behind
Grieveth.
HP 533 when any part of the bodie g. us
Cor. 97 for one man g. at anothers good
Ard. 507 it g. me so fair a creature should
Grievous.
HP 477 greevous unto me to harken thereunto
Ard. 1013 what g. groans and overlading woes
JB 18 committe most haynous and g. offences
JB 127 feeling also a g. griping of his inward partes
Grievously.
JB 60 understood of this thing, he was g. vexed
Grift.
HP 175 you see that I have gryft so many fruitfull Plants
Grim.
ST 2250 before g. Mynos and just Radamant
Grim-faced.
Ard. 1039 that g. fellow, pitiless Black Will
Grinning.
Ard. 1045 staring and g. in thy gentle face
Gripe.
ST 3039 let loose poore Titius from the Vultures g.
Griping.
JB 127 feeling also a grievous g. of his inward partes
Groan.
Cor. 1984 now (loaden) groane to feele the Romaine corses
Jer. 635 whose grone was that? what frightfull
ST 69 and murderers grone with never killing wounds
STA 2044 canst paint me a teare, or a wound, a groane or a sigh?
ST Bal. 80 filling the ayre with mournefull groanes
SP 585 villaine, thy brothers grones do call for thee
Ard. 1013 what grievous groans and overlading woes
Ard. 2155 what! groans thou? nay, then, give me the weapon!
Groaned.
Cor. 41 while th'earth, that gron'd to beare theyr carkasses
ST 1493 that ere gronde at my office doore
Groom.
Ard. 306 she's no companion for so base a g.
Ard. 578 to make recount of it to every g.
Ard. 660 a corporal, and thou but a base mercenary g.?
Gross.
HP 914 base of mind, grosse of vnderstanding, and
HP 1017 to see such grosse or homely kind of fare
HP 1552 may become so grosse and large in time
ST 2828 not to excuse grosse errors in the play
Ard. 426 this powder was too g. and populous
Ground.
HP 164 ministred unto me upon myne owne g.
HP 181 are they also growing upon your owne grounde?
Cor. 200 that (wastfull) shed their graine upon the g.
Cor. 714 that (torne in peeces) trayl'd upon the g.
Cor. 1193 hath left more Tombes then g. to lay them on
Cor. 1748 infected with the stench thereof surcloyes the g.
Jer. 681 why then rot off, and drop upon the g.
ST Bal. 96 and with my ponyard ript the g.
ST 148 on every side drop Captaines to the g.
ST 405 which pauncht his horse and dingd him to the g.
SP 368 overthrowne him and his Curtall both to the g.
SP 751 hinder my teares from falling on the g.
Ard. 118 these hands of mine should race it to the g.

Ard. 1771 the plat of g. which wrongfully you detain
Ard. 1790 that plot of g. which thou detains from me
Ard. 2038 and with a towel pull him to the g.
Ard. 2173 the blood cleaveth to the g. and will not out
Ard. 2429 Arden lay murdered in that plot of g.
HP 351 time so much as to surveigh his grounds
Cor. 216 and for faire Corne-g. are our fields surcloid
HP 172 the third is Meadowe g.
ST 563 come we for this from depth of under g.
Cor. 596 returne to springs by under-grounds
HP 1281 corne be some g. for bread, and othersome made
Cor. 1148 to sheathe our new-g. swords in Caesars throate?
VPJ 85 on thee we g. our hope, through thee we
ST 2341 whence growes the g. of this report in Court?
ST 2455 thus worldlings g., what they have dreamd, upon
SP 832 the g. of her unkindnes growes, because I
Grounded.
Cor. 964 there is nothing in the soule of man so firmely g.
Grove.
Cor. 408 mine haire grew bristled, like a thornie g.
Grovelling.
Jer. 1133 thou groveling under indignation of sword and ruth
Grow.
HP 194 olde men, or they that g. in yeeres
HP 301 made of the Grapes that g. in Greece
HP 304 that growe in colde Countries
HP 1495 g. the better, and in which the worse
Cor. 352 will never cease, but still g. worse and worse
Cor. 1285 the fairest flowers that g. in Rome
Cor. 1329 while gazing eyes at crownes g. dim
ST 237 our peace will g. the stronger for these warres
ST 1477 and I hope you will never g. so high while I am in the office
STA 1764 in very little time, will g. to some good use
ST 2000 and when our hot Spaine coulde not let it g.
Ard. 33 but through his favour let him not g. proud
Ard. 53 but, being kept back, straight g. outrageous
Ard. 753 that murder would g. to an occupation
Ard. 983 makes her vice to g. as Hydra's head
Ard. 1362 weeds in gardens, roses g. on thorns
Ard. 1754 when words g. hot and blows begin to rise
Ard. 2067 she like me would g. love-sick
Puck 78 and thus (for nowe I feare me I growe teadious)
HP 1469 it growes not other-where so plentiously
ST 688 for love resisted growes impatient
ST 748 ambitious villaine, how his boldenes growes
STA 1765 the more he growes in stature and in yeeres
STA 1945 growes lunaticke and childish for his Sonne
ST 2341 whence growes the ground of this report in Court?
SP 832 the ground of her unkindnes growes, because I
SP 1488 nay, then, Perseda growes resolute
Groweth.
HP 707 g. not so hastilie upon a man
HP 1604 g. to be infinit, and in exchange is not
Growing.
HP Ind. 82 grapes g. in Greece, of what collour
HP 180 are they also g. upon your owne grounde?
HP 1551 for as the nose upon some mans face, g. by disorder
SP 945 now am I g. into a doubtful agony
Grown.
HP 813 « But bigger growne, they tende the chase »
Cor. 181 (now growne so great with Souldiers-bodies that
Cor. 372 growne great without the strife of Citizens
Jer. 1035 war knows I am to proud a scholler g.
ST 345 my hart growne hard gainst mischiefes battery
STA 2943 and in that sight am growne a prowder Monarch than

Ard. 353 were to confirm the rumour that is *g.*
Ard. 603 and haply we be *g.* unto a match
Ard. 1819 God knows she is *g.* passing kind of late
Ard. 2385 she is *g.* so stout she will not know her
Cor. 222 and wil ye needs bedew my dead-*g.* joyes
Cor. 1777 when they have vomited theyr long-growne rage

Growth.
HP 217 before themselves were come unto their groweth

Grudge.
ST Bal. 104 hearing then how I did *g.* still at his sonne
ST 2432 and that, I hope, olde grudges are forgot

Guard.
Cor. 671 with fearles harts do *g.* our Romaine hopes?
Cor. 1323 or their people have devis'd, or their guarde, to
Cor. 1481 maintaine a watchfull *g.* about your gate
Cor. 1665 except some fewe that stayd to *g.* the Trench
Jer. 718 mark, mark, Horatio : a villaine *g.* a villaine
ST 214 talke with our brave prisoner and his double *g.*
ST 276 but, Nephew, thou shalt have the Prince in *g.*
ST 1243 strongly to *g.* the place where Pendringano
Ard. 584 lends him a sword to *g.* himself withal

Guarded.
SP 903 yes, sir, a garded sute from top to toe
Cor. 775 gates, fast-*g.* by a fell remorceles Monster

Guelpio.
SP 848 desire *G.* and signior Julio come speake with me
SP 1346 and *G.*, rather then denie his Christ
SP 1375 nor *G.*, nor signior Julio

Guerdon.
ST 280 and that just *g.* may befall desert
ST 343 Speak on. Ile *g.* thee what ere it be
ST 383 and hope for *g.* of my villany
ST 643 yet speake the truth, and I will *g.* thee
SP 1443 which ile not *g.* with large promises

Guess.
Jer. 321 brave, stout Andrea, for soe I gesse thee
SP 1467 thoughts may gesse, but tongue must not prophane
Ard. 588 a man, I *g.*, of great devotion?

Guest.
HP 457 I have entertained a greater *g.* then I expected
Jer. 95 lordes, let us in : joy shalbe now our *g.*
Jer. 719 the King may thinke my newes is a bad *g.*
ST 277 for thine estate best fitteth such a *g.*
ST 288 and feast our prisoner as our friendly *g.*
ST 511 sit downe, young Prince, you are our second *g.*
ST 519 he promised us, in honor of our *g.*
ST 2590 who at the marriage was the cheefest *g.*
HP Ind. 102 meate wanting upon sudden entertainment of guests
HP 393 having honorable guests he cannot commende his
 Supper
Ard. 1961 and as thou goest, tell John cook of our guests
Ard. 2086 he shall be murdered, or the guests come in
Ard. 2112 we shall have guests enough, though you go hence
Ard. 2169 mistress, the guests are at the duors
Ard. 2196 now, Mistress Arden, lack you any guests?
Ard. 2203 you may do well to bid his guests sit down

Guide.
HP 34 not to arrogat anie superioritie, but as your *g.*
HP 67 the youth that was my *g.*
HP 1532 nor greater then the Mariner can *g.*
Jer. 419 therefore, sly policy must be youre *g.*
SP 351 I go, and Fortune *g.* my Launce
SP 1368 to *g.* the praises of the Rhodian knight
Ard. 1541 path wherein he wont to *g.* his golden car
Ard. 1708 to go without a *g.* such weather as this
Ard. 1741 he needs would follow them without a *g.*

Cor. 574 that gouverneth and guides our dayes
SP 584 what dismall Planets guides this fatall hower?

Guided.
HP 923 and to be ruled, tamed, and *g.* by man
Cor. 349 then, as the Heavens (by whom our hopes are *g.*)

Guider.
ST 101 then blest be heaven, and *g.* of the heavens

Guideth.
Cor. 1300 for high Jove that *g.* all, when he

Guidress.
SP 912 ah, fickle and blind guidresse of the world

Guileful.
SP 785 that we therein might read their guilefull thoughts
SP 814 what are thy words but Syrens guilefull songs

Guilt.
ST 888 and in my bower, to lay the *g.* on me

Guiltless.
Cor. 31 soyl'dst our Infant Towne with guiltles blood
ST 1072 my guiltles death will be aveng'd on thee
ST 2912 my guiltles Sonne was by Lorenzo slaine
STA 2955 my guiltles Sonne was by Lorenzo slaine
Ard. 2318 and you shall find part of his *g.* blood

Guilty.
ST 1114 my guiltie soule submits me to thy doome
ST 1321 a guiltie conscience, urged with the thought of
ST 1806 that leadeth from a guiltie Conscience unto
Puck 77 suspect me guiltie of the former shipwrack

Guise.
Jer. 438 thinke, tis your love makes me create this *g.*

Gulf.
ST 3005 to Silla's barking and untamed gulfe

Gummed.
ST 2258 thy eies are gum'd with teares, thy cheekes are wan

Gunpowder.
Ard. 1302 or whether I love the smell of *g.*

Gush.
ST 920 O, *g.* out teares, fountaines and flouds of teares

Gusheth.
Cor. 1825 crusht in a Wine-presse, *g.* out so fast, as

Gushing.
Ard. 2350 this blood condemns me, and in *g.* forth

Guts.
SP 2177 and boyles, like Etna, in my frying *g.*

H.

Ha.
Jer. 34 *h.* : dare he still procrastinate with Spaine?
Jer. 665 his garments, *h.*, like mine ; his face made like
Jer. 723 *h.*, Andrea, the foore runner of these newes?
Jer. 725 *h.*, Andrea, speake ; what newes from Portugale?
Jer. 778 trybute denide us, *h.*?
Jer. 781 so daring, *h.*, so Peremptory?
Jer. 790 *h.*, soe peremptory, daring, stout?
Jer. 996 *h.*, Vullupo?
Jer. 1187 *h.*, soft, Jeronimo ; thou hast more friends
STA 852 *h.*, are they not great perswasions?
STA 2965 shuld ha'e been married to your daughter : *h.*, wast
 not so?
Ard. 1293 *h.*, Mosbie ! 'tis thou has rifled me of that
Jer. 259 dare I? *H.*, *h.*
Jer. 893 trybute, *h.*, *h.* ; what elles?
STA 947 *h.*, *h.*, Saint James, but this doth make me laugh
ST 1822 *H.*, *h.*, *h.* — *H.*, *h.*, *h.*
ST 1823 Why, *h.*, *h.*, *h.* Farewell, good *h.*, *h.*, *h.*
SP 1070 *h.*, *h.*, *h.*

Habeat.
HP 564 ille *h.* secum servetque sepulchro

Habent.
HP 822 Et tunicae manicas, et *h.* redimicula mitrae
Habes.
ST 2106 Fata si miseros juvant, *h.* salutem
ST 2107 Fata si vitam negant, *h.* sepulchrum
Habet.
ST 303 Qui jacet in terra non *h.* unde cadat
Habit.
HP 3 (in the habitte of an unknowne Pilgrim)
HP 760 taking uppon her the person of a Lover, and deposing the *h.* of a Wife
ST 1458 wouldst faine furnish me with a halter, to disfurnish me of my *h.*
SP 1136 under the *h.* of some errant knight
SP 1163 his habite argues him a Christian
SP 1406 still in black habite fitting funerall?
Cor. 2002 are mournfull habits may be deckt no more
Habitabit.
HP 1640ª David : Qui *h.*, &c. qui pecuniam
Habitation.
ST 1817 murderers have built a *h.* for their cursed soules
SP 253 each place is my *h.*
Hackney-man.
SP 452 a Hackney man should have ten shillings for
Haemonia.
Cor. 181 Th' Ausonian fame to reare in warlike Emonye
Hag.
Cor. 1731 a fearfull Hagge, with fier-darting eyes
ST 2206 a troupe of furies and tormenting hagges
Haggard.
ST 575 in time all *h.* Hawkes will stoope to lure
Hail.
Cor. 314 beat backe like flyes before a storme of hayle?
Cor. 1838 pesle-mesle pursued them like a storme of hayle
ST 144 thicke stormes of bullets ran like winters haile
SP 690 All haile, brave Cavelere. God morrow, Madam
Hair.
HP Ind. 88 hayre a great ornament of nature
HP Ind. 89 hayre cut from Wemens heads, and why
HP 118 the whiteness of his hayre and beard
HP 690 youthes, uppon whose faces hayre never came
HP 706 but hayre (which is a great orname[n]t of Nature)
HP 708 women, who delight in theyr hayre as Trees doo in theyr leaves
HP 712 they use yet in some place of Italie to cut away theyr hayre
Cor. 408 mine haire grew bristled, like a thornie grove
Cor. 712 hys hayre and beard deform'd with blood and sweat
Cor. 1750 blood-thirstie Discord, with her snakie hayre
Cor. 1998 and let your haire, that wont be wreath'd in tresses
Jer. 31 confesse, Beard, thou art fifty full, not a haire lesse
Jer. 358 not bate an inch of courage nor a haire of fate
ST Bal. 65 and rent and puld my silvered haire
STA 2029 whose least unvallued haire did waigh a
STA 2075 and let my haire heave up my night-cap
SP 277 not an hayre, not an excrement
Ard. 692 long *h.* down his shoulders curled
HP 1435 « We hide our gray haires with our helmets »
Cor. 1675 whose silver hayres and honorable front were
Cor. 1935 whose silver haires encouraged the weake
ST Bal. 15 age with silvered haires my aged head had overspred
Haired.
Cor. 59 for neither could the flaxen-haird high Dutch
Cor. 1120 and grave gray-haird men poynt at us
Jer. 1025 as sithmen trim the long haird Rufflan fields, so
Halberdiers.

ST 404 brought in a fresh supply of *H.*
ST 408 did finish what his *H.* begun
ST 412 and brought him prisoner from his *H.*
Hale.
ST 3035 this hand shall *h.* them downe to deepest hell
SP 1905 Lord Marshall, *h.* them to the towers top
Haleb.
SP 524 say, brother Amurath, and *H.*, say
SP 551 why, *H.*, didst thou not heare our brother sweare
SP 571 I take it, *H.*, thou art friend to Rhodes
SP 589 Oh, *H.*, how shall I begin to mourne
SP 604 I, I, and thou as vertuous as *H.*
SP 605 and I as deare to thee as unto *H.*
SP 606 and thou as neere to me as *H.* was
SP 609 and, *H.*, why did not thy harts counsell
SP 614 if love of *H.* forst me on to wrath
SP 637 I did accomplish on *H.* and Amurath
SP 600 in blood hath shortned our sweet Halebs dayes
Half.
HP 57 walked little more then halfe a mile
Cor. 32 and hongst (O Hell) upon a Forte halfe finisht thy
Cor. 247 for I am more then halfe your prysoner
Jer. 1005 meete me, Sir. — Just halfe way
ST 158 that, halfe dismaid, the multitude retirde
ST 2147 or will take halfe the paine that he will in
ST 2731 what, is your beard on? — Halfe on
SP 572 not halfe so much am I a friend to Rhodes
SP 1293 then take each one halfe of me, and cease to weepe
SP 1795 ah that Perseda were not *h.* so faire
SP 2115 the losse of halfe my Realmes, nay, crownes decay
Ard. 19 can any grief be *h.* so great as this?
Ard. 664 when I stole the *h.* ox from John the victualer
Ard. 1074 this negligence not *h.* contenteth me
Ard. 1651 *h.* drowned with new ale overnight
Ard. 1902 a fault confessed is more than *h.* amends
Ard. 1976 bears his sword-point *h.* a yard out of danger
Ard. 2070 not *h.* so lovely as Endymion
JB 223 two yeares and a halfe after the murder was committed
Half-cloven.
Cor. 1827 some should you see that had theyr heads halfe cloven
Half-heir.
ST 778 she is daughter and halfe heire unto our brother
Half-pike.
Cor. 1737 doe at the halfe pyke freely charge each other
Hall.
HP 84 we entred into a faire *H.*
HP 92 the *H.* was furnished with hangings
JB 219 condemned for the murder at the sessions *h.* nere new-gate
HP 1718 the care of Princes Halles belongeth not to private men
Halter.
VPJ 73 their scepter to a *h.* changde
SP 953 I doe not love to preach with a haulter about my necke
ST 1458 wouldst faine furnish me with a *h.*, to disfurnish me of my habit
Haltered.
SP 952 then the case is altered, I, and *h.* to
Halts.
Ard. 1436 back to Rochester : the horse *h.* downright
Hams.
Jer. 507 bending in the *h.* like an old Courtier
Jer. 524 bending in the *h.* enough, like a Gentleman usher?
Hand.
VPJ (Title) written with his owne *h.* in the Tower
VPJ (Title) written in the Towre with his owne *h.*
HP 282 Swine, or other Beastes that fatneth by the hande

HP 949 the right hande holdeth and disposeth any sort of
HP 1073 when the right *h.* is over labored, we can ease it wyth the left
HP 1090 as the *h.* is sturred to obey the mind
HP 1091 the *h.* is said to be The instrument of instruments
HP 1099 and heerein differeth from the *h.*
HP 1099 differeth from the *h.* for that the *h.* is fastned
HP 1309 to set her *h.* nowe and then to some work
HP 1373 she shall alwaies have them ready and at *h.*
Cor. 160 the heavens with their wrathful *h.* revenge
Cor. 400 not dead in fight, with pike in *h.*
Cor. 1047 and often helpst the helples hande
Cor. 1132 he lyft his *h.* imperiously o're us
Cor. 1139 and that thys *h.* (though Caesar blood abhor)
Cor. 1391 my *h.*, my hap, my hart exceeded his
Cor. 1677 in one *h.* held his Targe of steele embost
Cor. 1727 they ranne at ever-each other *h.* and foote
Cor. 1791 and subt'ly markt whose *h.* was happiest
Jer. 325 I kisse thy *h.*, and tender on thy throne my
Jer. 345 and, for my instance, this in your *h.* is one
Jer. 748 which this *h.* slew, pox ont, was a huge dotar
Jer. 793 I bad defiance with a vengfull *h.*
Jer. 1071 this *h.* and sword should melt him
ST Bal. 76 her owne *h.* straight doth worke her death
ST Bal. 152 unto my *h.* a pen did reach
ST 59 that on the right *h.* side was ready way unto
ST 63 the left *h.* path, declining fearefully
ST 246 this *h.* first tooke his courser by the raines
ST 351 I saw him, *h.* to *h.*, in single fight
ST 396 by yong Don Balthazar encountred *h.* to *h.*
ST 411 I with my *h.* set foorth against the Prince
ST 690 first, in his *h.* he brandished a sword
ST 850 then thus begin our wars : put forth thy *h.*
ST 851 that it may combate with my ruder *h.*
ST 1076 Ile lend a *h.* to send thee to the lake
ST 1296 who first laies *h.* on me, ile be his Priest
ST 1478 sirra, dost see yonder boy with the box in his *h.*?
ST 1805 there is a path upon your left *h.* side
STA 2054 and my *h.* leaning upon his head, thus, sir
STA 2069 my torch in my *h.*, and my sword reared up thus
ST 2731 halfe on ; the other is in my *h.*
ST 2919 for by her *h.* my Balthazar was slaine
STA 2951 for by her *h.* my Balthazar was slaine
STA 2970 this same *h.* twas it that stab'd his hart
STA 2971 stab'd his hart — doe ye see? this *h.*
ST 3035 this *h.* shall hale them downe to deepest hell
SP 359 he wore his *h.* in a scarfe, and said he
SP 393 give me thy *h.*, I vowe myselfe thy friend
SP 394 whose favourable *h.* hath entred such a
SP 503 and lookes for justice at her lovers *h.*
SP 612 withould thy *h.* from heaping bloud on bloud?
SP 622 bearing in either *h.* his hearts decay
SP 666 What pledge thereof? — An oath, a *h.*, a kisse
SP 667 O holy oath, faire *h.*, and sugred kisse
SP 672 when shall the graces, or Lucinas *h.*
SP 1109 to mar what Love or Fortune takes in *h.*
SP 1529 come, sit thee downe upon my right *h.* heere
SP 1570 fire, that lay with honours *h.* rackt up in ashes
SP 1804 and at Erastus *h.* let them receive the
SP 1896 what, is thy *h.* to weake? then mine shall helpe
SP 1997 and first Perseda shall with this *h.* die
SP 2092 but with thy *h.* first wounded to the death
Ard. 148 on that condition, Michael, here's my *h.*
Ard. 262 Clarke, here's my *h.* : my sister shall be thine
Ard. 436 and given my *h.* unto him in the church !
Ard. 515 and will not yield my lease into my *h.*

Ard. 529 tben here's my *h.*, I'll have him so dispatched
Ard. 535 a happy *h.* I wish, and so farewell
Ard. 866 till Arden's heart be panting in my *h.*
Ard. 917 we have devised a complat under *h.*
Ard. 937 and he whose kindly love and liberal *h.*
Ard. 944 on your left *h.* shall you see the stairs
Ard. 961 I that should take the weapon in my *h.*
Ard. 1305 ay, Fortune's right *h.* Mosbie hath forsook
Ard. 1391 how many pistols I have took in *h.*
Ard. 1405 and scarce a hurting weapon in their *h.*
Ard. 1616 now when serious matters are in *h.*?
Ard. 1802 and saw a dreadful southern flaw at *h.*
Ard. 1938 with a quart-pot in their *h.*, saying
Ard. 1974 now his way had been to have come *h.* and feet
Ard. 1980 a buckler in a skilful *h.* is as good as
Ard. 2209 peace, we have other matters now in *h.*
Puck 76 live & shake the uyper of my *h.* into the fier
HP 135 had provided water for our hands
HP 231 that ayde and comfort at theyr hands
HP 619 fallen into the handes of a perpetuall enemie
Cor. Arg. 29 fall alive into the hands of his so mightie Enemie
Cor. 10 and oft yee have your heavie hands with-held
Cor. 31 with guiltles blood by brothers hands out-lanched
Cor. 149 or that our hands the Earth can comprehend
Cor. 325 escapt not free fro thy victorious hands?
Cor. 608 and by a shephards hands erect
Cor. 789 now shalt thou march (thy hands fast bound behind thee)
Cor. 888 O faithles hands, that under cloake of love did
Cor. 1254 as if he wanted hands, sence, sight, or hart
Cor. 1297 that to free them fro the hands of a Tyrant
Cor. 1702 with blubbred eyes and handes to heaven uprear'd
Cor. 1754 encourageth the over-forward hands to bloode and death
Cor. 1832 with hands extended to the merciles
Jer. 117 whose hands are washt in rape, and murders bould
Jer. 372 for all Spaines wealth Ide not graspe hands
Jer. 661 lay hands on him ; [and] some reare up
Jer. 705 this letter came not to Andreas hands
Jer. 870 I vow to have it treble at thy hands
Jer. 1104 hand off, Lorenzo ; touch not my prisoner
ST 227 deserve but evill measure at our hands
ST 316 what helpe can be expected at her hands
ST 453 himselfe now pleades for favour at my hands
ST 1081 lay handes upon Villuppo
STA 2022 God hath engrossed all justice in his hands
ST 2136 thy hart to patience, and thy hands to rest
SP 318 I injoy my life at thy hands, I confesse it
SP 481 I pray you, sir, hold your hands, and, as I
SP 766 to win late conquest from many victors hands
SP 820 that plead for mercy at thy rigorous hands
SP 927 they will betray me to Phylippos hands
SP 1172 and liberall hands to such as merit bountie
SP 1324 what parle craves the Turkish at our hands?
SP 1376 nor rescue Rhodes from out the hands of Death?
SP 1492 and at my hands receive the stroake of death
SP 1534 and joyne their hands, whose hearts are knit already?
SP 1556 and both give me your hands
SP 1727 and gave Lucina into Brusors hands
SP 1733 and give Perseda to Erastus hands
SP 1859 both lay your hands upon the Alcaron
SP 1959 weepe and lament, and wring your hands
SP 2002 then will I yeeld Perseda to thy hands
Ard. 118 these hands of mine should race it to the ground
Ard. 774 « or rather impetrate mercy of your meek hands »
Ard. 939 I will deliver over to your hands

Ard. 1046 in their ruthless hands their daggers drawn
Ard. 1262 and I will cleanly rid my hands of her
Ard. 1947 why, I saw them when they both shook hands
Ard. 2032 my hands shall play you golden harmony
JB 203 « if I trust thee or hazard my life in thy hands »
SP 49 marking thy lilly hands dexteritie

Handfuls.
Jer. 59 shake the Kings hie court three *h.* downe

Handkercher.
ST 981 seest thou this *h.* besmerd with blood?
ST 2177 heere, take my *h.*, and wipe thine eies
ST 2864 and heere beholde this bloudie hand-kercher
Ard. 1468 then softly draws she forth her *h.*

Handle.
HP 1504 ought to *h.* these things like a Husbandman
SP 1788 Lord marshall, see you *h.* it cunningly
Ard. 1142 and then let me alone to *h.* him

Handled.
HP 1312 not to be manedged and *h.* by noble Matrons
HP 1527 cannot well be *h.*, managed, or lifted for their greatnes
ST 1629 me for thy freend Horatio *h.* thus

Handledst.
Ard. 1397 than e'er thou *h.* pistols in thy life

Handling.
HP 1192 in the manurance and *h.* of an ignorant

Handsel.
Ard. 757 a gallon of sack to *h.* the match withal

Handsome.
HP 663 wholesome, *h.*, or toothsome

Handsomely.
Ard. 846 where Arden may be met with *h.*

Hand-towel.
Ard. 2304 know you this *h.* and this knife?

Handwork.
Cor. 496 Carthage can witnes, and thou, heavens *h.*

Handy-blows.
ST 138 both battailes joyne and fall to handie blowes

Hang.
HP 191 which also *h.* upon the earth unripened
Cor. 1999 tresses, now *h.* neglectly, dangling downe your sholders
Jer. 746 Ile cut them downe, my words shall not be hong
Jer. 1102 and let revenge *h.* on our glittering swords
ST 1470 what, doe you *h.* by the howre?
ST 1843 for if I *h.* or kill my selfe, lets know who
ST 2729 well doon, Balthazar, *h.* up the Title
ST 3044 *h.* Balthazar about Chimeras neck
SP 88 over mine armour will I *h.* this chaine.
SP 1267 the Governour will *h.* you and he catch you
SP 1696 Ile *h.* my target there
Ard. 376 thou that wouldst see me *h.*, thou, Mosbie, thou
Ard. 684 if law will serve him, he'll *h.* me for his plate
Jer. 116 upon whose eie browes hangs damnation
SP 1357 their lives priviledge hangs on their beautie
Ard. 238 coming into the chamber where it hangs, may die
Ard. 348 upon whose general bruit all honour hangs

Hanged.
ST 887 a man hangd up and all the murderers gone
STA 961 it was a man, sure, that was *h.* up here
ST 1413 but if I should be *h.* with thee, I cannot weep
STA 2973 a youth, one that they *h.* up in his father's garden
ST 3013 false Pedringano hangd by quaint device
Ard. 1502 thou wilt be *h.* in Kent, when all is done
Ard. 1503 not *h.*, God save your honour
Ard. 1724 I hope to see him one day *h.* upon a hill
Ard. 1916 though we be *h.* at his door for our labour

Ard. 2212 I care not though I be *h.* ere night
Ard. 2426 Greene was *h.* at Osbridge in Kent
JB 221 the man to be *h.* in the same place before her eyes

Hanging.
HP 185 *h.* alwaies on the earth and
HP 1268 the *h.* up in smoke or baking of some kinds
STA 2061 *h.* upon this tree
ST 2853 where *h.* on a tree I found my sonne
SP 411 *h.* her head as partner of my shame
HP 93 the Hall was furnished with hangings and

Hangman.
ST 1407 scorne the audience, and descant on the *h.*
ST 1460 but, Hang-man, nowe I spy your knavery
ST 1474 dost thou mock me, hang-man?
ST 1489 why, sirra *H.*, I take it that that is good for

Hannibal.
Cor. 833 why from Molossus and false Hanibal have yee
Cor. 1981 especially that proudest Hanniball

Hannons.
Cor. 1980 the *H.*, the Amilcars, Asdrubals

Hap.
VPJ 42 thy good God knowes thy hope, thy *h.* and all
HP 1731 if my hart or happe would give me leave
Cor. 326 since thy hard *h.*, since thy fierce destinie
Cor. 335 where thy *h.* none others hopes with mischiefe may
Cor. 511 can wee be over-hastie to good *h.*?
Cor. 722 such *h.* (as ours) attendeth on my sonnes
Cor. 1391 my hand, my *h.*, my hart exceeded his
Cor. 1835 he that had *h.* to scape, doth helpe
Cor. 1891 by whom I am assurde this *h.* to have
Jer. 271 come then, how ere it *h.*, Andrea shall be crost
ST 1654 and if she *h.* to stand on tearmes with us
ST 2674 hard is the *h.* of olde Hieronimo
SP 133 wish me good *h.*, Perseda, and Ile winne
Ard. 516 I'll pay him home, whatever *h.* to me
Cor. 2005 widdowed of all my hopes, my haps, my husbands
ST 1256 dye, then by their life to hazard our good haps

Hapless.
Cor. Arg. 35 these crosse events and haples newes of Affrique
Cor. 211 must seeke in Hell to have a haples roome?
Cor. 258 lesse haples, and more worthily thou might'st
Cor. 332 O haples wife, thus ominous to all
Cor. 609 (with haples brothers blood besmear'd)
Cor. 878 the ashie reliques of his haples bones
Cor. 921 this is the hope that feeds my haples daies
Cor. 1976 now is our haples time of hopes expired
Jer. 747 that haples, bleeding Lord Alcario
ST Bal. 7 *h.* Hieronimo was my name
ST 1156 « me hath my haples brother hid from thee »
ST 1244 this night shall murder *h.* Serberine
ST 2712 the haplesse brest, that gave Horatio suck
ST 2826 the hopeles father of a *h.* Sonne
ST 3001 take up our haples sonne, untimelie slaine
SP 917 to cross me with this haplesse accedent?
Ard. 1297 woe worth the *h.* hour and all the causes that
Ard. 1908 and salve this *h.* quarrel if I may

Haply.
VPJ 5 it happ'ly pleasd our highest God in safety to preserve
HP 19 « you might happily get thither » (quoth he)
HP 199 happily lookes to be invited
HP 240 shall happily conforme him selfe thereunto
HP 306 albeit happilie the manner of their making
HP 413 unlesse it happilie be in respect onely of the motion
HP 462 that coulde not happily blazon mine estimation
HP 527 happily is termed by a tytle more effectuall
HP 660 as happily those other artificiall Oyles and

HP 751 but hapely so much the more by how much
HP 776 he may be happily employed better in some other action
HP 912 though he be happily Davus, Syrus, or Geta
HP 1018 happilye purveighed or provided for thy servaunts
HP 1196 and hapely the house it selfe, and money
HP 1462 shoulde happilie therein do nothing unworthye
HP 1541 he happely had reference unto those ryches which
HP 1545 and happely superfluous for many men in Rome
Cor. 390 bravely he died, and (haplie) takes it ill that
Cor. 501 Death (h. that our willingnes doth see)
Cor. 1064 and Pompey, whose dayes h. led so long
Cor. 1155 yet h. he (as Sylla whylom dyd)
Cor. 1598 h. the newes is better then the noyse
Cor. 1615 will h. comfort this your discontent
Cor. 1950 O see mine anguish ; haplie seeing it
ST 755 happelie the gentle Nightingale shall carroll
ST 1921 happily Hieronimo hath need thereof
ST 2317 the day that I have longd so happely to see
ST 2818 happely you thinke (but booteles are your thoughts)
SP 1613 shee happely might he woone by thy perswades
Ard. 608 and h. we be grown unto a match
Ard. 676 wherein h. thou mayest pleasure me
Ard. 905 if neither of these two do h. fall
Ard. 1398 ay, h. thou hast picked more in a throng
Ard. 1488 removing of a shoe may h. help it
Ard. 1700 they may h. lose their way as we have done
Ard. 1818 my wife may h. meet me on the way
Happed.
ST 1909 what accident hath hapt Hieronimo?
Happen.
HP 611 now if it h. that the Husband take
HP 1275 if it h. that by some mischance
Ard. 220 and h. what will, I am resolute
Happened.
HP 129 hee is h. on a place, where, to
HP 245 I have h. on an honest advocat
Jer. 567 though it had happend evill, he should have
SP 225 as I remember, there h. a sore drought
Ard. 228 I h. on a painter yesternight
Happeneth.
HP 161 (It lightlie h. not) (quoth hee) (that I
HP 189 it h. that there are few good mellons
HP 392 when it h. that having
HP 583 but when it h. yet that, by some
HP 912 but when it h. that some one is found
HP 1069 it sometime h. that one is too much charged
HP 1739 when it h. that, in comparison of number
Happier.
HP 573 h. are they that have but once
ST 2382 and thou art graced with a h. Love
Jer. 837 what h. fortune, then, my selfe can move ?
Jer. 982 never had father a more h. boy
Happiest.
Cor. 1791 and subt'ly markt whose hand was h.
Happily, *see* **Haply.**
Happiness.
HP Ded. Maister Thomas Reade Esquier Health and all Happines
Cor. Ded. 25 and another of the night in wishing you all happines
Cor. 648 afford no hope of future happinesse
Cor. 1934 whose hopefull life preserv'd our happines
Cor. 1941 I cannot looke for further happines
Jer. 159 respective deere, O my lives happines
Jer. 706 twas happines indeed
ST 110 unto the height of former happines
ST 1507 passages that intercepts it selfe of hapines
ST 2319 should intercept her in her happines ?

SP 493 and lost with hir is all my happinesse
SP 494 and losse of happines is worse than death
SP 646 for, in conclusion of his happines
SP 1440 my gratious Lord, rejoyce in happinesse
SP 2198 I give worlds happines and woes increase
Happy.
HP 158 (I hold it) (quoth I) (a h. thing to
Cor. 992 thrise h. were I dead
Cor. 1489 is not alonely h. in this world
Cor. 1508 vary not thy grace from Julus h. race
Cor. 1682 for now (quoth he) is come that happie day
Cor. 1944 now as for h. thee, to whom sweet Death hath
Cor. 2034 the happie vessels that enclose your bones
Jer. 22 O fortunate houre, blessed mynuit, h. day
Jer. 1051 thou art a wondrous friend, a h. sperit
Jer. 1059 come, h. mortall, let me ranke by thee
Jer. 1172 I am a h. Ghost
Jer. 1185 the day is ours and joy yeelds h. treasure
ST 485 Signior Horatio stoopt in happie time
ST 1090 are happie witnesses of his highnes health
ST 2100 then hast thou health, and h. shalt thou be
ST 2778 thrice happie in Erasto, that thou livest
SP 408 therefore, Erastus, h. laude thy fortune
SP 694 marry, thrise h. is Persedas chance
Ard. 535 a h. hand I wish, and so farewell
Ard. 1290 ay, to my former h. life again
Ard. 1381 Ah, would it were ! Then comes my h. hour
Ard. 1823 h. the change that alters for the best !
Harborough.
Ard. 2163 and if she will not give me h.
Harbour.
ST 447 but how can love find h. in my brest
ST 606 which pleasing wordes doe h. sweet conceits
SP 75 should linde a h. for my hart to dwell
SP 1181 this face of thine shuld h. no deceit
SP 2072 how could thy heart h. a wicked thought
Ard. 2289 why, Master Mayor, think you I h. any such ?
Ard. 2337 I came thither, thinking to have had h.
Hard.
HP 1273 become both h. and naught to eate without some
HP 1332 (Hard at their distaffe doth she hold her maids)
HP 1639 perilous evils as are h. or never to be cured
Cor. 326 since thy h. hap, since thy fierce destinie
Cor. 649 but what disastrous or h. accident
Cor. 996 there is no death so h. torments mee so
Cor. 1616 discourse the manner of his h. mishap
Cor. 1638 resolv'd by force to hold us h. at work
Cor. 1949 my h. mishap in marrying after thee
Jer. 88 I will be h. like thunder, and as rough as
Jer. 99 h. fate, when villaines sit not in the highest state
ST 225 young prince, although thy fathers h. misdeeds
ST 345 my hart growne h. gainst mischiefes battery
ST 580 no, she is wilder, and more h. withall
ST 1354 tis h. to trust unto a multitude
ST 2674 h. is the hap of olde Hieronimo
SP 827 h. doome of death, before my case be knowne
SP 932 ah, h. attempt, to tempt a foe for ayde
SP 1480 Adamant, too h. to take an new impression
Ard. 487 but wonder not though he be h. to others
Ard. 496 h. words and blows to mend the match withal
Ard. 593 did I not plead the matter h. for you ?
ST Bal. 85 the streets, h. by the Duke of Castiles house
ST 1224 thou knowest tis heere h. by behinde the house
ST 1798 O, h. by : tis yon house that you see
SP 1844 the fleete that lyes h. by us heere
Ard. 150 I understand the painter here h. by

Ard. 2071 mistress, my master is coming *h.* by
Harden.
HP 804 to indurat and *h.* them against the cold
Hardened.
Cor. 1683 with heavy Armor on theyr hardned backs
Hardest.
ST 576 in time small wedges cleave the *h.* Oake
Hardly.
HP 22 is so overflowen that you can hardlie passe it
HP 514 did *h.* compasse with much sparing
HP 533 grieveth us the mind can *h.* be content
HP 1627 beeing hardlie to be doone without great discomoditie
HP 1777 time and good manners will *h.* give us leave
Cor. 973 my griefes are such, as *h.* can be worse
Cor. 1296 *h.* then they them reward
Cor. 1430 those that your kindnes *h.* will requite
ST 1342 or els his Highnes *h.* shall deny
ST 2657 and *h.* shall we all be understood
HP 836 bring them up so *h.* or severely as the Lacedemonians
Hardness.
SP 911 least you pertake the *h.* of my fortune
Hardy.
HP 733 so bold and *h.* that she lay aside honest shame
Cor. 17 yet Brutus Manlius, hardie Scevola
ST 166 friendship and hardie valour, joynd in one
SP 99 and English Archers, *h.* men at armes
SP 516 call home my hardie, dauntlesse Janisaries
Hare.
ST 1850 and heere, 1 heere — there goes the *h.* away
Ard. 1346 and heard as quickly as the fearful *h.*
ST 263 so Hares may pull dead Lyons by the beard
Harebrained.
Ard. 1846 jealous *h.* man, what hast thou done !
Hark.
Jer. 838 harke, the drum beckens me ; sweet deere, farwell
Jer. 871 *h.*, Portugales : I heare their Spanish drum
ST 842 harke, Madame, how the birds record by night
ST 1293 harke, Gentlemen, this is a Pistol shot
SP 1508 harke, Brusor, she cals on Christ
Ard. 2084 but, Michael, *h.* to me a word or two
Ard. 2281 *h.*, *h.*, they knock ! go, Michael, let them in
Harlots.
Ard. 785 a crew of *h.*, all in love, forsooth
Harm.
ST 2900 upon mine honour, thou shalt have no harme
Ard. 1850 hurt thy friend whose thoughts were free from *h.*
VPJ 18 health of thy Countrey, helpe to all our harmes
Cor. 1539 to defend himselfe from harmes
ST 1273 will stand betweene me and ensuing harmes
ST 1312 and inexpected harmes do hurt us most
ST 2844 with pitchie silence husht these traitors harmes
Cor. 196 head-long to runne and reck no after harmes
Harmless.
Cor. 1205 against a harmeles Nation, kindly given
ST 754 there none shall heare us but the harmeless birds
ST 897 beene glutted with thy harmeles blood
ST 2804 which seazd on my Erasto, harmelesse Knight
ST 2922 can Kings affoord then harmeles silence ?
Ard. 957 ah, *h.* Arden, how hast thou misdone
Ard. 1873 the heavens can witness of our *h.* thoughts
Harmony.
ST 1615 rare hermonie to greet his innocence
Ard. 2032 my hands shall play you golden *h.*
Harness.
HP 1043 Harnes and implements of houshold
Harp.

ST 2212 and if thou canst no notes upon the Harpe
Harping.
Jer. 306 what, *h.* still upon Andreas death ?
Harriot.
Puck 39 *H.*, Warner, Royden and some stationers in Paules
Harsh.
ST 586 the lines I send her are but *h.* and ill
SP 282 O *h.*, un-edicate, illiterate pesant
SP 544 to sound a homeward, dull, and *h.* retreate
Hart.
HP 689 the *H.* with his fayre and bushie braunched hornes
HP Ind. 91 harts not bredde in Affrick
HP 268 Aeneas that in Affrick slew seaven Harts
HP 270 for in Affrick are no Harts bred
Harvest.
ST 12 but in the *h.* of my sommer joyes
ST 1017 thou talkest of *h.*, when the corne is greene
Ard. 1244 to make my *h.* nothing but pure corn
Ard. 1286 our *h.* else will yield but loathsome weeds
Harvest-corn.
SP 1603 that thrust his sickle in my harvest corne
Haste.
HP Ded. worth more then this, digested thus in *h.*
Cor. 210 for the fatall dombe the Fates make hast enough
Cor. 1147 why hast we not, even while these words are uttred
Cor. 1346 hast to tell the foming Seas the honour
Jer. 125 whether in such hast, my second selfe ?
Jer. 579 your quiek returne and speedy hast from Portugale
ST 96 and posting to our presence thus in hast ?
ST 1343 meane while ile *h.* the Marshall Sessions
ST 1512 nay, soft, no hast
ST 2700 Hieronimo, make *h.* to see thy sonne
ST 2703 make *h.*, Hieronimo, to hold excusde thy
ST 3053 then *h.* we doune to meet thy freends and foes
SP 125 here comes a Messenger to *h.* me hence
SP 1575 mervaile not that all in hast I wish you to depart
Ard. 620 I'll do it, and with all the *h.* I may
Ard. 778 what *h.* my business craves to send to Kent !
Ard. 1647 we have great *h.* ; 1 pray thee, come away
Ard. 2381 come, make *h.* and bring away the prisoners
JB 92 to make speedy *h.* to the heart, without any
Hasted.
ST 2852 with soonest speed I *h.* to the noise
Hasten.
ST 1338 to exasperate and *h.* his revenge
Ard. 412 in hope you'll *h.* him home, I'll give you this
Hastily.
HP 707 groweth not so hastilie upon a man
Hasty.
Jer. 482 I pray you, pardon me ; twas but youths *h.* error
SP 63 to *h.* lovers whose fancy soone is fled
SP 1762 what hastie news brings you so soone to Rhodes
JB 88 so importunate and hastie to have it done
Cor. 511 can wee be over-hastie to good hap ?
Hat.
SP 1382 unwise that you weare not the high Sugerloafe *h.*
HP 828 ‹ and your high Priests hats are made like hoods ›
Hatches.
Cor. 85 thy sides sore beaten, and thy *h.* broke
Hate.
HP 730 least she *h.* or feare thee with the dread
HP 736 as easily accompanied with love as servile feare with *h.*
Cor. 988 t'is pollicie to feare a powerfull *h.*
Cor. 1308 feare that doth engender *h.*
Cor. 1309 (*h.* enforcing them thereto)
Cor. 1562 spightfull *h.* so pecks their brest

Cor. 1769 with burning *h.* let each at other flie
Jer. 106 I *h.* Andrea, cause he aimes at honor
Jer. 254 deny his gifts, be all composd of *h.*
ST 569 their love to mortall *h.*, their day to night
ST 1025 and oft supplanted with exceeding *h.*
ST 1034 by *h.* deprived of his dearest sonne
ST 1037 had beene envenomde with such extreame *h.*
ST 1172 draw thy life in question and thy name in *h.*
ST 1716 in whose melancholie thou maiest see thy *h.*
STA 1778 none but a damned murderer could *h.* him
STA 2014 and then they *h.* them that did bring them up
ST 2413 such as love not me, and *h.* my Lord too much
ST 2486 with what dishonour and the *h.* of men
ST 2487 from this dishonour and the *h.* of men?
ST 2599 she, stirde with an exceeding *h.* therefore
ST 2840 the cause was love, whence grew this mortall *h.*
ST 2841 the *h.* : Lorenzo and yong Balthazar
ST 2886 but love of him, whom they did *h.* too much
ST 3034 against the rest how shall my *h.* be showne?
SP 21 did not I change long love to sudden *h.*
SP 812 and all my former love is turnd to *h.*
SP 863 unto Lucina, neither for love nor *h.*
SP 2098 a kisse I graunt thee, though I *h.* thee deadlie
Ard. 189 incurred my husband's *h.*, and, out alas!
Ard. 271 rather than you'll live with him you *h.*
Ard. 1403 zounds, I *h.* them as I hate a toad
SP 1299 see, see, Lucina hates me like a Toade
ST 684 sad, that I feare she hates me whome I love
SP 689 all the world loves, none hates but envie
Hated.
Cor. 93 now we are *h.* both of Gods and men?
Ard. 1129 *h.* and spit at by the goers-by
Hatedst.
Cor. 1085 because thou ever *h.* Monarchie
Hateful.
Eng. Parn. 2 It is an hell in hatefull vassalage
Cor. 416 thrice (to absent me from thys hatefull light)
Cor. 890 O barbarous, inhumaine, hatefull traytors
Cor. 907 a hatefull race, mongst whom there dooth abide
Cor. 1438 the hatefull crue that, wanting powre in fielde
Cor. 1930 what hatefull thing (unthought of) have I done
ST 2503 my selfe should send their hatefull soules to hell
ST 2703 whose hatefull wrath berev'd him of his breath
Ard. 1809 than the *h.* naming of the horn
JB 1 how hatefull a thing the sinne of murder hath beene
JB 225 to shunne the hatefull sinne of murder
Hater.
HP 672 shewing himselfe a *h.*, contemner, and carelesse of
Hateth.
Cor. 2028 Cornelia must live (though life she *h.*)
Hating.
Cor. 1219 teaching a people *h.* servitude to
Hatred.
HP 466 *h.*, dispraise of others, or superfluous conceit
Cor. 96 *h.* accompanies prosperitie
Cor. 658 and stil (unsatisfide) more *h.* beares
Cor. 854 the shame, the griefe, the rage, the *h.* that
Cor. 1484 there is no *h.* more, if it be mov'd
SP 22 and then rechange their *h.* into love
Ard. 340 the deadly *h.* of my heart's appeased
JB 64 it kindled such a *h.* in her heart against
JB 78 conceived such deadly *h.* against him
Haught.
Cor. 1388 Pompey, that second Mars, whose *h.* renowne
Haughtiest.
VPJ 2 sprowt higher then the hautiest of their heads

Haughty.
Jer. 1062 we may meete this haughtie prince, and
Jer. 1067 and break our *h.* sculs downe to our feete
Jer. 1103 this proud prince, the *h.* Balthezer
SP 185 hit the haughtie challenger, and strooke him dead
SP 2220 I, now will Death, in his most haughtie pride
Ard. 1636 and buries all his *h.* pride in dust
Haul.
ST 3004 and let the winde and tide hall me along to
JB 174 he wold so haule and pull her as was pittie to
Haunt.
Cor. 759 that wont to *h.* and trace by cloistred tombes
Ard. 799 to the Nag's Head, there is this coward's *h.*
Ard. 955 the hunger-bitten wolf o'erpries his *h.*
Haven.
HP 346 in the Winter is enforced to keepe the *H.*
Cor. 1861 trots to the *H.*, where his ships he finds
ST 1726 wherein I see no *h.* to rest my hope
SP 993 weele lay the ports and havens round about
Hawk-nosed.
Ard. 600 *h.* and very hollow-eyed
Hawks.
ST 575 in time all haggard Hawkes will stoope to lure
Hay.
Cor. 1087 lyke cocks of *H.* when July sheares the field
Hazard.
Cor. 725 farre from the common *h.* of the warrs
ST 1175 then *h.* not thine owne, Hieronimo
ST 1256 dye, then by their life to *h.* our good haps
SP 575 Ile *h.* dutie in my Soveraignes presence
SP 843 and like it is in play sheele *h.* it
JB 18 to the great *h.* of their soules and the destructions
JB 203 ‹ if I trust thee or *h.* my life in thy hands ›
Hazarded.
Cor. 16 our fathers *h.* their derest blood
Cor. 829 *h.* against the Samnites, Sabins, and
Cor. 1204 and *h.* our Cittie and our selves
ST 1117 thus have I shamelessly *h.* his life
Head.
HP 374 that she blushing held downe her *h.*
Cor. 284 that I should heape misfortune on theyr *h.*
Cor. 604 crowne, that now the Tyrans *h.* doth deck
Cor. 692 why suffer you vayne dreames your heade to trouble?
Cor. 732 I mov'd mine *h.*, and flonge abroade mine armes
Cor. 790 thy *h.* hung downe, thy cheeks with teares besprent
Cor. 1406 and crowne thy *h.*, and mount thy Chariot
Cor. 1740 runne *h.* to *h.*, and (sullen) wil not yeeld
Cor. 1806 what e're makes *h.* to meet them in this humor
Jer. 596 make it confused ere it come to *h.*
Jer. 815 that I may see your Gray *h.* crownd in white
Jer. 1080 Ile top thy *h.* for that ambitious word
Jer. 1082 see, a revengfull sword waves ore my *h.*
ST Bal. 16 age with silvered haires my aged *h.* had overspred
ST 130 heere falles a body scindred from his *h.*
ST 1596 this hearbe will purge the eye, and this the *h.*?
STA 2055 with my hand leaning upon his *h.*, thus, sir
STA 2085 ‹ the house is a fire, as the torch over my *h.* ›
ST 2528 for why the plots already in mine *h.*
SP 386 he shall helpe your husband to arme his *h.*
SP 411 hanging her *h.* as partner of my shame
SP 1238 or hide my *h.* in time of dangerous stormes
SP 1950 your turkish bonnet is not on your *h.*?
SP 2143 off with his *h.*, and suffer him not to speake
Ard. 14 the earth hung over my *h.* and covered me
Ard. 161 and fling the dagger at the painter's *h.*
Ard. 704 where I broke the tapster's *h.*

Ard. 818 what 'mends shall I have for my broken *h.*?
Ard. 823 my broken *h.* grieves me not so much as
Ard. 836 I pray thee, how came thy *h.* broke?
Ard. 840 boy let down his shop-window and broke his *h.*
Ard. 984 grow as Hydra's *h.* that plenished by decay
Ard. 1013 now will he shake his care-oppressed *h.*
Ard. 1799 which falling down light on the shooter's *h.*
Ard. 1932 the notches of his tallies and beat them about his *h.*
Ard. 1935 I have broken a sergeant's *h.* with his own mace
Ard. 1971 he in a bravery flourished o'er his *h.*
Ard. 2359 his purse and girdle found at thy bed's *h.*
Ard. 2375 and had not I with my buckler covered my *h.*
Ard. 2418 my blood be on his *h.* that gave the sentence
VPJ 2 sprowt higher then the hautiest of their heads
HP Ind. 89 hayre cut from Womens heads, and why
Cor. 65 lift theyr humbled heads, in presence of proud Rome
Cor. 88 see how the Rocks do heave their heads at thee
Cor. 1803 stooping their heads low bent to tosse theyr staves
Cor. 1827 some should you see that had theyr heads halfe cloven
STA 1768 strikes care upon their heads with his mad ryots
STA 2938 let us lay our heades together
Ard. 799 to the Nag's *H.*, there is this coward's haunt
Ard. 889 at the Nag's *H.*, at the eighteen pence ordinary

Headed.
ST 2208 least the triple *h.* porter should denye my passage

Headlong.
Cor. 196 head-long to runne and reck no after harmes
Cor. 1901 *h.* he threw himselfe into the seas
SP 1906 and throw them *h.* downe into the valley

Heady.
HP 323 that sharp and heddie taste which he calleth bitter

Heal.
HP 1516 the honest Phisitian will heale as much as hee can

Healed.
ST 1613 dauncing about his newly *h.* wounds

Health.
VPJ 18 *h.* of thy Countrey, helpe to all our harmes
VPJ 84 thy subjects *h.* and mirth
HP Ded. Maister Thomas Reade Esquier *H.* and all Happines
HP Ind. 64 exercise of Housekeepers for *h.*
HP 1030 Cleanlines increaseth and preserveth the *h.*
HP 1571 should have regarde unto his *h.*
HP 1573 gayne which most preserveth *h.*
HP 1576 are great helps to *h.*
Cor. 1043 where *h.* or wealth, or vines doe stand
ST 498 and learne my Father and my Countries *h.*
ST 1090 are happie witnesses of his highnes *h.*
ST 1488 methinks you should rather hearken to your soules *h.*
ST 2109 then hast thou *h.*, and happy shalt thou be
ST 2334 in his behalfe, and to procure his *h.*?
SP 1004 was in good *h.* at the sending hereof
SP 1765 great affaires, importuning *h.* and wealth of Soliman
Ard. 762 « hoping in God you be in good *h.* »
Ard. 1522 ay, in *h.* towards Feversham, to shame us all
Jer. 587 I tooke a boule and quaft a *h.* to him

Heap.
Cor. 284 that I should heape misfortunes on theyr head
Cor. 1986 and on theyr Tombes we heape our bodies
Jer. 991 now death doth *h.* his goods up all at once
SP 1831 a huge heape of our imperiall coyne
Cor. 495 have we not seene them turn'd to heapes of stones?
Cor. 1086 bodies (tumbled up on heapes, lyke cocks of Hay
Cor. 1717 may by our horse in heapes be over-throwne
Cor. 1823 and wretched heapes lie mourning of theyr maimes

Heaped.
HP 1620 easily may a great quantity of mony be *h.* up

Cor. 1007 when shee hath heap't her gifts on us
Cor. 1610 the heavens are heapt with rage and horror
Cor. 2018 (which both the world and Fortune heapt on him)

Heaping.
SP 612 withould thy hand from *h.* bloud on bloud?

Hear.
HP 475 to heare the dyscourse your Father made unto you
Cor. 422 till (griefe to heare, and hell for me to speake)
Cor. 913 I feare the heavens will not heare our prayer
Cor. 985 Madam, beware; for, should hee heare of thys
Cor. 1363 but trembleth if he once but heare of mee
Cor. 1536 when they heare another prais'd
Cor. 1599 let's heare him speake
Cor. 1601 me thinks, I heare my Maisters daughter speake
Cor. 1833 that stopt their eares, and would not heare a word
Jer. 146 nay, heare me, deere
Jer. 274 come hether, boy Horatio, didst thou here them?
Jer. 334 what newes, my Lord, heare you from Portugale?
Jer. 699 the King must heare; why should I
Jer. 774 away with him, I will not heare him speake
Jer. 871 hark, Portugales: I heare their Spanish drum
Jer. 934 I long to heare the musick of clashed swords
Jer. 935 why, thou shalt heare it presently
ST 313 and could she heare, yet is she wilfull mad
ST 347 then heare that truth which these mine eyes have seene
ST 376 vouchsafe, dread Soveraigne, to heare me speake
ST 609 hinder me not what ere you heare or see
ST 726 be deafe, my eares, heare not my discontent
ST 729 heare still, mine eares, to heare them both lament
ST 754 there none shall heare us but the harmeless birds
STA 942 doe ye heare me, sir?
ST 1681 have patience, Bel-imperia; heare the rest
ST 1828 the King sees me, and faine would heare my sute
ST 1861 to heare his Sonne so princelie entertainde
ST 1935 his Majestie, that longs to heare from hence
ST 1936 on then, and heare you, Lord Embassadour
ST 2339 to heare Hieronimo exclaime on thee?
ST 2399 I *h.* you find your selfe agrieved
ST 2701 hath scited me to heare Horatio plead with
ST 2830 I heare his dismall out-cry eccho in the aire
STA 2976 be deafe, my senses, I can heare no more
SP 51 when didst thou sing a note that I could heare
SP 141 heavens heare my harty praier, and it effect
SP 296 naye, but here you, sir; I must talke with you
SP 354 it is a world to heere the foole prate and brag
SP 531 didst thou not heare our brother sweare
SP 813 ah stay, my sweete Perseda; heare me speake
SP 875 I, but heare you, Maister, was not he a foole that
SP 1026 ah stay, no more; for I can heere no more
SP 1068 I, but heere you, sir; I am bound
SP 1169 yet have we eares to heare a just complaint
SP 1271 come, follow me, and I will heare the rest
SP 1470 now, faire Virgin, let me heare thee speake
SP 1604 pleaseth your Majestie to heare Brusor speake?
SP 1609 here me, my Lord: let me go over to Rhodes
SP 1639 and heere them play, and see my minions dance
SP 1688 then here my opinion concerning that point
SP 1722 I cannot be well till I heare the rest of the
SP 1844 heavens, heer you this, and drops not vengeance on them?
SP 1976 to heere and see the matter well convaid
SP 2087 I, but heere you, are you so foolish to fight with him?
Ard. 155 the which I *h.* the wench keeps in her chest
Ard. 327 *h.* me but speake: as I intend to live
Ard. 446 which, as I *h.*, will murder men for gold
Ard. 531 now, Alice, let's *h.* thy news

Ard. 554 let's *h.* them, that I may laugh for company
Ard. 575 'twere cheerful news to *h.* the churl were dead
Ard. 786 sirrah, let me *h.* no more of this
Ard. 901 we *h.* you have a pretty love in Feversham
Ard. 1050 methinks I *h.* them ask where Michael is
Ard. 1116 knock with thy sword, perhaps the slave will *h.*
Ard. 1190 first, Will, let's *h.* what he can say
Ard. 1329 nay, *h.* me speak, Mosbie, a word or two
Ard. 1343 wilt thou not *h.*? what malice stops thine ears?
Ard. 1348 when I have bid thee *h.*, or see or speak
Ard. 1478 stand close, Will, I *h.* them coming
Ard. 1695 why, didst thou *h.* any?
Ard. 1733 yet did we *h.* their horses as they passed
Ard. 1859 did'st thou not *h.* me cry ‹ they murder thee? ›
Ard. 2367 Shakebag, I *h.*, hath taken sanctuary
HP 1247 he heares or feareth any dearth or scarcity
ST 312 so is she deafe, and heares not my laments
Ard. 1534 O, how she'll chafe when she hears of this!

Heard.
VPJ 27 my tale was *h.*, and yet it was not told
HP 7 I *h.* a confused cry of dogs
HP 292 makes mee remember that which I have hearde
HP 337 many times hearde much quest[i]oning of
HP 399 I remember I have hearde my Father saie
Cor. 751 I saw great Pompey, and I *h.* hym speake
Cor. 1639 Scipio no sooner *h.* of his designes
Jer. 130 I have hard of your honor, gentle brest
Jer. 568 he should have hard his name yokt with the divell
ST Bal. 60 a voyce I hard, whereat I rose
ST Bal. 163 here have you *h.* my Tragicke tale
ST 1565 what have I *h.*, what have mine eies behelde?
ST 1648 my Lord the Duke, you *h.*, enquired for her
ST 1649 I hope you *h.* me say sufficient reason why
STA 2046 Sir, I am sure you have *h.* of my painting
ST 2327 I tell thee. Sonne, my selfe have *h.* it said
ST 2850 he shrikes : I *h.*, and yet, me thinks, I heare his
ST 2993 what age hath ever *h.* such monstrous deeds?
SP 164 our word of courage all the world hath *h.*
SP 256 I have seen much, *h.* more, but done most
Ard. 66 I *h.* thee call on Mosbie in thy sleep
Ard. 78 I *h.* you name him once or twice
Ard. 459 I *h.* your husband hath the grant of late
Ard. 1069 so great a cry for nothing I ne'er *h.*
Ard. 1346 and *h.* as quickly as the fearful hare
Ard. 1781 rail on me, as I have *h.* thou dost
Ard. 2225 or else I should have *h.* of him ere now
Puck 23 when he had *h.* of his conditions
SP 1653 having forehard of Basilicoes worth
JB 210 was over *h.* of some that revealed it to the

Hearest.
Ard. 1776 Franklin, *h.* thou this fellow speak?

Hearing.
Jer. 610 that her hart *h.* may relent and yeeld
ST Bal. 103 *h.* then how I did grudge
ST 240 for in our *h.* thy deserts were great
SP 1689 *h.* that you have lost a capitoll part of
JB 190 *h.* the great mone shee made unto him

Hearken.
HP 196 to harken to their speeches with attention
HP 478 greevous unto me to harken thereunto
HP 1171 to harken after the prices that are sette
Cor. 1587 but hope the best, and harken to his newes
ST 1221 and harken to me, thus it is devisde
ST 1488 methinks you should rather *h.* to your soules health
ST 2895 O *h.*, Vice-roy — holde. Hieronimo
Ard. 1146 and afterwards go *h.* for the flood

Ard. 2170 *h.*, they knock : what, shall I let them in?
Hearkening.
ST 1179 and harkening neere the Duke of Castiles house
Hearse.
Jer. 1160 see, he points at his owne *h.* — mark, all
Jer. 1176 my Funerall rights are made, my herse hung rich
Cor. 2029 to make your Tombes, and mourne upon your hearses
Heart.
HP 239 cannot yet find in his hart to be married
HP 941 that made impressions in my hart, and printed
HP 1731 if my hart or happe would give me leave
Cor. 113 wag'd further warre with an insatiate hart
Cor. 229 as my displeased soule may shunne my hart
Cor. 298 one while the hart, another while the liver
Cor. 300 nor spareth it what purely feeds the hart
Cor. 410 my frightfull hart (stund in my stone-cold breast)
Cor. 529 to force us doe that goes against our hart
Cor. 934 mine eyes have seene what I in hart desir'd
Cor. 971 can stoope the hart resolv'd to tyrannize
Cor. 979 for when, to ease th' oppression of my hart
Cor. 1168 did breake into the hart of Italie
Cor. 1254 as if he wanted hands, sence, sight, or hart
Cor. 1391 my hand, my hap, my hart exceeded his
Cor. 1456 good deeds the cruelst hart to kindnes bring
Cor. 1542 Envies dart (pricking still their poysoned hart
Cor. 1550 to choller doth convart purest blood about the *h.*
Cor. 1594 is this th' undaunted hart that is required in
Cor. 1844 whose stony hart, that nere dyd Romaine good
Cor. 1919 that th' extreame fire within my hart may
Cor. 1919 fire within my hart may from my hart retyre
Cor. 1946 O envious Julia, in thy jealous hart
Cor. 1952 and urge thee (if thy hart be not of flynt
Cor. 1955 revenge in Caesars hart upon so slight a cause
Jer. 9 I have a hart thrice stronger then my years
Jer. 189 tis fixed upon my hart ; adew, soules friend
Jer. 199 and, madam, in this circle let your hart move
Jer. 282 I like thy true hart, boy ; thou lovest thy friend
Jer. 328 thy masters hy prized love unto our hart is
Jer. 610 that her hart hearing may relent and yeeld
Jer. 647 I to the King with this unfaithfull hart?
Jer. 703 I, villaine, for thou aym[ed]st at this true hart
Jer. 843 Andreas bosome bears away my hart
Jer. 895 and receive the somes of many a bleeding hart
Jer. 903 O, in thy hart, waigh the deere dropes
Jer. 1016 the glory of our foe, the hart of courage
Jer. 1057 else his unpitying sword had cleft my hart
Jer. 1132 point at the rich circle of thy labouring hart
Jer. 1147 just at this instant her hart sincks and dies
Jer. 1163 to thank Horatio, and commend his hart
ST Bal. 54 the place where they should joy their *h.*
ST Bal. 72 it allwayes at my hart I kept
ST Bal. 108 although in *h.* I never meant
ST Bal. 134 with weeping eyes and mournefull hart
ST 211 nor fild my hart with overcloying joyes
ST 234 his Sonne distrest, a corsive to his hart
ST 345 my hart growne hard gainst mischiefes battery
ST 468 what, if conceite have laid my hart to gage?
ST 480 in whose translucent brest my hart is lodgde
ST 699 and through her eares dive downe into her hart.
ST 700 and in her hart set him where I should stand
ST 714 my hart (sweet freend) is like a ship at sea
ST 720 my hart, with feares and hopes long tost
ST 727 dye, hart : another joyes what thou deservest
ST 730 live, hart, to joy at fond Horatios fall
ST 821 although my fainting hart controles my soule
ST 829 and yet my hart foretels me some mischaunce

ST 879 and chill my throbbing hart with trembling feare
ST 911 my husbands absence makes my *h*. to throb
ST 918 for in revenge my hart would find releife
ST 1036 I had not thought that Alexandros hart
ST 1147 and feare my hart with fierce inflamed thoughts
ST 1207 my griefe no hart, my thoughts no tung can tell
ST 1597 ah, but none of them will purge the hart
STA 1944 should sleepe in rest, his hart in quiet
ST 2136 thy hart to patience, and thy hands to rest
ST 2532 she hath my hart, but you, my Lord, have hers
ST 2761 the warlike *h*. to wait
ST 2833 heere lay my hart, and heere my hart was slaine
ST 2836 but hope, hart, treasure, joy, and blisse
ST 2868 and never hath it left my bloody hart
ST 2871 which now perform'd, my hart is satisfied
ST 2932 first take my tung, and afterwards my hart
STA 2971 this same hand twas it that stab'd his hart
STA 2982 first take my tongue, and afterward my *h*.
SP 75 should finde a harbour for my hart to dwell
SP 77 let in my hart to keep thine company
SP 79 to equall it : receive my hart to boote
SP 522 till it have prickt the hart of Christendome
SP 745 I must unclaspe me, or my *h*. will breake
SP 755 here comes the Synon to my simple *h*.
SP 813 that please the eare but seeke to spoile the *h*.?
SP 824 my perplexed *h*. hath no interpreters but wordes
SP 858 Perseda, whom my *h*. no more can flie then
SP 1028 my *h*. had arm'd my tongue with injury
SP 1046 for, till we meete, my hart shall want delight
SP 1134 these praises, Brusor, touch me to the *h*.
SP 1179 that what my *h*. desires, mine eyes may view
SP 1192 thoughts should dare attempt, or but creepe neere my *h*.
SP 1298 my *h*. is full ; I cannot laugh at follie
SP 1371 to countercheck his hart by turning Turke
SP 1392 my *h*. is overwhelmd with thousand woes
SP 1477 how dooth thy hart admit the pure affection of
SP 1486 why, thats the period that my *h*. desires
SP 1749 my *h*. was purposd once to do thee wrong
SP 1787 come, Lucina, lets in ; my *h*. is full
SP 2072 how could thy *h*. harbour a wicked thought
SP 2116 could not have prickt so neere unto my *h*.
SP 2149 « To plague thy hart that is so full of poyson »
Ard. 65 this night, sweet Alice, thou hast killed my *h*.
Ard. 98 sweet Mosbie is the man that hath my *h*.
Ard. 153 but he hath sent a dagger sticking in a *h*.
Ard. 160 as she shall eat the *h*. he sent with salt
Ard. 326 the rancorous venom of thy mis-swoll'n *h*.
Ard. 332 I could not choose, her beauty fired my *h*. !
Ard. 639 Mosbie, you know, who's master of my *h*.
Ard. 713 this cheers my *h*. ; Master Greene, I'll leave you
Ard. 866 till Arden's *h*. be panting in my hand
Ard. 1272 breaks my relenting *h*. in thousand pieces
Ard. 1276 a *h*. that dies when thou art sad
Ard. 1316 that showed my *h*. a raven for a dove
Ard. 1448 a heavy blood is gathered at my *h*.
Ard. 1474 this fighting at my *h*. makes short my wind
Ard. 1515 even when my dag was levelled at his *h*.
Ard. 1886 ne'er shall my *h*. be eased till this be done
Ard. 1996 sweet Mosbie, hide thy arm, it kills my *h*.
Ard. 2108 but for yourself, you speak not from your *h*.
Ard. 2188 my husband's death torments me at the *h*.
Ard. 2222 ah, neighbours, a sudden qualm came o'er my *h*.
JB 64 it kindled such a hatred in her *h*. against
JB 92 to make speedy haste to the *h*., without any
JB 101 « find in my *h*. to doe so small a matter »
JB 133 « now I feele my selfe sicke at the very *h*. »

Puck 30 he was intemp[er]ate & of a cruel hart
Jer. 1089 my other soule, my bosome, my harts friend
ST 2213 the burden of thy sore harts greife
SP 61 the meaning of my true harts constancie
SP 622 bearing in either hand his hearts decay
SP 760 well, now Erastus, my hearts onely joy
SP 1286 and here my tongue dooth stay with swolne hearts greefe
SP 1287 and here my swolne harts greef doth stay my tongue
SP 1589 repent that ere I gave away my hearts desire
SP 1733 to worke each others blisse and hearts delight
SP 2066 first let my tongue utter my hearts despight
SP 2119 and with her love my hearts felicitie
Ard. 259 a weeping eye that witnesses heart's grief
Ard. 340 the deadly hatred of my heart's appeased
Ard. 990 my heart's grief rends my other powers
Cor. 21 our bastard harts lye idely sighing
Cor. 27 and teares our freedom from our franchiz'd harts
Cor. 158 farre from our harts, for stayning of our face
Cor. 624 as tyrannie shall yoke our basterd harts
Cor. 671 with feareles harts do guard our Romaine hopes ?
Cor. 793 thy bravest Captaines, whose coragious harts
Cor. 842 if yet our harts retaine one drop of blood
Cor. 851 or think'st thou Romains beare such bastard harts
Cor. 1619 Caesar, that wisely knewe his souldiers harts
Cor. 1709 theyr harts and eyes lye hovering over us
Jer. 246 I know womens harts what stuffe they are made of
ST 58 or pennes can write, or mortall harts can think
ST 897 their harts were great, their clamours menacing
ST 2165 may moove the harts of warlike Myrmydons
SP 15 twas I that made their harts consent to love
SP 609 harts counsell bridle the fond intemperance of thy tongue ?
SP 638 thou canst not teach their eyes to wound their hearts
SP 684 so both our hearts are still combind in one
SP 761 is come to joyne both hearts in union
SP 1534 and joyne their hands, whose hearts are knit already ?
JB 15 yet doth the Divell so worke in the hearts of a number
SP 195 and put the flint *h*. Perseans to the sword

Hearted.
Cor. 14 faint-harted do those liberties enthrall
SP 1305 Erastus, that faint *h*. run away
Ard. 2053 tush, you are too faint-*h*. ; we must do it
Cor. 1381 the stony-harted people that inhabite where

Heartily.
HP 373 and therwithall hee laughed so hartilie

Heartless.
ST 471 a hartles man and live ? A miracle

Hearty.
SP 141 heavens heare my harty praier, and it effect
SP 1003 after my most *h*. commendations
Ard. 505 as every day I wish with *h*. prayer

Heat.
HP 342 the Sommer with extreame heate, and the
HP 348 constrained to retyre from the heate
HP 369 our bodies resolved with the exceeding heate
HP 607 in whom naturall heate is not aportioned unto
HP 799 that first age aboundeth in naturall heate
HP 800 for restraining the naturall heate within
HP 801ᵃ Antiperistasis, where heate expels cold, or cold
HP 801ᵃ where heate expels cold, or cold expulseth heate
HP 801ᵃ the heate withdraweth to the lower parts
Cor. 228 and spunge my bodies heate of moisture so
Cor. 354 the spring, whom Sommers pride (with sultrie heate) pursues
Cor. 982 nor dryes the heate the moysture of mine eyes

Cor. 1069 swolne with honors heate
Cor. 1798 doth breathe new heate within Orestes brest
Jer. 928 to meete me single in the battailes h.
ST 2373 but not too fast, least heate and all be done
Ard. 861 whose lips are glued with summer's parching h.
HP 266 so many mishaps and heates of the Sunne
Heave.
Cor. 88 see how the Rocks do h. their heads at thee
STA 2075 and let my haire h. up my night-cap
Heaven.
VPJ 20 long maist thou live, and h. be thy home
HP 208 h. hath not graunted me a maiden Child
HP 410 you shall understand that H. is round
HP 1672 of whom both h. and Nature doe depend
Cor. 55 ore whom (save h.) nought could signorize
Cor. 56 and whom (save h.) nothing could afright
Cor. 108 h. heretofore (enclinde to do us good)
Cor. 126 for-h. delights not in us, when we doe
Cor. 144 whose mournfull cryes and shreekes to h. ascend
Cor. 166 the wrath of h. (though urg'd) we see is slow in
Cor. 268 if (as some believe) in h. or hell be heavenly powers
Cor. 280 for tis not h., nor Crassus (cause hee sees
Cor. 283 that I receiv'd from h. at my birth
Cor. 341 for H. and Time have faild in power to
Cor. 419 (with armes to h. uprear'd) I gan exclaime
Cor. 56 reacht from deepest hell, and with their tops tucht h.
Cor. 541 for h. it selfe, nor hels infectious breath
Cor. 556 till h. it selfe commaund it
Cor. 561 upon the will of H. doth waite
Cor. 570 from h. and heavens varietie
Cor. 786 the force of h. exceeds thy former strength
Cor. 911 will h. let treason be unpunished?
Cor. 918 for our chastisement that h. doth with wicked men
Cor. 1093 yet are there Gods, yet is there h. and earth
Cor. 1125 I sweare by h., th' Immortals highest throne
Cor. 1358 tyll h. unlock the darknes of the night
Cor. 1403 and rendring thanks to h., as we goe
Cor. 1466 ascend to h. upon my winged deeds
Cor. 1476 H. sets our time ; with h. may nought dispence
Cor. 1479 Fortune is fickle, H. imperious
Cor. 1493 and, if h. were pleas'd, I could desire
Cor. 1702 with blubbred eyes und handes to h. uprear'd
Cor. 1883 and H. it selfe conjur'd to injure him
Cor. 1902 O cruell Gods, O h., O direfull Fates
Jer. 108 which are as different as h. and hell
Jer. 163 and fears ill fate which h. hath yet withstood
Jer. 343 answer at next birth our fathers fawltes in h.
Jer. 483 he meanes to send you to h., when
Jer. 714 angels of h. forefend it
Jer. 812 O, my sweet boy, h. shield thee still from care
Jer. 814 and h. blesse you, my father, in this fight
Jer. 913 for h. can be revenged on their dust
Jer. 933 answere at next birth our Fathers faults in h.
Jer. 1130 h. and this arme once saved thee from thy foe
Jer. 1134 O then stept h. and I betweene the stroke
ST 101 then blest be h., and guider of the heavens
ST 122 and h. it selfe was frighted with the sound
ST 1056 Yet hope the best. — Tis h. is my hope
ST 1504 the soule, that shoulde be shrinde in h.
ST 1521 choked or infect with that which h. contemnes
ST 1577 they did what h. unpunisht would not leave
ST 1611 to h. : I, there sits my Horatio
ST 1633 till h., as I have hoped, shall set me free
STA 1784 well, h. is h. still
STA 1936 dive in the water, and stare up to h.
STA 2087 make me curse hell, invocate h., and

ST 2096 I, h. will be revenged of every ill
ST 2113 h. coureth him that hath no buriall
ST 2162 with mournefull eyes and hands to h. upreard?
ST 2303 to thinke how strangely h. hath thee preserved
ST 2366 sith h. hath ordainde thee to be mine
ST 2502 for heere I sweare, in sight of h. and earth
ST 2509 why then I see that h. applies our drift
STA 2977 fall, h.., and cover us with thy sad ruines
SP 275 O h., she comes, accompanied with a child
SP 669 when shall the gates of h. stand all wide ope[n]
SP 835 but how she got it, h. knows, not I
SP 972 seeing he was going towards h.
SP 1442 first, thanks to h.; and next to Brusors valour
SP 2129 as firme as are the poles whereon h. lies
SP 2189 but I, that have power in earth and h. above
Ard. 13 wish that for this veil of h. the earth hung
Ard. 39 (for dear I hold her love, as dear as h.)
Ard. 328 live with God and his elected saints in h.
Ard. 1110 and if I do not, h. cut me off!
Ard. 1193 for here I swear, by h. and earth and all
Ard. 1526 the Lord of H. hath preserved him
Ard. 2132 yet, Arden, I protest to thee by h.
Ard. 2328 God and h. can tell I loved him
Ard. 2355 and frown not on me when we meet in h.
Ard. 2336 in h. I'll love thee, though on earth I did not
Ard. 2416 seeing no hope on earth, in h. is my hope
Eng. Parn. 14 At last to be extol'd in heavens high joyes
Cor. 164 thou dost not seeke to calme heavens ireful king
Cor. 357 Heavens influence was nere so constant yet
Cor. 391 that (envious) we repine at heavens will
Cor. 496 Carthage can witnes, and thou, heavens handwork
Cor. 510 and our time is knowne to be at heavens dispose
Cor. 570 from h. and heavens varietie
Cor. 966 not heavens feare, nor Countries sacred love
Cor. 1100 have neither helpe nor grace in heavens sight
Cor. 1333 hath fild heavens fierie vaults with fright-full horror
Cor. 1336 and you brave walls, bright heavens masonrie
Cor. 1411 I call to witnes heavens great Thunderer, that
Jer. 972 be all as fortunate as heavens blest host
ST 2369 wherein my hope and heavens faire beautie lies
SP 526 great Soliman, heavens onely substitute
SP 1199 for looking but a scue at heavens bright eye
SP 1480 quick lampelike eyes, like heavens two brightest orbes
SP 2227 whose life is heavens delight, and Cynthias friend
Ard. 1538 see how the hours, the gardant of heaven's gate
Cor. 160 the heavens with their wrathful hand revenge
Cor. 230 Heavens, let me dye, and let the Destinies admit me
Cor. 349 then, as the Heavens (by whom our hopes are guided)
Cor. 378 Heavens did theyr favors lavishly bestow
Cor. 379 tis true, the Heavens (at least-wise if they please)
Cor. 399 but hee is dead (O heavens), not dead in fight
Cor. 431 O heavens, what shall I doe? alas, must I
Cor. 547 daughter, beware how you provoke the heavens
Cor. 597 and yet those seas (as heavens please)
Cor. 622 that earst was cleere as heavens Queene
Cor. 623 but, heavens, as tyrannie shall yoke our basterd harts
Cor. 667 and will the heavens, that have so oft defended
Cor. 685 the frowning heavens oppose themselves against
Cor. 894 cryme that gainst the heavens might bee imagined
Cor. 912 heavens will performe what they have promised
Cor. 913 I feare the heavens will not heare our prayer
Cor. 1478 but Fortune and the heavens have care of us
Cor. 1529 for high Jove the heavens among
Cor. 1600 the heavens are heapt with rage and horror
Cor. 1735 and with a duskish yellow chokt the heavens
Cor. 1924 say, freatfull heavens, what fault have I committed

Cor. 1988 O heavens, at least permit of all these plagues
ST 101 then blest be *h.*, and guider of the heavens
ST 831 and heavens have shut up day to pleasure us
ST 901 O heavens, why made you night to cover sinne ?
ST 987 the heavens are just, murder cannot be hid
ST 1066 whereof, as heavens have knowne my secret thoughts
ST 1134 O sacred heavens, if this unhallowed deed
ST 1151 eies, life, world, heavens, hel, night and day
ST 1419 that I may come (by justice of the heavens)
ST 1534 beat at the windowes of the brightest heavens
ST 1566 O sacred heavens, may it come to passe
ST 1610 wings, that mounts me up unto the highest heavens
ST 1808 then myrrh or incense to the offended heavens
STA 1976 the heavens are gracious, and your miseries and
ST 2320 heavens will not let Lorenzo erre so much
ST 2672 wrought by the heavens in this confusion
ST 2753 Bashaw, that Rhodes is ours, yield heavens the honour
ST 2915 upon whose soules may heavens be yet avenged
STA 2946 as many Heavens to go to, as those lives
STA 2958 upon whose soules may heavens be yet revenged
SP 141 heavens heare my harty praier, and it effect
SP 719 by favour and by justice of the heavens
SP 782 if heavens were just, thy teeth would teare thy tongue
SP 784 if heavens were just, men should have open brests
SP 786 if heavens were just, that power that forceth love
SP 788 yes, heavens are just, but thou art so corrupt
SP 1187 heavens brought thee hether for our benefit
SP 1278 returne him backe, fair heavens, or let me die
SP 1548 witnesse the heavens of my unfeined love
SP 1550 that heavens and heavenly powers do manage love
SP 1594 what was it but abuse of heavens that gave her me ?
SP 1595 and therefore angric heavens will be revengd
SP 1596 Heavens, Love, and Fortune, all three have decreed
SP 1746 and thanks to gratious heavens, that so
SP 1813 I heere protest by heavens unto you all that
SP 1841 heavens, heer you this, and drops not vengeance on them ?
SP 2113 ah heavens, that hitherto have smilde on me
SP 2120 even for Erastus death the heavens have plagued me
SP 2121 ah no, the heavens did never more accurse me
Ard. 195 the heavens can witness, and the world can tell
Ard. 1018 now will he cast his eyes up towards the heavens
Ard. 1873 the heavens can witness of our harmless thoughts

Heavenly.
Cor. 269 be *h.* powers, or infernall spirits
ST 1614 singing sweet hymnes and chanting *h.* notes
ST 1740 led by the loadstar of her *h.* lookes
SP 110 Ile be the glasse and thou that *h* Sun
SP 840 ah, Love, and if thou beest of *h.* power
SP 1550 that heavens and *h.* powers do manage love
Ard. 253 make *h.* gods break off their nectar draughts

Heavily.
Cor. 123 is *h.* return'd upon our selves

Heaviness.
JB 151 made a shewe of great heavines and sorrow

Heavy.
HP 617 to lighten and exonerat that ponderous and heavie loade
HP 1533 the Chizzel should not be so ponderous and heavie
Cor. 10 and oft yee have your heavie hands with-held
Cor. 174 that breaths her heavie poisons downe to hell
Cor. 1633 with *h.* Armor on theyr hardned backs
Jer. 722 what *h.* sounds are these, neerer, and neerer ?
Jer. 1023 tis now about the *h.* dread of battaile
ST 390 I nill refuse this heavie dolefull charge
ST 1021 Ile shew thee Balthazar in *h.* case
Ard. 1093 I am so *h.* that I can scarce go

Ard. 1448 a *h.* blood is gathered at my heart
Hebrews.
HP 404 tne opinion of some Doctors of the Hebrues
Hecat.
Cor. 1905 O triple titled Heccat, Quene and Goddesse
He-cat.
STA 1969 and yonder pale faced Hee-cat there, the Moone
Hector.
ST 48 where wounded *H.* lives in lasting paine
STA 2093 were he as strong as *H.*, thus would I teare and drage him
SP 137 fortune as the good Andromache wisht valiant *H.*
SP 1913 great Hectors sonne, although his age did plead for innocence
Hedged.
Ard. 1240 is *h.* behind me that I cannot back
Heed.
Jer. 300 O, then, take *h.* ; that Jest would not be trim
SP 184 and I, with single *h.* and levell, hit the
Ard. 2145 not yet, Will ; take *h.* he see thee not
Heifer.
Cor. 1739 Bulls, that (jealous of some Heyfar in the Heard)
Height.
Jer. 260 I have no hope of everlasting *h.*
Jer. 990 sweat now to find me in the hight of bloud
ST 110 unto the *h.* of former happines
ST 1024 first we are plast upon extreamest *h.*
ST 1536 but they are plac't in those empyreal heights
Heinous.
JB 18 committe most haynous and grievous offences
Heir.
HP 505 and heyre of a small patrimonie
Jer. 322 Portugalles eire, I thanke thee
Jer. 763 to make the heire of honor melt and bleede
Jer. 1015 Prince Balthezer, Portugals valliant heire
ST 778 she is daughter and halfe heire unto our brother
Cor. 134 what, were they the heires to Persia or the Medes
Ard. 3 hath freely given to thee and to thy heirs
Held.
HP 289 heerewithall I held my peace
HP 374 that she blushing *h.* downe her head
HP 1496 where they are helde deerest, and where best cheape
Cor. 143 whom we by force have *h.* in servitude
Cor. 288 and let theyr double losse that *h.* me deere
Cor. 1677 in one hand *h.* his Targe of steele embost
ST 206 *h.* him by th' arme, as partner of the prize ?
ST 2331 I helde him thence with kind and curteous wordes
ST 2594 one of his Bashawes whom he *h.* full deere
SP 199 along the coasts *h.* by the Portinguize
SP 228 I *h.* it pollicie to put the men children of
Ard. 1928 *h.* him by the ears till all his beer hath
Ard. 2430 which he by force and violence *h.* from Reede
JB 173 appoint her, *h.* hee up but his finger at any time
Helen.
HP 713 an auncient custome, as we read of Hellen in Euripides
Hell.
Eng. Parn. 2 It is an *h.* in hatefull vassalage
Cor. 32 and hongst (O *H.*) upon a Forte halfe finisht thy
Cor. 174 that breaths her heavie poisons downe to *h.*
Cor. 211 must seeke in *H.* to have a haples roome ?
Cor. 268 if (as some believe) in heaven or *h.* be heavenly powers
Cor. 334 what foule infernall, or what stranger *h.*
Cor. 422 till (griefe to heare, and *h.* for me to speake)
Cor. 466 and *h.* it selfe is deafe to my laments
Cor. 489 reacht from deepest *h.*, and with their tops tucht heaven
Cor. 773 descends to *h.*, with hope to rise againe

Cor. 906 els earth make way, and *h.* receive them quicke
Cor. 1797 as when Alecto, in the lowest *h.*, doth breathe
Cor. 1882 his people put to sword, Sea, Earth, and *H.*
Cor. 1907 confound me quick, or let me sinck to *h.*
Jer. 108 which are as different as heaven and *h.*
Jer. 216 as many waies as there are paths to *h.*
Jer. 294 I, ist not wondrous to have honesty in hel?
Jer. 309 Lorenzo has a reach as far as *h.*
Jer. 798 so, so, I have sent my slave to *h.*
Jer. 839 this scarfe shall be my charme gainst foes and *h.*
Jer. 1167 secrets in *h.* are lockt with doores of brasse
Jer. 1180 I never want a fare to passe to *h.*
ST Bal. 130 and eke his soule to *h.* did send
ST 27 then was the Feriman of *H.* content to
ST 64 was ready dounfall to the deepest *h.*
ST 377 away with him; his sight is second *h.*
STA 966 confusion, mischiefe, torment, death and *h.*
ST 1145 the ougly feends do sally forth of *h.*
ST 1151 eies, life, world, heavens, hel, night and day
ST 1295 now by the sorrowes of the soules in *h.*
ST 1530 and broken through the brazen gates of *h.*
ST 1837 that leades unto the lake where *h.* doth stand
ST 1903 for Ile goe marshall up the feendes in *h.*
STA 2086 make me curse *h.*, invocate heaven, and
STA 2092 there's the torment, there's the *h.*
ST 2203 Ile downe to *h.*, and in this passion knock at
ST 2442 for neere, by Stix and Phlegeton in *h.*
ST 2451 have yet the power or prevailance in *h.*
ST 3035 this hand shall hale them downe to deepest *h.*
SP 1347 then stab the slaves, and send their soules to *h.*
SP 1355 I would follow her, though she went to *h.*
SP 2069 accursed homicide, for whome *h.* gapes
SP 2221 fetch his imperiall Carre from deepest *h.*
Ard. 919 to send thee roundly to the devil of *h.*
Ard. 1011 ah, what a *h.* is fretful jealousy!
Ard. 2392 how long shall I live in this *h.* of grief?
Cor. 236 hels horror is mylder then mine endles discontent
Cor. 541 for heaven it selfe, nor hels infectious breath
Jer. 1174 come, Charon; come, hels Sculler, waft me ore
Ard. 1683 here, Shakebag, almost in hell's mouth
Hell-fire.
Ard. 337 *h.* and wrathful vengeance light on me
Hellish.
Jer. 288 unfould their *h.* practise, damnd intent
Helmet.
HP 1420 the curasse and the *H.* to the Souldiour
Cor. 312 thy *H.* deckt with coronets of Bayes?
HP 1455 ‹ We hide our gray haires with our helmets ›
Helms.
Cor. 675 bring from Affrique to our Capitoll, upon theyr helmes
SP 117 that carry honour graven in their helmes
Help.
VPJ 18 health of thy Countrey, helpe to all our harmes
HP Ind. 2 for the helpe and ease of one another
HP 288 satisfied of the helpe you have
HP 616 a companion that shold helpe to lighten
HP 1071 one should so helpe another as wee see
HP 1076 to *h.* and ease the weary and the well imployed
Cor. 1100 have neither helpe nor grace in heavens sight
Cor. 1855 he that had hap to scape, doth helpe a fresh to
Cor. 1960 gainst his mishap, as it my helpe had bin
Jer. 1084 O, I am slaine; helpe me, Horatio
ST 316 what helpe can be expected at her hands
ST 876 murder, murder: helpe, Hieronimo, helpe
ST 883 no, no, it was some woman cride for helpe
ST 913 heere, Isabella, helpe me to lament

ST 1303 helpe me here to bring the murdred body with us too
ST 1363 ‹ To stand good L[ord] and *h.* him in distres ›
ST 2534 to entreate your helpe. — My helpe?
ST 3033 but say, Revenge, for thou must helpe or none
SP 385 he shall helpe your husband to arme his head
SP 618 come, Janisaries, and helpe me to lament
SP 1896 is thy hand to weake? then mine shall helpe
SP 2125 come Brusor, helpe to lift her bodie up
Ard. 726 a little more I needs must use your *h.*
Ard. 1057 he comes, he comes! ah, Master Franklin, *h.*!
Ard. 1438 removing of a shoe may haply *h.* it
Ard. 1703 *h.*, Will, *h.*, I am almost drowned
Ard. 1704 who's that that calls for *h.*?
Ard. 1706 I came to *h.* him that called for *h.*
Ard. 1773 yet it will *h.* my wife and children
Ard. 1842 *h.*, *h.*! they murder my husband
Ard. 1843 *h.*, Will! I am hurt
Ard. 1860 called I not *h.* to set my husband free?
Ard. 1991 patient yourself, we cannot *h.* it now
Ard. 2011 and rather than you shall want, I'll *h.* myself
Ard. 2246 stay, Susan, stay, and *h.* to counsel me
Ard. 2251 come, Susan, *h.* to lift his body forth
HP 1576 are great helps to health
Cor. 68 what helps it that thou ty'dst the former World
Cor. 70 what helps thee now t'have tam'd both land and Sea?
Cor. 71 what helps it thee that under thy controll the
Cor. 1829 here one new wounded helps another dying
SP 1390 but what helps gay garments, when the minds oprest?
Helpest.
Cor. 1047 and often helpst the helples hande
Helpeth.
Cor. 94 what *h.* us the things that they did then
Helpless.
Cor. 1047 and often helpst the helpeles hande
ST 1023 seated amidst so many helpeles doubts
Helplessly.
ST 1922 but if he be thus *h.* distract
Hem.
Jer. 609 move and *h.* perswasion tweene her snowy paps
Hemisphere.
HP 452 is in the midst of our Hemysphere
SP 743 that ere sunne saw within our hemyspheare
Hemmed.
Ard. 1470 then *h.* she out, to clear her voice should seem
Hence.
ST 161 heere-*h.* the fight was eagerly renewd
Henceforth.
Cor. 287 hence-forth forbeare to seeke my murdring love
Cor. 835 or what stranger hell hence-forth wilt thou inhabite
Cor. 1351 that hence-forth Tyber shall salute the seas
Cor. 1507 *h.* vary not thy grace
Ard. 1863 *h.* I'll be thy slave, no more thy wife
Ard. 2125 *h.* be you as strange to me as I to you
Ard. 2130 *h.* frequent my house no more
Henceforward.
Ard. 185 there let him be; *h.* know me not
Ard. 191 and dost thou say, ‹ *h.* know me not? ›
Hendecasyllabon.
VPJ (Title) Hendacasyllabon: T. K. in Cygneam Cantionem
Hens.
HP 693 with more variety of collours the[n] those of theyr *H.*
He-one.
Jer. 209 Ile be the hee one then, and rid thee soone of
Herb.
ST 1595 so that you say, this hearbe will purge the eye
ST 2686 no, not an *h.* within this garden Plot

HP 173 reserved for hearbes, flowers, and rootes
HP 177 garden full of all sorts of sallet hearbes
Herbarum.
ST 1003 Quicquid & h. vi caeca nenia nectit
Herbas.
ST 997 O aliquis mihi quas pulchrum ver educat h.
Hercules.
SP 1660 aspire to purchase Godhead, as did H.
SP 2003 let me see : where is that Alcides, surnamed H.
Ard. 116 were he as mad as raving H.
Herculean.
SP 242 [I], all on foote, like an Herculian offspring
Herd.
Cor. 310 feard then Summers thunder to the silly Heard ?
Cor. 1739 Bulls, that (jealous of some Heyfar in the Heard)
Ard. 1151 whistly watching for the herd's approach
HP 172 whereon the Heards and little flocks
HP 1182 numbred by Algorisme (as Flocks and Heards)
HP 1211 and some with life, as Flocks and Heards
HP 1439 flocks, Heards, and droves compact
HP 1488 his flocks, heards, and such like
HP 1565 from the Earth, Heards, and Flocks
Herdman.
Ard. 1159 and at the noise another h. came
Hereabouts.
HP 124 « I have never seene him h. or elswhere »
Hereafter.
HP 1696 in so precise a sort as thou heereafter not forget them
Jer. 728 doth presage what shall h. follow
Ard. 416 h. think of me as of your dearest friend
Ard. 431 sworn never h. to solicit thee
JB 29 (as the sequell h. will shewe)
Here-hence.
ST 161 heere-hence the fight was eagerly renewd
Herein.
HP 232 and h. I remember that apt forme of
HP 634 and heerein it hath beene conveniently ordeined
HP 684 notwithstanding h. much may be attributed to use
HP 1099 and heerein differeth from the hand for that
HP 1362 and heerin seemeth it that in some sort
HP 1370 ought above all things to be diligent heerein
HP 1447 and heerein will I not conceale what
HP 1715 and heerein onely fayled his discourse
Jer. 1087 yet heerein joy is mingled with sad death
ST 771 yet heerein shall she follow my advice
SP 703 h., Lucina, let me buckler him
Ard. 298 hath any other interest h. ?
Puck 56 w^{thout} h. be somewhat donn for my recoverie
Puck 74 their lyves that h. have accused me
Hereof.
HP 1470 and heereof speaketh Tully in his Booke of Offices
SP 1004 was in good health at the sending h.
Ard. 763 « as I Michael was at the making h. »
JB 35 Brewen was h. very joyfull, and
Heretofore.
HP 41 but h. going into Fraunce I
HP 542 as to the soule it hath beene h. attributed
HP 1149 whatsoever others heertofore have spoke[n] to this purpose
Cor. 108 heaven h. (enclinde to do us good)
Hereupon.
HP 1129 and heereupon was that Treatise of under officers
Herewithal.
HP 289 heerewithall I held my peace, and
Cor. 310 alas, and here-withall what holpe it thee that
Cor. 981 yet herewithall my passion neither dyes

Heroic.
Cor. Ded. 8 your noble and heroick dispositions
Cor. 1287 o're his heroique kingly Tombe
Jer. 324 what thou art, a prince, and an heroycke spirit
Heroical.
SP 931 renownd for all heroyicall and kingly vertues
SP 1152 and, all in all, their deedes heroicall
SP 2136 affable ; and, all in all, his deeds heroyacall
Herrings.
JB 118 to fetch mee a penny worth of red h.
Hesiodus.
HP Ind. 111 oxen placed by H. in steede of servaunts
HP 602 (according to the testimony of H.)
HP 942 the authority of H., that auncient Poet
Hew.
Cor. 1745 they hewe their Armour, and they cleave their casks
Hewn.
Jer. 48 the eares of rough heawn tyrants more then blowes
Hexasticon.
VPJ (Title) caeterorumque conivrationem H.
Hid.
Cor. 409 my voyce lay h., halfe dead, within my throate
Cor. 487 hath h. them both embowel'd in the earth
ST Bal. 168 though long it be h. from man's sight
ST 987 the heavens are just, murder cannot be h.
ST 1156 « me hath my haples brother h. from thee »
SP 1047 my petty fellow, where hast thou h. thy maister ?
SP 1496 O Brusor, thou hast not h. her lippes
Ard. 1080 black night hath h. the pleasures of the day
Hidden.
ST 709 our h. smoke is turned to open flame
Hide.
HP 45 he could no longer h. what he desired
HP 765 a Clowde shoulde bee sent to h. her
HP 1455 « We h. our gray haires with our helmets »
SP 1238 or h. my head in time of dangerous stormes
SP 1495 Brusor, h. her, for her lookes withould me
Ard. 701 'twas bad, but yet it served to h. the plate
Ard. 1382 nothing shall h. me from thy stormy look
Ard. 1996 sweet Mosbie, h. thy arm, it kills my heart
ST 833 and Luna hides her selfe to pleasure us
Hideous.
STA 2036 will range this hidious orchard up and downe
Hie.
Cor. 213 must h., hopeles to hide them in a haples tombe ?
Jer. 647 I to the King with this unfaithfull hart ?
Jer. 1019 passe the leaft wing squadron ; h.
ST Bal. 160 for I to see my son did hye
ST 2469 but after them doth Himen h. as fast
SP 399 and let us h. to tread lavolto
Hied.
HP 143 « Hyed home at night and fild his bord with delicats unbought »
Hieronimo, see **Jeronimo.**
High.
Eng. Parn. 14 at last to be extol'd in heavens h. joyes
HP 59 swoln so h. as it farre surpast the
HP 79 it was as h. as on the outside we might
HP 584 a man marrieth a woman of so h. a birth
HP 801^a because, the hygh parts of the ayre being cold
HP 828 « and your h. Priests hats are made like hoods »
HP 829 scale you h. Ida hyl, where
HP 1129 observed and maintained in more h. degree
Cor. 24 poysoned Ambition (rooted in h. mindes)
Cor. 482 that Romes h. worth to Affrique did extend
Cor. 1109 the conquering Tyrant, h. in Fortunes grace

Cor. 1300 for *h.* Jove that guideth all, when
Cor. 1529 for *h.* Jove the heavens among
Jer. 8 with this *h.* staffe of office
Jer. 59 shake the Kings hie court three handfuls downe
Jer. 83 we make thee our Lord hie imbassador
Jer. 558 as the faire cheeke of *h.* authority
ST 1477 and I hope you will never grow so *h.* while I am in the office
SP 324 their Launces were coucht too hie, and
SP 654 he was overthrowne by Fortunes *h.* displeasure
SP 883 hie men and low men, thou wouldst say
SP 1382 unwise that you weare not the *h.* Sugerloafe hat
SP 1458 smooth forhead, like the table of *h.* Jove
SP 1968 for nothing but hie treason
Ard. 184 'tis now *h.* water, and he is at the quay
Ard. 853 offering me service for my *h.* attempt
JB 36 but no man was so *h.* in her books as Parker

High-Dutch.
Cor. 59 for neither could the flaxen-haird high Dutch

Higher.
VPJ 2 sprowt *h.* then the hautiest of their heads
HP 425 our Pole is the *h.*
HP 439 the Pole Antartick is the *h.* by Nature
HP 1006 controld, and at commaundment of those *h.* officers
HP 1414 compared it to some *h.* matter then an Armorie
Cor. 688 O no, our losse lyfts Caesars fortunes hyer
Jer. 21 rise *h.* and greater in thy Soveraines eies
ST 208 yet this is *h.* then my fortunes reach
ST 1721 the Prince is meditating *h.* things

Highest.
VPJ 6 it happ'ly pleasd our *h.* God in safety to preserve
HP 1118 friendship which by Aristotle is applied in the *h.*
Cor. 1125 I sweare by heaven, th' Immortals *h.* throne
Jer. 100 hard fate, when villaines sit not in the *h.* state
ST 875 yet is he at the *h.* now he is dead
ST 1027 and at our *h.* never joy we so
ST 1610 wings, that mounts me up unto the *h.* heavens

High-honoured.
Jer. 105 and we rejected that were once high honored

Highly.
HP Ded. of that which Tassos pen so *h.* gracde
HP 105 highlie favoured of the good Cardinall Vercellis
HP 107 in these quarters *h.* are accou[n]ted
ST 1934 your highnes *h.* shall content his Majestie
Ard. 737 Arden of Feversham hath *h.* wronged me
Ard. 1400 ay, my good lord, and *h.* bound to you

High-minded.
SP 139 orecome with valour these high minded knights

Highness.
Jer. 43 I thanke your highnes. Then, my Gracious leedge
Jer. 62 I humbly thanke your highnes
Jer. 84 your highnes cirkels me with honors boundes
Jer. 772 your highnes may doe well to barre his speech
ST 1342 or els his Highnes hardly shall deny
ST 1676 his highnes and my father were resolv'd
ST 1695 least that his highnes should have found you there
ST 1883 now last (dread Lord) heere hath his highnes sent
ST 1934 therein your highnes highly shall content his
ST 2308 or heere, or where your highnes thinks it good
SP 556 after his Highnes sweares it shall be so?
SP 561 his highnes gave me leave to speake my will
SP 567 but gave my censure, as his highnesse bad
SP 580 your Highnesse knowes I speake in dutious love
SP 581 your Highnesse knowes I spake at your command
SP 1766 his highnes by me intreateth you, as
Jer. 4 my knee sings thanks unto your highnes bountie

Jer. 39 stand firme within your highnes thoughts
ST 1085 your highnes sonne, L[or]d Balthazar doth live
ST 1090 are happie witnesses of his highnes health
ST 1095 these are his highnes farther articles
ST 1329 your Highnes man, my Lord
ST 2793 and lets thee wit by me his highnes will
SP 566 and for his highnesse vowe, I crost it not
SP 1925 lord Marshal, it is his highnes pleasure

High-prized.
Jer. 328 thy masters hy prized love unto our hart is

Hight.
ST 11 which *h.* sweet Bel-imperia by name

Highway.
HP 1225 neere to any high way or common street

Hill.
HP 829 ‹ scale you high Ida hyl, where ›
Ard. 672 I see more company coming down the *h.*
Ard. 1150 and I upon a little rising *h.* stood
Ard. 1500 one of you stay my horse at the top of the *h.*
Ard. 1725 I hope to see him one day hanged upon a *h.*
HP 1219 or whether they be guirt or environed with hylles
HP 1223 or whether it lie steepeward downe the hyls
ST 121 that vallies, hills, and rivers made rebound

Hilts.
Ard. 1970 when he should have locked with both his *h.*

Hind.
Ard. 1123 the next time that I meet the *h.*
HP 1011 the rest, that are thy Hyndes and meaner servaunts
Ard. 1323 go, get thee gone, a copesmate for thy hinds

Hinder.
ST 391 yet teares and sighes, I feare, will *h.* me
ST 609 *h.* me not what ere you heare or see
ST 1894 away, Lorenzo, *h.* me no more
SP 751 *h.* my teares from falling on the ground
Ard. 136 *h.* our meetings when we would confer
Jer. 618 for company hinders loves conference

Hinderance.
HP 345 not onely a hynderaunce to the Mariner
HP 1275 by some mischance or hynderaunce whatsoever

Hindered.
HP 1314 may not thereby be anoyd or hyndered
ST Bal. 94 by Lorenzos bad intent I hindred was

Hinderer.
ST 683 glad, that I know the *h.* of my love

Hindereth.
Ard. 1450 as *h.* the passage of my speech

Hindering.
Ard. 2156 take this for *h.* Mosbie's love and mine

Hippon.
Cor. Arg. 26 that drave him backe to *H.*, a Towne in Affrique

Hire.
VPJ 70 as their purpose bloody was, so shamefull was their *h.*
Jer. 635 I had my hier, and thou shalt have thy due
Jer. 755 to kill Andrea, which *h.* kild himselfe
SP 1908 Your selfe procured us. — Is this our hier?
Ard. 522 but *h.* some cutter for to cut him short
Ard. 567 I gave him ten pound for to *h.* knaves

Hired.
Jer. 478 well, Sir; — ‹ and has *h.* one to murder you ›
Jer. 484 ‹ and has *h.* one to murder you ›
Jer. 514 ‹ and has *h.* one to murder you ›
Jer. 754 then *h.* me with gold — O fate, thou elfe
Ard. (Title) *h.* two desperate rufflans, Black Will and
Ard. 2302 I *h.*-Black Will and Shakebag, rufflans both

Hireling.
HP 30 giving my Horse to a hyreling that came with me

Histories.
HP 972 if thou hast perused *H.*, and redd of that
History.
HP 1448 what Theucidides hath observed in the proem of his Historie
ST 2492 be not a historie to after times
SP 13 the historie of brave Erastus and his Rodian Dame?
SP 1740 for the historie prooves me cheefe actor in this tragedie
Hit.
Jer. 702 I hot, yet mist; twas I mistooke my part
Jer. 739 for had I hot it right, Andrea had line tbere
SP 184 *h.* the haughtie challenger, and strooke him dead
Ard. 1413 and he supposed a cannon-bullet *h.* him
Jer. 431 all fals out for the purpose : all hits jumpe
Hitherto.
SP 951 hetherto all goes well; but, if I be taken
SP 1433 for hetherto have I reaped little pleasure
SP 2113 ah heavens, that *h.* have smilde on me
Hive.
SP 106 though like a Gnat amongst a *h.* of Bees
Ard. 1245 and for his pains I'll *h.* him up a while
HP 174 some store of hyves for Bees
Ho.
Jer. 174 *h.*, Pedringano
ST 612 *H.*, Pedringano. — Signior. — Vien qui presto
STA 929 Roderigo, *h.*
SP 422 *h.*, God save you, sir
SP 846 *h.*, Piston
Hoard.
Ard. 478 so he may scrape and *h.* up in his pouch
Ard. 221 my saving husband hoards up bags of gold
Hoist.
SP 1923 and then will thou and I *h.* saile to Rhodes
Hold.
VPJ 12 admire, and daily *h.* thy name in reverence
HP 157 « I *h.* it » (quoth I) « a happy thing to
HP 237 you ought to *h.* your selfe no less satisfied
HP 256 I holde it rather a trouble to the stomack
HP 406 one of them that *h.* the contrary
HP 588 holde her his superior
HP 872 ought to holde them satisfied with labor
HP 1332 « Hard at their distaffe doth she *h.* her maids »
Cor. 844 nor longer *h.* us in this servitude
Cor. 1638 resolv'd by force to *h.* us hard at work
Cor. 1672 that tyer'd would nere *h.* out, if once they
Jer. 44 I *h.* it meete, by way of Embassage, to
Jer. 207 mischiefe within my breast, more then my bulke can *h.*
Jer. 1041 I can *h.* no longer : come, come
Jer. 1044 I *h.* three wounds to one. — Content : a lay
Jer. 1054 for by this act I *h.* thy arm devine
ST 361 holde thou thy peace
ST 573 let reason holde you in your wonted joy
ST 832 the starres, thou seest, *h.* backe their twinckling shine
ST 1079 stay, *h.* a while
ST 1260 now, Pedringano, bid thy Pistoll holde
ST 1261 and holde on, Fortune, once more favour me·
ST 1350 thus hopefull men, that meane to holde their owne
STA 1776 the very arme that did *h.* up our house
STA 2026 I, sir; no man did *h.* a sonne so deere
ST 2703 to *h.* excusde thy negligence in
ST 2895 O hearken, Vice-roy — holde, Hieronimo
STA 2939 see, here's a goodly nowse will *h.* them all
SP 481 I pray you, sir, *h.* your hands, and, as I
SP 529 I *h.* it not good pollicie to call your forces home
SP 776 I can no longer hould my patience
SP 1680 Pistoll proofe? ile trie if it will *h.* out pin proofe

SP 2025 but I love Basilisco, as one I hould more worthy
SP 2105 for kissing her whom I do hould so deare
Ard. 39 (for dear I *h.* her love, as dear as heaven)
Ard. 1341 and *h.* no other sect but such devotion
Ard. 1568 but that I *h.* thee dearer than my life
Ard. 1905 I pray thee, gentle Franklin, *h.* thy peace
Ard. 2013 and *h.* him with a long tale of strange news
VPJ 49 her thred still holds, thine perisht though unspun
ST 1836 and twixt his teeth he holdes a fire-brand
SP 1679 I tell thee, my skin holds out Pistoll proofe
Puck 7 that yor Lp holds me in concerning Atheisme
Puck 57 holdes yor honors & the state in that dewe reverence
Holdest.
Jer. 927 thy valiansie, and all that thou holdst great
Jer. 989 by all that thou holdst deere upon this earth
Holdeth.
HP 949 the right hande *h.* and disposeth any sort of
Cor. 1224 for Caesar *h.* signiorie too deere
Holding.
ST 243 but tell me (for their *h.* makes me doubt)
SP 349 why, my Page stands *h.* him by the bridle
Hole.
SP 369 it will be better then the Fox in the *h.* for me
Holidays.
SP 54 when didst thou goe to Church on hollidaies
Holloed.
Ard. 1412 when he that gave it him *h.* in his ear
Hollow.
Cor. 711 but all amaz'd, with fearefull, *h.* eyes
Hollow-eyed.
Ard. 690 hawk-nosed and very *h.*
Holp.
Cor. 302 Pompey, what holpe it thee, (say, deerest life)
Cor. 303 what holpe thy warlike valiant minde t'encounter
Cor. 305 what holpe it thee that under thy commaund thou
Cor. 311 what holpe it that thou saw'st, when thou wert young
Cor. 319 alas, and here-withall what holpe it thee that
ST 1352 he runnes to kill whome I have holpe to catch
ST 1560 « I holpe to murder Don Horatio too »
ST 1561 holpe he to murder mine Horatio?
Holpen.
HP 1262 may be *h.* many waies, and made to keep long
Holy.
Cor. 1704 that they will blesse our *h.* purposes
ST 2754 and *h.* Mahomet, our sacred Prophet
ST 3052 blaspheming Gods and all their *h.* names
SP 513 for by the *h.* Alcaron I sweare
SP 560 what twere to thwart a Monarchs *h.* oath
SP 667 O *h.* oath, faire hand, and sugred kisse
SP 1141 I wish that fortune of our *h.* wars would
SP 1401 if captivate, then forst from *h.* faith
SP 2225 for *h.* fates have graven it in their tables
Ard. 1237 and *h.* Church rites makes us two but one
Ard. 1336 the *h.* word that had converted me
Ard. 1517 Arden, thou hast wondrous *h.* luck
JB 2 the *h.* Scriptures doe manifest
Homage.
Cor. 868 earth, did *h.* to it with his deerest blood
Jer. 37 but his slack *h.*, that we most repine
Jer. 338 and find it much dishonord by base *h.*
ST 100 tribute and wonted *h.* therewithall
ST 181 that, if with *h.* tribute be well paide
Home.
VPJ 20 long maist thou live, and heaven be thy *h.*
HP 143 « Hyed *h.* at night and fild his bord with delicats unbought »

Jer. 653 welcome *h.*, Lord embassador
Jer. 974 ride [*h.*] all Conquerours, when the fight is done
Jer. 975 especially ride thee *h.* so, my son
ST Bal. 17 then left I warre, and stayde at *h.*
ST 753 that summons *h.* distresfull travellers
STA 940 and bid my sonne Horatio to come *h.*
SP 514 Ile call my Souldiers *h.* from Persia
SP 516 call *h.* my hardie, dauntlesse Janisaries
SP 518 call *h.* my Bassowes and my men of war
SP 530 not good pollicie to call your forces *h.*
SP 711 weele bring you *h.*
SP 711 no, I shall soone get *h.*
SP 1736 brought him *h.* unto his native land
Ard. 108 be not afraid ; my husband is now from *h.*
Ard. 412 in hope you'll hasten him *h.*, I'll give you this
Ard. 452 I am sorry that your husband is from *h.*
Ard. 495 when he's at *h.*, then have I froward looks
Ard. 499 and when he's weary with his trugs at *h.*
Ard. 637 I hope, now Master Arden is from *h.*
Ard. 789 come I once at *h.*, I'll rouse her
Ard. 999 then stay with me in London ; go not *h.*
Ard. 1002 at *h.* or not at *h.*, where'er I be
Ard. 1441 for 'twill be very late ere we get *h.*
Ard. 1491 you and your friend come *h.* and sup with me
Ard. 1586 how doth my mistress and all at *h.* ?
Ard. 1817 now that our horses are gone *h.* before
Ard. 2014 that he may not come *h.* till supper-time
Ard. 2015 I'll fetch Master Arden *h.*, and we like friends
Ard. 2027 take no care of that ; send you him *h.*
Ard. 2087 husband, what mean you to bring Mosbie *h.* ?
Ard. 2231 and if you find him, send him *h.* to me
Ard. 2282 Master Mayor, have you brought my husband *h.* ?
Ard. 2293 were my husband at *h.*, you would not offer this
Ard. 1156 and rounded me with that beguiling *h.*
Ard. 1550 *h.* is a wild cat to a wandering wit
JB 137 husband she must needs goe *h.* to her lodging
Ard. 1582 they'll be your ferrymen to long *h.*
Cor. 920 with usurie for all misdeeds pay *h.* the penaltie
Ard. 447 they shall be soundly fee'd to pay him *h.*
Ard. 516 I'll pay him *h.*, whatever hap to me
ST 2101 strike, and strike *h.*, where wrong is offred thee

Home-born.
Cor. 676 then, home-borne houshold gods, and ye good spirits

Homely.
HP 1017 to see such grosse or *h.* kind of fare
Jer. 538 much doth your presence grace our *h.* roofe
ST 2420 Hieronimo, frequent my *h.* house
Ard. 1868 if *h.*, I seem sluttish in thine eye

Homer.
HP Ind. 85 *H.*, why he called Wine sweete and why bitter
HP Ind. 86 *H.*, what properties he gave to Wine
HP 263 the banquets of Agamemnon, as we read in *H.*
HP 292 which I have hearde observed of *H.*
HP 309 the Wines were termed sweete of *H.*
HP 325 that it is called sweete of *H.*
HP 326 afterward *H.* calleth it black
HP 738 spake *H.*, saying : « O my beloved father in law
HP 755 when *H.* faigned that Juno, taking away Venus garter
HP 1348 in which example he followed *H.*, who

Homeward.
Jer. 1184 march we now *h.* with victory
SP 544 to sound a *h.*, dull, and harsh retreate

Homicide.
Cor. 908 there dooth abide all treason, luxurie, and *h.*
ST 1078 injurious traytour, monstrous *h.*
SP 2068 thou wicked tirant, thou murtherer, accursed *h.*

ST 2675 tell me no more : — O monstrous homicides

Honest.
HP Ind. 90 *h.* recreation not to be with-held from Women
HP 245 an *h.* advocat to pleade my cause
HP 675 of *h.* women desirous to content their Husbands
HP 683 fitter for a stage or Theater then the person of an *h.* Matron
HP 725 where other *h.* women and those of credit doo assemble
HP 729 to forbid her those *h.* recreations and desires
HP 734 so bold and hardy that she lay aside *h.* shame
HP 734 *h.* shame (a decent thing in *h.* wome[n])
HP 747 that which moderatly springs of *h.* Matrimonie
HP 771 wyth *h.* and enterchaungable love
HP 1477 and calleth that order of the Publicans most *h.*
HP 1481 that forme of merchandize is just and *h.*
HP 1516 the *h.* Phisitian will heale as much as hee can
Jer. 208 my names an *h.* name, a Courtiers name
Jer. 281 murder Andrea, *h.* lord ? Impious villayns
Jer. 292 strang newes : Lorenzo is becom an *h.* man
Jer. 297 « Lorenzo is become an honnest man »
Jer. 312 knaves longer reaches have then *h.* men
Jer. 469 « yet I speake not this of Lorenzo, for hees an *h.* Lord »
Jer. 470 'S foot, write him « *h.* Lord »
Jer. 472 what, write him « *h.* Lord » ? ile not agree
Jer. 477 « Lorenzoes an *h.* Lord »
Jer. 488 « yet hees an *h.* dukes son »
Jer. 490 « but not the *h.* son of a Duke »
Jer. 491 « but not the *h.* »
Jer. 513 « hees an *h.* Lord, and has hired one to »
Jer. 515 « yet hees an *h.* Dukes sonne :
Jer. 516 « but not the *h.* son of a Duke »
SP 481 and, as I am an *h.* man, Ile doe the best I can
SP 779 are there no *h.* drops in all thy cheekes
SP 954 for this once, ile be *h.* against my will
SP 1527 yet give me leave in *h.* sort to court thee
SP 1878 where filthie lust must murther *h.* love
Ard. 248 oh, you are an *h.* man of your word !
Ard. 1292 to *h.* Arden's wife, not Arden's *h.* wife
Ard. 1307 I left the marriage of an *h.* maid
Ard. 1488 my *h.* friend that came along with me
Ard. 1494 a gentleman, my *h.* friend
Ard. 1497 and bring your *h.* friend along with you ?
JB 77 although the *h.* young man loved hir tenderly
JB 155 esteemed her a very *h.* woman, although

Honester.
ST 1485 to trusse up many an *h.* man then either thou or he

Honestly.
HP Ind. 80 gaine *h.* made by the Mistresse of the house
HP 1306 but *h.* gaine, which is as requisite in her as

Honesty.
HP 865 better their estate with praise and *h.*
Jer. 294 I, ist not wondrous to have *h.* in hel ?
Jer. 298 for *h.*, spoken in derision, points out knavery
Jer. 494 « and *h.* in the bottome of a seller »
Jer. 495 « and *h.* »
Jer. 517 « and *h.* in the bottome of a seller »
Jer. 519 to say, knavery in the Court and *h.* in a cheese house
ST 1401 by my bare *h.*, heeres nothing but the
Puck 29 for p[er]son, quallities, or honestie, besides he

Honey.
Jer. 215 my sweet mischiefe ? hunny damnation, how ?
SP 1472 the sound is hunnie, but the sence is gall
SP 550 whose Hunny is not worth the taking up

Honey-sweet.
ST 760 but, honie sweet and honorable love

Honied.

Jer. 51 if friendly phraises, *h.* speech, bewitching accent
Jer. 606 and so bewitch her with my *h.* speech
ST 30 there, pleasing Cerberus with *h.* speech
Honour.
Eng. Parn. 10 who neither fayth, *h.*, nor right respects
Eng. Parn. 11 *H.* indeede, and all things yeeld to death
HP 130 *h.* and service alwaies hath beene used
HP 136 who desired to doo me honor, beeing a straunger
HP 585 more honor and esteeme of her then of his equall
HP 589 which honor is not yet accompanied with reverence
HP 628 to knowe howe to honor and obey her husband
HP 861 feare and love of God, honor of their Parents
Cor. Ded. 16 president of *h.*, magnamitie, and love
Cor. 387 till, fraught with yeeres and honor both at once
Cor. 1113 leades the conquered honor of the people yok't
Cor. 1218 to grace themselves with honor of the game
Cor. 1283 and honor him with hymnes therefore
Cor. 1332 whose honor, got by famous victories, hath
Cor. 1347 tell the foming Seas the *h.* of our fight?
Cor. 1538 so wrong'd of the honor him belong'd
Cor. 1668 bravely to fight for honor of the day
Cor. 2010 (a house of *h.* and antiquitie)
Jer. 30 age ushers honor; tis no shame; confesse
Jer. 106 I hate Andrea, cause he aimes at honor
Jer. 130 I have hard of your honor, gentle brest
Jer. 132 what, not to have honor bestowed on me?
Jer. 133 O yes: but not a wandring honor, deere
Jer. 135 could honor melt it selfe into thy vaines
Jer. 144 and will leane much to honor
Jer. 190 all honor on Andreas steps attende
Jer. 194 it is for honor; prethee let him goe
Jer. 305 could choke bright honor in a skabard grave?
Jer. 318 and do him all the honor that belonges him
Jer. 573 now, by the honor of Casteels true house
Jer. 624 resolved to loose both life and honor at one cast
Jer. 763 to make the heire of honor melt and bleede
Jer. 780 he will redeeme his honor lost with swordes
Jer. 819 to be denide our honor, why, twere base
Jer. 829 prove honor to sore above the pitch of love
Jer. 855 honor, your countries reputation, your lives freedome
Jer. 864 to die with honor, scorne captivity
Jer. 926 I bind thee, Don Andrea, by thy honer
Jer. 1126 come, noble rib of honor, valliant carcasse
Jer. 1143 smeard with foes bloud, all for the maisters honer
ST Bal. 14 and wonne great *h.* in the fielde
ST Bal. 18 and gave my *h.* to my sonne
ST Bal. 23 and with great *h.* did present him to
ST 458 without respect of *h.* in the fight?
ST 519 he promised us, in honor of our guest
ST 789 I hope his presence heere will *h.* us
ST 1124 and, Alexandro, let us honor thee with
STA 1197 I reserve your favour for a greater honor
ST 1314 if ought concernes our *h.* and your owne?
ST 1579 is this the *h.* that thou didst my Sonne?
ST 1672 I sought to save your *h.* and mine owne
ST 1673 mine *h.*? why, Lorenzo, wherein ist that
ST 1680 and wherein was mine *h.* toucht in that?
STA 1781 and his great minde, too ful of *H.*
ST 2337 what *h.* wert in this assemblie
ST 2753 Bashaw, that Rhodes is ours, yield heavens the *h.*
ST 2900 upon mine *h.*, thou shalt have no harme
SP 104 in *h.* of the Prince of Cipris nuptials
SP 117 that carry *h.* graven in their helmes
SP 151 for in thy honor hither are they come
SP 373 the prize and honor of the day is his
SP 488 take thou the honor, and give me the chaine

SP 640 each one by armes to honor his beloved
SP 641 nay, one alone to honor his beloved
SP 1050 why so? I am in honor bound to combat him
SP 1083 I, upon my *h.*
SP 1125 at tilt, who woone the honor of the day?
SP 1193 *h.* should force disdaine to roote it out
SP 1220 and spare me not, for then thou wrongst my *h.*
SP 1359 the greatest honor Fortune could affoord
SP 1416 newes to our *h.*, and to thy content
SP 1912 interd with *h.* in a kingly sepulcher
SP 2195 their bodies buried, yet they *h.* me
Ard. 190 made shipwreck of mine *h.* for thy sake?
Ard. 348 upon whose general bruit all *h.* hangs
Ard. 1407 it is not for mine *h.* to bear this
Ard. 2030 next unto Mosbie do I *h.* thee
Cor. 1069 now Caesar, swolne with honors heate
Jer. 84 your highnes cirkels me with honors boundes
SP 143 assembled heere in thirsty honors cause
SP 643 came short in reaching of faire honors marke
SP 935 whom honors title forst me to misdoe
SP 1246 whom I in honours cause have reft of life
SP 1396 of honors titles, or of wealth, or gaine
SP 1570 fire, that lay with honours hand rackt up in ashes
Ard. 1552 that honour's title nor a lord's command
Cor. 265 Pompey, the fame that ranne of thy frayle honors
Cor. 327 destinie (envious of all thine honors) gave thee mee
Cor. 370 return'd due honors to our Common-wealth
Cor. 661 our Common-wealth, our Empyre, and our honors
Cor. 1698 our goods, our honors, and our auncient lawes
Jer. 182 you drowne my honores in those flowing watters
Jer. 1098 honors in bloud best swim
ST 1094 « For both our honors and thy benefite »
Cor. Ded. 18 I shall beseech your *H.* to repaire with
Cor. Ded. 25 in some kind service to your *H.*
STA 1201 I ha' been too slacke, too tardie, too remisse unto your honor
Ard. 1492 I beseech your *h.* pardon me
Ard. 1499 to-morrow we'll wait upon your *h.*
Ard. 1503 not hanged, God save your *h.*
Ard. 1548 for so his *h.* late commanded me
Ard. 1558 I am sure his *h.* will welcome her
Cor. Ded. 27 yours Honors in all humblenes T. K.
ST 667 your Honors liberalitie deserves my duteous service
Ard. 1485 your honour's always! bound to do you service
Puck 4 reteyning me wᵗʰout yᵒʳ honoʳˢ former pryvitie
Puck 57 holdes yᵒʳ honoʳˢ & the state in that dewe reverence
Honourable.
Puck 5 so is it nowe R[ight] Ho[nourable] that
Puck 51 but whatsoever I have felt R[ight] Ho[nourable]
HP Ind. 5 arte of weaving *h.*
HP 393 having honorable guests he cannot commende his
Cor. Ded. 9 perfectly assur'd of your *h.* favours past
Cor. 1675 whose silver hayres and honorable front were
Cor. 1701 thinke how this day the honorable Dames
Jer. 249 indeede Andrea is but poore, though honorable
ST 228 yet shalt thou know that Spaine is honorable
ST 760 but, honie sweet and *h.* love
ST 1879 an argument of honorable care to keepe his freend
ST 2278 and welcome all his honorable traine
ST 2283 so is it that mine honorable Neece
ST 2409 the hope of Spaine, mine honorable freend?
Ard. 491 your *h.* friends, nor what you brought?
Ard. 669 for I keep that same *h.* mind still
Honourably.
Cor. 930 yet Caesar speakes of Pompey honourablie
Honoured.

VPJ 13 honour'd art, Princely behaviour, zeale to good
Cor. Ded. To the vertuously noble, and rightly *h.* Lady, The
Cor. 863 whom I have honored with true devotion
Cor. 881 to interr within his Elders Tombe that *h.* her
Jer. 200 honord promotion is the sap of love
Jer. 345 we may redeeme with honored valiansie
Jer. 988 by thy worthy bloud, thy honored faith
Jer. 1140 prepare for honord Funerall for thy melting corse
Jer. 1181 these honord rights and worthy duties spent
ST 424 I saw him *h.* with due funerall
ST 514 for well thou hast deserved to be honored
SP 93 the Knight of Malta, *h.* for his worth
SP 389 Erastus, be thou *h.* for this deed
SP 417 thus to disgrace thy honored name
SP 998 and honored with Balme and funerall
SP 1133 so well I loved and *h.* the man
Jer. 105 and we rejected that were once high honored
Honouring.
Jer. 7 and thank my leedge for honering me
Hoods.
HP 828 ‹ and your high Priests hats are made like *h.* ›
Hook.
Jer. 310 to hooke the divell from his flaming cell
Hope.
VPJ 24 and al my good is but vaine *h.* of gaine
VPJ 42 thy good God knowes thy *h* , thy hap and all
VPJ 85 on thee we ground our *h.,* through thee we
HP 382 inferior to Autumn as *h.* is to effects
HP 1398 may without impeach (I *h.)* bee profitablye recounted
HP 1670 ‹ For in their Gold their *h.* beguiled lies ›
Cor. 469 with *h.* to have him to be reviv'd by them
Cor. 648 afford no *h.* of future happinesse
Cor. 687 our losse (I *h.)* hath satis-fide theyr ire
Cor. 773 descends to hell, with *h.* to rise againe
Cor. 921 this is the *h.* that feeds my haples daies
Cor. 999 deprive me wholy of the *h.* of death
Cor. 1042 in *h.* he shall his wish obtaine
Cor. 1587 but *h.* the best, and harken to his newes
Cor. 1890 yea, thee, my latest fortunes firmest *h.*
Jer. 260 I have no *h.* of everlasting height
Jer. 439 and willing *h.* to see your vertue rise
Jer. 948 I *h.,* boy, thou wilt gaine a brother too
Jer. 1195 I *h.* thers never a Jew among you all
ST Bal. 49 the Villaine then, for *h.* of gaine
ST 116 both furnish well, both full of *h.* and feare
ST 209 my loving thoughts did never *h.* but hope
ST 319 why waile I then, wheres *h.* of no redresse?
ST 371 thou hadst some *h.* to weere this Diadome
ST 383 and *h.* for guerdon of my villany
ST 570 their *h.* into dispaire, their peace to warre
ST 661 in *h.* thine oath is true, heeres thy reward
ST 789 I *h.* his presence heere will honour us
ST 1033 the onely *h.* of our successive line
ST 1056 Yet *h.* the best. — Tis heaven is my *h.*
ST 1058 to yield me *h.* of any of her mould
ST 1116 but for reward and *h.* to be preferd
ST 1232 when thinges shall alter, as I *h.* they wil
ST 1476 and I *h.* you will never grow so high while I am in the office
ST 1513 why, wherefore stay you ? have you *h.* of life ?
ST 1649 why, and my Lord, I *h.* you heard me say
ST 1726 wherein I see no haven to rest my *h.*
ST 2369 wherein my *h.* and heavens faire beautie lies
ST 2404 Hieronimo, I *h.* you have no cause
ST 2409 the *h.* of Spaine, mine honorable freend ?
ST 2432 and that, I *h.,* olde grudges are forgot

ST 2882 heere lay my *h.,* and heere my *h.* hath ende
ST 2836 but *h.,* hart, treasure, joy, and blisse
ST 2994 the whole succeeding *h.* that Spaine expected
SP 648 whereon depended all his *h.* and joy
SP 1398 no, no ; my *h.* full long agoe was lost
SP 1519 but, if thou love me, and have *h.* to win
SP 1614 but whilst he lives there is no *h.* in her
SP 2081 didst thou misdoe him in *h.* to win Perseda ?
SP 2094 that Soliman slew Erastus in *h.* to win Perseda
Ard. 106 I *h.* he brings me tidings of my love
Ard. 144 I *h.* you'll think on me
Ard. 211 would I had never tried, but lived in *h.* !
Ard. 357 and then, I *h.,* they'll cease, and at last confess
Ard. 412 in *h.* you'll hasten him home, I'll give you this
Ard. 415 I *h.* he is not jealous of me now
Ard. 449 I *h.* 'tis one that comes to put
Ard. 637 I *h.,* now Master Arden is from home
Ard. 685 now I am going to London upon *h.* to
Ard. 1434 and in that *h.* I'll leave you for an hour
Ard. 1619 then this, I *h.,* if all the rest do fail
Ard. 1724 I *h.* to see him one day hanged upon a hill
Ard. 1995 that will, I *h.,* invent some surer means
Ard. 2416 seeing no *h.* on earth, in heaven is my *h.*
Ard. 2433 Gentlemen, we *h.* you'll pardon this naked tragedy
JB 43 and seeing no *h.* of her good will and favour
Cor. 112 but we, soone tickled with such flattring hopes
Cor. 141 what toucheth us the treasure or the hopes
Cor. 291 and all your hopes with hap may be effected
Cor. 336 none others hopes with mischiefe may entrap ?
Cor. 349 then, as the Heavens (by whom our hopes are guided)
Cor. 671 with feareles harts do guard our Romaine hopes ?
Cor. 794 harts (joyn'd with the right) did re-enforce our hopes
Cor. 1072 and will not see that Fortuue can her hopes defeate
Cor. 1887 since all our hopes are by the Gods beguil'd
Cor. 1940 sith in this widdow-hood of all my hopes I
Cor. 1976 now is our haples time of hopes expired
Cor. 2005 widdowed of all my hopes, my haps, my husbands
Jer. 234 how we may crose my Sisters loving hopes
Jer. 258 what dares not hee do that neer hopes to inherit ?
ST 595 I, but her hopes aime at some other end
ST 597 I, but perhaps she hopes some nobler mate
ST 720 my hart, with feares and hopes long tost
ST 1381 but let him wisely keepe his hopes unknowne
STA 1777 our hopes were stored up in him
ST 3009 I, now my hopes have end in their effects
SP 1055 but hopes the coystrell to escape me so ?
SP 1996 I know the letcher hopes to have my love
Hoped.
ST 486 I reapt more grace then I deserv'd or hop'd
ST 1633 till heaven, as I have *h.,* shall set me free
Hopeful.
Cor. 1934 whose hopefull life preserv'd our happines
ST 1350 thus hopefull men, that meane to holde their owne
ST 1559 ‹ wonne by rewards and hopefull promises ›
Hopeless.
Cor. 214 must hie, hopeles to hide them in a haples tombe ?
Cor. 1862 and hopeles trusteth to the trustles windes
ST 1104 sav'd the hopeles life which thou, Villuppo, sought
ST 2826 the hopeles father of a hapless Sonne
Hoping.
Jer. 502 ‹ thus *h.* you will not be murdred, and you ›
Jer. 503 ‹ thus *h.* you will ›
Jer. 522 ‹ thus *h.* you will not be murdered ›
Ard. 761 ‹ *h.* in God you be in good health ›
Ard. 773 ‹ thus *h.* you will let my passions penetrate ›
Horatio.

Jer. 5 come hether, boy *H.*; fould thy joynts
Jer. 61 Ide rather choose *H.* were he not so young
Jer. 164 *H.* knowes I go to knit friends
Jer. 178 *H.*, be in my absence my deare selfe
Jer. 193 O, good *H.*, no
Jer. 274 come hether, boy *H.*, didst thou here them?
Jer. 443 come, write, *H.*, write
Jer. 455 fie, fie, *H.*: what, is your pen foule?
Jer. 480 art thou a scholler, Don *H.*
Jer. 506 boy *H.*, write ‹ leave › bending in the hams
Jer. 524 *H.*, hast thou written ‹ leave › bending in the hams
Jer. 525 'S foote, no, *H.*; thou hast made him straddle
Jer. 531 wax, wax, *H.*: I had neede wax too
Jer. 570 send it with speede, *H.*, linger not
Jer. 669 son *H.*, see Andrea slaine
Jer. 704 *H.*, twas well, as fortune stands
Jer. 718 mark, mark, *H.*: a villaine guard a villaine
Jer. 804 with whome I rancke spritely *H.*?
Jer. 966 *H.*
Jer. 970 worthy Rogero, sprightly *H.*
Jer. 973 but blame me not, Ide have *H.* most
Jer. 1058 had not *H.* plaid some Angels part
Jer. 1084 O, I am slaine; helpe me, *H.*
Jer. 1112 *H.*, you tender me part
Jer. 1163 to thank *H.*, and commend his hart
ST Bal. (Title) containing the lamentable murders of *H.* and
ST Bal. 19 *H.*, my sweet onely childe
ST Bal. 26 desir'd *H.* to relate the death of
ST Bal. 48 sayd with *H.* shee's combinde
ST (Title) containing the lamentable end of Don *H.*, and
ST 25 by Don *H.*, our Knight Marshals sonne
ST 167 prickt forth *H.*, our Knight-Marshals sonne
ST 224 and thou, *H.*, thou art welcome too
ST 273 *H.*, thou didst force him first to yeeld
ST 284 that Don *H.* beare us company
ST 286 *H.*, leave him not that loves thee so
'ST 384 Signior *H.*, this is the place and houre
ST 436 and (Madame) Don *H.* will not slacke
ST 441 I, goe, *H.*, leave me heere alone
ST 444 from whence *H.* proves my second love?
ST 450 Ile love *H.*, my Andreas freend
ST 484 thanks, good *H.*, take it for thy paines
ST 485 Signior *H.* stoopt in happie time
ST 513 Signior *H.*, waite thou upon our Cup
ST 649 oh stay, my Lord, she loves *H.*
ST 650 what, Don *H.*, our Knight Marshals sonne?
ST 689 I thinke *H.* be my destinde plague
ST 731 why stands *H.* speecheles all this while?
ST 800 it was *H.*, our Knight Marshals Sonne
ST 840 I, but if Flora spie *H.* heere
ST 872 I loved *H*, but he loved not me
ST 891 alas, it is *H.*, my sweet sonne
ST 905 O poore *H.*, what hadst thou misdonne
ST 910 in leesing my *H.*, my sweet boy
ST 915 what world of griefe; my sonne *H.*!
STA 940 and bid my sonne *H.* to come home
STA 946 it is my Lord *H.*
STA 951 that this had beene my soone *H.*
STA 974 O sweet *H.*, O my deerest sonne
ST 1013 but tis my freend *H.* that is slaine
ST 1163 what cause had they *H.* to maligne?
ST 1318 touching the death of Don *H.*
ST 1560 ‹ I holpe to murder Don *H.* too ›
ST 1561 holpe he to murder mine *H.*?
ST 1573 both her, my selfe, *H.*, and themselves
ST 1600 *H.*, O, wheres *H.*?

ST 1602 with outrage for your sonne *H.*
ST 1611 to heaven: I, there sits my *H.*
ST 1618 the murderers, that slew *H.*?
ST 1629 me for thy freend *H.* handled thus
ST 1686 found Bel-imperia with *H.*
ST 1693 to thrust *H.* forth my fathers way
STA 1772 O, but my *H.* grew out of reach of these
ST 1885 his ransome due to Don *H.*
ST 1886 *H.*, who cals *H.*?
ST 1888 heere, see it given to *H.*
ST 1912 pride conceived of yong *H.* his Sonne
ST 1920 for what he hath, *H.* shall not want
STA 1942 distraught, since his *H.* dyed
STA 1947 he speakes as if *H.* stood by him
STA 1949 cryes out: *H.*, Where is my *H.*?
STA 1957 yet cannot I behold my sonne *H.*
STA 1982 that same night when my *H.* was murdered?
STA 1997 where my *H.* dyed, where he was murdered?
STA 2053 with a speaking looke to my sonne *H.*
STA 2082 finde it to be my sonne *H.*
ST 2175 oh my Sonne, oh my Sonne *H.*
ST 2180 O no, not this; *H.*, this was thine
ST 2201 to neglect the sweet revenge of thy *H.*?
ST 2227 and art thou come, *H.*, from the deapth
ST 2239 but let me looke on my *H.*
ST 2244 *H.*, thou art older then thy Father
ST 2269 for with a cord *H.* was slaine
ST 2392 my Lords, I thanke you for *H.*
ST 2459 Hieronimo cannot forget his sonne *H.*
ST 2478 is this the love thou bearst *H.*?
ST 2514 and in that letter how *H.* died
ST 2702 to heare *H.* plead with Radamant
ST 2712 the haplesse brest, that gave *H.* suck
ST 2847 upon my Sonne, my deere *H.*
ST 2858 tis like I wailde for my *H.*
ST 2910 as deare to me was my *H.*, as yours
ST 2927 hath done in murdring my *H.*
STA 2953 as deare to me was my *H.*, as yours
STA 2972 for one *H.*, if you euer knew him
ST 3011 *H.* murdered in his Fathers bower
ST 3025 Ile lead my freend *H.* through those feeldes
Jer. 17 my ledge, how like you Don Horatios spirit?
Jer. 1151 by Spaniards force, most by Horatioes might
ST Bal. 88 which show'd Horatios wofull end
ST Bal. 164 which on Horatios death depends
ST 260 my tongue should plead for young Horatios right
ST 278 Horatios house were small for all his traine
ST 435 she will be Don Horatios thankfull freend
ST 730 live, hart, to joy at fond Horatios fall
ST 845 to frame sweet musick to Horatios tale
ST 1159 ‹ Hieronimo revenge Horatios death ›
ST 1211 that hath, I feare, revealde Horatio's death
STA 1747 these slippers are not mine, they were my son Horatios
ST 1839 heele doe thee justice for Horatios death
ST 1844 who will revenge Horatios murther then?
ST 2252 and seekes not vengeance for Horatioes death
ST 2525 joyne with thee to revenge Horatioes death
ST 2865 which at Horatios death I weeping dipt within

Horn.
ST 82 and bad thee lead me through the gates of *H.*
SP 1666 even as a Cow for tickling in the horne
Ard. 1158 with that he blew an evil-sounding *h.*
Ard. 1895 why, Mosbie taunted your husband with the *h.*
Ard. 1899 the hatefull naming of the *h.*
Cor. 633 doth sing to see how Cynthia shrinks her horne
HP 690 the Hart with his fayre and bushie braunched hornes

Ard. 1607 put horns to them to make them become sheep
Ard. 1840 and yet no horned beast ; the horns are thine
Horned.
Cor. 1722 lyke Northern windes that beate the *h.* Alpes
Ard. 1840 and yet no *h.* beast ; the horns are thine
Hornsby.
Ard. 1757 shall wound my husband *H.* to the death
Horrible.
Cor. 1929 but mongst the rest, what *h.* offence
Horror.
Cor. 236 hels *h.* is mylder then mine endles discontent
Cor. 306 thou saw'st the trembling earth with *h.* mazed ?
Cor. 728 a trembling *h.*, a chyl-cold shyvering
Cor. 1333 have fild heavens fierie vaults with fright-full *h.*
Cor. 1610 the heavens are heapt with rage and *h.*
Cor. 1705 me thinks I see poore Rome in *h.* clad
Cor. 1796 him he enflam'd, and spur'd, and fild with *h.*
Jer. 666 an omynous *h.* all my vaines doth strike
STA 968 my cold bosome, that now is stiffe with *h.*
Horse.
Cor. 1717 may by our *h.* in heapes be over-throwne
SP 1157 their *h.*, I deeme them fiftie thousand strong
HP 6 to raine, I began to set spurs to my *H.*
HP 30 giving my *H.* to a hyreling that came with me
Cor. 1729 arose, and over-shadowed *h.* and man
Cor. 1831 here *h.* and man (o're-turnd) for mercy cryde
Cor. 1860 he spurrs his *h.*, and (breaking through the presse)
ST 170 but straight the Prince was beaten from his *h.*
ST 247 but first my launce did put him from his *h.*
ST 271 nephew, thou tookst his weapon and his *h.*
ST 272 his weapons and his *h.* are thy reward
ST 405 which pauncht his *h.* and dingd him to the ground
SP 95 the Moore upon his hot Barbarian *h.*
SP 131 bid my men bring my *h.*, and a dosen staves
SP 157 what is thy motto, when thou spurres thy *h.* ?
SP 232 else had my Frize-land *h.* perished
SP 331 the baye *h.* with the blew taile, and the
SP 344 it is the fury of his *h.*, not the strength of his arme
SP 348 but, syrra, wheres thy *h.* ?
SP 434 why, then, thy *H.* hath bin a Colt in his time
Ard. 50 but, as securely, presently take *h.*
Ard. 92 for yet ere noon we'll take *h.* and away
Ard. 93 ere noon he means to take *h.* and away !
Ard. 95 in the shape and likeness of a *h.* gallop
Ard. 364 sirrah Michael, see our *h.* be ready
Ard. 385 do so, and let us presently take *h.*
Ard. 711 he's now in Newgate for stealing a *h.*
Ard. 1436 back to Rochester : the *h.* halts downright
Ard. 1444 therefore have I pricked the *h.* on purpose
Ard. 1500 one of you stay my *h.* at the top of the hill
Ard. 1573 ay, your *h.* are ready, but I am not ready
Ard. 1732 that neither *h.* nor man could be discerned ?
HP 814 « to frame their horses fit for service and their »
HP 922 they differ from Horses, Mules, and other Beastes
HP 1002 to whom the busines of the stable and of horses
HP 1035 the Horsekeeper rubbe the horses and clense the stable
Cor. 1233 the stiffneckt horses champe not on the bit
Cor. 1821 every where lay Armed men, ore-trodden with theyr horses
SP 132 you shall have your horses and two dosen of staves
Ard. 88 whilst Michael fetch our horses from the field
Ard. 1572 come, Michael, are our horses ready ?
Ard. 1694 but, sirrah Will, what horses are those that passed ?
Ard. 1733 yet did we hear their horses as they passed
Ard. 1817 now that our horses are gone home before
Horseback.

HP 113 anon there came the Father on horsebacke
SP 236 I fought on *h.* with an hundred Kernes
Ard. 772 « as a plaster of pitch to a galled horse-back »
Horse-colt.
STA 1761 a young Bacon, or a fine little smooth *H.*
Horsed, *see* **Unhorsed.**
Horsekeeper.
HP 1010 that may be Stewardes, *H.*, and Bailieffe
HP 1035 the *H.* rubbe the horses and clense the stable
Horsemen's.
ST 131 Don Pedro, their chiefe Horsemens Corlonell
Horsing.
SP 453 should have ten shillings for *h.* a Gentlewoman
Hose.
Jer. 877 thou man, from thy *h.* downe ward, scarse so much
Jer. 886 my *h.* will scarse make thee a standing coller
Jer. 1117 I could whip al these, were there *h.* downe
Ard. 698 a pair of thread-bare velvet *h.*, seam rent
Hospital.
HP 1401 I entred the Hospitall, wherein, though
Jer. 220 from rich that die and build no hospitals
Host.
HP 75 so well accomplished an Hoste
Cor. 1161 against both Cynnas *h.* and Marius
Cor. 1661 an hoste of men to Affrique meanely Arm'd
Jer. 825 why it would raise spleene in the *h.* of Angels
Jer. 972 be all as fortunate as heavens blest *h.*
SP 194 have I been chiefe commaunder of an hoast
HP 976 those fearefull Hostes which the great Turke mustereth
Cor. 50 and civill furie, fiercer then thine hosts
Cor. 1272 and past the pikes of thousand hostes
Cor. 1632 and got hys willing hosts to march by night
Hot.
Cor. 1544 made his envious foe so hote
Jer. 142 and yet this is not all : I know you are to *h.*
Jer. 379 when we have drunke *h.* bloud together
Jer. 391 heere let the rising of our *h.* bloud set
Jer. 411 O entire is the condition of my *h.* desire
Jer. 750 who replide in scorne, and his *h.* suite denide
Jer. 985 to pierce Andreas ears throgh the *h.* army
ST 137 while they maintaine *h.* skirmish too and fro
STA 2000 and when our *h.* Spaine coulde not let it grow
SP 95 the Moore upon his *h.* Barbarian horse
SP 429 a *h.* piece of servise where he lost his taile
Ard. 1754 when words grow *h.* and blows begin to rise
Jer. 702 I *h.*, yet mist ; twas I mistooke my part
Jer. 739 for had I *h.* it right, Andrea had line there
Hough-Monday.
Ard. 1721 why, sir, this is no *H.*
Hought.
Ard. 1719 a fool as will rather be *h.* than get his way
Hound.
Jer. 641 leane like a court *h.* that liks fat trenchers cleane
HP 9 overtaken by two swift Grey-hounds
Hour.
Cor. Ded. 24 spend one howre of the day in some kind service
Cor. 862 both in his life, and at hys latest houre
Cor. 1548 in them poure sundry passions every houre
Cor. 1684 brave Romains, know this is the day and houre
Jer. 22 O fortunate houre, blessed mynuit, happy day
Jer. 367 twill keepe his day, his houre, nay minute ; twill
Jer. 1029 O long wished for houre
ST 384 Signior Horatio, this is the place and houre
ST 507 wrapt every houre in pleasures of the Court
ST 721 each howre doth wish and long to make resort
ST 752 our howre shall be when Vesper ginnes to rise

ST 759 till then each houre will seeme a yeere and more
ST 819 and there in safetie passe a pleasant hower
STA 950 I would have sworne, my selfe, within this houre
ST 1238 but, sirra, let the houre be eight a clocke
ST 1470 what, doe you hang by the howre ?
SP 584 what dismall Planets guides this fatall hower ?
SP 734 and come an houre hence unto my lodging
SP 2127 Is she not faire ? — Even in the houre of death
Ard. 286 and he shall die within an *h.* after
Ard. 991 worse than the conflict at the *h.* of death
Ard. 1086 as loth to give due audit to the *h.*
Ard. 1090 and at some *h.* hence come to us again
Ard. 1093 and so I'll leave you for an *h.* or two
Ard. 1297 woe worth the hapless *h.* and all the causes
Ard. 1381 Ah, would it were ! Then comes my happy *h.*
Ard. 1434 and in that hope I'll leave you for an *h.*
Ard. 2283 I saw him come into your house an *h.* ago
ST 2641 in one houres meditation they would performe any thing
ST 154 in all this turmoyle, three long houres and more
SP 243 endured some three or foure howers combat
Ard. 1538 see how the hours, the gardant of heaven's gate
Ard. 921 marked in my birth-*h.* by the destinies
Hourly.
HP 739 « O my beloved father in law whom I have hourely feard »
Cor. 923 I trust the gods, that see our hourely wrongs
Cor. 1869 did hourely keepe their ordinary course
ST 1044 that howerly coastes the center of the earth
House.
HP Ind. 36 thinges that are brought into the *h.*
HP Ind. 80 gaine honestly made by the Mistresse of the *h.*
HP 78 he ledde me to his *h.*
HP 81 before the *h.* there was a little Court
HP 97 « well placed » (quoth I) « is this goodlie *h.*
HP 120 the good man and maister of the *h.*
HP 157 and lodged in the *h.* of a poore Host
HP 207 and the good man of the *h.* beganne againe
HP 371 but the goodwife of the *h.* also
HP 471 giving up the government of his *h.* and
HP 771 (as a Father or Mother, Maister or Maistres of a *h.*)
HP 919 may well furnish his *h.*, seeking no
HP 993 Servaunts whereof a *h.* or familie in deede should
HP 1000 to whom by the Maister of the *h.* should the
HP 1032 everie thing that belongs to the keeping of a *h.*
HP 1037 the carefull Steward or surveighor of the *h.*
HP 1041 to have a speciall care that in the *h.*
HP 1082 nor should the Maister of the *h.* dysdaine, or
HP 1153 expences, wherewith he is to keepe his *h.*
HP 1196 and hapely the *h.* it selfe, and money
HP 1236 that whatsoever is necessarye for the use of his *h.*
HP 1238 and to leave his *h.* there furnished of so
HP 1253 such things whatsoever as are brought into the *h.*
HP 1306 necessary and fitt for the ability and credite of her *h.*
HP 1317 furnish any sufficie[n]t *h.* or dwelling
HP 1335 not of base women, but of a Mistres of a *h.*
HP 1353 forbad the Mistres of the *h.* all other works
HP 1358 to returne to the Mistres of the *h.* or huswife
HP 1393 we may well report that the forme of a *h.* is the order
HP 1394 the reformation of the *h.* or familie none other then
HP 1508 forgets his *h.*, his Children, and his Wife
HP 1688 concerning Husbandry and Keeping of a *h.*
HP 1733 that private *h.* of mine should farre surpasse that Pallace
HP 1750 governments or dispensations of a *h.* are devided into
Cor. 279 I am that plague, that sacks thy *h.* and thee
Cor. 808 blaze that fiercely burnes a *h.* already fired

Cor. 1610 are heapt with rage and horror gainst this *h.*
Cor. 2009 and must I live to see great Pompeys *h.*
Cor. 2010 (a *h.* of honour and antiquitie)
Jer. 573 now, by the honor of Casteels true *h.*
ST Bal. 86 the streets, hard by the Duke of Castiles *h.*
ST 278 Horatios *h.* were small for all his traine
ST 1179 and harkening neere the Duke of Castiles *h.*
ST 1224 thou knowest tis heere hard by behinde the *h.*
ST 1236 at S. Luigis Parke, behinde the *h.*
ST 1280 so neare the Duke his brothers *h.*
STA 1776 the very arme that did hold up our *h.*
ST 1797 to his *h.*, we meane
ST 1798 O, hard by : tis yon *h.* that you see
STA 2084 « the *h.* is a fire, the *h.* is a fire »
ST 2420 Hieronimo, frequent my homely *h.*
SP 449 lost her selfe betwixt a taverne and a bawdie *h.*
Ard. 29 is now become the steward of his *h.*
Ard. 117 and were thy *h.* of force, these hands of mine
Ard. 175 who would not venture upon *h.* and land
Ard. 203 being descended of a noble *h.*
Ard. 244 this is the painter's *h.* ; I'll call him forth
Ard. 317 the next time that I take thee near my *h.*
Ard. 334 and, Arden, though I now frequent thy *h.*
Ard. 349 forbear his *h.*
Ard. 352 to warn him on the sudden from my *h.*
Ard. 640 he well may be the master of the *h.*
Ard. 790 I'll rouse her from remaining in my *h.*
Ard. 940 this night come to his *h.* at Aldersgate
Ard. 998 my *h.* is irksome ; there I cannot rest
Ard. 1111 but let that pass, and show me to this *h.*
Ard. 1140 at the alehouse butting Arden's *h.*
Ard. 1494 my honest friend, to meet him at my *h.*
Ard. 1528 and bids him to a feast to his *h.* at Shorlow
Ard. 1562 if I should go, our *h.* would run away
Ard. 1656 'tis like to a curst wife in a little *h.*
Ard. 1658 then looks he as if his *h.* were a-fire
Ard. 1763 at his *h.* he never will vouchsafe to speak
Ard. 1955 will come and sup with you at our *h.* this night
Ard. 2130 henceforth frequent my *h.* no more
Ard. 2135 I'll have no such vows made in my *h.*
Ard. 2162 the widow Chambly ; I'll to her *h.* now
Ard. 2261 are coming towards our *h.* with glaives and bills
Ard. 2276 my *h.* is clear, and now I fear them not
Ard. 2283 I saw him come into your *h.* an hour ago
Ard. 2313 I fear me he was murdered in this *h.*
JB 82 till he had gotten her a better *h.*
JB 85 lodged never a night but the first in his *h.*
JB 94 secretly caried with her to her husbands *h.*
JB 148 « sweare I would not stay in the *h.* one night »
JB 165 being a continuall resorter to her *h.*
Puck 24 devyne praiers used duelie in his Lᵖˢ *h.*
HP Ind. 46 conserves necessary in houses
BP 90 prettie lodgings for servaunts, and houses for Corne
HP 1002 as in great houses it hath beene accustomed
HP 1008 our houses so distinguished and multiplyed with offycers
HP 1288 which custome is not gueason in some houses
HP 1716 the government of private houses and of Princes Courtes are different
HP 1754 those houses of the Viceroyes of Naples, Sicilie
HP 1756 to those Royall houses as were of olde
HP 1758 the houses of the Dukes of Savoy, Ferrara
Cor. 1694 by stuffing of our tropheies in their houses
Ard. 1923 the bawdy-houses have paid me tribute
Jer. 224 [one] from dicing houses
Jer. 519 to say, knavery in the Court and honesty in a cheese *h.*

HP 255 the Pigeons, them I have from my owne Dovehouse
Ard. 2018 locked within the counting-*h*. shall at a
Ard. 2050 give me the key : which is the counting *h*.?
Ard. 2075 stand before the counting-*h*. door
Ard. 2166 first lay the body in the counting-*h*.
SP 1979 to leade a Lambe unto the slaughter-*h*.?
Ard. 964 as unsuspected, to the slaughter-*h*.
Jer. 992 and crams his store *h*. to the top with bloud
Ard. *see* **Alehouse.**
Household.
HP Ind. 39 care of houshold is
HP Ind. 93 instruments of housholde to be kept cleene
HP Ind. 113 orders in housholde busines
HP 169 and other instruments of houshold
HP 498 to disgrade me of this petit government of houshold
HP 997 labor, countrey busines, and *h*. exercise
HP 1000 should the housholde care bee commended
HP 1043 Harnes and implements of houshold
HP 1095 he keepeth all the instruments of houshold occupied
HP 1108 in care of families and housholde busines
HP 1196 Arteficiall are moveables or houshold implements
HP 1281 all her houshold corne be some ground for bread
HP 1289 of houshold necessaries as all things els
HP 1412 disposd the *h*. of his glorious Sig. Capitano
HP 1512 object directed unto *h*. government
HP 1713 whether houshold care or housholde government be all one
HP 1722 wee found that there is difference in houshold governments
HP 1740 the houshold of a poor Prince is as little as
HP 1747 to governe a Princes houshold
HP 1764 wholy hee applies him to his housholde care
Cor. 676 then, home-borne houshold gods, and ye good spirits
Cor. 819 and kindly layd it by his houshold fire
Cor. 1644 and as a houshold Campe of creeping Emmets
HP Ind. 68 families or housholdes, of what sorte
Householder.
HP Ind. 136 times of the yeere to bee considered of a housholder
HP 517 the care of a good *h*. is devided into two thinges
HP (Title) The Housholders Philosophie. Wherein is perfectly
HP (Sub. Title) The Housholders Philosophie
HP Ind. 122 regard of householders
Housekeeper.
HP Ind. 37 cares necessary for a *h*.
HP Ind. 48 how farre it dooth concerne a *h*.
HP 349 but to the *h*. also, who
HP 388 one of the cheefest cares the *H*. should have
HP 398 most acceptable to the *H*.
HP 525 the good *H*., then, ought principally
HP 855 the care of a Father and good *H*.
HP 889 the *H*. shall so governe hys familie
HP 918 the good *H*. (that woulde have such
HP 1139 a Husband, a Maister, or a *H*.
HP 1151 the *H*. that is desirous to preserve his
HP 1211 whereof the good *H*. (oftentime) receiveth profit
HP 1490 naturall gayne necessary for a houskeeper
HP 1504 notwithstanding the *H*. ought to
HP 1511 the care of the Husbandman or *H*. doth
HP 1519 but the *H*. hath his desires of riches
HP 1536 limitted unto the *H*. and the family
HP 1564 conserning this naturall gaine convenient for a *H*.
HP 1570 the Husbandman and carefull *h*.
HP Ind. 64 exercise of Housekeepers for health
HP 1439 necessarye that Housekeepers have knowledge of
Housekeeping.
HP (Title) the true Oeconomia and forme of *H*.

HP Ind. 31 care of *h*. of divers sortes
HP Ind. 42 clenlines in *h*.
HP Ind. 98 weaving necessary in *h*.
HP 502 (a thing most needful and appropriate to *h*.)
HP 860 from the rest which I will speake of *h*.
HP 871 antiquities written of *h*. and
HP 943 who, reckoning up the properties of *h*.
HP 1417 whether this arte of encreasing be *h*. wholy
HP 1423 the art of *h*. and getting is not all one
HP 1426 whether to get be a forme or part of *h*.
HP 1584 although it be impertinent to Husbandry and *h*.
HP 1727 so shoulde the care of either houskeeping be one
Housewife.
HP Ind. 29 how it should bee used by a good huswife
HP Ind. 35 care of the Huswife concerning thinges
HP 1142 make mention of the duetie of a Huswife
HP 1259 a good huswife well considering, shold cause
HP 1274 a good Huswife makying store for her provision
HP 1308 neither ought a good Huswife to dysdaine or scorne to
HP 1316 wherewith a good Huswife may furnish
HP 1358 to returne to the Mistres of the house or huswife
HP 1370 the good Huswife ought above all things to be diligent
Housewifery.
HP Ind. 87 huswifry consisting much in spinning
Housewives.
HP 1338 been ascribd or attributed to privat huswifes
Hovering.
Cor. 1709 theyr harts and eyes lye *h*. over us
ST 1533 passions, that winged mount, and, *h*. in the aire
How.
Ard. 56 *h*.! Alice !
Ard. 247 *h*.! Clarke !
Ard. 730 *h*.? twenty angels? give my fellow
Jer. 32 *h*. now, what news for Spain? tribute returned?
Jer. 800 *h*. now, what means this trumpets sound?
ST 1184 *h*. now, whose this? Hieronimo? — My Lord
STA 1202 *h*. now, Hieronimo?
ST 1308 *h*. now, my Lord, what makes you rise so soone?
ST 1326 but heeres the Page-*h*. now, what newes with thee?
STA 1958 *h*. now, Who's there, sprits, sprits?
ST 2139 *h*. now, what noise? what coile is that you keepe?
ST 2377 and welcome, Bel-imperia. *H*. now, girle?
ST 2530 *h*. now, Hieronimo? what, courting Bel-imperia?
ST 2713 *h*. now, Hieronimo, where's your fellows
SP 468 *h*. now, sirra, what are you crying?
SP 861 *h*. now, Erastus, wherein may we pleasure thee?
SP 1405 why, *h*. now, Erastus, alwaies in thy dumpes?
Ard. 107 *h*. now, Adam, what is the news with you?
Ard. 142 *h*. now, Michael, whither are you going?
Ard. 588 *h*. now, Alice, what's the news?
Ard. 592 *h*. now, Clarke? have you found me false?
Ard. 654 *h*. now, fellow Bradshaw? whither away so early?
Ard. 885 *h*. now, Michael, whither are you going?
Ard. 890 *h*. now, Master Shakebag? what, Black Will !
Ard. 1097 *h*. now, Will? become a precisian?
Ard. 1264 *h*. now, Alice? what, sad and passionate?
Ard. 1371 *h*. now, Bradshaw, what's the news with you?
Ard. 1586 *h*. now, Michael? *h*. doth my mistress
Ard. 1707 why, *h*. now? who is this that's in the ditch?
Ard. 2178 *h*. now? what's the matter? is all well?
Ard. 2191 *h*. now, Mistress Arden? what ail you weep?
Ard. 2253 *h*. now, Alice, whither will you bear him?
Ard. 2282 *h*. now, Master Mayor, have you brought my husband home?
Howard.
JB 212 carried before Alderman *H*. to be examined

Ingram Content Group UK Ltd.
Milton Keynes UK
UKHW031808080523
421401UK00009B/713

9 781179 571270